CITY MATTERS

Competitiveness, cohe[illegible] urban governance

Edited by Martin Boddy and Michael Parkinson

First published in Great Britain in May 2004 by

The Policy Press
University of Bristol
Fourth Floor
Beacon House
Queen's Road
Bristol BS8 1QU
UK

Tel +44 (0)117 331 4054
Fax +44 (0)117 331 4093
e-mail tpp-info@bristol.ac.uk
www.policypress.org.uk

British Library Cataloguing in Publication Data
A catalogue record for this book is available from the British Library.

Library of Congress Cataloging-in-Publication Data
A catalog record for this book has been requested.

ISBN 1 86134 444 9 paperback

Reprinted 2005

A hardcover version of this book is also available

Martin Boddy is Associate Dean and Professor of Urban and Regional Studies at the University of the West of England, Bristol and **Michael Parkinson** is Director of the European Institute for Urban Affairs, Liverpool John Moores University.

Cover design by Qube Design Associates, Bristol
Front cover: photograph supplied by kind permission of CABE
Printed and bound in Great Britain by MPG Books, Bodmin

Contents

List of tables and figures

Tables

Figures

Foreword

For anyone interested in the economic and social role of our major cities the last 15 years have been an exciting time. We have re-discovered their potential as hubs of communication, as market places and as centres of fusion and innovation. The prospect of terminal decline in favour of a proliferating suburbia has been challenged by consumers and policy makers alike. We can now more clearly see that cities have much to offer an increasingly diverse population in an age where proximity, concentration and exchange continue to have economic and social value. That was the background against which the ESRC launched it's 'Cities: Competitiveness and Cohesion' Research Programme in 1997.

The proposition was simple. The new positioning and characterisation of cities needed fuller explanation and a new body of thought and evidence. There were lessons to be learned about the new competitive position of our cities. Were the emerging changes in the structures of employment and housing patterns fundamental or just a footnote for history?. There were lessons to be learned about the relative performance of different cities and the factors behind notable variations. There was an appetite to explore the consequences of different policies and governance regimes. Equally important there was an interest in the interaction between those forces shaping the new competitive position of our cities and the unchanged role they continued to play as homes for the poor and migrants seeking low cost housing, ready work, and the comfort of kin folk.

Martin Boddy and Michael Parkinson expertly draw together the wide-ranging product of that Programme in this book. It represents a fascinating array of scholarship and exploration, which has already had a significant impact on policy makers at local and national levels. As intriguing as any part of the book is the authors' concluding attempt to reach a balanced judgement on the original core question of whether there are links between competitiveness and cohesion and, if so, do these confirm the prospect for a continuing revival in the prosperity and well being of our cities. This collection provides a rich diet and vital reading for anyone interested in the future of urban life in the UK, and the wider lessons to be drawn from this

Sir Michael Lyons
Director, Institute of Local Government Studies,
University of Birmingham

Acknowledgements

Chapter Two: the study on which this chapter is based was part of the Central Scotland Integrative Case Study under the Economic and Social Research Council (ESRC) 'Cities' Programme (award number L130251040), with additional support from the Scottish Executive, Scottish Enterprise, Communities Scotland and Glasgow, Edinburgh, West Lothian and North Lanarkshire Councils.

Chapter Three: based on research carried out under ESRC award number L130251032.

Chapter Four: based on research carried out under ESRC award number L130251006. The chapter's authors would like to acknowledge the contribution to the early stages of the project of Nick Oatley and Nigel Taylor at the University of the West of England.

Chapter Five: research reported here was supported by the ESRC under grants L130251027 and L220252003. Figure 5.1 uses boundary data, copyright of the Crown and ED-LINE consortium. Among fellow members of the London research community, the chapter's authors particularly wish to acknowledge their debt to participants in the ESRC 'London' seminar series (1994-97) and Principal Investors on other London-related and 'integrated city study' projects in the 'Cities' programme. They are also indebted to several hundred Londoners who contributed their time and insights through extended interviews for this project.

Chapter Six: based on research carried out under ESRC award number L130251005.

Chapter Seven: based on research carried out under ESRC award number L130251013. Newcastle City Council part-funded the Newcastle case study.

Chapter Eight: based on research carried out under ESRC award number L130251015.

Chapter Nine: the author acknowledges the support of the ESRC under grants number L130251016 ('Urban Networks as Innovative Environments') and number R000238356 ('Social Capital and SME Performance') in enabling the research, on which this chapter was based, to be conducted. All respondents to surveys and interviews are gratefully acknowledged for their patience and time. For research support, Clare Davies, Rob Wilson and Nick Clifton deserve many thanks.

Chapter Ten: based on research carried out under ESRC award number L13025051. The author is very grateful for the collaboration, help and encouragement of his very congenial colleagues James Sennett (Oxford Brookes University), Peter Wood (University College London), Doug Hart (Reading University), Walter Manshanden (Universitaet van Amsterdam), Roberta Capello (Politecnico di Milano), Jeanine Cohen (Universite de Paris I) and Simone Strambach (Universitaet Stuttgart), and their colleagues who also worked on this project.

Chapter Eleven: based on research carried out under ESRC award number L130251045.

Chapter Twelve: based on research carried out under ESRC award number L130251034.

Chapter Thirteen: based on research carried out under ESRC award number L130251010.

Chapter Fourteen: based on research carried out under ESRC award number L130251046.

Chapter Fifteen: based on research carried out under ESRC award number L1302I5101. Dr Garry Robson, who co-authored many of the papers on which this chapter draws, undertook much of the research for this project.

Chapter Sixteen: based on research carried out under ESRC award number L130251025. This chapter reflects the collective effort of Elizabeth Bicler, Jane Lewis, Josephine Ocloo and Stephen Thalle, as well as the authors. We also acknowledge the support of the Development and Diversity research funding programme at the University of North London.

Chapter Seventeen: this chapter's authors are grateful to the ESRC for funding this study (award number L130241049) and the financial contributions of Birmingham Business Link, Birmingham Enterprise Link, Birmingham Partnership for Change and Birmingham and Solihull Training and Enterprise Council. They also appreciate the assistance of Balihar Sanghera and Gerald Barlow for their contribution to the project. The usual disclaimers apply.

Chapter Eighteen: based on research carried out under ESRC award number L130251008.

Chapter Nineteen: based on research carried out under ESRC award number L130251031.

Chapter Twenty: ESRC support for the research (grant number L130251044) is gratefully acknowledged. The research was led by the author of this chapter and the research team included, at different times: Noel Castree (now Department of Geography, University of Manchester); Karen Hibbitt (now Chief Executive's Department, Manchester City Council); Peris Jones (now Norwegian Institute of Human Rights, University of Oslo); Peter Lloyd and Alison Mitchell (Department of Geography, University of Liverpool); and Michael Samers (now School of Geography, University of Nottingham).

Chapter Twenty One: based on research carried out under ESRC award number L130251052 and draws on earlier published work, Malorey et al (2000, 2001).

Notes on contributors

Tahir Abbas is Lecturer in Sociology, University of Birmingham.

Mark Andrew is Lecturer in Economics, University of Reading.

Rowland Atkinson is Research Fellow in the Department of Urban Studies, University of Glasgow.

Nick Bailey is Research Fellow in the Department of Urban Studies, University of Glasgow.

Keith Bassett is Senior Lecturer in Geography in the School of Geographical Sciences, University of Bristol.

Iain Begg is Professor of Economics at South Bank University.

Martin Boddy is Associate Dean and Professor of Urban and Regional Studies at the Faculty of the Built Environment, University of the West of England (UWE) Bristol.

Sophie Bowlby is Senior Lecturer in Human Geography at the University of Reading.

Glen Bramley is Professor of Planning and Housing at Heriot Watt University.

Nadia Joanne Britton is a Lecturer in Applied Sociology at the University of Sheffield.

Belinda Brown is Research Fellow, Institute of Community Studies.

Nick Buck is Professor, Director of the UK Longitudinal Studies Centre, and Associate Director, Institute for Social and Economic Research, University of Essex.

Tim Butler is Reader in Human Geography at King's College London.

Tony Champion is Professor of Population Geography at the University of Newcastle.

Paul Cheshire is Professor of Economic Geography at the London School of Economics and Political Science.

Philip Cooke is Professor of Regional Development at the University of Cardiff.

Iain Deas is Senior Lecturer in the Department of Planning and Landscape at the University of Manchester.

Fiona Devine is Professor of Sociology at the University of Manchester.

Iain Docherty is Research Fellow in the Department of Urban Studies, University of Glasgow.

Richard Evans is a Reader at the European Institute for Urban Affairs at Liverpool John Moores University.

Tania Fisher is a Researcher at the British Medical Association, Health Policy and Economic Research Unit.

Jo Foord is Senior Lecturer in the Cities Institute, London Metropolitan University.

Shaun French is Lecturer in Geography in the School of Geography, University of Nottingham.

Ken Gibb is a Reader in the Department of Urban Studies, University of Glasgow.

Norman Ginsburg is Professor of Social Policy, London Metropolitan University.

Robina Goodlad is Professor of Housing and Urban Studies, in the Department of Urban Studies, University of Glasgow.

Ian Gordon is Professor of Human Geography and Director of LSE London, London School of Economics and Political Science.

Ron Griffiths is Principal Lecturer in Urban Planning in the Faculty of the Built Environment, UWE.

Simon Guy is Professor of Urban Development in the University of Newcastle.

Peter Halfpenny is Professor of Sociology at the University of Manchester.

Peter Hall is Professor of Planning, Bartlett School of Architecture and Planning, University College, London, and Director of the Institute of Community Studies.

Robin Hambleton is Dean of the College of Urban Planning and Public Affairs at the University of Illinois, Chicago, and Professor of Urban Planning, Policy and Public Administration.

Alan Harding is Professor of Urban and Regional Governance and Co-Director of the Centre for Sustainable Urban and Regional Futures (SURF) at the University of Salford.

Michael Harloe is Vice Chancellor and Professor of Sociology, University of Salford.

Annette Hastings is Lecturer in Urban Regeneration in the Department of Urban Studies, University of Glasgow.

John Henneberry is Professor of Town and Regional Planning, University of Sheffield.

Chris Huxham is Fellow of the Advanced Institute of Management Research and Professor of Management, University of Strathclyde Graduate School of Business.

Trevor Jones is Visiting Professor, Small Business and Enterprise Research Group, Business School, De Montfort University.

Keith Kintrea is Senior Lecturer in the Department of Urban Studies, University of Glasgow.

Karryn Kirk is Research Associate in the Centre for Research into Socially Inclusive Services at Heriot Watt University.

Mark Kleinman was at the time of writing Professor of International Social Policy, University of Bristol, and is now Head of Housing and Homelessness, Greater London Authority.

Christine Lambert is Reader in Urban Planning in the Faculty of the Built Environment, UWE.

Joe Leibovitz is Research Fellow in the Department of Urban Studies, University of Glasgow.

Bill Lever is Professor of Urban Studies in the Department of Urban Studies, University of Glasgow.

Andrew Leyshon is Professor of Economic and Social Geography in the School of Geography, University of Nottingham.

Sally Lloyd Evans is Lecturer in Human Geography at the University of Reading.

Stefano Magrini is a Lecturer in the Department of Economics, University of Venice.

William Maloney is Reader in the Department of Politics and International Relations, University of Aberdeen.

Francesca Medda is a Lecturer in the Department of Economics, University of Reading.

Richard Meegan is Reader in the European Institute for Urban Affairs, Liverpool John Moores University.

Geoffrey Meen is Professor of Applied Economics, University of Reading.

Rosemary Mellor was a Senior Lecturer in Sociology at the University of Manchester until her untimely death in March 2001.

Vassilis Monastiriotis is a Lecturer in Economics at Royal Holloway, University of London.

Barry Moore is Reader in Economics in the Department of Land Economy, and Fellow of Downing College, University of Cambridge.

Jimmy Morgan is a Lecturer in the School of the Built Environment, Heriot Watt University.

Karen O'Reilly is Senior Lecturer in Sociology, University of Aberdeen.

Michael Parkinson is Director of the European Institute for Urban Affairs, Liverpool John Moores University.

Ronan Paddison is Professor of Geography in the University of Glasgow.

Gareth Potts is an independent consultant.

Monder Ram is Professor of Small Business at De Montfort University.

Clare Roche is a PhD student at the University of Limerick.

James Simmie is Professor of Innovation and Urban Competitiveness in the School of Planning at Oxford Brookes University.

Laura Smethurst is Senior Research Officer, Department for Work and Pensions.

Graham Smith is Senior Lecturer in the Department of Politics, University of Southampton.

Ian Smith is Senior Research Fellow in the Faculty of the Built Environment, UWE.

Jo Sparkes works in the Social Exclusion Unit, Office of the Deputy Prime Minister.

Murray Stewart is Visiting Professor of Urban and Regional Governance, Cities Research Centre, Faculty of the Built Environment, UWE.

Gerry Stoker is Professor of Political Science in the Department of Government at the University of Manchester.

David Sweeting is Research Fellow in the Cities Research Centre, Faculty of the Built Environment, UWE.

Nigel Thrift is Head of the Life and Environmental Sciences Division, University of Oxford.

Ivan Turok is Professor of Urban Economic Development in the Department of Urban Studies, University of Glasgow.

Siv Vangen is Lecturer in Management, The Open University Business School.

Stuart Wilks-Heeg is a Lecturer in the Department of Sociology and Social Policy at the University of Liverpool.

Stephen Young is a former Senior Lecturer in the Department of Government, University of Manchester.

ONE

Introduction

Michael Parkinson and Martin Boddy

Cities are now back firmly on the UK policy agenda. Between the 1960s and the early 1990s, the focus was all on urban problems and the challenges posed by 'those inner cities', as Margaret Thatcher disparagingly referred to them in 1987. Following two or more decades of decline, it seemed that cities were synonymous with economic decline, physical decay, shrinking populations and social deprivation. The 1990s, however, saw a sea change in how our towns and cities were viewed. The idea that cities were the dynamos of the UK national economy, vital to the competitiveness of 'UK plc', rather than economic basket cases as they were sometimes portrayed, seized the imagination of politicians, pundits, academic researchers and business leaders alike. Cities are now increasingly seen as economic assets rather than urban liabilities. There have been very real signs of renewed investment, cultural development and an appetite for urban lifestyles. Urban living and the quality of urban life, culture and environment have been increasingly recognised as cornerstones of a civilised and progressive society, much as they always had been in continental Europe. Even the problems of inner-city areas were recast in the language of social exclusion and social cohesion alongside growing recognition that economic success has often been associated with continuing or worsening problems in terms of social equity.

Reflecting this, the future of our towns and cities has been increasingly central to national government policy, particularly since Labour's return to power in 1997. There has been a whole raft of enquiries, reports and policies designed explicitly to promote and enhance the interests of our urban areas. The most significant include the 1999 report of the Urban Task Force led by Sir Richard Rogers (Urban Task Force, 1999), the government White Paper, *Our towns and cities: The future* (DETR, 2000), the government's Neighbourhood Renewal Strategy and related policy measures that built on the work of the Cabinet Office Social Exclusion Unit. Following these came the government's 'Communities Plan'[1] (ODPM, 2003), which set out strategies for managing pressures of urban growth in booming southern England alongside plans for the renewal of low-demand areas elsewhere in the country.

Much of this new thinking was presented at the government's high-profile Urban Summit held in Birmingham in 2002. The summit was opened by the Deputy Prime Minister, John Prescott, and included an address from the Prime Minister (via a live video link) and with a finale from the Chancellor, Gordon

Brown. Alongside this wholesale rethinking of our towns and cities from a policy perspective, the whole landscape in which they operate has undergone profound change. This has reflected increasingly intense competition in an increasingly globalised economy, rapid shifts in technological capacity and innovation and the increasing predominance of the 'knowledge economy' in the production of both goods and services.

This, then, was the context for the *Cities: Competitiveness and Cohesion Research Programme*, reported here. Set up in 1997 by the Economic and Social Research Council (ESRC), with additional support from the Department of the Environment, Transport and the Regions, the programme set out to address major questions and issues around the key ideas of economic competitiveness and social cohesion in an urban context. It addressed many of the concerns that have been central to government thinking on our towns and cities and the issues which confront them. And it also set out to look explicitly at the role of policy, government and governance in relation to competitiveness and cohesion. At its core, the research programme set out to explore and explain:

- the processes that shape and determine economic competitiveness in UK cities. What makes for competitive success?
- the relationship between social exclusion and social cohesion, on the one hand, and economic competitiveness, on the other. Does social exclusion impact negatively on competitiveness? Does social cohesion boost economic success? And what, in turn, are the impacts of economic competitiveness on cohesion and exclusion?
- the role of government and governance in relation to economic competitiveness and the links between competitiveness and cohesion. What role (if any) do they play in boosting economic competitiveness? And what impacts can government and governance have on the links between competitiveness and cohesion?

The programme set out to explore why cities matter, in what ways and to whom. Clearly the answers to these questions have important policy and political implications. And the programme was able to feed into the policy process and ways of rethinking cities and the significance of cities along the way, contributing to the evidence base for urban policy in general and the White Paper and subsequent initiatives in particular.

The programme itself included 23 different projects, involved 30 universities and almost 100 researchers. It was also diverse, exploring both the headline questions outlined earlier in this chapter and a wide range of related issues. The individual projects also varied in their scale, geographical focus and methodology, ranging from local case studies to broad-ranging national and European-scale analysis. This volume provides a summary of the main arguments and findings from these various studies. It is also designed to encourage further exploration of the issues and arguments raised in the individual research projects. To this end, the individual chapters include extensive references to these other outputs. Details of the programme's other outputs can also be accessed via the ESRC's own database, www.regard.ac.uk[2].

Overarching issues

A key objective of the research programme as a whole was to explore issues around competitiveness, cohesion and governance and the relations between these broad domains. As many of the contributions to the programme make clear, none of these domains is very straightforward either in conceptual terms or in terms of empirical research. Nevertheless, they have provided a key focus for research and policy over recent years. And while in practice they have undoubtedly proved complex and at times confused and inconclusive, they have nevertheless proved very fruitful as a means of thinking through both urban issues and urban policy. Both competitiveness and cohesion have been central, moreover, to policy goals at local, regional and national levels, and effective 'governance' has been seen as vital in supporting and securing these goals.

Competitiveness

It is now widely accepted that 'place' and local context matter in terms of competitive strength; that is, some cities clearly offer a better mix of attributes for business and business success than others over relatively extended periods of time (Begg, 1999, 2002). In strict economic terms, it may be correct to argue that it is businesses that compete, not cities or regions as such. The business environment can, however, have significant impacts on the capacity of businesses to compete effectively. The potential for policy and governance to affect this may be quite highly constrained, dominated as they are by the effects of competition, structural change in the economy and technological developments. Nevertheless, they can also have very real impacts at the margin – the margin often being what makes the difference between different places.

There have been many different attempts to define competitiveness and the factors which promote or underpin competitive success. In terms of outcomes, evidence of competitive strength is typically associated with economic indicators such as the level or change in the level of output, productivity or value-added per head. More tangible outcomes include levels of personal or corporate earnings, income and spending power. They might also include overall levels of employment, economic activity or unemployment. These outputs or outcomes are in effect the end result in economic terms of competitive success.

At the level of regions or urban areas, competitive strength can also be seen in terms of employment growth, in-migration and the attraction of inward investment. At one level, these are also outcomes in the sense that they reflect economic success: population, employment and investment tend to be sucked in to more competitive cities and regions. They are, however, also important drivers of continuing economic success in their own right.

Beyond this, in terms of inputs, there have been many different attempts to identify those factors most closely associated with competitive strength or critical to competitiveness. Different studies have assembled lists of indicators or more complex, derived indices or 'scorecards', seeking to capture and quantify the determinants of competitiveness and, hence, of economic success (Local Futures Group, 2002, 2003; Robert Huggins Associates, 2002; see also Chapter Nine of this volume). These include a wide range of statistical measures such as education and skills, research and development (R&D) expenditure, and numbers of patents filed. They have also been incorporated into more general concepts such as 'the knowledge base' or 'innovative capacity' that are seen as fundamental in explaining economic performance at national, regional or more local levels.

Some approaches have stressed the role of a wider set of 'urban assets' (Deas and Giordano, 2002; Kresl, 2002). These typically include, for example, accessibility and connectedness, the supply of land and premises, quality of life and the capacity to attract in technical and professional labour, and less tangible concepts such as leadership or strategic capacity, embracing both public and private sectors. Some cities, as Begg (2002) has argued, manifestly offer a better mix of attributes for business operations than do others. The stock of assets in different places, some tangible and some less so, provides in effect the environment within which economic activity takes place.

It is also evident, however, that existing industrial structure is a key determinant of economic performance in the short to medium term. Many aspects of competitive strength are, in a sense, embedded in a city's or region's sectoral make-up. There are exceptions, but the hierarchy of different cities or regions whether at national or European levels tends to remain relatively unchanged over periods of many years. Many of the factors, however, which impinge on particular cities and which impact on urban competitiveness in terms of outputs and outcomes clearly derive from national and international economic circumstances and are essentially beyond local influence. There remain, however, aspects of the local 'business environment', as Begg (1999) has termed it, in different towns, cities and regions which, crucially, remain open to policy influence whether at the local, regional or national level.

Social cohesion

Social cohesion and social exclusion have, similarly, been widely debated and have been used in a variety of ways in different contexts. Without revisiting these debates at length, the main dimensions can usefully be summarised (Boddy, 2002). At one level, the term 'social exclusion' has frequently been used as an alternative to poverty, inequality or social deprivation. In this sense, it has been used in a largely descriptive way. Beyond the purely descriptive level, social exclusion has also been used to capture some idea of the processes or mechanisms of exclusion or inclusion. It has been used to try and capture the idea that there are active processes or mechanisms that cut people off from the mainstream of society. It is these processes that are then, in turn, reflected in the observed levels of poverty and deprivation based on a range of different indicators. In addition, empirical work has focused on the dynamics and duration of these effects, both over time and between generations. Longitudinal studies in particular have pointed to the crucial impact of child poverty and of educational attainment on later outcomes (Burchardt et al, 1999; Hobcraft, 2003).

Cohesion and exclusion have also been used in the sense of relationships and networks, and of exclusion from the 'normal' activities of mainstream society. This includes exclusion and distancing from the common values, attitudes and behaviour of the mainstream. While it can be argued that there is no single set of norms, rules and values, this sense of cohesion or exclusion does carry some notion of dominant or mainstream; otherwise, the question 'Exclusion from what?' is left begging. Lack of cohesion may thus, for example, be manifest in a lack of attachment to paid work, restricted social contacts, attitudes to education, substance abuse or propensity to crime. It might also extend to a propensity to social disorder.

Finally, there is common ground between social cohesion and the idea of 'social capital', which is addressed in a number of this volume's chapters. This emphasises, in particular, participation in social activities and active involvement in 'civil society'. It has also been linked to what are seen as desirable attributes at the level of community or society such as active citizenship and political participation.

Competitiveness, cohesion and governance

As noted earlier in this chapter, one aim of the programme was to explore the possible relationships or interaction between economic competitiveness on the one hand, and social cohesion or exclusion on the other. The desirability of competitive success in terms of rising levels of output, productivity and incomes, high levels of investment and economic activity coupled with low unemployment are usually taken as self-evident. Pressures may result in terms of population and employment growth, but problems of managing growth pressures are generally seen as preferable to managing those of decline. The relationship between competitiveness, cohesion and exclusion are not, however, quite so clear.

Questions can be posed at two levels. First, to what extent and in what way does competitiveness impact on social cohesion and social exclusion? In particular, is competitive success necessarily a prerequisite for and reflected in increased cohesion or reduced levels of social exclusion, as is frequently argued? Alternatively, might the impacts of competitive success on the structure of the labour market, for example, lead to increased social exclusion? And if so, what are the implications?

Second, what impact does cohesion or exclusion have, in turn, on levels of competitiveness in particular urban areas? Do high levels of social exclusion threaten or undermine competitive strength, and are high levels of social cohesion necessary to competitive success? In a sense, this raises the question of the business case for addressing social exclusion. Levels of social exclusion could potentially impact adversely on competitiveness and the strength of the 'business environment' in particular places were this to lead to lower levels of investment or higher costs of doing business. It could also impact adversely were it perceived as reducing the quality of life locally and deterring better-off and/or more highly skilled households from moving in.

A second general aim was, therefore, to explore the role of policy and 'governance' in relation to the goals of competitiveness and cohesion. The concept of *governance* – as distinct from that of *government* – is used to describe the wider set of institutions and interrelationships which play a role in shaping or steering economic and social processes than the formal bodies and processes associated with the latter. The idea of governance emphasises the part played by a wider set of bodies, organisations or associations beyond the formal structure of local, regional and central government.

This extends not only to a range of non-elected public and voluntary sector bodies, but also private sector businesses and organisations. The term also places particular emphasis on relations between such bodies including, for example, more formal partnership, collaboration and leadership, but also the importance of less formal networks and cooperation. In this sense, it also captures something more nebulous and systemic in the nature and quality of institutional structures within different urban areas and, importantly, their impacts on capacity for action.

The structure of this volume

All the chapters of this volume are based on recent and original empirical work conducted by leading UK researchers. From different perspectives and using a diversity of approaches, they address a range of issues focused around the core themes of the research programme outlined earlier in this chapter.

Part One presents findings from four 'integrated city studies' that formed a major component of the programme as a whole. The aim of these four studies was to try to understand in some detail how different processes, including broad questions of competitiveness, cohesion and governance, interact in particular and contrasting urban areas. The programme supported four such large studies. Ivan Turok and colleagues (Chapter Two) focus on Glasgow and Edinburgh, the two largest cities in Scotland. They analyse the contrasting performance and very different trajectories of these two neighbouring cities over the last two decades and on the relationship between them. Glasgow has experienced major economic decline, the effects of which are still very apparent, but more recently has shown significant evidence of urban renaissance. Edinburgh, on the other hand, has emerged as an highly economically successful 'capital city'.

Alan Harding and colleagues (Chapter Three) focus on the neighbouring cities of Liverpool and Manchester, the largest urban areas in the North West of England. Each one, like Glasgow, has suffered from major economic decline and job loss, in the context of a region which has underperformed relative to the national economy as a whole. Also like Glasgow and Edinburgh, they have experienced somewhat different fortunes. Manchester, more recently, however, seems to have capitalised more effectively on opportunities to boost its competitive strength, and the chapter focuses in particular on the degree to which governance, government and politics have contributed to the relative performance of the two cities.

Martin Boddy and colleagues (Chapter Four) and Ian Gordon and colleagues (Chapter Five) focus on Bristol and London respectively. Both are cities in prosperous southern England and both have demonstrated considerable competitive strength. London, however, is in many ways unique given its sheer scale, complexity and intense internationalisation. Bristol, on the other hand, is a free-standing city which, while by no means immune from the impacts of wider economic forces, has nevertheless demonstrated considerable adaptive capacity and competitive strength over recent decades. Both chapters explore the roots of competitive strength, the interaction between competitiveness and cohesion, and the difference that governance has made.

Part Two of this volume looks at competitiveness and urban change at the level of the urban system as a whole. Each chapter presents original and innovative analysis based on large-scale data sets. Barry Moore and Iain Begg (Chapter Six) look at the sources, nature and location of economically successful towns and cities, and identify the long-term winners and losers in the UK urban system. They also look at the factors that explain their relative success. They ask, in particular, what are the factors that help shape the competitiveness of cities and allow some to grow more rapidly than others? Tony Champion and Tania Fisher (Chapter Seven) look more specifically at demographic patterns in the UK and explore what attracts and binds people to the nation's larger cities and their inner areas. They show that while some of the larger cities have arrested the worst losses of the past 20 years, they are still losing ground to smaller places lower down the urban hierarchy. Paul Cheshire and colleagues (Chapter Eight) then focus on UK urban areas in the wider European setting. This detailed work explores how cities located near each other affect one another, and in particular the impacts of economically more successful cites on their near neighbours.

Part Three focuses on innovation and the competitive strength of urban areas. The two chapters by Philip Cooke and James Simmie (Chapters Nine and Ten) explore these issues analytically and empirically, using evidence from both the UK and continental Europe. Cooke looks at the meaning of 'place competitiveness' and the extent to which social capital in areas and between firms can be exploited to encourage increased competitiveness. James Simmie poses three key questions: how does innovation lead to growth? Why is innovation so concentrated in a minority of urban regions? And, how can public policy contribute to increased innovation in less successful cities and regions? He explores these questions through a comparative study of five of the most innovative urban regions in Europe.

Part Four focuses on housing and property. The chapters by Geoffrey Meen and Mark Andrew, and by Simon Guy and John Henneberry both focus upon the role of property and the built environment, including housing, in relation to competitiveness and the economic performance of cities. Meen and Andrew (Chapter Eleven) use formal economic modelling techniques to analyse aggregate data of economic performance. They explore the relationship between housing demand, residential preferences and workforce implications and the potential for housing-based policies to improve city competitiveness. Guy and Henneberry (Chapter Twelve) are interested in the ways in which decision-making processes in the property market affect the shape and distribution of investment in different property markets across the UK. They identify the impacts of the wider economic and social context on property markets and property market trends, assess how different development agents and business actors have different strategies within different cities, and examine the different ways in which urban policy interacts with local property development in different cities.

Part Five looks at the role of space, place and location in relation to social exclusion and cohesion and at the internal structure and function of urban areas at neighbourhood level. Nick Buck and Ian Gordon (Chapter Thirteen) explore the question of how much 'place' matters and in particular whether living in a deprived area makes the life chances of poor people even worse, as is frequently assumed. This clearly has implications for much of formal urban policy and neighbourhood renewal with their explicit emphasis on 'area-based initiatives'. Peter Halfpenny and his co-researchers (Chapter Fourteen) explore whether 'place' matters from the rather different perspective of the role of 'good suburbs' and whether they can make a difference to the performance of a city's economy. Their work in Manchester explores the role of prosperous neighbourhoods in attracting a skilled workforce to urban areas and also the impact of city development upon prosperous suburbs and the implications. Tim Butler (Chapter Fifteen) then looks at the social roles and relationships within different kinds of middle-class areas in London. He teases out the different patterns of gentrification in different parts of the capital in what is an increasingly middle-class city, and some of the consequences of these processes.

Part Six explores different aspects of the economic and social experiences of ethnic communities in UK cities. Jo Foord and Norman Ginsburg (Chapter Sixteen) explore two contemporary themes in the regeneration of poor urban areas. The first is the extent of social capital to be found in poor communities. The second is the emergence, scale and significance of multicultural and creative enclaves within some inner-city locations. Trevor Jones and colleagues (Chapter Seventeen) also focus on ethnic enterprise and entrepreneurs in an inner-city context – that is, the independent restaurant sector in Birmingham. They look at the economic trajectory of the sector, strategies for breaking free from some of the constraints this implies, and the impact of these pressures upon family businesses and relationships. Sophie Bowlby and colleagues (Chapter Eighteen) then look at the experience of ethnic groups in the labour market. Their work focuses upon the school and labour market experiences of young people from different ethnic and class backgrounds in localities that are economically buoyant.

Part Seven, finally, examines issues of governance, leadership and social capital. David Sweeting and his co-researchers (Chapter Nineteen) explore the nature and operation of leadership, particularly in relation to partnership, an issue that is increasingly to the fore given the proliferation of partnership working in a wide range of urban initiatives. This is again the case with Local Strategic Partnerships where success is likely to depend in part at least on clear and effective leadership that articulates the relationships between the various stakeholders. Richard Meegan (Chapter Twenty) provides a detailed examination of governance, participation and the nature of social capital. These are explored through an evaluation of a particular neighbourhood partnership in Liverpool. Then, Gerry Stoker and colleagues (Chapter Twenty One) take a critical look at the concept of social capital as developed by Robert Putnam and others. They argue the need to focus not only on relations between people but also on the relationship between associations and organisations and the role of corporate actors. Chapter Twenty Two presents our own summary of key findings from the Programme as a whole together with the policy implications.

Notes

[1] This was outlined by the Deputy Prime Minister in a speech to Parliament in July 2002 and again at the Urban Summit in October 2002. It was then fleshed out in an Action Plan (ODPM, 2003) and a series of regional strategies.

[2] Project details and programme outputs can be accessed by clicking on ESRC Ref No, then entering reference number L130251. Outputs from particular projects can be found by entering the relevant project reference number, detailed in each individual chapter of this volume, see pages ix to xi.

References

Begg, I. (1999) 'Cities and competitiveness', *Urban Studies*, vol 36, no 5/6, pp 795-809.

Begg, I. (ed) (2002) *Urban competitiveness: Policies for dynamic cities*, Bristol: The Policy Press.

Boddy, M. (2002) 'Linking competitiveness and cohesion', in I. Begg (ed) *Urban competitiveness: Policies for dynamic cities*, Bristol: The Policy Press, pp 33-53.

Burchardt, T., Le Grand, J. and Piachaud, D. (1999) 'Social exclusion in Britain, 1991-95', *Social Policy and Administration*, vol 33, no 3, pp 227-44.

Deas, I. and Giordano, B. (2002) 'Locating the competitive city in England', in I. Begg (ed) *Urban competitiveness: Policies for dynamic cities*, Bristol: The Policy Press, pp 191-209.

DETR (Department of Environment, Transport and the Regions) (2000) *Our towns and cities: The future. Delivering an urban renaissance*, Cm 4911, London: DETR.

Hobcraft, J. (2003) *Continuity and change in pathways to young adult disadvantage: Results from a British birth cohort*, CASE Paper no 66, London: London School of Economics and Political Science.

Robert Huggins Associates (2002) *The state of urban Britain: UK competitiveness index 2002, city, metropolitan and ward benchmarking*, Cardiff: Robert Huggins Business and Economic Policy Press.

Kresl, P. (2002) 'The enhancement of urban economic competitiveness', in I. Begg (ed) *Urban competitiveness: Policies for dynamic cities*, Bristol: The Policy Press, pp 211-31.

Local Futures Group (2002) *A regional perspective on the knowledge economy in Great Britain*, Report for the DTI, London: Local Futures Group.

Local Futures Group (2003) *State of the nation: A geographical perspective on Britain*, London: Local Futures Group.

ODPM (Office of the Deputy Prime Minister) (2003) *Sustainable communities: Building for the future*, London: The Stationery Office.

Urban Task Force (1999) *Towards an urban renaissance*, Final Report of the Urban Task Force chaired by Lord Rogers, London: E&FN Spon.

Part One: Competitiveness, cohesion and urban governance

TWO

Sources of city prosperity and cohesion: the case of Glasgow and Edinburgh

Ivan Turok, Nick Bailey, Rowland Atkinson, Glen Bramley, Iain Docherty, Ken Gibb, Robina Goodlad, Annette Hastings, Keith Kintrea, Karryn Kirk, Joe Leibovitz, Bill Lever, Jimmy Morgan and Ronan Paddison

Although only 45 miles separate Edinburgh and Glasgow, the two largest cities in Scotland, they exhibit striking contrasts in their historic performance and social conditions. Severe deindustrialisation and decentralisation have left Glasgow with some of the most serious social and environmental problems in Britain. In recent years, however, there has been an economic turnaround, the extent and consequences of which have not been analysed in detail before. Edinburgh, on the other hand, has experienced accelerated growth over the last decade, causing tighter labour and property markets and displacement of population and jobs towards the urban edge and beyond. Congestion, high house prices and labour shortages arouse concern within the business and residential communities.

Integrative case studies of Glasgow and Edinburgh sought to explore issues of competitiveness and cohesion and to question the validity and underlying assumptions of these multifaceted concepts. Key questions that were addressed included, how important are local sources of competitiveness and cohesion in an increasingly open economy? Do social justice and economic success really go hand-in-hand in a modern economy? Is cohesion a significant source of economic prosperity, or exclusion a drag on long-term development prospects? The study involved unpacking the apparently simple concepts of competitiveness and cohesion and exploring their determinants and interrelationships through research on a variety of substantive issues. One strand of work, for example, involved identifying the main urban assets that facilitate or frustrate economic performance, including physical infrastructure, housing and social institutions. Another analysed the influence of deprived neighbourhoods, citizen participation and the labour market on social cohesion and prosperity. The study also sought to assess the strategic capacity of urban governance; that is, its ability to mobilise resources and negotiate a coherent vision for the city in the context of institutional fragmentation, micromanagement tendencies and intensified competition.

The Scottish study used a range of methods and data sources according to the questions addressed. Considerable effort went into assembling and manipulating existing public statistics to provide consistent data for comparable areas. An interim report analysed the changing economic, social and institutional structure of Central Scotland over the last two decades (Bailey et al, 1999). Three new data sets were also created and analysed using advanced statistical methods. First, a survey was carried out of almost 1,700 businesses in key sectors to assess the significance of local factors and forces for their performance (Docherty et al, 2001a). Second, there was a survey of 800 households in two pairs of neighbourhoods (deprived and socially mixed) located close together in each city to test the significance of 'area effects' on quality of life and social cohesion (Atkinson and Kintrea, 2001; Docherty et al, 2001b). Third, a survey of 570 occupiers in 15 new private housing schemes was undertaken to identify their social and economic consequences (Bramley and Morgan, 2003). During the course of the research, several hundred interviews were also undertaken with employers, officials, professionals, community representatives and local residents.

Competitiveness

Competitiveness has become a powerful mantra in economic and spatial policy during the last decade. Yet the concept is far from straightforward and has been interpreted in a variety of ways and contexts. Indeed, the very idea of a city, region or nation as a competitive unit is contested (Castells, 1996; Krugman, 1996). At its simplest, the term is often equated with the level of prosperity of an area, so a competitive city is one with high average incomes or low unemployment. The term also features as a prominent goal of development agencies, although typically as an end in itself rather than as a specific guide to how economic development might be accelerated. These uses add nothing to our understanding of how and why cities prosper, focusing as they do on the outcomes of economic processes rather than the sources or causes of prosperity.

Other uses of the term have, after careful elucidation, more insights to offer. The notion can point to some important drivers of local economic development, particularly the relative position of cities and their firms in contested external markets (issues of trade performance), the value of their products and the efficiency with which they are produced (productivity) and the extent to which local resources are used (for example, the employment rate). Against this, the term risks representing the determinants of city prosperity too narrowly, overstating the importance of *international* trade and explicit competition between city authorities, and diverting attention from other sources of development. It also conceals important diversity between the performance of different sectors within cities and the uneven consequences of competitive success for different social groups.

One way of unpacking the idea is to distinguish between two key dimensions of place-based prosperity (or output [GDP] per capita). They are productivity (GDP per employee) and the employment rate (the proportion of the population in work) (Begg, 1999). Productivity is widely considered to be the single most important determinant of competitiveness. However, it needs to be considered alongside the employment rate, which affects average living standards more directly and is an important aspect of economic and social inclusion (one of the dimensions of cohesion discussed later in this chapter). New Office for National Statistics (ONS) data on GDP for local authorities was analysed at the city scale for the first time, with appropriate adjustments made for commuting imbalances between cities and their hinterlands. Edinburgh emerged as the second most prosperous major city in Britain after London (Bailey et al, 2002).

A more general finding from this analysis was the weak relationship between the level of productivity and employment rate across all cities. Cities such as London and, to a lesser extent, Glasgow have relatively high average productivity but a relatively low employment rate, whereas the opposite appears to be the case in Leeds and Sheffield. So, raising productivity is no simple panacea for ensuring city prosperity (especially if it comes about by shedding labour). Another implication is that there is a degree of independence between productivity (and therefore competitiveness) and employment (and, therefore, inclusion and cohesion). The two objectives do not necessarily go together in the way suggested by some current thinking (see, for example, HM Treasury, 2001). The policy message is that different cities face different basic priorities to improve their overall prosperity. In Glasgow's case, it is clearly to raise the employment rate, which is one of the lowest in the UK at some 61·3% of the working-age population.

Employment emerged from the study as a crucial link between competitiveness and cohesion. The labour market transmits competitive shocks and restructuring of the economy to the job prospects, incomes and quality of life of communities (Turok, 1999). The ability of local labour markets to adjust through migration, commuting and reskilling may affect several aspects of social cohesion, including inequality and stability (discussed later in this chapter). The labour force is also a crucial urban asset influencing economic performance through its productivity, creativity and sheer agglomeration advantages. Labour shortages are an increasing concern of Edinburgh's businesses, partly as a result of growth outpacing new housing supply, high house prices limiting in-migration and transport bottlenecks constraining in-commuting (Turok and Bailey, 2002).

The competitiveness concept can be unpacked further by distinguishing between the different kinds of markets or systems in which cities are in competition with each other (Gordon, 1999; Turok et al, 2003). A single all-encompassing notion or measure of competitiveness cannot reflect the diversity of city economies. The markets in which cities compete may be defined in terms of spatial scale (such as regional, national or international) or type of commodity (for example, products, services or resources such as finance or labour). The form and intensity of competition and the structure of incentives will vary between them, so the way cities gain a competitive advantage will differ too: it may be through knowledge and innovation, supply of higher quality resources, lower costs or more efficient infrastructure. Understanding these dynamics is important for local development strategies and projects to be consistent and to have a cumulative effect. As with other cities, Glasgow and Edinburgh generally compete far more in regional and national markets than internationally. For example, only 7-10% of sales by firms in key externally traded sectors in both cities are exports (Docherty et al, 2001a). There are at least five kinds of markets in which cities compete.

First, city cores have a distinct competitive advantage as *regional service centres* for retailing, leisure, entertainment and related uses. They offer economies of scale and scope, including greater diversity and choice to consumers than surrounding towns. For businesses, they offer greater market access and awareness of the behaviour of consumers and competitors, which reduces risk. A high-quality urban environment (good design, cleanliness, security, and so on) adds to the consumer experience and an efficient radial transport network connecting city cores and suburbs reinforces these advantages. Glasgow city centre performs well in these respects, together with its complementary cultural attractions (for example, modern cinemas, nightclubs, museums, art galleries and architectural heritage) and higher education institutions drawing people into the area (Turok and Bailey, 2004a: forthcoming). It has reinforced its position as the second largest retail centre in the UK by adding a million square feet of floor space, attracting specialist retailers to the region, developing distinctive bars and restaurants and investing heavily in urban design and the public realm. It has a very large regional catchment for comparison shopping and even manages to attract customers from other Northern British cities through concerted marketing of city breaks, although the net increase in Glasgow's retail and related employment has been surprisingly modest in recent years. Retail development in Edinburgh has had less of a city-centre focus because of various developments permitted around the perimeter of the city, arguably to the detriment of the centre. Disadvantages of city cores for regional service functions include increased congestion, parking difficulties, higher property costs and, for some business sectors, competition for customers and labour.

Second, cities compete indirectly for *nationally and internationally traded products and services* through the cost and quality of local resources, knowledge and business infrastructure. Sectors producing externally traded goods and services tend to be the fundamental drivers of urban performance since they generate additional income for the city to offset imported goods and services and government transfers. The business survey confirmed the importance of straightforward agglomeration economies (Marshall, 1920; Gordon and McCann, 2000), including access to shared transport infrastructure, external connectivity (for access to wider markets, suppliers and collaborators) and a large labour pool (Docherty et al, 2001a). General assets such as an effective supply of land and property were also significant. Yet, these inherent advantages of cities cannot be taken for granted. They are fragile and can be offset by higher costs, greater congestion and in some cases inferior quality and poorer access to the motorway network and airports compared with outlying areas and smaller towns.

Glasgow has sought to create the conditions for a new economic base in traded services to replace traditional industries (Turok and Bailey, 2004a: forthcoming). The first phase of call centres and 'back-office' activities attracted to the city represented relatively low-value products. Glasgow's main advantage here lay in its modest costs and ready availability of spare buildings and labour, especially in the context of the upturn in the economic cycle and constrained labour and property markets elsewhere in the UK. Other activities are higher value and may prove more durable in the long term, including certain software activities, more sophisticated call centres and creative industries, where Glasgow's advantage includes the availability of qualified graduates, technical expertise and the presence of key institutions. Over the last decade, Edinburgh and Glasgow have experienced the fastest rates of growth in financial services of all British cities (Bailey and French, 2004: forthcoming). This has had some spin-offs for local software firms and call centres. Edinburgh is probably the stronger of the two in qualitative terms, with major headquarters of international banks, life assurance companies and fund managers. This is attributable in part to historical accident and individual business successes giving it critical mass and a supply of skilled labour and entrepreneurs. The quality of fixed urban assets and property schemes initiated by the City Council at Edinburgh Park and the Exchange District have also facilitated growth, although the future may be less secure should labour shortages and congestion worsen. Glasgow is planning a major new international financial district at the Broomielaw to encourage further growth.

A third market is for *inward investment* of various kinds. An explicit responsive approach towards external opportunities is an essential attribute of a competitive location, including an ability to deliver bespoke property, financial incentives and a trained workforce reasonably quickly. For many years, Glasgow lost out to the surrounding New Towns and Enterprise Zones with their focused one-stop approach and substantial public resources to develop infrastructure, strategic sites, industrial premises and new housing. Between 1994 and 2000, Glasgow secured less than 3% of the 29,500 manufacturing jobs attracted to Scotland through inward investment (Turok and Bailey, 2004a: forthcoming). More effort has gone into competing for inward investment in office-based services and consumer services related to tourism, hospitality and leisure. Several of these sectors have dedicated marketing teams geared to promotional activities and targeted industry support. There was belated recognition of the importance of redeveloping some of Glasgow's substantial vacant and derelict land through a programme of strategic industrial sites in the late 1990s, although such efforts have been constrained by a lack of resources and institutional focus (Gibb, 2002). There are also stronger incentives (in the form of income from council taxes and sales of public land) for allocating brownfield sites to housing.

Fourth, cities may compete with outlying areas and other regions for the *skilled mobile population* in order to enhance their labour supply, replace out-migration and increase council taxes. New and refurbished housing assists in-migration by managers, professionals and other mobile workers because of its relatively simple purchase process compared with second-hand property (Bramley and Morgan, 2003). This applies to new suburban housing for families and to the increasingly popular loft apartments for young professionals seeking city-centre living close to workplaces and amenities. Glasgow has seen the biggest change in this respect with many successful conversions of redundant Victorian and Edwardian commercial buildings and warehouses to residential use, actively encouraged for the first decade or so by public bodies. With their expansion over the last decade, universities have also become increasingly important catalysts for attracting young adults from beyond the region. The proportion that stays on in the city after graduating appears to be influenced by the size and dynamism of the local jobs market (available career opportunities), as well as the quality of life and the environment. Edinburgh is a particularly successful net-importer of human capital in this respect, drawing in a much higher proportion of students from beyond the region than Glasgow and retaining more of them afterwards (Scott, 2004: forthcoming). Students also contribute to the economy of both cities through their spending power and by filling part-time jobs in bars, restaurants and call centres. Their contribution to workforce expansion appears to be particularly important in Edinburgh's tight labour market.

Fifth, city authorities compete explicitly in a range of *'episodic markets'* to host international conventions, cultural festivals, sporting fixtures and other hallmark events. They also compete for government challenge funds, lottery money and other periodic opportunities to finance major capital projects. The basis for competitive success is often unclear because of the variable rules of the game (Taylor et al, 2001). Glasgow's public agencies have a reputation for some important qualities, including basic organisational ability, entrepreneurship and imagination. This has enabled them to host a series of prominent events and to develop a range of distinctive physical attractions (Turok and Bailey, 2004a: forthcoming). Rivalry with Glasgow has prompted authorities in Edinburgh to become more opportunity-oriented, too. Effort devoted in Glasgow to discrete events and facilities has sometimes been justified as 'pacing devices' to give people a sense of achievement and to maintain morale and momentum during the long process of city regeneration. Sustaining momentum is a challenge if and when popular interest begins to diminish and maintenance proves costly to the local public purse. There is clearly a balance to be struck between developing new assets and making best use of existing ones through active marketing and management. Agencies in both cities have sought to extend and fill gaps in the calendar of events through additional festivals to improve continuity for hotels and restaurants. Capacity constraints during peaks and discontinuities at other times imply scope for greater cooperation between the cities (Turok and Bailey, 2004b: forthcoming). Collaboration could also assist the development and marketing of complementary attractions and avoid duplication.

Economic interactions

Competitiveness within one market is not necessarily independent of performance in another since interactions and spillovers may occur. Success as a regional service centre can create important visitor attractions (distinctive shops, music venues, hotels and restaurants) and encourage institutions to plan and manage city centres that support the growth of urban tourism through city breaks and international conventions. Success in securing international cultural and sporting events and winning challenge funds can alter external perceptions of cities and improve their ability to attract investment and mobile population. There is some evidence of both phenomena in Glasgow in recent years (Turok and Bailey, 2004a: forthcoming). Similarly, stronger international business linkages can reinforce tourism by improving transport services, such as direct flights to European cities. Edinburgh's growth as an international financial centre stems partly from its history as a strong financial centre serving its region. Well-established linkages also exist through income flows or multipliers. For example, success in external markets increases export demand that stimulates local consumption and strengthens the city as a regional service centre.

Economic interactions can also be negative, in the sense that poor performance in one market undermines the competitive position in another. Weakness in external product markets damages income and employment opportunities, and makes it more difficult to retain skilled population, as Glasgow's post-war history shows only too clearly. Poor performance as a regional service centre may undermine a city's image, dampen positive sentiment and hamper its ability to attract productive investment. It may prove very difficult for cities to stem and reverse a cumulative process of decline, partly because the confidence of investors and other key agents can suffer. Cities like Glasgow are also burdened with the substantial tangible costs of addressing the legacy of vacant and derelict land, outdated skills and extra needs of a poorer, more dependent population. Core city authorities lack the direct incentive and resources to promote economic growth by reinvesting in their business infrastructure because the national funding system pools local business rates and redirects a substantial share to other areas. Despite these constraints, Glasgow's economic turnaround appears to be genuine, although it is rather narrowly based and dates back only to the mid-1990s, a decade after the 'Miles Better' campaign (Turok and Bailey, 2004a: forthcoming).

Our research suggests that sustained competitiveness depends on a balance being maintained between the key variables of employment, housing, infrastructure and skills (Turok et al, 2003). This does not appear to happen sufficiently smoothly or automatically through self-adjustment by property or labour market mechanisms, nor through adaptation by the transport and education and training systems. These processes are either too slow or create problems of their own. Coordinated action on the part of local organisations ('strategic capacity') is also important, backed by the powers and resources of central government; that means actions based on a common understanding of the situation, sensitive to markets but also able to anticipate and respond to imbalances, in recognition of the wider costs. Edinburgh's economic growth risks constraint because of increasing shortfalls in the workforce, inflated house prices and traffic congestion (Turok and Bailey, 2002). There is pressure for major transport improvements, greater housing land allocation and more affordable housing to accommodate lower paid service workers squeezed out of the current market (Bramley and Morgan, 2003).

Until the mid-1990s, Glasgow's employment decline increased worklessness and encouraged out-migration, which reduced housing demand and required a substantial programme of demolition, including housing, schools, hospitals and other social infrastructure, some of which continues to this day. The recent turnaround has created a narrower range of job opportunities compared with the skills of residents, resulting in greater in-commuting from the suburbs and a smaller reduction in worklessness than might have been the case (Turok and Bailey, 2004a: forthcoming). According to the New Earnings Survey, only a quarter of full-time jobs in Glasgow are now manual, compared with a third in Britain as a whole. This is a striking transformation for what was one of Britain's pre-eminent industrial cities, causing considerable dislocation costs and social problems for the working-class population.

The coincidence between Edinburgh's constrained property and labour markets, and Glasgow's spare capacity in land, labour and infrastructure, prompts an obvious question about the relationship between the two cities. They do not appear to be functionally well-integrated at present, at least in terms of labour market interactions. Business connections are stronger and there are increasing cross-boundary housing movements and shopping patterns. There is also a range of opportunities for pursuing complementary policies and projects. Consequently there is some justification for suggesting that closer institutional collaboration within a strategic development framework focused on housing, transport and jobs would facilitate growth by helping Central Scotland to function better as an economic unit (Turok and Bailey, 2004b: forthcoming).

Within Glasgow and Edinburgh, the research identified strong links between physical assets and competitiveness, and revealed the uneven impact of land-use planning controls in current circumstances. There is considerable restriction on new housing development and far less control over certain forms of business location (Bramley et al, 2001). This is partly linked to local decision making in a competitive territorial environment, as well as pressure to contain suburban sprawl. The current fragmented and underfunded system for providing serviced land and infrastructure also fails to ensure sustainable or integrated developments, causing increased reliance on private cars, limited use of public transport and a growing dislocation between jobs and housing. Edinburgh Park is an example of how lack of prior transport planning in a new edge-of-city business park can create serious congestion.

Dimensions of social cohesion

Social cohesion is a nebulous concept and is difficult to pin down. Its popular use signifies a general concern that society is becoming more unequal and divided, which threatens the collective well-being through conflict, crime and other forms of disruption. The positive interpretation is that a cohesive society 'hangs together'; each element fits in and contributes to the general welfare though interaction and mutual obligation. To go beyond these loose ideas, it is clear that the term encompasses several distinctive issues that warrant separate consideration. Five dimensions of cohesion can be identified to assist analysis of the social processes at work and their implications for individual life-chances and the prosperity of the wider community (Kearns and Forrest, 2000; Turok et al, 2003). Although there are links between them, there are also fundamental differences and contrasts in the issues involved. A particular interest was in exploring the relationship between different aspects of social cohesion at the neighbourhood and city scales.

First, according to certain uses of the term, cohesion implies something about the level of *inequality* in society. 'Inclusion' means some degree of social solidarity and possibly redistribution to limit inequalities in income, access to jobs and other resources. Narrower social and economic disparities may give people greater security, hope for the future and better personal relationships. The extent of upward mobility is also important, since some inequality may be more acceptable if individuals have good prospects of improvement in the future. Long-term or recurrent poverty or unemployment with low expectations of progress is an important feature of *social exclusion*; that is, the opposite of inclusion. Our research on labour markets found that Glasgow has the highest level and proportion of the working-age population on sickness and disability benefits of any city authority in Britain (72,000, or 19%) (Turok and Bailey, 2004a: forthcoming). Flows onto these 'inactive' benefits have been substantial over the last two decades as a result of manufacturing job loss and discouragement. Flows off have been much weaker because of the slack labour market for most of this period, the predominantly non-manual character of the opportunities created, and disincentives in the benefit system to rejoin the workforce. Edinburgh's steady employment growth, on the other hand, and tightening labour market have been more effective at absorbing long-term unemployment and inactivity.

Glasgow has some of the largest and most severe spatial concentrations of poverty and exclusion in Britain. Our research on 'area effects' sought to examine whether living in these neighbourhoods worsens people's life-chances: can place exacerbate exclusion? A conceptual framework was developed identifying a range of potential mechanisms, including the effects of concentration, location, milieu, socialisation, physical environment and public services. Many of these were tested in the neighbourhood survey. This provided tentative evidence of selected area effects. People in poor areas have more localised social networks that may limit their knowledge of – and links into – job opportunities. They also feel disadvantaged by stigma affecting their areas. This may exacerbate their vulnerability to unemployment and inactivity. Interestingly, some of these effects were overcome by the more buoyant labour market in Edinburgh: "neighbourhoods are lifted by a wider tide of relative prosperity" (Atkinson and Kintrea, 2001, p 2293).

Second, cohesion implies something about *social connectedness*; that is, the strength of social relationships and networks. Cohesion means a high degree of social interaction within communities. This can provide social support, give people a sense of identity and promote cooperation and trust in each other and in wider authority. This idea can be applied to residential communities or communities of interest covering business or other sectional concerns. Our research found that poor neighbourhoods in fact tend to have a stronger sense of community, mutual aid and bonds between family, friends and neighbours than mixed neighbourhoods, although the pattern is not clear-cut. They also appear to have a greater sense of belonging to the area and there is solidarity among residents. The stronger social support, combined with the difficulties poor people may have in negotiating their way in a more affluent mainstream, means that being poor in a poor area is seen by some as preferable to being poor in a more affluent area (Atkinson and Kintrea, 2004: forthcoming). However, these are not all positive features since they arise partly from adversity, namely the sense of stigma that residents believe tarnishes their areas (Goodlad et al, 2001).

One converse of connectedness is segregation or isolation, in a social and/or spatial sense. Cohesion at the neighbourhood scale may coexist with segregation at the city scale. The research on area effects confirmed that relative isolation is a feature of deprived areas for many residents. Barriers to external movement include location (distance from the city centre), poverty (the cost of transport and participating in mainstream consumption), low skills (inability to engage in a labour-market seeking qualifications and credentials) and a lack of confidence. For young people, territoriality is further supported by the institution of gangs, which means it can be dangerous to stray outside one's immediate area (Atkinson and Kintrea, 2004: forthcoming).

The research on new housing found that market-led development promotes segregation rather than balanced or integrated neighbourhoods (Bramley and Morgan, 2003). There have been very few attempts by house-builders or planning authorities to introduce diversity into new suburban or central city developments, either through affordable housing, atypical house types or different social or demographic groups. Use of public subsidies to lever private development into poorer single-tenure estates has managed to introduce some middle-income households, and they appear to provide stability by remaining attached to the area. More tenure mixing in poor areas is also welcomed by most existing residents as evidence that they are "no longer at the end of the world" (Atkinson and Kintrea, 2004: forthcoming). While little social mixing appears to occur with incoming owners, there are advantages for existing residents in improvements to the area's image and environment. However, many of these local housing markets in former council estates are fragile and have not yet proved self-sustaining since new development still requires a subsidy.

Third, the concept implies certain *common values* which enable members of an urban society to support common objectives and to share moral principles and codes of behaviour through which they interact. One example would be support for, and participation in, political institutions (a 'civic culture'), rather than indifference, disaffection or exclusion. Our research on citizen participation found that only a small minority of local residents in the poorest communities actually take part in neighbourhood governance, although the majority do appear to offer tacit support for government institutions at the local, city and national levels (Docherty et al, 2001b). People in poor neighbourhoods tend to be less trustful of political institutions than people in mixed neighbourhoods (that is, they display less civic engagement and are less likely to vote in elections), but only a small minority appears to be seriously disaffected. Public authorities can engender more positive attitudes towards participation, as long as opportunities for community involvement are genuine and lead to tangible improvements in neighbourhood conditions.

Fourth, cohesion implies a degree of *social order*, or an absence of conflict, unrest and social disorder. This may reflect a pragmatic acceptance of the existing order and system on the part of some sections of urban society, rather than active citizenship. Similarly, there may be respect for difference and tolerance between groups and communities rather than positive cooperation. Unemployment and poverty in Glasgow and Edinburgh have, in fact, caused little visible conflict and unrest over the years, certainly there has been nothing like the street disturbances that occurred in some English cities. Hardship, however, has had a range of other personal and social consequences, including poor health, drug and alcohol addictions and crime (Bailey et al, 1999).

Our research in the poorest neighbourhoods found little evidence of antisocial subcultures, conflict or crime being considered acceptable by local residents (Atkinson and Kintrea, 2001). Nevertheless, some of our respondents seemed to think that the level of informal social control in poor communities had diminished over time. There is a sense that people tend to 'keep themselves to themselves' or are too afraid of retaliation to intervene in incidents of trouble. There was also a tendency among some respondents to deny that their neighbourhoods are different from anywhere else, despite the fact they suffer disproportionate crime, occasional difficulties with gangs and manifestations of disorder such as vandalism and graffiti.

Fifth, the concept of social cohesion implies some degree of *place attachment* or territorial identity. People learn certain ways of life and form identities through their experiences in particular places. Should these areas be too confined and spatial mobility limited, people can become isolated, place attachment can become introspective and parochial, and the stability and diversity of the wider society can be undermined. Our research found evidence that social networks in poor neighbourhoods are more inward-looking than in mixed neighbourhoods (Atkinson and Kintrea, 2001, 2004: forthcoming). Residents of poor areas also express a stronger sense of attachment to the neighbourhood in ways that may be puzzling to outsiders who perceive few advantages in living there. Yet, the significance of this is offset by the survey finding that residents in all areas seem to have a slightly stronger attachment to the city than the neighbourhood.

The research found connections between some dimensions of cohesion. For instance, there was evidence from the neighbourhood survey of a mutually reinforcing link between participation, trust in local institutions and effective governance (Goodlad et al, 2001). Where citizens felt their involvement made no difference to service delivery, and conditions on the ground were not improving, this seemed to create distrust, disillusionment and alienation from wider political processes. The policy implication is that resident involvement in neighbourhood decision making must be meaningful or it will damage engagement within wider communities and institutions. There was also some evidence of place attachment being associated with sectional social networks at the level of the city-region, for example among selected retired business people keen to help increase enterprise and economic development in their areas (see also discussion later in this chapter).

The research also found tensions between some aspects of cohesion. Upward social and residential mobility of households often meant weakening attachment to particular neighbourhoods and less stability for the community (Bramley and Morgan, 2003). Over time, this process could worsen social and environmental conditions in poorer areas, especially where the demand for housing was already low. The work on area effects confirmed that, for many people, getting on meant getting out. Social networks in the particular deprived areas studied had been fractured by selective out-migration of the most skilled and able. This may have contributed to low esteem and low expectations among remaining residents (Atkinson and Kintrea, 2004: forthcoming). Better housing, schools and other amenities would be needed to retain upwardly mobile households.

Links between cohesion and competitiveness

Determining the strength and direction of causality between competitiveness and cohesion is not straightforward because of the potentially multifaceted, indirect and circular nature of the relationships. In examining the pattern of economic and social change in Central Scotland over the last two decades, there is strong support, however, for a causal relationship linking economic performance to social conditions, especially through the labour market. In Glasgow, sustained deindustrialisation caused a severe loss of manual jobs, resulting in higher unemployment, inactivity and selective out-migration. Lack of work caused a decline in household incomes and greater stress within working-class communities, contributing to family breakdown, poorer educational performance, homelessness, higher mortality, increased debt, awkward neighbours, and so on (Bailey et al, 1999; Webster, 2000). Widening income inequalities have also contributed to increasing neighbourhood segregation. There is also evidence of positive economic performance contributing to improved social conditions, especially in Edinburgh's tight labour market where employers have been forced to recruit from among disadvantaged groups and where, even in the city's poorest areas, poverty seems less entrenched than Glasgow.

The research suggests that relationships in the reverse direction are weaker. There are at least two possibilities: that the existence of cohesion promotes competitiveness, and that lack of cohesion erodes competitiveness. To explore the former, we tested the concept of industrial clusters through the business survey and interviews with firms in key sectors. The theory holds that clustering of interconnected firms and related institutions make places more competitive because dense personal networks and collaborative relationships foster creativity, trust and long-term decision making. In practice, we found more evidence to support the existence of traditional agglomeration economies, whereby firms compete more than cooperate and are attracted to cities by virtue of their labour pool, shared infrastructure and amenities, and greater awareness of their market (Docherty et al, 2001a). Major publicly funded institutions such as specialised colleges, research units and broadcasters also act as urban anchors for particular kinds of activities.

There were some modest exceptions to this. For instance, we found an active network of 'business angels' (informal investors in small firms) in and around Edinburgh. Their commitment to nurturing local technology-based companies, especially in computer software, goes beyond commercial considerations. Their cooperation, and commitment of personal savings, time and technical expertise to support the start-up and growth of high-risk innovative firms stems from their attachment to the city-region and their close identification with the local scientific and business communities. Their sustained assistance has helped to produce several successful companies.

In the film and television industry, several aspects of cohesion have economic effects (Turok, 2003). Strong images of Scotland have provided rich material for successful film narratives with some spin-offs for production, distribution and tourism. They range from traditional 'kailyard' representation of cohesive communities on the rural periphery, to more contemporary images of social disorder and exclusion in urban Scotland, including human despair, drugs, gangs and heavy drinking. There is understandable debate within the industry about the real economic and cultural value of these images. The fragmented structure of the industry also relies to a greater extent than most on social networks among actors, producers, technicians and intermediaries to exchange ideas and coordinate projects. Yet, localised networks are not the driving force; rather, external connections and key institutions such as the BBC are much more important. The shared amenities and infrastructure found in a major city like Glasgow also play a part.

In financial services, there was evidence of fairly high levels of networking between actors, but this did not seem particularly important for business competitiveness (Bailey and French, 2004: forthcoming). Most financial services firms are large, often with external ownership ties, and they operate in national or international markets. Connections to the local milieu seem less important than for sectors dominated by smaller firms. There are some positive examples where collective action has emerged from a sense of common interest to benefit economic development. The best example is the effort of fund management firms to maintain the sector's critical mass or to tackle recruitment problems in investment administration. Strong local networks are thought to be a disadvantage if they make the sector inward-looking and discourage incomers.

On the other hand, there are several ways in which a lack of cohesion may erode competitiveness. Government policy suggests that social exclusion in the form of long-term unemployment limits the potential workforce and thereby inflates wage costs and constrains economic expansion. Our evidence questioned the significance of this, bearing in mind the spatial and skills mismatch between the tight local labour markets and the areas and groups vulnerable to high worklessness. The availability and cost of labour emerged as growth constraints in the business survey, and about a third of firms reported unfilled vacancies and recruitment difficulties (especially in Edinburgh). However, these were predominantly for skilled and intermediate posts requiring formal qualifications. Only one in eight firms reported any loss of orders or trade as a result of not being able to fill them. Most companies coped by asking existing staff to work overtime and/or accepting slight inefficiency (Docherty et al, 2001a).

It is also possible that disaffection and crime may damage the image of a place and reduce its attractiveness as somewhere to move to, visit or invest in. Thresholds seem important, and this effect is likely to be stronger at the small area scale than at city level, and therefore less damaging to the urban economy as it affects where *within* the city resources are located, not whether they come to the city at all. The physical distance between the most deprived, peripheral housing estates and the city centres probably limits adverse spillover effects on the image of the latter as places to do business or visit. Yet, pedestrian security and area reputation are ongoing concerns of commercial interests within the city centres, partly as a result of homelessness, begging, litter and graffiti. Of course, antisocial behaviour exists across all social classes. Measures have been taken to manage the issue through street wardens and surveillance cameras. Adverse publicity has been limited to date and does not appear to deter many visitors, shoppers or investors, as should be apparent from the strong growth in city-centre commercial investment. Crime and disorder may divert a small amount of energy and resources of city authorities away from directly economic concerns, but policing is funded centrally through a dedicated budget that would not be available for other purposes. The point applies even more so to the main costs of poverty and exclusion in national welfare and health programmes. The financial burden is borne centrally, so is no particular constraint on the local economy. Indeed the expenditure contributes to local consumer demand. The many rules and restrictions governing welfare spending are a source of frustration to cash-strapped local organisations seeking a better solution to inactivity and hardship, through social economy projects, for example, supported work experience or more substantial training schemes to develop advanced skills (Turok et al, 2003).

Another possible mechanism involves administrative boundaries undermining the territorial identity, functional integration and overall cohesion of a city. This could weaken its economic position by promoting unproductive competition for resources, population and jobs between core and surrounding authorities. Such divisions make it more difficult for areas to recognise their interdependence and complementary roles (for example, as employment centres or dormitory suburbs), and inhibit strategic planning and decision making across the functional city-region. There may be unnecessary duplication of facilities and fragmentation of services, and additional costs involved in coordination. In the case of Glasgow, achieving closer cooperation between three local authorities and three local enterprise companies is an issue for the coherent regeneration of the River Clyde Corridor. The metropolitan core also experiences higher costs from providing environmental services for people travelling in from surrounding areas to work, shop or socialise. There is evidence of this in both cities, particularly in Glasgow where the city boundary is tightly drawn (Bailey et al, 1999).

There are some relationships with unclear outcomes that are likely to depend on the specific circumstances of each situation and the timescale considered. For instance, new suburban housing seems to have made a particular contribution to Edinburgh's competitiveness by providing ready access to quality accommodation for skilled mobile labour. However, it may undermine the city's longer-term economic position by adding to the road traffic and worsening congestion. It has also increased social segregation and reduced cohesion in that respect. Urban policy-makers and planners are familiar with the difficulties involved in balancing these sorts of economic, social and environmental considerations.

Conclusion and policy implications

The study's conclusion is that there is no simple, direct or all-encompassing relationship between cohesion and competitiveness *at the level of the city*. The two do not necessarily go together, particularly in the direction from cohesion to prosperity. Economic success supports some forms of cohesion (particularly inclusion/equality and social order/stability) provided it is broad-based enough to create a sufficient range and quality of job opportunities suitable for the resident population. Narrowly focused economic growth that excludes part of the population from improvements in economic well-being may well undermine cohesion by increasing social disparities, stress and insecurity, with detrimental consequences for average health conditions, violent crime and the overall quality of life.

Social cohesion does not seem fundamental to economic growth in the short term. At least the lack of cohesion in these cities across various dimensions does not appear strong enough to have threatened their recent economic performance in ways that are easily detected. There are some positive and negative links between specific aspects of both phenomena in particular circumstances, but there do not seem to be strong, systematic or generalised causal connections from the various forms of cohesion to economic success. It is in this sense that we have referred to Edinburgh and Glasgow as 'twin track' cities (Turok et al, 2003). In addition, cities are not closed systems. There are many external forces that impact on both cohesion and competitiveness. These include national and international economic relationships and business connections, since cities are relatively open economies exposed to many wider influences. They also include the role of central government in protecting cities and their residents from more extreme social inequalities and cumulative processes of decline that might otherwise arise from economic shifts and systematic disparities in the quantity and quality of economic resources between areas. This occurs through universal systems of social protection, public sector employment, urban and regional policies and other measures involving a degree of redistribution and counter-cyclical support. It is important that the capacity of government in Westminster to pursue these fundamental roles is not diminished as decentralisation and devolution are pursued.

One implication for policy of the relative independence of cohesion and competitiveness is that local and central governments need to promote both, and for somewhat different reasons. They cannot rely on a trickle-down approach involving growth of any kind to deliver jobs and higher living standards for all. The current fashion for enhancing social capital is not in itself a reliable route to prosperity for neighbourhoods and cities. Broadening and expanding the economic base of cities is fundamental to provide sustainable jobs and incomes for a higher proportion of residents and to generate the resources to fund public services. Policies to reduce poverty, hardship and inequality directly are important to improve people's quality of life, particularly for those who are too young, too old or too sick to work, or who may be outside the labour market for other reasons such as bringing up children. They should not need to be justified on the grounds that they support economic growth somehow.

There are complicated choices to be made about what degree and forms of social justice to pursue, and what kinds of economic development to prioritise. There are also certain policies that can help to link the goals of cohesion and competitiveness, and generate gains all-round. The best example is probably employment creation and associated measures to bring inactive people of working age into the workforce, given the wide-ranging economic and social benefits that flow to individuals and the wider community from having a higher employment rate. Local economic strategies should promote industrial diversity and balance, rather than narrow specialisation on, say, knowledge-intensive services, in order to reflect the broad assets of cities, and the need for a wide range of job opportunities in view of the diverse social structure and skills of the population.

Finally, the research generally found physical assets to be an important but somewhat neglected influence on city competitiveness. The availability of an effective supply of land and premises (for economic *and* residential uses), the quality of the surrounding environment and public realm, and the state of the transport system (roads, rail *and* air services) tend to frustrate economic development in cities to a greater extent than elsewhere. Their infrastructure is generally older and more congested, the pattern of land ownership is more complex and fragmented, and redevelopment tends to be a more complicated and conflicting process because of the diverse interests and stakeholders involved. This is another important message for national and local policy after a long period during which investment in physical infrastructure, derelict land and public transport services has tended to be downplayed in relation to other, 'softer' issues.

References

Atkinson, R. and Kintrea, K. (2001) 'Disentangling area effects: evidence from deprived and non-deprived neighbourhoods', *Urban Studies*, vol 38, no 12, pp 2277-98.

Atkinson, R. and Kintrea, K. (2004: forthcoming) '"Opportunities and despair, it's all in there": practitioner experiences and explanations of area effects and life chances', *Sociology*, vol 38, no 3.

Bailey, N., Docherty, I. and Turok, I. (2002) 'Dimensions of city competitiveness: Edinburgh and Glasgow in a UK context', in I. Begg (ed) *Urban competitiveness: Policies for dynamic cities*, Bristol: Policy Press, pp 135-59.

Bailey, N. and French, S. (2004: forthcoming) 'Cities and financial services', in N. Buck et al (eds) *Changing cities*, Basingstoke: Palgrave.

Bailey, N., Turok, I. and Docherty, I. (1999) *Edinburgh and Glasgow: Contrasts in competitiveness and cohesion*, Glasgow: Department of Urban Studies, University of Glasgow.

Begg, I. (1999) 'Cities and competitiveness', *Urban Studies*, vol 36, no 5/6, pp 795-809.

Blair, T. and Schroder, G. (1999) 'Europe: the Third Way', reprinted in *The Spokesman*, vol 66, pp 26-37.

Bramley, G., Kirk, K., Morgan, J. and Russell, J. (2001) 'Planning Central Scotland: the role of infrastructure, urban form and new development in promoting competitiveness and cohesion', *Policy Paper 2*, Scottish Executive, Glasgow: Department of Urban Studies, University of Glasgow.

Bramley, G. and Morgan, J. (2003) 'Building competitiveness and cohesion: the role of new housing in central Scotland's cities', *Housing Studies*, vol 18, no 4, pp 447-71.

Castells, M. (1996) *The rise of the network society*, Oxford: Blackwell.

Commission on Social Justice (1994) *Social justice: Strategies for national renewal*, London: Vintage.

Docherty, I., Bailey, N. and Turok, I. (2001a) *Central Scotland business survey: Preliminary report*. mimeo, available from the authors on request.

Docherty, I., Goodlad, R. and Paddison, R. (2001b) 'Civic culture, community and citizen participation in contrasting neighbourhoods', *Urban Studies*, vol 38, no 12, pp 2225-50.

Gibb, K. (2002) 'Land, property and economic competitiveness in Central Scotland', *Policy Paper 5*, Scottish Executive, Glasgow: Department of Urban Studies, University of Glasgow.

Giddens, A. (2000) *The Third Way and its critics*, Cambridge: Polity Press.

Goodlad, R., Docherty, I. and Paddison, R. (2001) 'Citizen participation in urban governance', *Policy Paper 4*, Scottish Executive, Glasgow: Department of Urban Studies, University of Glasgow.

Gordon, I. (1999) 'Internationalisation and urban competition', *Urban Studies*, vol 36, pp 1001-16.

Gordon, I. and McCann, P. (2000) 'Industrial clusters: complexes, agglomeration and/or social networks?', *Urban Studies*, vol 37, no 3, pp 513-32.

HM Treasury (2001) *Productivity in the UK. 3 – The regional dimension*, London: HM Treasury.

Kearns, A. and Forrest, R. (2000) 'Social cohesion and multi-level urban governance', *Urban Studies*, vol 37, pp 995-1017.

Krugman, P. (1996) 'Making sense of the competitiveness debate', *Oxford Review of Economic Policy*, vol 12, no 3, pp 17-25.

Marshall, A. (1920) *Principles of economics* (8th edn), London: Macmillan.

OECD (2001) *Devolution and globalisation: Implications for local decision-makers*, Paris: OECD.

Scott, A. (2004: forthcoming) 'Graduate retention in cities and regional development', PhD Thesis, University of Glasgow.

Taylor, P., Turok, I. and Hastings, A. (2001) 'Competitive bidding in urban regeneration: Stimulus or disillusionment for the losers?', *Environment and Planning C: Government and Policy*, vol 19, pp 45-63.

Turok, I. (1999) 'Urban labour markets: the causes and consequences of change', *Urban Studies*, vol 36, no 5/6, pp 893-915.

Turok, I. (2003) 'Cities, clusters and creative industries: the case of film and TV in Scotland', *European Planning Studies*, vol 11, no 5, pp 549-65.

Turok, I. and Bailey, N. (2002) 'A development strategy for Central Scotland?', *Scottish Affairs*, vol 39, pp 57-81.

Turok, I. and Bailey, N. (2004a: forthcoming) 'Glasgow in the 1990s: divided growth and its consequences', *Urban Studies*.

Turok, I. and Bailey, N. (2004b: forthcoming) 'The theory of polycentric urban regions and its application to Central Scotland', *European Planning Studies*.

Turok, I., Bailey, N., Atkinson, R., Bramley, G., Docherty, I., Gibb, K., Goodlad, R., Hastings, A., Kintrea, K., Kirk,. K., Leibovitz, J., Lever, B., Morgan, J., Paddison, R. and Sterling, R. (2003) *Twin track cities: Linking prosperity and cohesion in Glasgow and Edinburgh*, Glasgow: Department of Urban Studies, University of Glasgow.

Webster, D. (2000) 'Scottish social inclusion policy: a critical assessment', *Scottish Affairs*, vol 30, pp 30-50.

THREE

Reinventing cities in a restructuring region? The rhetoric and reality of renaissance in Liverpool and Manchester

Alan Harding, Iain Deas, Richard Evans and Stuart Wilks-Heeg

Governing urban change in England's North West

The cities of Manchester and Liverpool in England's North-West region have historically had a symbiotic, if fractious, relationship with each other that was critical to the UK's early industrial ascendancy. Manchester was the key manufacturing centre, and Liverpool was the distributive hub providing a crucial link with the (colonial) trading world. By the closing decades of the 20th century, both were beset by the precipitous decline in 'traditional' industries that was typical of UK cities in crisis (Turok and Edge, 1999). In both cities, new political leaderships elected during the mid-1980s followed a course of practical and symbolic opposition to virtually every attempt by a Conservative national government to tackle its understanding of 'the British disease' (Parkinson, 1985; Harding, 2000). And yet, by the end of the 20th century, Liverpool and Manchester were popularly seen as divergent in both their development trajectories and the manner in which they were managed. On the one hand was Manchester, a now 'pragmatic' but still Labour-dominated city that has been seen as a paragon of renaissance and policy innovation by successive Conservative and Labour national administrations and which feels justified in proclaiming itself the de facto regional capital. On the other was Liverpool, a city that struggled to overcome the legacy of the militant-led, Trotskyite-influenced Labour administration of the mid-1980s and was beset by political indecision and lack of strategic direction. Arguably, as a result, it lost ground to its regional neighbour 30 miles along the M62 motorway.

The core objective of the Liverpool-Manchester Integrated Case Study (LMICS) was to assess the extent to which the effectiveness (or otherwise) of the structures and processes of urban governance had an independent impact, over time, upon the economic, social and environmental fortunes of the North West's two principle metropolitan areas. While the study team remained resolutely sceptical about the anthropomorphic and heroic theory of history, which has it that cities can 'pull themselves up by their own bootstraps', this line of enquiry was useful in setting the context for the study. This was the case, not least, because the conventional wisdom about the development trajectories of the two cities over the last two decades strongly suggests that 'governance makes a difference'.

The historic similarities of the two cities and the extent of recent divergence are, of course, overdrawn for the purposes of argument. This stark conventional wisdom nonetheless provided useful hypotheses for the LMICS team to test. The team's findings on the cities' alleged convergence then divergence are the main subject of this chapter. Two dangers of contrasting Liverpool and Manchester in this way, however, need to be noted. First, and most important, irrespective of any differences that governance might make, there are clearly many similarities that have made the promotion of urban renaissance as challenging, in Liverpool and Manchester, as it has been anywhere in the country. This has reflected the historic dominance of declining sectors and the location of the two cities within an underperforming region. The study team attempted to clarify the degree of difficulty that faced key decision makers in and for the two cities and city-regions by placing these particular urban areas in the context of broad changes within the key English metropolitan areas. Second, while the project focused primarily on governance within the two central cities, it is clear that the economic and social changes they experienced are intimately interconnected to those taking place within wider, city-regional employment and housing markets. These more localised, contextual factors were recognised in both the quantitative and qualitative research.

The remaining sections of this chapter pose three broad questions, each related to hypotheses emerging from the received wisdom. The first asks: how significant was (or has been) the alleged convergence, followed by divergence, between the two cities/metropolitan areas? It also explores whether or not recent patterns of change accord with the idea that there was a transformation in the effectiveness of governance in Manchester from the late 1980s onward but not in Liverpool. The second seeks to clarify how governance made a difference in the thematic areas covered by project case studies. The final section of this chapter distinguishes between rhetoric and reality in the 'convergence–divergence' thesis and summarises the extent to which differences in urban governance have contributed to the 'real' contrast between the two cities.

The nature of change: competitiveness and cohesion

Conventional readings of the recent fortunes of the cities suggest a breakpoint in the late 1980s. Apparent convergence, based upon common experiences of large-scale economic restructuring and the social problems that inevitably accompany it, gave way to increasing divergence as Manchester adapted more swiftly and effectively to the demands of an evolving 'information economy'

(Castells, 1989, 1996). Evidence from the LMICS, however, shows that degrees of convergence and divergence are indeed both overstated. Beginning with overall employment figures, the period 1971-96 witnessed steep employment decline in both cities and metropolitan areas but of an emphatically greater order in Merseyside. While crude job numbers fell by 12% in Greater Manchester and by 30% in the core Manchester local authority area during that period, the parallel figures for Merseyside and Liverpool were a massive 35% and 53% (Figure 3.1).

When the figures for the core cities are taken out of the equation, employment in the rest of Greater Manchester grew by around 2.5% in the period compared to an increase of 0.5% in the rest of Merseyside. At this level of generality, then, the picture is of differentially declining central cities located within sub-regions that benefited only to a limited extent – and far less than the UK's most successful urban areas – from alternative location choices by employers. Even if 1971-96 trends are broken down into smaller time periods (1971-81, 1981-91, 1991-96), the picture is still one in which continued central-city employment decline, while it slowed over time, was more pronounced in Liverpool than in Manchester. The one notable difference that shows up in the last of these periods is at the metropolitan scale where it appears that Liverpool's decline continued to be a bigger 'drag factor' on Merseyside's performance than was Manchester's within Greater Manchester. Indeed, during the 1990s, Manchester was one of only two of the ten relevant metropolitan districts that lost employment within a sub-region where overall employment growth began to match the national average. While suggestive of recently divergent *metropolitan* fortunes, however, this observation offers no evidence of differential rates of renaissance within the core cities.

Figure 3.1: Employment change in Greater Manchester, Manchester, Merseyside and Liverpool (1971-96)

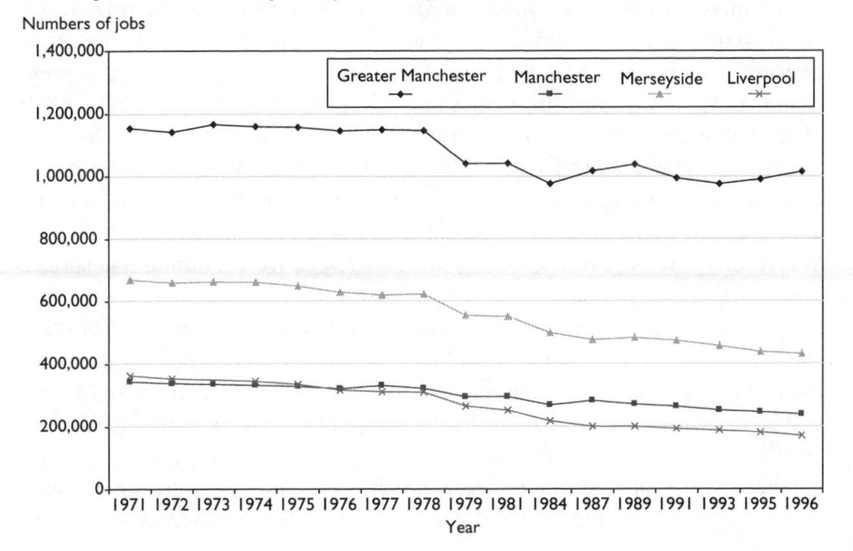

Crude employment change figures, however, tell only part of the story. On the one hand, they hide a more complex underlying picture of sectoral employment losses *and gains*, thereby underplaying positive trends in areas that were centres of declining economic activity while magnifying their importance in areas where 'traditional' employment had previously been less densely concentrated. On the other hand, particularly when they are based upon arbitrary administrative districts that lack any economic rationale, they fail to appreciate linkages across districts within the metropolitan area. Once these two factors are taken into consideration, the picture becomes significantly more positive for both conurbation cores, but particularly for Manchester.

The Liverpool-Manchester Vision Study (Charles, 2001; DTZ Pieda Consulting, 2001; Wilks-Heeg, 2001; Wong et al, 2001), led by LMICS team members after the 'Cities' project concluded, focused in more detail upon the sectoral components of employment change and the way their spatial implications were felt within and between Greater Manchester and Merseyside. Its analysis of trends in key national growth sectors in particular (financial and business services, creative and cultural industries, new media and ICTs, sports, tourism and life sciences) illustrated the two core cities' growing importance within sub-regional and regional economies while also demonstrating Manchester's stronger performance. The Vision Study showed that, in 1998, 31% of employment in Manchester's regional centre – the central city together with contiguous growth areas in Salford and Trafford – was in these high-value, knowledge-intensive industries, compared to 19% in the rest of Greater Manchester, 21% in the North West of England and 26% in the country as a whole. The parallel figure for the city of Liverpool (27%) was closer to the national average but still significantly above that of the region and the rest of Merseyside (17%).

Together, the two conurbations accounted for 79% of all employment growth within these sectors in the North West in 1991-98, new jobs being particularly concentrated in and around the two city centres and close to their respective airports. It is because of such trends that a subsequent study of employment change in English conurbation cores between 1995 and 1999 (Hutchins, 2002) identified growth rates in Liverpool (10.4%) and Manchester (8.5%) that compare favourably with Bristol (9.8%) and Leeds (8.2%); that is, cities that are more usually considered economically dynamic. For the most part, sectoral developments in the two cities proceeded in parallel and were complementary. Where there was significant overlap in their respective economic specialisms, however, the evidence suggests that Manchester had become the more strongly favoured location. Corporate rationalisation in banking, insurance, accounting and legal services, for example, benefited Manchester at Liverpool's expense to the extent that employment in financial and business services increased by 8% in Manchester between 1991 and 1999 but fell by 1% in Liverpool (Charles, 2001).

Finer-grained analysis, then, suggests that each core city increasingly acted as the motor for sub-regional and regional growth in key 'knowledge' sectors, but that Manchester maintained a competitive edge over its regional neighbour, Liverpool. Just as these trends had different geographical employment implications for areas within and beyond the central city boundaries, however, so the benefits that flowed from them for different urban social groups also varied substantially. The uneven way in which the costs of decline and the benefits of growth were shared among city residents is underlined by demographic and housing trends. In tandem with city-centre employment growth, both cities witnessed a remarkable fourfold increase in the number of city-centre residents during the 1990s, facilitated by the conversion of warehouses, selective new build programmes and a growing preference – largely among professional, childless households – for more 'urban' lifestyles. While similar trends occurred elsewhere, the rate of growth in Liverpool and Manchester exceeded that of other English core cities (DTZ Pieda Consulting, 1998; Chesterton, 1999).

Despite the increased attractiveness of urban living for some of the more privileged beneficiaries of economic renaissance, however, headline results from the 2001 Census indicate that the two central cities, overall, continued to lose population at comparatively heavy rates between 1991 and 2001. The fact that evidence of selective economic renaissance and booming niche housing markets can exist alongside problems in the overall attractiveness of the two cities as places to live reflects falling demand for the least-desired housing stock in the two conurbations. This includes social rented housing and poorer quality pre-First World War and interwar private terraces which are disproportionately concentrated within the core city areas. While the boom in city-centre living caused the average price of central Liverpool and Manchester homes to rise to over £100,000 by 2000, property values elsewhere in the urban core areas stagnated (Robson et al, 2000) or even collapsed (Nevin et al, 2001) during the 1990s as swathes of previously popular housing were abandoned.

These housing market developments suggest that improvements in urban economic competitiveness have not translated straightforwardly into reduced levels of social exclusion in contemporary Liverpool and Manchester. Despite the positive trends noted earlier in this chapter, there is still a tendency for better-off family households, in particular, given the premium they attach to reasonably spacious accommodation, good schooling and safe, attractive local environments, to either desert the central cities or not to move within their boundaries in the first place. In the process, the least affluent and mobile residents are left behind in what have become increasingly divided central cities. Two-thirds of the 30 most-deprived wards in the Index of Multiple Deprivation for England (DETR, 2000) are still found in Merseyside or Greater Manchester, particularly in north Liverpool and east-central Manchester.

In line with Sassen's (1992) argument in respect of 'global cities', polarisation between households on the highest and lowest incomes has actually grown rather than shrunk in Liverpool and Manchester as economic performance has improved. Ignoring the fact that there is substantial 'leakage' of economic benefits caused by cross-district commuters accessing many of the more lucrative 'knowledge economy' jobs, average weekly wages are above the national average in Manchester. The fact remains, however, that as recently as 2001, 14% of Manchester residents (that is, double the national average, in fact) were in receipt of income support (DTZ Pieda Consulting, 2001). Equally, growth in professional employment has helped increase the proportion of Manchester residents qualified to degree level to 23% (2% higher than the national average), and yet 26% lack any qualifications (compared to 19% nationally).

There is even evidence to suggest that problems related to social exclusion are, if anything, more pronounced in Manchester than they are in 'less competitive' Liverpool. Seventy-nine per cent of Manchester residents, for example, live in wards ranked among the 10% most deprived in England, compared to 72% in Liverpool (Robson et al, 2000). Levels of recorded crime are also higher in Manchester, and educational attainment levels lower. Crimes per capita against property, in particular, are nearly 40% higher in Manchester than they are in Liverpool, and only 31% of Manchester secondary school children achieved five or more GCSEs in 2001, compared to 35% in Liverpool and 50% nationally.

Does governance matter?

The analysis thus far has been useful in reassessing the 'convergence–divergence' narrative. However, it has said little about whether, and how, the governance of the two cities made any difference to the more nuanced picture it described. As part of the LMICS, the study team modelled the relationship between 'competitive assets' and 'competitive outcomes' in a sample of major English core cities and metropolitan areas in order to put the two case study locations into perspective (Deas and Giordano, 2001, 2002). This work operationalised a conceptual schema (Figure 3.2) that indicated the role that governance, in principle, might play in improving competitive outcomes. Predictably, this element of the research identified a clear association between the respective strengths of asset bases and outcomes. Thus, at the broader sub-regional scale, Merseyside's relatively weak asset base compared to that of Greater Manchester, for example, translated straightforwardly into stronger outcomes in the latter than the former. For the core urban areas, however, the aggregate quantity and quality of local assets provided a relatively poor predictor of the competitive performance of their constituent firms. Manchester and Liverpool provided contrasting examples. While the data confirmed that both cities had reasonably similar asset bases in relation to the sample as a whole, the difference between the two is more marked in terms of outcomes. The results of a regression model (Figure 3.3) suggested that, while competitive outcomes in Liverpool were somewhat lower than might be expected in light of the city's asset base, in Manchester outcomes exceeded expectations. Indeed, Manchester was the most marked outlier in the sample; it was the city where assets were the weakest predictor of competitive outcomes.

These findings suggest that key urban assets have been mobilised more

Figure 3.2: The relationship between assets and outcomes

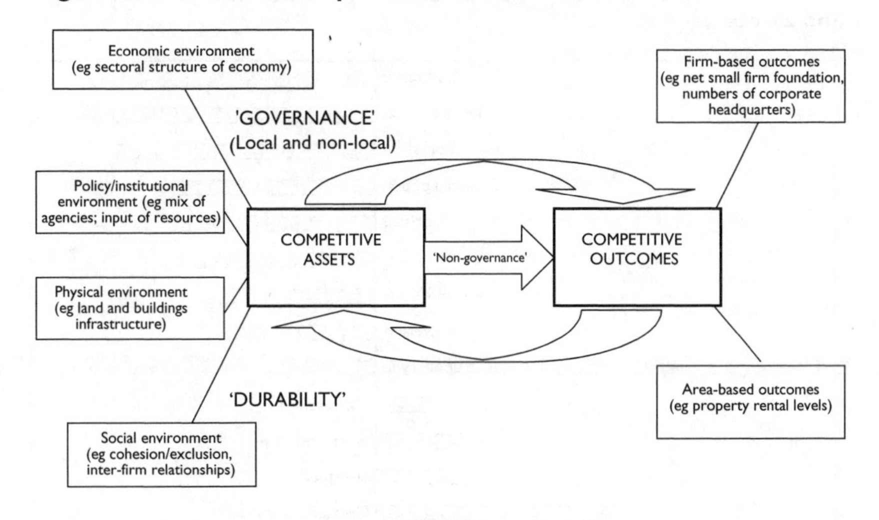

effectively in Manchester than in Liverpool. Part of the explanation of this linkage, as suggested in Figure 3.2, can be put down to market-driven feedback mechanisms, whereby improved outcomes selectively enhanced the value of assets independent of overt public sector interventions. However, some of the difference might, logically, be ascribed to processes of governance. Of course, it is one thing to argue that governance seems to make a difference; it is quite another to demonstrate how. Any effort to do so runs up against the conceptual difficulty posed by the fact that (a) public agencies are engaged in a very wide range of activities that do not impact directly upon the competitiveness of firms, but (b) almost everything the public sector does – from determining fiscal policy to organising street cleansing – has an indirect, often unplanned and even, sometimes, unintentionally discriminatory effect on the environments in which firms operate.

Local authorities in particular, given their primary role in delivering 'social consumption' services, play a very indirect role in determining competitive urban outcomes. However, they do so, through complex arrangements involving higher levels of government, other public agencies and partners in the private and voluntary sectors, across a huge range of activities. The challenge for the LMICS, therefore, was to devise manageable, and inevitably selective, research that tested the degree to which programmes and projects had been devised and implemented locally that, whether intentionally or not, promoted competitiveness and, in so doing, had an impact upon patterns of social cohesion and exclusion. This was attempted through six case studies, four of which 'worked forwards' from policy intentions to external effects while two 'worked backwards' from market outcomes to the way in which public investments and policies supported them. These studies, outlined in Table 3.1, are reported at length elsewhere (Harding, 1999a, 1999b; Wilks-Heeg et al, 1999; Evans, 2000a,

Figure 3.3: Residual values from regression of aggregate outcomes and assets

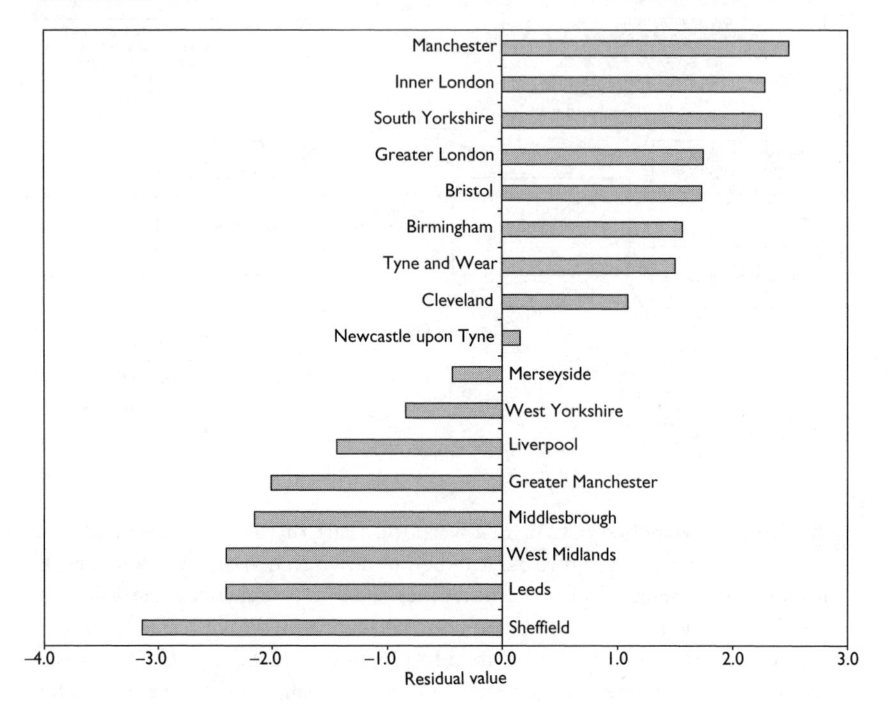

2000b, 2000c; SURF Centre, 2002). Here, there is space only to sketch out the key governance, as distinct from substantive impact, issues.

The study of Manchester International Airport and the Port of Liverpool explored the way that the resources and powers of the public sector had been harnessed to underpin the development of major infrastructure, which has played crucial roles in local economic fortunes. It found that recent commercial success in both cases stemmed more from market opportunities, managerial innovation, bargaining strength and serendipitous national and European policy change, rather than from local interventions. While the broad context within which the two operated was externally determined, however, differences in local governing arrangements clearly made the airport a more central player in city affairs.

In retrospect, Manchester is fortunate that, unlike Liverpool's, its airport was not requisitioned by the Ministry of Defence after the Second World War. That afforded the opportunity for it to develop into a major civil aviation hub as a municipal enterprise. Over time, the Greater Manchester local authorities that own the airport developed a keen appreciation of its economic value and saw it as a natural ally in efforts to develop the sub-regional economy and enhance visitor potential. The authorities' willingness to forego dividends and invest heavily – with key private partners – in airport facilities and infrastructures was critical in enabling the company to overcome public-sector borrowing restrictions and secure its place as the busiest UK airport outside London. In return for that investment (that is, the operational freedom given to company executives and constructive treatment under local planning regimes), they sought extensive community consultation and engagement in broader civic projects. This 'deal' has provided a workable balance between environmental protection and crucial airport expansion programmes. For example, it has seen the airport underwrite some of the costs of the city's Olympic bids, become a key partner in new institutional initiatives to promote tourism and inward investment in Greater Manchester and cooperate with national and metropolitan transport providers to improve public transport access to the airport.

The independent Mersey Docks and Harbour Company, by contrast, is less engaged in local development initiatives. While 7% of its recent capital spending has come from public-sector regeneration programmes, its dealings with local authorities have been more instrumentally focused on short-term operational needs. The relationship has worked well in some cases, for example in the modernisation of dock infrastructures in Bootle and the development of new ferry services. At times, however, the company's conservative approach to the sale and reuse of redundant tracts of its estate has brought it into conflict with development authorities and slowed the pace of regeneration, particularly along the city's extensive waterfront.

The strategic metropolitan frameworks project tested the extent to which 'visions' had been developed for the two cities and surrounding areas to guide key programming decisions related to competitiveness and social cohesion. The Merseyside Objective 1 (MOb1) and Manchester City Pride (MCP) programmes, while radically different, provided an opportunity for local partners to improve governance at the metropolitan scale where institutional capacity

Table 3.1: The case study framework for testing the interplay between governance, urban competitiveness and social exclusion

Case study theme	Case study	Orientation
Major infrastructures – transport gateways	Manchester airport/ Port of Liverpool	Assets
Strategic metropolitan policy frameworks and partnerships	Manchester City Pride (MCP) (inner Greater Manchester) Merseyside Objective 1 (MOb1)	Sub-regional strategy and governance
Attractiveness to external investors	Inward investment	Outcomes
Area-based regeneration programmes	Hulme City Challenge/ Moss Side SRB, Speke Garston Development Company/SRB	Local governance
Propulsive industries (two studies)	Financial services E-commerce	Market

Note: SRB = Single Regeneration Budget.

and coherence had been lacking since the abolition of the metropolitan county councils in 1986. Merseyside Objective 1 (1995-2004) initially comprised a five-year, £1.5 billion sub-regional package of government, Economic Research Development Fund (ERDF)/European Social Fund (ESF) and private funds – later extended to ten years – focusing on corporate and indigenous business development, key growth sectors, and the (then) innovative 'Pathways' programme, a mixture of counselling, guidance, training and community development initiatives for residents of Merseyside's most deprived areas (Meegan, 2003). The MCP programme (1994 onwards) developed through two strategic prospectuses, incorporating indicative projects relating to business support, asset development, marketing and promotion, area regeneration, the linkages between economic development and social need and, latterly, support programmes for the 2002 Commonwealth Games. Initially, it covered the inner metropolitan areas of Manchester, Salford and Trafford, but neighbouring Tameside was added in a second phase. Although it guaranteed no additional resources, the Conservative government that launched MCP signalled that convincing City Pride strategies could enhance subsequent attempts to secure discretionary resources.

Essentially, the programme's prospectuses were marketing rather than planning documents. Nonetheless, they provided member authorities with sufficient ammunition to procure substantial additional public and private sector resources, occasionally on an inter-authority basis, in support of a loosely interrelated set of development projects and activities focused around the 'regional centre'. Manchester City Pride partners' entrepreneurial and flexible approach contrasted with Merseyside partners' struggle, despite the greater substance and formal inter-district coherence of MOb1's delivery structures, to reach a consensus over economic development priorities. The availability of substantial resources through MOb1, paradoxically, encouraged a short-term, parochial resource procurement mentality rather than a more strategic long-term view. However, MOb1 partners devoted greater attention to social inclusion both in terms of programme participation and linking economic benefits with social need. They also gained in terms of closer engagement of higher educational institutions (HEIs) and the private sector, additional venture capital, physical infrastructure improvements and better marketing. In neither case, however, did a move towards 'metropolitan' policy machinery have a substantial independent impact upon district level approaches to regeneration, the more strategic use of mainstream resources or local capacity to envision and respond to future changes in the environment in which the partners were likely to operate.

In the case of inward investment, a similar picture emerged. Again, Merseyside arrangements had greater formal coherence, not least because MOb1 resources helped create the Mersey Partnership, an inter-district, public–private body covering all of Merseyside and charged with inward investment promotion, tourism development and public relations for the sub-region in general. Arrangements in Manchester, by contrast, split these functions across two agencies; MIDAS, covering the MCP area, and the airport-sponsored Marketing

Manchester, which covers all of Greater Manchester. Below the surface, however, intense rivalry between the district authorities remained.

This rivalry – along with differences in access to regional grants, the quality of the local 'product' (serviced sites, premises, communications, skills, attractive working and living environments) and the degree of local sophistication in working with regional inward investment bodies, the Department for Trade and Industry, private-sector mentors and overseas agents – was more decisive than any coherent metropolitan view of priorities in determining the pattern of inward investment. Such data as was available demonstrated that both metropolitan areas – and particularly Merseyside (Knowsley and, latterly, Liverpool) – were increasingly successful in attracting inward investors in the 1990s, although the figures, which tend to concentrate on industrial uses of large sites, systematically underestimate Manchester's success in attracting service-based property investment. It was only with the appearance of the Northwest Development Agency, which subsumed the pre-existing, voluntarily supported regional agency (INWARD), however, that a more selective approach on issues such as strategic sites began to emerge.

The area regeneration study focused upon two sets of wards – Hulme/Moss Side in Manchester, Speke-Garston in Liverpool – that are generally viewed as the neighbourhoods that have undergone the most radical transformation in the last decade. The study found little evidence to support the proposition that approaches adopted in Manchester were significantly more sophisticated or effective than those in Liverpool. Both programmes, indeed, were as successful as any in the country at tackling the rather different problems faced by residents and businesses in the two areas and turning them into strategic assets for the two cities. These outcomes were delivered, in both cases, through highly effective institutional arrangements that put a premium on partnership with the private sector, public agencies and voluntary sector providers and provided opportunities and support for community involvement.

These exemplary projects, however, were not easy to replicate for somewhat different reasons. The study found that the key to the success of the regeneration of Speke-Garston was the high level of autonomy achieved by the key delivery agencies active in the area and their ability to pioneer new ways of working in the face of (and despite occasional overt hostility within) what was then a less innovative and more ponderous city council. In Manchester, despite the ostensible similarity in 'arm's-length' delivery arrangements, the reverse was true; it was the very high level of engagement of senior council members and a core of particularly proactive council officers that drove the regeneration programmes. While neither approach could easily be sustained politically in the longer term, the evidence at the time of the study suggested that the lessons of Hulme/Moss Side were being applied effectively on a much larger scale in east Manchester whereas the shift of focus to the city centre in Liverpool presented challenges that seemed set to take a long time to address.

The last two case studies attempted to understand the extent to which public services, policies and investments helped underpin the development of two key strands of the 'new' urban economy – financial services and e-commerce. Here, it was clear that like was not being compared with like. Manchester is indisputably the region's leading finance centre, containing most of the major banks, accountancy and law firms; Liverpool's specialisms, on the other hand, are in niche areas such as private fund management and legal support services for the insurance industry. Similarly, Manchester contains the major information and communication technologies (ICT), multimedia and music technology companies and others offering facilities management (for example, TeleCity) and secure hosting services (XTML). Liverpool's ICT strengths are in niche markets such as computer games, boutique software, graphics, multimedia, fulfilment and logistics; but the city contains few firms providing business-orientated internet services.

The study found that market factors and changes in national regulatory regimes had been more important to firms in these sectors than more localised factors. That said, the reconstruction of Manchester city centre after the IRA bombing in 1996, paradoxically, helped trigger the development of 'off-centre' production spaces for new and relatively risky arts, multimedia and independent IT ventures and the consumption outlets – bars, cafes, restaurants, and so on – that appeal to their staff. In the medium term, it also facilitated the development of a more attractive environment for the mainstream financial services industry. Manchester's HEIs, with a combined student population of 80,000, along with the city's reputation as a centre for youth culture, also generate a ready supply of young people who are keen to remain in the city in sectors that are able to provide rewarding and/or attractive work. Similar sorts of processes have been at play in Liverpool, which, like Manchester, was a centre for the early development of new telecommunications infrastructures. The greater density of career options in Manchester, however, means it has retained an edge in terms of business support services and networks and the quality and quantity of graduates it can retain. Its ICT training infrastructure is more highly regarded than Liverpool's and its regeneration bodies have generally catered more for the special property and other requirements of e-commerce businesses in particular.

Two cheers for effective governance

To recap, the 'headline' evidence from the study showed that there had been no simple convergence in the development trajectories of the two cities in the period leading up to the 1990s. The degree of difficulty in promoting the renaissance of Liverpool, even in the more promising economic context of the 1990s, continued to be greater than it was in Manchester. Neither was there consistent case-study evidence that Manchester City Council was significantly more visionary, on the surface, than its counterpart in Liverpool during this later period. In certain respects, indeed, it was simply more fortunate. Nor had the benefits of any recent contrasts in economic performance resulted in significant differences between the two core cities when it came to the incidence and severity of social exclusion. Improved competitiveness clearly had a positive impact in higher value property markets in both cities. The evidence suggests, however, that high concentrations of lower-value private and social rented housing in the two core cities continued to encourage the leakage of benefits to residents elsewhere in the metropolitan area (and beyond) and to limit the direct value that Manchester, in particular, derived from urban economic renaissance. In all these respects, the evidence for recent divergence based on the differential effectiveness of governance was more limited than the conventional wisdom suggests.

That said, however, more subtle differences are apparent in Manchester's ability to trade upon what initially were real but comparatively marginal advantages. The council used these to construct better quality relationships of trust and credibility with stakeholders beyond the local authority, which, through a number of essentially opportunistic projects, cumulatively demonstrated a better capacity to deliver. As a result, the level of external confidence in the city rose over time, resulting in greater ambition within the council and a greater preparedness on the part of private investors – once markets had been demonstrated and economic conditions improved – to take risks on projects that were able to rely less upon public funding. The fruits of these advantages are visible in a series of developments that have added to Manchester's attractiveness to residents, 'users' and investors – the country's first modern tram system, a booming airport, a more buoyant retail environment within and beyond a reconstructed city centre, new sporting facilities and a broader range of facilities supporting visitor and night-time economies.

From the case study evidence, it is possible to identify three main factors that distinguish the governance of urban change in Manchester from that in Liverpool, in these more subtle respects, from the late 1980s.

Stability in local political and executive leadership

Manchester remains a Labour-dominated city wherein effective party political opposition is minimal and there is strong continuity and internal discipline within the Labour group. Manchester City Council has had just two leaders in the period since 1984, both of whom quickly realised the limitations of any development strategy that could not trigger external support within public and private sectors. During this crucial period, they oversaw an administrative elite in which key, long-serving officers who 'cut their teeth' on complex regeneration issues came to occupy leading positions. Liverpool City Council, by contrast, 'lost' an entire Labour leadership in the mid-1980s and was politically divided for most of the subsequent period because there was either no overall party control or there was such tension between official and unofficial Labour and/or left-of-centre councillors that no stable majority could be constructed. Only towards the end of the study period – in a development outsiders find surprising but is perfectly consistent with Liverpool's fluctuating party political history and voter frustration at the preceding period of drift and indecision –

did the Liberal Democrats win a workable majority within the council and begin, with a new chief executive, to radically restructure the executive. Before that, five Labour leaders had come and gone in a period in which the post of chief executive at one point remained unfilled for two years, so poor had the council's reputation become in the professional local government community.

As ratepayers in other municipal 'one-party states' have found to their cost, no automatic benefit accrues from stable local leadership. What stability meant in Manchester's case, however, was that at a particularly critical juncture in the city's history, the municipal leadership was able to take a longer term, tactical view of its position and needs and, insofar as the council's powers and resources allowed, to follow it through, confident that it could bear any electoral cost. Councillors in Liverpool in that period, by contrast, could never plan with any certainty beyond a single electoral cycle and were much more likely to see their ability to deliver short-term 'spoils' for their particular wards (or service departments) as central to their political career prospects. As a result, the energies of Liverpool's executive leadership were more often turned inward and focused more narrowly upon things they could control rather than how they could use their resources to influence others.

Manchester's superior capacity to generate and pursue 'the big idea'

The council's biggest idea – to stage the Olympic Games in the city – was, paradoxically, the failure upon which much of its subsequent success rested. Manchester's two Olympic Games bids are emblematic of a change in the council's approach from one that focused upon how to stem decline through the use of locally-controlled resources to one that emphasised how future potential could be unlocked, indirectly, through a radically different understanding of how to redevelop the most problematic areas of the city. The second bid, in particular, was the basis of a long-term strategy to underpin the regeneration of ex-industrial east Manchester, backed by a short-term drive to provide the sporting and related facilities and infrastructure improvements needed to make the bid credible. By sharing the leadership of the bid with the private sector and the city's government-appointed Development Corporation, the council presented a politically acceptable face to government while at the same time limiting the bill for local ratepayers. As a result, it acquired a level of credibility with government, public sports and regeneration bodies and the business community that resulted, eventually, in both short- and long-term successes; the first through discretionary investment in pre-games facilities by government and other public agencies, the second as a result of winning and staging the 2002 Commonwealth Games – a natural fallback after the Olympic bid failed – and using it to build and legitimise a broader regeneration programme for east Manchester.

There was simply no equivalent to Manchester's Olympic and Commonwealth Games effort in Liverpool, where the pursuit of 'mega-projects' is much more recent and has yet to bear significant fruit. What Manchester's leadership gained from its experience was the confidence to compare itself and the city it served with European, rather than domestic, counterparts. It also gained access to a network of potential supporters within government, other public bodies and the investment community who could find more self-interested reasons to associate themselves with risky but adventurous projects in Manchester than was the case elsewhere. It is this that underlies Manchester's other main advantage over Liverpool in the study period, dealt with next.

Manchester's ability to adopt and realise a 'horses-for-courses' approach to intergovernmental and public–private sector partnership

Partly this is a reflection of the previous two points. Manchester would not at one time have had a unique and dedicated line within the government's urban block of expenditures, for example, had the council not had the confidence to mount the second Olympic Games bid and had the government not felt it had something to gain from supporting it. Neither would the council leadership have been able to mobilise the level of support for projects listed in MCP prospectuses or in the rebuilding of the city centre following the IRA bombing so readily had it not had previous experience of dealing with key partners on other regeneration projects in the city.

At the same time, however, the pool of potential partners that could be drawn upon was always more likely to be larger in Manchester than in Liverpool. As noted in the section on key sectors, Manchester benefits from the greater range and density of career options available within the city, particularly within sectors whose profits rely upon modifications to the physical environment. This continues to mean that key private sector decision makers are more likely to work in Manchester, to have built their careers there and, at some point, to be interested in 'putting something back into the community' in a slightly less instrumental fashion. Liverpool's key private sector partners, by contrast, are fewer in number. They tend to come either from the branch plants of multinationals, whose managers are inevitably less concerned with the city as a whole than they are with immediate issues of company profitability, or from long-established Liverpool firms in sectors where any gains from improvements in the local economy are relatively tenuous (for example, Littlewoods, the pools and mail order retailer).

Urban governance, then, makes a difference in a relatively indirect but cumulatively significant way. However, to paraphrase Marx, it does so in circumstances that are not chosen by the main participants.

One final observation from the study is that the impact of local initiatives in Liverpool and Manchester could have been greater during the study period had the 'urban mission' of successive national governments extended to departments beyond the predecessors to the current Office of the Deputy Prime Minister, and had resources been grouped together to grapple with the issues of urban economic competitiveness and social cohesion at the city-regional rather than district scale. It would also have helped if there had not been constant changes in the huge number of relatively lightly resourced but time-consuming government area-based initiatives, each with their own regulations, delivery structures and auditing procedures. It would have been good, as well, had regional development agencies with a better understanding of the importance of the new urban economy to regional development trajectories appeared on the scene and developed coherent sub-regional strategies earlier.

References

Begg, I. (1999) 'Cities and competitiveness', *Urban Studies*, vol 36, no 5/6, pp 795-809.

Boddy, M. (1999) 'Geographical economics and urban competitiveness: a critique', *Urban Studies*, vol 36, no 5/6, pp 811-42.

Castells, M. (1989) *The informational city*, London: Edward Arnold.

Castells, M. (1996) *The rise of the network society*, Oxford: Blackwell.

Charles, D. (2001) *Liverpool-Manchester vision study: Building the region's knowledge economy*, Centre for Urban and Regional Development Studies, University of Newcastle.

Chesterton (1999) *City centre living in the North: A study of residential development within the city centres of northern England*, Manchester: Chesterton.

Deas, I. and Giordano, B. (2001) 'Conceptualising and measuring urban competitiveness: the relationship between assets and outcomes in major English cities', *Environment and Planning A*, vol 33, pp 1411-29.

Deas, I. and Giordano, B. (2002) 'Locating the competitive city in England', in I. Begg (ed) *Urban competitiveness: Policies for dynamic cities*, Bristol: The Policy Press, pp 191-210.

DTZ Pieda Consulting (1998) *Manchester city centre homes report*, Manchester: DTZ Pieda.

DTZ Pieda Consulting (2001) *Liverpool-Manchester vision study: Benchmarking the city-regions*, Reading: DTZ Pieda.

Evans, S.R. (2002) 'The Merseyside Objective One programme: exemplar of coherent city-regional planning and governance or cautionary tale?', *European Planning Studies*, vol 10, no 4, pp 495-517.

Evans, S.R. (2002) 'E-commerce, competitiveness and local and regional governance in Greater Manchester and Merseyside. A preliminary assessment', *Urban Studies*, vol 39, no 5/6, pp 947-75.

Evans, S.R. and Hutchins, M. (2002) 'The development of strategic transport assets in Greater Manchester and Merseyside: does local governance matter?', *Regional Studies*, vol 36, no 4, pp 429-38.

Harding, A. (2000) 'Regime-formation in Manchester and Edinburgh', in G. Stoker (ed) *The new politics of British local governance*, Basingstoke: Macmillan, pp 54-71.

Harding, A. (1999a) *Hulme city challenge: Did it work?*, Manchester: Manchester City Council.

Harding, A. (1999b) 'Strategic metropolitan frameworks, urban competitiveness and social exclusion: a case study of Manchester City Pride', *Working Paper for LMICS, ESRC Cities programme*, Liverpool: European Institute for Urban Affairs.

Hutchins, M. (2002) *Are big cities getting better? Socio-economic trends in England's core cities*, Liverpool: European Institute for Urban Affairs, Liverpool John Moores University.

Nevin, B., Lee, P., Goodson, L., Murie, A. and Phillimore, J. (2001) *Changing housing markets and urban regeneration in the M62 corridor*, Birmingham: Centre for Urban and Regional Studies, University of Birmingham.

Parkinson, M. (1985) *Liverpool on the brink*, Hermitage: Policy Journals.

Robson, B., Parkinson, M., Boddy, M. and MacLennan, D. (2000) *The state of the English cities*, London: DETR.

Sassen, S. (1992) *The global city: London, New York, Tokyo*, Princeton: Princeton University Press.

SURF Centre (2002) *Hulme: Ten years on*, Manchester: Manchester City Council.

Turok, I. and Edge, N. (1999) *The jobs gap in Britain's cities: Employment loss and labour market consequence*, Bristol: The Policy Press.

Wilks-Heeg, S. (2001) *Liverpool-Manchester vision study: Composite report*, Manchester: Centre for Sustainable Urban and Regional Futures, University of Salford.

Wilks-Heeg, S., Deas, I. and Harding, A. (1999) 'Does local governance matter to city competitiveness? The case of inward investment in Merseyside and Greater Manchester', *Working Paper for LMICS, ESRC Cities programme*, Liverpool: European Institute for Urban Affairs, Liverpool John Moores University.

Wong, C., Brown, P., Marsden, J., Batey, P. and Coombes, M. (2001) *Liverpool-Manchester vision study: Mapping the city-regions*, Liverpool: Department of Civic Design, University of Liverpool.

FOUR

Competitiveness and cohesion in a prosperous city-region: the case of Bristol

Martin Boddy, Keith Bassett, Shaun French, Ron Griffiths, Christine Lambert, Andrew Leyshon, Ian Smith, Murray Stewart and Nigel Thrift

A large, free-standing city in prosperous southern England, Bristol has demonstrated considerable competitive strength and capacity for economic adaptation over recent decades. This has been reflected in significant expansion in both population and employment and has contributed to rapid growth in household numbers. Unemployment rates across the area as a whole has generally been low compared with national rates. However, there are significant concentrations of high unemployment and deprivation both in the core inner city and outer social housing estates of Bristol District. Five Bristol wards are among the worst 10% nationally in terms of the government's composite indicator of deprivation.

In the context of the ESRC 'Cities' Research Programme and the other studies reported in this volume, Bristol thus represents a specific example of competitive success. However, it also raises particular issues relating to poverty and social exclusion within what is in many other respects a highly successful city-region. It is a particularly useful vehicle, therefore, through which to explore issues of competitiveness, cohesion and the relationship between the two. As with the other city case studies in the programme, the study as a whole covered a wide range of themes and issues and generated an extensive range of outputs. This chapter presents an overview of key findings linked to the core questions addressed by the overall research programme.

First, it presents a brief account of patterns of economic and social change and shifts in the spatial structure of the city-region, including edge-of-city expansion. It looks at the role of financial services and the cultural and media sector both of which are prominent locally and which have often been seen as key drivers of competitive strength both nationally and internationally. It then looks in turn at the core issues of competitiveness and cohesion, before finally discussing the role of policy and governance in shaping the city-region and the broader implications that can be drawn from this[1].

Figure 4.1: Bristol city-region

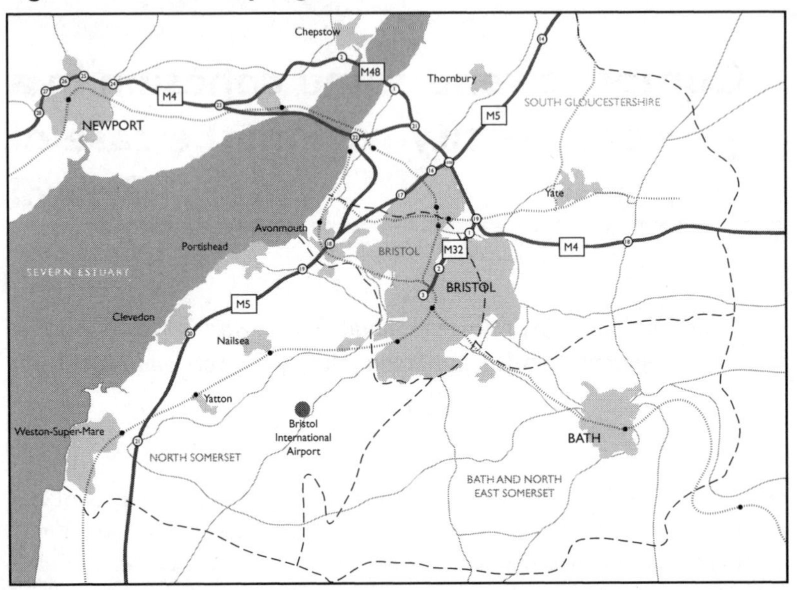

The changing city

On the economic front, the Bristol economy has performed well both in a regional context and compared with national and international benchmarks (Boddy, 2003b). Cheshire et al (2002) ranked Bristol 26th out of 121 large city-regions across Europe in terms of annual growth in per capita GDP over the period from 1978-80 to 1992-94. Although not quite in the same league as the top performers among the larger European cities, such as Dublin (3rd), Frankfurt (4th) or Munich (7th) it was however the best performing UK city after Edinburgh (5th) and in the top quarter all European city-regions[2]. Reflecting this, Bristol has also seen significant growth in population and employment, key indicators of competitive strength (see Chapter Two of this volume). In terms of population, the city-region's population as a whole grew by some 2.9% 1991-2001, slightly ahead of national rates.

Table 4.1: Population change (1981-91 and 1991-2001)

	Change 1981-91		Change 1991-2001	
	abs.	%	abs.	%
Bath & NE Somerset	1,644	1.0	6,028	3.7
Bristol City	–9,020	–2.2	–11,421	–2.9
North Somerset	16,349	10.0	9,614	5.4
South Gloucestershire	19,007	9.4	23,846	10.7
Bristol city-region	27,980	3.0	28,067	2.9
Great Britain	1,016,863	1.9	1,317,332	2.4

Source: National Statistics, NOMIS, mid-year estimates, revised in line with 2001 Census

Table 4.2: Estimated household change (1991-99)

	1991	1999	Change 1991-99	Change 1991-99 (%)
Bath and NE Somerset	65,626	71,000	5,374	8.2
Bristol City	158,588	174,000	15,412	9.7
North Somerset	70,786	79,000	8,214	11.6
South Gloucestershire	84,466	99,000	14,554	17.2
Bristol city-region	379,466	423,000	43,554	11.5

Source: Census of Population 1991, DTLR statistics on housing and households, estimated household numbers by local authority district 1999

The booming 'north fringe' grew at more than three times this rate, up by 10.7% over the same period. Economic expansion has also attracted net in-migration from the rest of the country, a further indicator of competitive success. Combined with other demographic factors, this has resulted in rapid expansion of household numbers, up by almost 12% in the period 1991-99 across the city-region as a whole and by over 17% in the north fringe.

In terms of employment across the city-region as a whole, employment in the 1980s grew just ahead of the national rate. Employment decline in the 1970s in the City of Bristol itself was reversed in the 1980s. Jobs growth in South Gloucestershire and the booming north fringe was spectacular, up by almost a quarter in the decade to 1991.

Significantly, it has also to be remembered that these were decades of major change in the structure of the economy nationally, with major losses in manufacturing across the country's urban areas – losses from which many cities have been slow to recover (Turok and Edge, 1999). Bristol shared in this loss of traditional manufacturing which, locally, hit the food, drink and tobacco, paper and packaging and aerospace sectors in particular. Almost half the city-region's manufacturing jobs disappeared in just two decades. This, however, was more than offset by the growth of finance and business services, public sector jobs and other service industries (Table 4.4). Bristol's economy thus

Table 4.3: Total employment (1981-2001)

	1981	1991	2001	1981-91 (%)	1991-2001 (%)
Bristol city-region	411,110	462,500	530,260	12.5	14.7
Bath & NE Somerset	67,900	77,124	81,200	13.6	5.3
Bristol City	211,170	224,258	228,500	6.2	1.9
North Somerset	51,780	61,866	79,250	19.5	28.1
South Gloucestershire	80,260	99,252	141,310	23.7	42.4
Great Britain (000s)	435,598	488,460	556,973	12.1	14.0

Notes: Includes employees and self-employed.

Source: Joint Strategic Planning and Transportation Unit, Bristol, estimates based on Annual Employment Statistics and Annual Business Inquiry, National Statistics, adjusted for known errors

Table 4.4: Employment specialisation by sector, Bristol city-region (2001)

Industry		Employment	Index of specialisation
752	Provision of services etc	14,815	1.59
803	Higher education	12,825	1.44
353	Manufacture of aircraft and spacecraft	10,632	5.31
747	Industrial cleaning	9,661	1.24
660	Insurance and pension funding	9,237	2.23
641	Post and courier activities	7,833	1.4
742	Architectural/engineering activities etc	7,723	1.31
642	Telecommunications	6,392	1.34
672	Activities auxiliary to insurance/pension funding	4,620	1.79
222	Printing etc	4,347	1.22
285	Treatment and coating of metals etc	3,880	1.54
746	Investigation and security activities	3,842	1.4
726	Other computer related activities	3,206	1.45
922	Radio and television activities	2,229	1.49
744	Advertising	2,126	1.22
713	Renting of other machinery and equipment	1,996	1.31
212	Manufacture: articles of paper/paperboard	1,874	1.41
300	Manufacture: office machinery/computers	1,769	2.14
711	Renting of automobiles	1,142	1.92
266	Manufacture of articles of concrete etc	1,126	1.94
921	Motion picture and video activities	1,042	1.38

Notes: Shows all sectors at 3-digit SIC level with more than 1,000 employees and with a location quotient of 1.2 or above. The location quotient measures the percentage share of employment in a given sector locally relative to the percentage share nationally (LQ = Local %/National %). A location quotient of more than 1.0 for a given sector thus indicates a higher proportion of total employment in that sector locally than nationally.

Source: NOMIS, National Statistics, Annual Business Inquiry, 2001

proved highly resilient precisely at the time that many urban areas across the country suffered the severe consequences of industrial restructuring.

Employment growth across the city-region as a whole accelerated in the 1990s – up by nearly 15% in the decade to 2001. Growth on the north fringe was even more spectacular, up by over 40% over the same period. Growth in the core urban area represented by the City of Bristol actually fell back a bit over the decade to 2001, but ongoing developments in the city centre may have countered this more recently.

In terms of the geography of population and employment change across the city-region as a whole, the core urban area (City of Bristol) saw a reduction in jobs in the 1970s and in population in the 1970s and 1980s. Growth rates since then have lagged well behind the north fringe and other outer areas in the city-region. This has not, however, constituted 'counter-urbanisation' at the level of the city-region as a whole in the sense of significant out-migration or the movement of substantial numbers of people and jobs down the urban hierarchy (Robson et al, 2000; see also Chapter Seven of this volume). At the same time, there was major growth in people and jobs concentrated in the three outer districts adjacent to the City of Bristol. And crucially, for any discussion of broader trends towards counter-urbanisation, these districts are an integral part of the functional city-region and constitute a largely contiguous developed area. Again, in-migration and inward investment rather than large-scale movement out (that is, decentralisation or 'hollowing out') from the urban core itself fed this growth.

This rapid growth in the outer districts included a particularly marked concentration of population and employment growth on the northern edge of the existing urban area, adjacent to the M4 and M5 motorways. Significantly, although contiguous with the existing built-up area, this was beyond the administrative boundary of Bristol City Council. It represented essentially a new focus of competitive advantage within the city-region. Developments here have included over 10,000 housing units, major business parks, a retail mall and leisure complex, large-scale investments including Hewlett Packard and, most recently, the Ministry of Defence, which relocated some 6,000 employees from the rest of the UK to a purpose-built complex (discussed later in this chapter).

It is also important to recognise that despite major economic restructuring, the core urban area of Bristol saw little in the way of the urban decline that hit major cities in the midlands and north. Actually, employment in Bristol City itself grew: by just under 4% in the 1980s and just over 4% in the 1990s. Population in the urban core, in common with other large urban areas had been falling. The rate of loss was lower than in most other cities, however; it slowed in the 1980s and slowed further in the 1990s. And there has been significant expansion in household numbers in the urban core reflecting in particular growth in numbers of single person households – up by 8% in the 1990s and an estimated 12% over the decade to 2001.

This turnaround in Bristol's central area also saw major lottery-funded cultural facilities on the harbourside. There was new housing development and conversion of former commercial and industrial premises to residential use including waterfront schemes (mainly for higher-income niche markets), a significant revival more recently in central area commercial property and hotel development, and approval of a large mixed-use development on the last remaining major site in the city centre.

New urban forms

The spatial structure of UK urban areas has seen significant shifts over recent decades and the emergence of new urban forms: re-urbanisation replacing earlier decades of counter-urbanisation, the emergence of polycentric urban regions, and the growth of new suburban or ex-urban centres. Bristol itself, as noted, saw rapid 'edge-of-city' expansion on its north fringe (Lambert and Smith, 2003). This was driven by shifts in economic structure and business locational preferences, and in the spatial logic of growth pressures in the economy and housing market in southern England. These provided the context in terms of demand for development. The process itself, however, was mediated by the particular local policy context in terms of planning and development in the city-region. Edge-of-city expansion reflected strategic planning policy decisions in the 1970s, identifying a major growth node in what was a highly marketable location. This marketability itself reflected to a significant extent the limited supply of such development opportunities in equivalent or near equivalent locations elsewhere in southern England.

The scale and speed of development also reflected the particular configuration of local government boundaries and political attitudes to development and its regulation. A pro-growth, urban-fringe planning regime under Conservative-dominated North Avon Council (later incorporated into South Gloucestershire) contrasted strongly with a conservationist-minded Bristol City Council right through to the mid-1990s, impacting both on local planning policy frameworks and the investment strategies of developers and house builders. This permissive policy framework, in tune with the deregulatory agenda at national level, did little to control or effectively manage the rapid rate of development. This resulted in typically low-density residential and employment areas, all car-dependent, with poor community service provision (particularly early on) and badly served by public transport. The long-term consequences of this type of policy regime continue to be played out some 20 to 25 years later both in terms of continuing levels of development and the consequences of the type of development encouraged in earlier years. This was also, however, a key factor underpinning the competitive strength of the city-region as a whole and its ability to attract a continuing flow of growth and investment.

From the mid-1990s, however, there was growing resistance to further housing development or land release for employment in the north fringe. This reflected a shift in party political control in South Gloucestershire, the perceived negative impacts of growth on this scale, and growing problems of sub-regional imbalance in economic development. The process of structure plan review saw the local authorities arguing in a somewhat mechanistic way, to restrain development in those locations where market demand was strong with the objective of diverting investment and growth to other parts of the city-region.

The scale of edge-of-city growth and investment in the business and retail sectors here had also for some time been seen as a threat to the city centre – particularly through out-of-town retail development and relocation from the city centre. The major insurance company, Axa Sun Life, had moved out from the city centre and the Bristol and West Building Society was for a time seriously considering a similar move. Commercial development in the 1990s slumped in central Bristol while continuing to boom on the north fringe. As already noted earlier in this chapter, actual 'hollowing out' of the city centre to the benefit of the fringe was not a major factor. The Axa Sun Life move, although significant, particularly in symbolic terms, was the exception rather than the rule; rather, it was differences in rates of inward investment and in terms of in situ growth rates which largely account for the contrast in economic trajectories between the two locations at the time.

Bristol's urban core remains the dominant employment centre in overall terms. It retains its concentration of financial and business services and has a growing leisure and residential role. Commercial property investment in the urban core has also recovered, albeit based on earlier public subsidy supporting key city-centre flagship schemes. The north fringe is now established, however, as a major employment centre in its own right, with growth continuing to outpace the urban core. It has attracted a diverse mix of activity, in terms of both sectors and types of production process. There are, however, significant concentrations of high technology manufacturing and research and development (R&D) in aerospace, computing and telecommunications. The overall spatial structure of the city-region thus shifted fundamentally over this 25-30-year period, and the growth of the north fringe has been a major factor in the overall competitive strength of the city-region as a whole.

Thus, the case of Bristol exemplifies a number of broad shifts in terms of urban spatial structure, policy responses to these and some of the tensions that result. It demonstrates, in particular, the emergence of edge-of-city locations as competitive business locations to rival core urban locations. More broadly, it illustrates the emergence of more fragmented urban forms. Central urban locations retain an important economic role, but are no longer the exclusive or primary focus of economic activity in the city-region. Significant concentrations of activity can be seen developing elsewhere, notably adjacent to the motorway network.

Bristol also exemplifies the sort of rapid expansion of new housing development and conversion of former commercial and industrial premises seen more generally across larger urban areas in the UK. This has been one component of the new vitality at the heart of these urban areas. At one level this is in line with the government's vision of 'urban renaissance', focusing development on previously used sites and contributing to the quality of the urban environment. As the case of Bristol shows, however, much of this represents high-cost developments for niche markets. Wider benefits in terms of the provision of low-cost housing or promoting socially mixed communities have been very limited, and the impacts have been largely confined to a relatively small area of the urban core and to key development opportunities in terms of prestigious sites.

The culture and media sector

Increasing attention has focused on the role that the cultural domain can play in fostering economic competitiveness and social cohesion in urban areas, both nationally and internationally (Bassett et al, 2003). Cultural development and the arts and media sector have commonly been cited as one of Bristol's distinctive assets. A cultural strategy and a new leading agency, the Bristol Cultural Development Partnership, were established in the early 1990s, and in 2002 the city was shortlisted as a contender to become 'European City of Culture 2008'.

The study, therefore, took the opportunity to use Bristol as a case study of the role of cultural industries and cultural development strategy in underpinning competitiveness and cohesion. It examined the structure of cultural industries in the city, the development of cultural strategy, the extent of local media industry clusters, the role of cultural infrastructure in city-centre regeneration and of the arts in community development and social inclusion.

In terms of the broadly defined cultural production and media sector, employment locally totalled some 8,500 jobs in 2000. As a share of total employment locally this was nearly two and a half times that for the sector nationally. There is an even higher concentration in the more narrowly defined film, radio and TV production with employment locally accounting for nearly three times the share it does nationally. In absolute terms, total employment numbers are not very great – financial services, for example, account for nearly 28,000 jobs. The degree of local concentration, however, is particularly high. There is a relative concentration of employment around regional television and radio production and distinctive, functional clusters of international status in natural history film-making and animation. The sector has also been prominent in symbolic terms, with significant employers including the BBC Natural History Unit and Aardman Animations. The local concentration of activity, and prominent employers such as these, largely reflects historic locational decisions, and the local origins of animation expertise, for example, rather than local cultural industries strategy as such.

The city was in fact slow to develop its cultural profile and assets, and explicit cultural strategy remained underdeveloped until the early 1990s. Emergence of the business-led Bristol Initiative, a commissioned Strategic Review, establishment of a Cultural Development Partnership and increasing involvement from the City Council (prompted in part by economic downturn), then, contributed to more effective cultural strategy through the 1990s and to developments 'on the ground'.

Major cultural infrastructure projects were slow to get off the ground and suffered early setbacks linked to problems with external funding. More recently, there has been considerable success in securing cultural projects (with lottery funds an important factor) as one component of wider harbourside development. Their catalytic or spillover effect has been relatively limited, however. There is increasing awareness of the role that cultural activity can play in community-based regeneration and specific examples demonstrating how this can be achieved. Their wider implications, however, remain to be demonstrated.

While limited in terms of its specific economic impact overall, the development of some elements at least of cultural and media activities demonstrates the potential role of policy and strategic development at the local level – within opportunity structures set by the national context. Development of the cultural and media sector has also contributed in a significant if less tangible way to the overall image and attractiveness of Bristol to business investment and to key labour market groups. It is likely, therefore, to have had positive impacts in terms of competitiveness.

Financial services

Bristol was one of a number of places that benefited from the major expansion and relocation of financial services in the UK from the early 1970s along with cities such as Leeds and Edinburgh (French and Leyshon, 2003). Relocation of London-based banks and insurance companies and their subsequent expansion saw Bristol established as a major provincial centre for financial services, employing over 22,000 by 1981. Finance and business services have been a key driver of economic restructuring and a major generator of new jobs in urban areas since the early 1970s.

From the mid-1980s, however, there has been major restructuring of the financial services sector across the whole of the UK, reflecting a sea change in the regulatory framework. The latter part of the 1980s saw rapid expansion, diversification and corporate restructuring in a context of fierce competition. Rapid employment growth continued in the Bristol city-region, which by 1991 was the fourth-largest provincial financial services centre (behind Manchester, Birmingham and Edinburgh) with over 30,000 jobs.

Economic slow-down and rising interest rates then saw a period of retrenchment in the early 1990s accompanied by mergers and acquisitions, branch closures and redundancies. Recovery in the latter part of the 1990s has seen renewed expansion but also major innovation including centralised credit-scoring, telephone and internet banking and a range of new corporate actors entering the field. Bristol just about held its own through the turbulent 1990s in terms of total numbers employed. Rival centres, on the other hand, did rather better and, while Bristol did not actually lose jobs over the 1990s, it lost ground in relative terms, being overtaken by Glasgow in the overall rankings and virtually caught up by Leeds.

While losing out somewhat relative to its rivals, then, activity and employment in Bristol proved resilient nevertheless in the face of intensifying merger and takeover activity and rapid innovation. The accumulated skills and experience of the local workforce together with sunk costs in premises and IT systems were cited as powerful factors underpinning operations in the local area. Bristol was also able to attract newer call-centre based activities that were commonly grafted on to existing operations rather than simply located in least-cost locations. There was also significant innovation in socially responsible investment activity, for example.

Financial services, therefore, remain a very significant sector locally, with direct employment of a little over 30,000 representing nearly a quarter of all jobs in the city-region in 1999, compared with 19% nationally. A proportion of the total employment is in effect locally oriented, servicing local people and businesses. Much of it, however, relates to national markets and represents an important 'export' sector driving the local economy. It is one of the sectors that makes Bristol 'different'.

Key influences on the competitive success of Bristol in terms of financial services include the relatively conventional set of locational factors contributing to the overall business environment of the city-region (outlined in the next section of this chapter), including proximity to London, the area's relocation potential and its ability to recruit and retain labour. However, the overall trajectory of the sector has been largely driven by national sectoral trends combined with the particular structure and corporate strategy of businesses located locally. National policy has impacted heavily in this respect through the impacts of financial deregulation. The effects of policy as such, beyond those impacting on the cost and availability of premises at crucial junctures, have been largely absent.

With reference to recent work on locational economics, agglomeration effects resulting from clustering or networking, however, were found generally to be only weakly developed in the financial services sector, reflecting the dominance of vertically integrated, export-oriented activities. There was no real evidence for the role of 'untraded interdependencies' based on collaboration or relationships of trust. Evidence of spatial clustering based on 'traded interdependencies' was strongest in the case of those firms using Bristol to serve local and regional demand, particularly for corporate and commercial financial services. Employers generally cited the scale of the local labour market in financial services and Bristol's reputation as a financial services centre as a distinct advantage. This could be seen as evidence of 'labour market pooling' in the 'Marshallian' sense. There was evidence as well of what Krugman among others has termed 'path dependence' whereby sunk costs, 'bounded rationality' and inertia have led to the embedding of earlier, historic location decisions.

Competitiveness

As indicated in Chapter One of this volume, the basis of urban competitiveness was a key issue for the project and the programme as a whole. Various accounts of the competitive advantage of urban areas have stressed the role of different forms of clustering as the basis for agglomeration economies and scale effects. Clustering, it has been argued, results from a range of things including labour market pooling, specialist inputs and services, and knowledge and information flows and the key role of untraded interdependencies including trust, cooperation and the transfer of tacit knowledge. Other approaches have focused on the role of particular lead sectors as economic drivers including, variously, high technology, financial services, the 'creative', cultural and media sector (or, more generally, 'the knowledge economy'), and more specifically innovation and entrepreneurship. Begg (1999) distinguishes the influences on urban performance of sectoral trends including the inherited mix of activities; company characteristics; the business environment including various factors of production, social and environmental factors and the variety of agglomeration effects; and capacity for innovation and learning.

Evidence from the Bristol study supports the argument that more traditional locational factors and the overall business environment do much to explain levels of inward investment and the competitive success of businesses in the city-region. Businesses emphasise three sets of factors, in particular. First, good motorway and rail links including access to London and Heathrow facilitate contact and networking with collaborators and customers within and outside companies, both domestic and international. Second, the local labour market combined with a wider labour catchment for technical and professional staff extending along the M4 corridor provides a large and multilayered labour pool offering a wide range of skills and experience. Third, the city and its surrounding area are particularly attractive to professional, technical and managerial staff. It ought to be attractive, therefore, in terms of inward investment and businesses seeking to relocate. It also enables businesses already located in the city-region to recruit staff from elsewhere in the country and to retain those they already employ. The particular success of the north fringe can be attributed to these same factors, coupled with the volume and variety of sites and premises made available with flexible tenure terms, generous parking provision and the sort of image and environment which many expanding businesses wanted to project to customers, clients, and employees or potential employees. The context established by the permissive planning regime of the 1970s was a key factor with continuing impacts over successive decades.

This supports the importance, therefore, of a fairly traditional set of locational factors rather than more currently fashionable accounts of the process. The latter would include, for example, the role of business clusters, the importance of key sectors such as high technology or financial services or the impacts of local growth coalitions. However, there is little evidence (from employer surveys and interviews) to suggest that clustering as the basis for collaboration, innovation and knowledge transfer or untraded interdependencies has played any major role in terms of location, investment flows or competitive strength. There are parallels here with the findings related in Chapter Two of this volume, that traditional agglomeration economies were more significant than industrial clusters in explaining concentrations of business activity.

There is, as noted, a particular concentration of firms in finance and business services locally. They share a common location and investment locally has been prompted by common factors. There are also links with particularly smaller businesses locally, in the sense of normal subcontractor and supplier relationships. The larger firms in this sector operate essentially independently, however, and clustering in the sense of interaction between these businesses is of little importance in business terms. The best example of a functional cluster is the media sector. This, however, is small in scale and relatively unimportant in terms of the overall functioning of the city-region economy and its competitive success. Again, it is financial services that, in Chapter Two of this volume, display higher levels of cohesion – although again, that chapter concludes, the implications in terms of competitive strength are slight.

Nor does it appear that particular key sectors have played a dominant role in the overall strength of the city-region economy. Financial services clearly represent a prominent sector but in terms of employment or output still only amount to a relatively small proportion of overall economic activity. The media sector and a number of 'high technology' employers have a high profile in local and regional terms but account for a small share of employment or output. They have played a significant but by no means dominant role. Historically, it would seem to be the diversity of economic structure, and relatively strong performance of a number of industrial sectors, that accounts for the competitive success of the city region. This reflects the co-location and common investment strategies of a number of diverse sectors in response to the particular bundle of assets offered by the city-region.

Nor, finally, is there evidence of a governing elite or public–private coalition of interests, a local 'growth regime' as such, seeking to mould and marshal the overall business assets of the city-region and to attract and retain investment and sustain competitive advantage. The enduring impact of the 1970s' planning regime on the north fringe has perhaps been the major single policy influence over recent decades. As argued earlier however, it reflected a political and ideological take on the planning system at the time rather than any form of explicit long-term growth strategy for the sub-region. Subsidised redevelopment of key sites in the core urban area and the emerging cultural strategy and harbourside developments have played an important role more recently in securing specific developments. Political and administrative fragmentation have inhibited, if anything, strategic initiative and leadership at the level of the city-region.

Inner city and social cohesion

Overall lack of demand and the gap between the number of jobs available in the local labour market and the size of the labour force have typically been seen as generating high levels of poverty and social exclusion (Turok and Edge, 1999). This is undoubtedly an important factor in the case of many of the more peripheral cities in the UK. The case of Bristol (and indeed London; see Chapter Five of this volume) emphasises the fact that competitive success in overall terms does not in itself serve to combat what are by national standards quite marked concentrations of poverty, deprivation and social polarisation within an otherwise prosperous urban area.

In the case of Bristol, there are significant levels of deprivation by national standards in both the inner city and outer estates (Boddy, 2003c). Five Bristol wards are among the worst 10% of wards nationally (DTLR composite indicator). Lawrence Hill in the core inner city ranks 133rd out of 8,414 wards nationally, and Filwood (an outer estate), 221st. There is also a high degree of polarisation between neighbourhoods with very marked differences in ranking over short distances within the city. Southmead ward (628th nationally), for example, sits next to Westbury (7,363rd) while Ashley (756th) is adjacent to Redland (7,367th).

It is also worth looking at how this picture has changed over time. Has the situation improved with the long-term economic success of the city-region as a whole? Discontinuities in data and boundaries impede longitudinal analysis. Over the period 1981-91, however, the three *inner-city* wards with the highest unemployment rates in 1981 in fact significantly increased their share of total unemployment. The three *outer estates* with the highest levels of unemployment in 1991 did, however, significantly decrease their share.

Over the five-year period 1991-96, the share of total unemployment accounted for by the three inner-city wards changed little. The share accounted for by the three outer wards continued to decline. Again, South Bristol in particular seems to have improved its position relative to the core inner city. Over the period as a whole, therefore, the situation in the core inner city got worse, if anything, with an increasing concentration of unemployment there. The situation on the outer estates improved to some extent. Overall, however, patterns of poverty and deprivation proved particularly persistent.

It seems likely that low levels of educational attainment are a reinforcing factor in the case of Bristol. The city-region as a whole is highly polarised in terms of educational outcomes, reflecting both the characteristics of local populations and the strength of the educational infrastructure. Pupils in state-sector schools in the City of Bristol generally perform well below the national average and those from schools in the three surrounding districts considerably better than average. Only 63% of pupils in Bristol City gain Level 4 (or above) in Maths at Key Stage 2, compared with the national average of 72%, and 78% for pupils in the adjoining district of Bath and North East Somerset. Only 31% of 15 year olds in Bristol City gained five or more A*-C grades in GCSEs compared with 47% nationally, and 57% in Bath and North East Somerset. No fewer than 16 of Bristol City's 34 wards are among the worst 10% of wards nationally in terms of the government's indicator of educational attainment. Filwood in South Bristol is actually 7th from bottom out of 8,414 wards in the country as a whole and three other neighbouring wards are in the worst 100 nationally.

Again, however, there is marked polarisation within Bristol City itself. Three wards in the north west of the city are in the best 5% of wards nationally. Contributing to this polarisation, Bristol City has a particularly high concentration of pupils in private schools, in itself a reflection of historical endowment from the city's age of mercantile capitalism but also reflecting the purchasing power of the city-region's population. Here, results contrast sharply with those of the poorly performing state sector. The mean score of 15 year olds taking GCSEs in Bristol City in the private sector was nearly twice that of pupils in the state sector. In Chapter Fifteen of this volume, Tim Butler points to the very focused educational strategies of middle-class parents in London. In the case of Bristol, it would seem that those parents in Bristol who can afford it send their children to private schools. Those who cannot attempt to locate in the catchment areas of the small number of better performing schools in the Bristol local authority, almost exclusively in the north of the city. Many, however, locate in or move out to the catchment areas of the strongly performing schools in the three surrounding local authorities. This process tends to increase demand for housing in the three districts beyond Bristol City's boundary. It also undermines attempts to raise standards in Bristol City's state sector as parents seek to avoid or move out of areas with poor levels of educational performance, impacting as we have seen on South Bristol in particular.

Despite the strong economic performance of the city-region as a whole and rapid expansion of the north fringe in particular, there are nevertheless persistent concentrations of poverty and disadvantage both in the core inner city and the outer local-authority estates. This would seem to reflect the sort of processes identified in Chapter Thirteen of this volume: that is, patterns of housing allocation in both the social and market sectors serve to concentrate those who are most deprived in the worst housing which is itself spatially concentrated. To the extent that individuals succeed in securing employment and/or lifting themselves out of severe poverty, they tend to move out of these worst areas, which therefore tend to be reproduced over time. The overall context for this, as many commentators have noted, is the increasing polarisation of the labour force and of income levels. Added to this is the significant proportion of the population in a city the scale of Bristol, living on benefit and unable to take up the government's preferred route out of poverty, namely from welfare into paid employment.

On the other hand, in common with findings from the other city-based case studies in the research programme, there was little if any evidence to suggest that the scale and pattern of social exclusion and concentrated disadvantage in parts of the city in any way impacted negatively on competitiveness. There was no evidence from business surveys or interviews that employers and investors considered social exclusion or concentrated disadvantage to be a threat to their competitive advantage. There has been major business investment immediately adjacent to areas of concentrated disadvantage both in the core inner-city area and the outer estates.

It might be thought that low levels of educational attainment in Bristol City schools in particular would have negative impacts on business locally. Less than half of Bristol employers surveyed in 2001 were satisfied with a range of young people's key skills, including problem solving, numeracy and literacy. Employers in Bristol were less satisfied in this respect than those in the three surrounding districts and levels of satisfaction among Bristol employers have declined over time. Educational underperformance in the state sector was not however specifically identified by businesses in Bristol as something that concerned them. When interviewed, moreover, in relation to education they tended to single out the scale of private education in the city plus the quality of state provision in the surrounding districts as positive factors. The strength of the higher education sector was seen as a positive factor. In-migration also provided a ready supply of better-educated and more skilled or experienced staff making businesses less reliant on 'home-grown' sources.

Shaping the urban future

Bristol, as elsewhere, has in recent years seen a whole succession of policy initiatives, including specific urban policy and area-based initiatives. There has also been a proliferation of institutional structures at different spatial scales from the neighbourhood to the regional level. This has brought, in turn, an increasing emphasis on partnership and 'network governance', both local and citywide, across public, private and voluntary sectors (Stewart, 2003). In terms of formal structures of government, local government reorganisation led to the abolition of Avon County Council, the second tier of local government. This had been roughly coterminous with the economic 'city-region' defined as the official travel-to-work area. Abolition left formal government across the functional city-region split between the four unitary authorities with the City of Bristol at the core.

The rhetoric from central government in terms of changing governance structures has been that of devolution, decentralisation and engagement at the local level. Evidence from Bristol, however, indicates that central government departments retain strong control over main programmes including education, health, policing and social services. They also exercise considerable influence through 'locally' based initiatives such as Sure Start, New Deal for Communities and Education Action Zones.

There has been something of a shift towards participative democracy through a number of area-based initiatives: New Deal for Communities, the Neighbourhood Renewal Strategy and proposals for Neighbourhood Partnerships. These might be expected to strengthen social cohesion. Executive-style government, on the other hand, is widely viewed locally as having led to more remote decision making within local government and a lessening of the role of back-bench members. There is also a widely perceived tension between the role of the Bristol City Council and that of the Local Strategic Partnership. At a more local level, there are also some tensions between the elected community members of the New Deal for Communities Board and elected council members.

Conceptually, what has been termed the 'new urban governance' combines competition for resources, hierarchy within multi-level structures, and networks. In the case of Bristol, there are instances where partnership and network-based governance has successfully addressed specific issues. Overall, however, the complex proliferation of partnerships and networks is weakly integrated and is lacking in collaborative capacity and strategic direction. Lines of accountability and scrutiny in relation to the proliferation of partnership organisations are also potentially weak.

Bristol City Council itself has participated in a wide range of partnerships. It has not intervened, however, to provide much in the way of leadership and coherence across these structures as a whole. It has remained relatively distanced, for example, from issues of regeneration and social exclusion. The proposed model for a Local Strategic Partnership with 70 members, a core executive group and (informally) an 'inner core' of key partners again seems, at the time of writing, to illustrate these tensions between 'involvement' and strategic capacity. The Bristol case indicates that effective partnership working and the development of collaborative capacity cannot simply be externally imposed. It will vary with the local context, the perceived policy challenges and the historic legacy of local political structures and culture. It takes time to develop but also requires active engagement on the part of partners and potential partners to develop collaborative capacity as the basis for network governance.

Leadership and strategic direction within local government more generally across the city-region remains relatively weak. Bristol City Council has not generally been perceived as providing 'strong leadership' or strategic direction within the city itself. Fragmentation combined with political diversity (see later in this chapter) have also frustrated the development of leadership and strategic direction at the level of the city-region as a whole. And Bristol does not – and has not sought to – provide leadership within the region as a whole, reflecting contrasts and conflicting agendas between the city-region and much of the rest of the south west region. There are also new tensions between the demand for a more community-based focus on the one hand and the 'new regionalism' on the other, pulling the City Council in two directions at once.

As already noted, local government across the functional city-region as a whole (defined in terms of the travel-to-work area) is fragmented between Bristol City at the geographical core, surrounded by three other districts that include both parts of the functional city-region and a more rural hinterland. Other work suggests that this 'under-bounding' or fragmentation of formal governance structures is likely to impact adversely on economic efficiency and competitive strength (Cheshire, 2002). Local research supports the case that fragmentation and conflict, exacerbated by differences in political control across the constituent districts undermines the capacity for strategic planning and coordination across the city-region. This is particularly the case in terms of planning and transportation and educational provision, but possibly also the image and wider representation of the city in regional and national forums. Joint planning mechanisms have failed to compensate for this fragmentation and have tended to 'manage' the tensions towards mutually acceptable but strategically suboptimal outcomes.

The joint structure plan, for example, aimed to 'cool down' growth on Bristol's north fringe rather than provide for the proactive management of future growth based on the competitive advantage of this part of the city-region. Long-delayed investment in any form of mass public transit system has repeatedly been obstructed by inter-district disagreement over even the simple first steps and more generally by a lack of strategic vision and commitment across the city-region as a whole. The West of England Strategic Partnership, a 'sub-regional' partnership covering the four districts, has similarly struggled to articulate any wider strategic vision or to identify goals at the level of the city-region. Nor has the regional level been able to instil much in the way of sub-regional vision or coherence from above. Regional Planning Guidance (RPG 10, 2001) does identify Bristol as a key focus for growth within the south west. The four unitary authorities, however, have resisted any meaningful implementation of this. The Regional Development Agency (RDA), meanwhile, has struggled to reconcile its objectives in terms of competitiveness and the development of an overall spatial strategy for the region to follow through on this, which would again focus attention on Bristol, and issues of cohesion and spatial strategy which emphasise needs across the region as a whole including rural areas and the far south west.

Local planning policy could thus represent a threat to competitiveness by restricting employment growth and expansion of the labour force in locations clearly favoured by business. Planning reform as outlined in the recent bill currently before Parliament (ODPM, 2003b), however, could shift the balance of influence to the regional level. This will do away with the current system of structure and local plans. It also introduces the requirement to develop regional spatial strategies in which Regional Assemblies, RDAs and regional government offices will play a key role.

Project findings, as reported to the Structure Plan Examination in Public, moreover, specifically questioned the capacity of planning policy to cool down growth in the north fringe with the idea of steering investment to central and south Bristol. The alternative for businesses considering investment or expansion in the north fringe would not be other parts of the Bristol sub-region but rather locations elsewhere in the UK or mainland Europe which could offer a comparable set of attributes to the north fringe. Attempts to squeeze growth out of the north fringe would be likely to reduce future levels of business investment in Bristol and the south west.

This raises the question of the potential impacts of planning policy on competitiveness more generally, particularly across those parts of southern Britain which, as development and labour market pressures clearly demonstrate, are considered by business to be the most competitive locations. Issues of local impact and inequality at sub-regional levels remain. Pressures to support competitive places for business in the context of global competition, however, remain strong.

The case of Bristol thus suggests the difficulty of achieving effective collaboration towards common strategic goals in a context of relative economic success. In economically less buoyant areas, local governments may be more willing to adopt common goals at the level of economic strategy and infrastructure provision. Bristol has clearly been economically successful. Laissez-faire planning in the 1980s led to the development boom in north Bristol. It did not provide, however, for the effective management of that growth or ensure the quality of development. More effective strategic governance at the level of the city-region could in fact have further enhanced the competitive strength and success of the sub-region. It might also have facilitated more sustainable outcomes and ensured more effective provision of infrastructure and services on the back of that success.

Notes

[1] A much fuller presentation of the findings of the project as a whole can be found in Boddy (2003a).

[2] Considerably smaller places such as Porto (1st) and Padua (2nd) tended to have the fastest growth rates rather than the larger urban areas.

References

Bassett, K., Griffiths, R. and Smith, I. (2003) 'City of culture?', in M. Boddy (ed) *Urban transformation and urban governance: Shaping the competitive city of the future*, Bristol: The Policy Press, pp 52-65.

Begg, I. (1999) 'Cities and competitiveness', *Urban Studies*, vol 36, no 5/6, pp 795-809.

Boddy, M. (1999) 'Geographical economics and urban competitiveness: a critique', *Urban Studies*, vol 36, no 5/6, pp 811-42.

Boddy, M. (2002) 'Linking competitiveness and cohesion', in I. Begg (ed) *Urban competitiveness: Policies for dynamic cities*, Bristol: The Policy Press, pp 33-54.

Boddy, M. (ed) (2003a) *Urban transformation and urban governance: Shaping the competitive city of the future*, Bristol: The Policy Press.

Boddy, M. (2003b) 'The changing city', in M. Boddy (ed) *Urban transformation and urban governance: Shaping the competitive city of the future*, Bristol: The Policy Press, pp 4-19.

Boddy, M. (2003c) 'Social exclusion and the polarised city', in M. Boddy (ed) *Urban transformation and urban governance: Shaping the competitive city of the future*, Bristol: The Policy Press, pp 66-75.

Cheshire, P. and Magrini, S. (2002) 'Competitiveness in European cities – what can we learn?', Urban governance, economic competitiveness and social cohesion workshop, Worcester College, Oxford, 7-9 April (mimeo).

French, S. and Leyshon, A. (2003) 'City of money?', in M. Boddy (ed) *Urban transformation and urban governance: Shaping the competitive city of the future*, Bristol: The Policy Press, pp 32-51.

Lambert, C. and Smith, I. (2003) 'Reshaping the city', in M. Boddy (ed) *Urban transformation and urban governance: Shaping the competitive city of the future*, Bristol: The Policy Press, pp 20-31.

ODPM (Office of the Deputy Prime Minister) (2003a) *Creating sustainable communities: Building for the future*, London: ODPM.

ODPM (2003b) *Planning and Compulsory Purchase Bill*, London: ODPM.

Robson, B., Parkinson, M., Boddy, M. and Maclennan, D. (2000) *The state of English cities*, London: DETR.

Regional Planning Guidance 10 (2001) *Regional planning guidance for the south west*, London: Department of Transport, Local Government and the Regions.

Stewart, M. (2003) 'Towards collaborative capacity', in M. Boddy (ed) *Urban transformation and urban governance: Shaping the competitive city of the future*, Bristol: The Policy Press, pp 76-89.

Turok, I. and Edge, N. (1999) *The jobs gap in Britain's cities: Employment loss and labour market consequences*, Bristol: The Policy Press.

FIVE

London: competitiveness, cohesion and the policy environment

Ian Gordon, Belinda Brown, Nick Buck, Peter Hall, Michael Harloe, Mark Kleinman, Karen O'Reilly, Gareth Potts, Laura Smethurst and Jo Sparkes

Introduction

For its sheer scale, the wide array of service activities in which it possesses competitive advantage by both national and international standards, and for its cosmopolitanism and international connections, London clearly stands out among British cities. It is also, in simple terms that can too easily be lost sight of in an era of self-conscious globalisation, the national capital of the UK: economically, socially and culturally, as well as politically. As such, it plays a crucial role in the British urban system, with important implications, both complementary and competitive, for the way in which other city-regions can function and develop. Understanding how its role and performance are evolving in the new kind of intense internationally competitive economic environment that has been emerging over the past 20 years or so, has an importance that goes well beyond both the rather privileged areas of south east England, or what it has to show about the development of 'global cities'.

The things which make London most distinct in a British context, however, namely its sheer scale and diversity, both physically and in population terms, also mean that an unusually wide cross-section of urban situations, environments and issues can be found (and observed) somewhere within its functional region. Often this is on a scale which makes them more visible, statistically and politically, than in smaller places. There are obvious exceptions in that London had little of the kind of heavy industries, whose demise has been so traumatic in many northern cities, and has benefited from the general strength of the southern regions since the 1920s. Comparison with Glasgow, Liverpool and Manchester in particular among cities studied in this programme highlights ways in which these basic regional economic and structural facts matter. But equally, a London study can display rather clearly a number of processes which are underway in some parts of (or affecting some groups in) all city-regions, producing similar kinds of outcome and giving rise to what may be very similar policy issues.

The research reported here, like that of the Bristol, Liverpool–Manchester and Edinburgh–Glasgow teams (see Chapters Two to Four of this volume), was designed to be 'integrative', rather than to be focused on a specific theme or activity (as projects reported in the remaining chapters of this volume are). In other words, the aim was to try to understand how a range of different processes (including those addressed in specific thematic studies) interact, within particular city-regions, to produce varying patterns of economic, social and political outcome. At the broadest level, this involved an interest in possible interrelations in cities between the domains of 'competitiveness', 'cohesion' and 'governance' with which the programme as a whole is concerned[1]. In the London case, because of its extreme scale, there was a particular interest in understanding the interrelation between overall patterns of development in the city-region and local processes and outcomes of more immediate relevance to the lives, business and choices of individuals. Alongside the other integrative studies, it was hoped that comparison with London would illuminate questions about the difference that sheer scale, complexity and more intense internationalisation make to urban economic, social and governance processes – and how far urban competitive success serves to resolve problems of social cohesion.

As a case study area, London presented some clear advantages as well as some particular difficulties. Among the advantages are that the city is big enough to show up as a visible entity both in published statistics and unpublished survey databases, and of sufficiently wide interest to have generated much previous research including quite a number of major studies over the years[2]. The intention with this project was not to simply replicate or extend this work, but to concentrate as much as possible on addressing new issues, particularly those relating to the core themes of the programme. A special concern was with the question of how far there had been a fundamental break in patterns of development since around the start of the 1980s – which could be linked to growing internationalisation and/or 'flexibilisation'. The first of these two processes had been discussed in comparative studies of London and other centres published in the early 1990s (Sassen, 1991; Fainstein et al, 1992), but only limited evidence was then available about its impacts. In this study, we took a longer-run view, starting with an open mind as to how far either process and other factors, old or new, might have been responsible for key aspects of social and economic change in London during the 1980s and 1990s.

The particular difficulties of studying London also stem, however, from its sheer size and diversity and start with the question of where the city really begins and ends. This question of definition can make a big difference to the characteristics which the city as a whole seems to display. We have taken the view that the modern city has to be seen in terms of the functional economic region; that is, the area within which people and businesses are effectively integrated into the agglomeration. This has been operationalised in terms of the London metropolitan region defined by 1960s planners[3], including an Outer Metropolitan Area (OMA) as well as Greater London. Together, these cover some 4,400 square miles, with a population of about 14 million, and 86 separate local authorities.

By any standards, this is a very large geographical and institutional canvas on which to work, adding further challenges to those set by the substantive breadth of the 'integrative city study' brief. In order to address these, a distinctive style of research was required. First, priority was given to understanding in a rather holistic way how significant economic, social and political relationships processes work out, at various spatial scales, rather than trying to investigate each of the more specific relationships with equal rigour (or picking off a few as self-evidently key to understanding how the city worked). Indeed, a strong message of this study is that attempts to explain developments in this region in terms of a few key factors or sectors always involve serious distortion. Within the project, entirely new pieces of *in-depth* research on particular issues were only attempted where there were both significant gaps in understanding and readily available data sources.

Second, we made a determined effort to integrate region-wide analyses of secondary data (including large-scale survey data sets) with more qualitative interview-based local investigations. In order to pursue this, work was organised in two phases. The first phase spanned the city-region as a whole and relied on secondary sources, while the second involved intensive work in a number of small areas, where interviews with residents, business people, educationalists and political actors could be placed in a known local context. These locally based investigations were focused on eight pairs of residential localities/ employment centres (each typically involving a couple of wards) together with an additional employment area within the City of London (Figure 5.1). These were chosen both to provide interesting contrasts and comparisons, and, when taken together, to be reasonably representative of the regional population and its employment structure[4]. A rationale for this approach was that while people and organisations operate in very different kinds of locales across the city-region, these are strongly linked by sets of flows and overlapping markets. Hence, life in all areas and sectors is affected in some way by various aggregate characteristics, potentials and constraints of the metropolitan region, lying outside the immediate experience of individual firms, people or local public actors, as well as by those immediate connections that they recognise.

In each phase of the work, our analyses focused on a number of key themes: spatial structures and change; competitiveness and business milieus; labour market processes; schooling; social capital; inequality and social exclusion; the role of neighbourhoods; and governance. These also provide the framework for a fuller account of our findings in the project book, *Working capital* (Buck et al, 2002). Here, however, we shall concentrate on a set of four broader questions towards which the research was directed:

- What do competitiveness and cohesion actually mean for the residential and business communities of a city such as London?
- How substantially have these changed as a result of internationalisation and intensified competition since the early 1980s?

Figure 5.1: Sub-regions and case study areas

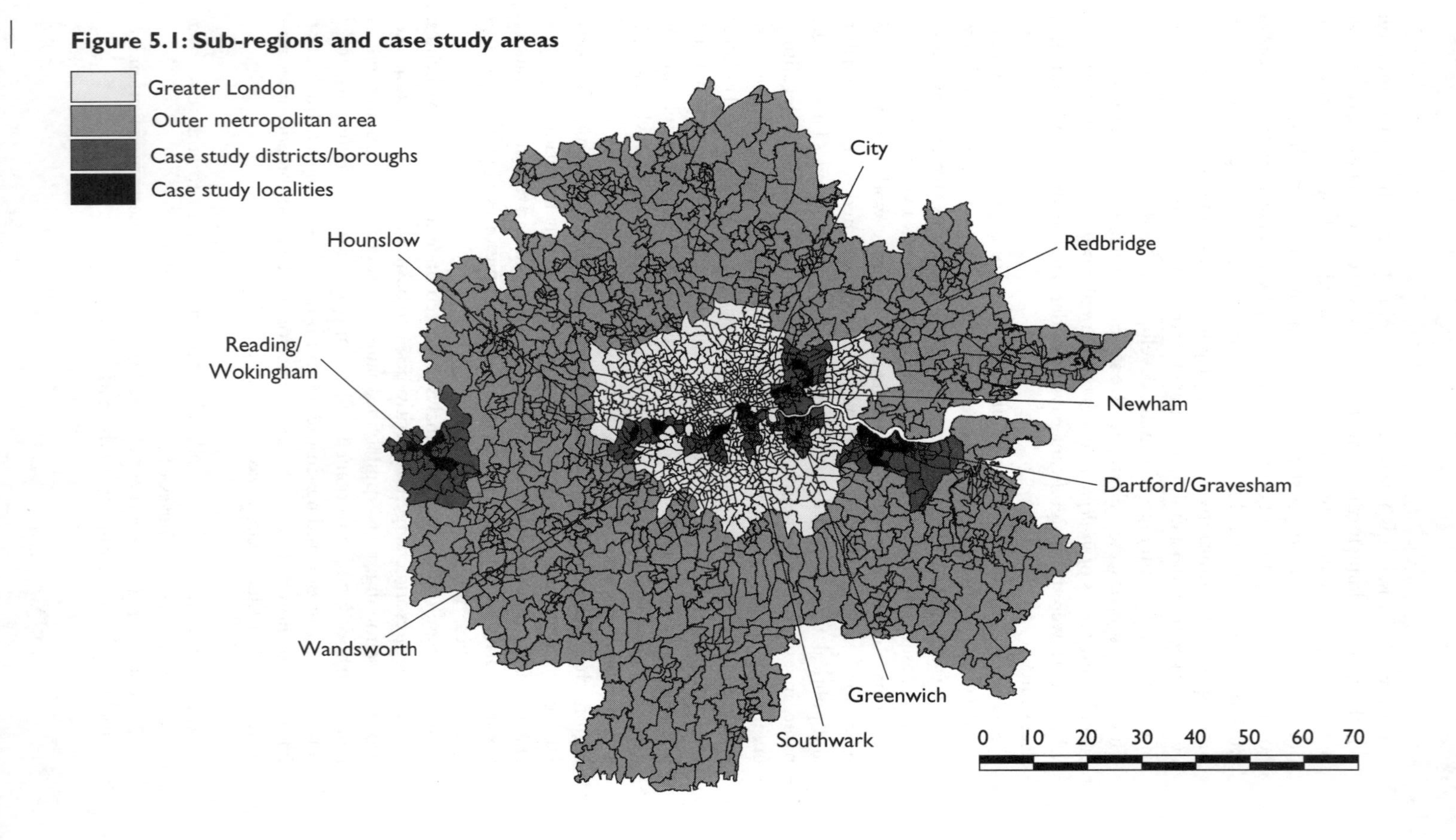

- How important are different aspects of 'social cohesion' (and policies for these) to sustaining urban economic success in this new context?
- What role does urban governance play in achieving competitiveness and cohesion goals[5]?

The remainder of this chapter summarises for each question in turn what we have found out, both substantively and conceptually, including ways in which we have found key terms and hypotheses to be oversimplified.

Competitiveness and cohesiveness in the London region

Competitiveness and cohesion, sometimes linked with governance and sometimes with sustainability, have become key terms in a policy discourse about processes of change in advanced capitalist societies – the 'new liberal formulation' or 'new conventional wisdom' (Harloe, 2001; Gordon and Buck, 2004: forthcoming). In this context, they are offered as a new language in which to express a consciously consensual set of economic, social, institutional and environmental aims, appropriate to 'new times' in which competitive pressures have become both more intense and much more pervasive. However, each of these ideas contains substantial ambiguities, with elements in each that are not necessarily very closely associated. This presents problems in mobilising evidence to assess how areas are performing in terms of each of them, or how they affect an area's development. To get more clarity, we have found it necessary to disaggregate each of these concepts. Thus, within the blanket term 'social cohesion', we distinguish aspects of inequality, connectedness and order; under the umbrella of 'competition' we likewise distinguish different kinds of markets: for products, inward investment, desirable residents and governmental favours.

In the case of *competitiveness*, we find that the most important issue concerns the ability of London firms to sell their products in open, contested markets, and the characteristics of the city's economic and social environment that help or hinder them in this task. We have taken the growth, productivity and export success of London business establishments as the key indicators of product market competitiveness. In these terms, the region's performance is somewhat mixed: distinctly strong by British standards on the second and third criteria, but only average in terms of growth over the last couple of decades. Productivity and earnings levels are substantially higher than in any other UK city-region, while across the range of service trades, plus publishing and printing, export propensities are double those in the rest of the UK. In terms of product innovation, London also scores well, although the real areas of strength are outside Greater London, and a number of the most innovative areas are actually beyond the boundary of our region, in the fringes of the Greater South East[6]. The region's growth record is held back by an inelastic supply of space, rather than weak demand, partly reflecting the maturity of core areas, but also planning constraints, which bite especially strongly in the OMA. Within the region there seem to be substantial differences in competitiveness, with the eastern half clearly doing worse on all criteria. By European standards, London's overall economic performance has been on a par with the group of leading cities, but not generally ahead of them, despite its position as the most internationally oriented of these cities (and arguably of all major cities).

It is less clear precisely how a London location contributes to this competitive success. For most individual firms, the key factors affecting performance are (almost inevitably) bound up with their specific company strengths, including the technologies they can access, with the strength of the market sector they operate in, and also with much wider economic factors. This does not mean that regional factors are unimportant; as we aggregate across the London economy, many firm-specific influences will cancel out, while the wider influences can be seen as just defining the playing field on which firms and city-regions compete. Making such allowances, some of the relevant regional influences are very clear (deteriorating public transport, for example). For others, however, including many broad agglomeration economies, this is not the case: firms only have to take notice of them if and when they consider relocation out of the region, which very few actually do. Nevertheless, the fact that market rents are so high – particularly in central areas of the region – and that firms thrive despite such higher costs suggests that agglomeration economies are really important, even if London firms habitually take them for granted.

Urban competitiveness involves more than successfully producing and selling goods or services. It is also a matter of developing, or somehow securing, both the high-quality human assets and the more routine skills necessary to sustain a successful service economy. At graduate level, the region is currently very successful in attracting well-qualified and ambitious candidates from both home and abroad, even though the high cost of living absorbs much of the nominal difference in earnings compared with the rest of the country. In part, this clearly reflects the opportunities for personal development (building both human and social capital) in the responsible leading-edge jobs that the city offers, together with the strong prospects for advancement through inter-firm movement in a flexible, high turnover labour market. This 'up escalator' is one key aspect of the region's competitive performance. However, it is clear that the city also attracts talent for other reasons, including the vibrancy of its cultural life (of all kinds) and a level of tolerance and open-mindedness – in social as well as economic settings – that is particularly valued by a more highly-educated workforce, as well as by migrants and minorities.

In terms of the education of its own young residents, London's performance is less clear. Overall, school results for the region are a little above average by British standards. But this is probably not good enough for a region specialising in service functions where the great majority of jobs require at least a basic level of academic and interpersonal skills, including those jobs filled almost entirely from within the local population. In much of inner London and Thameside, school-level performance actually appears very poor. Basically, this reflects concentrations of disadvantaged groups within catchment-area populations, including relatively high proportions of lone-parent families. In value-added terms, the average school does not seem to be doing a bad job, in difficult circumstances. However, the degree of variation between schools points to clear room for improvement, both in achievement levels and in behavioural factors such as truancy rates, which mediate the effects of social disadvantage. There has been progress in reducing actual failure rates, but this remains one of the weak areas in the region's competitive performance and in the assets it has to offer.

In the case of *social cohesion*, we gave more or less equal attention to the three dimensions of (in)equality, connectedness and social order. On the first dimension, it is clear that the London region is one of particularly sharp inequality, with much more than its share of the really affluent, and rather more than its share of the poor. Poverty here, in real income terms, is particularly associated with a high cost of living (especially for housing and transport); but it also reflects an above-average concentration of many vulnerable groups, together with unemployment rates, which have tended to remain somewhat above the national average. All of these characteristics are exaggerated when we focus on the inner areas. This is principally because of the way that the region's housing market (or the quasi-market of the social sector) generates patterns of residential segregation. For this reason, it cannot be taken as evidence of area effects on poverty and inequality, although there are processes operating within the region which tend to increase both the risks for vulnerable groups and the rewards for those who have the assets, determination and luck to succeed in this competitive environment.

For connectedness, the second dimension of cohesion, we have focused on a number of particular aspects. These include: 'getting on' and 'getting by' forms of social capital; the effects of London's relatively fragmented family structures; and the question of how far individuals suffering from various forms of material deprivation are effectively 'excluded' from participation in normal social relations. We found that Londoners, in the main, get about as much social connectedness as they want. Against many expectations, survey findings show that Londoners are just as connected in terms of friends, family, organisations or trust, as similar sorts of people in any other part of the country, although physical distances separating people from family and friends are much greater. However, because the population composition is different in London, average levels of connectedness are lower on some indicators of social capital, and this may have some negative consequences. Some groups, such as the long-term sick and disabled and the retired, clearly do experience substantial social isolation, while those lacking qualifications, income or networks (quite reasonably) perceive themselves to be isolated and remote in the midst of a successful, global city. However, we found few people who were 'truly excluded', in the sense that they concurrently experience all forms of exclusion: from the labour market, from communal support and from citizenship entitlements, as hypothesised by Kesteloot (1997) and found in Afro-American ghettos (Wilson, 1987).

On the third dimension of cohesion, namely order, Londoners report many worries – about incivility, crime and social disorder. For most, this is an inconvenience, but for some it is a major blight on their lives. Across the entire region, general crime rates are actually close to the national average (except for mugging, which is much more common) but, as elsewhere, there are great variations, and the risks of crime are clearly greater in inner areas. Maintaining social order is an issue that increasingly impinges on local institutions, particularly schools in socially stressed areas, where it can form one of the key constraints on raising performance.

Although most Londoners felt comfortable where they were, an appreciable minority did not: in some inner areas, in particular, they felt a general sense of menace and fear. Here, many reported that they wanted to move away, and that others had already gone. And this was reinforced by some of those living more comfortable lives in quieter and more secure areas, who told us that they had moved from places they regarded as distinctly less secure. However, the comfortable ones were the great majority, and we were struck by the large numbers who liked not merely the physical qualities of their neighbourhoods but also the social relationships: the small courtesies done by or for neighbours, the sense that help would be at hand in a sudden emergency, the general sense of security that all this brought. This was not a city where anomie or alienation loomed very large.

All the same, the exceptions were important, and they seemed to fit one principal stereotype: they occurred in places of transition, where new residents with different ways of life were disturbing a settled order. There was sometimes a racial (or racist) component here, as in Bermondsey, but it was confusingly mixed with other elements such as age (the old people's block invaded by young people with different lifestyles) and economic status (a settled Indian population facing an influx of refugees). Yet sometimes these transitions seemed to work quite satisfactorily for almost everyone, as in Battersea for example. Generally, London does not seem to be a city with very high tension levels; rather, people of different ages, different incomes and lifestyles, different races live well together, and even celebrate the fact.

Internationalisation and intensified competition since the early 1980s

In terms of social and economic outcomes, a lot changed in London during the 1980s and 1990s which was not a simple continuation of trends established in the 1960s and 1970s. Among our three competitiveness indicators, we lack any measure as to how export performance may have changed. However, there were strongly positive developments in both growth and productivity. For growth, the actual degree of progress is somewhat obscured by a great increase in the volatility of the regional economy, both absolutely and relative to other parts of the UK. So far, this has involved two unprecedented strong 'boom' phases – the late 1980s and 1990s – separated by a 'bust' phase, also (for London) of unprecedented strength (Figure 5.2). Another 'bust' now seems on the cards, with employment having peaked in late 2001. Comparing this with

Figure 5.2: London region employment (1971-2000) (millions, full-time equivalent, log scale)

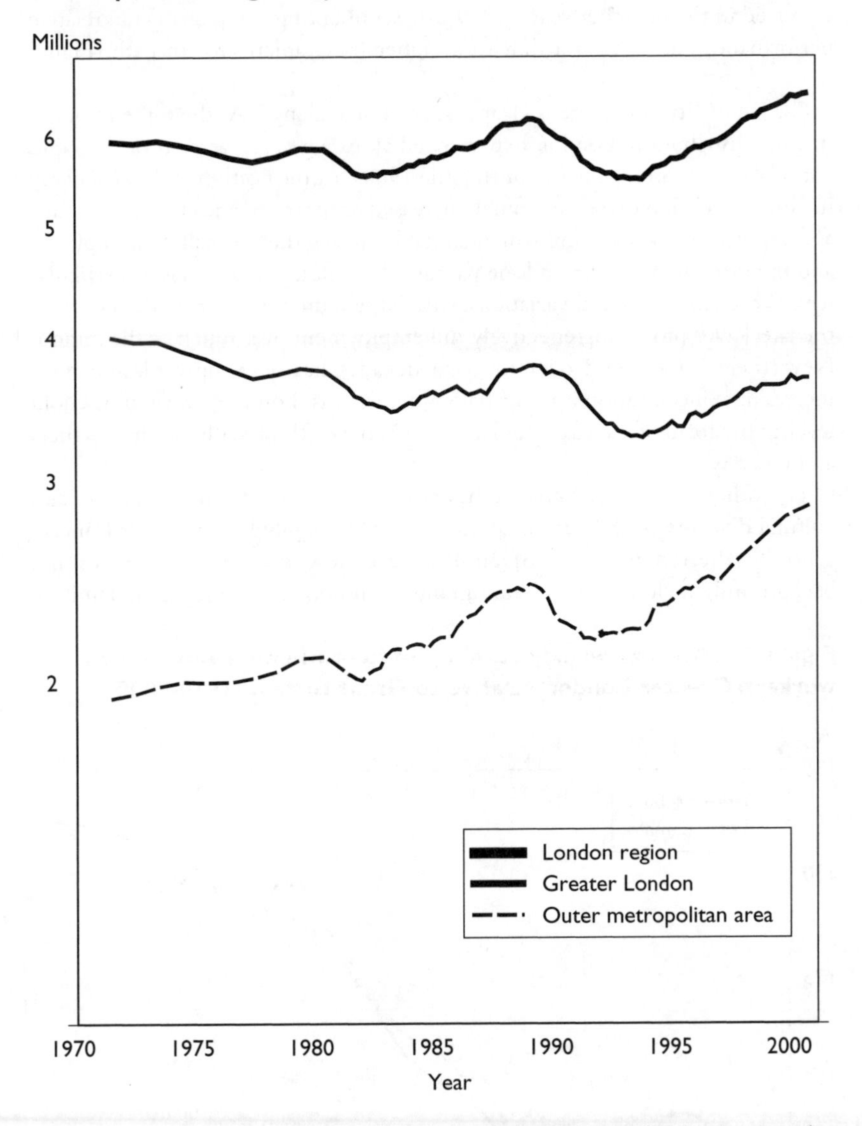

earlier peaks in London employment levels, the indications for Greater London are that the downward trend which marked the 1960s and 1970s has been replaced by effective stabilisation. In the OMA, an established growth trend has been given a further boost – although the change in trends is less there.

In relation to productivity levels, evidence of an upward shift is also clear, and much easier to quantify, at least in terms of earnings differentials, with which they are strongly associated. Basically, the gap between Greater London and national performance doubled during this period (in the case of earnings moving from a differential of around 15% to about 30%): the OMA's smaller gap also more or less doubled. However, virtually all of the shifts seem to have occurred in the Thatcher years (1979-90), representing a step change in relative performance, rather than a shift to a higher (per capita) growth path (Figure 5.3).

For inequality, also, there is clear evidence of a change. At the top end of the income distribution, London experienced an exaggerated version of the rapid national growth in top salaries during the 1980s. At the bottom end, particularly in Greater London there were much increased proportions among the working-age population outside employment, notably among the (formally) unemployed and the growing numbers of lone parents. Unemployment levels in particular have shown great cyclical variations, with large reductions during the boom of the late 1990s producing effectively full employment over much of the region. Nevertheless, the trend over the two decades has been upward, and with increasing concentration both spatially (in inner east London) and at household level, in the form of increasing polarisation between those with multiple earners and those with none.

The other major social change has been a great increase in the ethnic and cultural diversity of the city since the late 1980s, highlighted in inner London schools where a majority of children are now from non-white ethnic backgrounds, including many immigrants from non-English speaking families.

Figure 5.3: Average weekly earnings of full-time men and women workers: Greater London relative to Great Britain (1970-2000)

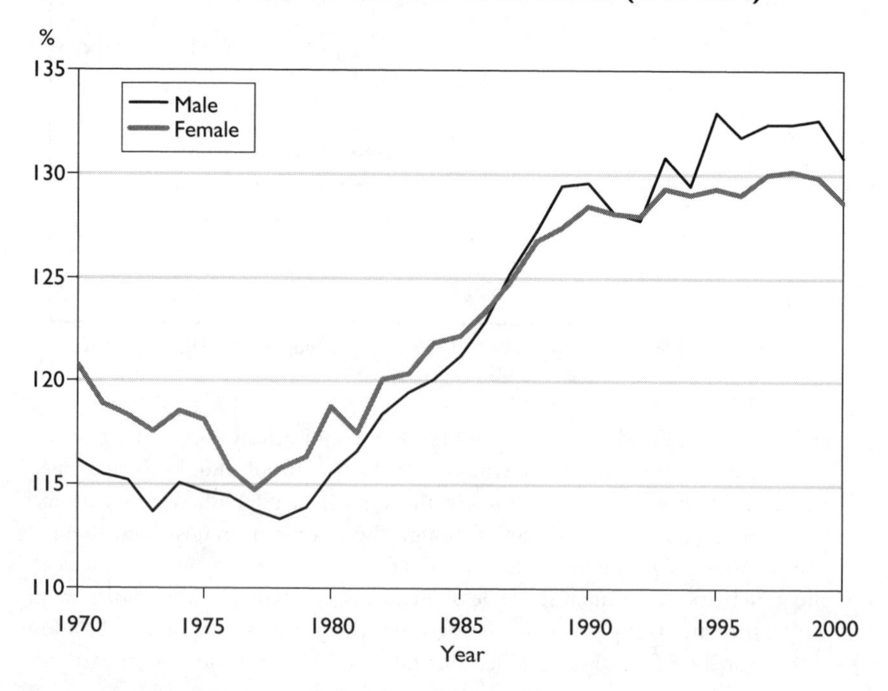

This has not, however, been accompanied by further spatial separation, although other trends have brought some increase in segregation of the employed from the non-employed and of couple-based from non-couple-based households. In terms of social order, there have been short- and medium-term swings in both actual crime rates and perceptions of insecurity, but, although concerns over incivilities and drug dealing have risen, Londoners are actually no more worried about crime than they were 20 years ago.

Identifying how far these changes are a consequence of internationalisation and/or 'flexibilisation' is more complicated, since neither of these are simple, single processes. In the first case, there are four important ways in which London has been affected, through:

- simple removal of barriers to trade (particularly in services) and factor mobility (particularly for capital);
- increasing flows of refugees and asylum seekers;
- adjustment of national policies to respond to the challenges of international competition, notably through financial deregulation and 'rolling back' of state activity;
- growth of specialised urban service functions to facilitate other forms of internationalisation; that is, 'globalcityisation' (Gordon, 2002).

The last of these processes has tended to be seen as key to recent social and economic change in London (as in Sassen, 1991), because it represents London's most distinctive economic role. Indeed, by most criteria this is one of the most 'global' of the major cities of the world, with advanced services that are only comparable in their international orientation with those of New York City, and a much stronger third-party role in support of international activities by foreign firms. Significant new business for London has clearly been created by the growth of these activities since the early 1980s. However, it is important not to exaggerate the role of such 'global city' functions as the 'driver' of the London economy or their responsibility for the upturn in its performance. Data on employment by sector and market area shows that the city's global and European roles together remain much less significant than its role in the national economy. And although the international ('global city') sector contributed greatly to the ups and downs of London activity during the 1980s and 1990s, over the period as a whole, it is not clear that it has grown much faster than comparable nationally oriented activities.

Two other aspects of internationalisation, however, have been important for the growth of these activities:

- the continuing shift of British comparative and competitive advantage away from goods-related sectors;
- policy responses to internationalisation, in the form of privatisation and deregulation.

Both of these have boosted demand for those financial and business services in which London is pre-eminent within the UK.

At the top end of the income distribution, internationalisation has clearly contributed to increased inequality in London, both through boosting demand for the most highly-paid types of business professional, and through a levelling-up of their salaries towards American norms. However, at the bottom end, as we have seen, it is unemployment rather than lower wages which kept personal incomes down. This cannot be directly blamed on globalisation, either in terms of Sassen's (1991) thesis about global cities' burgeoning demand for low-paid service activities, or in terms of a 'race to the bottom', driven by competition from new producers in cheap-labour economies. Different trends in New York during the 1980s may have reflected the fact that it had a more elastic supply of immigrants from low-wage economies. (Whether London's recent influx of asylum seekers could have a similar effect cannot yet be judged, however.)

Overall, we can see that internationalisation has intensified the processes discussed in answer to the first question that I posed earlier in this chapter. It has created for talents of all kinds, more spaces and opportunities, and it has added both to the city's diversity and to recognition that this is an asset. However, it has also helped to make it a more volatile city, with more risks, larger gaps, and further to fall for those firms and individuals that do not succeed. These outcomes reflect a variety of processes both direct and indirect, and are not simply a reflection of the growth of command and control, or finance and business service functions. Nor are all of them peculiar to London since they also reflect ways in which the country as a whole has accommodated to internationalisation.

In the case of 'flexibilisation' the main hypotheses were that vertical disintegration and an increased emphasis on markets would work to London's competitive advantage, but with greater insecurity, turbulence and volatility impacting negatively on social cohesion. In terms of competitiveness, the strongest supporting evidence comes from earnings and productivity measures, with the sharp widening of London's (positive) differential during the Thatcher era of market deregulation. We cannot tell how far it was labour rather than product market changes that were responsible. However, a major part must reflect the impact of widening earning differentials, passed on via prices to measured productivity – as distinct from those gains which more productive London businesses may have achieved in more open markets, and passed on in higher earnings to their key workers. In terms of employment growth, London's improved performance is not specifically linked to this period of deregulation. It seems, rather, to reflect the boost to demand for the various business services in which it specialises, stimulated both by outsourcing and by a shift from state to self-provisioning in pensions, health insurance and other personal financial arrangements.

In relation to social cohesion, increasingly competitive labour market behaviour during the 1980s, did clearly contribute to growing inequalities in earnings within London (as well as a higher average). At the bottom end of the income distribution, however, where higher unemployment was the key factor, the contribution of intensified competition is less evident. London does have higher levels of job turnover (compared with other cities) which increase the risks of underemployment – but turnover rates do not actually seem to have increased during the period. And, while in more industrial cities local business failures in the face of heightened competition were clearly a significant factor in raising unemployment, these seem to have been much less relevant in London.

Instead, we find that both the general increase in levels of unemployment across the region experienced during this period, and the much greater increases experienced in eastern parts of inner London have their origin in national recessions and the loss of competitive advantage by older manufacturing activities mostly located in other regions. Their impact on the London region reflects the openness of the regional economy and labour market more than competitive forces acting directly on the region. Although the initial causes were largely external, the way that unemployment developed in the region, particularly its concentration and persistence within parts of inner London, reflected processes operating within the regional labour market. In particular, we find that conditions of slack demand within that labour market as a whole (prevailing for most of the period up to the mid-1990s) exacerbated long-established sources of labour market inequality and led to both downward mobility and marginalisation of vulnerable groups. Beyond this there were important knock-on effects on other components of deprivation, notably sickness and lone parenthood. Similar factors would have operated in most other parts of the country, and continued beyond the mid-1990s in regions of weaker demand. However, the scale and structure of the London region meant that the pattern of deprivation was particularly concentrated and statistically more visible. These developments are likely to have had substantial implications both for connectedness and order, although the major changes here appear to be those associated with shifting family and household structures, rather than direct repercussions of deprivation or rising inequality.

Interrelations between competitiveness and cohesion

In this study, we spent much effort on investigating how one or other dimension of social cohesion might feed back into economic success or failure. This was stimulated both by an academic literature suggesting an increasing dependence of the economy on social relations, and a policy literature questioning whether neoliberal policies, which promoted increasingly individualistic and deregulated forms of behaviour, were compatible with sustained economic success.

In searching for evidence of such links, however, we encountered two main difficulties. The first was that connections between aspects of social cohesion and economic performance are likely to be quite indirect, rather than things which would be directly recognised either subjectively by economic actors or objectively through analyses of statistical data. The second difficulty is that some of the more powerful arguments for the importance of social conditions and relationships imply thresholds beyond which some key processes or sources of order start to break down. Available evidence, however, tends to relate to conditions inside these thresholds where little evidence of such potential breakdowns is likely to be found.

We attempted to deal with the first of these difficulties by identifying a series of hypothetical paths along which one or other dimension of social cohesion could feed through to business competitiveness, and then looking for evidence on the various causal links involved. In the project book (Buck et al, 2002), we explored six paths through which cohesion (or its absence) might plausibly be seen as impacting on competitiveness within a city or region – via selective migration, education, image, crime, business networks and workforce morale. We deal with these only briefly here, because we actually found little strong evidence that most were operationally significant in the London region.

To take one example, we found no real evidence that either business performance or the presence of highly-skilled workers in London were threatened by perceived risks of crime or disorder – because of the defensive strategies which could be deployed (including residential segregation), the opportunities on offer and positive evaluations of other aspects of the social order, including diversity and tolerance. These are issues, however, where thresholds are clearly important, and problems can be triggered by quite specific incidents. Hence, we cannot know reliably how far social inequality and connectedness would need to deteriorate in order to have major negative impacts on London's image as a business centre, as occurred in New York in the late 1960s. Our judgement, however, is that the city is not approaching any of these thresholds.

In relation to potential gains from local social networks, involvement in local institutions and the development of relations of trust within spatial clusters of businesses (much emphasised in recent academic and policy literatures), London businesses generally appeared sceptical. The main exception was the City of London financial services cluster, although here the key issue was one of access to current intelligence rather than a greater potential for collaboration (Gordon and McCann, 2000). There were two key reasons why local social capital of this kind was not more widely valued. First, the value of London as a location consists largely in the array of possible business links available to be pursued in shifting market circumstances, rather than in building more restricted and durable partnerships: agglomeration promotes weak rather than strong ties. And secondly, London firms are outward-looking and where stronger relations with customers or partners were critical to successful innovation, these were as likely to be with non-local (including international) businesses as with those based in the city.

One real source of concern to businesses, particularly in east London, was the quality of labour available for posts filled from local young people. Formal qualifications did not appear to be the issue here, although they are among the few signals available to employers, and schooling is clearly relevant to both the basic and soft skills with which employers are concerned. Such complaints are not new and some of the issues seem to reflect subcultural differences along age and class lines more than conventional notions of skill. However, these are much more salient issues in a post-industrial economy where workers' performance has a more direct relevance to competitiveness. Although the key response may be through employers' personnel practices, they are at root issues of social cohesion, since subcultural differentiation among young people in particular seems to be largely about means of achieving and sustaining 'respect'. And it is an educational issue, since achievement of formal qualifications is – together with equal opportunities policies – a critical route for reconciling these aspirations with those of employers. The reasons, however, why achievement levels in parts of inner London, in particular, are poor, are not simply to be found in what happens in school, or in poor attendance; they also reflect background social factors, notably the impact of family fragmentation, both on those directly affected and at neighbourhood level.

The fact that we have not been able to trace more clear effects from cohesion to competitiveness does not decisively prove that these do not exist, or that levels of inequality, disconnectedness and disorder can be allowed to drift without any regard for possible economic consequences and thresholds which may be crossed. However, it should redirect attention to the basic point that poverty, isolation and insecurity are bad in themselves. Our findings suggest that it is quite easy to overdramatise both the possibility and the implications of social exclusion, and particularly the extent to which these are tied to specific neighbourhoods in urgent need of targeted 'regeneration'; but there is a very great deal of old-fashioned poverty and poor housing conditions, together with newer problems of racism and family fragmentation – and a lot of Londoners who simply have difficulty getting by or exerting much control over their situation. Some, but by no means all, of the victims are concentrated in poor neighbourhoods, which makes some problems worse, but most of their difficulties relate to who they are, and what their past experiences have been, rather than where they are within the region.

Connections in the reverse direction, running from economic competitiveness to social cohesion, are rather more obvious. We have found much evidence of the negative impacts of economic deprivation on social relations, while in the medium term, at least, economic growth does seem to lower the incidence of many kinds of crime. However, there are two important qualifications to be made. One is that what is likely to be critical is the economic position of the bottom quartile or so of the population, who have clearly not benefited to the same degree from the generally rising prosperity and economic success of the region over the past couple of decades, when a very large share of the gains have accrued to those with access to high-status jobs. The second qualification is that, even for this disadvantaged group, the spatial scale at which economic competitiveness matters is not local, nor even sub-regional, but closer to that of the Greater South East, since labour markets are so strongly interconnected across this region. Thus, while neighbourhood level unemployment rates have a strong bearing on rates of single parenthood, for example, these unemployment rates are much less sensitive to whether employment in surrounding areas has been growing than to growth and the pressure of demand across the extended region. From a social as well as economic perspective, it is appropriate, therefore, to address issues of competitiveness in a regional rather than local context. And, although the vast majority of Londoners are better off as a result of living in an economically successful region, rather than one of those struggling with the legacy of declining heavy industry, it also means that their welfare is heavily dependent on the competitive success and economic management of the national UK economy. Inner-city Londoners suffered heavily from national recessions and weak demand during much of the last 20 years – although less than those living in inner Strathclyde or Merseyside – and they have clearly benefited from the more sustained growth achieved over the past eight or nine years.

The role of governance

Within both the policy and academic literatures, recent emphases on ideas of urban 'governance' (rather than 'government'), imply both:

- a particular concern with strategic objectives, often expressed in terms of competitiveness, cohesion and sustainability (rather than routine service delivery); and
- forms of active cooperation cutting across public–private and geographical borders.

While this language was quite often used, two of our general findings are that adequate delivery of basic services (particularly education, housing and transport) is still key to meeting economic and social goals in the region, and that in practice the governance role remains weak and limited. In the inner areas this may change, but beyond there, it may well not.

The general capacity of local government in the region to respond to economic and social challenges has been reduced, not enhanced, over the past 20 years: both by loss of powers and responsibilities to other bodies (market and non-market) and by reduced resources. Policies within Labour's modernisation agenda seem to offer resources to address some of the key issues, as well as incentives to improve performance levels. However, these appear too 'provisional' (in coverage, resources and time-limits) to give authorities the capacity they require, while shifts towards network governance can actually reduce this capacity, without effectively bringing in resources from other partners.

For authorities in inner areas at least, a key change during the last decade has been recognition that they face real issues of competitiveness as well as cohesion, and cannot simply ignore or resist the former (as most Labour authorities unsuccessfully attempted during the 1980s). For those authorities that are well-placed in terms of location, inherited assets and political directions, there is a strong temptation to compete by working with the grain of those powerful market-based forces which favour closure and exclusion as routes to social upgrading of their areas. In the process, they may be able to purchase local social cohesion as well as competitiveness: in Wandsworth, for example, some real benefits do seem to have trickled down to those less advantaged groups that survived the exclusionary phase of area change. Inevitably, however, there are knock-on effects for neighbouring areas, which have to deal with poorer population groups displaced from these successful areas. A more even balance between competitiveness and cohesion goals is desirable, but harder to achieve, and the outcome of attempts at this – by boroughs such as Newham and Greenwich – is not yet apparent.

Such competition between boroughs is intensified in the London region because of the combination of sheer scale and political fragmentation. Two major challenges for urban governance here are to mitigate the negative effects of local competition, and to provide some coherence in managing change and investment across the functional region. In the interregnum between the Greater London Council's abolition in 1986 and the new Greater London Authority's (GLA) inception in 2000, only a weak system of network governance was available to attempt this. The GLA and its agencies do not wholly replace this: their key functions are strategic rather than operational; and in such a huge, complex, polycentric place as London, government will always be fragmented. It is too soon really to assess the new arrangements, but the new system of 'regional' authorities (three of which are responsible for parts of the functional region) has evident flaws. It remains to be seen whether they can achieve much in the way of redistribution and building positive externalities, or whether their competitive instincts may generate new negative externalities. Early signs are not encouraging. Internally, London's complex and diverse interests have been too readily condensed into a drive to accommodate growth in order to secure its 'world city' status (MoL, 2002). Externally, the London Mayor's strategies assume that 'London' ends at the GLA boundary, which, as we have shown, is far from the case – while those for the south east and eastern regions turn their back on London. The fact that both central and decentralised government each operates at the Greater London level exacerbates this situation and also leads to a confusion of roles at this level, especially when the GLA's major 'diplomatic' concerns are either with 'ministries' which are not themselves regionalised (that is, the Treasury) or with ministers personally. And so far, the GLA's priority objective, to exercise effective control over upgrading of its inadequate public transport system, has been thwarted by central government.

The key point emerging from our work, however, is the continuing centrality of actual service delivery to what is expected and required of authorities in the region. Efficiency and responsiveness of performance remain highly variable, but this (rather than strategising) proves to be the key not only to quality of life for residents, but also to both competitiveness and cohesion.

Conclusions

A number of clear findings emerge from this study as to the scale and character of change over the past 20 years in the London region, which is one of those places whose inherited strengths fit it particularly well for the new competitive, international and post-industrial economy. Economically, some of its gains are quite closely related to increases in social inequality within the country as a whole, and inequality has grown particularly sharply within London itself, exacerbating some old-established social problems. By contrast with Manchester, Liverpool and Glasgow (among the other cities discussed in this volume) – if not with other leading European city-regions – it has become a strikingly successful city in the past 20 years. However, it also has some similar problems to these cities, in terms of: the kind (if not the intensity) of social problems; unmet needs for infrastructure provision; and (to a greater degree than these) the difficulty of achieving an effective form of governance to deal with competitiveness and cohesion issues across the city-region.

In terms of the analytic questions that we posed, the answers are less straightforward. In part, this is because some of the key terms (such as 'social cohesion'), taken from the language of current policy debate, are deceptively oversimplified. This is also true of some of the newer models of how cohesive urban systems might be expected to function (including ideas about the role of 'clusters'), especially when applied to a major agglomeration. And, crucially, it is because London is a very complex city containing a large number of different elements that may be only loosely linked, in relation to which the questions may be answered in quite different ways. Some of the elements and sources of change that are most distinctive (notably the 'global city' role) turn out to be only part of the story, and substantially less important than others which are less remarkable (including both the 'capital city' economy and the impact of national economic developments). At the most general level, however, we do find evidence that internationalisation and flexibilisation have had significant impacts, both on the London economy (generally positive though with greater instability) and on social relations (much more mixed), although much that has happened in the city has reflected older and/or national trends. We find very limited evidence, however, that any of the aspects of social cohesion are critical to the city's competitiveness or likely to become so in the foreseeable future. Nor does it seem that evolving systems of governance yet have much capacity to influence economic and social outcomes. We also find that in a generally prosperous (but expensive) city there is substantial poverty, many Londoners that have difficulty getting by, and substantial unmet needs for basic public services.

Notes

[1] Only the first two of these terms appear in the programme's title. This may be due to another recent ESRC initiative on 'governance'; however, it clearly was always a third important element in the programme's research agenda.

[2] Recent studies include Donnison and Eversley (1973), Wilmott and Young (1973), Buck et al (1986), Hall (1989) and Fainstein et al (1992). Important works with a historical perspective include King (1970), Hebbert (1998) and Porter (2000).

[3] Previously used by Hall (1963), Young and Willmott (1973), Buck et al (1986) and Fainstein et al (1992).

[4] Although with a deliberate down-weighting of the highest status groups, for whom locally based processes were thought to be less significant.

[5] To keep our chapter as concise as possible, we have omitted a discussion of a fifth, more speculative question, concerning prospects. This is covered in Buck et al (2002).

[6] This extended region, defined by Hall (1989), stretches from Cambridgeshire to Dorset.

References

Buck, N., Gordon, I. and Young, K. (1986) *The London employment problem*, Oxford: Oxford University Press.

Donnison, D. and Eversley, D. (1973) *London: Urban patterns, problems and policies*, London: Heinemann.

Fainstein, S., Gordon, I. and Harloe, M. (eds) *Divided cities: New York and London in the contemporary world*, Oxford: Blackwell.

Gordon, I. and Buck, N. (2004) 'The new conventional wisdom: city competitiveness, cohesion and governance', in N. Buck, I. Gordon, A. Harding and I. Turok (eds) *Changing cities: Rethinking urban competitiveness, cohesion and governance*, Basingstoke: Palgrave, Ch 1.

Gordon, I. and McCann, P. (2000a) 'Industrial clusters: complexes, agglomeration and/or social networks?', *Urban Studies*, vol 37, pp 513-32.

Hall, P. (1963) *London 2000*, London: Faber and Faber.

Hall, P. (1989) *London 2001*, London: Unwin Hyman.

Harloe, M. (2001) 'Social justice and the city: the new "liberal formulation"', *International Journal of Urban and Regional Research*, vol 25, no 4, pp 889-97.

Hebbert, M. (1998) *London: More by fortune than design*, Chichester: Wiley.

Kesteloot, C. (1997) 'The geography of deprivation in Brussels and local development strategies', in S. Musterd and W. Ostendorf (eds) *Urban segregation and the welfare state*, London: Routledge.

King, A.D. (1990) *Global cities: Post-imperialism and the internationalization of London*, London and New York: Routledge.

Porter, R. (2000) *London: A social history*, Harmondsworth: Penguin Books.

Sassen, S. (1991) *The global city: New York, London and Tokyo*, Princeton, NJ: Princeton University Press.

Wilson, W. (1987) *The truly disadvantaged*, Chicago, IL: University of Chicago Press.

Young, M. and Willmott, P. (1973) *The symmetrical family: A study of work and leisure in the London region*, London: Routledge & Kegan Paul.

Part Two: Competitiveness and urban change

SIX

Urban growth and competitiveness in Britain: a long-run perspective

Barry Moore and Iain Begg

Introduction

What factors underpin the competitive success or otherwise of different urban areas? This question, clearly, is central to any debate over the fortunes of different towns and cities in the British urban system. Taking a long-term view, over the past 50 years, say, some cities have consistently prospered, maintaining or increasing their share of national employment and population; others have lost ground and have struggled to attract new investment and jobs. Generally speaking, it is the major conurbations and large cities that grew rapidly in the 19th century that have typically lost both population and employment. The smaller towns and new towns[1] (particularly those in the south of England and close to London) have, on the other hand, gained both population and employment.

Many of these shifts in population and employment have persisted over decades, in fact, rather than years. In the 1970s and 1980s, these trends received much attention as inner-city areas in the declining conurbations experienced worsening economic and social problems and intense difficulties in adapting to a rapidly changing economic environment (Hall, 1981; Gudgin et al, 1982; Begg et al, 1986; Robson, 1988; Breheny, 1999). And despite the proliferation of highly targeted area-based regeneration policies, many of these problems remain. Arguably, in some cities they have actually intensified and spread to other parts of the city, including outer estates and suburbs.

In parallel with these processes of geographical restructuring, there have been major shifts in the economic base of different towns and cities. This includes the well-documented decline in manufacturing employment and the rise of new sectors including finance and business services, high technology and the new 'knowledge economy'. These, in turn, have impacted differentially on different towns and cities as new patterns of locational preference have impacted on investment and disinvestment.

This study set out to establish fundamental information about the factors that help shape the competitiveness of cities and which determine patterns of growth and decline. The aim was to identify the particular attributes of different urban areas – what can be termed the 'asset base' of the city – that create competitive advantage. This asset base sets the context within which businesses and other economic agents operate and interact and, it is argued, has major implications for the competitiveness or otherwise of different urban areas and the businesses which operate within them. There have been several attempts to specify these contextual factors (see, for example, Kresl, 1995) and to assess their relative importance for the growth of cities (Glaeser et al, 1995). Here we look in particular at the impacts of a city's industrial inheritance and specialisation, the types of companies in the city, the locational characteristics of the city and the quality of its infrastructure and the capacity of the city to support innovation and learning. Public policy is also seen as an important contextual influence, conditioning and regulating private sector activities and providing resources to support and renew different elements of a city's portfolio of assets. A key objective of the research was to assess the relative importance of these different characteristics in determining the competitiveness of the city.

Research programme

The research programme consisted of three main strands of work. First, it developed a conceptual framework for understanding the notion of urban competitiveness and the factors that differentiate successful from less successful cities. Specifically, the project sought to develop the concept of 'investability' (that is, conditions conducive to increasing the rate of investment in an area) to underpin an approach to policy that focuses on the competitive position of cities. Four main sources of competitive advantage are distinguished: the inherited mix of industries; the degree of specialisation and diversity; the characteristics of companies in the city; and the business environment and factors that inhibit or encourage firms to innovate.

Second, the research established a number of city performance indicators reflecting long-run trends in urban competitiveness. These performance indicators focused primarily on employment and population and a number of intermediate measures such as new company formation and economic restructuring. A starting point was to define a city's constitution. The approach followed was to identify all built-up areas with a population in excess of 65,000 using boundaries shown in Key Statistics for Urban Areas from the 1991 Census of Population, and matched as closely as possible to Local Authority Districts (LADs). Over 100 urban areas (UAs) were distinguished – some defined to cover single LADs, others to encompass certain adjacent districts, reflecting the spread of a city into what might once have been rural areas or adjacent cities. Thus, Bristol UA includes Bath and Weston-Super-Mare, while Cambridge UA includes the City of Cambridge and South Cambridgeshire. Although the initial database was based on the 1992 definition of LADs, a complementary data set based on the 1996 Unitary Authority areas has also been developed. The empirical work involved drawing on a variety of different sources including the 1951, 1971, 1981, 1991 and 2001 Censuses of Population, the Censuses of Employment, the Annual Business Inquiry and the Labour Force Surveys. Considerable effort was made to ensure consistent definitions of cities and sectors through time.

Thirdly, a variety of different city-attributes or characteristics were identified and measured to explore the relative importance of different factors influencing city competitiveness and performance. A data set of over 30 indicators was established reflecting a range of factors and city characteristics. These included, for example, city industry diversity and specialisation (to capture potential inter- and intra-industry externalities), location attributes (such as proximity to London or different types of airport), the knowledge and skill base of the city and the residential attractiveness of the city.

The empirical research included descriptive work documenting past economic and demographic trends in individual cities and a range of city types or groupings, shift-share analysis and econometric modelling. Inevitably, the results and key findings below can only be presented in a very concise form (see also Begg et al, 2002).

Population

In the 50 years from 1951 to 2001, Britain's urban population increased from 35.7 million to 39.3 million. However, with Britain's total population also increasing over this period from 48.8 million to 57.1 million, the proportion of the population in UAs fell from 73.1% to 70% (Table 6.1). Underlying these broad demographic trends, three important features of the changing settlement pattern stand out. The first is an urban–rural shift, the second is a shift in population from larger cities to smaller cities, and the third is a shift from the north to the south of the country. Thus, the share of the population resident in the seven conurbations declined from just under 40% to 32% with

Table 6.1: The growth of population by city type (1951-2001) (% pa and % share)

	Population 1951 (000s)	% pa 1951-2001	% pa 1951-1971	% pa 1971-1981	% pa 1981-1991	% pa 1991-2001	% share 1951	% share 2001
Conurbations	19,395	–0.15	–0.08	–0.51	–0.09	–0.01	39.7	31.0
Free-standing cities	7,761	0.22	0.57	–0.08	0.12	–0.07	15.9	15.0
Northern cities	2,391	0.31	0.20	1.27	–0.07	–0.04	4.9	4.0
Southern cities	3,350	0.85	1.42	0.70	0.44	0.27	6.9	9.0
Expanded cities	1,202	0.83	1.28	0.99	0.44	0.20	2.5	3.0
New towns	701	1.82	2.40	2.79	1.05	0.49	1.4	3.0
Coastal towns	903	0.53	0.81	0.26	0.58	0.18	1.8	2.0
Rural	13,137	0.61	0.97	0.16	0.57	0.41	26.9	31.0
Great Britain	48,841	0.31	0.54	0.08	0.25	0.16	100.0	100.0

Source: Census of Population 1951 to 2001; Local Authority Districts (1991) based Urban Areas definition

a population loss of 1.4 million. The smaller cities and rural areas gained 4.2 million and 4.9 million residents respectively and southern smaller cities increased their population at three times the rate of the northern cities.

Within each of the city classes, there are also important differences which are masked by the aggregate figures. For example, the striking feature revealed by the disaggregation of the overall figures for the conurbations is the recovery of London's population since 1981. With the exception of the West Yorkshire conurbation, which perhaps surprisingly steadily gained population, the other conurbations continue to lose population, although there is evidence that the decline is attenuating in Manchester and to a lesser extent in Glasgow.

A diversity of experience is also found in the other city groupings. While many of the smaller northern cities lost populations over the period, the population of Harrogate and Chester increased. Within the group of smaller Southern cities significant differences in growth performance were also identified.

Employment

In the 50-year period 1951 to 2001, total employment in Britain has increased by nearly 6 million (or, that is, 0.5% per year) (Table 6.2). Despite this very substantial expansion of national employment, both the conurbations and the smaller northern cities experienced a fall in employment. By 2001, the share of total employment located in the conurbations had fallen to 34.3% from 45.3% in 1951. Employment in the conurbations shows signs of recovering in

Figure 6.1: The growth of population in the seven major conurbations of Great Britain (1981-2001) (1951 = 100)

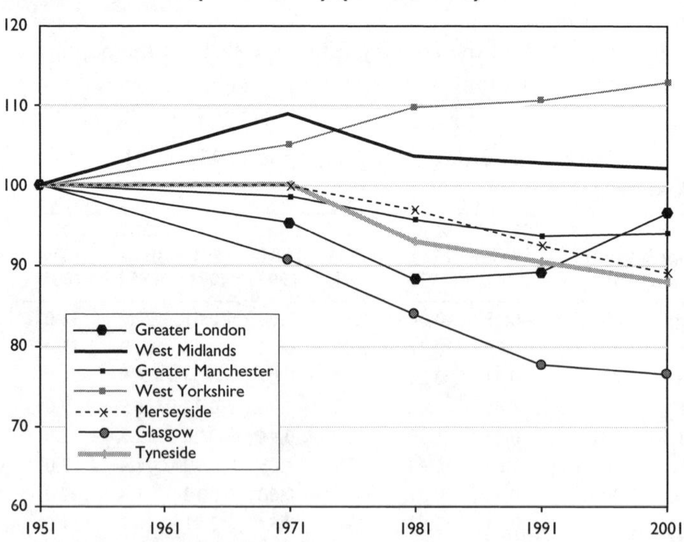

Note: Definition of London Conurbation is wider than Greater London.
Source: Census of Population, Local Authority District (1991) based estimates

Table 6.2: The growth of employment by city type (1951-2001) (% pa and % share)

	Employment (000s)	% pa 1951-2001	% pa 1951-1971	% pa 1971-1981	% pa 1981-1991	% pa 1991-2001	% share 1951	% share 2001	Employment 1951-2001 (000s)
Conurbations	9,721	–0.07	–0.11	–1.13	–0.06	–1.07	45.3	34.3	–325
Free-standing cities	3,652	0.24	0.29	–0.45	0.61	0.48	17.0	15.1	+475
Northern cities	1,238	–0.05	–0.1	–0.91	0.34	0.52	5.8	4.4	–32
Southern cities	1,580	0.93	1.09	0.09	1.52	0.89	7.4	9.2	+934
Expanded cities	576	0.8	0.51	0.47	1.15	1.43	2.7	3.2	+287
New towns	352	1.99	2.2	0.85	2.59	2.12	1.6	3.4	+592
Coastal towns	387	0.29	0.37	–0.5	1.6	–0.35	1.8	1.6	+61
Rural	3,961	1.38	1.48	1.66	0.88	1.39	18.5	28.7	+3,900
Great Britain	21,467	0.49	0.45	–0.11	0.6	1.05	100.0	100.0	+5,893

Source: Census of Population, Labour Force Survey, Local Authority District 1991 definition.
Includes employees in employment and self-employed

the 1990s. Figure 6.2, however, shows that this is accounted for principally by the turnaround in the fortunes of London and the West Yorkshire conurbation. Liverpool and Glasgow are shown to be the worst performers, but even for these cities the evidence indicates a bottoming out of the long-run post-war decline in employment. Major employment increases are to be found in the southern smaller cities (934,000+) and the new and expanded towns (879,000+); but the really substantial gains in employment have taken place in the rural areas outside the urban system, and here employment increased by nearly four million. Moreover employment growth was much greater in the southern rural areas than in the rural areas in the north.

Our research also reveals considerable stability in the rankings of city performance with the same group of cities performing well across periods. Excluding new and expanded towns[1], Cambridge, Cheltenham/Tewksbury, Gosport/Fareham, Swindon, Slough/Windsor and Wycombe appeared in the twenty fastest-growing urban areas in each decade from 1951 to 2001. Equally, many of the same cities remained in the worst performing group for long periods, with relatively few cities making the transition from persistent relative decline to growth. Given the economic problems linked to persistent decline of some cities and to the accommodation of growth by others this finding raises important questions concerning the efficacy of either market adjustment mechanisms or past policies to shift the balance of growth across the urban system.

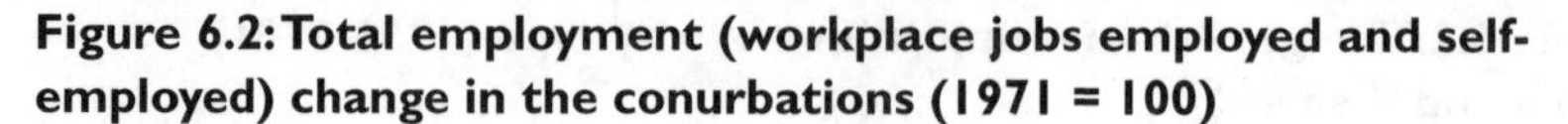

Figure 6.2: Total employment (workplace jobs employed and self-employed) change in the conurbations (1971 = 100)

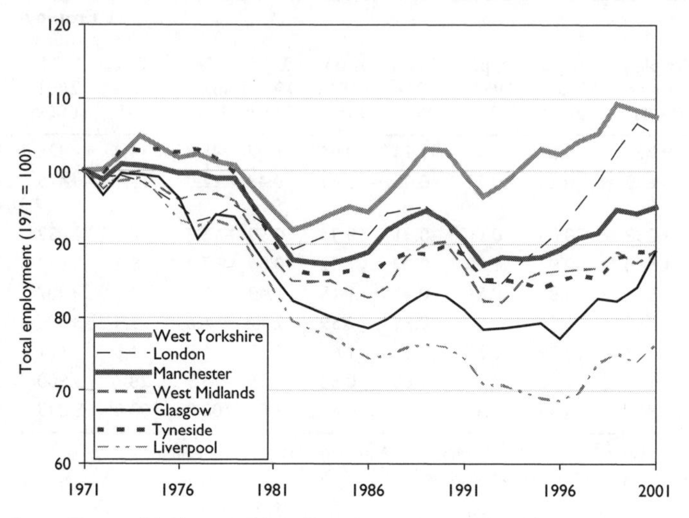

Source: Census of Employment, Labour Force Survey, Estimates for 2001

Unemployment

Despite significant changes in the share of population and the share of employment across the urban system, the share of unemployment across different city types has remained relatively stable over 50 years (Table 6.3). Over half of Great Britain's unemployment is located in the seven major conurbations and free-standing cities and their share of unemployment has changed very little over the period. The unemployment rate has risen across each of the city types with the greatest increases in the conurbations and new towns. The worsening unemployment predicament of the conurbations is also highlighted by the rise in their unemployment rate relative to that experienced nationally. The analysis of unemployment by duration and city type also reveals that the long-term unemployed are disproportionately concentrated in the conurbations, most importantly, London, Birmingham and Merseyside. These findings reveal the failure of unemployment rates to converge even over very long periods of time and expose significant limitations of market adjustment mechanisms in resolving unemployment disparities across the city system.

Structural adaptation and the changing role of cities

The ability of a city to adapt to structural change is an important facet of its performance and reflects the city's 'investability'. Behind the broad trends in urban performance identified earlier in this chapter, important shifts in the structure of industry nationally have been taking place that have profoundly influenced not only the relative performance of different cities but also their

Table 6.3: Resident unemployment across the urban system (1951-2001)

	Unemployment as a % of total population		Unemployment % relative to GB %		Unemployment share	
	1951	2001	1951	2001	1951	2001
Conurbation	1.033	2.223	106	130	42.1	41.5
Free-standing	0.962	1.72	99	101	15.4	15.4
Northern smaller	1.108	1.713	114	100	5.4	4.8
Southern smaller	0.672	1.287	69	75	5.1	6.7
Expanded	1.081	1.547	111	91	2.7	2.9
New towns	0.509	1.282	52	75	0.8	2.2
Coastal	1.623	1.802	167	105	3.0	2.2
Rural	0.927	1.346	95	79	25.6	24.4
Great Britain	0.793	1.709	100	100	100.0	100.0

Note: The definition of unemployment used is the Census definition of 'out of work' and the 2001 figures are estimated. All rates are expressed as a share of total population and are therefore lower than alternative definitions but changes similarly.
Source: Census of Population, ONS

role in the wider national economy. The 'deindustrialisation' of the British economy, meaning the decline of manufacturing industry, is a familiar story. In the three decades since 1971, the manufacturing sector in Britain halved with a loss of some four million jobs. Over the same period employment in the business services sector expanded by 3.5 million jobs, and by 2001 employed more than 5.5 million workers. Perhaps less frequently recognised is the expansion of the distribution and leisure sector by over 2.3 million and the expansion of public service employment by over two million.

These structural changes in the national economy have impacted very unevenly across the urban system. Here we summarise the impact of these structural shifts by presenting results for the economy broken down into six sectors and also for the high technology sector and computing services. Our starting point is the urban impact of the long-run decline of national manufacturing employment that gathered momentum in the 1970s. From 1971 to 2001, the seven major conurbations experienced a loss of over two million manufacturing jobs and, at the end of this period, manufacturing employment was only one third of its level in 1971. The free-standing cities and the northern and southern smaller cities declined broadly in line with the national decline in manufacturing employment losing close to half their manufacturing jobs over the period. New towns, expanded cities and rural areas also lost manufacturing jobs but to a much smaller extent than the conurbations and larger cities. These findings are very much in line with earlier work (see, for example, Fothergill and Gudgin, 1982; Gudgin et al, 1982; Gudgin, 1995; Breheny, 1999). The outcome of these trends is that the relative concentration of manufacturing has increased in the rural areas in both the north and the south but declined significantly in the conurbations and to

Table 6.4: Growth and specialisation in manufacturing employment change across the urban system (index 1971 = 100; change 000s)

	Index				Employment change 1971-2001	LQ 1971	LQ 2001
	1971	1981	1991	2001			
Conurbation	100	65	42	33	–2,154	102	79
Free-standing city	100	77	57	48	–692	104	105
Northern cities	100	76	62	53	–273	121	142
Southern cities	100	84	66	54	–274	94	90
Expanded cities	100	85	68	59	–83	104	103
New towns	100	83	73	65	–78	126	115
Coastal towns	100	85	66	66	–30	67	96
Northern rural	100	83	77	70	–159	87	118
Southern rural	100	89	85	82	–177	89	116
Great Britain	100	75	58	50	–3,920	100	100

Source: Census of Employment, Annual Business Inquiry and Labour Force Survey, Unitary Authority 1996 definition of Urban Area (employees in employment and self-employed)

a lesser extent in the new towns. In Table 6.4, the conurbations have moved from close to the national share in 1971 with a Location Quotient (LQ) of 102 to well below average specialisation with an LQ of 79[2].

The broad city groupings hide very substantial differences in the relative concentration of manufacturing between individual cities. Thus, some traditional manufacturing urban areas such as Burnley/Nelson, Redditch and Blackburn/Darwen still today have more than double the national share of manufacturing and have experienced persistent specialisation in this sector for three decades or more. By comparison St Albans, Chester, Harrogate, Reading/Woking and the London UA have consistently had less than the national share of manufacturing, and by 2001 their LQs indicated that they had less than half the national share of manufacturing.

As manufacturing employment has declined across the urban system other sectors have expanded their employment, notably the financial and business services (FBS) sector. In the conurbations, FBS employment has increased by just fewer than 1.5 million in the three decades since 1971. This increase makes a significant contribution towards offsetting the loss of 2.2 million manufacturing jobs in the conurbations. Much of this increase, however, has been concentrated in the London conurbation where employment has risen by one million, more than double the increase in all the other six conurbations in aggregate, although the greatest percentage increase in FBS has been experienced in the West Yorkshire conurbation that includes Leeds. London has far and away the greatest specialisation in this sector, with an LQ of 165 in 2001 (compared with 170 in 1971) and, with the exception of the Glasgow conurbation with an LQ of 107 in 2001, is the only conurbation with an LQ exceeding 100. Outside of London, the evidence indicates specialisation in cities in the hinterland of London, particularly in new towns and expanded cities. Beyond the south, specialisation is apparent in only Chester, Edinburgh

Table 6.5: Growth and specialisation in Financial and Business Services employment (employees in employment and self-employed) across the urban system (index 1971 = 100; change 000s)

	Index				Employment change	LQ	LQ
	1971	1981	1991	2001	1971-2001	1971	2001
Great Britain	100	136	199	269	+3,482	100	100
Conurbation	100	127	171	241	+1,457	125	131
Free-standing city	100	138	210	254	+479	93	92
Northern cities	100	137	209	272	+130	59	65
Southern cities	100	144	232	302	+371	108	106
Expanded cities	100	150	244	369	+123	88	100
New towns	100	147	250	402	+154	110	114
Coastal towns	100	133	172	163	+21	93	59
Northern rural	100	141	212	243	+149	64	55
Southern rural	100	161	264	370	+579	72	78

Source: Census of Employment, Annual Business Inquiry and Labour Force Survey, Unitary Authority 1996 definition of Urban Area

and Aberdeen. However, the broad picture is for specialisation in this sector to be relatively stable over time by city type. What is also clear from the disaggregated analysis is that specialisation in FBS exists in a relatively small number of cities, with only 19 cities showing an LQ greater than 120 in 2001 (compared with 36 for manufacturing).

Distribution and leisure industries have provided an additional 2.3 million jobs since 1971. Much of this activity, however, meets the needs of the local population and the scale of activity, therefore, is related fairly closely to population size. There is, therefore, only limited concentration of such employment across the city groups with the exception of the coastal cities and here specialisation has been steadily declining. An analysis of specialisation across individual cities in 2001 confirms the specialisation of this sector in coastal cities with Great Yarmouth, Harrogate, Eastbourne, Torbay and Gravesend with LQs exceeding 125 – at the other end of the spectrum of specialisation are the urban areas of Cambridge, Hartlepool, Inverclyde, Torfaen and the Rhondda with LQs in the low 80s.

Although the utilities, construction and communications sector provided close to four million jobs in 2001, this was very close to the number employed three decades earlier. There is some evidence of a weak urban–rural shift with growth of jobs in southern rural areas and declines in conurbations and free-standing cities. Differences in specialisation are not pronounced across the city grouping and the highest specialisation is found in the expanded cities (LQ=112) although southern rural areas experienced an increase in specialisation from an LQ of 96 in 1971 to 109 in 2001.

The distribution of public service employment across the city system is to a significant extent determined by the distribution of population across cities. However, changes in the relative concentration of public services across cities do occur as a result of the decline or growth of the other sectors and regional policy motivated relocations such as the move of the Driving Vehicle Licence office from London to Wales. The relative concentration of public service jobs has increased in the free-standing cities, the northern cities, the coastal towns and northern rural areas. These are typically areas that have experienced a significant relative loss of manufacturing without a parallel increase in other sectors. The position of the conurbations has changed only marginally but there have been important shifts in specialisation in individual conurbations not revealed by the aggregate of this group. The main finding is the decline in public service specialisation in London and its rise in the other six conurbations. Thus, whereas in 1971 the LQ for London was 108, by 2001 it was only 79. The LQ for this sector increased in each of the other conurbations with particularly striking increases in Liverpool and Tyneside.

Within the broad industrial groupings discussed earlier in this chapter, a number of key industries were identified as especially significant for the long-run evolution of a city economy. High technology is commonly thought to offer prospects of expanding domestic and overseas markets and high quality jobs associated with the so-called knowledge economy. Earlier research suggests distinct locational preferences for high-technology industry (HTI) (Begg and Cameron, 1988; Begg, 1991; Fingleton, 1994). Is there evidence that HTIs continue to favour some cities rather than others? And what are the long-run trends in specialisation? The 'Butchart' (1987) definition of high technology was enhanced to include other sectors such as higher education and engineering services known to include a relatively high proportion of professional and scientific staff and where research and development (R&D) is significant. The results are quite striking. The new towns and expanded towns show the highest degree of specialisation in high-technology manufacturing, with LQs of 1.55 and 1.48 respectively in 1998 (in contrast to an LQ of 0.58 in the conurbations).

Table 6.6: Growth and specialisation in Public Services employment across the urban system (index 1971 = 100; change 000s)

	Index				Employment change	LQ	LQ
	1971	1981	1991	2001	1971-2001	1971	2001
Great Britain	100	115	130	148	+2,088	100	100
Conurbation	100	108	112	123	+393	99	95
Free-standing city	100	114	133	153	+397	106	115
Northern cities	100	122	138	165	+158	89	109
Southern cities	100	119	129	145	+194	120	103
Expanded cities	100	122	141	168	+75	100	95
New towns	100	126	152	189	+82	93	83
Coastal towns	100	124	173	183	+61	97	120
Northern rural	100	126	152	175	+251	97	110
Southern rural	100	122	154	181	+477	93	90

Source: Census of Employment, Annual Business Inquiry and Labour Force Survey, Unitary Authority 1996 definition of Urban Area (employees in employment and self-employed)

Rural areas, smaller northern cities and smaller southern cities have LQs of 1.32, 1.17 and 1.1 respectively. For HTI services, the greatest specialisation is in the smaller southern cities (LQ=1.4) and the lowest in the smaller northern cities (LQ=0.58). The conurbations show some specialisation in HTI services with an LQ of 1.07, although within this group Merseyside and West Yorkshire lag behind the average.

Within the HTI sector, computing services is a particularly dynamic sector and in 2001 provided over 500,000 jobs. It provides an instructive example of changing specialisation across the city system (Table 6.6). The number of jobs in this sector increased by nearly half a million in the period 1971 to 2001 approximately 40% of which were located in the conurbations. The pattern of specialisation changed sharply over the 30-year period, falling in the conurbations (with only London with an LQ>1) and free-standing cities, and increasing in the other city groupings and southern rural areas. A more disaggregated analysis at the individual city level shows specialisation ranging from LQs>3 in southern cities such as Stevenage, St Albans and Reading/Woking, to 0.25 or less in Doncaster, Barnsley and Rhondda.

What makes a city more or less competitive?

Although there is a considerable body of economic theory concerned with increasing our understanding of the forces underpinning long-run differences in urban growth and competitiveness, there is a relative dearth of empirical research on the subject, particularly research that focuses on the urban system as a whole. A review of the theoretical literature produced a number of key hypotheses relating to both demand- and 'supply-side' influences (the latter representing essentially inputs such as skill levels and other characteristics of

Table 6.7: Growth and specialisation in Computing employment (employees in employment and self-employed) across the urban system

	Jobs change 1971-2001	% GB 1971	% GB 2001	LQ 1971	LQ 2001
Great Britain	487	100	100	100	100
Conurbation	197	56	42	139	122
Free-standing cities	49	18	11	109	71
Northern cities	11	4	3	69	45
Southern cities	68	8	13	92	140
Expanded cities	30	2	6	97	188
New towns	19	3	4	115	120
Coastal towns	6	0	1	19	63
Northern rural	17	3	3	40	41
Southern rural	89	6	17	38	92

Source: Census of Employment, Annual Business Inquiry and Labour Force Survey, Unitary Authority 1996 definition of Urban Area

individual cities). On the demand side, a 'shift-share' analysis provides an initial assessment of the influences of changes in demand and the significance of a city's industrial structure in influencing growth[2]. The significance of entrepreneurship is explored through an analysis of new firm formation rates. A multivariate regression analysis of industry growth by city examined the relationship between a variety of city supply-side factors and the industry growth performance in the subsequent period, after controlling for the growth of national industry demand. Drawing on research on city growth in the US (for example, Glaeser et al, 1992) supply-side factors included proxies for inter- and intra-industry knowledge externalities and human capital concentration[3]. Other factors investigated included, inter alia, locational advantages of the city such as proximity to London, accessibility and communications, the residential attractiveness of the city and eligibility for urban and regional policy assistance.

Industrial structure

Shift-share analysis suggests that the initial industrial structure played a role in the subsequent growth performance of many cities. In aggregate, conurbations inherited a relatively favourable industrial structure at the beginning of the post-war period, although the contribution of this to overall growth was quite small (5% between 1959 and 1997). The most unfavourable industrial mix was in the smaller northern cities, accounting for about 15% of their long-run decline. Perhaps rather surprisingly, new towns and expanded towns suffered an unfavourable industrial structure of a similar order of magnitude to the smaller northern cities, but in both cases this structural effect was overwhelmed by positive competitiveness (differential) effects associated in part with the policy driven growth of these cities. Focusing on the role of particular sectors also suggested structural explanations for trends in employment growth. For example, a high concentration of 'traditional' industry (mining, textiles and basic metals) significantly disadvantaged certain cities in the north, whereas a specialisation in some of the new and growing service industries favoured the growth of smaller cities in the north. With the exception of smaller northern cities, competitiveness effects dominated structural effects for all city types.

New firm formation

Gudgin (1995) argues that spatial differences in new firm formation rates are not only important in their own right for a region's performance but also provide a useful indicator of 'attitudes to business entrepreneurship'. Evidence on birth rates and death rates across the urban system is provided by VAT registration data[3]. The gross formation rate per employee indicates the propensity of individuals in a city to set up in business, and the net formation rate (births minus deaths) the propensity to stay in business. The analysis shows considerable variation in the registration rate, with northern cities experiencing the lowest rate and the registration rate for conurbations confirming the conventional

Table 6.8: Birth and death rates of companies per 1,000 employees across the urban system

	Birth rate (registration)	Death rate (deregistration)	Net formation rate
Great Britain	6.14	6.53	–0.39
Conurbation	6.62	6.58	0.04
Free-standing cities	4.86	5.27	–0.41
Northern cities	4.76	5.65	–0.90
Southern cities	6.09	6.28	–0.19
Expanded cities	5.38	5.60	–0.22
New towns	5.37	5.32	0.05
Coastal towns	5.19	7.34	–2.15
Northern rural	5.80	6.81	–1.02
Southern rural	7.35	8.08	–0.74

Source: NOMIS, VAT registrations and deregistrations

wisdom that they act as incubators for new start-ups. Southern rural areas stand out as experiencing the highest birth rates but also the highest deregistration rates.

Recent results from Dale and Morgan (2000) that demonstrate the crucial significance of the birth rate for net job creation find support from our analysis of birth rates by city. A scatter plot for the nine city types of birth rate in 1995 against employment growth in the period 1995 to 2001 shows a positive correlation.

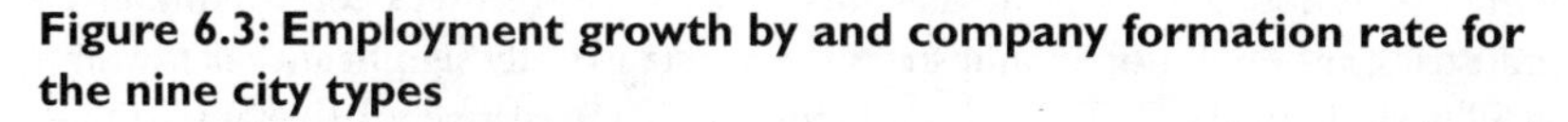

Figure 6.3: Employment growth by and company formation rate for the nine city types

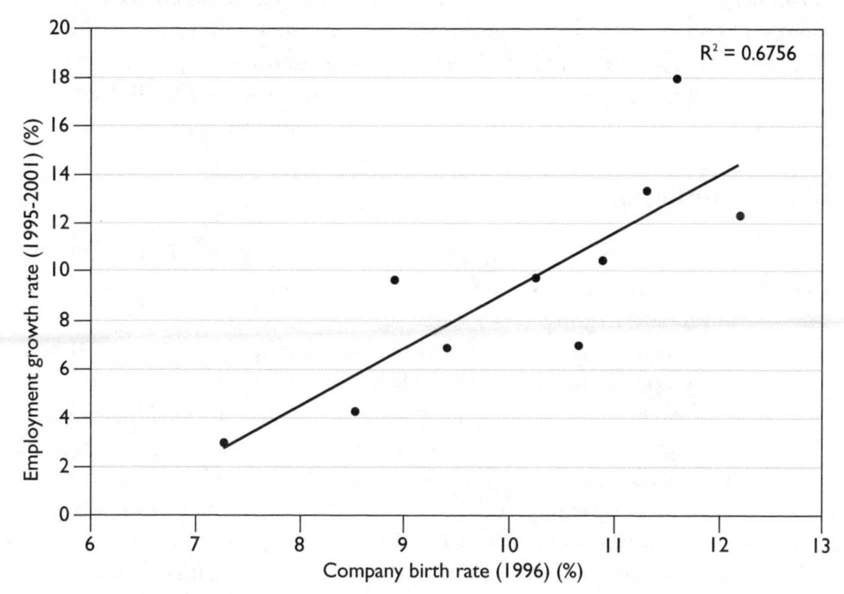

Supply-side factors

Statistical research exploring the relative importance of different supply-side factors is still underway at the time of writing and only a brief summary is provided here to give a flavour of the analysis and point to some of the more robust preliminary findings. First, the analysis suggests that industry specialisation (indicating potential intra-industry spillover benefits) has a negative influence on the subsequent growth of industry in the city. This negative influence is fairly clear-cut for a number of industries, including, for example, resource-based industries such as traditional and high-technology manufacturing, utilities/ construction and distributive industries across a range of different periods. This is very much in line with the results for the US (Glaeser et al, 1992). For business services, the results are somewhat less clear. Specialisation in this sector has a negative influence on subsequent employment growth in some periods and a positive influence in other periods; moreover, the results would also seem to depend on the degree of industrial disaggregation of the sector. There is some limited support for the Jacobs' (1969) diversification hypothesis and the potential positive influence of inter-industry knowledge spillovers and this is particularly the case for the growth of high-technology manufacturing and business service in the 1980s and 1990s. Higher concentrations of human capital in the city at the beginning of the period are associated with faster city growth and the results are robust for different time periods and for a breakdown into ten industry groups, although further industrial disaggregation reveals more mixed results. The important location factors are new town designation, which is almost always positively linked with city growth for a number of industries, although not all industries show a statistically significant relationship in all periods analysed. There is no evidence of a pervasive north–south divide across all sectors but northern locations are associated with slower growth in the distributive sector and the business services sector for some periods. Perhaps not surprising, proximity to airports tends to be associated with faster city growth and some city industries clearly benefit from proximity to London.

Policy implications

Urban policy, narrowly defined, has tended to focus on the regeneration of specific local areas within individual cities, addressing particular problems of market failure and manifestations of urban decline, often in a piecemeal way and uncoordinated with other policies impacting on the urban system (DETR, 2000). A key conclusion of our research is that government policy will only provide lasting solutions to the plight of Britain's lagging cities (and the pressures faced by the rapidly expanding cities in the south), if these urban problems are addressed in the context of change in the urban system as a whole. The evidence reveals powerful long-run trends increasing the concentration of relatively successful cities in the south. Even London would seem in the 1990s to have reversed its long-run loss of population and jobs. Many cities in the north, however, struggle to attract investment, to retain skilled labour and continue to face problems associated with persistent relative decline. The implication for policy making is that strategic urban policy has to meet the challenges of problems linked to both urban decline and urban growth and has therefore to consider the evolution of the overall urban system. Moreover, by taking account of developments affecting the urban system as a whole, policy makers are more likely to avoid strategies for individual cities that are in conflict with one another.

Evidence of a shift in the location of population and economic activity towards smaller towns and rural areas in the hinterland of the conurbations and larger cities suggests that within the national urban system, important adjustments are also taking place at a regional level. For example, the growth of the smaller cities in the south east and east regions, and the growth of the rural areas and smaller towns in these regions, are inextricably linked to economic and demographic change in London. While London may retain or strengthen its competitive advantages for some industries, it will be losing it for other industries that perceive locational advantages in the hinterland towns and cities. Equally, shifting migration patterns and changing residential preferences within sub-regional urban systems are changing the spatial distribution of different population segments. That these changes impact unevenly on the city system and are closely linked to many urban problems is well established. The message for policy makers is that cities cannot be uncoupled from their regional and sub-regional context and that careful consideration must be given to the appropriate spatial scale for intervention when designing urban policy.

Our analysis of the different and changing roles of cities as reflected in their changing industrial structures over the past 50 years and in their response to differential patterns of growth and decline, signals that the urban system is adjusting to market forces. A striking feature of our results, however, despite these adjustments, is the long-run stability of the city rankings with relatively few examples of cities reversing their fortunes or significantly changing their position in the urban hierarchy of economic performance. At the same time, the evidence reveals a strong tendency for Britain's new and growing industries to favour locations in the cities of the south. These findings imply that the sources of urban competitive advantage and disadvantage are deep-seated, not easily dislodged and that the long-run market adjustments (and policies) that have taken place have fallen short of resolving many of the problems cities face. The danger for policy in responding to this challenge is to encourage a zero-sum game in which one city's gain is another city's loss. The recognition that cities play different roles at both a regional and national level and that cities both compete and collaborate in a variety of ways supports an 'investability' approach. This would recognise the diversity of cities and seek to upgrade those city characteristics and competencies that improve the capacity of the city to attract and retain investment. The obstacles to raising urban competitiveness, however, extend well beyond the urban characteristics of improved design and built quality emphasised by the Urban Task Force. In our view, it would be wrong to focus urban policy largely on these factors or to follow their suggestion that cities should concentrate on promoting 'informational' activities. Our research emphasises the scale and persistence of urban problems and the need to tackle these problems at the national and sub-regional level, and embrace the full spectrum of conurbations, smaller cities, towns and rural areas. This argues the need for an urban strategy that, crucially, draws on and coordinates mainstream national functional programmes rather than simply resources devoted to 'urban policy' as such.

Notes

[1] New towns were new settlements established under the formal powers of the English New Towns Act (1946) and initiated over the period from 1946 to 1970 (Schaffer, 1972).

[2] The location quotient (LQ) is obtained by dividing the employment share of a particular sector in the city type by the national sector share.

[3] There are some weaknesses with VAT registrations as a measure of entrepreneurial activity, including the exclusion of businesses below the size threshold for registration. It remains, however, the best available comprehensive indicator available.

References

Begg, I. (1991) 'High technology location and the urban areas of Great Britain', *Urban Studies*, vol 25, no 6, pp 961-81.

Begg, I. (1999) 'Cities and competitiveness', *Urban Studies*, vol 36, no 5/6, pp 795-810.

Begg, I. and Cameron, G. (1988) 'High technology and the urban areas of Great Britain', *Urban Studies*, vol 25, pp 361-79.

Begg, I., Moore, B. and Rhodes, J. (1986) 'Economic and social change in urban Britain and the inner cities', in V. Hausner (ed) *Critical issues in urban economic development. Volume 1*, Oxford: Clarendon Press.

Begg, I., Moore, B. and Altunbas, Y. (2002) 'Long-run trends in the competitiveness of British cities', in I. Begg (ed) *Urban competitiveness: Policies for dynamic cities*, Bristol: The Policy Press, pp 101-34.

Begg, I. and Moore, B. (2000) *Memorandum of evidence: Proposed urban White Paper*, House of Commons Environment, Transport and Regional Affairs Committee, HC 185-1, House of Commons Papers.

Breheny, M. (ed) (1999) *The people: Where will they work?*, Town and Country Planning Association.

Butchart, R.L. (1987) 'A new UK definition of the High Technology Industries', *Economic Trends*, no 400, February, pp 82-8.

Dale, I. and Morgan, A. (2000) *Job creation: The role of new and small firms*, Sheffield: Small Business Service.

DETR (Department of the Environment, Transport and Regions) (2000) *The state of English cities*, London: The Stationery Office.

Fingleton, B. (1994) 'The location of high-technology manufacturing in Great Britain: changes in the late 1980s', *Urban Studies*, vol 31, no 1, pp 47-57.

Fothergill, S. and Gudgin, G. (1982) *Unequal growth, urban and regional employment change in the UK*, London: Heinemann.

Glaeser, E.L., Kallal, J.A., Scheinkman J.A. and Shleifer, A. (1992) 'Growth in cities', *Journal of Political Economy*, vol 100, no 6, pp 1126-52.

Glaeser, E.L., Scheinkman J.A. and Shleifer, A. (1995) 'Economic growth in a cross-section of cities', *Journal of Monetary Economics*, no 36, August, pp 117-43.

Gudgin, G., Moore, B. and Rhodes, J. (1982) 'Employment problems in the cities and regions of the UK: prospects for the 1980s', *Cambridge Economic Policy Review*, vol 8, no 2, Aldershot: Gower Publishing.

Gudgin, G. (1995) 'Regional problems and policy in the UK', *Oxford Review of Economic Policy*, vol 11, no 2, pp 18-63.

HM Treasury (1995) *A framework for the evaluation of regeneration projects and programmes.*

Jacobs, J. (1968) *The economy of cities*, New York, NY: Vintage Books.

Rowthorn, R. (1986) 'De-industrialisation in Britain', in R. Martin and R. Rowthorn (eds) *The geography of de-industrialisation*, London: Macmillan.

Schaffer, F. (1972) *The new town story*, London: Paladin.

SEVEN

Migration, residential preferences and the changing environment of cities

Tony Champion and Tania Fisher

Perhaps the feature of British cities that has been given the most consistent attention in recent years by the media and policy makers alike is population loss through migration to other parts of the country. Once seen in a positive light as a key mechanism for reducing urban development pressures and supported by policy initiatives such as the New Towns programme, the urban exodus has, for the past three decades, been viewed as one of the nation's biggest planning challenges. This is clear, most recently, in the Urban White Paper and supporting documents setting out and supporting central government's latest efforts at securing an 'urban renaissance' (Urban Task Force, 1999; DETR, 2000; Robson et al, 2000). Urban exodus is seen both as the haemorrhaging of human capital from cities and towns and as the source of pressures for growth and unacceptably high house-building requirements elsewhere. Stemming this tide is portrayed as a crucial factor in the success of urban regeneration policy, as well as potentially assisting the achievement of wider environmental sustainability objectives. Better intelligence about the dynamics of this phenomenon and the motivations of the people involved, therefore, is a vital element in deciding on the best approach to be taken towards reviving the social and economic life of our cities.

This chapter presents the findings of a 'Cities' programme project that aimed at improving our understanding of the factors that bind and attract residents to, and (not least) that repel people from, the nation's larger cities and their inner areas. That project included aggregate analyses of population trends and migration patterns and investigations of social differences in migration behaviour and residential preferences. The chapter begins by examining the extent of a demographic renaissance in urban Britain, based on official population estimates and data on within-UK migration. It then probes the characteristics of people moving from, to and within Britain's main conurbations, and goes on to look at the factors influencing people's migration decisions, drawing principally on evidence collected in a case study of Newcastle upon Tyne. In the final section, it concludes that, while the extent of the urban exodus has not been significantly dented by policy interventions up to now, the analyses of migration behaviour reveal a number of promising signs. Even so, given what is reported here about prevailing residential preferences, the task of increasing housing densities at the same time as improving cities' attractiveness as places to live may be a balancing act that is difficult to sustain in the longer term.

The extent of demographic renaissance in urban Britain

Population change, and especially the migration component within this, is commonly viewed as a key indicator of urban performance and prospects. This is partly because the population shifts experienced by a place tend to reflect its circumstances relative to other places, notably its employment situation but also aspects relating to cost of living and quality of life. It is also partly due to the fact that demographic trends impact on the characteristics of places by altering the size and composition of the residential population, with knock-on effects on local purchasing power, on size and quality of the labour force and on confidence in the future of businesses and house prices. More practically, official population estimates made on an annual basis provide a readily accessible source for monitoring and projecting these trends. Unfortunately, however, population estimates produced since the 2001 Population Census cast doubts over the accuracy of original estimates for the 1990s and portray a picture of the extent of demographic renaissance since the early 1980s that is less sanguine than was previously thought to be the case, especially for the provincial cities.

In general, the picture before the release of 2001 Census data, as portrayed by the results of this 'Cities' programme project among other studies, was fairly rosy (Champion, 2002). In particular, all the larger conurbations were found to have recorded a substantial upswing in population trend between the 1970s and 1980s. Analysis of population estimates indicated that London's Local Labour Market Area (LLMA) had switched from an overall population loss of 8.4% in 1971-81 to a gain of 1.1% in 1981-91 and the five next largest LLMAs had in aggregate reduced their rate of loss from 8.6% to 3.8%. At the other end of the settlement hierarchy, the pace of population growth had slowed conspicuously, against the national trend of a rise in growth rate from 0.8% to 2.5%. Between these two decades, LLMAs classified as Rural Areas saw their rate fall from 9.6 to 6.0%; and those classified as Towns from 7.0% to 4.7%. While there remained a clear urban–rural gradient in growth rates, it was much less steep in 1981-91 than in the previous decade (Champion, 2003).

This population recovery appeared to have continued through the 1990s, although even the contemporary population estimates suggested that this recovery was less impressive than previously, both in its overall scale and its coverage. Greater London, the six English metropolitan counties and the Clydeside conurbation, having in aggregate lost just under a quarter of a million people in 1981-91, looked set to have *gained* twice this number by the time that the population estimates for 2001 were produced. By comparison, their overall loss for 1971-81 had been around 1.25 million. In terms of geographical coverage, the most notable feature was the widening gap between London and the rest. On the one hand, London's population was estimated to have grown by 395,000 between 1991 and 1999, an annual rise of 0.72% that was markedly higher than its 0.12% average growth rate during the 1980s. By contrast, the other six conurbations were still losing population in the 1990s, with an upward shift in average annual growth rate from the 1980s of only 0.19 percentage points, less than one third of London's (Champion, 2002).

According to the 2001 Census, however, the extent of demographic recovery since the early 1980s appears considerably less. Nationally, even after the imputation of people believed to have been missed by the Census enumeration on 29 April 2001, the final UK Census figure was well over one million smaller than the estimate for June 2000. Indications are that possibly as much as one third of the overestimation relates to before 1991; that is, that the adjustments made to allow for undercounting by the 1991 Census were too large. Inadequacies in the mechanisms for monitoring migration to and especially from the UK are identified as the main culprit. As the larger cities had been treated as the main beneficiaries of the UK's estimated net gains from overseas, these were the subject of the largest proportionate reductions between the estimates for 2000 and the 2001 Census. Subsequently, however, the Office for National Statistics (ONS) identified some 213,000 people missed by the Census, 193,000 being added to the 2001 population estimate for England and Wales (in September 2003) and a further 20,200 added to the population of Manchester (in November 2003). Nevertheless, even with these amendments, the estimates for 2001 still mean a substantial reduction compared with the pre-census estimates.

Table 7.1 shows for England's main conurbations and principal cities the rates of population change since 1981 indicated by the now-obsolete estimates for June 2000 and compares them with the picture portrayed for 2001 at the time of writing (November 2003). Greater London and England's six metropolitan counties have had 353,000 people sliced from their combined populations by the latest figures. Both these components of metropolitan England have thereby seen a cut in their estimated post-1981 population changes. London's growth, although still much greater than for any other conurbation, is pegged back to 7.4% for the 20-year period, while the six metropolitan counties have experienced an overall loss two and a half times larger than previously indicated. Their principal cities appear even more badly affected, with their total population estimate cut back by nearly 3 percentage points, signalling an overall loss of 6% of their population since 1981. All six are now reckoned to have lower populations in 2001 than in 1981, with Liverpool sustaining the largest percentage loss, followed by Manchester, Newcastle and Sheffield.

In sum, there remains no question about the existence of an upturn in the demographic dynamism of our cities since the 1970s. In that decade, Greater London and England's six metropolitan counties saw their combined population fall by 1.25 million people, whereas in the last 20 years the overall change was an increase of 25,000 people, according to the latest estimates for 2001. Nor is there any question about London's remarkable recovery since the 1970s, with

Table 7.1: Population change since 1981 for England's main conurbations and principal cities, based on original estimate for 2000 and revised estimate for 2001

	Population (000s)			Change (% for period)		
Area	1981	2000	2001	1981-2000	1981-2001	Difference
Greater London	*6,805.6*	*7,375.1*	*7,307.9*	*8.4*	*7.4*	*–1.0*
Metropolitan counties	*11,353.5*	*11,161.6*	*10,876.0*	*–1.7*	*–4.2*	*–2.5*
Greater Manchester	2,619.1	2,585.7	2,512.3	–1.3	–4.1	–2.8
Merseyside	1,522.2	1,403.4	1,365.6	–7.8	–10.3	–2.5
South Yorkshire	1,317.1	1,301.5	1,266.5	–1.2	–3.8	–2.7
Tyne and Wear	1,155.2	1,103.6	1,077.9	–4.5	–6.7	–2.2
West Midlands	2,673.1	2,619.0	2,570.1	–2.0	–3.9	–1.8
West Yorkshire	2,066.8	2,121.4	2,083.6	2.6	0.8	–1.8
Principal cities	*3,550.1*	*3,433.9*	*3,336.6*	*–3.3*	*–6.0*	*–2.7*
Birmingham	1,020.6	1,010.4	985.9	–1.0	–3.4	–2.4
Leeds	717.9	726.1	715.6	1.1	–0.3	–1.5
Liverpool	517.0	457.3	442.3	–11.5	–14.4	–2.9
Manchester	462.7	439.5	418.6	–5.0	–9.5	–4.5
Newcastle upon Tyne	284.1	270.5	261.1	–4.8	–8.1	–3.3
Sheffield	547.8	530.1	513.1	–3.2	–6.3	–3.1

Note: Data for 2000 are original mid-year estimates. Data for 2001 are revised in the light of the 2001 Census and the further changes published by ONS on 26 September 2003 and 4 November 2003. Figures may not sum exactly as they have been rounded after calculation.
Source: ONS website www.statistics.gov.uk, and authors' calculations. Crown copyright.

a loss of 750,000 in that decade giving way to a 20-year gain of half a million. However, the post-census revelations that the six metropolitan counties lost 478,000 people over the previous 20 years rather than the 192,000 indicated by the pre-census estimates, and their principal cities lost 214,000 rather than 116,000, will be disappointing to those who had been led to believe that these areas were beginning to stabilise in demographic terms.

Finally, the evidence currently available on within-Britain migration affecting the larger cities tends to emphasise the more gloomy features of the picture presented above. As shown in Figure 7.1, net migration between England's main conurbations and the rest of the UK has involved a flow from the former to the latter averaging some 90,000 people a year over the past 20 years – equivalent to a reduction in their combined populations of around 0.5% a year and adding up to a full 10% loss over the period. Moreover, although the scale of net out-migration from the conurbations has fluctuated somewhat over time, there does not appear to be any sign of a long-term diminution. Indeed, since the early 1990s the level has again been moving upwards. Urban regeneration activity would not seem to have fed through into a reduction in the population exodus from cities, hence the value of a more detailed examination of this component of migration.

Figure 7.1: Net out-migration from Greater London and six English metropolitan counties to the rest of the UK (1981-2000)

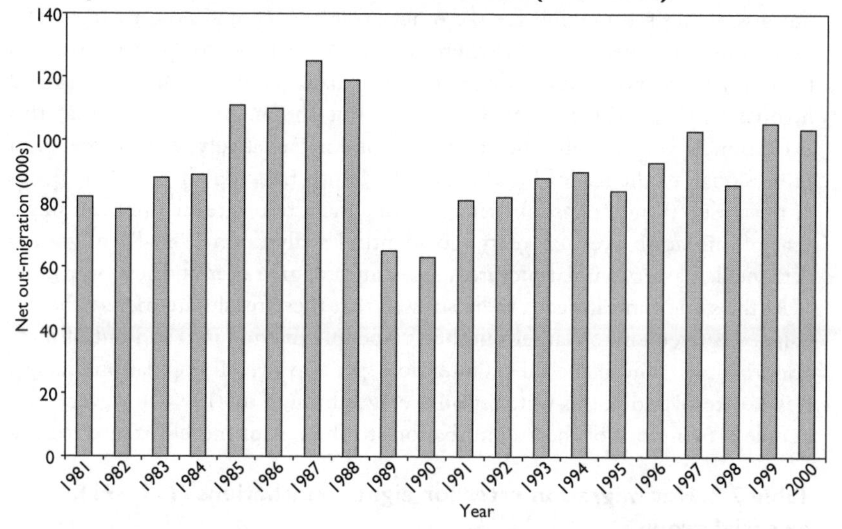

Characteristics of people moving from, to and within the large cities

Examining the characteristics of migrants can tell us a great deal about the nature of the population movements that are affecting British cities, although, as we shall see later in this chapter, additional insights can be obtained from data on people's reasons for moving, levels of satisfaction with their current circumstances and aspirations for the future. Given the anecdotal evidence of the urban exodus primarily involving better-off households and families with children, with important implications for the socio-demographic profiles of city populations, the project gave particular attention to the occupational distribution of migration affecting the large conurbations. Additionally, because of its major importance in Britain's overall urban exodus, London was the subject of a special study. In both cases, the analyses were based on the Population Census, because this is the only large-scale data set that provides information on migrants' other characteristics besides sex and age. This part of the project (Champion, 2002) was thus restricted to the examination of people changing address in the 12 months leading up to the 1991 Census. On a positive note, however, the results were very clear-cut and they also provide a novel benchmark against which the 2000-01 migration patterns can be set, once the relevant data sets from the latest Census are available for analysis.

The occupational composition of the net exodus from Britain's eight largest conurbations in 1990-91 is shown in Table 7.2. This demonstrates very clearly that better-off people are the more likely to be involved in these places' net migration losses to the rest of the UK. The overall rate of net loss of professional, managerial and technical workers is much higher than the rates for the other three named categories for all but one of the eight places. Indeed, Greater Manchester exhibits a perfect ranking of the six main social groups by rate of net loss, while the ranking for six other areas also comes close to this. The exception is Greater London, where the rate of net loss for professional and technical workers is much lower than for managerial staff and also skilled manual workers. Further analyses (data not shown here) reveal that this exception is very largely due to Inner London's relatively low net losses of professionals to the rest of London and the South East, together with net gains of this group from the rest of Britain. While these results relate only to a single year of migration over ten years ago, identical analyses on 1980-81 migration data yielded a very similar picture, suggesting a degree of robustness over time.

At the same time, it needs to be stressed that these results are merely the net balance between much larger numbers of people moving into and out of these conurbations. Given the media attention given to overall population change, it is easy to overlook this fact. Yet on average, through the 1990s, for every four people moving out of these conurbations to the rest of the UK, there were at

Table 7.2: Net migration rates for eight conurbations (1990-91), by social group

Social group	Greater London	Greater Manchester	Merseyside	South Yorkshire	Tyne and Wear	West Midlands	West Yorkshire	Strathclyde
All groups	–0.66	–0.26	–0.53	–0.37	–0.35	–0.57	–0.29	–0.22
Professional	–0.45	–1.59	–0.89	–0.41	–0.96	–1.31	–1.00	–1.59
Managerial	–1.14	–0.61	–0.45	–0.26	–0.71	–1.33	–0.44	–0.28
Technical	–0.40	–0.40	–0.73	–1.31	–0.61	–0.79	–0.75	–0.11
PMT sub-total	*–0.75*	*–0.67*	*–0.63*	*–0.71*	*–0.70*	*–1.12*	*–0.63*	*–0.40*
Other non-manual	–0.36	–0.14	–0.49	–0.35	–0.34	–0.46	–0.19	–0.16
Skilled manual	–1.05	–0.04	–0.23	–0.04	+0.01	–0.43	–0.18	–0.03
Other manual	–0.44	+0.08	–0.53	–0.28	–0.20	–0.16	–0.02	–0.14
Other	–1.57	–3.41	–3.14	–1.58	–2.46	–1.64	–3.40	–1.10
Ranking of six social groups in each area								
Professional	3	1	1	2	1	2	1	1
Managerial	1	2	5	5	2	1	3	2
Technical	5	3	2	1	3	3	2	5
Other non-manual	6	4	4	3	4	4	4	3
Skilled manual	2	5	6	6	6	5	5	6
Other manual	4	6	3	4	5	6	6	4

Note: Rate per 100 residents in Social Group in 1991. Ranking: 1 for highest rate of net out-migration, 6 for lowest rate of net out-migration or highest rate of net in-migration. 'Technical' refers to 'Associate professional and technical'.

Source: Champion (2002). Originally calculated from 1991 Census Regional Migration Tables. Crown copyright

least three moving in the opposite direction to take up residence in them (Champion, 1999). In order to understand better the dynamics of the net exodus, it is important to examine, therefore, the characteristics of the migration flows in both directions. As has already been mentioned, London was used for this part of the study, beginning with a set of single-variable analyses of its in-migrants and out-migrants for 1990-91. Interestingly, the two sets of flows were broadly similar in their composition, with the majority of migrants in both directions being young, single, white, economically active and in non-manual occupations and, also worth noting, being more distinctive in all these respects than London's population as a whole (Table 7.3). When the two flows are compared in detail, however, it is found that those moving into London from the rest of the UK tended to be younger, more single, less white and more economically active than those leaving. As is clear from Table 7.3, out-migrants were less likely to be aged 20-24, single, in work and ending up in non-family households and rented accommodation, and more likely to be white, married, retired and living in owner-occupied housing.

Subsequently, advantage was taken of the 1991 Census 2% Sample of Anonymised Records to classify London's individual residents and migrants into ten groups (Ford and Champion, 2000). Cluster analysis was used to see which types of people were most commonly represented in migration into and out of London, and also in those moves which took place entirely within London where the capital was able to hold on to residents despite the fact that they were moving home. Table 7.4 summarises the main findings of this analysis, showing the typical characteristics of each group, the overall propensity of group members to change address and the dominant types of migration for each group.

Table 7.3: Selected characteristics of London's residents, in-migrants and out-migrants (%)

Characteristic in 1991	In-migrants 1990-91	Out-migrants 1990-91	Residents 1991
Age: 20-24 years	38.2	17.3	8.4
Marital status: single	72.5	51.4	47.4
Marital status: married	18.9	34.3	36.8
Ethnic group: white	90.0	92.9	80.1
Family type: non-family	50.5	24.6	21.8
Economic status: active	82.6	72.9	60.2
Economic status: in work	72.7	62.6	55.0
Economic status: retired	2.2	10.8	16.9
Occupation: non-manual	78.0	84.3	62.1
Tenure: owner-occupied	41.1	68.2	61.3
Tenure: private renting	48.4	24.7	11.4

Note: Migration refers to changes of address within Great Britain only. Figures are percentages of the relevant population indicated in column headings. Economic status is for people aged 16+, Occupation is for those in the labour force and with a job in the previous ten years (ROGB) Rest of Great Britain.
Source: calculated from 1991 Census 2% Sample of Anonymised Records (ESRC/JISC purchase). Crown copyright

Table 7.4: Profiles of 10 clusters of London's residents by 1991 socio-demographic characteristics and 1990-91 migration behaviour

	Cluster 1	Cluster 2	Cluster 3	Cluster 4	Cluster 5
Typical characteristics	Older females in 'couple with dependants' families, employed in non-manual occupations, owner-occupiers	Older non-family one person households, with diverse socio-economic characteristics	Older heads of 'other family' households, owner-occupiers, diverse socio-economic characteristics	'Couple only' families employed in non-manual occupations, owner-occupiers	Older females in 'couple only families, economically inactive, owner-occupiers/renting
Overall mobility	Low	Medium	Very low	High	Low
Dominant migrant type	Out-migrants	Local movers Out-migrants In-migrants	–	Out-migrants In-migrants Local movers	Out-migrants
	Cluster 6	**Cluster 7**	**Cluster 8**	**Cluster 9**	**Cluster 10**
Typical characteristics	Young 'other relatives' of 'other family' households, diverse socio-economic characteristics	Older males in 'couple with dependants' families, in non-manual and manual occupations, owner-occupiers	Older males in 'couple only' families, employed in manual occupations, owner-occupiers/renting	Young 'other relatives' of 'other family' households, employed in non-manual occupations, owner-occupiers	Young 'couple with dependants' families, diverse socio-economic characteristics, renting
Overall mobility	Medium	Low	Medium	Medium	High
Dominant migrant type	Local movers	Out-migrants	Local movers	Out-migrants In-migrants	In-migrants Local movers Out-migrants

Note: 'Local movers' refers to people moving within Greater London.

Source: Ford and Champion (2000). Originally calculated from 1991 Census 2% Sample of Anonymised Records (ESRC/JISC purchase). Crown copyright

Focusing on the latter, it can be seen that out-migration is significant for seven of the ten groups and is typified by middle-aged or older people from a range of family types, largely home owners and in non-manual occupations, together with their adult children where still at home. In-migration is clearly a weaker and more selective process, being a notable feature of only four groups. As such, in-migration is most prevalent among members of young renting families, non-manual couples without children at home, other family households and non-family households especially people living alone. Finally, within-London movement is most typical of young renting families, other-family households and their grown-up children, non-family households including those containing only one person and couples without children at home, the last of these including older male manual workers as well as owner-occupiers (broadly the same as the composition of in-migrants apart from including older male manual workers).

The implications for British cities of these findings on the characteristics of their migrants do not appear, at least at first glance, very encouraging. In net terms, London appears to lose virtually all types of people except younger adults, while the large conurbations in general tend to lose their better-qualified people more quickly than their less skilled. On a more positive note, however, only one of London's ten types of resident declined by more than 2% in size as a result of the one year's migration examined, and only one of the eight conurbations lost more than 0.75% of its professional, managerial and technical population. Also, much more encouraging than the bottom-line figure of a net exodus of some 90,000 people a year is the fact that, in terms of gross flows, more than three times this number are moving into the conurbations each year. In terms of the basic arithmetic, only a fairly small increase in this volume of arrivals – or a small reduction in the 400,000-odd leaving them each year – would be sufficient to reduce these net losses substantially. On top of this, large numbers of city residents change address each year but choose to remain in these places, and moving home involves barely one in ten people in an average year. To discover the chances of seeing a shift in residential mobility patterns in favour of Britain's cities, however, it is necessary to probe the factors that affect people's migration behaviour.

Factors influencing people's migration behaviour

There are two main ways of investigating the factors that influence people's migration behaviour. One is to examine how places vary in their attractiveness for migrants and then identify the characteristics that correlate with higher and lower levels of attractiveness. The other is to survey residents in order to find out from them the reasons why they have chosen to leave one place and move to another and learn about their attitudes to their current situations and what their future aspirations and intentions are. The project probed both these avenues, first through the analysis of patterns of migration at a national scale and, second, through a local, survey-based case study.

Modelling migration at a national scale

The main work on analysing migration patterns involved the calculation of an index of 'Relative Intrinsic Attractivity' (RIA) for the 451 local authority districts of mainland Britain, using data from the 1991 Census on in-migration to each district from the rest of the country (Fotheringham et al, 2000). This particular index was used in preference to a simple in-migration rate because it takes into account the proximity of each district to the rest of the population – an important consideration given that most migrants move only short distances. Allowing also for the population size of the individual districts, the results for this pre-census year 1990-91 revealed a very wide difference between places. At the extremes, as shown in Table 7.5, the RIA score for the district with the highest attractivity, Badenoch and Strathspey (in the Scottish Highlands), was almost 45 times that for the lowest district, Sandwell (in the West Midlands conurbation). The prominence of rural Scotland in the top ten can probably be attributed to the stage reached in the UK's economic cycle at this time. Even so, the full set of results confirmed the importance of the rural dimension in general, as would be expected from what has already been said about the net migration losses from the larger conurbations. At the other extreme, Britain's ten least attractive places according to this index are a set of industrial districts, mainly in Britain's north but with the London Borough of Barking and Dagenham reinforcing the apparent effect of a manufacturing legacy.

In terms of the features most strongly correlated with variance in migration attractivity, exploratory work using census-based variables in stepwise regression analysis (Fotheringham et al, 2000) identified a strong negative association with population potential, confirming that districts located in the more built-up areas of the country are less attractive to migrants. The places with the greatest pulling power for migrants were those with the highest proportions of

Table 7.5: Relative Intrinsic Attractivity (RIA) scores standardised by population: top and bottom 10 districts of mainland Britain

District *Top ten*	RIA score	District *Bottom ten*	RIA score
Badenoch & Strathspey	44.6	Sandwell	1.00
Nairn	38.8	Walsall	1.13
Sutherland	37.0	Dudley	1.33
Lochaber	24.6	Knowsley	1.42
Caithness	22.8	St Helens	1.50
Ross and Cromarty	18.4	Stoke-on-Trent	1.57
Tweedale	18.0	Wigan	1.57
Moray	17.6	Oldham	1.63
Kincardine & Deeside	16.8	Wolverhampton	1.65
Berwickshire	16.0	Barking & Dagenham	1.68

Note: Scores are scaled to the lowest of 451 RIAs, which is set at 1.00.
Source: after Fotheringham et al (2000, p 402). Originally calculated from 1991 Census Special Migration Statistics Set 2. Crown copyright

people in Social Classes I and II, people without long-term limiting illness, recent immigrants from outside Britain and households renting unfurnished private accommodation. These all made statistically significant independent contributions to explaining the differentials in migration attractivity across the 451 districts. According to the parameters derived from this analysis, a doubling of the proportion of people without long-term limiting illness is associated with an increase in RIA score by a factor of 1.7. Similarly, a doubling of the proportion of people in the top two Social Classes raises it by a factor of 1.6, with factors of 1.2 for the other two variables. Clearly, a major element of Britain's between-district migrants is opting for its better-off and healthier places, but the last two variables also reflect strong movement into places that especially attract what is the most mobile section of the population. This comprises young adults with their well-documented preference for the 'bright city lights', which are also among the main reception areas for international immigrants, not least because of the availability of relatively cheap rented accommodation.

Subsequent modelling work undertaken for the former Department of Transport, Local Government and the Regions (Fotheringham et al, 2001) has provided more detailed and up-to-date evidence of the factors influencing the destination choice of people moving between places. This analysis was based on migration for 1996/97, using data from the NHS Central Register on flows between shire counties, metropolitan districts and groupings of London Boroughs. Characteristics which contributed to making places attractive for migrants included low unemployment rate, low council tax, low reported crime, little vacant and derelict land, low proportions of new house building on brownfield sites, high house prices, high household incomes, presence of listed buildings and a warmer drier climate. These results thus confirmed many expectations, although in the final analysis it is debatable how far a measured characteristic is proxying for another not included in the multiple regression (although a substantial range of explanatory variables was tested) and also whether some variables are more the cause or the effect of migration (although time lags were included where time-series data were available).

A local case study of Newcastle upon Tyne

Information on migration behaviour can, of course, be obtained most directly from surveying and interviewing the people involved. As part of the overall project, a local, survey-based case study was carried out focusing on the City of Newcastle and surrounding localities[1]. The context for this was the particular concern of the City Council over the net loss of residents to surrounding areas of north-east England as well as further afield. The council, therefore, had initiated a regeneration programme entitled 'Going for Growth' (Newcastle City Council, 2002). A key concern focused on people moving into the new private housing estates being built in these nearby areas. A particular policy concern was whether this exodus could be stemmed in the future if the scale of new house building within the city boundaries could be increased. This might include building on greenfield sites within the city but also, given green-belt restrictions, by recycling brownfield land yielded up by former industrial sites and cleared council housing. The case study provided the opportunity to examine the detailed factors impacting on patterns of migration and residential choice at a local level.

Survey work was undertaken in ten localities, five within the city boundary and five outside it, with completed questionnaires being obtained from 727 households and follow-up interviews being held with 22 households representing different types of 'move' and personal circumstance. In the analysis, particular attention was given to the 73 residents of the five survey areas outside Newcastle who had moved from an address in the city during the five years preceding the time of the survey (summer 2000). These comprised nearly one in five of all the residents surveyed in these areas, with the remainder comprising people who had moved from everywhere else besides Newcastle as well as some residents of more than five years' standing, a proportion of the housing stock dating from before the mid-1990s. The characteristics, motivations and intentions of this group were compared with a smaller group who had moved from the surrounding region into one of the five survey areas in the city over the same time period and with those recent movers who had chosen to remain within the city boundary.

The findings for those moving out of Newcastle to one of the five survey areas in the surrounding regions largely confirmed the stereotypical images provided by previous studies of this nature (for a review, see Champion et al, 1998). As Table 7.6 illustrates, the majority comprised younger couples, mostly with at least one child or planning to start a family. Only a quarter of the household heads were aged 45+ at the time of the survey, very few were retired, and two out of three were professional or managerial in occupation. Housing reasons dominated their decisions to leave their previous address in the city, notably wanting a bigger house, a different type of house and to buy a house; however, one in nine gave a better neighbourhood as their main reason. The main reasons given for choosing a house outside Newcastle were the general availability of housing, access to good schools and simply liking the house and the area, while price featured very strongly in the selection of the house itself. Relatively few (only one in eight) had plans to move again within the next five years, reflecting the generally high satisfaction ratings that people gave about their present housing circumstances. In the latter context, among the most frequently mentioned 'best features', besides the house itself, were the area's quiet and peaceful nature and its easy access to the facilities that people considered most important in their daily lives. Of the nine households proposing to move again soon, only one intended to move back to Newcastle, although two others were undecided about their destination.

Much less expected, however, was the finding that the people moving in the opposite direction – into one of the five survey areas in the city from the surrounding region – were not far different in their characteristics and attitudes.

Table 7.6: Selected characteristics of households that moved out of, into and within the City of Newcastle upon Tyne in the five years before the survey

Characteristic/ Type of mover (N)	Moved out of Newcastle (73)	Moved into Newcastle (39)	Moved within Newcastle (111)
Household type			
Couple only	37.0	30.8	27.0
Couple with child(ren)	47.9	53.8	58.6
Lone person	9.6	15.4	9.0
Age of household head (years)			
25-34	28.8	17.9	34.2
35-44	45.2	46.2	34.2
45-64	20.5	17.9	27.0
65+	4.1	15.4	3.6
Work status of household head			
In full-time employment	74.0	76.9	73.0
In part-time employment	13.7	7.7	9.9
Retired	4.1	12.8	4.5
Occupation of household head			
Professional/managerial	68.5	69.2	63.0
Main reason for leaving previous residence			
Bigger house	31.5	35.9	42.3
Different type of house	9.6	0.0	1.8
Wanted to own	8.2	2.6	3.6
Marriage/divorce/retirement	4.1	10.3	3.6
Better neighbourhood/school	13.7	5.1	7.2
Main reason for choosing new area			
Housing/land availability	15.1	5.1	6.3
Access to good schools	11.0	2.6	9.0
Closeness to family/friends	2.7	10.3	7.2
Access to work	4.1	17.9	7.2
Access to shops/facilities	1.4	5.1	2.7
Liked area	11.0	15.4	11.7
Main reason for choice of house			
Price of house	31.5	23.1	23.4
Style/quality of house	12.3	17.9	13.5
Migration intentions			
Planning to move in next five years	13.0	32.5	20.7
of whom, stay in Newcastle	11.1	46.2	56.5

Note: Not all values of each variable are shown, so the figures for each variable do not necessarily sum to 100. Moves out of and into Newcastle are with respect to the surrounding region only.

Source: Newcastle case study, as reported in Ford and Champion (2001)

Over half these households comprised couples with one or more children, again almost 70% were professional and managerial, and a similar proportion of around one third listed the desire for a bigger house as the main reason prompting their move. Similarly, simply liking the area was also one of the most frequently cited reasons for choosing their new area of residence, and style of house featured prominently in their choice of particular house. Moreover, among the most cited 'best features' of their local area were its quiet and peaceful nature and easy access to open space and parks.

Nevertheless, there were some differences between these two groups. Those moving into the city included a somewhat higher proportion of one-person households and retired people than those moving out. More cited life-stage change (such as marriage, divorce/separation, retirement) as the main reason for leaving their previous home, while fewer cited the search for a better neighbourhood or school. More mentioned closeness to work, shops and family/friends as the main reason for their selection of their new area. House price was less important in choice of house, although it was still mentioned as the main reason by nearly one in four. Finally, while the majority were generally satisfied with their new circumstances, around one third (more than twice the proportion of those moving out) planned to move again within the next five years, with under half of these expecting to remain in the city.

The general similarity between those moving in both directions between the city and the surrounding region is broadly repeated with respect to the Newcastle residents moving but choosing to remain within the city, as evidenced by the 111 households moving into one of the five survey areas there from somewhere else in the city. Over half were couples with one or more children and almost two thirds were professional or managerial, while the desire for a bigger house was again the key factor prompting the move. The most commonly cited reasons for staying in Newcastle were simply liking the area in which their new home is situated, the access to good schools and the general availability of suitable new housing. Yet again, peace and quiet and access to open space and parks featured strongly among the perceived benefits of living in these areas. The proportion planning to move again within the next five years, at one in five, was higher than for those moving out of the city but lower than for those moving into it. Also, while over half of these intending movers envisaged continuing to stay in Newcastle, this means that a substantial proportion of them were considering moving out.

A fairly consistent picture thus emerges for these three groups of movers. Irrespective of whether people were moving from, to or within the city, a clear preference was expressed in favour of newly-built detached housing situated on a quiet street with adequate car parking and with a feeling of spaciousness helped by local greenery, if not a view over open land. On the one hand, this degree of conformity is perhaps not surprising, given the way in which the survey was targeted on areas of recent private house building. Even so, the findings underlined the fact that for many people it is the character of the housing and the estate that is most important, not so much the broader geographical location within the region. The availability of suitable housing was frequently cited as a reason for the particular choice of area. Given this, it is likely that if the balance of this type of house building were to shift more towards Newcastle and away from the surrounding region, more people would choose Newcastle as the destination of their move than do so currently.

Less promisingly for the city's 'Going for Growth' strategy, however, the study also found that many people had consciously chosen to live outside Newcastle. As confirmed by the in-depth interviews, much of this was to do with house price. This set of people largely comprised young families and pre-family couples who are on the lower-paid rungs of their professional and managerial career ladders and are thus quite sensitive to the size of mortgage needed. Indeed, several of them cited house price as a key consideration in choosing their new home. At the same time, it would be wrong to portray everyone in this group as a reluctant mover, as a good number of them cited among their main reasons for moving out of the city the desire for a better neighbourhood, access to a good school and being close to open space and countryside.

In sum, the survey results, together with the insights gained from the in-depth interviews, provide general support for Newcastle's 'Going for Growth' strategy. This would certainly seem to be the case to the extent that the strategy can, as intended, deliver additional opportunities for people to buy newly built detached homes within the city boundary. At the same time, judging by the evidence collected, this housing must be able to compete on price with that on similar estates in the surrounding region, whilst ensuring that standards of peace and quiet and feelings of openness are not compromised. Access to good shops, schools and public transport is also valued. People who have consciously chosen to live outside the city but not mentioned affordability as a key factor probably pose the main challenge to this policy, because presumably other aspects of city life would have needed to be different for them to have been persuaded to stay; crime, traffic, parking and school quality feature strongly in this context.

Conclusion

This chapter provides insights into the patterns and processes of migration affecting British cities, drawing on the results of a project that examined this topic using a variety of sources including census data, other migration data and a local case study. It is very clear that the urban exodus continues apace, with no sustained diminution in net migration losses from the major conurbations to the rest of the country since the early 1980s in spite of the variety of urban regeneration initiatives pursued by successive governments over this period. The study has also confirmed that, in net terms, this urban exodus has involved disproportionately large numbers of better-off households with strong representation of professional and managerial occupations. These parts of the project's results, therefore, paint a rather negative picture of recent trends and provide little comfort for those currently committed to securing an urban renaissance in Britain.

Set against such results, however, is a number of more positive signs. In the first place, it has been emphasised that the most frequently quoted figures on the urban exodus merely represent the net balance between far larger gross outflows and inflows. At any time, there are normally nearly as many people moving into Britain's larger cities as are moving in the opposite direction. Secondly, through the analysis of previously neglected data from the 1981 and 1991 Censuses, the study has been able to reveal that London seems to be able to attract and retain people working in professional and technical jobs much better than do the major provincial centres. Indeed, its net loss rates for these high-skilled categories are lower than for all its other broad social groups except for less skilled manual workers. A key challenge, therefore, is how to achieve an increase in the level of inward movement to cities without there being a concomitant rise in the level of outflow, and vice versa. In particular, future research should try to shed more light on the factors behind London's relative attractiveness to residents working in the professions and see if these can provide any pointers for action both in relation to the other social groups there and also more generally in terms of the approach to be taken to other cities.

The findings on migration behaviour have also provided some grounds for believing that current policy initiatives are broadly on the right track, although also sounding something of an alarm bell. Admittedly, both the migration modelling and the Newcastle case study have pointed to the continuing attraction of smaller towns and more rural areas. Nevertheless, both suggest that success, among other things, in reducing unemployment and crime in cities and improving the availability of suitable housing and the quality of schools and other amenities there would help to redress the balance. Particularly striking was the finding that the people who have been moving into newly built private housing in Newcastle were not much different in their characteristics, reasons for moving and levels of satisfaction with their decision from those moving to similar housing elsewhere in the region. Greater provision of such housing within cities could well help to bring about the hoped-for urban renaissance. As a cautionary note, however, such policies should not ignore the importance attached to peace and quiet and to proximity to parks and other open space, suggesting that there may well be limits to the degree of land-use intensification that these sought-after residents will feel comfortable with.

Finally, however, one of the biggest uncertainties currently surrounding British cities concerns the question of exactly how fast they have been growing or declining in recent years, and indeed whether or not they have remained on an upward trajectory since their impressive recovery of some 20 years ago. While the data on within-Britain migration has continued to indicate significant weaknesses, some consolation could be gained from the belief that net immigration from overseas was compensating for these deficits, almost completely in the case of London and partially elsewhere. Given the conclusion drawn from the 2001 Census that this no longer appears to have been the case, a major reassessment of the demographic dynamics of urban Britain is clearly in order.

Note

[1] This part of the study was carried out in collaboration with Newcastle City Council who part-funded the research.

References

Champion, T. (1999) 'Migration and British cities in the 1990s', *National Institute Economic Review*, vol 170, pp 60-77.

Champion, T. (2002) *Migration, residential preferences and the changing environment of cities: ESRC Cities programme project end of award report*, Newcastle upon Tyne: University of Newcastle.

Champion, T. (2003) 'Testing the differential urbanization model: Great Britain, 1901-1991', *Journal of Economic and Social Geography (TESG)*, vol 94, pp 11-22.

Champion, T., Atkins, D., Coombes, M. and Fotheringham, S. (1998) *Urban exodus*, London: Council for the Protection of Rural England.

DETR (Department of the Environment, Transport and the Regions) (2000) *Our towns and cities: The future. Delivering an urban renaissance*, Cm 4911, London: DETR.

Ford, T. and Champion, T. (2000) 'Who moves into, out of and within London? An analysis based on the 1991 Census sample of anonymised records', *Area*, vol 32, pp 259-70.

Ford, T. and Champion, T. (2001) *Who moves where and why? A survey of residents' past migration and current intentions*, Report to Newcastle City Council, Newcastle upon Tyne: University of Newcastle.

Fotheringham, A.S., Champion, T., Wymer, C. and Coombes, M. (2000) 'Measuring destination attractivity: a migration example', *International Journal of Population Geography*, vol 6, pp 391-422.

Fotheringham, A.S., Barmby, T., Brunsdon, C., Champion, T. et al (2001) *Development of a migration model*, Report to the Department of Transport, Local Government and the Regions, Newcastle upon Tyne: University of Newcastle.

Newcastle City Council (2000) *Going for Growth*, Green Paper, Newcastle upon Tyne: Newcastle City Council.

Robson, B., Parkinson, M., Boddy, M. and MacLennan, D. (2000) *The state of English cities*, London: DETR.

Urban Task Force (1999) *Towards an urban renaissance*, Final Report of the Urban Task Force chaired by Lord Rogers, London: E & FN Spon.

EIGHT

Cities are not isolated states

Paul Cheshire, Stefano Magrini, Francesca Medda and Vassilis Monastiriotis

Introduction

We know that neighbourhoods within cities do not exist in isolation: that they are part of the interactive whole that constitutes 'a city'. Neighbourhoods cannot be viewed as isolated from the wider metropolitan region either in housing terms or as labour markets. Should new jobs be created as part of a local area regeneration effort, people who live outside the community that is the target of the regeneration will take many of these jobs. Moreover, people from outside the neighbourhood who take the jobs create opportunities to be filled elsewhere (either because they have left a job, thus creating a vacancy, or because they have not taken an alternative job elsewhere in the city). Unemployment rates for people of given employability even out, therefore, over the city's whole labour market area quite quickly. The speed with which this equalisation of opportunities happens varies with the size of the community concerned relative to the city as a whole and its self-containment in commuting terms. An early and still credible estimate for areas as open to cross commuting as London boroughs was about one year (Gordon and Lamont, 1982).

More recently, it has been realised that neighbourhood housing markets interact in rather similar ways within a city. Neighbourhoods within cities have different socio-economic compositions. There are rich neighbourhoods and poor ones and how rich or poor a household or neighbourhood is, is closely correlated with indicators of labour market success: indeed it directly reflects them. The result is that rich neighbourhoods have concentrations of better educated, more highly qualified, healthier residents with lower probabilities of experiencing unemployment, fewer discriminated against groups and fewer of those groups with low labour market success or inactivity. The residents of poor neighbourhoods have essentially the reverse set of characteristics. However, 'residents' are not fixed. Neighbourhoods continuously experience inward and outward movement of households and most of such movements are within a given city. Nor is such movement random: those moving out of the most deprived areas are biased towards those who have improved their position and employability within the labour market ('get on and get out') while those moving in tend to have even less favourable employability characteristics than those who do not move at all.

The paradox is that even successful attempts to improve the skills of the residents of the most disadvantaged neighbourhoods are likely to lead to an increase (not reduction) in the level of unemployment and poverty in the neighbourhood relative to others. The improved labour market prospects of those whose skills improve leads them to differentially move away to be replaced by more disadvantaged residents (Cheshire et al, 2003).

In broad terms, much of the research from the 'Cities' programme has reinforced this conclusion. It has important policy conclusions. It means that efforts to reduce differences between neighbourhoods – reduce polarisation or social segregation – by simply localised regeneration policies are doomed to failure. It does not mean that they are necessarily a waste of resources. Successfully delivering enhanced labour market prospects to disadvantaged groups by geographically targeted training programmes may be quite an effective way of improving their life chances. However, its success is not sensibly measured by looking at the relative incidence of neighbourhood unemployment after the policy has been implemented. It is likely to have become more unequal and the more effective the policy, the more inequality will have increased because it will have generated more out movement of the previously disadvantaged.

These processes and our increasing understanding of how they operate, focus on relationships between neighbourhoods within particular urban areas. The research reported here was an exploration of the extent to which similar processes of spatial adjustment and labour market interaction exist *between* cities as well as *within* them. It focuses on the interaction between cities within regions of Europe. Although the definition of 'city' that underlay the proposal was intentionally one which generated areas as self-contained as possible in economic terms[1], nevertheless there are regions within Europe which are heavily urbanised and interaction between them is possible – even likely. One of the factors prompting the initial curiosity was the observation in the 1990s that:

> Dramatic contrasts such as those between the centre and the outlying regions are being overtaken by a more complex pattern.... [T]his diversification of disparities is generating a patchwork in which privileged areas border directly on depressed areas. (Millan, 1993)

Recent work on the determinants of urban growth in the EU had also shown that, other things being equal, a city-region with a faster growth rate grew faster the closer it was to other, less rapidly growing city-regions. Similarly, a slower growing city-region grew more slowly the closer it was to faster growing city-regions. Cheshire and Magrini (2000) named this tendency the 'growth shadow effect'. The hypothesis which triggered the initial investigation was that, just as commuting patterns adjusted to even out differences in labour market opportunities between neighbourhoods, within cities so they might, too, where cities were densely packed. Examples might include the Ruhr region of Germany, much of the Benelux countries, the English London/ Birmingham–Bristol/Cambridge axis, or central Scotland. It is possibly of direct relevance to understanding some aspects of the interactions between Liverpool and Manchester and of Glasgow and Edinburgh reported in Chapters Two and Three of this volume.

The findings are that commuting between cities behaves exactly as would be predicted on the basis of the inter-regional migration literature. It responds both to economic push factors and to pull factors. It does so, however, with rather more of a lag than findings on the speed of adjustment of intra-urban commuting might lead one to expect. Again, complementing the findings in the migration literature, the responsiveness of commuting flows to differential opportunities between cities diminishes with the commuting time between them.

This chapter concludes by considering some of the welfare and policy implications of what has been shown to be a process of real economic interaction and systematic adjustment between the economies of the EU's major cities where such cities are a part of larger urbanised regions. The overall approach is rooted in regional science or spatial economics. Our hypotheses are generated on the basis of essentially economic theory and we analyse patterns of interaction between spatial variables using large enough samples to apply statistical methods and tests of significance. In this sense, it provides a valuable complement to more detailed case studies based on a variety of different methodologies and data sources.

Background and basic hypothesis

The natural starting point is to restate the mechanism by which adjustment occurs between spatially defined labour markets. Empirical work in the late 1970s and early 1980s demonstrated that local labour markets which are integrated into wider urban regions tend to interact with each other primarily through adjustment of commuting patterns (Cheshire, 1979; Burridge and Gordon, 1981; Evans and Richardson, 1981; Gordon and Lamont, 1982; Gordon, 1985; Morrison, 1999). Indeed, this work has shown that the more densely crowded are sets of local labour markets and the more they are open to cross commuting, the more important are changes of those flows as a source of adjustment.

This *seamlessness* (Morrison, 1999) is produced not because all workers in any part of a metropolitan area compete for all jobs, but mainly by 'chain interdependence'. Only the highest skilled workers have effective search areas (employment fields) covering the whole metropolitan area. Less-skilled workers have smaller search areas and the least skilled the smallest search areas. However, while it may be useful for modelling purposes to represent origins of workers as points that is not how they are in actual metropolitan areas. Residential neighbourhoods occupy space – they are not points! – so workers are more or less continuously distributed over urban space. Despite social segregation which results in workers of given skill levels not being randomly distributed across urban space, nevertheless, workers of all skill levels are so widely distributed that it is better to think of search areas for all skills groups as being continuous. Despite each individual unskilled worker's employment field being relatively local they more or less all have substantial overlap.

Similarly demand even for unskilled workers is continuous across urban space. This is because, first, employers are relatively widely distributed and, second, the demand for personal services done by unskilled workers – cleaners, window cleaners, odd-jobbers and so on – is widely distributed across residential areas. There is substitution by would-be workers both between areas of search/ employment and across job categories and by employers between skill categories of workers and where those workers come from. This results in a form of 'chain interdependence' across the whole of the larger metropolitan labour market even though most workers do not search or take jobs far from where they live. This produces an effectively seamless metropolitan labour market for all groups. The essential mechanism that achieves this effect is commuting pattern adjustment. The necessary condition to achieve this outcome, therefore, is a sufficiently high connectivity via commuting patterns.

The question now is the extent to which in highly urbanised regions changes in commuting patterns may similarly adjust to changes in the spatial distribution of opportunity between separate city-regions. Insofar as they do this provides a consistent explanation for the previous findings on the growth interdependence of neighbouring cities in the EU urban system and the emergence of apparently less prosperous cities in close proximity to successful ones.

This chapter is divided into four sections. The following section explores in rather more detail how commuting patterns might be expected to adapt to changes in the pattern of spatial job opportunity between city-regions in densely urbanised wider regions. This is followed by a section summarising the findings of an analysis of the changes in commuting patterns in the EU. The results of this show that changes in commuting flows between cities not only occur over time but that they do respond to changing patterns of economic opportunity. Such changes are also sensitive to the time distance between cities. The final section presents our conclusions. Throughout the chapter the empirical analysis is undertaken on data relating to Functional Urban Regions (FURs). These are defined on the basis of a core city identified by concentrations of employment and a dependent economic hinterland defined according to commuting patterns observed in 1971. The original FURs were defined in Hall and Hay 1980[2], and it is this definition which supported the assertion made earlier that the cities which were the subject of this research were as self-contained as possible in economic terms. Despite this, because they occupy space and their residents are distributed over that space, opportunities exist for the adjustment of commuting patterns between them in densely urbanised regions. It is to this we now turn.

Adjustment mechanisms between urban labour markets

Changes in flows of commuters between FURs could affect the transmission of economic growth and influence, the pattern of spatial disparities in per capita income and mean (un)employment rates. Should a more rapid growth of income, or of job opportunities, in a particular urban region have the effect of attracting additional commuters from surrounding areas, there would be three impacts:

- *Statistical effect:* it would change measured per capita income in each FUR since income and output are measured at workplaces and so would rise in the gaining FUR and fall in the one that was losing economically active commuters. Resident population would remain the same in both regions leading to an (additional) apparent growth of per capita GDP in the faster growing region but to an (additional) apparent fall in the slower growing.
- *Composition effect:* it would change the average level of labour productivity if the average productivity of the workers induced to change their commuting patterns differed from the average productivity of existing workers. The additional members of the workforce attracted to the faster growing FUR would be relatively long-distance commuters. Workers who travel longer distances to work tend to have higher human capital and productivity than short-distance commuters. As a consequence, the 'composition effect' is likely to be positive for the more rapidly growing FUR and negative for its less rapidly growing neighbour(s).
- *Dynamic agglomeration effects:* it could change the average level of labour productivity as a consequence of the absolute increase in human capital in the regional labour force. If there are increasing returns to human capital (Cheshire and Carbonaro, 1996; Magrini, 1998), the increase in high human capital workers in the faster growing FUR(s) may trigger a dynamic mechanism that increases productivity of all workers in the region even further. In addition, if over relevant ranges there are increasing economies of urbanisation (agglomeration), then growth could itself lower costs leading to further growth in the faster growing city or cities.

Bearing in mind that conventions of statistical measurement are such that income and output are measured at workplaces but people are enumerated where they live, consider a system of two regions – Region A and Region B – and two types of workers: skilled (high human capital) workers and unskilled (low human capital) workers. In Region A, skilled workers represent a higher proportion of the labour force than in Region B. As a consequence, Region A has a higher level of per capita income than Region B. However, labour markets are assumed to be in equilibrium and unemployment rates and wage levels are assumed to be similar in both Regions A and B for workers of a given skill level. There is, therefore, no incentive for net changes in cross commuting or migration to occur. For simplicity's sake, it is also possible to assume that productivity grows at the same rate for all workers in all regions, so that the equilibrium is stable over time.

The first adjustment phase

Suppose now that the system is affected by a spatially asymmetric shock, which generates faster productivity growth in Urban Region A than in Urban Region B, and/or determines the creation of new job opportunities in Urban Region A. This underlying process of asymmetric growth could result from a number of different sources, which we will ignore for the present.

For the moment, no adjustment mechanisms between the labour markets exist. This implies that adjustment takes place essentially through intra-regional changes. Suppose each FUR is composed of a core city and a set of sub-centres as in Figure 8.1. Given the absolute concentration of activities in the core, the creation of new job opportunities determined by the upsurge in economic activity in FUR A is likely to be relatively concentrated in its core.

Job searching is assumed to be a costly activity where the cost is a positive function of the physical size of the search area. At this stage, it is likely that the differences existing between the two FURs in terms of wages and/or job opportunities are not sufficient to offset the higher search costs faced by workers residing in FUR B. As a consequence, the underlying process of growth is expected to give rise to a process of intra-regional adjustment, whereby some

Figure 8.1: First phase of adjustment to growth in FUR A

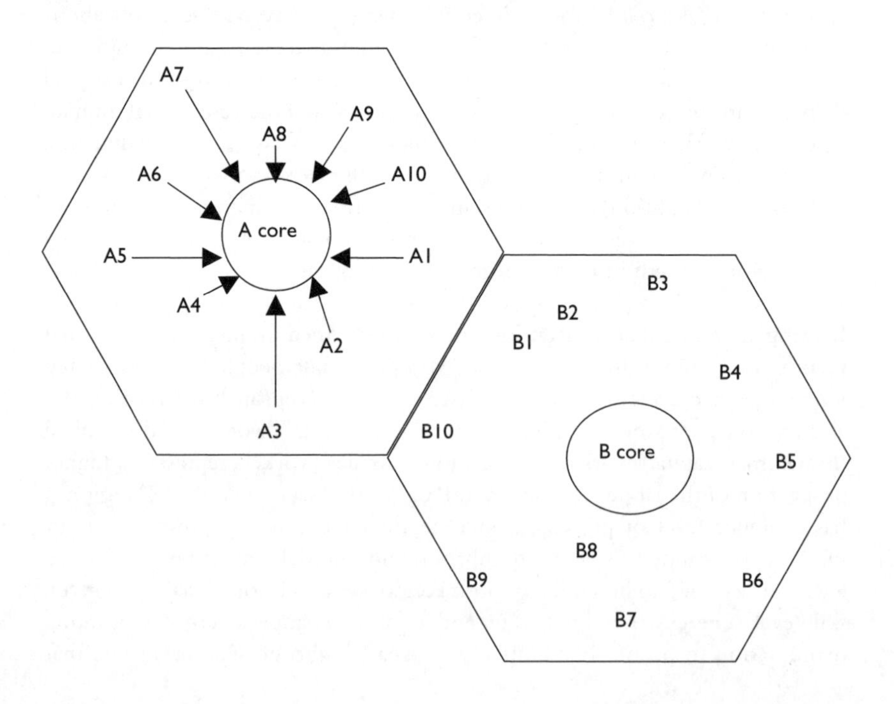

workers previously employed in one of the sub-centres are now able to improve their position should they be able to find a job in the region's core. At the same time, it will also be easier for previously inactive or unemployed workers residing in the faster growing FUR A to find employment. In this FUR, therefore, there will also be falling unemployment and rising activity rates.

A representative situation is summarised in Table 8.1. Wage-rate differentials are likely to develop due to the difference in labour productivity growth. At the same time, the creation of new jobs in FUR A reduces unemployment rates for both skilled and unskilled workers.

It is also possible that this would produce a shortage of labour supply and, as a consequence, wage differentials could rise even further. As a result of the combined effect of all these forces, FUR differentials in skill-specific wages and average per capita income will appear and would be expected to widen.

A second adjustment phase

The combination of the process of economic growth favouring FUR A and the process of intra-regional adjustment described above implies that job opportunities and skill-specific wages in sub-centres A1, A2, and A3 are likely to improve. This fact, coupled with the widening of inter-regional differentials in terms of job opportunities and wages, will trigger a mechanism of adjustment between the FURs. Workers resident in B1, B2 and B10, who were previously commuting to the core of FUR B or to one of its sub-centres, might now find a job in one of the nearby sub-centres of FUR A (Figure 8.2).

Although this implies inter-regional commuting, actual commuting distances may not increase, so that the incentive for a costly adjustment such as migration does not necessarily arise. Cross-commuting flows are likely to represent the dominant labour market adjustment mechanism since they are much cheaper than migration (which involves both a change of job location and of residence).

Unemployment levels, which are measured at place of residence, are expected to decrease in FUR B since some workers residing in it find a job in FUR A. However, FUR unemployment rates are still not in equilibrium. Those for both skill groups in FUR A are still generally lower than in FUR B. As noted earlier in this chapter, it is assumed that skilled workers search for, and travel to, work over longer distances and so manifest a greater propensity to respond to changes in spatial opportunities. Consequently, unemployment rate disparities are likely to be smaller for skilled workers than for unskilled ones.

Table 8.1: First phase of adjustment to growth in FUR A

FURs	Underlying growth phenomenon	Statistical effect	Composition effect	Agglomeration effect	Wage rates Skilled	Wage rates Unskilled	Unemployment rates Skilled	Unemployment rates Unskilled
A	>B	na	na	na	>B	>B	<B	<B
B	>A	na	na	na	<A	<A	>A	>A

Figure 8.2: Second phase of adjustment to growth in FUR A

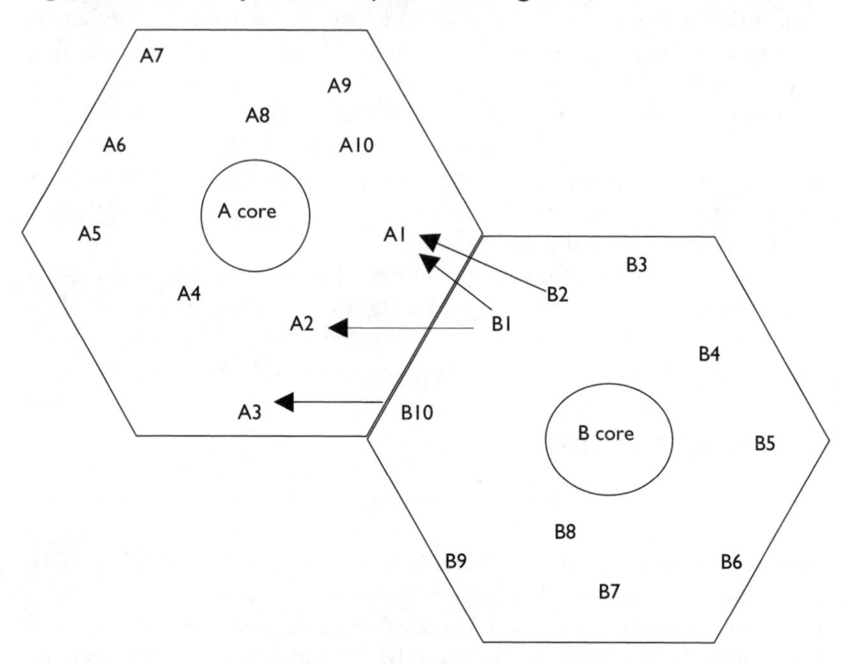

Whether skill-specific FUR wage differentials disappear, persist or widen depends essentially on the strength and the nature of any 'agglomeration effects'. The possible outcome ranges between two extremes. Let us examine the upper limit case first. This would be where positive 'agglomeration effects' related to the mass of skilled labour exist, and are dynamic in nature. In this case, the net inflow of skilled workers will accelerate the process of productivity growth and so generate a further increase in wage disparities for skilled workers.

The evolution of the wage differential for unskilled workers depends on the overall effect on the demand for unskilled labour of the concentration of skilled workers, and on the elasticity of supply of unskilled workers in both FURs. For instance, should the concentration of skilled workers in FUR A stimulate demand for unskilled labour (that is, production is characterised by a relatively high degree of complementarity between skilled and unskilled labour) and the supply of unskilled workers is relatively small and inelastic (implying among other things that FUR B's unskilled workers are relatively immobile), existing regional wage disparities for unskilled workers are likely to widen.

In this situation, the main effects induced by this additional adjustment mechanism are described in Table 8.2a.

Although inter-regional unemployment rate disparities might have decreased with respect to the outcome of the previous adjustment phase, wage disparities might have further increased both for skilled and unskilled workers.

As for differentials in average per capita incomes, it is quite clear that the particular mechanism of adjustment fosters existing disparities even further.

Table 8.2a: Outcome of second phase: with dynamic agglomeration economies

FURs	Underlying growth phenomenon	Statis-tical effect	Compo-sition effect	Agglo-meration effect	Wage rates		Unemployment rates	
					Skilled	Unskilled	Skilled	Unskilled
A	=B	Positive	Positive	Positive	>B	>B	<B	<B
B	=A	Negative	Negative	Negative	<A	<A	>A	>A

Indeed, the 'statistical effect' the 'composition effect' and any 'dynamic agglomeration effects' are all positive for FUR A and negative for FUR B, increasing the gap in measured average per capita income. Moreover, the hypothesised evolution of inter-regional wage and unemployment rate differentials is likely to enhance this tendency even further.

The lower limit case for the outcome of the second adjustment phase would be where the accumulation of high skill, high human capital workers has no agglomeration effects on labour productivity and, instead, commuting flows interact with 'conventional' diminishing returns to scale effects. In this case, cross commuting by skilled workers tends to reduce productivity differentials, so that inter-regional wage differentials for skilled workers also tend to fade away as adjustment proceeds.

As with the previous case, the evolution of unskilled labour productivity depends also on the degree of 'complementarity' between the two types of workers and on the characteristics of the supply of unskilled workers. A high degree of complementarity between skilled and unskilled labour coupled with a low degree of elasticity of unskilled labour supply implies that FUR differentials in wage rates for unskilled workers are likely to persist for some time before being absorbed. In contrast, the combination of a low degree of complementarity between skilled and unskilled labour (leading to a smaller increase in the demand for unskilled labour) coupled with a large and elastic supply of unskilled labour would imply that the demand increase for unskilled labour in FUR A could be met and inter-regional wage disparities for unskilled labour would be likely to be rapidly eliminated.

As for per capita income disparities, it is clear from Table 8.2b that the major source of disparities is now represented by the 'statistical effect'. Indeed, a comparison with Table 8.1 shows that productivity effects, either due to the underlying growth phenomenon or to the adjustment mechanism, have faded away. This, coupled with a gradual convergence of skill-specific wage rates

Table 8.2b: Outcome of second phase: without agglomeration economies

FURs	Underlying growth phenomenon	Statis-tical effect	Compo-sition effect	Agglo-meration effect	Wage rates		Unemployment rates	
					Skilled	Unskilled	Skilled	Unskilled
A	=B	Positive	na	na	>B	>B	<B	<B
B	=A	Negative	na	na	<A	<A	>A	>A

across FURs, tends to eliminate one of the sources of per capita income disparities previously identified. On the other hand, the statistical effect brought about by the change in commuting patterns is even more important than at phase one, and its effect is enhanced by residual differences in measured unemployment rates. As a consequence, the actual level of per capita income differentials between the two regions depends on the relative magnitude of these two opposing tendencies.

It is also worth emphasising that the general situations summarised in Tables 8.2a and 8.2b are not necessarily mutually exclusive over time. Indeed, even if a situation characterised by positive dynamic agglomeration effects actually occurred, it is quite possible that congestion problems in FUR A and the abundance of idle immobile resources in FUR B will at some point become significant enough to limit the unfettered growth of FUR A and slow down, if not halt, the tendency towards 'catastrophic' decline in FUR B.

A third adjustment phase

The natural evolution of the previous phase(s) is the attainment of a new steady-state situation, in which no further adjustment is necessary (Table 8.3). It is clear that all the forces stimulating adjustment have faded away, although small differentials in wages and unemployment rates may still persist in the presence of positive costs of adjustment via changes in commuting patterns. However, even if differences in productivity, wages and unemployment levels had completely disappeared, this does not imply that per capita income disparities have also disappeared. On the contrary, the presence of a 'statistical effect' implies that 'observed' disparities in average per capita income levels between the regions have increased with respect to even the second phase of adjustment. Part of this increase in disparities might be due to the presence of 'true' disparities originating from the structural differences between the FURs; however, part owe their existence to the fact that output and income are measured at workplace rather than at residence. They are, moreover, essentially induced by the particular mechanism – changes in commuting – dominating the adjustment to spatial changes in job opportunity.

It is worth noting, however, that they could be in reality non-trivial. For instance, the growth rate of per capita GDP of the urban region of Bremen (defined so as to be largely self-contained with respect to commuting) was only 72% of that of the much smaller administratively defined NUTS[3] region of Bremen between 1981 and 1991. Similarly, the level of per capita GDP of

Table 8.3: Outcome of third phase: a new steady state

FURs	Underlying growth phenomenon	Statistical effect	Composition effect	Agglomeration effect	Wage rates Skilled	Wage rates Unskilled	Unemployment rates Skilled	Unemployment rates Unskilled
A	=B	Positive	na	na	=B	=B	=B	=B
B	=A	Negative	na	na	=A	=A	=A	=A

the urban region of Brussels in 1980 was only 50% of the level for the corresponding NUTS region.

The size of these disparities depends on the composition of the cross-regional commuting flows induced by the adjustment mechanism. Clearly, the larger the share of skilled labour within these commuting flows, the larger the induced increase in 'observed' disparities since the larger will the effect be on the recipient FUR's total income.

In addition, the size of the 'statistical effect' also depends on the definition of 'region' being adopted. Indeed, the use of a functionally defined set of regions, the boundaries of which are defined on commuting patterns, such as FURs used for the analysis presented in this chapter (see Hall and Hay, 1980; Cheshire and Hay, 1989), should substantially reduce – even eliminate – the effect if boundaries were regularly redefined. Let us suppose that as a consequence of the adjustment in commuting patterns, the majority of the workers residing in some localities of FUR B now commute to employment centres in FUR A rather than to employment centres in FUR B. Then, if fixed (or administrative) definitions of regional boundaries are used, it is clear that the output of these workers will be counted in FUR A while they will still be enumerated as residents of FUR B. This is precisely the 'statistical effect' described above. In contrast, if FUR boundaries were redrawn on the basis of commuting patterns, a change in commuting patterns would require an adjustment in their delimitation along the lines indicated in Figure 8.3. The spatial sphere of

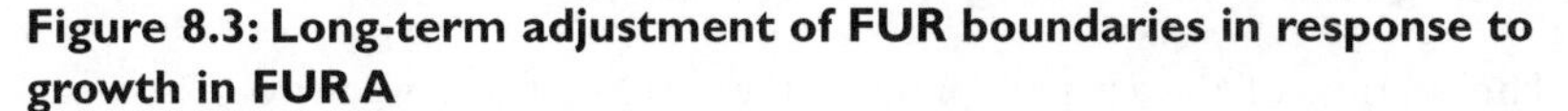

Figure 8.3: Long-term adjustment of FUR boundaries in response to growth in FUR A

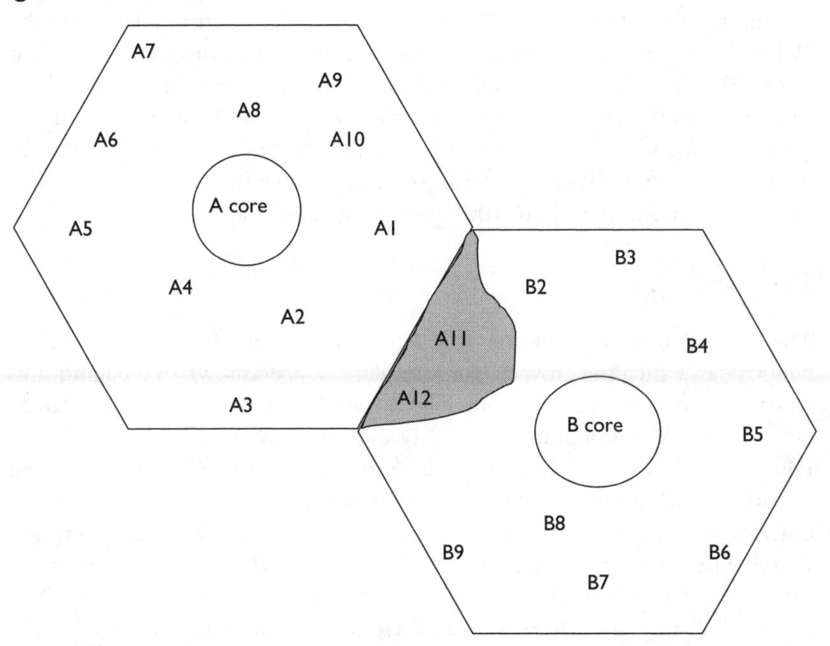

influence of FUR A would now be enlarged to include localities that were previously contained in FUR B.

A change in regional boundaries such as this would therefore reduce the 'statistical' component of the 'observed' per capita income disparities between the two regions. It would not eliminate it if the induced changes in commuting patterns only increased the flow of commuters into FUR A from the nearest zones of FUR B but did not produce a situation in which a majority of the active population in those zones now worked in FUR A. Redefining boundaries on the basis of (changes in) commuting patterns, however, would certainly be beneficial to the analysis of regional disparities in per capita incomes. As a result, observed disparities would be closer to 'true' disparities arising from structural factors rather than to disparities originating from the way in which data are measured. The size of these disparities depends on the composition of the cross-regional commuting flows originated by the adjustment mechanism. Clearly, the larger the share of skilled labour within these commuting flows, the larger the induced increase in 'observed' disparities since the larger will the effect be on the recipient region's total income.

Opting for a functional definition of regions does not, even in principle, eliminate the 'statistical effect', therefore; rather, it just reduces its importance. Since the definitions of FURs used in the analysis in this chapter are 'frozen' at 1971 patterns of commuting, even this qualification does not apply.

Changes in commuting flows over time

This section of the chapter presents the results of a new analysis of actual commuting flows between FURs and changes in them over the decade of the 1980s. It took advantage of parallel work on urban growth and development in the EU, the most recent results of which are summarised in Cheshire and Magrini (2002). This not only confirmed the statistical significance of the 'growth shadow' effect, but also suggested that the most relevant measure of distance between FURs was in terms of time, and that the effect disappeared if FURs were more than about 100 minutes travel time apart.

The data

The aim was to collect data for two dates – 1981 and 1991 – and for all the countries in which the growth shadow effect had been shown to be significant. The choice of dates was determined by the availability of data. This needed to be a matrix of commuting flows only available from national Censuses of Population. Since the FURs are built from the smallest spatial units in each country for which the relevant data are available, commuting data had to be obtained for these small units. In fact, the analysis had to be confined to the FURs of just three of the six countries where the growth shadow effect appeared to exist: France, Italy and the UK[4]. There has been no census in Germany since 1987. The only alternative source of German commuting data (for all the kreise, there have been one-off studies in a number of Länder) derived from the social security records[5]. These relate only to private sector workers and suffer from the problem that the place of record is frequently the location of the headquarters of the employing company rather than the actual place of employment. This produces significant distortions in recorded commuting flows and as a result it proved impossible to construct a time series for German FURs on a consistent basis. It proved impossible to find a Dutch source of commuting data relating to units small enough to reconstitute to FURs. The only available potential source was a sample survey undertaken on behalf of the Dutch Ministry of Transport, but this is unpublished. Belgium data have been collected but have not yet been integrated into the pooled database. Since there are only four Belgian FURs, this means that only six data points are missing which could be incorporated, so the results are not likely to change in any significant way when the Belgian data are included.

In order to generate true commuting data for FURs, it is necessary to obtain a matrix of flows between all the component spatial units on the basis of which the FUR boundaries are defined. Since the boundaries of such small spatial units are subject to change over time, the original boundaries have to be re-approximated on units for each census for countries where such changes occur. For example, in the UK the units on which the boundaries of the FURs used in this data set were originally analysed related to the pre-1974 local government units; that is, the old urban and rural districts and boroughs. The original boundaries had to be re-estimated, therefore, on the basis of 1981 and 1991 Census Wards (there were small changes in the boundaries of these between 1981 and 1991). In addition, because in France (where Commune boundaries have been comparatively stable) the Census years were 1982 and 1990, the changes in commuting flows over time for all countries have been converted into annualised rates and re-estimated to simulate a change between 1981 and 1991.

The analysis

The dependent variable to be 'explained' is the change in gross commuting – or the best approximation thereof in the case of France – between each pair of FURs over the ten-year period 1981-91. The data for all countries has been pooled yielding a total 114 observations[6].

The model tested reflects the arguments set out in the introductory sections of the chapter. There is an expectation that commuting adjustment would react with a lag to changes in economic conditions; however, there is no a priori way of identifying what the appropriate lag should be. Table 8.4 shows the result of experimentation with alternative periods over which the growth differentials were also measured (see Cheshire and Magrini, 2002). It was found that the identical period to that which works best in the growth model performs best when changes in commuting flows are the dependent variable. That is the result reported as Model (3) in Table 8.4.

Table 8.4: Pooled regressions with country fixed effects: dependent variable – log of adjusted change in in-commuting (1981-91)

Independent variables	Model (1)	Model (2)	Model (3)	Model (4)	Model (5)	Model (6)
Difference between the two FURs in their population densities in 1981	–0.00001 (–0.09)	–0.00005 (–0.55)	0.00001 (0.11)	–1.49e–06 (–0.013)	–1.99e–06 (–0.017)	5.55e–06 (0.049)
Growth differential; calculated as the difference between two FURs in their average annual growth rates over the period 1981-91	0.9903 (1.20)	–	–	–	–	–
Growth differential; calculated as the difference between two FURs in their average annual growth rates over the period 1978-82	–	4.116 (1.4)	–	–	–	–
Growth differential; calculated as the difference between two FURs in their average annual growth rates over the period 1978-86	–	–	9.89[a] (2.11)	9.825[a] (2.03)	9.765 (1.45)	9.144 (1.403)
Change in growth differential for each pair of FURs: difference between average annual growth rates of 1978-82 and average annual growth rates of 1987-92	–	–	–	–	–0.04 (–0.013)	–0.505 (–0.165)
Distance (minutes)	–0.0091[b] (–3.40)	–0.0087[b] (–3.30)	–0.009[b] (–3.47)	–0.00354[b] (–4.14)	–0.0035[b] (–4.08)	–0.009[b] (–3.44)
Employment in FUR of destination in 1981	4.14e–07[b] (5.20)	4.15e–07[b] (5.23)	4.04e–07[b] (5.13)	3.63e–07[b] (5.18)	3.63e–07[b] (5.12)	4.05e–07[b] (5.10)

Table 8.4 contd .../

Table 8.4: contd.../

Change in unemployment rate in the FUR of origin between 1987 and 1992	0.1212[b] (3.17)	0.123[b] (3.22)	0.127[b] (3.39)	0.147[b] (3.97)	0.1477[b] (3.95)	0.127[b] (3.37)
Population of FUR of origin (1981)	–9.03e–09 (–0.26)	–5.13e–09 (–0.14)	–2.05e–11 (–0.001)	–3.18e–08 (–1.03)	–3.18e–08 (–1.027)	–9.61e–11 (–0.003)
Log of in-commuters (1981)	–0.0133 (–0.30)	–0.0093 (–0.22)	–0.011 (–0.261)	–	–	–0.0108 (–0.255)
Dummy for France	7.471[b] (16.22)	7.39[b] (16.4)	7.423[b] (16.66)	6.95[b] (44.17)	6.956[b] (43.9)	7.420[b] (16.56)
Dummy for Italy	7.387[b] (22.39)	7.339[b] (22.81)	7.398[b] (23.11)	7.072[b] (39.5)	7.071[b] (0.180)	7.40[b] (22.9)
Dummy for Britain	6.891[b] (24.20)	6.90[b] (24.27)	6.89[b] (24.64)	6.57[b] (49.66)	6.57[b] (49.08)	6.90[b] (24.5)
R–square	0.994	0.994	0.994	0.994	0.994	0.99

Notes: t values in parenthesis; [a]significant at 5%; [b]significant at 1%.

In addition to the pull factor of faster growth in GDP per capita in one FUR compared to others, it is necessary to reflect changing opportunities in the FUR(s) of origin. This is done by including the change in the unemployment rate in the FUR of origin. The result reported in Table 8.4 uses the change in unemployment in the FUR of origin over the period 1987-92[7].

As well as these two measures of changes in economic opportunities in FURs of destination and origin, it is necessary to take account of the distance between the FURs and of their size. It will be seen that the results are as expected. The sensitivity of commuting flow adjustments to any given change in economic opportunities falls with distance but increases with the absolute size of the labour market opportunities in the FUR of destination. Although alternative models were estimated in which distance was measured in kilometres rather than estimated travel times, these performed worse. This is further evidence that commuting flows are sensitive not just to distance but to transport connectivity.

The models reported in Table 8.4 show the results of including three other economic variables although none of these is 'significant' in statistical terms. The additional variables are: the difference in the density of population between the two FURs; the population of the FUR of origin; and the log of the commuting flow between the two FURs at the start of the period. The rationale for including the size of the FUR of origin is straightforward: not only might the size of the labour market affect the attractiveness of a destination FUR but so might the size of the FUR of origin. This, however, appears not to be the case.

The difference in population density between the two FURs was included on the grounds that, other things being equal, this would be reflected in differences in housing costs. Thus, other things being equal, lower density cities might provide cheaper locations than higher density cities (adjusting for size and income). The result, therefore, would be that any difference in economic opportunities between the FURs would be (partially) offset by differences in housing costs. Such arguments underlie the approach of the 'quality of life literature' (Blomquist et al, 1988; Gyourko and Tracey, 1991) and the argument proposed by Glaeser et al (1995) that the best measure of the growth of a city's welfare is the growth of its population. The density of population is a very crude proxy, however, and appears from the results reported in Table 8.4 to be not significant. Whether this is because of the noise in the data or because such effects are too small to have any impact on residential location and so commuting flows is not clear.

When the variables measuring the labour market size and the time distance between the pairs of FURs are omitted, the size of the commuting flow at the start of the period tends to be significant and positive. It is correlated both with the measures of size and the time distance. However, when these underlying variables are included its significance disappears.

The final variables are the dummies for individual countries. These estimate differences in rates of change in commuting between different countries. Since the dependent variable is the log of the change in in-commuting over the study period, these tell us about the differential rates of autonomous change in each country. Inter-FUR commuting flows in all three countries showed large positive trends. The order of magnitude of the increase in commuting was similar in all three countries but somewhat smaller in Britain than in France or Italy.

Conclusions

These results are consistent with previous findings reported in Cheshire and Magrini (2000, 2002) that there is a systematic interaction between the rates of growth of European FURs and that the strength of this interaction diminishes with time distance between them. The variable capturing this effect – the sum of differential growth – was designed to reflect the expected interaction of urban economies when they are spatially clustered. It was expected that not only would the faster growing FUR(s) attract commuters in from surrounding regions, boosting their measured GDP relative to the size of their resident populations, but also such differential commuting would attract more highly skilled and productive workers. In addition there might be a dynamic agglomeration effect of such differential growth performance[8].

The expectation that induced changes in commuting flows were the mechanisms giving rise to the observed interaction in the growth performance of neighbouring FURs in the EU is consistent with the results reported in Table 8.4 above. Changes in commuting flows between FURs behave remarkably like migration. They respond to changes in the spatial pattern of opportunities, both to 'push' and to 'pull' factors, and commuting responses induced by a given change in differential opportunities also decline with (time) distance. These interactions between urban growth rates seem both to represent and to reflect a fundamental mechanism of spatial economic adjustment. They reflect the way that commuting acts as a spatial adjustment mechanism. Moreover, they represent more than just an accident of statistical measurement, because the sum of growth differences variable continues to be highly significant even if the dependent variable is the rate of change of output per employee (rather than per resident)[9]. The most plausible explanation for this would seem to be that such changes in commuting flows produce composition effects in the skill mix of the labour forces of the neighbouring FURs, adverse in the case of the slower growing FUR, and beneficial in the case of the faster growing FUR. Some form of dynamic agglomeration economies may accompany such composition effects. On this basis, it is worth giving at least some preliminary consideration to what the policy implications of these results might be.

As was noted in the introduction to this chapter, one of the stylised facts of European urban and regional development has been that some of the worst-performing cities/regions in Europe are located in close proximity to some of the most dynamic and prosperous ones – this is known as the 'patchwork of disparities' phenomenon, and has both excited considerable comment and influenced the development of policy. The findings reported in this chapter suggest two things. First, the 'patchwork of disparities' phenomenon is neither isolated nor does it arise by chance. Assuming – as the evidence now strongly suggests – it is produced by changes in commuting patterns induced by changing patterns of spatial opportunity generated by the growth process itself, then it is a systematic feature of the European spatial economy. The evidence also shows that the emergence of this 'patchwork of disparities' is not just the result of a quirk of statistical measurement (although that may contribute to the phenomenon as observed).

Even so the policy implications are not as clear-cut as one might expect at first glance. There is a paradox: the divergence of mean differentials in per capita incomes between city-regions is not necessarily inconsistent with the convergence (or stability) of marginal differentials for specific groups, with common characteristics (Table 8.2b). Should this be correct, this would have non-trivial consequences for urban and regional research but (perhaps equally significant) important welfare and policy consequences also. Should the divergence of growth rates and mean per capita and per employee GDP reflect only the composition effect, then it is consistent with returns for skill (and other characteristics for individuals affecting employability) being equal or at least in equilibrium allowing for commuting costs. The same would be true for unemployment rates. These conclusions would only relate to the 'patchwork of disparities' phenomenon; that is, where the disparities exist between FURs which are located in wider densely urbanised regions.

The situation in terms of its implications for welfare and policy becomes more complicated if dynamic agglomeration economies are involved in the process of interactive FUR growth. In that case, there might be persistent differentials in the wage and unemployment rates of equivalent individuals between neighbouring urban regions (Table 8.2a). Thus, disparities emerge and grow and will not disappear unless or until some diseconomies of agglomeration intervene. On the other hand, there is an efficiency gain from the process of differential growth. Since growth is more concentrated in one among a cluster of interacting urban regions, the income of the cluster as a whole (and by implication the country and the EU as a whole) will be increased since it is possible to exploit economies of agglomeration which would not otherwise exist. Intervention to remove the initial disparities would result in the non-exploitation of potential agglomeration economies. The case for intervention would be strengthened if some other mechanism (perhaps of social exclusion and consequent welfare losses) were involved. However, even then it would appear to be a classic problem of trading off gains in equity against losses of efficiency.

Second, in densely urbanised regions, differences in the mean values of indicators such as unemployment rates or income per capita bear a significant parallel to such differences as measured over the neighbourhoods of a large metropolitan area. In order to obtain a measure of such indicators of welfare capable of a reasonable interpretation one should relate them to individuals of constant characteristics.

This discussion is not meant to be conclusive. Rather, it is intended to raise some not so obvious complexities for policy makers to address given the findings about the importance and source of interaction between the economies of neighbouring FURs and the way in which commuting flows adjust to, and produce adjustments to, economic differences between neighbouring cities. Some questions can be addressed directly. For example, it is possible to see whether the unemployment rates of skill-specific groups tend to converge relative to aggregate unemployment rates across interacting city-regions[10]. It is also possible to investigate the extent to which the degree of convergence varies with skill level. The results reported here, therefore, answer one significant question but suggest others. One particular implication is that they provide a new piece of information hinting at the existence of that elusive phenomenon – urban agglomeration economies.

Notes

[1] Empirical analysis is undertaken on data relating to Functional Urban Regions (FURs). These are defined on the basis of a core city identified by concentrations of employment and a dependent economic hinterland defined according to commuting patterns observed in 1971. The original FURs were defined in Hall and Hay (1980).

[2] Commuting data were not available in all countries and other data – such as retail catchment areas in Italy – were resorted to in some countries to delimit the FURs.

[3] NUTS (Nomenclature des unités territoriales statistiques) are the official administrative regions of the EU for which Eurostat publish data. In Germany, for example, the Federal Länder represent the largest regions, the NUTS Level 1. Bremen is for historical reasons a Land and so a NUTS 1 region even though the NUTS 1 region of Bremen is only half the size of the FUR of Bremen in terms of population.

[4] One interesting by-product of the work was the discovery that the official analysis of commuting flows in Italy from the 1981 Census was incorrect because of a programming error. This only emerged when changes in flows between 1981 and 1991 were calculated and in many cases nonsense emerged. After a significant delay, ISTAT traced the problem and re-estimated all small area commuting flows for the 1981 Italian Census.

[5] These were kindly made available by Professor F.-J. Bade of the University of Dortmund.

[6] A dummy is included for each country effectively as an alternative estimate of the constant. This dummy is highly significant as can be seen from the results reported in Table 8.4. There are distinct different national patterns to commuting.

[7] Estimated from the Labour Force Survey, so giving comparable results over countries.

[8] The variable was designed to minimise the possibility of estimation bias arising from endogeneity by measuring the sum of differential growth only over the first part of the period. Such an implicit lag is also economically plausible since commuting patterns are likely to react to changes in the spatial distribution of opportunities only with some delay. In Cheshire and Magrini (2002), additional models are estimated which measure the growth interaction variable in terms of employment instead of income growth further reducing the possibility of endogeniety problems. The main results are replicated.

[9] See Cheshire and Magrini (1998). That it continues to be observed when the dependent variable is the rate of growth of output per worker rather than GDP per capita, rules out the possibility that it arises just from the accident of measuring output or GDP where people work while population is measured at place of residence, of course, because both output and employment are measured at workplace.

[10] Lack of data precludes this for wages/incomes.

References

Blomquist, G.C., Berger, M.C. and Hoehn, J.P. (1988) 'New estimates of the quality of life in urban areas', *American Economic Review*, vol 78, pp 89-107.

Burridge, P. and Gordon, I. (1981) 'Unemployment in the British metropolitan labour areas', *Oxford Economic Papers*, vol 33, pp 274-97.

Cheshire, P.C. and Carbonaro, G. (1996) 'Urban economic growth in Europe: testing theory and policy prescriptions', *Urban Studies*, vol 33, no 7, pp 1111-28.

Cheshire, P.C. and Hay, D.G. (1989) *Urban problems in Western Europe: An economic analysis*, London: Unwin Hyman.

Cheshire, P.C. and Magrini, S. (1998) 'Investigating the causes and effects of localised income divergences in the EU', *39th European Regional Science Association Congress*, Dublin, August.

Cheshire, P.C. and Magrini, S. (2000) 'Endogenous processes in European regional growth: implications for convergence and policy', *Growth and Change*, vol 31, no 4, pp 455-79.

Cheshire, P.C. and Magrini, S. (2002) 'The distinctive determinants of European urban growth: does one size fit all?', *Research Papers in Spatial and Environmental Analysis*, no 73.

Cheshire, P.C., Monastiriotis, V. and Sheppard, S. (2003) 'Income inequality and residential segregation: labour market sorting and the demand for positional goods', in R. Martin and P.S. Morrison (eds) *Geographies of labour market inequality*, London: Routledge, pp 83-109.

Evans, A.W. and Richardson, R. (1981) 'Urban employment: interpretation and additional evidence', *Scottish Journal of Political Economy*, vol 282, pp 107-24.

Glaeser, E.L., Scheinkman, J.A. and Shleifer, A. (1995) 'Economic growth in a cross-section of cities', *Journal of Monetary Economics*, vol 36, pp 117-43.

Gordon, I. (1985) 'The cyclical sensitivity of regional employment and unemployment differentials', *Regional Studies*, vol 19, pp 95-109.

Gordon, I. and Lamont, D. (1982) 'A model of labour-market interdependencies in the London region', *Environment and Planning A*, vol 14, pp 238-64.

Gyourko, J. and Tracy, J. (1991) 'The structure of local public finance and the quality of life', *Journal of Political Economy*, vol 99, pp 774-806.

Hall, P.G. and Hay, D.G. (1980) *Growth centres in the European urban system*, London: Heinemann Educational.

Magrini, S. (1998) 'Modelling regional economic growth: the role of human capital and innovation', Unpublished PhD thesis, London School of Economics and Political Science.

Millan, B. (1993) *Memorandum to the Informal Council of Ministers responsible for Regional Policy and Spatial Planning*, November, mimeo.

Morrison, P.S. (1999) *Unemployment and urban labour markets*, mimeo.

Part Three: Competitiveness, innovation and the knowledge economy

NINE

Competitiveness as cohesion: social capital and the knowledge economy

Philip Cooke

Introduction

Competitiveness at the spatial level is a questionable concept (Begg, 2002; Camagni, 2002) despite 'the competitive advantage of nations' having proved an influential slogan in the 1990s (Porter, 1990). What can be said with confidence is that firms are more or less competitive depending on the kinds of competition they are set up to engage in (quality, time and price being distinctive kinds of competitiveness) and that places that have high concentrations of firms in any or all of these are 'competitive'. This means 'competitive' in terms of influencing other firms to co-locate, either to compete or to exploit localisation or agglomeration economies. This will, in turn, boost secondary markets for housing, utilities, healthcare and the like, and drive up property rentals to points where these may eventually be deemed 'uncompetitive'.

The observation about competitive places being so because of being the location for many successful, competitive businesses will be developed later in this chapter, save to say that convincing evidence of its veracity arose in research conducted to examine small- and medium-sized enterprise (SME) performance in the 'knowledge economy' (Cooke and Clifton, 2002). In brief, the best performing UK SMEs are *innovative*, having introduced products new to the market, new processes or organisational reforms up to three years before being surveyed. This is true in weakly performing and strongly performing local or regional economies. The difference between weakly and strongly competitive *areas* is that the latter have high densities of innovative firms.

The aim of this chapter is to show how, by creating a competitiveness index based on regions and localities, one can arrive at a method for assessing the competitiveness of firms. As will be shown, important to firm competitiveness, at least at SME level, are forms of collaboration, networking or *social capital*. Thus, the relative economic competitiveness of regions and localities in the UK, and presumably many if not most market economies where SMEs predominate, will be argued to depend, ironically, on possession by firms, and relevant support organisations, of a sophisticated understanding and use of cooperation. This is an argument that was developed conceptually at the regional level some years ago (see, for example, Cooke, 1994, 1999; after Dei Ottati, 1994; Franchi, 1994; Körfer and Latniak, 1994) as 'the cooperative advantage of regions'; however, now it can be extended conceptually and empirically to localities. So this chapter will show, by constructing a single index that reflects, as fully as possible, the measurable criteria constituting 'area competitiveness', that this happy state rests on inter-firm and firm-organisation collaboration.

The global importance of the concept of competitiveness has increased rapidly in recent years, with the issues surrounding it becoming both more empirically refined and, at the same time, theoretically complex. It was the research of Freeman (1987), Lundvall (1988) and Porter (1990) that first defined national competitiveness as an outcome of a nation's ability to innovate in order to achieve, or maintain, an advantageous position over other nations in a number of key industrial sectors. However, while the first two authors stressed the importance of interaction to innovation, Porter (1990) downplayed it but could not ignore it in composing his widely cited and critiqued 'diamond' of competitiveness. Further work by Thurow (1993) argued that national competitiveness is primarily achieved through *knowledge-based* industries within which a nation needs to specialise in order to obtain a world-class standard of living for its citizens. Examples of these industries include microelectronics, biotechnology, new materials science industries, telecommunications, civil aviation, robotics/machine tools, computers and software, as well as knowledge-based service sector activities. These sectors can be categorised as strong-demand activities, typically with a high technological composition and forming the basis of the competitiveness of most industrialised nations. Conversely, weak-demand sectors are characterised by low technological content, high natural resources and/or labour input and low wage levels.

Area competitiveness – at both the local and regional level – is defined as the capability of a sub-national economy to attract and maintain firms with stable or rising market shares in an activity, while maintaining stable or increasing standards of living for those who participate in it (Storper, 1997). Although low labour costs may initially contribute to the attraction of business investment to an area, such costs are in many ways a double-edged sword, resulting in employees working for lower wages than their counterparts in other localities and regions. Therefore, it can be argued that true local and regional competitiveness occurs only when sustainable growth is achieved at labour rates that enhance overall standards of living. A key factor in achieving such growth is the possession of a critical stock of firms – indicated by firm density – that are able to generate new entrepreneurs and innovations in developing sectors and markets, and ultimately new jobs (Gallagher et al, 1994). As Porter's (1990) work makes clear, business density is important since firm concentration and competitive performance are related. Low business density results in a lack of firms creating wealth and jobs, with those firms that are in existence operating in a competitive environment ill-suited to enhancing efficiency and effectiveness.

The competitiveness of localities or regions and the competitiveness of firms are interdependent concepts as we have already stated. For example, at the core of US competitiveness in the 1990s was its ability to grow using innovations, quickly taking advantage of breakthroughs in new technologies to create new business opportunities. Despite the post-2000 downturn, the stock of knowledge generated means it remains a leader in transforming computer, biotechnology and telecommunication knowledge into innovations (IMD, 1999). Measuring such competitiveness, however, is no easy matter and, as attempts to develop indicators of national competitiveness have shown, cannot be reduced solely to notions of gross domestic product (GDP) and productivity. Similarly, area competitiveness cannot be measured by ranking any one variable in isolation, since competitiveness is the result of a complex interaction between input, output and outcome factors. Clearly, not all of these factors are readily measurable, given that as well as economic variables they also include political, social and cultural parameters. However, since the focus here is on relative competitive performance within the UK, the assumption can be made that these factors will have an identifiable effect on key economic measures. For example, the cultural differences between a traditional manufacturing economy and a knowledge-based economy should have an obvious bearing on their relative economic performance. Also, factors such as the effect of the prevailing regulatory regime will be common. Whether the political asymmetries of devolved governance in parts of the UK are important will be commented on later in this chapter.

Existing work on competitiveness within the UK, particularly that undertaken by the Department of Trade and Industry (DTI, 1999), has recognised that area performance must be assessed via a balanced picture of the available statistical information. The DTI's business competitiveness indicators, therefore, have consisted of: business formation and survival rates, employment levels, gross value added per employee in manufacturing, average earnings and per capita GDP. In its work on regional competitiveness, which the DTI (2002) defines as the ability of regions to generate high income and employment levels while remaining exposed to domestic and international competition, the number of indicators has been expanded to take account of education, training, land and infrastructure factors. However, the DTI has continued to measure each factor in relative isolation and has not sought to produce an overall composite index at either a regional or local level. The principal objective of this study was to go some way towards filling this gap.

Constructing a UK competitiveness index

A key objective was to facilitate local, especially city-level, competitiveness comparisons. This clearly requires an index incorporating data available and comparable at the local, regional and national levels, and which goes some way to reflecting the link between macroeconomic performance and innovative business behaviour. The overall 'value', and thus relative weight, of indicators and their effectiveness as performance measures demand attention, as do the interrelationships between the 'measure chain' of inputs, outputs and outcomes, and also the capacity for the index to be updated. After experimentation, an index reflecting the model for measuring competitiveness as shown in Appendix One (p 169) was adopted. This model consists of a framework of competitiveness based on three key input factors:

- business density (firms per capita);
- the number of knowledge-based businesses (as a proportion of all businesses);
- overall economic participation (economic activity rates).

These three variables are conceptualised as contributing to the output-productivity of an area (measured by per capita GDP). Finally, the impact of these measures, in terms of tangible outcomes, is seen as the level of average earnings (full-time wages) and the proportion of people seeking work who are in work (Appendix One).

Regional competitiveness

The most striking feature of the Index of Regional Competitiveness in the UK is the continuance of a North–South divide in economic fortunes (Table 9.1). While London, the South East, the South West and the East all perform above the UK average, the East and West Midlands, Scotland, the North West, Northern Ireland, Yorkshire and the Humber, Wales and the North East are all significantly underperforming when compared to the UK as a whole.

As the index makes abundantly clear, it is the southern regions of England that are driving economic growth in the UK. It is these regions that are home to the highest density of firms, the most knowledge-intensive firms and the highest levels of economic activity, which in turn gives firms based in these areas a higher than average level of productivity, resulting in higher average wages and less unemployment.

Table 9.1: Index of regional competitiveness in the UK (UK = 100)

Rank	Region	Index
1	London	115.5
2	South East	105.6
3	South West	100.8
4	East	100.8
5	East Midlands	96.1
6	West Midlands	95.5
7	Scotland	95.1
8	North West	94.5
9	Northern Ireland	93.7
10	Yorkshire and the Humber	93.4
11	Wales	90.7
12	North East	88.8

Source: Derived from ONS data for 1999

It is unsurprising that London and the South East head the rankings, since these geographic areas represent the UK's most advanced metropolis and best national example of knowledge regions. At the lower end of the table, it is interesting to note that Scotland and Northern Ireland, which are usually viewed as 'peripheral', are actually significantly more competitive than either Wales or the North East. In simple terms, this allows for the possibility that grant-aid in the first two regions has been applied more effectively and has had a higher impact. Also, it should be noted that in the 1990s Scotland and Northern Ireland received high levels of UK and EU funding assistance. As in the case of the Republic of Ireland, this suggests that grant-aid can substantively assist firms in raising their own competitiveness, through improving their capacity to innovate, and thus that of the economy within which they are situated.

However, as will be shown in this chapter, it would be unwise to perceive the South East as solely market-driven, untouched by the effects of public intervention and support. It is a well-established fact that government expenditure massively assisted this region's growth profile, whether through defence, cultural, or transport investment subsidies of all kinds (Breheny, 1988). Much is made also of the fact that the 'golden triangle' of London–Oxford–Cambridge attracts the lion's share of scientific research funding, even benefiting from discretionary Treasury subsidy, as occurred when Cambridge University received £68 million to bolster its academic entrepreneurship link with Massachusetts Institute of Technology in 1999 (Baty, 1999). However, the South East's 'economic business environment' (Porter et al, 2000) had been assisted by local training and enterprise agencies long before the establishment of Regional Development Agencies (RDAs) in April 1999. Indeed, strong partnership networking has been responsible for installing key facilities that market logic could not sustain. Three such instances are Reading College's Media and Computing degree courses, Newbury College's Inpaq software facility for advanced Printed Circuit Board design, and Oxford Brookes' Masters degree in Motor Sport Engineering. Each was set in motion by local training councils and/or economic development partnerships. Each benefited firms like Hewlett Packard, Microsoft, Oracle, Vodafone, Williams and Benetton Racing confronted with skilled labour shortages and human capital 'poaching'. Finally, to this should be added a propensity among 'knowledge economy' SMEs, if not their larger brethren, that are a pronounced feature of the South East's business landscape, to network locally and globally to a greater extent than the norm (Cooke et al, 1999).

Without seeking to make the more economically advantaged parts of the UK sound like beneficiaries of a grant-aided life-support system, it may be that this hitherto underemphasised feature of the institutional 'governance' of business life through conventions and 'rules-of-the-game' favouring the exploitation of social capital requires far more thorough attention when considering reasons for lower economic performance in less favoured regions. Paradoxically, because of a perception by South Eastern enterprise support staff speaking for their organisations, and indeed the wider regional constituencies, of low 'natural' social cohesiveness compared to perhaps idealised pictures of the opposite 'up North', they work effectively at networking and partnership activities. This assists the competitiveness of firms through intermediation indirectly and directly, in ways already noted. A more complex narrative is hypothesised for differences among peripheral parts of the UK, which is that Northern Ireland and Scotland, with reasonable competitiveness indicators, exploit social capital in an enterprise support 'milieu' that is 'sociable and trustful', whereas Wales and North East England are 'sociable but not trustful'. The meaning of this is enlarged upon later in this chapter.

Even before policy began to recognise the potential future importance of the knowledge economy (DTI, 1998), authors such as Nonaka and Takeuchi (1995), Castells (1996) and Stewart (1997) had argued conclusively the indispensability of knowledge-based business to economic competitiveness. This stimulated construction of a 'knowledge economy' index for the UK to compare localities and regions with the outcomes from the UK Competitiveness Index already discussed in this chapter. It consisted of calculating the proportion of knowledge-based businesses in an area as a proportion of all businesses. The OECD (1999) definition of knowledge-based business was employed, which covers all high technology manufacturing and knowledge-based service sector activities such as IT, computer technology and telecommunications, financial and business services, media and broadcasting.

The Regional Knowledge-Based Business Index (Table 9.2) illustrates the massive differentiation between the South and North of the UK. Outside of southern England, the next best region is the North West, which itself has 16.4% less than the average proportion of knowledge-based business.

The strong correlation between the 'Knowledge' rankings and the 'Competitiveness' rankings indicates the rapidly dawning reality that in the future the concentration of competitive firms will be further consolidated in

Table 9.2: Index of regional knowledge-based business in the UK (UK = 100)

Rank	Region	Index	Competitiveness rank
1	London	146.7	1
2	South East	130.3	2
3	South West	124.2	3
4	East	107.6	4
5	North West	83.6	8
6	East Midlands	78.4	5
7	West Midlands	76.4	6
8	Yorkshire and the Humber	76.0	9
9	Scotland	73.3	7
10	Wales	64.5	10
11	North East	62.6	11

Note: Excludes Northern Ireland due to lack of data.

the South of England, leading to the gap with the rest of the UK widening even further. As knowledge-based business becomes an increasing prerequisite for achieving area competitiveness and growth, less-favoured regions and localities will fall further behind unless they learn some of the more tractable methodologies for stimulating 'knowledge economies' of their own (Cooke, 2002). At the UK level, the South of England possesses a highly significant competitive advantage over other regions since an expanding core of growth businesses is already sited there. These businesses cannot be expected to relocate in large numbers to more peripheral regions. Economic development policies need, therefore, to focus on expanding indigenous business growth through new initiatives enhancing knowledge-based entrepreneurial opportunities, as the ubiquitous 'cluster' aspirations of the RDAs signify (Martin and Sunley, 2003).

Local competitiveness

Although the discussion so far has confirmed the relatively strong competitive performance of the southern regions of the UK, the Index of Local Competitiveness is a useful indicator of the specific parts of these regions that are driving growth, as well as pinpointing the weakest areas of those regions that are underperforming. The index of the top 20 performing localities is shown by Table 9.3, which illustrates, for instance, the competitive strength of inner west London.

This is due to the enormously large concentration of businesses in this area and the subsequent high levels of employment and GDP that are achieved. Outside of this part of London, Table 9.3 shows that the chief concentrations of competitive firms (with the notable exception of Aberdeen oilfield areas) are situated around the eastern end of the M4 corridor and the wider Thames Valley areas including parts of Surrey, Buckinghamshire and Milton Keynes.

It is no surprise that the M4 corridor and Thames Valley localities are the home of significant business clusters in the knowledge-intensive sectors of IT, electronics and communications, publishing, biotechnology and motor sports, as well as having a larger than average quotient of multinational headquarter establishments (Gordon and Lawton Smith, 1998). The Local Knowledge-Based Business Index, the top 20 of which is shown in Table 9.4, confirms this dominance and highlights the adjacent localities of Bracknell and Wokingham as having the strongest concentration of knowledge-intensive businesses in the UK, with approximately double the national average.

At the other end of the UK local competitiveness scale, Table 9.5 highlights that the least-competitive localities of the UK are virtually all situated within the lagging regions, along with a small number of coastal resorts.
A very similar picture is evident from the bottom end of the rankings in terms of local knowledge-based businesses (Table 9.6).

The statistical differential between the competitiveness of areas such as Bracknell and Wokingham compared to Blaenau Gwent and Merthyr Tydfil is

Table 9.3: Index of local competitiveness in the UK: top 20 performers (UK = 100)

Rank	Locality	Index	Rank	Locality	Index
1	Inner London – West	155.4	12	Aberdeenshire	109.4
2	Bracknell Forest	117.9	13	Outer London – West and North West	108.7
3	Wokingham	116.1			
4	West Berkshire (Newbury)	115.7	14	Edinburgh, City of	108.5
5	Surrey	113.1	15	Hertfordshire	107.3
6	Windsor and Maidenhead	112.5	16	Slough	106.6
7	Aberdeen City	111.4	17	Inner London – East	106.2
8	Buckinghamshire County	111.3	18	Oxfordshire	106.0
9	Milton Keynes	111.1	19	Bristol, City of	105.6
10	Swindon	110.2	20	Cambridgeshire County	105.5
11	Reading	109.8			

Table 9.4: Index of local knowledge-based business in the UK: top 20 performers (UK = 100)

Rank	Locality	Index	Rank	Locality	Index
1	Bracknell Forest	202.6	12	Outer London – West and North West	142.4
2	Wokingham	197.5			
3	Inner London – West	182.1	13	Aberdeen City	137.4
4	Windsor and Maidenhead	165.9	14	Hampshire County	136.6
5	Surrey	157.3	15	Slough	131.3
6	Reading	152.5	16	Bedfordshire County	125.9
7	Milton Keynes	148.9	17	Southend-on-Sea	125.8
8	Buckinghamshire County	147.8	18	West Sussex	123.3
9	Outer London – South	147.2	19	Brighton and Hove	122.7
10	Hertfordshire	145.7	20	Bristol, City of	120.1
11	West Berkshire (Newbury)	143.1			

Table 9.5: Index of local competitiveness in the UK: bottom 20 performers (UK = 100)

Rank	Locality	Index	Rank	Locality	Index
130	Conwy	85.9	140	Isle of Anglesey	83.5
131	Torbay	85.4	141	North Ayrshire	83.5
132	South of Northern Ireland	85.2	142	East Ayrshire	82.3
133	East Dunbartonshire	85.2	143	North Lanarkshire	82.2
134	Clackmannanshire	84.9	144	West Dunbartonshire	81.7
135	Torfaen	84.8	145	Caerphilly	81.2
136	Durham County	84.6	146	Rhondda Cynon Taff	80.1
137	Blackpool	84.2	147	Midlothian	79.8
138	West of Northern Ireland	84.0	148	Blaenau Gwent	78.8
139	East Lothian	83.6	149	Merthyr Tydfil	78.6

Table 9.6: Index of local knowledge-based business in the UK: bottom 20 performers (UK = 100)

Rank	Locality	Index	Rank	Locality	Index
126	Clackmannanshire	52.1	136	Dumfries and Galloway	43.0
127	Torbay	51.1	137	Blaenau Gwent	42.7
128	Cornwall and the Isles of Scilly	51.1	138	East Ayrshire	42.3
129	Conwy	50.7	139	Caerphilly	41.9
130	North Lanarkshire	49.5	140	Isle of Anglesey	41.5
131	Merthyr Tydfil	48.4	141	Scottish Borders	41.3
132	Neath Port Talbot	47.9	142	Shetland Islands	40.2
133	Moray	46.0	143	Argyll and Bute	38.7
134	Pembrokeshire	45.3	144	Orkney Islands	35.6
135	Gwynedd	43.9	145	Eilean Siar (Western Isles)	32.1

evidence that economic competitiveness and prosperity does not and will not organically spread itself in a relatively even manner across the UK, and that policy intervention, despite its well recorded limitations, is required to be continually targeted at creating a more evenly balanced UK economy. However, such policies should not compromise the relative global strength of those localities responsible for driving forward UK competitiveness.

Competitiveness and knowledge-based economies

The analysis so far has shown how the geographic spread of economic competitiveness in the UK is strongly related to the location of knowledge-based business activity. Now we draw on the results of two studies that sought to move beyond the bare bones indicators of economic competitiveness, which this chapter shows to be intimately associated, to extract the 'missing ingredient'. This ingredient, it is hypothesised, is heightened by capabilities in exploiting social capital both by firms and enterprise support agencies. In brief, the proposal is that competitiveness and cohesion are two sides of the same coin, and that uncompetitive firms or areas are insufficiently cohesive.

However, it is important to state that this is a partial not a total explanation. It is presented because the analysis of small and medium 'knowledge intensive' firm practices, in particular, resonate well with the hypothesis. Further, it can be argued, the hypothesis is somewhat heterodox. Other approaches to explaining the spatial competitiveness divide in the UK are not incompatible, however, with a 'social capital in the knowledge economy' approach. For example, a different starting point is to recognise that every locality and/or region can be conceptualised in terms of its own distinctive *skills economy*, whereby the interplay between economic and social structures incorporates the means by which the expectations of employers, employees and those outside the workforce influence the existing and potential skills and knowledge base of an area. Analysing areas in terms of a skills economy provides the crucial link between the economic competitiveness of an area and its human capital resource.

For instance, the McKinsey Global Institute's (1998) report on low productivity in the UK specifically points to poor managerial practices as one of the root causes of an underperforming national economy on the global stage. Taking this assertion further downstream, it is evident that the UK as a whole has under-invested in its skills economy, which has accentuated problems in already underperforming and deprived areas. This lack of long-term investment in the education and training system has resulted in the majority of UK companies adopting lower skill strategies than their rivals in other countries, suppressing demand for training and trapping the UK economy in a low-skill equilibrium with low levels of innovation (Finegold, 1996). The key feature of this low-skill equilibrium, or skills trap, therefore, is that there has not been an overwhelming requirement for an overly effective education and training system. However, without an effective education and training system, the number of potential entrepreneurs and dynamic leaders and managers who enter their respective skills economy will continue to be restricted.

Furthermore, even if there are individuals with this potential entering the skills economy, their human capital – in terms of their own skills and knowledge – must be economically mobilised if they are going to positively enhance wider competitive performance. In other words, the 'raw human asset' must tacitly learn the culture of business and entrepreneurship at both a generic and more sector-specific level. It is here that *social capital* and *business network* building have a vital role to play in developing competitive knowledge-based economies. While the most competitive firms appear to continually reposition themselves and their networks to maintain growth, less competitive firms are often caught in a vicious circle. Such firms are not usually members of established business networks and are subject to a significantly high degree of insularity and a lack of externally based social capital, which in turn makes them sceptical of actually joining networks.

Social capital in the knowledge economy

Part of the research focused on patterns of collaboration and SME performance. This compared OECD-defined knowledge-intensive and high technology firms with the rest. These results relate to 450 (14%) useably responding SMEs across the UK out of 3,600 targeted in a stratified sectoral and spatial sample (Cooke and Clifton, 2002). Table 9.7 shows average magnitudes of current collaborating partners for knowledge- and non-knowledge-based SMEs, across seven categories of actor.

At first glance knowledge companies appear to collaborate with many more other firms than do non-knowledge SMEs. In reality, they have many more collaborations per firm, nearly three times the non-high technology/knowledge-intensive rate.

With regard to collaboration involving actors other than firms, in the area of finance no significant differences were observed in terms of contact with either investors or advisors (Table 9.8).

Table 9.7: SME inter-firm/organisation collaboration: number of collaborations

	Mean number	
	Hi-tech and knowledge	Non-hi-tech and knowledge
Collaborate other companies	34.39	13.53
Collaborate financial investors	0.36	0.56
Collaborate financial advisors	1.79	1.66
Collaborate HE/FE	1.24	0.43*
Collaborate other research institution	0.82	0.19*
Collaborate business support	0.79	0.40*
Collaborate business consultant	1.04	0.29*

Note: * significant at the 99% level.
Source: ESRC Social Capital and SME Performance Project (Cooke and Clifton, 2002)

Table 9.8: Percentages of SMEs with specific collaborations

	High-tech or knowledge firms	Non-high-tech or knowledge firms
Other companies	85.2	82.2
Investors	26.1	24.2
Financial advisors	80.4	81.7
HE or FE institution*	45.1	30.5
Other research institution*	26.6	14.2
Business Support Agency*	40.8	34.6
Business consultants*	35.3	19.7

Note: * significant at the 99% level.
Source: ESRC Social Capital and SME Performance Project (Cooke and Clifton, 2002)

Conversely, knowledge firms were on average collaborating with significantly more sources of technical and business expertise than non-knowledge firms. This was true across both private and public agencies. It should be noted that we are dealing with small numbers here – that is, an average of around one current collaborator across the four categories. The picture is explored further in the discussion later in this chapter; the analysis is similar to that outlined earlier, but with a 'yes we collaborate'/'no we do not' dichotomy across each category, rather than an average number of collaborators.

This reinforces the evidence from Table 9.7, namely that most SMEs collaborate to some degree with other firms. Other findings from the study suggest strongly that a certain level of social capital is necessary for markets to function for SMEs. That is, SMEs are unlike 'blind' atoms of rational utility maximisation as conceptualised in the neoclassical economics perspective; rather, they mostly trade with firms whom they know by repute to be worthy of doing business with. Hence 'collaborations' here include relationships involving monetary exchange as well as the minority that would fall under the heading of 'untraded interdependencies' (Storper, 1997). Striking, of course, is the relatively much higher collaboration of knowledge-intensive and high-technology firms with higher education institutions (HEIs), research institutes, (public) business support organisations and business consultants. To repeat, this is true for such firms whatever their spatial location. High knowledge-intensive areas are distinctive for the *density* of these firms, that are also innovative (measured in output new to the market during the past three years from date of survey) and, as the Competitiveness Index data show, competitive.

Finally, it can be seen that, whatever existed before the RDAs by way of enterprise and innovation support in the most competitive and knowledge-intensive areas of the UK was seemingly fully utilised, if the Thames Valley is any guide (Cooke et al, 1999). The Thames Valley Economic Partnership (TVEP, formed in May 1994) was experienced in supporting collaboration among diverse public and private sector actors. Private sector representatives on the TVEP board included British Airports Authority (Heathrow), PricewaterhouseCoopers, Southern Electric Ltd, Thames Valley Chamber of Commerce, Slough Estates Ltd and Equitable Life Assurance Society. Public bodies involved were Thames Valley Enterprise (TEC, Business Link), Slough, Wycombe, Bracknell Forest, Buckinghamshire, and Cherwell local councils, the Association of Councils in the Thames Valley Region (ACTVaR), and West Berkshire Council. This mix of public and private representation and experience of coming to consensus on a wide range of economic development issues made this and other economic partnerships valued local points of reference for the new regional development agency for South East England (SEEDA).

The role of TVEP was to act on economic development activities more effectively and efficiently conducted at a supra-local authority level. One was Foreign Direct Investment, something pursued with vigour since the onset of downsizing among established overseas investors in the local economy such as Ampex and Digital during the period since TVEP was established. At that time (1994), TVEP's area had 10% unemployment; by 1999 it was 2% ranging from 2.2% at Slough to 0.7% at Wokingham. New inward investors such as Oracle, the software firm whose sales and distribution functions employed in 1999 some 3,500 in Reading and a further 1,000 in Birmingham, had grown quickly. The Thames Valley Economic Partnership claimed the arrival of ACER Peripherals, Oracle and forging links concerning banking software with Bangalore software development companies among projects in which help had been provided. Encouraging the formation of a sub-cluster of Enterprise Resource Planning (ERP) software, involving firms such as Oracle, Peoplesoft, Baan (now Invensys) and JD Edwards in Reading, had also been a feature of this approach. Reading College of Further Education had been sponsored by Hewlett Packard to offer a computing degree course and Newbury Further Education College received £27 million of sponsorship led by firms such as Mentor Graphics to set up Inpaq, a unique software engineering course for advanced Printed Circuit Board design. Other Newbury sponsors include the Training and Enterprise Council (TEC), Periodical Contents Index (PCI) Federation, the engineering trades unions and the Atomic Weapons Establishment (AWE).

Other than inward investment-led cluster-building and inter-firm or firm-organisational institution-building through strengthening network interactions, TVEP saw the need for an indigenous business development strategy and pursued this through support for the Great Eastern Investment Forum, a group that met regularly to put entrepreneurs in contact with investors assisting with business planning, management and financial engineering. The Thames Valley Economic Partnership had hosted discussion and consensus formation about future economic development of the area, particularly indigenous development, and recognised this would proceed more vigorously from 1999 onwards led by SEEDA.

A different body, Thames Valley Enterprise, an umbrella banner encompassing the activities of the TEC, Business Link and Chamber of Commerce, had a less sanguine view of the partnership and networking capabilities of the Thames Valley sub-region than TVEP. Here, the view was presented that this was not an area that worked very well together. It was perceived to be a somewhat disconnected area, where, for example, the TEC had nine sub-boards, a lack of identity was expressed in there being 15 separate weekly newspapers, one daily newspaper for Reading, ten or 12 radio stations and three separate TV broadcasters. "Here, there is no focal point" was the view expressed by the TEC Director of Corporate Development. These judgements were being made in light of the imminent demise and dismemberment of the TEC. The new Learning and Skills Councils for the Thames Valley area was to mirror those for the Small Business Administration, focused on a Milton Keynes–Oxfordshire–Buckinghamshire axis. Remarkably, attracting a greater share of government resources away from areas in receipt of major regeneration grants like the North East of England, given the inner-city and outer estate problems of Reading, Slough and Oxford, was seen as necessary, although, for obvious reasons, difficult.

A constant stress in the TVE perspective was placed, no doubt correctly, on the difficulties posed by an overheating region: how to find jobs for the less skilled in the absence of automotive assembly plants, for example. How to make the economy friendly to particular kinds of low-paid, low-skilled worker in retailing, distribution, catering, hotel work and the caring industries, remains a dilemma in Thames Valley. The example of nurses receiving a £14,000 annual income but being unable to afford to rent or buy a house or flat, in a context where the Health Trusts had recently sold hostel-type nursing accommodation to generate more funds for patient care, was used to argue that public services in growth areas were in serious danger of failing. These were the tasks facing the new Learning and Skills Councils and Small Business Administration franchises. As in the case of TVEP, the expectation that software would be reinforced as a key industry in future was pronounced. The TEC area had received IT excellence awards for its collaborative support for ICT software training. The next step was to develop training software for software management, along the lines offered by Peoplesoft, Baan, Oracle and JD Edwards.

Partnership was also relatively strong among the ACTVaR group of organisations, despite the apparent difficulties cited by Thames Valley Enterprise.

The ACTVaR group had a quite pronounced EU orientation as well as lobbying SEEDA on skills and economic development issues. Working with the esteemed Reading College media department with strengths in imaging, computer graphics and animation for course development, the promotion of Virtual Colleges has been a part of the lobbying process to attract SEEDA growth 'hub'-status to Reading in the media field. In a different dimension, Reading College was a partner with Reading University, TVEP and Thames Valley Chamber of Commerce to investigate and help to promote, along with the local authorities, an 'SME gazelles' (that is, very fast growing firms) strategy. Slough and Reading also sought to promote the idea of a 'social exclusion' hub with business development training and support for the socially excluded. Thus, the incentive of extra funding from the EU has been important in bringing the group together. This experience, however, placed them in a good position to become a stakeholder in deliberations on a broader regional canvas under the leadership of SEEDA.

Finally, the South East Regional Planning Network (SERPLAN) was close to SEEDA's 'hub' or 'corridor' thinking at the time. Both were unconvinced of the 'growth pole' and housing-driven approach associated with Stephen Crow (Crow, 1999). Despite this, a variant of Crow's proposal to concentrate growth in four key centres remains the UK governments favoured method of tackling housing demand in 2002. The key planning problem in the South East was perceived to be housing, seen as an emotive issue for many local authorities. The South East Regional Planning Network's view was that the housing issue needed to be detached from thinking about economic development and growth. Over 100,000 new jobs could easily be absorbed in knowledge-based industries, for example. Policy should seek to direct footloose industries to regeneration areas, either in the rest of the UK or within weaker parts of the South East. The South East Regional Planning Network had no difference with SEEDA on economic growth, growth axes and, importantly, integrated transportation to enhance mobility around the South East. Growth needed to be targeted in knowledge-based 'hubs'. Clearly, the 'economic business environment' in the South East (Porter et al, 2000) was the subject of great expenditure of energy and initiative among key enterprise support agencies even before the establishment of SEEDA. The emphasis on knowledge-intensive industry and employment was, and judging from SEEDA's strategic plans, remains, a core interest. Interactions of the kind described reveal the significance of the role of intermediaries even in the most competitive regions and localities.

Conclusion

This chapter consists of an initial attempt to measure economic competitiveness within the regions and localities of the UK in a manner that in future will be repeatable and replicable. The Index of Competitiveness has highlighted the unevenness of economic fortunes in the UK and, more importantly, the possibility of the gap widening even further. The economic and societal inequalities, divisions and segmentation that authors such as Hutton (1996) have argued are a highly negative feature of the UK's current make-up, are increasingly becoming geographically polarised as the most competitive firms and industries limit their activities to a relatively small number of localities. As Landes (1998, p 455) states, in his work on the wealth and poverty of nations, detractors of the use of measurable data sources often make the argument that "the business of an economy is to make people happy, not to perform statistical feats". This is not untrue, but it must also be recognised that analyses such as these must be used if certain localities are to avoid becoming so economically uncompetitive that it results in widespread deprivation and misery for the people who live there. One key insight that this chapter offers is that competitiveness relies on cohesion of the kind captured in the concept of social capital. In the knowledge economy, this is even more pronounced as a distributional feature. Relatively less competitive regions and localities are less cohesive in this socio-economic interaction and networking sense of the term 'social capital'. Simplistically speaking, firms in less favoured regions and localities could become stronger if they exploited social capital in the manner in which wealthier region's firms do. Some regions have public agencies that are more accomplished than others in embedding themselves to assist this process, while others may have important new lessons to learn.

References

Baty, P. (1999) 'Globalisation in the Fens', *The Times Higher Education Supplement*, 12 November, p 4.

Begg, I. (2002) 'Introduction', in I. Begg (ed) *Urban competitiveness: Policies for dynamic cities*, Bristol: The Policy Press, pp 1-10.

Breheny, M. (ed) (1988) *Defence and regional development*, London: Mansell.

Camagni, R. (2002) 'On the concept of territorial competitiveness: sound or misleading?', Paper presented to 42nd Congress of the European Regional Science Association, Dortmund, 27-31 August.

Castells, M. (1996) *The rise of the network society*, Oxford: Blackwell.

Cooke, P. (1994) 'The cooperative advantage of regions', Paper to Harold Innes Centenary Conference, Toronto, September.

Cooke, P. (1999) 'The cooperative advantage of regions', in T. Barnes and M. Gertler (eds) *The new industrial geography*, London: Routledge, pp 54-73.

Cooke, P. (2002) *Knowledge economies*, London: Routledge.

Cooke, P. and Clifton, N. (2002) *Social capital and SME performance*, Final Report, Swindon: Economic and Social Research Council.

Cooke, P., Davies, C. and Wilson, R. (1999) 'Economic development Hubs or a Spoke in the Wheel?', Working Paper no 2, ESRC Cities programme 'Urban Networks as Innovative Environments', Cardiff: Centre for Advanced Studies.

Crow, S. (1999) *Regional planning guidance for the South East of England: Public examination May-June 1999*, Report of the Panel, Department for the Environment, Transport and the Regions.

Dei Ottati, G. (1994) 'Cooperation and competition in the industrial district as an organisational model', *European Planning Studies*, vol 2, pp 463-84.

DTI (Department of Trade and Industry) (1998) *Our competitive future: Building the knowledge driven economy*, London: DTI.

DTI (1999) *Regional competitiveness indicators*, London: DTI.

DTI (2002) *Regional competitiveness indicators*, London: DTI.

Finegold, D. (1996) 'Market failure and government failure in skills investment', in A. Booth and D. Snower (eds) *Acquiring skills: Market failures, their symptoms and policy responses*, Cambridge: Cambridge University Press, pp 66-83.

Franchi, M. (1994) 'Developments in the districts of Emilia-Romagna', Paper to conference on 'Industrial Districts and Local Economic Development in Italy: Challenges and Policy Perspectives', May, Bologna, in F. Cossentino, F. Pyke and W. Sengenberger (eds) (1996) *Local and regional responses to global pressure: The case of Italy and its industrial districts*, Geneva: International Institute for Labour Studies, pp 17-36.

Freeman, C. (1987) *Technology policy and economic performance: Lessons from Japan*, London: Pinter.

Gallagher, C., Graves, A. and Miller, P. (1994) *TEC performance and firm demographics*, Newcastle upon Tyne: Trends Business Research Ltd.

Gordon, I. and Lawton Smith, H. (1998) *Economic structures and clusters in the Thames Valley*, Slough: Thames Valley Economic Partnership Ltd.

Hutton, W. (1996) *The state we're in*, London: Vintage.

IMD (International Institute for Management Development) (1999) *The world competitiveness yearbook*, Lausanne: IMD.

Körfer, H. and Latniak, E. (1994) 'Approaches to technology policy and regional milieux – experiences of programmes and projects in North-Rhine Westphalia', *European Planning Studies*, vol 2, pp 303-20.

Landes, D. (1998) *The wealth and poverty of nations: Why some are so rich and some so poor*, London: Abacus.

Lundvall, B. (1988) 'Innovation as an interactive process', in G. Dosi et al (eds) *Technical change and economic performance*, London: Pinter.

McKinsey Global Institute (1998) *Driving productivity and growth in the UK economy*, Washington, DC: McKinsey Global Institute.

Martin, R. and Sunley, P. (2003) 'Deconstructing clusters: chaotic concept or policy panacea?', *Journal of Economic Geography*, vol 3, pp 5-35.

Nonaka, I. and Takeuchi, H. (1995) *The knowledge-creating company*, Oxford: Oxford University Press.

OECD (Organisation for Economic Co-operation and Development) (1999) *OECD science technology and industry scoreboard 1999: Benchmarking knowledge-based economies*, Paris: OECD.

Porter, M. (1990) *The competitive advantage of nations*, London: Macmillan.

Porter, M., Sachs, J. and Warner, J. (2000) *The global competitiveness index*, Boston: Harvard Business School Press.

Robson, B., Bradford, M. and Tye, R. (1995) *1991 deprivation index: A review of approaches and a matrix of results*, London: HMSO.

Stewart, T. (1997) *Intellectual capital*, London: Nicholas Brealey.

Storper, M. (1997) *The regional world: Territorial development in a global economy*, New York: Guildford.

Thurow, L. (1993) *Head to head: The coming economic battle among Japan, Europe and America*, London: Nicholas Brealey.

Appendix One: Competitiveness index model specifications

Figure A9.1: A model for measuring local and regional competitiveness

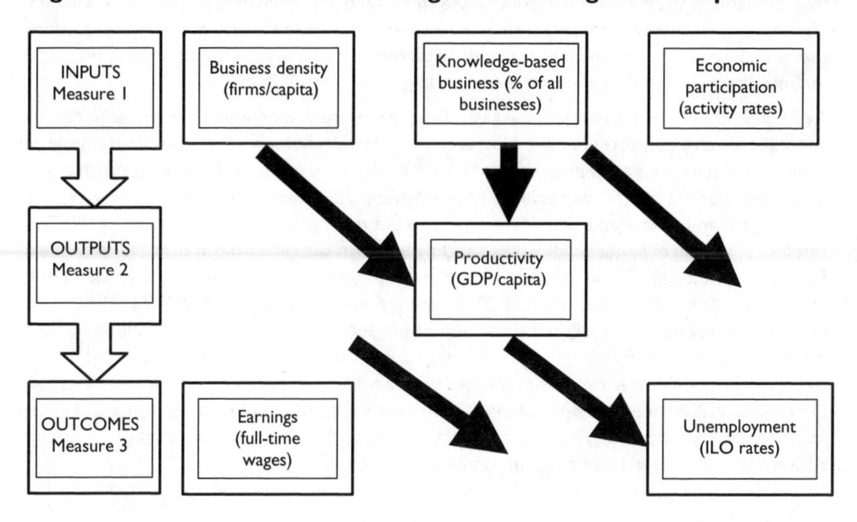

Data on these measures are available at the required area levels (with the exception of statistics for knowledge-based business in Northern Ireland) and in this case were gathered from 1999 Office for National Statistics and NOMIS sources. It was concluded that this data set consists of the best currently available representation of area competitiveness, in particular:

- **GDP per capita** is the most important measure of the economic activity of an area, indicating the historical impact of competitiveness.
- **Average earnings** reflect the pay levels of employed workforce earnings, with high earnings being an indicator of area competitiveness if they are also supported by high productivity.
- **Business density** is a strong measure of the potential for sustainable economic growth through the generation of new entrepreneurs and new firms.
- **Knowledge-based business** is now recognised as the key driver of economic growth at all levels and provides a crucial link between firm-based competitiveness, in terms of innovation, and aggregated geographic-based competitiveness.
- **Economic activity rates** currently provide the most robust measure of the 'raw' human capital available at an area-level.
- **Unemployment** is a key measure of labour market performance, with the unemployment rates measuring the 'tightness' of a labour market.

In order to achieve a valid balance between each of the indicators, in terms of their overall significance to the composite index, each of the three measures – Measure 1: Inputs; Measure 2: Output; and Measure 3: Outcomes – were given an equal weighting, since it is hypothesised that each will be interrelated and economically bound by the other. Fundamentally, each of the three measures are strongly correlated, with outcomes being an impact of the output, which is itself a result of the inputs. Therefore, the overall weightings given to each of the six indicators are as follows (within a total weighting ratio of 1.0): Business Density (0.111); Knowledge-based Business (0.111); Economic Participation (0.111); Productivity (0.333); Earnings (0.166); and Unemployment (0.166).

For each measure an index was calculated with a UK average base of 100, and the distribution range for each calculated. As was expected, it was found that some of the ranges had both a skewed and long distribution range, the result being that these variables had an overly strong influence on the composite index. This feature was similar to that experienced by Robson et al (1995) in their calculation of the UK Deprivation Index undertaken for the then Department of the Environment. Robson et al (1995) undertook a normalisation procedure transforming each variable into a standard form so that their distributions are as similar as possible. It was decided that the same procedure would produce the most valid and realistic Competitiveness Index. Therefore, each data series was transformed into its logarithmic form to produce distributions that are closer to the 'normal' curve, and that dampen out extreme values so that no single variable distorts the final composite score.

As Robson et al (1995) argue, it is the case that the untransformed values are no more real or 'natural' than the transformed ones. However, in order to reflect as far as possible the scale of difference in area competitiveness the composite scores were finally 'anti-logged' through exponential transformation. This was achieved by calculating the exponential difference between the mean logged and un-logged index of the fifty localities nearest the overall UK mean of 100. This resulted in a mean exponential difference slightly less than the cubed-mean of the logged index. For example, a logged index of 104 produced an un-logged index of approximately 112.5 (104^3 divided by 100^3) and a logged index of 90, an un-logged index of approximately 73 (90^3 divided by 100^3). Therefore, bearing in mind the aim of producing a frequently repeatable index, the exponential cube transformation approach was adopted. Give the above criteria and methodology, a composite Competitiveness Index was calculated for all regions and localities of the UK. Data were available for all regions of the UK with the exception, as already highlighted, of information on knowledge-based business in Northern Ireland, with the factor weightings for this region adjusted to take account of this omission.

TEN

Innovation clusters and competitive cities in the UK and Europe

James Simmie

Introduction

International competition, particularly from low-wage, newly industrialising countries (NICs), is forcing many changes on the advanced economies in terms of business strategy. It is becoming increasingly difficult for the latter to compete in international markets, particularly in manufacturing, on the basis of price alone. For them, competitive advantage is to be found more in the quality of their goods and services. Much of this quality is based on sophisticated scientific, technical and managerial knowledge. The transfer of this knowledge into commercial products and services via the crucial process of innovation is therefore becoming one of the main ways for 'first world' economies to develop their competitive capabilities in international markets.

Innovation is so important because:

> At the level of the economy, innovation is the single most important engine of long-term competitiveness, growth and employment. The OECD estimates that between 1970 and 1995 more than half of the total growth in output of the developed world resulted from innovation, and the proportion is increasing as the economy becomes more knowledge-intensive. (Innovation and Technology Transfer, 2000)

While there is widespread agreement that innovation drives economic growth, there is very little analysis of why this is the case. Thus, one of the key questions of this research was: 'How does innovation lead to growth?'

For the purposes of this research, innovation was defined as:

> the commercially successful exploitation of new technologies, ideas or methods through the introduction of new products or processes, or through the improvement of existing ones. Innovation is a result of an interactive learning process that involves often several actors from inside and outside the companies. (EC, 1996, p 54)

The growing importance of innovation is recognised by the fact that it is now monitored on a European-wide basis by the Community Innovation Survey that is conducted every four years. EUROSTAT also compiles the European Trend Chart on Innovation that aims to build a comprehensive picture of innovation and innovation policies across Europe. A picture is emerging from this data of the strengths and weaknesses of different urban regions across Europe with respect to innovation. Low innovation rates are one of the three major weaknesses to be found in a number of European regions. These include most of the southern European countries: Spain and Portugal, southern Italy and Greece stand out in this analysis. Low rates of innovation are also to be found in Eastern Germany and much of the non-core metropolitan areas of the UK and Ireland. Partly as a result of such low rates of innovation, urban regions in these areas are associated with a lack of competitiveness, low or even negative growth rates and high rates of unemployment and social security claimants.

Conversely, there is also strong international evidence that innovation is highly concentrated in a minority of key regions. Feldman (1994) and Audretsch and Feldman (1996) used a 1982 database compiled by the US Small Business Administration to analyse the spatial distribution of innovation in the US. As a result of analysing this data, Feldman (1994) showed that innovation was particularly concentrated in the New England megalopolis of New Jersey, Massachusetts, New Hampshire and New York. A further major concentration was also shown to exist in California.

In Europe, Ulrich Hilpert (1992) conducted a study of the geography of innovation for the Commission of the European Communities (CEC) DG XII for Science, Research and Development, reported in *Archipelago Europe: Islands of innovation*. In this study, he identified ten major islands of innovation in Europe according to the following criteria:

> Islands which are specialised in more than one of the three studied techno-scientific fields; islands which are covering more than 20% of public R&D expenditures in the country; strong presence in the islands of both research institutions and enterprises; islands which are European 'knots' in the web of cooperation links. (Hilpert, 1992, p 2)

The ten islands of innovation identified according to these criteria are Greater London, Rotterdam/Amsterdam, Ile-de-France, the Ruhr area, Frankfurt, Stuttgart, Munich, Lyon/Grenoble, Turin and Milan.

The second key question addressed by this research, therefore, was: 'Why is innovation so concentrated in a minority of urban regions?' Taken together, the two main questions add up to the main focus of the research, which was to seek explanations of what it is about a minority of cities that leads to exceptional concentrations of innovative activities in them and how this contributes to their collective competitiveness and economic growth. This led on to further questions as to the roles public policy can play not only in enabling continual innovation in these successful cities but also in the less successful and more peripheral regions.

Explanation and methodology

There are four main bodies of theory that seek to explain directly or indirectly the reasons why innovation is relatively concentrated in some places rather than others. These alternative explanations are:

- traditional agglomeration theory;
- networked and embedded production theory;
- knowledge economy theory;
- new trade theory.

It is argued that each offers a partial explanation of what makes Europe's ten islands of innovation so successful. As a result, elements of each of them need to be woven together to provide a more comprehensive explanation of what makes them so. In what follows, the main elements of each are outlined briefly. Their key elements are then identified and used to explain the empirical results of the research.

Schumpeter and traditional agglomeration theory

In his pre-war explanation of innovation, Schumpeter (1939) argued that exogenous inventions are sought out by entrepreneurs, brought into their (usually small) companies and turned into commercial innovations. Swarms of these inventions emerge around the depression and recovery periods of long waves of economic change. This process, it is argued, is pushed along by new technological inventions. This formed the basis of early attempts to explain the spatial concentration of innovations. It was combined with the traditional agglomeration theory of Marshall (1919) and Scitovsky (1963) by Hoover (1948), Vernon (1966) and Peroux (1950) to form the basis of product life cycle and growth pole theory. These theories formed the conventional wisdom of the relationships between innovation and space up to the 1970s. From this perspective, the main reasons why innovations are concentrated in larger cities are because those cities provide more encouraging environments for the formation of new firms and therefore their early incubation phase. This is partly because of the variety of possible inputs to innovation and partly because of the high birth rate of new firms.

Networked and embedded production

During the 1970s and 1980s, two main alternatives to these original arguments emerged. The first of these was inspired by the work of Piore and Sabel (1984). They argued that there was a sea change taking place in firm structures and relationships. The key features of this were the breakdown of vertically integrated corporations and the adoption of flexible specialisation among the resulting networks of smaller firms. The two main critiques, inspired by these arguments, of the traditional innovation agglomeration theories were the 'new industrial districts' thesis Becattini (1990), along with the concept of 'innovative milieu' developed by the GREMI, and institutional analyses also drawing on the work of Coase (1937) and Williamson (1975). Both argued the need for smaller innovative firms to concentrate in local production systems in order to accommodate continuous change and minimise networking and transaction costs. From these perspectives, it is argued that mainly smaller firms concentrate together in order to facilitate local supply chains. By doing so they can reduce their transaction costs. They can also take advantage of beneficial externalities, such as skilled labour pools for which they do not have to pay directly.

The importance of networks and linkages is also a key feature of Porter's (1990) notion of competitive regional clusters. He argues that their success is based on four key characteristics. First, these include factor conditions such as infrastructure, regulation and training; many of these are the responsibility of government at all levels. Second, are sophisticated demands from local and national consumers who can work together with producers to develop innovative products. Third, are related and supporting industries; these may be international suppliers transferring global experience. Innovation may be accelerated if suppliers and producers are located in the same area. Finally, there is firm strategy, structure and rivalry. Larger firms are more likely to have at least medium-term innovation strategies whereas smaller firms tend to react more to market conditions. Both are argued to be more innovative when there is local rivalry among competitors combined with mutual cooperation over particular projects.

The knowledge economy

The implications of modern evolutionary theory and new trade theory have also been developed in order to provide some explanation of why innovation is particularly concentrated in world cities and other large metropolitan international trading nodes. This starts with the post-war Schumpeter (1942) model. This recognises the growing significance of large corporations and the systematic research and development (R&D) carried out within them.

Following Schumpeter, Nelson and Winter (1982) and Dosi et al (1988) developed the modern version of evolutionary economic theory. Collectively, they emphasise the significance for innovation of uncertainty, selection and path dependency confronting firms both in terms of the difficulties facing them and the circumstances in which they must operate for most of the time. From this perspective, innovation is argued to be a crucial element in the developing knowledge economy. National systems of innovation have been identified (Lundvall, 1992). These are based on how good local innovation systems are at acquiring and using new economic knowledge. Their relative capabilities in doing this are argued to be an important selection mechanism sorting the more from the less innovative cities.

From this perspective, the main reasons why innovative firms group together in space is that some places are better at supporting learning than others. This is because they have a combination of adaptable innovation systems and labour markets that provide supplies of highly qualified and knowledgeable labour. In addition, the movement of labour between firms creates a learning system as in Silicon Valley or the UK's Motor Sport cluster.

Audretsch and Feldman (1996) hypothesised that such concentrations arise where new economic knowledge plays an especially important role. They argued that many small firms in innovative cities do not conduct much R&D of their own. Despite this, they produce relatively high rates of innovation. The explanation, according to Audretsch and Feldman (1996), is that local knowledge spillovers take place in such areas from the larger companies that conduct R&D to the smaller firms that do not have the same scale of resources. They went on to demonstrate that the main sources of new economic knowledge were industry R&D, skilled labour and the size of the pool of basic science for a specific industry.

New trade theory

There is a tendency in both traditional evolutionary theory and the more recent alternatives to focus on local supply-side production systems. However, in order to be commercially successful, innovations need to be internationally competitive and to be traded successfully around the globe. Markets, competitiveness and trade are therefore important requirements for successful innovation, emphasising the importance of both demand-pulls and the globalisation of economic activity.

This was recognised by Vernon (1979) and Utterback (1988) in their updating of Vernon's original (1966) formulation of the product life-cycle theory.

This was subsequently developed by Krugman (1991) in terms of 'new trade theory', which emphasises the significance of international trade in driving the specialisation and success or failure of particular regions. While Krugman does not address the question of innovation specifically, his analysis of the role of international trade in the competitive success of regions provides insights into demand-led innovation. His basic argument is that the advanced economies are losing their comparative trading advantages in routine production to less developed countries where labour is much cheaper. The main route out of this dilemma is to develop absolute competitive advantages based on products and services that are geared to the specific needs of international customers. Generally these need to be based on knowledge and quality that are not readily available or possible in the less-developed economies.

Specialisation and greater division of labour is one route by which regions in the advanced economies may achieve absolute international competitive advantage. Innovation is clearly a key basis for the achievement of absolute trading advantage. The city-regions in the advanced economies that can provide high levels of specialisation, sophisticated and highly qualified labour, together with international trading capabilities, are therefore likely to be both those where high levels of innovation take place and those with international competitive trade advantages.

In these theories, the reasons why innovation is concentrated in space are a complex mixture of international trading capabilities, combined with regional specialisations, high-quality local factor conditions, sophisticated local and national customers, supporting industries and innovation oriented firm strategies. These combine to create a virtuous circle of innovation and international competitiveness for the minority of city-regions in which they are found.

Research design and methods

Elements of these four groups of theory were combined to form the basis of the empirical investigations designed to answer the two main questions outlined above. These investigations consisted of a major pilot survey of innovative firms in five of Europe's most innovative cities followed by a modified and more detailed survey of innovative firms in the London Metropolitan Region.

In the first pilot survey, a cross-section of five of the most innovative city-regions as defined by Hilpert (1992) were selected, one from each country. The reason for this was to attempt to take account of both national and regional differences in facilitating innovation. The five city-regions selected for investigation were Amsterdam, London, Milan, Paris and Stuttgart.

A common sample frame of innovative firms in these five cities was then identified. This was achieved in the first instance by compiling a list of firms that had won grants from the Brite-EuRam III Programme. Basic Research in Industrial Technologies for Europe (Brite) awards were presented to firms, academia and research organisations for pre-competitive collaborative and cooperative research in materials, design and manufacturing technologies, using consistent criteria across Europe. The main aims of the programme were to stimulate technological innovation, encourage traditional sectors of industry to incorporate new technologies and processes, promote multi-sectoral and multidisciplinary technologies and to develop scientific and technological collaboration.

The total sample frame derived from this source consisted of all the firms winning Brite awards between 1996 and 1997 in the five countries where the cities to be studied were located.

Each local team also investigated the possibility of using local sample frames of innovative firms in addition to the Brite award winners. As a result, a total of 238 separate innovative firms were also identified of whom 160 were interviewed successfully. Some 79 of these firms were Brite winners and 81 were drawn from local data sets of innovative companies, a response rate of 67%.

The responses gained from these interviews were analysed and used to develop a questionnaire, which was used to interview innovative firms in the Greater London region. In this instance, a composite sample frame of innovative small- and medium-sized enterprises (SMEs) was drawn from among firms winning two types of innovation awards. The selected awards were the Department of Trade and Industry's (DTI's) SMART/SPUR for 1995-96 and the Design Council's Millennium Products awards for 1998-99. The SMART/SPUR awards are for pre-competitive research for the development of innovative projects in firms with less than 250 employees. The Millennium Product awards were for firms that had demonstrated technological and design excellence in their new products. The majority of the innovations studied came on to the market during 1997-99.

The total sample frame consisted of 310 firms of which 228 were still in existence and pursuing their award-winning innovations during 1999-2000 when the fieldwork was conducted. Out of this overall sample, a total of 128 interviews were conducted successfully by telephone. These included 69 SMART/SPUR winners, a response rate of 59%, and 59 Millennium Products award winners, a response rate of 54%. The summary of key findings from this work draws on the results of both these surveys. Where international comparisons are made, the data is taken from the European sample. Where international comparisons are not made, the data is drawn from the Greater London sample unless specifically stated otherwise.

Key findings

The key findings of the research are grouped under the four alternative theoretical positions outlined earlier in this chapter. They show that there is still some importance attached to urbanisation economies in larger cities by innovative firms. These seem to lessen the advantages of forming interlinked clusters that are found in the smaller regional capitals studied here. Local knowledge spillovers do make contributions to innovation for a minority of firms. Nevertheless, many firms are highly reliant on their own internal resources for innovation. Finally, it is shown that one of the key reasons why innovation contributes so much to economic growth is because of its importance to exports. Trade also brings advantages in terms of international knowledge spillovers. These arguments are illustrated for each of the theoretical positions identified at the start of the research.

Traditional agglomeration theory

Traditional agglomeration theory starts with the classification proposed by Hoover (1937, 1948). He grouped the sources of agglomeration advantages into three categories. These were: internal returns to scale; localisation economies; and urbanisation economies. Contrary to much of the more recent analyses of clusters, the "pure model of agglomeration presumes no form of cooperation between actors beyond what is in their individual interests in an atomised and competitive environment" (Gordon and McCann, 2000, p 517). The key variable is the size of the agglomeration. Greater size increases the chances of profitable local interactions through chance, the law of large numbers and natural selection of the businesses that can benefit from the multiple opportunities on offer.

Urbanisation economies are of particular interest in the analysis of the relationships between cities and innovation because they consist of external economies available to all firms irrespective of sector. Therefore, they are external to both the firm and industry but largely confined or internal to the urban region. The main dynamic characteristics of urbanisation economies are that:

> Firms and other actors will change who and what they buy from and sell to, simply in response to current advantage and their very specific requirements. The system is without any particular observable organisation or inter-agent loyalty, and simply functions as an ecology of activities benefiting from proximity, and developing emergent forms of specialisation – possibly including distinct forms of economic culture. (Gordon and McCann, 2000, p 517)

The significance of urbanisation economies for innovation was also recognised early on by Vernon (1966). His seminal work relates different stages of product life cycles to their location in space.

Firms in the European sample were asked to rate a list of some 27 possible urbanisation advantages with respect to their choice of location for their innovation. Figure 10.1 shows the most important of these grouped statistically into sets of closely related factors.

Among the most important urbanisation economies for innovative firms across the European sample was a group consisting of labour and services. Among these, the innovative firms surveyed rated the availability of professional experts and skilled manual labour most highly. Specialised labour pools remain an important reason why innovative firms locate and remain in certain cities. The presence and proximity of specialised and general private business services also back up the knowledge and skills possessed by these individuals. Taken together, they form key elements of the knowledge base of city economies.

Figure 10.1 also shows that a group of traditional transport systems contribute significantly to the reasons why innovative firms chose to locate and remain in the five European cities studied. International connections through hub airports complemented by good access to the national road network and central city were all rated as quite important to the locational decisions of the innovative firms interviewed.

Finally, Figure 10.1 also shows the relative importance attached to factor costs by innovative firms in the five European cities. It may be seen that, although capital, premises and labour availability and costs were considerations for the innovative firms, they were not rated as so important as labour pools or air and road networks. This indicates a distinctive feature of innovation in that it is not initially so cost sensitive as products that are further along their life-

Figure 10.1: Agglomeration economies and factors costs

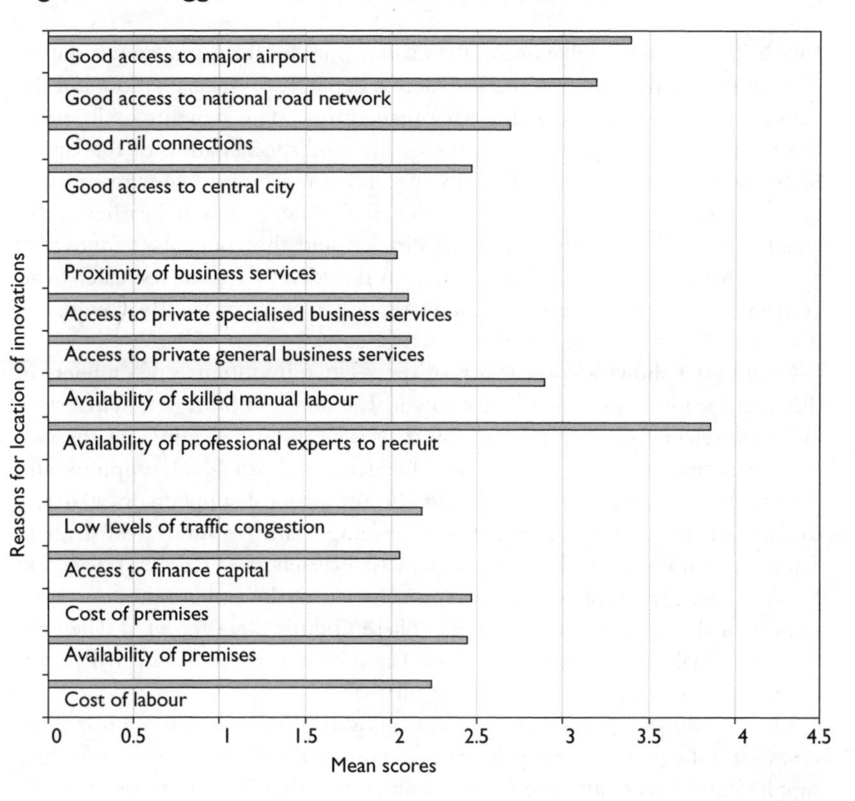

cycle paths. Thus, the often high costs of operating in the five cities studied can be born by innovative firms because of the other advantages offered by the cities to innovators combined with the economic success gained from innovation.

The elements contributing to urbanisation economies shown in Figure 10.1 were in effect considered to be important 'urban assets' by the firms interviewed. Although this did not form part of this investigation, it could be argued that such assets could be of benefit to all firms located in the cities and not just to the more innovative ones. This is probably the case. This leads to two observations at this stage of the analysis. First, is that innovative firms appear both to benefit from the specified urbanisation economies and to be in a better position to pay for their higher costs than non-innovative ones. More of the latter are likely to die because of a combination of lack of innovation, lower profits and consequential lower ability to pay higher locational costs. Second, while urbanisation economies may be assumed to benefit all the firms that can pay the required locational costs they cannot at the same time be argued to explain specifically the concentration of innovative firms in particular cities. They form important enabling conditions for innovative firms but are not the most significant reasons for their high levels of geographic concentration.

Networked and embedded production theory

Marshall (1952) argued that one of the main reasons for the spatial concentration of industries is the fact that market success depends on specialisation and the development of effective industrial organisation. The benefits of localised specialisation include increases in the quality and specialisation of the labour force and the increased use of highly specialised machinery. Much was made of these ideas during the 1970s and 1980s, including, as outlined earlier in this chapter, the rediscovery of industrial districts and the concept of innovative milieu. Much of this argument rested on the idea that mainly smaller firms concentrate together in order to facilitate local supply chains. By doing so, it is argued, they can reduce their transaction costs.

Figure 10.2 shows a comparison of the relative importance of suppliers in different locations for innovative firms in London and Stuttgart. These two cities are selected from the European survey because they represent the two most extreme cases of the use and location of both local suppliers and collaborators. Figure 10.2 shows that the use of local suppliers located at a distance of up to 50 kilometres was more important for innovative firms in Stuttgart than it was for those in London. Conversely, the firms interviewed in London regarded suppliers located regionally, nationally and in Europe as more important than purely local suppliers. These findings were repeated when the other national capitals, Amsterdam and Paris, were compared with Milan, the other regional capital included in the survey.

These findings suggest that the most innovative firms in core metropolitan cities are not gathered there primarily because of the need to locate near their suppliers and thus reduce their transaction costs; rather, it seems to be more the case that they locate in these types of cities because they are well connected with their respective national economy and also other national economies. Innovative firms tend to use suppliers in all of these alternatives in addition to any that are based in close geographic proximity to them.

In contrast, innovative firms in regional capitals like Milan and Stuttgart are more likely to use local suppliers than those in Amsterdam, London or Paris. The reasons for this difference may be:

- that the regional capitals are normally not so well served by national and international communications systems and therefore longer distance transactions costs are higher for firms in regional as opposed to national capital cities;
- that there are fewer but stronger social/business networks in smaller cities and this leads to the development of stronger local supply chains.

A third possible reason is that the development of local supply chains is one way of overcoming relative geographic peripherality as compared with national capital cities.

Figure 10.2: Location of suppliers

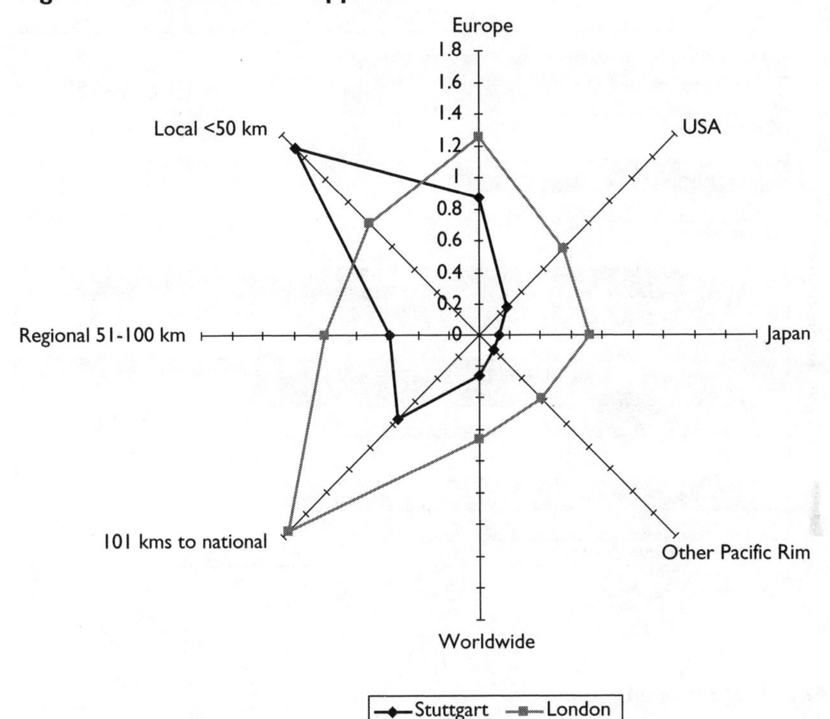

The relative importance of suppliers to innovative firms, however, needs to be put into the perspective of the overall importance of all types of collaborators. Figure 10.3 shows a comparison of the importance of all types of collaborators to the innovative firms interviewed in London and Stuttgart. It may be seen that clients or customers were rated as the most important collaborators for innovation by firms in both Stuttgart and London. Among other things, this indicates the importance of demand-pulls as drivers of innovation. It suggests that any explanation for the concentration of innovative firms in certain cities must consider simultaneously the significance of both demand and supply factors for innovation.

Figure 10.3 also shows that the sampled innovative firms rated collaboration with other firms within their own groups as nearly as important as collaborations with external suppliers. In both cases the geographic proximity of these collaborators was much more important for firms in Stuttgart than it was for firms in London.

We may conclude from this that transaction cost reductions based on the geographic proximity of suppliers is not the only or even the major reason why innovative firms develop and remain in certain cities. They are quite important for some firms, mainly in regional rather than national capitals. It has already been shown that other factors, such as collaborations with clients and customers, are more important for more innovative firms in both types of city.

Figure 10.3: Importance of collaborators

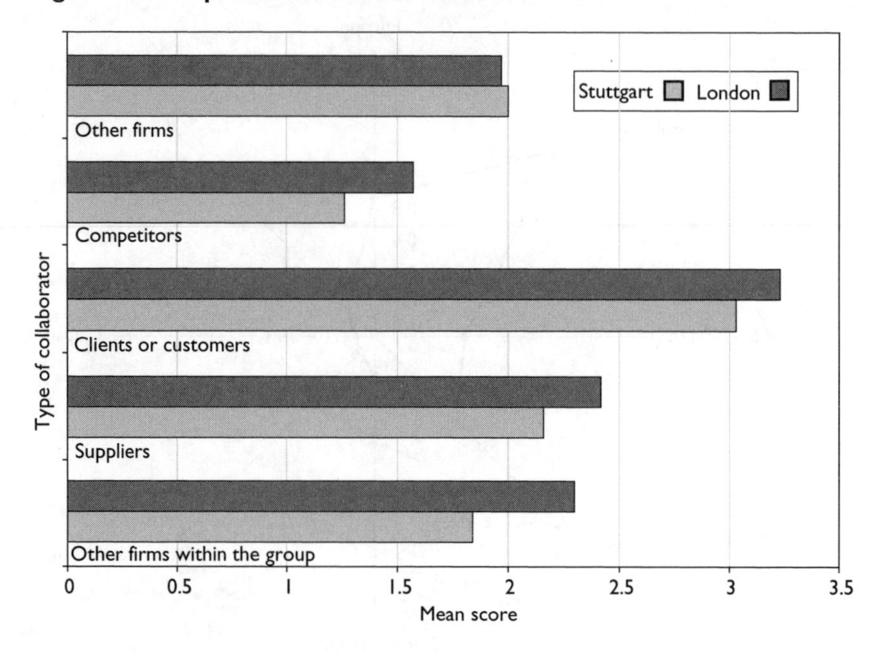

Knowledge economy theory

As outlined earlier in this chapter, Audretsch and Feldman (1996) have argued persuasively that concentrations of innovation arise where new economic knowledge is especially important to new products and services. They also argued that many small firms in innovative cities do not conduct much R&D of their own, yet still manage to produce relatively high rates of innovation based on local knowledge spillovers from larger companies.

Figure 10.4 suggests that this is a plausible hypothesis for innovative firms in the London Metropolitan Region. This figure shows an analysis of the degree to which the knowledge and experience used by firms for the specific innovation investigated in this study was found within the firm itself. Figure 10.4 shows that, for nearly two thirds of the firms, more than 75% of the knowledge and experience used to develop their award-winning innovation was present within the firm. However, for around one third of firms, much lower proportions of the knowledge used came from within the firms themselves. There is thus a prima facie case for arguing that these latter firms must have benefited from knowledge spillovers of one kind or another.

Audretsch and Feldman (1996) concentrated on R&D spillovers; however, innovation requires a greater range of knowledge than R&D alone. Indeed, one of the key features of innovative companies is their ability to recombine several different kinds of knowledge into new products or services. The range of these knowledge requirements is shown by the different types of uncertainty

Figure 10.4: Knowledge and experience located within firms

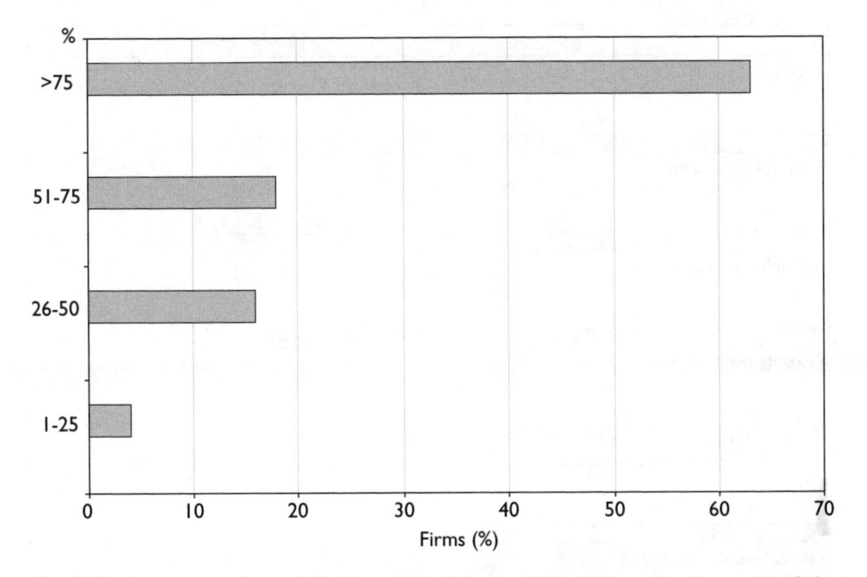

faced by innovators in producing new things. Uncertainty is also one of the most important characteristics of the process of innovation and therefore confronts firms with some of their major challenges.

Figure 10.5 shows the relative importance attached to different types of uncertainty confronting innovative firms in the London sample. It may be seen that finance for innovation is actually ranked as more important than technological difficulty. This is itself closely followed by demand factors such as market demand and price. Possessing the required knowledge and experience to innovate was also perceived as a fairly important uncertainty confronting innovators. Finally, government regulations could also create uncertainties.

Thus, Figure 10.5 shows the complex set of uncertainties facing innovators during the process of producing a new product or service. To the degree that all the knowledge and experience needed to overcome these uncertainties was not available from within the firms themselves, then a variety of spillovers are clearly important to many firms to enable them to innovate successfully. One reason for the relative success of firms in core metropolitan regions is the richness of these external sources of knowledge that are present within their functional areas.

Figure 10.6 gives some indication of the rich variety of sources of local knowledge employed by innovative firms in the London region. One surprise, perhaps, is the exceptionally high contribution made by the universities in the region. Overall, some 26% of firms made use of some kind of knowledge gathered from these sources. This is a much higher figure than is usually found in the UK. The rich concentration of research-oriented universities in the Greater South East combined with the high proportion of smaller firms thrown up by the sample may account for some of this phenomenon.

Figure 10.5: Types of uncertainty confronting innovating firms

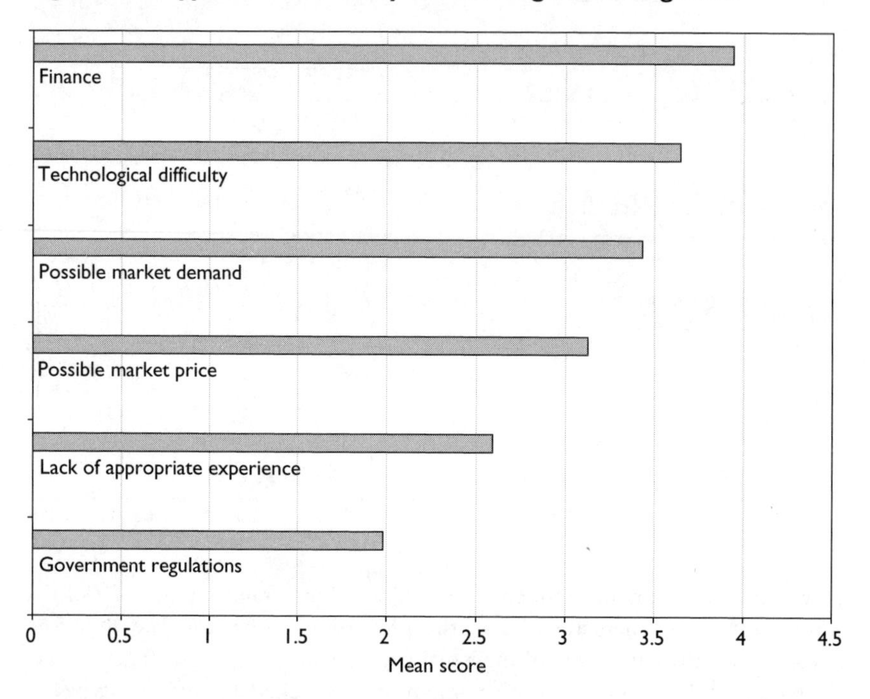

After universities, suppliers and collaborators proved to be significant local sources of knowledge for innovative firms. Industrial support organisations, specialist consultants and R&D organisations followed these. The high concentrations of this variety of knowledge sources within the region provides a rich mixture of potential spillovers and traded relationships that contribute to different stages of the development of particular innovations.

We describe this ability to draw on different sources of knowledge during the development of innovations as a 'pick-and-mix' economy. This phrase encapsulates the needs of firms developing new products or services to draw on different inputs during the development and initial production phases of the innovation. This involves fast-changing needs for different types of knowledge and experience through time. This also appears to be one of the reasons why regular supply-chain relationships do not tend to develop during the early stages of the innovation process.

One of the reasons why there is a distinctive geography of knowledge exchanges during the early phases of innovation is the need for face-to-face meetings for the elaboration and exchange of experience. This is often referred to as tacit knowledge: it is the un-codified, specialised and indeterminate knowledge that is gathered during the processes associated with 'learning by doing'. It is expertise that is embodied in particular people, and carried around by people in their heads and embodied in their skills.

Figure 10.7 shows the relative importance of face-to-face meetings for the

Figure 10.6: Main local sources of knowledge

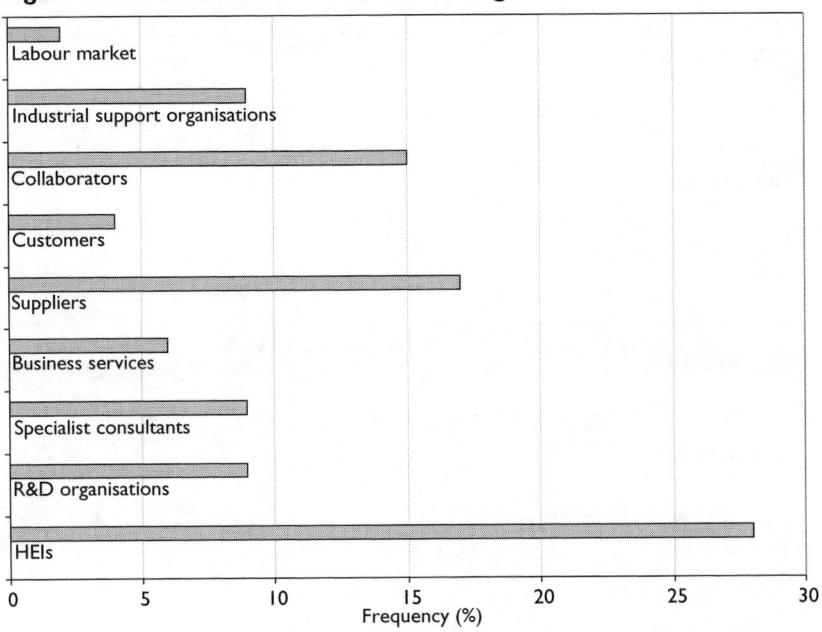

exchange of this type of knowledge. Project leaders were asked to say how often they met with others in the London region to exchange knowledge during the course of the development of a specific award-winning innovation. Over a third said that they met regularly – at least once per month. Slightly less than this said that they met at least once per quarter; just under one fifth met on a weekly basis. These data show two things:

- the relative importance of face-to-face meetings for the exchange of un-codified knowledge and experience during the development of innovation projects;
- the need for so many meetings of different kinds with different sources of knowledge puts a premium on either spatial or time proximity for the people involved.

Generally speaking, such meetings need to take place within the time frame of a single day. This may be achieved either by spatial proximity using land-based forms of transport or by time proximity facilitated by international hub airports. Either way, core metropolitan cities tend to score highly. They have both the advantages of large agglomeration economies with many sources of knowledge located in and around the conurbation, and major international hub airports with multiple destinations to international sources of good practice and cutting-edge expertise. This combination of local, national and international contact systems provides a powerful logic for the concentration of innovators in cities with these characteristics.

Figure 10.7: Local face-to-face meetings for exchange of knowledge

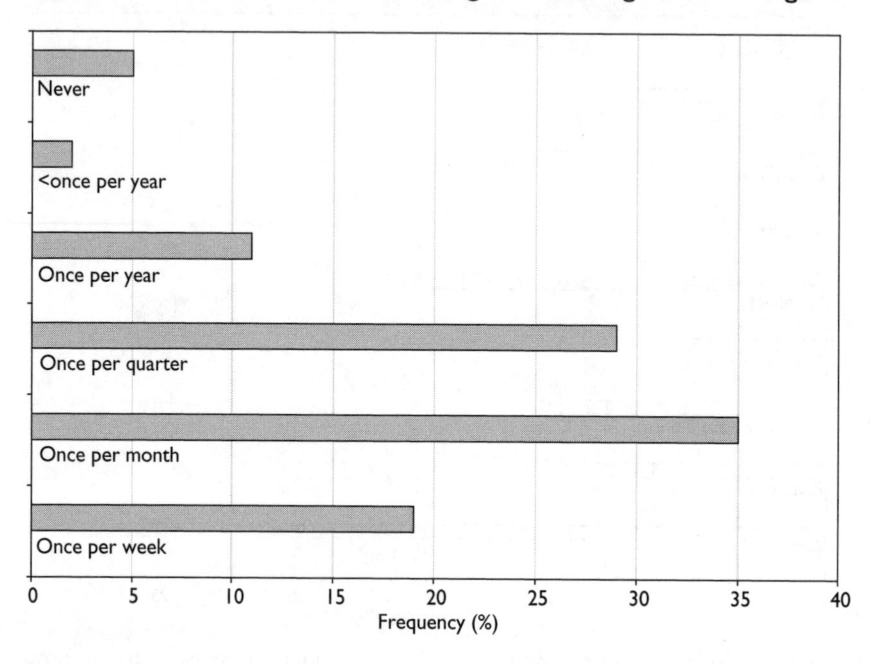

New trade theory

Up to this point, most of the theoretical explanation and empirical evidence has focused on local 'supply-side' production systems; that is, inputs to the process of innovation and development. In order to be commercially successful, however, innovations need to be internationally competitive and traded successfully around the globe. Demand factors and markets are therefore an equally crucial element in the explanation not only of how innovation contributes to economic growth but also of why the activity is overwhelmingly concentrated in international trading cities.

Much of the contemporary inspiration for the renewal of interest in trade, specialisation and economies of scale is derived from Krugman (1991). He argues persuasively that the main route to competitive advantage for the advanced economies is through the development of products and services that are geared to the specific needs of international customers. Generally, these need to be based on knowledge and quality that are not readily available or possible in the less-developed economies. Innovation is the major contributor to this process.

Figure 10.8 shows the importance of innovation and its degrees of novelty in the export success of innovative firms in the London region. First of all, it shows the significance of the degree of novelty to export success. Among those firms that had produced innovations that were new to the world, some 44% were exporting 76-100% of their total production of that innovation. Even among innovations that were new to the particular industry in which the firms were working, 36% were also exporting 76-100% of their total production. These figures indicate the competitive nature of these products and services. They show very successful export performance by the firms concerned.

Firms in these two categories may be considered as leaders of innovation. They are either leaders in an international context or leaders within their own domestic industries. In contrast, firms that were producing innovations that were only new to the firms may be considered followers. They are more likely to be the adopters of innovations first developed by other firms. Although this still makes an important contribution to the relative competitiveness of these firms, their export performance is generally weaker than that of the leaders of innovation. Thus, for example, only 14% were exporting between 76% and 100% of the production of their innovation. Conversely, around 72% were exporting less than 50% of their production.

International trade produces a double advantage for innovative firms and a major advantage for the cities in which they are located. As far as the innovative firms are concerned, it provides them with opportunities for increased economies of scale derived from success in much larger than purely domestic markets. These economies of scale are important in justifying the original risks involved in innovation. They make possible returns that can justify the sometimes long development times and major investment needed to translate world-leading ideas into commercial innovations.

Figure 10.8: Novelty of innovation and % exported

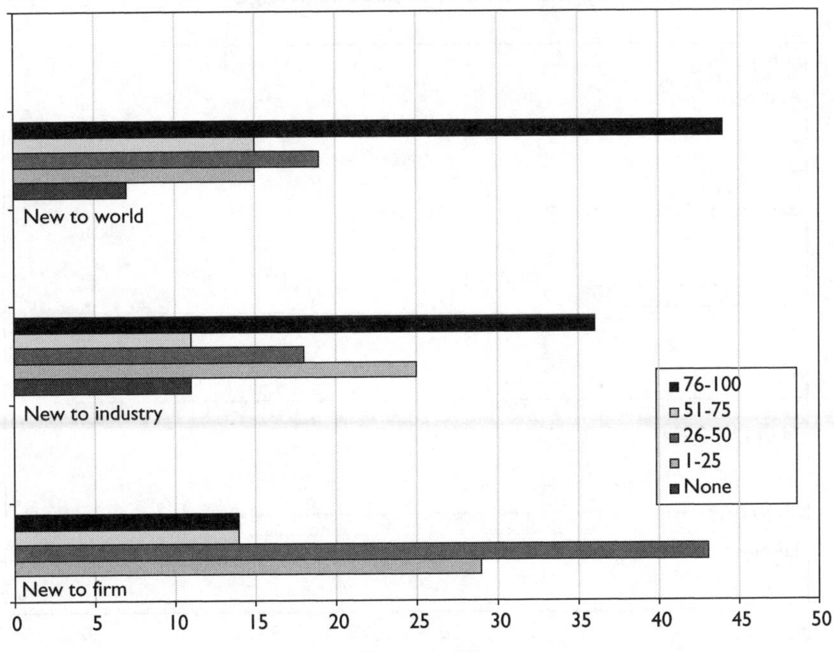

A second major advantage of international trade to innovating firms is that it provides access to sources and contact systems of cutting-edge knowledge and experience. Some 95% of all R&D, for example, is conducted outside the UK. It is not possible, therefore, for firms in the UK to rely solely on domestic sources of knowledge to become world-leading innovators. Traded and untraded international knowledge spillovers are a significant source of inspiration for innovation in the UK. Trade is an important channel of communication for cutting-edge knowledge.

Figure 10.9 shows the main geographic origins of the international knowledge and experience used by firms in the London region during the development of the innovations studied here. North America is the leading source of knowledge. Some 42% of firms in the London region had acquired some ideas or experience from this area for their innovations. This is not surprising as the US, in particular, conducts more R&D than any other single economy and is also the biggest single market for innovative products and services.

European Union countries also proved to be important sources of new knowledge for innovating firms in London. Some 33% of firms in the sample had used ideas and experience gained from the EU in the development of their award-winning innovations. Although in relative terms the EU lags behind both North America and Japan in terms of innovation outputs, collectively it is still one of the most significant sources of knowledge and experience for innovators in the London region.

Figure 10.9: Locations of international knowledge

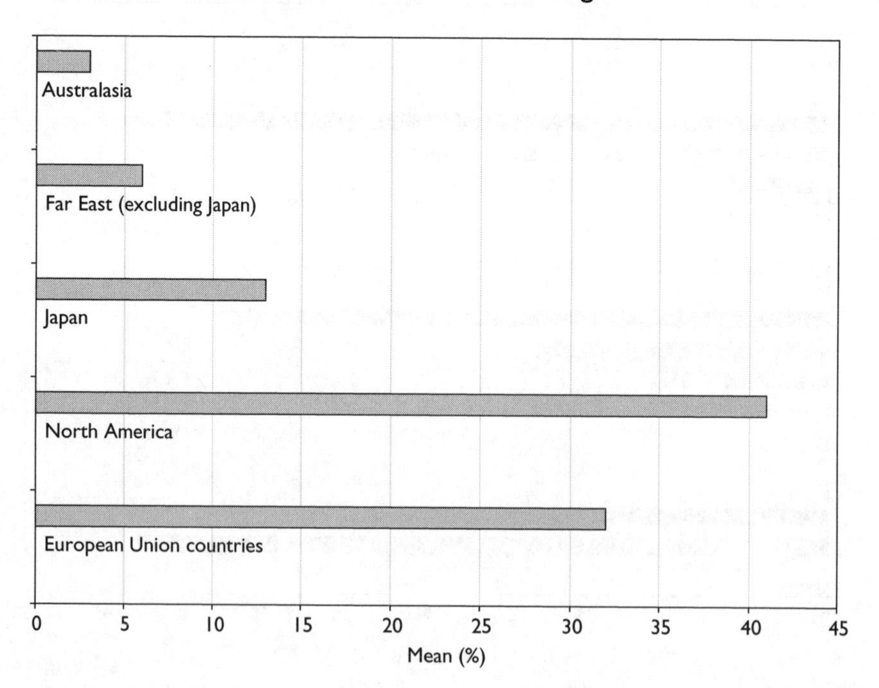

The advantage of trade to cities is that it contributes to their economic base. Basic industries, in terms of traditional economies, are those that export from the urban region. They form a crucial minority of all industries in the area. Export industries bring in new capital to cities. They are able to pay higher wages and so attract younger and better-educated workers who are an important requirement for innovation and growth. Export industries tend to be more competitive than non-exporting ones as exemplified by their ability to export into world markets. Thus for cities a virtuous circle of innovation, exports, new knowledge, social capital and competitive economic growth is a highly desirable interactive system to establish or maintain. It can be a major spearhead of urban prosperity.

The markets for the innovations studied here tended to be quite extensive for firms in all the European cities. This was partly because the size of local and regional markets on their own were generally not great enough either to justify the investment needed to produce innovations in the first place or to provide adequate economies of scale. Thus, Figure 10.10 shows that innovative firms in both London and Stuttgart rated the importance of customers in national, European and US markets as at least equal to or more important than their local and regional customers. For firms based in the London region, even their markets as far away as Japan were rated as important as their local customers.

These results are perhaps most significant for firms in Stuttgart. This is because, according to network and cluster theory, successful regions should exhibit not only strong local/regional supplier linkages (Figure 10.2) but also important linkages with local/regional demanding customers. The fact that even innovative firms in Stuttgart rated the importance of national and European customers as more important than their local or regional ones calls into question the preoccupation of these theories with production and supply-side transactions and linkages.

The importance of local competition in driving innovation is also limited in both London and Stuttgart. Figure 10.11 shows that, in the case of firms in Stuttgart, competitors in the rest of Europe, the US and Japan were regarded as equally important as those based in the local region. National competitors were seen as the most important of all.

The international trading orientation of firms in the London region is shown by the much greater importance attached to competitors located in Europe, the US and Japan. These are the three major markets for innovations and so export oriented companies need to be able to compete with the strong competition from domestic innovators in these areas.

Overall trade and exports are crucial to innovative firms and the cities in which they are located. It provides channels for the communication of cutting-edge knowledge, opportunities for economies of scale and the development of basic industries. In turn, the successful exploitation of these opportunities leads to economic growth and prosperity. Thus, export success provides a powerful explanation of why innovation leads to economic growth. The

Figure 10.10: Locations of customers and clients

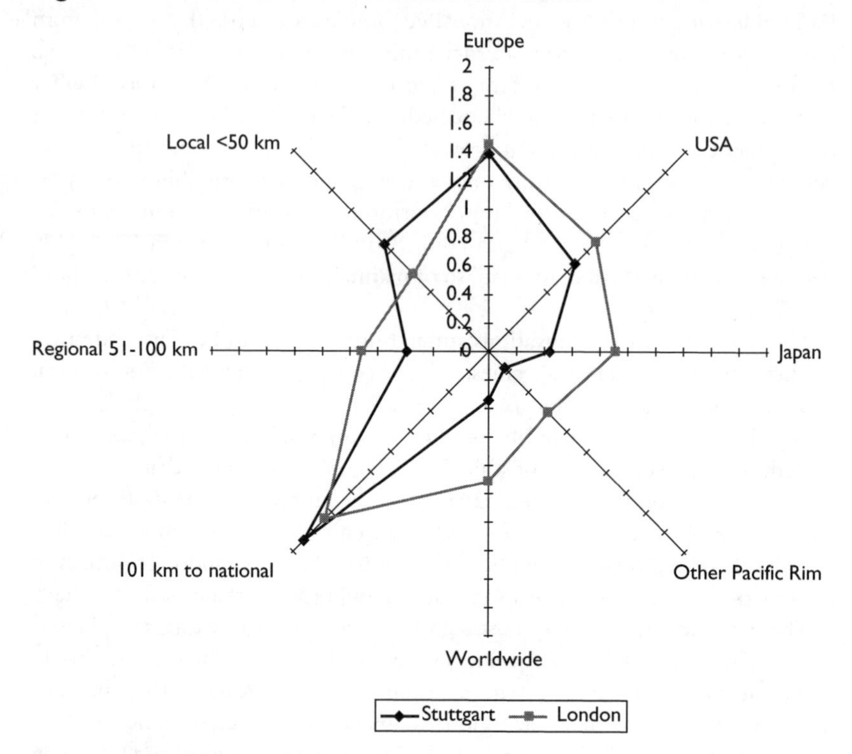

competitive export success of the most novel innovations shown in Figure 10.8 is a key explanation of the OECD observation quoted earlier that:

> At the level of the economy, innovation is the single most important engine of long-term competitiveness, growth and employment. (Innovation and Technology Transfer, 2000)

Lessons and implications for policy

Figure 10.12 sums up the main findings of the study. These have implications for policy mainly at the national and regional levels of governance.

The figure presents a simplified model that shows some of the key relationships between innovation and urban competitiveness and growth. It represents an iterative rather than linear model. Explanation could start with innovation or exports of capital but for clarity of exposition in this instance we shall start with innovation.

The data presented here have shown that the supply side of innovation is encouraged by urbanisation economies such as high- and quality labour pools and specialised and general business services. It is also facilitated by good transport and communications infrastructure particularly hub airports linked to national

Figure 10.11: Locations of competitors

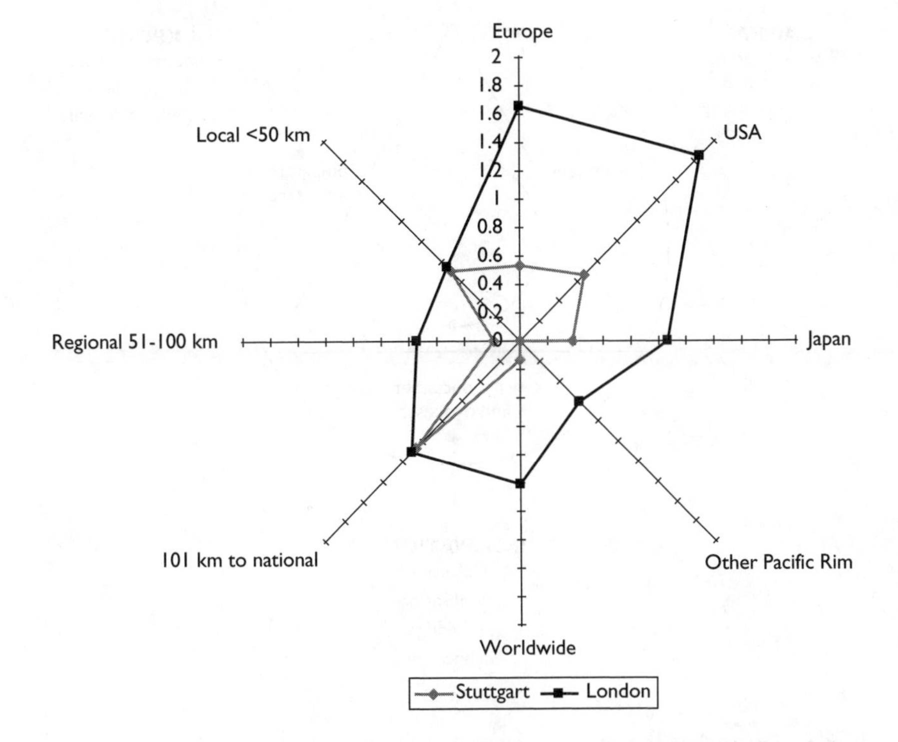

road networks. In addition, it has been shown that in the smaller regional and more peripheral capitals studied some advantages accrue to innovators from the development of regional supply linkages. The importance of these should not be overemphasised, however, as innovative firms seek suppliers that can match their demanding requirements wherever those suppliers may be located.

The most crucial asset for innovation has been shown to be cutting-edge knowledge. This may spill over from large firms conducting their own R&D to smaller firms in the locality that are not able to make such large investments. It should also be borne in mind that R&D is not the only type of new economic knowledge used by firms in the development of innovation. In practice, they call upon a rich mixture of different types of knowledge during the life cycle of each innovative project. Much of this external knowledge is transferred using face-to-face contacts. These may be facilitated either by spatial proximity within the region or by time proximity arising from the existence of multiple air links to international suppliers and customers.

The policy implications of these findings are first that size counts. The greatest ranges of urbanisation economies are normally found in core metropolitan cities. This provides the firms located in them with rich alternative sources of knowledge and communications systems that are particularly critical during the early incubation phases of innovation. This leads to the importance

Figure 10.12: Innovation urban economic growth engine

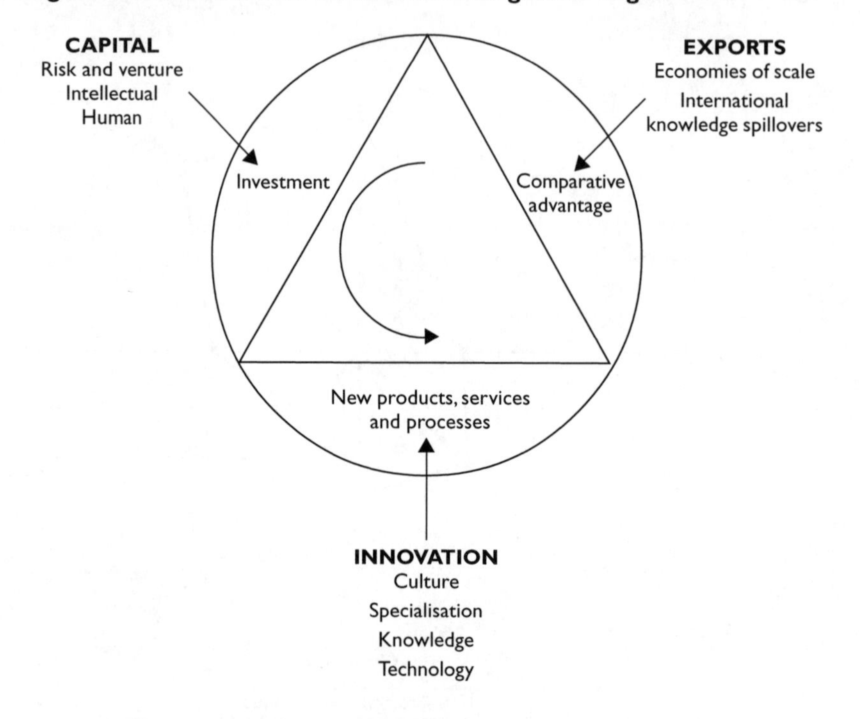

for policy makers of the promotion of hub airports and high capacity communications systems focused on them. It also suggests that in lieu of large-scale urbanisation economies attention should be paid to networks of both supply chains and cities in order to make up for the fact that most cities will not have the advantages enjoyed by core metropolitan capitals.

Policy makers should also consider establishing permanent institutional arrangements for the acquisition of international cutting-edge ideas, knowledge and experience. These are one of the most significant ingredients in the development of novel, world-leading innovations. Some of these may be found in the domestic knowledge base, but the majorities are much more likely to be generated in other national economies particularly in the US, Europe and Japan. Face-to-face contact systems are the main way in which such knowledge and experience is transferred. Web-based alternatives have not so far replaced this tried and tested method. Policy makers should therefore concentrate for the time being on facilitating institutionalised personal contacts between key players in different innovative sectors.

In Figure 10.12 innovation is seen as leading to exports. It has been argued that these are critical to both firms and cities. From a firm's point of view they provide opportunities for specialisation, economies of scale and the interchange of international cutting-edge knowledge and experience. From a city's point of view, exporting firms make up an important part of its overall competitiveness and form the crucial minority that constitute the economic base of the city. This innovative and exporting economic base of firms is often the key distinguishing feature between competitive and prosperous and stagnating and declining cities.

Policy makers therefore need to address the issues of markets and exports as well as supply chains and production. International trade policies linked to knowledge exchanges and novel innovations should be high on the agenda of those responsible for the overall prosperity of cities and regions. Again, permanent institutional arrangements with medium- to long-term time horizons need to be established in order to foster a virtuous circle of world-leading innovations, knowledge exchanges and international exports. In cities where virtuous circles of this type are already established, as in the five European cities studied here, the system also attracts and draws in different types of capital.

In the first place, it attracts funds from export success and inward investors that are attracted by the image of innovative success. This 'new' money produces significant multiplier effects in the regional economy. Second, innovative regions attract social capital in the form of younger and better-educated workers from the less successful regions. This benefits the importing regions but places further question marks over the future of the exporting regions who are essentially giving up some of their seedcorn for the future. Social capital in the form of highly educated professional and technical workers along with other skilled workers is the most important input to innovation. Third, virtuous innovation circles also create and draw in intellectual capital. This consists of ideas, knowledge and experience. It also forms one of the critical bases of innovation. The sources of intellectual capital may be both domestic and international. Universities and research institutes make significant contributions, as do the linkages between international firms based in different national economies.

Policy makers need to analyse what can be done to strengthen these three different types of capital in their particular regions. This will involve such things as: inward investment policies; generating high-quality public services, housing provision and cultural and leisure amenities to attract and retain highly paid professional and technical workers; and investing in the local knowledge base together with mechanisms for seeking and acquiring international cutting-edge ideas.

Competitive and prosperous cities contain rich mixtures of all these factors and policies; but they are never identical in any two cities. Each has its own specialisations and institutional arrangements for innovation, exporting and the development of the three different types of capital noted above. One of the key findings from the European study was that each of the successful cities tended to specialise in different economic activities. They all had long-standing traditions of international connections and trade. They were all richly endowed with finance, social and intellectual capital. The ways in which they achieved these virtuous circles tended to differ according to the particular histories of their development, their national systems of innovation and their institutional arrangements for securing competitive and innovative prosperity (Simmie, 2001).

References

Audretsch, D.B. and Feldman, M.P. (1996) 'R&D spillovers and the geography of innovation and production', *The American Economic Review*, June, vol 86, no 3, pp 630-40.

Becattini, G. (1990) 'The Marshallian industrial district as a socioeconomic notion', in F. Pyke, G. Becattini and W. Sengenberger (eds) *Industrial districts and inter-firm cooperation in Italy*, Geneva: International Institute for Labour Statistics, pp 37-51.

Coase, R.H. (1937) 'The nature of the firm', *Economica NS*, vol 4, pp 386-405.

Dosi, G., Freeman, C., Nelson, R., Silverberg, G. and Soete, L. (1988) *Technical change and economic theory*, Pinter: London.

EC (European Commission) (1996) *Dgs XIII and XVI RITTS and RIS guidebook: Regional actions for innovation*, Brussels: EC.

Feldman, M.P. (1994) *The geography of innovation*, Boston: Kluwer Academic Publishers.

Gordon, I.R. and McCann, P. (2000) 'Industrial clusters, agglomeration and/ or social networks?', *Urban Studies*, vol 37, no 3, pp 513-32.

Hart, D. and Simmie, J.M. (1997) 'Innovation, competition and the structure of local production networks: initial findings from the Hertfordshire project', *Local Economy*, November, pp 235-46.

Hilpert, U. (1992) *Archipelago Europe – Islands of innovation, synthesis report*, vol 18, Prospective Dossier no 1, Science, Technology and Social and Economic Cohesion in the Community, Monitor, FAST programme, Brussels: CEC, Science, Research and Development, XII/411/92.

Hoover, E.M. (1937) *Location theory and the shoe and leather industries*, Cambridge, MA: Harvard University Press.

Hoover, E.M. (1948) *The location of economic activity*, New York, NY: McGraw-Hill.

Innovation and Technology Transfer (2000) *Special edition, June*, Luxembourg: EC, Enterprise DG (www.cordis.lu/itt-en/00-4/intro1.htm).

Krugman, P. (1991) *Geography and trade*, Cambridge, MA: MIT Press.

Lundvall, B.-A. (ed) (1992) *National systems of innovation: Towards a theory of innovation and interactive learning*, Pinter: London.

Marshall, A. (1919) *Industry and trade*, London: Macmillan.

Nelson, R. and Winter, S.G. (1982) *An evolutionary theory of economic changes*, Cambridge, MA: Harvard University Press.

Perroux, F. (1950) 'Economic space: theory and applications', *Quarterly Journal of Economics*, vol 64, pp 89-104.

Piore, M.J. and Sabel, C.F. (1984) *The second industrial divide: Possibilities for prosperity*, New York, NY: Basic Books.

Porter, M.E. (1990) *The competitive advantage of nations*, New York, NY: The Free Press.

Schumpeter, J.A. (1939) *Business cycles: A theoretical, historical and statistical analysis of the capitalist process*, New York, NY: McGraw-Hill.

Schumpeter, J.A. (1942) *Capitalism, socialism and democracy*, New York, NY: McGraw-Hill.

Scitovsky, T. (1963) 'Two concepts of external economies', reprinted in A.N. Agarwala and S.P. Singh (eds) *The economics of underdevelopment*, Oxford: Oxford University Press, pp 295-308.

Scott, A.J. (1990) *New industrial spaces*, Pion: London.

Simmie, J.M. (ed) (1996) *Innovation, networks and learning regions?*, London: Jessica Kingsley.

Simmie, J.M. (ed) (2001) *Innovative cities*, London: Spon.

Simmie, J.M. (2002) 'Trading places in the global economy', *European Planning Studies*, vol 10, no 2, pp 201-14, February.

Simmie, J.M. (2002) 'Knowledge spillovers and the reasons for the concentration of innovative SMEs', *Urban Studies*, vol 39, nos 5/6, pp 885-902, May.

Simmie, J.M. (2002) 'Innovation, international trade and knowledge spillovers', *Italian Journal of Regional Science*, no 1, pp 73-91.

Simmie, J.M. (with J. Sennett, P. Wood and D. Hart) (2002) 'Innovation in Europe: a tale of knowledge and trade in five cities', *Regional Studies*, vol 36, no 1, February, pp 47-64.

Simmie, J.M. and Sennett, J. (1999) 'Innovative clusters: theoretical explanations and why size matters', *National Institute Economic Review*, vol 4/99, no 170, October, pp 87-98.

Storper, M. (1995) 'The resurgence of regional economies, ten years later: the region as a nexus of untraded interdependencies', *European Urban and Regional Studies*, vol 2, no 3, pp 191-221.

Utterback, J.M. (1988) 'Innovation and industrial evolution in manufacturing industries', in B.R. Guile and H. Brooks (eds) *Technology and global industry: Companies and nations in the world economy*, Washington, DC: National Academy Press.

Vernon, R. (1966) 'International investment and international trade in the product cycle', *Quarterly Journal of Economics*, vol 80, pp 190-207.

Vernon, R. (1979) 'The product cycle hypothesis in a new international environment', *Oxford Bulletin of Economics and Statistics*, vol 41, pp 255-267.

Williamson, O.E. (1975) *Markets and hierarchies*, New York, NY: Free Press.

Part Four: Housing, property and economic performance

ELEVEN

The role of housing in city economic performance

Geoffrey Meen and Mark Andrew

Introduction

The human capital or skill level of the urban population is frequently identified as the key factor determining urban growth and competitiveness. In the US, for example, the growth rates of cities in the 1990s were closely correlated with the level of residents' education (Glaeser and Shapiro, 2001). Crucial to this relationship is the link between human capital and housing. Housing plays a critical role in the economic performance of cities through its influence on the locational choices of the more highly skilled members of the labour force. There are links between housing, on the one hand, and social and environmental capital, on the other, and we comment on these in this chapter. The central concern of this chapter, however, is with this crucial relationship between housing and human capital.

The population structure of cities depends to a considerable extent on the housing choices of residents over their life cycle, and housing demand typically varies with both demographic and economic circumstances. From an analytical perspective, we need to understand the key factors that determine residential location and its impacts on the skills base of cities. Looked at from a policy perspective we need to assess the extent to which policy measures might impact on the locational choices of, in particular, more highly skilled members of the labour force. We need to examine what policies might serve to retain the more highly skilled within cities or attract those who have left back to cities. In addition to understanding the housing decisions and location choices of the high skilled, we need to consider the reasons why the low skilled become trapped in particular (usually inner-city) locations. Consequently, we need to understand segregation. The research set out to address the relative lack of quantitative evidence in this country that can be brought to bear on the extent to which housing markets actually contribute to or detract from the economic performance of cities. It also assesses the extent, in turn, to which policy can have any impact on this.

To anticipate, our conclusions do not make comfortable reading: our work suggests that the probability of attracting households back to cities once they have left is rather small. Internationally and in the UK, recent increases in the population in the central areas of cities have been primarily concentrated on young, small, high-income households without children, rather than on 'traditional' families. A challenge for the future is to retain these households in cities as they age so that they do not follow the route of their parents to the suburbs as they progress through their own life cycle. As things stand at the moment, however, there is little evidence that conventional patterns of housing demand will be challenged.

In order to comment on likely future household trends, particularly between urban and suburban locations, and to assess the likely success of government policy (for example, brownfield building targets or attempts to attract households back to cities), an appropriate quantitative framework is required. A large proportion of urban housing analysis still rests on the foundations of traditional residential location theory. Although this work is valuable, it does not cover all aspects that we might expect to be important for quantifying future trends. In particular, it does not provide an integrated empirical model of housing choice, industrial location, labour demand and supply, social cohesion and exclusion, and transport, all of which are required in an ideal world. There is, on the other hand, increasing evidence that these analytical problems are being recognised in policy circles. The background paper to the Urban White Paper, Robson et al (2000), for example, recognised the failings of traditional methods of empirical analysis.

The models put forward in this chapter begin to move towards a more complete framework. The chapter, therefore, has a number of objectives. It aims:

- to construct a framework for the analysis of housing dynamics, capable of explaining the emerging workforce skills base of cities;
- to provide quantitative estimates of the key factors that determine household residential moves and location choices, primarily for London and South East England (although we believe that the general principles are likely to hold for other major cities);
- to comment, in general terms, on the likely future distribution of households in London and the South East, with its implications for key workers in the South East, deprivation and segregation in some areas of the city and overall city competitiveness;
- to analyse some of the key local housing issues of the day, notably cumulative processes of urban decline, low demand housing, the absence of socially integrated neighbourhoods and the potential role of design-led policies in reinvigorating city centres;
- to discuss the impact of housing-based policies for improving city competitiveness.

The changing population structure of cities

Indicators suggest that the UK suffers from the highest degree of social exclusion in Europe. The UK has the highest percentage of children living in households with incomes below the US official poverty line and the highest proportion of households with children in which no adult is in employment. Only Spain fares worse in maths tests for 13 year olds. The UK also shows low levels of adult literacy, low rates of participation in learning at age 18 compared with the EU average, the highest teenage birth rate, the highest rate of drug usage by teenagers and high chances of being the victim of a crime (Social Exclusion Unit, 2001). These problems are also most heavily concentrated in urban areas. As the Social Exclusion Unit (2001, para 1.4) suggests, these problems are linked and are mutually reinforcing, creating "a fast-moving vicious circle".

Table 11.1, taken from Robson et al (2000), shows the regional pattern of the most and least deprived wards in England, based on the 2000 Index of Deprivation. With the exception of London, the most deprived wards are heavily concentrated in the North of England, whereas the most prosperous wards are primarily in the South. However, a simple representation of a North–South divide is misleading. London, in particular, has a high proportion of deprived wards and, as Table 11.2 indicates, the top three English districts with the highest proportions of deprived populations all lie in Inner London.

Since London is the basis of our modelling work later in this chapter, further comments are in order for the capital, concerning population trends and indicators of social conditions. Major cities, over the last ten years, have not all lost population. For example, after decades of population decline, London's population in 1996 stood at over seven million, a 4.6% increase from 1983 (ONS, 1998). Even the population of Inner London has increased slightly since 1983, although the population remains similar to that in the 1850s.

Table 11.1: The regional pattern of the most and least deprived wards

	Regional breakdown of 10% most deprived wards	Regional breakdown of 10% least deprived wards
North East	19.0	0.8
Yorkshire & Humberside	9.4	2.7
East Midlands	9.0	9.5
Eastern	3.7	17.4
London	18.0	5.6
South East (excluding London)	3.4	47.1
South West	3.6	9.4
West Midlands	8.2	3.4
North West	25.7	4.0
Total	100.0	100.0

Source: Robson et al (2000)

Table11.2: Districts with the highest proportions of deprived populations

	% of population living in one of the 10% most deprived wards in England
Hackney	100
Tower Hamlets	97
Newham	95
Manchester	79
Knowsley	79
Easington	79
Liverpool	72
Middlesborough	60
Islington	58
South Tyneside	58

Source: Robson et al (2000)

The gains in recent years in London have occurred partly as a result of natural population increases. London has both a high birth rate and low death rate as a result of its relatively young population compared with the country as a whole. Furthermore, London has gained significantly from international in-migration. In terms of internal migration, London continues to gain population from the northern regions, but loses population to the neighbouring South East and eastern regions. In terms of the age structure of migration, London benefits from the mobile 16-24 age group, but contracts in the other age groups. These trends have established distinct patterns of urban–rural drift. To caricature the movements, at early stages of an individual's life cycle, they tend to be drawn towards London (as a result of labour market opportunities). However, as they become older and household characteristics change, they tend to migrate short distances to Outer London or the South East and, in many cases, commute back to London to work. These patterns give rise to the population distributions shown in Table 11.3.

Inner London clearly has a younger population structure than the rest of the South East, particularly in the 16-24 and 25-39 age bands. The table also demonstrates that individuals tend to move away from the centre as they become older. However, an important element of current urban policy is concerned with how these deep-seated long-run trends might be reversed, since they

Table 11.3: Population age structure in London and South East England (% shares)

	0-15	16-24	25-39	40-59	60+
Inner London	19.2	14.0	28.5	20.6	17.8
Outer London	19.7	13.0	24.2	23.3	19.8
Rest of South East	*19.9*	*12.5*	*21.9*	*24.7*	*21.1*

Source: 1991 Census of Population

potentially undermine the asset base of the city. The question, however, is why households move away from London as they age. To answer the question, we need to look at the housing careers of households and to ask, first, what the factors are that cause households to move and, second, what the factors are that influence the choice of location? These are, of course, interlinked and we return to the issue later in this chapter.

London is not alone in its population increase. Cheshire (1995) has pointed to the increasing populations of many major cities in Northern Europe. Glaeser and Shapiro (2001) find that many US cities have experienced significant expansion over the last ten years – particularly on the West Coast and in sunbelt areas. In an analysis of the 2000 US Census, Sohmer and Lang (2001) found that, in a sample of 24 cities, 18 downtown areas experienced population growth over the previous ten years (although the absolute numbers remain small). Meen (2001) finds that some Australian cities have also experienced a revival. However, in each of these cases, the strongest growth is in areas of high educational attainment, such as university towns or cities of high-amenity value. Many of the major Northern British conurbations have continued to lose population albeit at a slower rate than in earlier decades (although there are certainly good examples of improving urban areas).

A further key factor is that population growth at the urban core – the Central Business District – has in most countries been concentrated on one socio-demographic group: young, small, high income, professional households. Robson et al (2000) provide a case study for Central Manchester. In their sample, 40% were single-person households and over 50% were two-person households (few contained children); most were employed in the professions in Central Manchester (so commuting distances were short), and 35% were drawn to the city from outside the North West. Similarly, between 1991 and 1996, Melbourne's 70-year population loss was arrested and, in 1999, the city was the strongest growing local government area in Australia (Department of Infrastructure, 2000). However, young households in the 20-29 age group dominated city growth. In 1996, 25% of inner-city residents were in this age group. Furthermore, inner-city residents are more highly qualified, work in managerial and professional occupations, typically in service industries, and earn more than the Melbourne Statistical Division average.

Internationally, therefore, many cities are experiencing a revival in population (although partly through international immigration), by appealing to a relatively small socio-demographic group possessing high levels of skills. Cities have facilities that are particularly attractive to this group. As noted above, the city's skill level, however, is a key element of the urban asset base. In the US, Glaeser (2000) indicates that the most reliable indicator of urban growth (apart from the weather) is the human capital in a city's workforce. Therefore, a challenge to the future economic performance of cities is the extent to which they are able to retain these households once they start to have children. We suggest later in this chapter that, once households have left cities, the probability of them ever returning is small. Empty nesting remains small in this country and, similarly, Frey (2000) indicates that, in the US, a significant return of older households to cities is unlikely. It should also be remembered that, although official projections suggest that 3.8 million new households will be created in this country between 1996 and 2021 and most will be single-person households, many of them are in older age groups. Only a small proportion is the young households, who are most likely to be attracted to cities.

Given our interest in the potential attractiveness of core London areas, Table 11.4 examines differences in housing conditions between Inner London, Outer London, the rest of the South East and England as a whole. The table shows that, for England in 1999, new *social* housing completions were approximately 12.5% of the total (and similar in the South East), but the share in London was approximately twice as large. Since the *stock* of social dwellings is also more heavily concentrated on inner areas, new building programmes tend to reinforce the existing segregation of low-income households. Table 11.4 also shows that the average household size is noticeably smaller in Inner London. This is unsurprising, perhaps, given the age distribution shown in Table 11.3, although it should be noted that in the deprived areas of Newham and Tower Hamlets the average size is 2.63 and 2.41 respectively (that is, above the national average). The high percentage of lone-parent and single-person households is also evident. The London Housing Federation (2002) also reports that 19% of households in London live in poor housing compared with 13% in England as a whole and that overcrowding is six times greater in London. There are also 237,000 unfit dwellings requiring major work, 52,000 households are living in temporary accommodation, 211,000 households are on housing waiting lists and the housing stock is old (60% of London's dwellings were built before 1944, compared with 34% nationally).

Modelling, social interactions and policy in urban housing markets

Constructing empirical models of local or city housing markets is conceptually more difficult than either national or regional models. Interactions between

Table 11.4: Housing conditions

	Private housing completions (1999)	Social housing completions (1999)	Average household size (no of people 1998)	Lone-parent households (% of all households 1998)	One-person households (% of all households 1998)
England	122,335	17,605	2.37	5.8	29.4
Inner London	4,533	1,322	2.18	10.2	38.7
Outer London	5,032	1,563	2.40	6.1	30.4
Rest of South East (excluding London)	20,004	2,958	2.38	4.6	28.2

Source: Regional Trends (note that South East refers to the old Standard Statistical Region)

agents in local markets are strong, social networks are established within neighbourhoods, peer group pressures (both positive and negative) become important and segregation and social exclusion occur. Although there is now a substantial literature on these interactions, as yet there remain few examples of empirical models incorporating them that can be used for policy purposes. Ideally, the models should be able to shed light on some of the key policy issues for local housing markets. These include, for example, the presence of increasing returns and cumulative processes of decline in some areas (see Keenan et al, 1999; Power and Mumford, 1999), areas of low demand housing (Bramley and Pawson, 2002), the failure of policy to promote socially integrated or balanced neighbourhoods, the role of design-led policies in reinvigorating city centres (DETR, 1999) and the possible effects of the recently announced fundamental changes to the land-use planning system.

Galster (2002) suggests that housing policy in the US and Europe is no longer an end in itself and is seen as a means to achieving the wider target of reducing social stratification and social exclusion. If, as suggested earlier in this chapter, social interactions are important, policy might aim both to raise social capital in the poorer neighbourhoods and attempt to disperse low-income households across the wider community. Dispersal policies have been adopted more widely in the US than in Europe, where the emphasis has been on trying to improve the conditions of low-income local residents in situ and on the creation of mixed communities, either through attracting higher-skilled residents to poor areas (for example, through improvements in infrastructure, amenities and social capital) or new building programmes with affordable housing components (see Kearns, 2002, for a discussion of the difference in emphasis between UK and European policies).

In the US, a variety of initiatives have been adopted to encourage the dispersal of low-income households. These include the replacement of high-rise public sector complexes, court-ordered dispersal programmes for minority populations in order to overcome past discriminatory practices, and the encouragement of spatial mobility by housing subsidy recipients, for example through Moving to Opportunity (MTO) programmes (Galster, 2002a). We might also note that, in Australia, where public housing is only a small percentage of the overall housing stock and low-income households rely primarily on the private rented sector, poorer households are less spatially concentrated and, indeed, high rental costs in cities have tended to drive poorer households to the outer suburbs.

Both dispersal and social capital initiatives emphasise the *externalities* that may be generated and models have to take them into account. In the UK, Buck (2001) provides one of the few UK empirical studies of the effects of neighbourhood externalities (see also Chapter Thirteen of this volume). Externalities may take the form of peer-group effects; that is, behaviour is influenced by those of similar social standing (see, for example, Glaeser et al, 1996, for a model of urban crime in which social interactions play a key role) and/or neighbourhood quality (location choices are influenced by school performance, crime rates, and so on). Neighbourhood externalities also play a central role in the models of Brueckner et al (1999), used to explain why wealthy households live in the suburbs in some countries, but towards the centre in others. Quality of life indicators have increasingly been emphasised in explaining location patterns. Furthermore, as soon as we include measures of externalities, our models can illustrate a range of processes including cumulative processes of growth and decline and neighbourhood 'tipping'.

We do, however, have to take seriously the possibility that segregation is the 'natural' city structure and that policy attempts to induce 'mixed' neighbourhoods are fighting against deep-seated trends. Cutler et al (1999) measured the persistent segregation of black US households between 1890 and 1990, and although Glaeser and Vigdor (2001) show that black–non-black segregation in US metropolitan areas is now at its lowest point since 1920, segregation remains extreme in the largest metropolitan areas. However, the fall in segregation has occurred as a result of higher-income black households moving into formerly white suburbs, rather than any integration in former black ghettos. Furthermore, certain classes of model, based on the work of Schelling (1971), imply that segregated communities are likely to arise, even if no one in the community wants segregation. Urban geographers working with models derived from complexity theory have more recently adopted these ideas. In these models, city structures are self-organising and there is little scope for action by policy makers and planners in influencing the social mix of neighbourhoods, which are likely to tend towards segregation.

Finally, it should be noted that dispersal policies or attempts to create mixed communities do not necessarily increase overall efficiency and the economic performance of cities, although there may still be good arguments in terms of equity. Galster (2002a) suggests that the necessary and sufficient conditions for justifying a deconcentration of the poor in terms of the net social benefits to the community as a whole are stringent. Policies that achieve only a modicum of deconcentration do not appear to bring efficiency gains.

Household dynamics and the city asset base

Changes in the number of households in any locality are determined by either natural rates of population increase (along with any associated changes in headship rates) or by moves between different locations. The former involves the creation of *new* households, whereas the latter involves a redistribution of *existing* households. Although this is true whatever the spatial dimension (nation, region or metropolitan area), the relative importance differs with each. Typically, the smaller the spatial scale, the more important is moving or migration relative to in situ change. At the metropolitan level, therefore, moving is the dominant manner by which areas expand or contract in terms of population.

This is because most moves by households are short distance. According to the Survey of English Housing (SEH), for example, for owner-occupiers, 55% of moves were for less than five miles in 1996/97 and 80% less than 20 miles. Furthermore, similar patterns emerge in other countries. Clark and Dieleman

(1996) and Dieleman et al (2000), for example, reach similar conclusions for both the US and the Netherlands. In contrast to regional flows, typically, short-distance moves are not primarily generated by labour market conditions. Rather, moves take place either to improve housing and environmental conditions or because of changes in family circumstances, for example marriage or family break-up. According to the SEH, only 9% of moves by owner-occupiers in 1996/97 were for job-related reasons.

Therefore, our central concern is to identify the factors that determine emerging patterns of spatial structure. Although new household formation is important and trends in the timing of leaving the parental home and tenure choice changed significantly in the 1990s (Andrew and Meen 2002), we concentrate primarily on changing housing choices of pre-existing households at different stages in their housing careers since these are quantitatively larger. More precisely, we wish to understand the factors that cause households to move home and where they move. Our models concentrate on London and the South East.

The dominant factors determining moving decisions are age of the household head and current tenure. The 20-35 age group is the most mobile in most developed economies, triggered by leaving home, changing jobs, marriage and the addition of children. After the age of 35, these triggers become less frequent, so that the requirement to move home becomes less, at least up to retirement age. Private renters are also more likely to move house than home-owners (although the mobile also have a higher probability of renting) – again this appears to be common across developed economies – since transactions costs are much greater for home-owners. In addition to demographic factors, economic factors also have a role in determining moving, particularly incomes.

Quantitative estimates of the relative importance of demographic and economic factors are given in Andrew et al (2002). The key findings are that moving probabilities are higher for young, high-income households, without children and who are renting. Moving by owner-occupiers was limited in the first half of the 1990s by the existence of negative equity (see Henley, 1998, for additional evidence). Table 11.5 takes a selection of household types and shows our estimates of their moving probabilities in any year, discriminating between income quartiles, tenure, the number of children and the age of the household head. The probabilities of moving for households in the upper income quartiles are significantly higher than for households in the lower quartiles. For example, from Row 1, a young renter with income in the first quartile has a 36% probability of moving each year, but this rises to 40% in the fourth quartile. Furthermore, moving propensities fall with age and with the presence of school-aged children. Those in the private-rented sector have considerably higher moving probabilities but, surprisingly, public tenants have higher moving probabilities than those in owner-occupation.

There are at least two explanations. First, estimation of the model is over the period 1991-96, a period over which the turnover rate of the owner-occupier housing stock is known to be very low by the standards of the 1970s and

1980s as a result of negative equity. Second, a survey by Keenan et al (1999) records rapid mobility in local authority housing in recent years. Turnover rates have doubled since the late 1970s. This has been attributed to "growing residential instability and a weakening of social cohesion" (Keenan et al, 1999, p 731). Recently, Hughes and McCormick (2000) also record higher mobility by social tenants in the 1990s.

In an ideal world, our modelling work would be able to distinguish between location choices at fine spatial levels. In fact, we looked at the choices of moving households between Inner London, Outer London, the Rest of the South East and the rest of England. In line with discussion earlier in this chapter, our results suggest that externalities are particularly important in determining the choice. Location is not determined purely by relative housing costs. The area's unemployment rate and overall level of deprivation are highly significant. Since, as Tables 11.2 and 11.4 show, conditions are notably worse in some of the Inner London boroughs, as we shall see, segregation and a cumulative run down of the city's skill base is one possible outcome.

Table 11.6 shows the location probabilities estimated from our models for moving households who begin the sample period living in either London or the South East. The probabilities are constructed conditional on the previous location. Despite the fact that moves are typically short distance, for those previously living in Inner London, we estimate that there is a 23% probability that moving households will relocate in the rest of the South East. By contrast, for those originally living in the South East, there is a less than 3% probability that they will move to Inner London. For this group, there is an 86% probability that any moves will be to another South-Eastern location, although there is a 6% chance that they will move out of the South East altogether. Moves by Outer London residents also show relocation outwards rather than back into Inner London. Note that the final row should be interpreted carefully: it gives the probability that a household, which was originally based in London and the South East and which moves to the rest of England, will move to each of the areas if it relocates once again.

Table 11.5: Probabilities of moving

Household type	Probabilities
Income quartile 1; private renting; 0 children; age <40	0.362
Income quartile 4; private renting; 0 children; age <40	0.403
Income quartile 1; owner-occupation; 0 children; age <40	0.097
Income quartile 4; owner-occupation; 0 children; age <40	0.114
Income quartile 1; public renting; 0 children; age <40	0.164
Income quartile 1; owner-occupation; 1 child; age 45	0.037
Income quartile 2; owner-occupation; 0 children; retired	0.097

Table 11.6: Location probabilities by previous location

	Inner London	Outer London	Rest of South East	Rest of England
Previously Inner London	0.395	0.184	0.228	0.193
Previously Outer London	0.041	0.769	0.103	0.087
Previously South East	0.028	0.057	0.856	0.059
Previously England	0.131	0.265	0.327	0.277

Note: 'Rest of South East' refers to the old Standard Statistical Region.

Some implications

The implications of these findings need stressing. On this evidence, and in the absence of policy intervention, the inner city is likely to experience a further erosion of its skills base, leading to enclaves of low-income households. This is an implication of Tables 11.5 and 11.6. Since high-income households have greater moving propensities, in any year, they are more likely to move (particularly if they are young and have no school-aged children). Furthermore, on moving, they are more likely to choose areas of low unemployment and low deprivation, typically outside London, adding to the housing pressures in those areas. However, if the high skilled move, unemployment and deprivation in the inner-city areas rise even further, adding to the pressures to move for those who can. Segregation between high- and low-income areas, therefore, is further enhanced. Furthermore, since older households have lower migration rates, once they have moved away from the city, the probability of them ever returning is low.

In fact, the outcome for cities is potentially even worse. First, if industry is more likely to locate close to sources of high-skilled labour, the population outflows will generate a loss of city jobs. Although the issue of whether workers follow jobs or jobs follow workers is still controversial, Meen (2002) presents evidence to suggest that, in South East England, the latter has occurred in manufacturing. If true, spatial mismatch occurs for low-skilled workers, so that even those previously employed are more likely to lose their jobs. Second, the position is worsened further for those in employment by the wage gap between the high and low skilled. Income distributions have widened sharply since the late 1970s. Third, the cumulative processes may be strengthened further if peer effects exist as well as the amenity effects identified and localities are subject to Schelling-type influences, generating segregation. Fourth, the low skilled suffer disproportionately from access to mortgage finance markets and from the existing tenure structure of housing.

This sounds like a council of despair – on this view of the world, deprivation and segregation in cities worsens in the future, whereas the rest of the South East experiences continuing housing shortages, rising house prices and consequent key worker problems. The processes are consistent with the findings on city decline by Power and Mumford (1999) and low demand estates (Bramley and Pawson, 2002). A worst-case scenario, perhaps, provides a suitable background against which to assess alternative outcomes. Two issues are particularly important: first, the role of newly forming, young households and migrants from other regions and, second, the potential role of policy in reversing the trends. Each is discussed in turn.

Young households and the future of cities

The models described in the last section of this chapter relate to the housing decisions of pre-existing households. As we have seen, there is very little evidence that this group will reverse its historic movement away from cities (at least on the basis of recent policies). It also appears to be the case that outward trends by 'traditional families' are continuing internationally, for example in the US and Australia. Moreover, we have suggested that once households have left cities they are unlikely to move back, even with improvements to cities, because moving probabilities decline with age. Although it is true that a proportion of these households commute back to London to work, adding to the skills base, many are likely eventually to adjust their employment patterns as well and seek jobs nearer home. As far as cities are concerned, these are lost generations.

However, cities can still grow, both by natural increase and by international and inter-regional migration. As noted, London in particular benefits from both. Andrew and Meen (2002) examine household formation and tenure choice among the under-30s. During the course of the 1990s, nationally, both household formation and owner-occupation demand fell, noticeably among the under-25s. Although there is no one reason for the decline, changes in the income distribution have been particularly important. Relative incomes of the under-25s compared with the older age groups fell sharply. Nevertheless, although the trends are beginning to be understood, a gap in research is the development of formal models of location choice among newly forming households. There is prima facie evidence, for example, that young households are attracted to the facilities (as well as the employment opportunities) that cities bring.

However, the policy implication for housing is not that we should be building homes for 'traditional families' in cities (on brownfield sites) in an attempt to attract lost families back – this is probably a lost cause. The concentration should be on building homes and facilities attractive to young, high-income potential city residents, who add to the skills base. As noted earlier, these policies have been successful internationally and in some UK cities.

Can housing policy reverse the population trend?

The final key question is the potential impact of housing policy. Urban growth requires the balanced development of human, physical, environmental and social capital and housing influences all of these aspects. Although housing policy is only one element of urban policy, it is, however, particularly important. Urban housing policies adopted in Britain can broadly be categorised into planning policies, area regeneration policies and fiscal policies, although the three have common elements.

Planning policy has recently come under review in England with the publication of a Green Paper (DTLR, 2001). Among the key issues that the Green Paper discusses are:

- the need to encourage urban regeneration by channelling development to existing town centres rather than adding to sprawl (current policy is that 60% of new homes should be constructed on Brownfield sites);
- simplification of the planning process, both in terms of the number of layers of control and in terms of the complexity of the regulations; and
- the need to increase the speed of decision making.

The Green Paper also proposes a change of focus. In particular, greater emphasis is to be placed on meeting the needs of industry, for example, through the creation of business zones where explicit planning permission is not required.

An earlier policy document, Planning Policy Guidance Note Three (PPG3), set out the current requirements for local planning authorities in terms of housing. The document highlighted:

- the need to create mixed communities through planning decisions;
- the need to provide sufficient housing land, but giving priority to reusing land in urban areas, bringing empty homes back into use and the conversion of existing buildings;
- the creation of sustainable development patterns; and
- the promotion of good design in new developments in order to create high-quality living environments.

Are, then, these ambitious objectives consistent with market demands and the findings of our earlier analysis? We would suggest that these objectives amount to a wish list, rather than a serious, evidence-based analysis of the most likely outcomes. Governments may wish demand to be concentrated in city centres, but there is no reason why planning by itself should be able to reverse the deep-seated demands for suburban locations found in this chapter; nor do our models suggest that mixed communities will readily emerge.

Area-based regeneration initiatives have been used widely throughout Europe. Skifter Andersen (2002) lists the most commonly used policy measures: physical neighbourhood improvement; active marketing and attempts to counteract bad reputation; change in tenure and dwelling disposals; support for private service facilities; efforts to combat crime; empowerment of local residents and communities; direct support for socially weak groups, including immigrants; attempts to attract new firms; and, finally, education and job training.

Skifter Andersen, however, suggests that although evaluations of policy initiatives have differed in their conclusions, most appear to be unfavourable in that they find only limited evidence that conditions have improved in the supported areas. In England, the stability of the deprivation rankings over the last ten years is striking, despite the fact that most, if not all, of the above policies have been tried at some stage. It remains to be seen whether the latest National Strategy for Neighbourhood Renewal, established in 2001, will be more successful. This has the aim that, within 10-20 years no one should be seriously disadvantaged by where they live. Housing policies are only one part, but the strategy recognises that the most deprived areas are dominated by poor quality, social housing, based on large estates and, in many cases, suffer from low demand and abandonment (Bramley and Pawson, 2002). Nine Northern areas, suffering from particularly low levels of housing demand, have recently been designated as 'Pathfinder' areas to receive special attention.

Traditionally, *fiscal incentives* have been used to attract industry to deprived areas, rather than attracting individuals to those locations. However, if deprived areas are simply those where low-skilled households choose – or are forced – to live, then a complementary approach might be to target incentives on high-skilled individuals in an attempt to promote integrated neighbourhoods. In fact, there are relatively few examples of such initiatives – the belief remains that integrated communities can be promoted either through physical development controls or by improving the quality of the environment through regeneration initiatives. Indeed, figures on Council Tax payments suggest that the fiscal system discourages population movements towards areas of greatest deprivation, since effective tax rates are generally lowest in the areas of highest property values, due to the regressive nature of the system.

Among the few initiatives to have been implemented is the exemption from Stamp Duty of property transactions of less than £150,000, introduced in November 2001 for designated disadvantaged areas. The exemptions are ward-based and cover not only the North of England, but also the most deprived wards of London (including parts of Kensington and Chelsea). It is still too early to assess the success of this initiative, although government estimates suggest that approximately 40,000 dwelling sales per annum will become exempt.

In summary, it is difficult to be optimistic that policy will produce fundamental changes to population location patterns. Brownfield targets suffer from the problem that they do not necessarily match market demand and we would question the value of building homes for 'traditional' families with children in cities. Except for a relatively small (although important) segment of the market, there is little evidence that 'traditional' families with children will reverse their historical outflows from urban areas as they approach middle age. Attracting older households back to cities once they have left is also a tall order. Although good urban design, as espoused by the Rogers Urban Task Force (DETR, 1999) and the New Urbanism movement, may be valuable in itself, we question whether this will be sufficient to change underlying market trends (see Bohl, 2000, for an analysis of the New Urbanism movement in the US). Nevertheless, there is evidence internationally that developing urban, brownfield sites aimed at young, high-income, small households acts as a valuable engine of growth and, although relatively small in absolute numbers, our judgement would be that they will be increasingly important in the future. For similar reasons, greenfield building is difficult to restrain – the targets are fighting against deep-seated market demands.

Our models suggest that the quality of the environment is extremely important in determining location. In principle, urban regeneration policies that lead to such improvements could contribute to reducing population outflows (but would be less effective in inducing inflows), but the problem is how to bring about changes in environment. The need to improve the physical infrastructure, raise inner-city education standards, lower crime rates and so on is recognised worldwide (and design-led policies may have a useful role to play here). However, the literature generally suggests that such policies have not as yet delivered long-lasting change and, indeed, deprivation indices in England continue to exhibit similar ward rankings over the years. The idea of using fiscal policies as an alternative to physical controls to overcome externality problems is hardly new in economics – pollution taxes are one example. As noted earlier in this chapter, limited moves towards the use of fiscal policies as a tool to combat deprivation in Britain have already been implemented but, in our view, the use of fiscal policies in this field remains underdeveloped.

References

Andrew, M. and Meen, G.P. (2002) 'House price appreciation, transactions and the decisions of young households in Britain: a micro and macro analysis', Paper presented to 'European Network for Housing Research' Conference, Vienna.

Andrew, M., Meen, D. and Meen, G.P. (2002) 'Markets and self-organisation: population change and location choice in London and South East England', University of Reading, mimeo.

Bohl, C.C. (2000) 'New urbanism and the city: potential applications and implications for distressed inner-city neighborhoods', *Housing Policy Debate*, vol 11, no 4, pp 761-801.

Bramley, G. and Pawson, H. (2002) 'Low demand for housing: incidence, causes and UK national policy implications', *Urban Studies*, vol 39, no 3, pp 393-422.

Brueckner, J., Thisse, J.-F. and Zenou, Y. (1999) 'Why is central Paris rich and downtown Detroit poor? An amenity-based theory', *European Economic Review*, vol 43, pp 91-107.

Buck, N. (2001) 'Identifying neighbourhood effects on social exclusion', *Urban Studies*, vol 38, no 12, pp 2251-76.

Cheshire, P. (1995) 'A new phase of urban development in western Europe: the evidence for the 1980s', *Urban Studies*, vol 32, no 7, pp 1045-63.

Clark, W.A.V. (1991) 'Residential preferences and neighborhood racial segregation: a test of the Schelling Segregation Model', *Demography*, vol 28, no 1, pp 1-19.

Clark, W.A.V. and Dieleman, F.M. (1996) *Households and housing: Choice and outcomes in the housing market*, Rutgers: Center for Urban Policy Research.

Cutler, D.M., Glaeser, E.L. and Vigdor, J.L. (1999) 'The rise and decline of the American ghetto', *Journal of Political Economy*, vol 107, no 3, pp 455-506.

Department of Infrastructure (2000) *Housing ourselves: The story behind housing in Victoria*, Victoria (Australia): Department of Infrastructure.

DETR (Department of the Environment, Transport and the Regions) (1999) *Towards an urban renaissance*, Final Report of the Urban Task Force Chaired by Lord Rogers of Riverside, London: The Stationery Office.

Dieleman, F.M., Clark, W.A.V. and Deurloo, C. (2000) 'The geography of residential turnover in twenty-seven large US metropolitan housing markets, 1985-95', *Urban Studies*, vol 37, no 2, pp 223-45.

DTLR (Department for Transport, Local Government and the Regions) (2001) *Planning: Delivering a fundamental change*, Planning Green Paper, London: The Stationery Office.

Frey, W.H. (2000) 'The new urban demographics: race space & boomer aging', *Brookings Review*, vol 18, no 3, pp 18-21.

Galster, G.C. (2002) 'Trans-Atlantic perspectives on opportunity, deprivation and the housing nexus', *Housing Studies*, vol 17, no 1, pp 5-12.

Galster, G.C. (2002a) 'An economic efficiency analysis of deconcentrating poverty populations', Paper presented to 'European Network for Housing Research' Conference, Vienna.

Glaeser, E.L. (2000) 'Demand for density? The function of the city in the 21st century', *Brookings Review*, vol 18, no 3, pp 10-13.

Glaeser, E.L. and Shapiro, J.M. (2001) 'City growth and the 2000 census: which places grew, and why?', Center on Urban and Metropolitan Policy, Brookings Institution Survey Series Census 2000.

Glaeser, E.L. and Vigdor, J.L. (2001) 'Racial segregation in the 2000 census: promising news', Brookings Institution Center on Urban and Metropolitan Policy Survey Series.

Glaeser, E.L. Sacerdote, B. and Scheinkman, J. (1996) 'Crime and social interactions', *Quarterly Journal of Economics*, vol 111, no 2, pp 507-48.

Henley, A. (1998) 'Residential mobility, housing equity and the labour market', *Economic Journal*, vol 108, no 447, pp 414-27.

Hughes, G.A. and McCormick, B. (2000) *Housing policy and labour market performance*, London: DETR.

Kearns, A. (2002) 'Response: from residential disadvantage to opportunity? Reflections on British and European policy and research', *Housing Studies*, vol 17, no 1, pp 145-50.

Keenan, P., Lowe, S. and Spencer, S. (1999) 'Housing abandonment in inner cities – the politics of low demand for housing', *Housing Studies*, vol 14, no 5, pp 703-16.

London Housing Federation (2002) *Housing: No 1 for Londoners?*, London: National Housing Federation.

Meen, G.P. (2001) *Modelling spatial housing markets: Theory, analysis and policy*, Boston: Kluwer Academic Publishers.

Meen, G.P. (2002) 'On the long-run relationship between industrial construction and housing', *Journal of Property Research*, vol 19, no 3, pp 191-211.

ONS (Office for National Statistics) (1998) *Focus on London*, London: ONS, London Research Centre, Government Office for London.

Power, A. and Mumford, K. (1999) *The slow death of great cities*, York: Joseph Rowntree Foundation.

Robson, B., Parkinson, M., Boddy, M. and Maclennan, D. (2000) *The state of English cities*, London: DETR.

Schelling, T. (1971) 'Dynamic models of segregation', *Journal of Mathematical Sociology*, vol 1, pp 143-86.

Skifter Andersen, H. (2002) 'Can deprived housing areas be revitalised? Efforts against segregation and neighbourhood decay in Denmark and Europe', *Urban Studies*, vol 39, no 4, pp 767-90.

Social Exclusion Unit (2001) *Preventing social exclusion*, London, available at: www.socialexclusionunit.gov.uk/publications/reports/html/pse.html/index.htm

Sohmer, R.R. and Lang, R.E. (2001) *Downturn rebound*, Fannie Mae Foundation and The Brookings Institution Center on Urban and Metropolitan Policy, Census Note.

TWELVE

Economic structures, urban responses: framing and negotiating urban property development

Simon Guy and John Henneberry

Property and urban development

> ... private property development is driven more by investment demand and suppliers' decisions than by final user demand – even less by any sort of final user needs. (Edwards, 1990, p 175)

Property development makes many contributions to urban economies (Turok, 1992; Gibb et al, 2002). There is the direct impact of construction activity as a major sector of the economy. Beyond this, however, it can have a range of effects that can be critical to the competitive success or otherwise of particular urban areas. The quality and operating costs of the local building stock affect directly occupiers' productivity and ability to expand. The availability of good accommodation may help to attract inward investment. In addition, property can support neighbourhood revitalisation via investment that upgrades the physical environment. Finally, large-scale redevelopment may be necessary to accommodate major changes in city functions in the face of economic restructuring.

In order to gain these benefits, however, cities need continuously to reproduce a stock of property that meets the requirements of local industry and the wider community. Significantly, however, a series of structural changes in the property sector and the wider economy has affected the capacity of particular urban areas to do this. Over the last 20 years, the private sector has increasingly assumed the role of the dominant supplier of buildings in Britain. It now accounts for more than three quarters of all new construction orders (Henneberry and Rowley, 2000). Construction projects have become larger and construction periods have become significantly shorter, increasing the elasticity of supply of new buildings (Ellison, 1998). The reduction in the public sector's relative and absolute contribution to building production has also diminished its stabilising effect on development. The property market, therefore, has become more volatile and less tractable to policy.

In parallel with these trends, renting of commercial and industrial property has grown at the expense of owner-occupation. By 1995, around 45% by value of the UK commercial and industrial property stock was held by investors of which about half (24% of the stock) was held by UK institutions (Callendar and Key, 1996). The value of the latter's commercial property portfolio was estimated to be £64.8 billion: they are major actors in the property market. Most UK institutions, property companies and property financiers are based in London and constitute a nexus of influential, metropolitan decision makers whose activities affect the whole of the UK commercial property market (for a general example, see Martin, 1995, for his discussion of pension funds). Since such a significant proportion of UK commercial property is in the control of the institutions, their investment decisions have important implications for the physical redevelopment of cities. Consequently, "levering private finance and investment in urban regeneration has been a central consideration of policy" (Adair et al, 1998, p 10).

Objectives

Against this context of the shifting dynamics of building production and the issues that this presents, our research had three main objectives. First, we wanted to identify the economic and social structures within the wider property market and to explore the way that they interact to produce property market trends. These trends set limits on and offer opportunities for development activity in cities and regions. Second, we wished to assess how the capacity of local development agents and business actors to negotiate different responses within wider market structures varies between cities and regions. Third, we aimed to examine the terms of engagement of urban policy with local property development in different urban contexts. We considered that the development 'path' of any city or region would be the product of the interaction of these influences.

The description and analysis of economic structures in the property market was based primarily on secondary data relating to rents, yields, employment, gross domestic product (GDP) and other factors. The spatial distribution of economic, development and investment activity was identified. The relative relationship between economic activity and that of property development and investment patterns was defined and the volatility of property market variables was measured. Financial modelling techniques were used to produce representations of property values and development profitability in different sub-markets and over time. These urban and regional development cycles were deconstructed to identify the various cost and value based influences on development profitability and their interaction. The long-run regional convergence or divergence of property development was estimated using a statistical variable[1].

The role of financial decision makers in structuring markets was examined through a case study of the City of London. The main element of this part of the study was a series of semi-structured, in-depth interviews with senior executives (directors, partners, department heads or equivalents) in relevant organisations, such as investment institutions, property agencies, UK and overseas banks, property companies and independent data providers. The main areas covered during the interviews were:

- the formulation of investment, development and lending strategies;
- property investment market characteristics and their influence on investment decisions;
- property market knowledge/familiarity and its impact on levels of investment; and
- the role of property analysis in investment decisions.

The way in which the development sectors of cities constructed and negotiated their responses within these economic and social structures was explored through a set of case studies. The cities examined were Newcastle upon Tyne, Manchester and the City of London. Shorter studies of Leeds and Reading also took place for comparative purposes and links were created with the Bristol project team in relation to their property-related research. The case studies employed a qualitative methodology to avoid any attempt to 'freeze' the development process into static economic typologies of role and action.

Each case study involved three stages of analysis: a general examination of the social organisation of property interests and the spatial patterning of development zones; a focused study of the sources and flows of investment capital into and within each city; and a selective study of local models of development which provided useful insights into the success or failure of urban regeneration strategies. Interviews took place with key development actors including developers, agents, architects and planners. Both wider urban dynamics and specific development ventures were analysed in order to differentiate between the institutional approaches, patterns of decision making and financial constraints and priorities informing different development practices in different cities. This fieldwork was supplemented by selected review of commercial property and planning literature covering the local context of operation and the development projects that formed a part of them.

Economic and social structuring in the property market

A comparison of the spatial pattern of development with the distribution of economic activity demonstrates that a significant mismatch between demand and new property supply exists. The relative distribution of development was most uneven in the office market (see Figure 12.1). The causes of this mismatch lie in the structure and behaviour of the property market and its relation to the wider economy.

Developers develop if they can make a profit. Profits are made when and

Figure 12.1: Level of office development relative to office-based activity (1985-93)

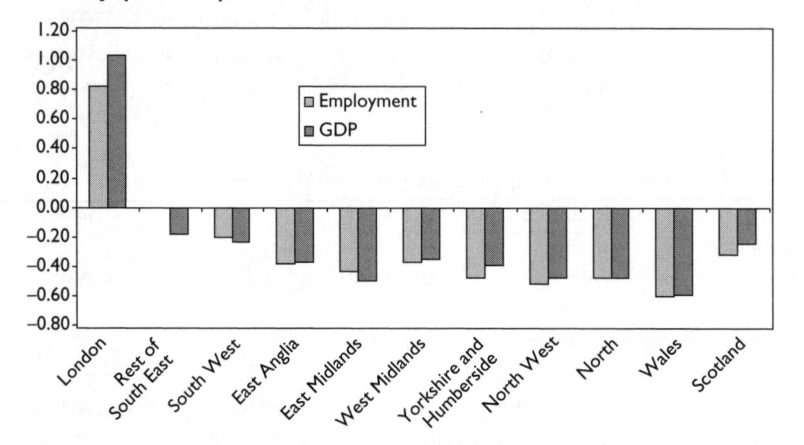

Note: Level of office development expressed as a location quotient relative to the distribution of employment and of GDP in the Banking, Finance and Business Services Sector.

where development values exceed development costs. Development values vary much more than development costs, so profit opportunities are value-driven. Property values are determined by two factors in the rented sector:

- the price (rent) that occupiers are willing to pay to use property;
- the price (capital value) that investors are willing to pay to own property and, therefore, to receive the rent paid by the occupier.

The link between the rent and the capital value is the yield (property jargon for rate of return).

Thus, property values incorporate, to an extent, the interplay between the local and the global (or, at least, the non-local). Rents are determined by the demand for accommodation of locally active, if not locally controlled, industrial and commercial occupiers in the face of local building supply. Yields, and hence capital values, are determined by the views on performance and risk held by investors. Since investors are based overwhelmingly in London, their pricing decisions represent an external influence on property values in other cities and regions. This influence is articulated in two ways. The first is through the level of yields. Yields are an indicator of property investment prices. They should reflect expectations of future rental growth (Barras, 1994). There is evidence of significant pricing inaccuracies in the office property market. Investment Property Databank (1996) conducted an analysis of investment pricing. They examined the relationship between yields at the end of 1981 and total return and its components for 68 office centres. There was a positive, statistically significant relationship between yields and income return ($r = 0.44$, $sig = 0.00$) and between yields and rental value growth ($r = 0.30$, $sig = 0.01$). Regional location had a powerful influence on returns, especially in the office sector where there was a marked differentiation in returns between northern and southern regions.

What this indicates is that yields are lower – and investment prices are higher – in locations where property investments perform relatively poorly: and vice versa. In effect, London-based property investors overprice property investments in London and the South East and underprice property investments elsewhere. Rowley and Henneberry (1999) sought to identify those factors that might explain this. London-based financial decision makers presented a formal logic which underpinned their choice and pricing of investment properties, especially with regard to their regional and urban location.

Three investment property and market characteristics were identified by investors as vital in shaping patterns of investment, primarily through their effect on risk: lot size, the nature of occupier demand and market liquidity. Larger markets with higher numbers of institutionally owned properties (larger buildings accommodating larger organisations with stronger covenants) are usually more liquid than smaller markets. The combination of these three characteristics limits the potential for property investment in peripheral regions and cities. Smaller markets can rarely offer properties of the size required by most institutions and the lack of these properties has a significant impact on market liquidity. In other words, the London market possesses characteristics not present, or present to a lesser extent, elsewhere which compensate for lower levels of return.

The second way in which investors influence property prices is through price shifts. This is articulated through the temporal relationship between yield trends and rent trends. The relationship is typically described thus (Figure 12.2):

> … the inverse relationship between yield and rent movements reinforced each other. This produced capital value cycles which were even more volatile than their corresponding rent cycles. The 1 year lead between the rise in yields and the onset of real rental decline at the end of each of these booms was translated into a similar lead between the downswings of the capital value and rent cycles…. (Barras, 1994, p 194)

Changes in yields are seen as an important influence on the turning point of the capital value and development cycles (McGough and Tsolacos, 1995). Key et al (1994) suggest that yields and investment allocations have, in some respects, acted as internal stabilisers in the property market.

Should yield trends lead rent trends by longer periods, then property market capital value trends will be more stable (Figure 12.3). Here, yields contribute modestly to capital value growth for part of the market upturn. From then to the peak in capital values, those values increase only because rental growth continues while yields remain unchanged. The initial and most marked part of the downturn is caused by yield growth exceeding rental growth. Capital values peak earlier and at a lower level than would otherwise be the case. Thus,

Figure 12.2: Standard view of rent, yield and capital value cycle

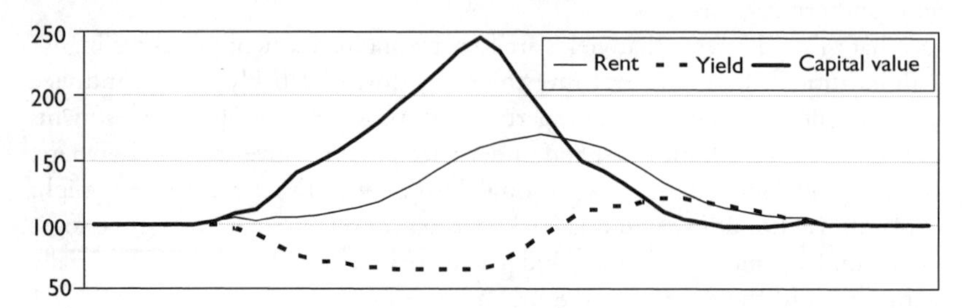

earlier changes in yields first reduce capital value growth and then precipitate the downturn in capital values. In other words, they dampen capital value volatility. In this way, the scale and duration of high property values and, hence, of profitable development conditions are constrained.

Significant variations in the relationship between yield trends and rent trends in the British property market exist (for a detailed exposition, see Henneberry and Rowley, 2000). Yield trends lead rent trends by longer periods in peripheral cities and regions. Moreover, this variation had a systematic effect on capital values: the greater was the yield lead, the less volatile were capital values. The extent of this price dampening effect is inversely related to market strength. Relatively weak and unprofitable markets are also markets where yield trends lead rental trends by comparatively long periods. That is, they are markets where such leads reduce market volatility and market strength and profitability. This feeds through into the pattern of development. Regions where the impact of yield leads on market strength is most marked tend also to be regions where offices are most underproduced in relation to underlying economic activity. Variations in the relationship between yield trends and rent trends therefore exaggerate inter-urban and inter-regional differences in the distribution of office development.

Figure 12.3: Impact of greater yield lead

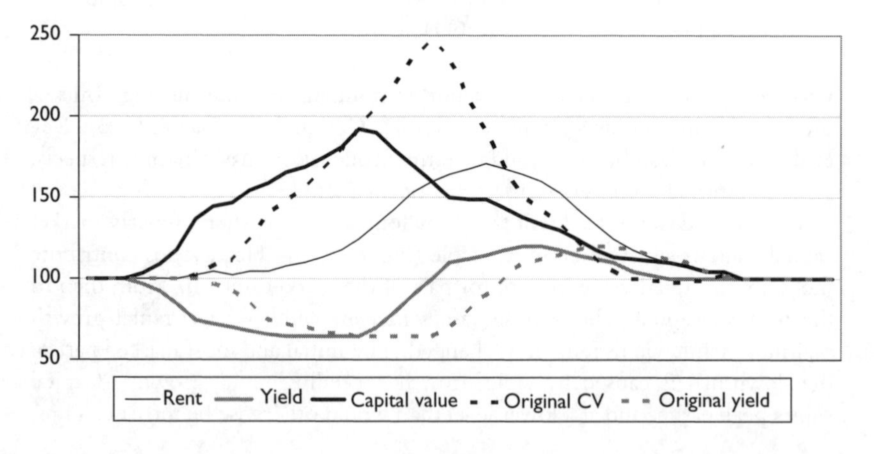

The variation in the relative timing of rent and yield trends is something of a puzzle. Why did investment prices better anticipate rent turning points in peripheral rather than core regions when the latter are larger, more transparent markets? There are competing explanations for this. Ball (2002) suggests that London may have acted as a leading cyclical indicator allowing investors to avoid the scale of overbuilding elsewhere. Guy and Henneberry (2002) agree with Ball that "the late 1980s commercial property bubble in the UK was particularly a 'London' phenomenon ... most UK regions simply did not count in such world city stakes" (Ball, 2002, pp 1460-1). Yields for whole-asset classes are set by the ebb and flow of funds in world capital markets of which London is a key node. Therefore, minor variations in rental trends in unimportant UK regions just do not signify (although the consequences of these mechanisms for the regions are important).

This fits with Leitner's (1994) arguments about the way in which changes in national and international political economy have differential effects on urban property markets and the character of their development cycles. On the supply side, capital markets have become more spatially integrated. Globalisation, deregulation and the development of new financial instruments have increased the availability of capital. Spatial integration of the development industry has also occurred. Developers with the resources necessary to undertake large-scale development can operate in all cities. Capacity is not a constraint on the ability of cities to reproduce their built environments. Each locality has a specific economic and political make-up and position in the settlement system. This conditions cities' responses to restructuring, producing inter-urban differences in demand for floor space and consequently in the attractiveness of locations for property development and investment.

Leitner (1994) identified office development cycles with a duration of 10-11 years whose amplitude increased between 1962 and 1986. Studying the cycles in the 30 largest US central cities, Leitner found "considerable divergence in the timing of peaks and troughs ... until the mid-1970s, followed by a dramatic convergence in the late 1970s and 1980s" (1994, p 792). The peaks of the set of urban cycles constituting the 1960s-1970s US office property boom occurred over a period of nine years. In the 1980s' boom, the peaks occurred within two years of one. The convergence was attributed to the aforementioned supply-side factors that made national trends a more important component of local cycles.

In comparison with the US, Britain has a highly integrated economy with much less marked regional differences. It has a truncated urban hierarchy, dominated by London. There are no other first rank cities: just a group of subordinate regional centres. Additionally, the City of London is the world's largest international capital market and Britain's property development and investment sectors are established, significant and in an advanced stage of development (Keogh and D'Arcy, 1994). In these circumstances, one might expect supply-side influences to swamp differences in regional and urban character and thereby to eliminate most variations in the character of office development cycles.

However, as we have seen, the British experience cannot be captured as simply as this. The influence of the capital market, articulated through the price setting and shifting of institutional investors, has had a significant and increasingly important impact on urban property markets. Development in peripheral markets has been reined in. However, while the character of local development cycles may have become more similar as a consequence, their product – new development – has become more unevenly spread relative to economic activity.

The differences between the pattern of economic activity and the distribution of office property development are persistent and growing. Using an alternative formulation of σ-convergence (see Henneberry and Rowley, 1999) the change in the regional dispersion of cumulative new orders was measured for two periods: 1970-82 and 1983-95. Each period covers roughly one major and one minor property cycle. The results of this exercise for the office sector are described in Figure 12.4. They provide evidence of significant divergence of regional development trends for offices over the last 25 years. The coefficient of variation for the relative regional distribution of office development increases from 0.129 in the first period to 0.291 in the second period. This strengthens claims for the property market to be considered a significant influence on regional and urban economic competitiveness.

Urban responses

By focusing on the structural elements of the property market, we have learned much about the framing of property markets. In particular, it has developed our understanding of the day-to-day pressures on, and limits to, the agency of

Figure 12.4: Change in relative distribution of office development (change: base LQ)

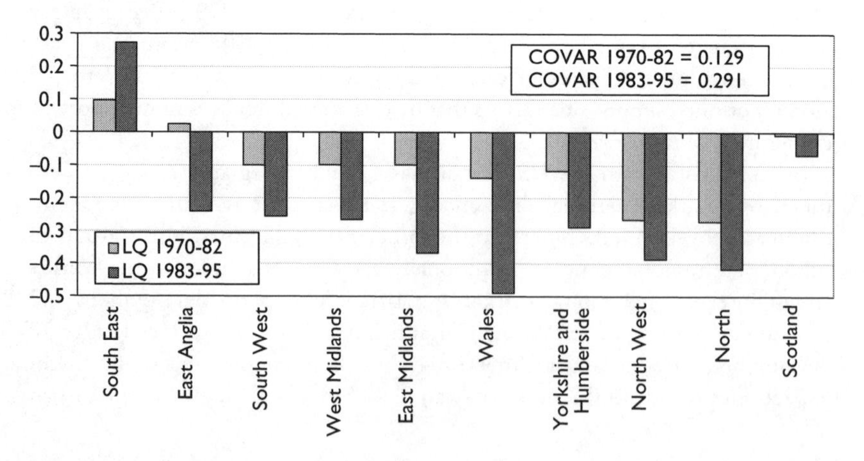

development professionals presented by economic processes. But, how are those economic conditions negotiated at the local level? By analysing how "key players, and their motives and methods of operation, are quite distinct" (Cundell and Harris, 1995, p 32) in different times and places we can begin to identify opportunities for property actors to influence the shape and direction of local property markets. Here, property actors, economic development organisations, planners and their relationships will provide the main focus of study as critical elements engaging with the economic frameworks that fashion the social context of local development activity.

The challenge of urban regeneration is often portrayed as one of identifying shared development opportunities for private, public and community organisations operating in local, national and even global contexts. Our research challenges the feasibility of developing a shared vision of urban development between property actors operating within widely diverging organisational worlds and with competing perspectives and strategies. In particular, we identified the tensions that can arise in the pursuit of a unified vision, and illustrated how competing assessments of local market value can result in diverse urban development strategies.

In each case study city – London, Manchester, Newcastle, Leeds and Reading – we explored the emergence of competing development pathways, in the process identifying what we term 'islands of development' (Guy and Coaffee, 1999). Within each city, we have analysed the construction of a range of these development islands, which have each evolved in specific ways as a result of the sometimes resonant, and sometimes dissonant, actions of local property actors, national and international investors, and local and national government policy. What is clear is that no single blueprint, vision or investment strategy can explain the evolution of these heterogeneous islands. Each island tends to be differently envisioned by competing development actors, embodies different histories and cultures, and has its boundaries maintained, threatened or extended by different assemblages of social, physical and organisational processes.

For instance, the effort to create a nationally recognised office centre in Newcastle has resulted in a patchwork of property islands. In Grainger Town, ideas to create an office core ran up against physical and design limitations which led to a new development pathway aiming to balance heritage with economic and cultural vibrancy. As a result, the Newcastle Quayside development replaced the central core (Grainger Town) as the city's main office centre. There are now proposals to develop Quayside still further, coupling it with the Gateshead Quays development on the other side of the River Tyne as an 'island of culture'. More recently, a new office centre has been proposed in Gallowgate, an edge-of-centre site, to the west of the city centre which will provide a linked focal point for commercial enterprise. As Table 12.1 illustrates, each of these different development logics is characterised by great diversity in terms of visions, social interests, funding regimes and design strategies.

Critically, the development of the islands cannot be viewed in terms of coherent and cooperative co-evolution. Development actors in Grainger Town

Table 12.1: Islands of development in Newcastle upon Tyne

	Grainger Town	Quayside	Gallowgate
Vision	Heart of a great city	Expanding the heart of the city	New commercial core
Key visionary	English Partnerships/ Heritage	Local/National Government	Local Government
Design strategy	Heritage centre	Waterfront renaissance	Commercial focal point
Location	City centre	Peripheral	Edge of centre
Ownership	Multiple and heterogeneous	Local Government	Public/Private
Funding	English partnerships/ RDA	National Government	Private
Developers	Local/Regional	National	Regional/National
Key economic sector	Mixed-use	Office/leisure	Commercial
Design	Classical/conserved	Postmodern	Urban integration
Services	Basic and inflexible	High grade but inflexible	Responsive
Floorplate	Small and irregular	Medium	Medium/large

are now attempting to win back office occupiers through a series of initiatives funded by English Partnerships and the regional development agency (RDA). Independent development initiatives there have been hampered by demands for a purity of vision. Transport initiatives to link Quayside to the city centre have so far failed to materialise, serving to isolate the two centres. Local estate agents have also warned that the type of large-scale schemes planned in Gallowgate are unviable in market terms.

Only in the City of London and in Reading was it possible to talk in terms of a coherent, consistent and a commonly legible property market. Here, the continued presence of a strong office market ensures the dominance of an institutional approach to property development resulting in a familiar uniformity in approach and style of development. In all the other case study cities, we found a diverse and dynamic patchwork of property development and investment. In the case of Manchester, we found property reproduced in a tightly prescribed island of development that conformed to institutional requirements. Traditionally, the office market in Manchester has been centred on what is referred to as the 'Square Half Mile', a compact portion of the central city. In morphological and design terms, this parallels the City of London's Square Mile. It is here that most new office development has traditionally taken place in Manchester.

In recent years, the market has been healthy and has been seen as a good investment opportunity. Hence, a number of new developments have come online. However, the letting of these landmark buildings in the core area has proved to be problematic. Closer inspection of the Manchester market reveals a high degree of localism. Most of the take up of space is the result of internal relocations, especially by companies in the financial services industry. The tendency for institutions to treat the local market as a 'statistical aggregate' blinds them to these secondary processes. Moreover, the character and performance of the Manchester office market is inherently – and importantly – linked to the changing nature of the urban scene in the city. Therefore, a holistic approach to envisioning the Manchester market is required as infrastructure improvements and growth in retail and leisure facilities are key features in maintaining the city's appeal for investors. Again, the particular cultural perspective of institutional investors that incorporates traditional descriptive and analytical practices tends to blind them to local specificity.

Interestingly, local Manchester developers have not simply accepted this institutional approach as the only way forward. Instead, over the past decade, a number of independent (some would say 'maverick') developers have begun to develop a new way forward. Critically, these developers have strayed far from the traditional institutional core. Working in the shadows of the institutions, they have trodden where institutions fear to tread, in the marginal development zones of empty buildings where rents fall below £10 per square metre. Recognition of the contribution of local vitality to the viability and value of local developments has been central to the approach of Urban Splash in Castlefields and the Northern Quarter, and other developers such as Carol Ainscow whose development of the now famous gay area of Canal Street triggered a mini development boom. Table 12.2 contrasts the main features of this type of independent development with the widely recognised features of institutional development, highlighting the interrelated physical, legal, aesthetic, social and economic elements of each approach.

We can begin to delineate the 'independent view' by noting a preference for fringe locations that tend to be ignored by institutions. Hall (1999, p 41) notes in his review of world cities how "innovative places ... were not at the centre

Table 12.2: Models of urban development: an ideal type

Models ⇒	**Institutional**	**Independent**
Features ⇓		
Location	Core	Fringe
Size	Large	Small/medium
Tenancy	Single	Multiple
Use	Fixed	Mixed
Lease	Rigid	Flexible
Image	Universal	Vernacular
Design	Blind	Sensitive
Knowledge	National/global	Local/regional
Risk	Averse	Positive
Vision	Retrospective	Future
Profession	Insiders	Outsiders
Value	Economic	Socio-economic

but neither were they off the edge of the world altogether". Echoing this, independents tend to work in the shadows of mainstream developers, counterbalancing low rental values with a close proximity to the city core as in the Northern Quarter. Working in such peripheral zones often necessitates dealing with smaller lot sizes, multiple tenancies and mixed-uses. While such property characteristics are anathema to institutional investors, independents appear to recognise the links between such social complexity and the urban vitality that is central to regeneration processes and ultimately to rising rental values. Engaging closely with a locality, which O'Connor (1999, p 85) highlights as the key to negotiating the relationship between cultural and economic capital, is central to the approach of independent developers:

> It is to some extent about location but it's about recognising the intrinsic qualities of a location that often property people don't, this is the soul of an area, or a sense of place of an area. (Local developer)

Independents also strive to add value through an emphasis on distinctive design, often with a preference for conservation of local vernacular styles through the reuse of former warehouses or department stores. As an independent developer suggests:

> I believed that good design doesn't cost more money as it actually generates value. (Local developer)

This aestheticisation of property contrasts with the overt ambitions of many investors to distance themselves from the visual impact of buildings, the better to value them 'objectively'. Attitudes to development risk also appear to differ. While institutions broker trust and mediate risk though national and international networks of advisors and researchers, independents are linked to more community-based networks of other cultural intermediaries who share investment and offset development risks through collaborative projects and initiatives (Banks et al, 2000). Most starkly, what is at stake here is a very different vision of prospective urban development. While institutions tend to base estimates of future investment performance on an extension of past trends when evaluating likely profiles of risk and return, independents strive to develop a different urban future.

In Manchester, committed to what Quilley (2000, p 613) terms a "post-industrial script" around cultural entrepreneurship, the service economy and city living, areas like the Northern Quarter have been symbolically as well as physically reconstructed. In this way, older buildings have been successfully adapted to new uses that blend with a distinctive local image and ambience, thereby highlighting "the potential for urban economies to avoid serial subjection to the 'universal force of capital circulation' (Harvey, 1989, p 351)" (Banks et al, 2000, p 463). Or as Tom Bloxham (1995, p 2), director of Urban Splash argues, the "missing ingredient for renewal in the urban core is developers with 'bottle', developers who have the vision and confidence to propose, finance, develop and market buildings to niche markets".

Through the concept of islands of development linked to alternative models of development, we can view regeneration in new ways that involve both social and economic processes. Different levels of development are negotiated within the wider structures of the market, subject to the complex interplay of local and national influences and competing assessments of local market value. They result in diverse urban development strategies and competing development pathways. While the strength of regional property markets is often viewed through the lens of levels of institutional activity, we would point to the need also to identify levels of independent development. While unevenly developed across our case studies, most strongly in Manchester, but also emerging in Leeds and to a lesser extent in Newcastle, 'independent development' represents a major contribution to the regeneration of urban spaces neglected by institutional investors and developers.

Seen this way, cities should not be viewed as homogeneous entities, defined either through a singular public vision, or in narrow commercial terms (the economically weak or strong market). Instead, cities should be viewed as comprising a series of heterogeneous islands which represent alternative logics of urban development.

Conclusions: towards independent development

> To contemplate public policy for our cities or to consider acting collectively requires not merely an analysis of the conditions available for success but also a reflective understanding of the language with which we represent those conditions. (Beauregard, 1995, p 77)

Wrapped up in the development of particular investment views is a particular way of seeing cities. These views clearly make cognitive and strategic sense to institutional development actors. Moreover, these views make cultural sense in that they correspond to a set of preconceived values and assumptions about the locations and building types that, on the basis of previous experience, are likely to generate surplus value. Given the highly risk-averse nature of institutional investors, it is perhaps not surprising that they tend to confine their activities to cities and sectors with which they are familiar. Innovation within these organisational confines is very difficult as new investment proposals will be evaluated with reference to established guidelines and to previous practice and experience. The "handing down of attitudes, habits, and rules is integral to the definition and coherence of a culture" (Davis, 1999, p 17). This occurs in property investment and development no less than elsewhere:

> That perspective is a direct function of people's background, in particular of their professional culture. One's professional culture gives one a pre-disposition to frame situations and problems in particular ways, that is, to

> analyse them according to specific categories, to synthesise them into specific structures, and to represent them in specific verbal, graphic, or numerical ways. (Fischler, 1995, p 21)

Seen this way, investment theory and practice (ways of seeing and doing) are not sensitive to challenge from outside their own terms of reference. If "People are subject to explicit constraints, and they are limited in their deeds and words by all that is taken for granted as belonging to the order of things, by their culture..." (Fischler, 1995, p 14), then simply shouting 'You're wrong! You don't understand!' will not be very productive. In contrast, we would argue that it is vital to recognise that "finance capital is not some passive actor in the construction of landscapes, but an active participant with a logic of its own" (Wharf, 1994, p 325). The problem is that if we evaluate inner cities in the 'language' of the institutional investor – as McNamara (1993) urges and Adair et al (1999) have done – we also adopt the particular, market-referenced, economic rationality that articulates itself through that 'language'.

By definition, institutional investors are only interested in institutional property. This limits the parts of the city that institutions 'see'. If a set of cities with building stocks made up of a wide variety of properties is considered (Figure 12.5a), only that element of the stocks which conforms to institutional investment criteria will be the subject of interest (Figure 12.5b). From this perspective, zones of the city such as the Northern Quarter in Manchester are unlikely to be visible. While it may be possible to extend the core market a little here and there, the use of policy to 'translate' a little more of cities' property into institutional 'language' will have a limited effect on the regeneration of the whole city:

> Personally the moment that institutions get interested in regeneration is the death of regeneration and it's much more to do with the local property market and this market keeps it alive and gives it a greater amount of freedom in terms of what happens. If they are not interested, accept this and go away and formulate ways in which you can work with the local property market, with the local entrepreneur because that's where the real innovation and freedom comes from. (Local developer)

In debates about the role of institutional investors in urban regeneration, the nature, construction and utilisation of investors' strategic rationality, and the ways in which these intersect with local development needs are rarely addressed. Nor are the cultures and operational rationalities or the potential contributions of other actors considered. What is needed is a way of conceptualising the physical reproduction of cities that recognises alternative forms of property development and investment processes. While no one would recommend discouraging institutional investment from taking an active role in urban regeneration, the experience of Manchester might suggest that we refocus

Figure 12.5a: Cities' property stocks

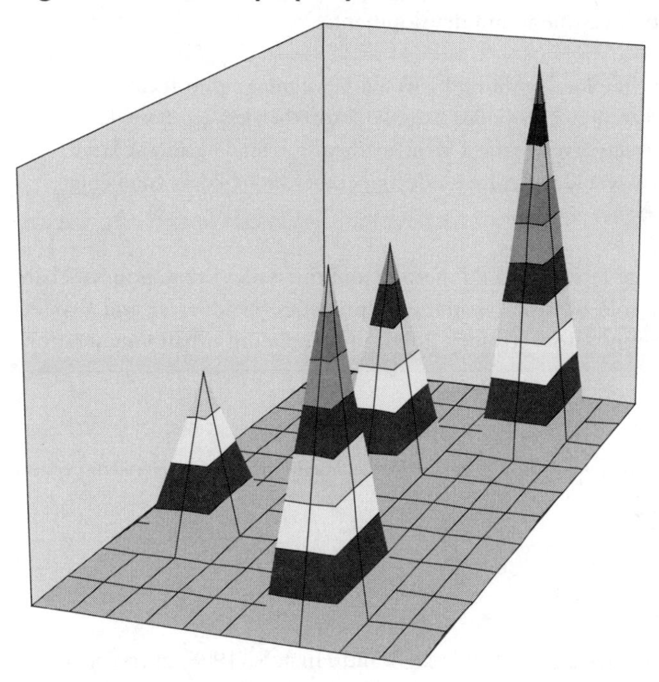

Figure 12.5b: What investors 'see'

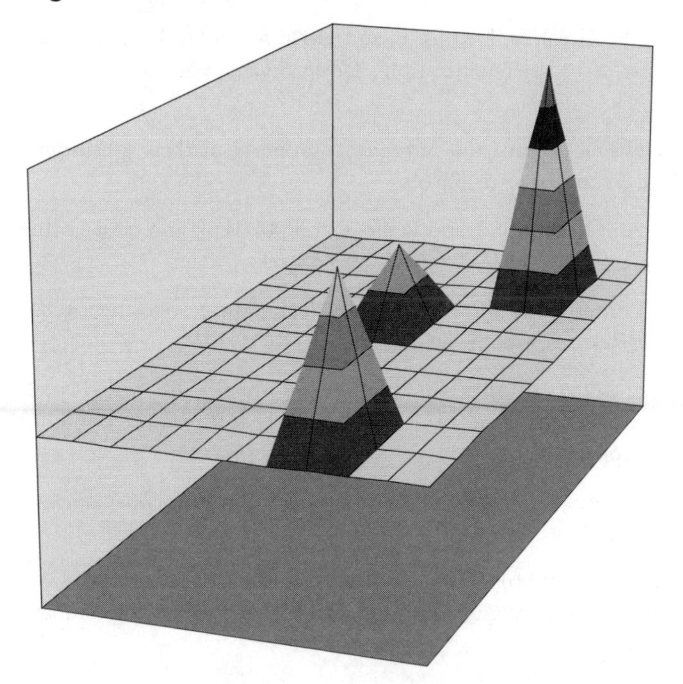

national and local policy efforts to encourage independent and locally based forms of property investment and development:

> If I was them [the local authority] I would be running up to them saying 'Come on, what more can we do? Lets work together, lets get more done'. Whereas, in reality, every time I went to them for funding it was 'Yeah, right', as if they would rather have a developer they didn't know coming in. (Local developer)

In this way property research could usefully join the wider urban policy debate as it explores the role of new cultural entrepreneurs (Leadbeater and Oakley, 1999) and urban innovators (Landry, 2000) in stimulating urban regeneration.

Note

[1] The basic measure used was σ-convergence: the decline in the cross-sectional dispersion of the subject variable.

References

Adair, A., Berry, J., Deddis, B., McGreal, S. and Hirst, S. (1998) *Accessing private finance: The availability and effectiveness of private finance in urban regeneration*, Research Report, London: RICS.

Adair, A., Berry, J., McGreal, S., Deddis, B. and Hirst, S. (1999) 'Evaluation of investor behaviour in urban regeneration', *Urban Studies*, vol 36, no 12, pp 2031-45.

Ball, M. (2002) 'Cultural explanation of regional property markets: a critique, *Urban Studies*, vol 39, no 8, pp 1453-69.

Banks, M., Lovatt, A., O'Connor, J. and Raffo, C. (2000) 'Risk and trust in the cultural industries', *GEOFORUM*, vol 31, pp 453-64.

Barras, R. (1994) 'Property and the economic cycle: building cycles revisited', *Journal of Property Research*, vol 11, pp 183-97.

Beaurgard, R.A. (1995) 'If only the city could speak: the politics of representation', in H. Liggett and D.C. Perry (eds) *Spatial practices*, London: Sage Publications, pp 59-80.

Bloxham, T. (1995) 'Regenerating the urban core', *Urban Design International*, vol 53, January, pp 1-3.

Callender, M. and Key, T. (1996) *The total value of commercial property in the UK*, Paper presented at the RICS 'Cutting Edge' conference, Bristol, September.

Cundell, I. and Harris, R. (1995) 'In what sense a forecast?', *Estates Gazette*, Issue 9501.

Davis, H. (1999) *The culture of building*, Oxford: Oxford University Press.

Ellison, L. (1998) 'Examining the implications for property development of the increased role of the private sector in domestic fixed capital formation', Paper presented at the RICS 'Cutting Edge' Property Research Conference.

Fischler, R. (1995) 'Strategy and history in professional practice: planning as world making', in H. Liggett and D.C. Perry (eds) *Spatial practices*, London: Sage Publications, pp 13-58.

Gibb, K., Mackay, D. and White, M. (2002) 'The property sector and its role in shaping urban competitiveness: a selective review of literature and evidence', in I. Begg (ed) *Urban competitiveness*, Bristol: The Policy Press, pp 81-100.

Guy, S. and Henneberry, J. (2002) 'Bridging the divide? Complementary perspectives on property', *Urban Studies*, vol 39, no 8, pp 1471-8.

Guy, S. and Coaffee, J. (1999) *Islands of development: The micro-production of space*, Proceedings of the RICS 'Cutting Edge' annual research conference.

Hall, P. (1999) 'The creative city in the third millennium', in J. Verwijnen and P. Lehtovuori (eds) *Creative cities: Cultural industries, urban development and the information society*, Helsinki: UIAH Publications, pp 36-57.

Henneberry, J. and Rowley, S. (1999) 'Regional convergence of commercial and industrial property development in Britain', Paper presented at the RICS 'Cutting Edge' Property Research Conference.

Henneberry, J. and Rowley, S. (2000) 'Property market processes and development outcomes in cities and regions', *RICS Foundation Research Papers*, vol 3, no 9, pp 1-59.

Investment Property Databank (1996) *Key centres report*, London: Investment Property Databank.

Keogh, G. and D'Arcy, E. (1994) 'Market maturity and property market behaviour: a European comparison of mature and emergent markets', *Journal of Property Research*, vol 11, pp 215-35.

Key, T., McGregor, B., Nanthakumaran, N. and Zarkesh, F. (1994) *Economic cycles and property cycles: Understanding the property cycle: Main report*, London: Royal Institution of Chartered Surveyors.

Landry, C. (2000) *The creative city: A toolkit for urban innovators*, London: Earthscan.

Leadbeater, C. and Oakley, K. (1999) *The independents: Britain's new cultural entrepreneurs*, London: Demos.

Leitner, H. (1994) 'Capital markets, the development industry, and urban office market dynamics: rethinking building cycles', *Environment and Planning A*, vol 26, pp 779-802.

McGough, T. and Tsolacos, S. (1995) 'Property cycles in the UK: an empirical investigation of the stylised facts', *Journal of Property Finance*, vol 6, pp 45-62.

McNamara, P. (1993) 'Parameters for institutional investment in inner city commercial property markets', in J. Berry, S. McGreal and B. Deddis (eds) *Urban regeneration: Property investment and development*, London: E. & F.N. Spon, pp 5-15.

Martin, R. (1995) 'Undermining the financial basis of regions: the spatial structure and implications of the UK pension fund system', *Regional Studies*, vol 29, pp 125-44.

O'Connor, J. (1999) 'Popular culture, reflexivity and urban change', in J. Verwijnen and P. Lehtovuori (eds) *Creative cities: Cultural industries, urban development and the information society*, Helsinki: UIAH Publications, pp 76-100.

Quilley, S. (2000) 'Manchester first: from municipal socialism to the entrepreneurial city', *International Journal of Urban and Regional Research*, vol 24, no 3, pp 601-15.

Rowley, S. and Henneberry, J. (1999) 'The London property nexus: Social interrelations and conventions within property investment decision-making', Paper presented at the RICS 'Cutting Edge' annual research conference.

Turok, I. (1992) 'Property-led urban regeneration: panacea or placebo?', *Environment and Planning A*, vol 24, pp 361-79.

Wharf, B. (1994) 'Vicious circle: financial markets and commercial real estate in the United States', in S. Corbridge, N. Thrift and R. Martin (eds) *Money, space and power*, Oxford: Blackwell, pp 309-26.

Part Five:
Space, place and social cohesion

THIRTEEN

Does spatial concentration of disadvantage contribute to social exclusion?

Nick Buck and Ian Gordon

Background and objectives

People assume as a matter of common sense that place matters. Estate agents assert that location is the prime attribute of a house in determining its price. Government policy and resources are targeted to particular areas on the basis that concentrating resources in this way will have the greatest pay-off. However, when it comes to considering the influence of space and place on the life chances of individuals, it is much less clear precisely why space should matter, or for what outcomes it is particularly important. It is far from clear how much spatial variations actually matter for outcomes, for example, compared with personal characteristics.

The aim of the research discussed in this chapter was to explore whether it is possible to identify negative effects on individual life chances from living in 'disadvantaged neighbourhoods' (that is, places with a concentration of people facing some form of social or economic disadvantage). It disentangles some of the possible meanings behind a policy goal such as that of the Social Exclusion Unit's *National strategy action plan for neighbourhood renewal*, that "within ten to twenty years, no-one should be seriously disadvantaged by where they live" (Social Exclusion Unit, 2001, p 5). The research aimed to test the widespread assumption that the substantial variation in individual and family disadvantage that exists between small areas, implied that area characteristics themselves had causal effects. In other words, it tests whether an individual with given characteristics would suffer worse outcomes living in a disadvantaged area than if they lived in a better area.

There is no question that there is substantial spatial variation in social and economic disadvantage at the individual and household level, and in social exclusion, however that is measured. However, this is what we expect from the operation of the housing market, which will tend to segregate people at least by their capacity to afford different types of housing. Poor people will tend to be concentrated in areas of cheaper, poorer quality housing. What we are interested in is whether this sorting, or compositional difference between areas, generates additional effects. Does living in a deprived area have an additional detrimental effect on people's life chances?

We are not only interested, however, in establishing whether there is an association between area conditions and individual life chances. We are also particularly interested in the 'shape' of any such relationship and what it can tell us. Much targeted policy tends to be focused on a narrow group of highly deprived areas. This rests on the assumption that the association is qualitatively different in such areas, and by implication that overall it is 'non-linear' in form; that is, the effects are more than proportionately greater in the worst areas. Perhaps even, there are thresholds of disadvantage above which effects become much stronger.

There has been a substantial body of research in the US around these questions, largely focused on child and adolescent development issues, and some work also on employment outcomes (for example, see Jencks and Mayer, 1990; Brooks-Gunn et al, 1997). This work has been based on a range of methods, including the analysis of individual level survey data, cross-sectional and longitudinal, matched to area data, the analysis of area level data on its own and policy experiments (for example, Ludwig et al, 1998). The US research has found *some* significant neighbourhood effects, but their scale was not particularly large, compared with the impact of a number of individual characteristics.

In the UK, work in this area has been less developed and has primarily used case study methods in small numbers of areas, normally restricted to more disadvantaged areas only. While such research may provide information on processes leading to disadvantage, without a systematic comparison with non-deprived areas it is impossible to assess the size and significance of neighbourhood effects. There has also been a more recent line of development in research on neighbourhood effects in relation to health outcomes.

In practice, there may be a number of different types of intrinsic area effects, some of which do not necessarily follow from population characteristics and which do not necessarily relate to social exclusion. These might reflect for example, environmental pollution, features of the built environment, quality of local services or the strength of labour demand within a local economy. Such factors are not a primary concern of this chapter, although we do introduce controls for the last of these.

Our focus is on factors affecting individual life chances and is informed by the current debates around the idea of social exclusion. While this concept has many problems of lack of precision and narrowing of policy agendas (Levitas, 1998), it does have certain advantages. The shift in conceptualisation, from the static language of 'deprivation' (current in the 1970s and early 1980s) to that of 'exclusion', implies identifiable and ongoing processes, with outcomes some of which may be affected by area-specific factors. This can lead, beyond traditional descriptive analyses of the incidence of 'multiple deprivation', to more direct and testable causal hypotheses about ways in which concentration may matter.

It also encourages a focus on processes indicative of life chances (for example, moves in and out of poverty or jobs) or factors affecting them (such as, perceptions of labour market opportunities), which can be more naturally related to a distinction between compositional and contextual effects than can static measures of deprivation.

It is likely that the causal mechanisms which link concentrated area disadvantage to negative outcomes for individuals are extremely complex. US research on child development has developed a range of possible models of neighbourhood effects. Buck (2001a) extends and adapts these for application to social and economic outcomes among an adult population, which is our focus. Among the models are ones suggesting that more disadvantaged people will do worse in *more* deprived areas (because of a contagion of pathological social norms, absence of information and other resources or overstretched services), and other quite plausible ones that suggest quite the opposite: that they might do worse in *less* deprived areas (perhaps through relative deprivation leading to discouragement, alienation or exclusion from opportunities by local 'gatekeepers').

This range of hypotheses about how neighbourhood effects may affect individuals' life chances suggests the need for rather careful specification of the models used to test for evidence of such effects. Among a range of statistical and conceptual difficulties in separating out the roles of individual level and neighbourhood factors (discussed in Buck, 2001a), three particular kinds of problem can be identified. The first of these involves the difficulty in some situations of distinguishing the effect of population mix (specifically the proportion with some supposedly disadvantaging characteristics) from other kinds of contextual effect. Second, since people generally have some choice as to where they live, there is a danger that effects will be attributed to an observed area characteristic, when really they arise from unobserved characteristics of the type of people choosing to live in these different kinds of area. For example, if employment success depends on motivation or other unmeasured personal characteristics, and successful people tend to leave 'disadvantaged' areas (perhaps because they can afford better housing), lack of success may erroneously be attributed to the area factor. And, finally, there is a problem of the quality or coarseness of measurement available both for individuals and for neighbourhoods, which may lead to misjudgements of the significance of area influences – in either direction, depending upon where the limitations of the data occur. For example, if individual data only distinguishes broad socio-economic categories (such as identifying someone simply as semi-skilled or unskilled), when an individual's socio-economic status actually has a continuous effect on outcomes, a spurious neighbourhood effect may be indicated if (say) areas with a greater proportion in the low-status category actually include more people from extremely low-status occupations. For these reasons, both researchers and policy makers need to be very cautious in drawing over-rapid conclusions from research findings in this field.

Research methods

The study used national survey and census data to address this question. Such data are often less rich than those arising from qualitative case study work, although in fact we had a very broad range of relevant indicators. Such methods also have the major advantage of allowing a comparison based on the full range of area conditions, including both deprived and non-deprived areas. We addressed the question in two different ways. First, we used individual level data about both outcomes and characteristics which might be expected to relate to those outcomes, and linked these to area data on the proportions of various disadvantaged groups in the local population. We investigated whether these 'population-mix' measures made a significant contribution to explaining the individual outcomes after individual characteristics had been taken into account. Many of these analyses exploited the existence of longitudinal data. Second, using aggregative data, we examined the 'shape' of the relationship between area measures of population composition, and area measures of outcomes (typically success and failure rates), looking for forms of relationship that would only be expected if contextual effects operated. In this part of the research, we also looked at the influence of urban size on the degree and scale of spatial segregation (since neighbourhood effects should be most important in segregated areas), and whether such segregation produced more unequal outcomes at an individual level. In both parts of the research, we were particularly concerned with the substantive importance of any association, as well as its statistical significance, and also with the possibility that area effects were particularly strong among the more deprived areas.

Analyses were carried out for a wide range of individual outcomes and attributes, which have been discussed in relation to social exclusion. The outcome measures included individual poverty and deprivation indicators, indicators of ill health, educational achievements, crime, family formation behaviour, subjective views and measures of flows in and out of poverty and work. The measures of potential influences included demographic and other control variables, together with indicators of (dis)advantage, constraint, educational qualifications and social capital formation. Here, we can only give a selective summary of findings from a large number of analyses. The next two sections of this chapter discuss these strands separately, and contain some further discussion of methods used in each strand.

Findings from individual level analyses

Individual level analyses examined a wide range of behaviour, attitudes, outcomes and characteristics. This section summarises results under four main headings: outcome indicators; subjective views related to social exclusion; transitions into and out of disadvantage; and measures of social capital which are hypothesised to form an intermediate link between area conditions and individual outcomes.

Most of the research reported in this section was based on the British Household Panel Survey (BHPS). Related analyses were also undertaken using the Census Sample of Anonymised Records and the National Child Development Study. In most analyses, area characteristics were measured using single composite deprivation indicators. A range of different indicators were used, including the Department of Transport, Local Government and the Regions' (DTLR, 2000) Index of Multiple Deprivation, and Townsend's area deprivation index (Townsend, 1979). The results suggested no clear advantage of one indicator over others (and, indeed, the ward unemployment rate was often as effective a predictor as any of the more complex indicators). Analyses explored the effects both of simple versions of these indicators, and of statistical transformation, in order to establish whether effects might be stronger in the worst areas. Most analysis was carried out at ward level, although we discuss some investigation of the associations at different scales later in this chapter[1].

One part of the study, reported in more detail in McCulloch (2001a), used the BHPS to analyse the associations between deprivation scores, using the Townsend (1979) area deprivation index, and a number of outcome indicators for individuals, associated with social exclusion. The indicators were: current subjective financial situation; financial expectations; health status; poverty; employment status; social support; mental health; and a measure of whether or not the respondent dislikes the neighbourhood. The analysis sought to test for effects of ward deprivation on these outcome measures. In the main analysis, four successive models were fitted. The first included, in addition to the area indicators, only the region of residence and the wave of interview. This showed significant area effects on all the dependent variables except financial expectations for both men and women. In the next model, a range of individual level *background* variables including age, ethnicity, education and household type were added. The scale of the area effects was reduced, but they all remained significant. However, when individual level *deprivation* indicators were introduced, including council tenure and unemployment, most of the area effects became non-significant. The major exception – not surprisingly – was dislike of the area. This analysis does not provide much support, therefore, for a direct model of influence from area deprivation to individual outcomes associated with social exclusion. It did, however, find some mixed evidence of interactions between individual deprivation and area deprivation, which suggested that for men, area deprivation tended to intensify the effects of individual deprivation. For women, on the other hand, the impact of individual disadvantage was greater in less deprived areas.

A second part of the analysis, reported in more detail in Buck (2001a), examined three indicators of subjective social exclusion: a non-monetary poverty score; an indicator of whether non-employed respondents expected to find a job in the next year; and whether they had any employed close friends. There were also three indicators of the probability of making transitions from one year to the next: whether or not non-employed respondents did in fact find a job; whether people in poverty left poverty in the next year; and whether people not in poverty entered poverty in the next year. In addition to neighbourhood deprivation scores, the statistical models included controls for individual demographic characteristics, employment status, social class, educational qualifications, income and local travel-to-work area unemployment. Table 13.1 provides an overall summary of the results.

The conclusions are rather diverse for different indicators. There is a clear and significant neighbourhood deprivation association with a non-monetary poverty indicator, which might arise from longer poverty durations in deprived areas, or perhaps a range of impediments to participation and consumption in such areas. There is evidence that, in deprived areas, both people's expectations of starting a job and their actual probability of starting a job are lower, controlling for individual characteristics; similarly, chances of leaving poverty are lower, and of re-entering poverty are higher than in non-deprived areas. The association with having no employed friends is weaker, and only on the margins of statistical significance. All of this is consistent with exclusionary processes placing barriers to exit from disadvantaged states, which are greater in deprived areas than in non-deprived areas. However, none of these effects would be very large substantively[2]. Area is a significant influence, but there are other equally and more important influences at the individual and household level. For example, having no qualifications (compared with O-level qualifications) has around one and a half times the effect on leaving poverty and twice the effect on entering poverty of the area deprivation score. It should also be noted that size of the area deprivation association is substantially reduced if housing tenure is also included in the models, although they remain significant. Housing tenure itself has substantial effects, but it is also strongly associated with area choice. These complex associations are still being investigated.

We suggested that policy often relied on the assumption that effects were non-linear, with area effects increasing in more deprived areas. However, in only one case – poverty exit – is there reasonably clear evidence that the association is non-linear with a marked deterioration in the worst areas. To illustrate the implications of this, Figure 13.1 plots predicted exit probabilities for a sample person: a female lone parent, aged 25, with one child, living in a moderately high unemployment travel-to-work area (alternative formulations will produce similar shapes, but at different levels). The graph suggests that the exit probability falls at below average unemployment rates, and is then relatively flat until rather high unemployment (around 23-4%) when it starts to fall rather more sharply. This turning point is at around the 95th percentile of the distribution of the sample in poverty; that is, 5% of the sample in poverty live in these extremely deprived areas, where deprivation appears to be associated with exceptionally low poverty exit. This result has to be treated with some caution since it is the only case where a clearly significant non-linear trend of this type is found, although there is some statistically non-significant evidence for such an association for the non-monetary poverty indicator and for entry into work. We shall see, however, that in the case of some outcomes the

Table 13.1: Summary of main individual level findings

Scale of linear effects		Non-linear effects		Spatial scale of deprivation effects
Effect of 1 standard deviation increase in Townsend area deprivation score measured in standard deviations of poverty score		Quadratic form significant?	Cubic form significant?	
Non-monetary poverty score	7.4%	Significant (increasing) for Townsend score	No	Steep decline with distance and population
Effect of 1 standard deviation increase in Townsend area deprivation on the odds ratio of experiencing outcome				
Do not expect to start work in next year	1.19	No (marginal decreasing effect)	No	Increase with distance and population
No close friends employed	1.05	Marginal (increasing) for Townsend	Marginal (increasing) for Townsend	Steep decline with distance, population effects weaker
Do not start work between one Wave and next	1.14	No	Marginal (increasing) for unemployment	Weak decline with distance, no population effect
Do not exit from poverty	1.12	No	Significant (increasing) effect for unemployment	Weak population effects, declines at longer distances
Enter poverty	1.10	No	No	Weak population effects, declines at longer distances

evidence tends to suggest that the differences are greatest between least-deprived areas and average areas.

We also investigated the neighbourhood scale at which effects operated. The results suggest that this varies with the nature of the outcome. Non-monetary poverty has the sharpest difference in effects based on differences in scale, with the coefficient for the smallest scale (measured in population terms) nearly 40% greater than that for the largest scale used. Not having employed close friends, poverty entry and poverty exit display smaller but appreciable differences in the same direction. For entry into work, the scale differences are minor, and for expectations of employment, they work in the opposite direction. This is the subject of further research based on a wide range of outcome variables to try to understand what influences the spatial scale at which these processes work.

It is sometimes argued that weak social capital (for example, limited social networks) may contribute to social exclusion, and that this may be associated with living in a deprived neighbourhood. This aspect of the study was investigated using BHPS data, with results suggesting a very mixed pattern of association. In particular, there was only weak evidence of greater social isolation in deprived neighbourhoods, and no evidence of fewer friend contacts in such areas, although the likelihood of such friends being employed was lower (Buck, 2001b). Further analysis was based on an indicator of neighbourhood social capital, and an indicator of social order, particularly associated with exposure to crime. This used a wider range of neighbourhood indicators. It suggests that concentrated affluence (but not deprivation), residential stability and ethnic homogeneity are predictive of social capital for women. Lower population density is the only characteristic to predict social capital for men. For both men and women concentrated disadvantage and population density are

Figure 13.1: Estimated poverty exit probability by ward unemployment

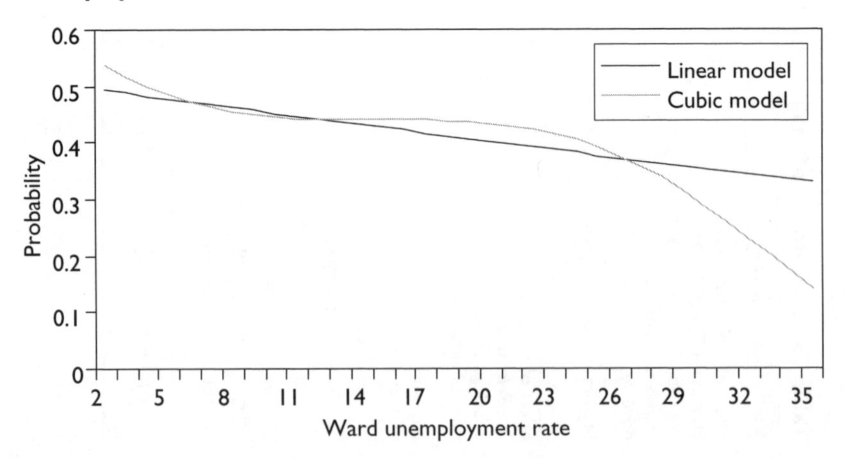

predictive of social disorder, and residential instability also predicts social disorder for women.

In summarising the individual level results, the first, and not unimportant, conclusion, is that findings are highly diverse across different indicators. We do not find consistently strong effects of area deprivation on individual outcomes, attitudes and behaviours once we have taken into account individual characteristics such as age, education level, employment status, social class and in some models income. There is some pattern to this diversity. Not surprisingly, subjective views on area quality and related factors, for example, crime incidence, are strongly related to area socio-economic deprivation. On the other hand, for outcome indicators such as subjective financial situation, poverty, health status, area effects appear extremely weak. There is also no clear association between weak social capital formation and neighbourhood disadvantage.

Indicators of flows in and out of disadvantage over time are however associated with neighbourhood disadvantage. This is consistent with exclusionary processes placing barriers to exit from disadvantaged states, which are greater in deprived areas than in non-deprived areas. However none of these effects would be substantively very large. Area is a significant influence, but there are other more important influences at the individual level.

Findings from aggregate spatial analyses

A second strand of the research focused entirely on cross-sectional analyses of aggregate spatial data. The key idea here was that the existence of significant neighbourhood/area effects should be signalled by evidence of *non-linearities* in the statistical relationship between the incidence of good/bad socio-economic outcomes in particular areas and aggregate characteristics of their population (such as the unemployment rate or the proportions from disadvantaged minorities); evidence, in other words, that socio-economic outcomes for individuals, for example, get increasingly worse compared to the aggregate characteristics of an area's population, as the latter gets worse. Evidence as to the existence of such non-linearities is also of direct interest in relation to spatial policies focused on reducing spatial disparities in the incidence of disadvantage, since only where such relationships apply can any changes in the spatial pattern of (dis)advantage be expected to affect the overall, national scale or intensity of outcomes.

The basic model around which this set of investigations was organised assumed that the probability of an individual experiencing some good/bad outcome was a function *both* of whether or not that individual possessed some (dis)advantaging characteristic *and* of the proportion of the local population with that characteristic. If there are no neighbourhood effects, this simply implies differing probabilities of success (independent of area) for those within/without the advantaged group, and a linear relation across areas between rates of success and proportions of the population in this group. Where there are significant neighbourhood effects, however, these would have an additional 'multiplicative' effect on success probabilities, *and* lead to some form of non-linearity in the aggregate relation between the incidence of disadvantage and success rates. This may involve *either* more *or* less than proportional relations with the size of the disadvantaged group.

Investigation of these relationships focused on three outcomes which have been central to a number of arguments (for example, from Wilson, 1987) about the effect of local population characteristics on processes of social exclusion and underclass formation, namely educational achievement, crime rates and the incidence of lone-parent families[3].

A final part of the work examined the extent to which segregation of disadvantaged, and more advantaged groups, was associated with urban size, and hence whether (for a given scale of 'neighbourhood') 'neighbourhood' effects would be more significant in big cities, and, if so, whether or not they contributed to more unequal outcomes for the individuals who lived there.

Educational achievement

In the education analyses reported in detail in Gordon and Monastiriotis (2004a), the focus was on performance in GCSE exams (normally taken immediately prior to the earliest permissible point for leaving school, at age 16). The dependent variables were the percentage of the cohort achieving three standard levels of achievement in 1999, with absence rates also being examined, both as an important intervening variable in exam success and as a distinct contributor to exclusion processes. All analyses were confined to schools in the state sector, and excluded 'special' schools for the educationally disadvantaged. The independent variables included both school-specific characteristics (size, type, control and gender composition) and population characteristics (social class, unemployment, lone parenthood, ethnicity, and so on) of wards in the potential catchment areas.

School characteristics play a major role in these analyses, not only in relation to selection (with predictably better results in those schools with selective admissions), but also size, gender and control (with worse results in smaller, co-educational schools under direct local authority control, and those with more 'problem' pupils). Population characteristics in the catchment area are also very important, although the relevant 'area' varies, being much more tightly drawn for low-status groups (whose effect is more localised) than for the professional and managerial classes, who can presumably both afford to travel further and know more about non-local opportunities. Relevant population characteristics include ethnicity, socio-economic groupings, unemployment and the proportion of lone parents. When all these are combined into an indicator of deprivation–advantage, there is evidence of a significant non-linear effect. The form of this implies, however, that it is concentration among the advantaged groups that has the greater effect on achievements than concentration of the disadvantaged. Closer analysis, however, indicated that this non-linearity was associated solely with lone parenthood, which has a strongly negative effect on results (at least in non-selective, local authority-controlled schools). This implied that starting from low levels, increasing the proportion of lone-parent families markedly reduces average exam success rates (beyond what is plausible as a purely individual effect), but that this effect is less at higher levels of lone parenthood. A large part of this effect was channelled through rates of absenteeism (both authorised and unauthorised), which were strongly and non-linearly related to exam success and (particularly) failure rates, and which were also strongly, but linearly, influenced by the proportion of lone parents (as well as some school characteristics). Of course, the effect attributed to these variables cannot be taken as simply reflecting effects of missing study, but may well also be indicative of other facets of behaviour and relations in school. It does suggest, however, that in relation to educational achievement, disciplinary issues may be a substantial element in neighbourhood effects, and may be indicated particularly by concentrations of lone-parent families.

Crime

Gordon and Monastiriotis (2004c), analysed crime rates at the level of Crime and Disorder Reduction Partnership areas (basically local authority districts) using Home Office measures for six types of recorded crime (burglary, thefts of cars, thefts from cars, robbery, violence against the person and sexual offences) in the year 1999/2000. The sum of the first three of these crime types was taken as an indicator of property crime rates, and that of the second three as an indicator of crimes of violence, although (as the analyses confirmed) the position of robberies was somewhat ambiguous. A series of cross-sectional regressions were undertaken for each of these measures with population-based measures (including ethnic, family, socio-economic, industrial, demographic, mobility and deprivation indicators) together with two control variables – a measure of urban service accessibility and of bar-employment per head of population. Both of these control variables proved to be generally significant, particularly that relating to bars, which appeared to have a clearly positive impact on all types of crime, except perhaps for burglary, and with a particularly strong association to rates of violent crime. A further measure (of earnings inequality across the relevant travel-to-work area) was intended to allow some distinction between effects of deprivation and inequality, in the light of Kelly's (2000) work suggesting (with US evidence) that the latter was particularly relevant to explaining the geography of violent crime. In fact, although always apparently positive in its effects, it was only statistically significant in relation to car thefts.

The analyses found significant associations (varying by type of crime) with a series of population characteristics, including employment rates, marital status, socio-economic and ethnic composition, together with the incidence of educational disadvantage and of children in poverty. There are also indications that the industrial structure of areas has some relevance, with significantly lower rates of several crimes in areas of old/heavy industries.

In relation to hypotheses specifically about neighbourhood effects, however, the key findings are that there are just four population variables with a significant *non-linear* association to crime rates, indicating possible area effects, and all relating to violent crimes. For two of these (the household mobility rate and a non-employment rate), this non-linearity implied a weakening of positive effects on crime rates at higher levels. For the other two (the proportion of personal service workers – the least stable of all SEG employment categories – and the incidence of educational deprivation), the effect is to intensify positive effects at higher levels: in the first case this applies to rates of personal violence, sexual offences and (especially) robbery; for educational deprivation it just applies to personal injury and sexual assaults. In each of these cases, there appears to be rather strong prima facie evidence for some kind of neighbourhood effect. However, there is a notable lack of support from these analyses for any simple expectations about accelerating effects on crime at higher levels of overall income/employment deprivation.

Lone parenthood

The third strand of the aggregate work, also reported in Gordon and Monastiriotis (2004b), analysed the incidence of lone parenthood among families with dependent children at both the ward and district levels. Since social exclusion (and the negative affects of lone parenthood on educational performance) appears to be particularly associated with non-working lone parents (who typically have lower levels of human capital themselves on which to draw), separate analyses were undertaken for this group. However, since in general these analyses tended only to identify the same relations in a stronger form, they can be discussed together.

In contrast to the two previous sets of analysis which could largely take the distribution of different population groups as given, any investigation of the incidence of lone parenthood clearly involves both factors influencing, first, *where* lone parents (or those at risk of becoming lone parents) choose, or are constrained, to live; and, second, *whether or not* residents of particular areas are liable to become lone parents. These have different salience at the two levels of analysis which we pursued, and it was not surprising to find that the distribution of tenure types (particularly public sector housing and furnished private renting) were more strongly associated with the ward level geography of lone parenthood. At this scale, negative associations with the tenure mix in nearby areas supported the hypothesis that these relations primarily reflected the influence of local housing opportunities on where lone parents come to live.

Ethnic origins of the local population (with positive association between lone parent rates for black groups and negative for those from South Asian origins) were also relatively more important at the ward level. In the case of socio-economic group, patterns were less consistent, but a common feature was that higher rates of lone parenthood were not associated in any simple way with higher proportions of manual workers or the unskilled. In fact, the one clear link with disadvantage was in relation to the unemployment rate for younger males, which was a strong influence at both levels (consistent with Wilson's 1987 hypotheses about the impact of a shortage of 'marriageable males'), and *much* the stronger factor at district level, accounting on its own for most of the variance.

Three or four forms of non-linearity were evident in these relations, suggestive of neighbourhood effects on the chances of being a lone parent. These included the proportion of rented accommodation in the area, to the proportion of personal service workers and the rate of population movement. None of these showed a clear tendency for increasing effects at higher levels. The most significant case, however, involved the male unemployment rate, where there was a general tendency for the effect on lone parenthood rates to be stronger at high levels of unemployment. At ward level, there actually appeared to be two thresholds, with very little effect at rates below 10% (or above 25%), but a strong one between these levels. At district level (where there were many fewer extreme cases), the relation was more simply convex, with each increment in local male unemployment raising lone-parent rates by an increasing margin.

Segregation, urban size and inequality

Finally, the research investigated the question whether neighbourhood effects would have more practical significance in big cities, because for any given scale of 'neighbourhood' there was likely to be a higher degree of segregation there – and whether this could be shown to produce more unequal outcomes for individuals in such places.

For the first part of this analysis, 'cities' were defined in terms of 'functional regions', representing the effective labour and housing market areas, within which residential segregation occurs (using the version of these defined by Coombes et al, 1982). Segregation measures were computed for a wide range of population groups, distinguished in terms of ethnicity, social class, unemployment, lone parenthood, old age, limiting illness, residential mobility and housing tenure, at three different spatial scales (enumeration districts, Census wards and parliamentary constituencies). Statistical tests were run with various control variables relating measured segregation to the population size of the functional regions. These demonstrated that there was a consistently strong size effect on segregation, especially for the more broadly defined area units. One implication of size alone is that big cities were always likely to have more of their population among the areas (wards) figuring among the most deprived in the country, although they were even more likely to have a disproportionate share of the least deprived areas also (Gordon and Monastiriotis, 2003a).

On an area basis, then, big cities appear to have substantially less equal outcomes, even if this is just a function of larger-scale clusters of the advantaged and disadvantaged. The question is, however, whether or not this actually makes a difference to outcomes for individuals, because area effects operating at a constant neighbourhood scale produce stronger positive and negative effects within the more segregated neighbourhoods of big cities. This might particularly be the case where institutions of a more or less fixed scale ensure that functional 'neighbourhoods' have a similar scale in both large and small settlements – as seems to be the case for (English) state schools.

A second part of this segregation work thus looked at the question of whether educational outcomes – good, bad and middling, measured in terms of university admission, failure to achieve any qualifications and median GCSE results – were affected by the degree of segregation in a functional region. Control variables were introduced relating to the degree of inequality among adults in the area, and institutional segregation in terms of the role of selective and independent schools in the area. Results from the regression analyses confirmed that more pupils in residentially segregated city-regions did have significantly more unequal results, as hypothesised. However, this was very largely because higher levels of segregation of the advantaged produced a greater incidence of 'good' performance (that is, more university entrants), not because segregation of the disadvantaged produced significantly more 'bad' results. And there was some indication that the more segregated areas enjoyed a higher average level of performance, since numbers achieving at least 'middling' levels of performance were greater there (Gordon and Monastiriotis, 2003a).

Conclusions and implications for policy

The analysis using aggregate data, on educational achievements, crime and lone parenthood suggested that in each case (except for property crimes) there were some significant contextual/neighbourhood effects. These, however, were linked to quite particular sets of population characteristics rather than generalised measures of deprivation. They were often stronger among relatively advantaged areas. Hence, it could not be assumed that reducing disparities between areas in terms of population mix or the incidence of unemployment would necessarily improve overall outcomes across broader areas. Thus, as with the individual level analyses, the emphasis is on diversity of potential effects, rather than a single uniform process of area disadvantage generating social exclusion.

Similarly, for the majority of outcomes, individual level analysis suggests either a continuous steady relationship across all levels of deprivation or – in the case of neighbourhood social capital – that the greatest differences are between affluent areas and average areas; that is, that the spatial concentration of affluence may actually contribute to social advantage for the average person. However, for one outcome, poverty exit, there is reasonably clear evidence of a non-linear association involving a markedly greater deterioration in the worst areas. This would support a view that in this case concentrations of disadvantage do contribute to social exclusion (if not to the degree that various individual characteristics do).

In principle, effects of spatial concentration might arise at a range of spatial scales, although 'neighbourhood effects' are usually assumed pragmatically to relate to areas about the scale of an electoral ward. The majority of our analyses focused on this level, although some work examined a range of spatial scales.

The conclusions varied across the indicators (and also across population groups). However, the tendency was for the scale at which neighbourhood effects appeared strongest to be considerably smaller than the average ward.

These findings are consistent with those of the integrated city-studies reported elsewhere in this volume. Turok et al (Chapter Two of this volume) found only tentative evidence for any neighbourhood effects in Glasgow and Edinburgh, although they suggest that limited social networks in the most disadvantaged areas did seem to have some impact. Other studies demonstrated the inequalities between neighbourhoods, but did not directly investigate whether these were caused by neighbourhood effects on individual outcomes. The Bristol study (Boddy et al, Chapter Four of this volume) identifies the particular concentration of educational disadvantage and the high level of contrast between best and worst areas in terms of outcomes. The Manchester/Liverpool study (Harding et al, Chapter Three of this volume) and Bristol study both emphasise the extent of variation between the best and worst areas in terms of disadvantage, often in close proximity one to the other. This may well drive the sorts of 'non-linear' effects identified in the current work.

One aim of this research has been to test the assumptions on which much spatially targeted policy has been based. The findings certainly do not suggest that such policies are entirely without foundations. We have discussed a range of significant associations between indicators of social exclusion area characteristics. However, the magnitude of these effects is not large in comparison with the effects of individual characteristics that generate disadvantage. Moreover, the evidence for threshold effects, that the effects are distinctly stronger in a subset of the most disadvantaged areas, is rather weak. The research has also highlighted how difficult it is to find conclusive evidence of the nature of the processes which may lead to these effects, and hence to guide appropriate policy interventions. Also, we must draw attention again to some of the problems of identifying neighbourhood effects. To give a concrete example, if people tend to leave disadvantaged areas as soon as they have enough resources, then we will get an exaggerated view of the size of the neighbourhood effect, since we will tend not to observe the people who succeed there. Paradoxically, this means that we may underestimate the success of a neighbourhood policy in the area, since we may not see the people who gain from it.

One conclusion from this, which may not be altogether welcome, is that social scientists and policy makers need to be reasonably modest about what can possibly be known about the magnitude and causes of neighbourhood effects. In developing future policy, it is important to move away from simple assumptions about neighbourhood effects, and consider more specifically what relevant processes may be generating these effects, and how policy might modify these. It also needs to recognise the greater importance of parallel policies that address the situation of individuals at risk of social exclusion wherever they live. This would include, for example, national-level policies such as the various New Deal programmes, Working Family Tax Credit (and its successor, Child

Tax Credit) and the various components of the National Childcare Strategy, including Sure Start. At present, we would conclude that there is no substantial general basis for claims that policies targeted at the worst (most disadvantaged) areas are a particularly effective way of tackling individual disadvantage.

Notes

[1] Statistical analyses used regression models including a range of individual characteristics. There were also controls for regional labour market effects. Much of the focus of our results is on the association between individual characteristics and with measured area characteristics. While for some analyses we did use multi-level methods, which aim to partition the unexplained part of the variance in the dependent variable into that associated with area, and that associated with the individual level, we did not treat the former as evidence of area effects. In this instance, the partitioning is suspect given area selection by individuals, and the potential for unobserved individual characteristics to be correlated within areas because of sorting.

[2] For the logistic regression models of probabilities of various outcomes, the effect of a one standard deviation increase in area deprivation ranges between a 5% and a 19% increase in the likelihood of the outcome.

[3] In each case, the methodology was essentially the same and this strand of the research focused more on *particular* population mix characteristics, rather than general indicators of area disadvantage.

References

Brooks-Gunn, J., Duncan, G.J. and Aber, J.L. (1997) *Neighbourhood poverty. Volume 1*, New York, NY: Russell Sage Foundation.

Buck, N. (2001a) 'Identifying neighbourhood effects on social exclusion', *Urban Studies*, vol 38, pp 2251-75.

Coombes, M.G., Dixon, J.S., Goddard, J.B., Openshaw, S. and Taylor, P.J. (1982) 'Functional regions for the population census of Britain', in D.T. Herbert and R.J. Johnston (eds) *Geography and the urban environment 5*, London: Wiley, pp 63-112.

DTLR (Department for Transport, Local Government and the Regions) (2000) *Measuring multiple deprivation at the small area level: The indices of deprivation 2000*, London: DTLR.

Gordon, I.R. and Monastiriotis, V. (2003) 'Urban size, spatial segregation and educational outcomes', LSE Research Papers in Environment and Spatial Analysis, 87, London School of Economics and Political Science.

Gordon, I.R. and Monastiriotis, V. (2004a) 'Spatial analyses of neighbourhood influences on examination performance', LSE Research Papers in Environment and Spatial Analysis (forthcoming) London School of Economics and Political Science.

Gordon, I.R. and Monastiriotis, V. (2004b) 'Using aggregate evidence to test for neighbourhood effects on social exclusion' LSE Research Papers in Environment and Spatial Analysis (forthcoming) London School of Economics and Political Science.

Gordon, I.R. and Monastiriotis, V. (2004c) 'Criminal behaviour and social context: the role of spatial effects', LSE Research Papers in Environment and Spatial Analysis (forthcoming) London School of Economics and Political Science.

Jencks, C. and Mayer, S.E. (1990) 'The social consequences of growing up in a poor neighborhood', in L. Lynn and M. McGeary (eds) (1990) *Inner city poverty in the United States*, Washington, DC: National Academy Press, pp 111-86.

Kelly, M. (2000) 'Inequality and crime', *Review of Economics and Statistics*, vol 82, no 4, pp 530-9.

Levitas, R. (1998) *The inclusive society? Social exclusion and New Labour*, Basingstoke: Macmillan.

Ludwig, J., Duncan, G. and Hirschfield, P. (1998) 'Urban poverty and juvenile crime: evidence from a randomized housing-mobility experiment', *JCPR Working Paper*, Chicago, IL: Northwestern University.

McCulloch, A. (2001) 'Ward level deprivation and individual social and economic outcomes in the British Household Panel Study Waves 1 to 8', *Environment and Planning A*, vol 33, pp 667-84.

Social Exclusion Unit (2001) *A new commitment to neighbourhood renewal: National strategy action plan*, London: Social Exclusion Unit, Cabinet Office.

Townsend, P., Phillimore, P. and Beattie, A. (1989) *Health and deprivation*, London: Routledge.

Wilson, W.J. (1987) *The truly disadvantaged*, Chicago, IL: University of Chicago Press.

FOURTEEN

The 'good' suburb as an urban asset in enhancing a city's competitiveness

Peter Halfpenny, Nadia Joanne Britton, Fiona Devine and Rosemary Mellor

Introduction

Along with other regional cities in the UK, Manchester grew during the Industrial Revolution into a major centre of manufacturing. However, employment in this sector declined at an increasing rate over the 20th century. Towards the end of this period, the city sought to reinvent itself as major regional centre for business, cultural and leisure services in the UK and indeed in Europe. This involved not only regenerating the city to make it an attractive place for high-level service industry professionals to work and play, but also promoting it as an enjoyable place for them to live. It is in this context that we raise the question of whether 'good' suburbs are 'assets' in maintaining and enhancing the city's competitiveness, by helping it to attract and retain a highly qualified professional workforce. The research thus addresses one of the key themes running through the Cities Research Programme around the bases of competitive advantage and the role or urban assets.

The chapter begins with a brief overview of the changing employment patterns within the city before focusing on the financial and business services sector and the experiences of people working within it. This is followed by an examination of two long-established leafy suburbs, and in particular the development pressures they have come under as the city centre's economy is revitalised, and the resistance offered by residents and others as they seek to preserve the exclusiveness of these neighbourhoods. The chapter ends with some observations about the lack of strategic planning for the future sustainable development of the good suburbs.

The study on which the chapter is based had two strands. The first examined the financial and business services sector located in Manchester city centre, and focused on six areas of professional employment: commercial law, accountancy, corporate banking and venture capitalists, actuarial services, architecture and creative design and advertising. These six areas were chosen because each had a significant presence in the city centre and each was widely acknowledged to be contributing to and benefiting from Manchester's regeneration. Semi-structured interviews were conducted with a senior partner or manager in 34 city-centre firms, large, medium and small, multinational and local, and with 10 key informants drawn from various professional and other organisations. The interviews explored professional and organisational changes in the service sector in Manchester, the client base, competition and cooperation between firms, reasons for being in Manchester and views on the recent regeneration of the city, as well as informants' assessments of the career paths, and the recruitment and retention, of those working in their professional areas. These were followed by interviews with 70 employees from a sample of the 34 firms. These interviewees were mostly in their late 20s or early 30s. There were more men than women (7:3), as would be expected given that it is only in the last decade or so that significant numbers of women have acquired the high-level qualifications necessary in order to enter professional occupations. The interviews examined career history, residential mobility and housing history, non-work activities, commitment to their current residential locale and to Manchester and the region. These two sets of interviews in the first strand of the research made it possible to understand differences in work-orientation, and more generally lifestyle, between generations and how suburban neighbourhoods are evaluated by this sector of the city's workforce.

The second strand of the study looked at reactions to the development pressures that the older suburbs have come under with the revitalisation of the city-centre economy. Interviews were conducted with some 40 key informants in two 'exclusive' suburbs, including property developers and estate agents, councillors and unsuccessful candidates in local elections drawn from all political parties active in the two areas, activists in civic societies, residents associations and conservation schemes, members of the Women's Institute, Soroptomists and Round Table, shopkeepers, religious leaders, community police officers, a youth worker and key actors in the field of education. The interviewees were selected partly because of the sorts of organisations and interests they represented and partly by 'snowball sampling' among the local 'influentials'. These interviews centred on the informants' assessments of changes occurring in the two localities, the main issues that had exercised people living there recently, the property market, the quality of life and community involvement in the area, and the effects of Manchester's regeneration on the suburb, as well as their reactions to contests over development proposals.

Alongside the primary research, there was a programme of secondary research. This included analysis of local and city-wide newspapers, documents from the Manchester City and Trafford Planning Departments and publications and websites maintained by professional associations. Except where otherwise specified, the evidence described in the remainder of this chapter is derived from the documentary materials and, especially, from the interviews conducted in the two strands of the study, all of which were tape recorded and fully transcribed. All our interviewees expressed themselves fluently, thoughtfully and perceptively and we are indebted to them for the time they gave us despite their busy schedules.

The city's decline and revival

The consensus about urban change in Britain 25 years ago was that major industrial cities were experiencing inevitable decline (Paris, 1977; Pascall, 1987). Manufacturing jobs were being lost in cities as new jobs in services were created in the suburbs and beyond. Between 1981 and 1996, the 20 biggest British cities lost half a million jobs, whereas the rest of the country gained 1.7 million (Turok, 1999). In Manchester, the visible indication of this was areas of dereliction close to the centre and a swathe of new office blocks and business parks on the city's southern edge, from Stockport to Warrington. Once the heart of the cotton industry, controlling the world textiles market, the city centre's early grandeur had become dilapidated and unkempt. Alongside the loss of jobs, cities were also losing their populations as the suburbs and the villages beyond increasingly attracted people seeking to escape urban decay and social breakdown. The population of the Manchester local authority district fell from 710,000 in 1951 to 420,000 in 1991.

More recently, however, prompted by changes in occupational structures, a different view of urban change has emerged, which maintains that the social success and economic competitiveness of cities now depend on the growth of a nexus of service industries, especially the advanced professions servicing the corporate institutions of the global economy (Castells, 1989; Sassen, 1994; Florida, 2002), and also on implanting the leisure, cultural, heritage and tourist industries into city centres (Amin and Graham, 1997). Technical and professional workers were thus central to the competitive success of the city. Accordingly, the policy priority in Manchester has become that of the remaking of the city centre (Mellor, 1997). Trading off its heritage, from its Roman amphitheatre to its Victorian architecture, the city centre is being restyled and refurbished. The palatial mercantile headquarters of the long-gone cotton firms have been converted into hotels, the oldest passenger railway terminus into an industrial museum, derelict canal sides into fashionable bars and the disused central station into the GMEX exhibition centre, all promoted and funded by partnerships between state agencies and private firms. Striking new buildings have been erected too, such as the Bridgewater Hall to rehouse the Hallé orchestra, Urbis Museum of City Living and the Sportscity stadium that played a central role in the 2002 Commonwealth Games.

The vision is that of a European city, vibrant and alive, and of public spaces thronged with affluent consumers and tourists from far and wide. The decline of population has been halted, with a modest rise in the Manchester local authority area from 420,000 in 1991 to 431,000 in 1999. Alongside this has been the growth of the city-centre financial and business services sector, in 1999 employing 23% of Manchester's 280,000 workforce, only slightly less than the 29% employed in public administration, education and health, this latter being the largest employment sector in the local authority area (National Statistics, 1999). Nationally, 18% of the workforce was employed in the financial and business services sector in 1999, compared with only 11% 20 years earlier (National Statistics, 1999). The concentration of specialised service industries in city centres has stimulated the demand for high-level jobs. Employment within Manchester City grew by 8.2% between 1995 and 2000, to a total of over 280,000 jobs, the most rapid growth being in financial and business services, alongside a continuing decline in manufacturing and traditional industries (Harrison, 2001).

The growth of the advanced service sector in Manchester city centre has benefited from the conjunction of several factors. One is the explicit policy of the city council to seek partnerships with the private sector to promote a service-sector led recovery, including property redevelopment, and to recapture the city centre for the middle classes (Quilley, 1999). This economic strategy became particularly prominent during the flurry of remodelling and rebuilding that followed the extensive damage to the core of the shopping district caused by the IRA bomb in 1996. Older properties that are no longer suitable for modern office work, especially the widespread use of IT and open floor plans, are being converted into fashionable shops, bars, restaurants and flats. At the same time, prestige office blocks are being constructed to meet the demand for modern workspaces. It has become important for professional firms to take up occupancy of these premium city-centre blocks in order to signal the success of their company to their clients and competitors. Another factor is the increasingly global outlook of the City of London, which has resulted in firms based there becoming disdainful about servicing clients in the UK regions, except through satellite offices. This led to branches of major international financial and business services companies being established in Manchester. The competition that this generated for local firms exerted pressures to consolidate through mergers and to diversify so as to be able to offer a full service across a variety of professional specialisms rather than just a single one.

The necessity to address the more competitive climate was also forcefully demonstrated by the recession of the early 1990s, which came as a shock to Manchester firms – especially because they had to make people redundant – and which exposed their lack of investment in information technology. Once they had introduced IT, not only did it improve productivity but it also allowed Manchester firms instant access to the same financial and other data that is available to national and international companies, and enabled them to offer better client-oriented services. In addition, restructuring of both private and public sectors over the past two decades has encouraged outsourcing to independent service companies, sometimes spun out of the original company. In this more intense business environment, smaller firms in surrounding towns and even the city suburbs have found it difficult to compete for the larger and more lucrative clients.

The entrepreneurial firms in the city centre now provide the financial and business services which maintain much of the region's economy. However, despite the sector's importance to the future of the city, it remains precarious. As it attempts to extend its client base beyond the North West, it comes into competition with other regional centres, such as Bristol, Birmingham and Leeds, which are also seeking to extend the geographical reach of their own business services sector (see French and Leyshon, 2003; also Chapter Four of this volume). London continues to dominate in servicing national and international companies, including those based in mainland Europe (Chapter Five of this volume), despite the aspirations of the Central Manchester Urban Development Corporation to establish Manchester as a European business city. What is left for Manchester are the few international companies with sites in and a commitment to the North West, together with small- and medium-sized businesses based in the regions: deals worth over £100 million are rare. Should the regional companies they service grow through mergers or be taken over by larger companies, they might transfer their custom to London. Indeed, some Manchester-based financial and business services firms have opened London offices and, should they be able to expand their activity in the capital, they could migrate there eventually. Moreover, much of the recent expansion of the Manchester city-centre economy is due to the buoyancy of the wider economy throughout the 1990s, and the global downturn that began in 2001 could have a severe effect. Since we completed our interviews in 1998, it has been reported that "some of the region's lawyers, accountants and venture capitalists have announced office closures, the reorganisation of corporate teams or even mergers with other firms" (Pysden, 2002). Any weakening of the North West regional economy has an adverse impact on the Manchester city-centre firms that service it; that is, they remain vulnerable to macroeconomic changes over which they have little, if any, control.

The Manchester financial and business services sector

Despite the long shadow of London, which circumscribes the work available in regional centres and drains talent away from them, Manchester-based financial and business services firms are often preferred by North West companies because of their local knowledge and the relations of trust developed through personal contacts. National and international companies might be serviced by London or other global cities but firms that have their offices in Manchester typically service the remaining small- and medium-sized companies based in the North West. The Manchester firms are responsive to the needs of local companies because it is from these companies' success that future fee income will derive: they have a direct stake in the economic regeneration of the region. The relatively circumscribed client base has sharpened competition between firms operating in the same field, intensifying the work of partners and managers as they seek to maximise the proportion of their time devoted to fee-earning activities – the leisurely long lunch has disappeared. At the same time, there is substantial cooperation between firms operating in complementary fields as they seek to source locally all financial and business services necessary to effect the deal. Collectively, they are keen to demonstrate that the Manchester business-services complex comprises a critical mass of specialised professional firms capable of providing a first-rate full service to coordinate investment in business development, without recourse to London.

The success of the city-centre financial and business services sector is sufficiently visible for recruitment not to be a problem. Despite the pull of London, there is an abundant supply of well-qualified labour. An important factor was applicants' allegiance – or their partners' allegiance – to Manchester or the North more generally (Devine et al, 2003). Some, originally from the region, had moved away to universities but returned to be near their family and friends. Others had come from elsewhere to study at the local universities and then found ample job opportunities to enable them to stay in an area they had found enjoyable. Some from both groups had taken their first job in London or elsewhere but then moved back to Manchester, on the basis that they could successfully develop their career there at the same time as enjoying a better quality of life than in London. Although their work had intensified and their working day lengthened, due to competitive pressures and through computerisation, Manchester was felt to be less frenetic and demanding than London. Even commuting into Manchester, the feature of their lives that attracted most adverse comment, compared well with London. At the time we interviewed them, all the professionals enjoyed job security and all were generously remunerated, including the younger interviewees, 11 of whom had already reached partner or senior management level.

The Manchester 'business community', as our respondents described it, achieves functional cohesion through mutual interdependence and the cross-referral of work between professional firms whose specialisms are complementary. It is this that keeps the financial and business services firms together in the city centre, rather than dispersing to the suburban business parks. There they would be cut off from vital circuits of activity conducted face-to-face: bumping into people on the streets and in the pub; informal meetings over a quick lunch; chat about opportunities for future contracts; people available to sign documents without delay; and the ease of working with the firm just along the street. Proximity – within what is known as the Square Half Mile – is to the firms' mutual benefit, enabling them collectively to deliver a full service to their clients and to monitor each other's performance. Immediate access to city-centre facilities is important too: the courts, the town hall, the legal and commercial sections of the city's central reference library and the support services like print-shops and suppliers of office equipment. These factors, and the prestige and credibility that derive from a city-centre location, outweigh poor accessibility, congestion and lack of parking. Rather than relocate to more accessible places, firms attempt to ameliorate the disadvantages of travel to the city centre by more flexible working practices, including homeworking, facilitated by IT.

Competition does not fracture the sector's cohesion because firms may be rivals over one deal but partners in the next. Since the business community is relatively small, it is important to maintain good relations: reputation is critical to being invited to tender or to join a consortium. Cohesion achieved through proximity and interdependence is reinforced through more formal mechanisms: professional associations' seminars and dinners, public lectures at the Manchester Business School and meetings of the Manchester Financial and Professional Forum. This last was formed in 1987 "to promote the wide range of professional skills available to any organisation doing business in Manchester" and now has over 165 firms as members (Pro-Manchester, 2002). Supporting Manchester's cultural and educational institutions further strengthens networks: serving on the management committees or acting as sponsors for the art galleries, the Literary and Philosophical Society, the Hallé Orchestra and other musical associations, the museums, universities, colleges and schools. The intricate web of affiliation engenders loyalty to Manchester and camaraderie among professionals, often expressed in terms of rivalry with London or with other regional centres which are also promoting regeneration around financial and business services, such as Leeds.

Nevertheless, profit is of prime importance. Although there is a sense of affinity and a collaborative determination to prevent firms from elsewhere, especially London, taking business away from those based in Manchester, work has intensified. Clients no longer remain loyal to their service providers if rival firms offer a better deal. Diversification into services beyond the core specialism of the firm (for example, accountancy firms offering legal services) widens the range of competitors. Employees no longer commit themselves to a lifetime with their current firm but seek out better opportunities for career development elsewhere. A balance has to be struck by firms between, on the one hand, collaborating to build trust in Manchester's capacity to provide good value, highly professional, full service support to the region's economy and, on the other, competing effectively with local rivals to retain clients and staff and, above all, maintain or increase profits. The outcome is that the people from the financial and business services responsible for the buoyancy of the city-centre economy use the shopping, leisure and cultural facilities that surround their workplaces rather less than expected. They work long hours, and the older senior managers and partners especially contrast their current hectic working lives with what they fondly remember as more relaxed and more sociable times when they first entered their professions, when they had time for leisurely lunches or for calling into the fashionable clubs or bars or shops on the way home. The junior employees, in contrast, do enjoy visiting the smart shops during their lunchtimes and do go drinking in the bars in central Manchester, especially on Friday evenings. These younger professionals, without family ties, more instrumental about their careers and more accustomed to the often frenetic pace of modern life, expressed relief that the old-fashioned 'gentlemanly' social side of work has faded, leaving them more time to focus on their jobs. Nevertheless, both age groups' lives are largely fashioned around work in the city centre and home in the suburbs or beyond, which is where they also spend most of their leisure time, particularly once they have families. The regenerated city centre offers a more pleasant place to work but its most important function is to attract new clients for their firms to service or more custom from their existing clients, rather than act as a focus for their non-working lives.

The 'good' suburbs

Having good places to live for its middle-class professional workers, we would argue, is important if Manchester is to secure its status as a competitive city. In the past, it has been the city's long-established 'exclusive' suburbs, with large, good-quality houses at relatively low densities, that have provided the homes for wealthy industrialists and professionals with well-paid careers. Our study examined two such residential neighbourhoods. One, Didsbury, is embedded in the Manchester city conurbation, inside the M60 orbital motorway, only five miles from the city centre. The other, Hale, is part of Trafford Metropolitan Borough and is further away, on the edge of the green belt, ten miles from the city centre. The two are similar in that both originally grew as railway suburbs, with a mixture of workers' terraces, middle-class villas and merchant-gentlemen's mansions. Today, they retain a core of large detached and semi-detached Victorian and Edwardian houses which attract high and rapidly increasing prices, especially if they are close to the shops in the 'village' centre. Hale's top-range prices exceed those of Didsbury, reflecting the former's more residential and suburban feel and the latter's more mixed-use and urban character. Both have good access to the city centre and to open green spaces; they are close to the motorway network and the airport without either of these intruding overly on their peacefulness; and excellent state and public schools, leisure facilities and NHS and private hospitals are within easy reach.

All those interviewed about these two suburbs maintained that they are good places in which to live: Didsbury is seen as the best area within the city and Hale the best in the region or even in the whole country. However, neither suburb is homogeneous: they are stratified by housing type and quality; by residents' age (which differentiates households markedly); by lifestyle preferences, even within age cohorts; by ethnic and religious variations; and by differences in outlook between the business and professional segments of the middle class. Nevertheless, there is tolerance of heterogeneity among neighbours, facilitated by middle-class values of domestic privacy and respectability: people there keep themselves to themselves. Conversely, there is little evidence of overall community cohesion. In general, the residents are 'suburban consumers', in that they use but do not contribute greatly to local organisations. The churches, synagogues and mosques attract large numbers of worshippers every week but many of these are from outside the neighbourhood. They are also one of the very few loci of social concern and voluntary action, although much of this focuses on limited client groups or is directed outside the locality, in addition to which its religious base reduces its appeal to many.

In general, most residents' level of involvement in local life is low and they offer little support for local campaigns. Those who do speak for local interests are relatively few in number and they are older, long-term residents known to each other. They are strongly committed to the locality as it is or, increasingly, was: spacious with mature trees and green spaces, respectable neighbours with well-maintained houses in well-kept gardens, and a centre with a village character, within walking distance and comprising small, specialist shops whose staff and customers know each other by sight or by name. It is threats to their immediate physical locality and not the community that prompts protest from the small number of activists among the residents: issues to do with the development of adjoining properties, however minor, or the state of their own street or the loss of a favourite shop. Preservation, rather than sustainable development, is their watchword. They resist every change and deplore the loss of amenity and heritage without regard for the potential gains from new facilities or the replacement of obsolete buildings.

Renewed growth in the city economy has triggered strong development pressures in both suburbs, with builders and property developers constantly seeking sites and planning permission: any new development in these localities is highly marketable. The development pressures are fuelled by the dearth of greenfield sites across the city, a strong demand for housing helped by low-cost mortgages, and changes in both family formation patterns and leisure pursuits resulting in more time spent outside the home, especially by single and childless people in their 20s and 30s with considerable spending power. The large old houses are targets for conversion into multi-occupation or replacement by luxury blocks of flats. Pockets of land formerly serving commercial purposes, such as the milk bottling plant in Didsbury, are redeveloped intensively for housing. Small shops are bought out and converted into wine bars, restaurants and pubs. Trafford's tight planning controls have checked such pressures in Hale and the broad areas covered by its designated conservation areas. New developments have been largely limited to substantial detached houses that are modern versions of the suburban mansion and small, select apartment blocks that mimic, externally, the surrounding century-old villas, both of which preserve the character of the area.

In Didsbury, the city planning authority has been more sympathetic to development and the area has experienced a surge in investment in housing and leisure facilities. There has been more in-filling on the remaining open spaces, including the gardens of privately owned houses, and more replacement of large houses with often characterless blocks of flats, both developments aimed at small households, young or old, rather than families. There has been extensive change of use of outlets in the village centre, from specialist shops to bars, pubs and restaurants. Younger professionals from within and outside the locality view the changes positively, since they add a new vibrancy to the area and make it an attractive place in which they can pursue their favoured lifestyles outside their work time. However, the change from shopping village to leisure site is a threat, even a crisis, in the eyes of the older, established residents, undermining the 'exclusivity' of the locality, in terms of both its facilities and its users. The contests between developers and long-established home-owners, and the older residents and the younger incomers, for control over the 'suburban estate' are central issues in local politics in both areas, frequently featured on the front pages of the local newspapers.

Interestingly, crime was not identified as a major concern in either suburb. Thefts and burglaries are regarded as a fact of life but, for well-insured households, they are not a significant source of worry. Most homes have private security systems, often sophisticated on the more expensive properties. There was some comment about growing public order problems in the late evenings resulting from increasing numbers of outsiders attracted to the cafes and bars, especially in Didsbury where there are more of these facilities than in Hale. However, for some residents, having more people out and about made them feel safer on the streets at night and community safety officers confirmed that no extra police resources were required, even at weekends.

Broader changes in housing markets are affecting the two suburbs and they are no longer the automatic first choice of good places to live among the younger generation of professionals. The interviews with employees in the city-centre financial and business services firms revealed that the very large majority lived in the towns or villages surrounding Manchester, the quality of life available there being one of the main factors that attracted them to working in the North West. Because of their local allegiances, they had a sophisticated understanding of the region's housing hierarchy. Although Didsbury and Hale might be staging posts as they move up the housing ladder, the pinnacle for them, unlike the older generation of professionals, was not the traditional good suburb, but rather a place in the countryside. They complained about the time it took to commute to work in the city centre by car on congested roads but this did not deter them from living, or aspiring to live, beyond the suburbs. In central Manchester, conversion of Victorian business premises into stylish apartments and construction of new luxury blocks of flats continues apace, offering alternative 'good' places to live in the heart of the 24-hour city, but surprisingly very few of our respondents had any interest in living there.

Political disenchantment

The perceived failure of both national and local government to support the rights of the residents of these suburbs (especially the older residents) to live undisturbed in their neighbourhood of choice with easy access to good local services and facilities has nurtured their disenchantment with the political process. There is dissatisfaction with the local authorities, which is expressed in terms of complaints about town hall ignorance of the area, the imposition of city-wide policies that are insensitive to local circumstances, the unresponsive and inappropriate town-planning system and bureaucratic inefficiency. For example, in Hale, the local authority introduced car-parking charges in the village centre, which provoked critical comment about the failure to recognise that this interfered with locals' convenience when doing their day-to-day shopping. In general, there were accusations of class discrimination in that residents of these good suburbs are highly taxed both on their properties and on their incomes, but their suburbs are given low priority in the allocation of public resources because they are middle-class areas. The very poor state of the roads and pavements in the two suburbs was an oft-cited example.

There is also dissatisfaction directed at central government about changes that have more subtle impacts that are perceived to undermine the exclusiveness of the locality. One example is provided by national educational policies that weaken local state schools or restrict access to public schools – the selective state grammar schools in Hale are seen to be under threat and the abolition of assisted places has made fee-paying schools less affordable. Another example is the uniform business rate that many owners believe imposes excessive burdens on small, local shops and firms. Local MPs, even if supportive of campaigns (such as the attempt to prevent the closure of the hospital on the fringe of Didsbury) have been ineffective in resisting unwelcome developments pursued by central government. Overall, there is a sense among residents of a loss of influence which is channelled into resentment at the perceived dominance of non-local business interests and at the unwillingness or inability of government to protect the locality from changes seen as detrimental to the quality of life available to residents. Resistance to development pressures is forcibly articulated but felt to be unavailing. Even the local key players feel estranged from the system of governance.

What future for the good suburbs?

Young professionals with successful, well-paid careers before them see their moves up the local housing hierarchy culminating not in the exclusive suburbs but in a home in the countryside, beyond the city's boundaries, especially when they reach the family-building stage of their lives. They are attracted by well-entrenched images of rural life and the pastoral landscape, which entice them to believe that the countryside offers them a better quality of life than available within the city and its immediate suburbs. Many have moved to or stayed in the North West to benefit from this possibility. Car-ownership provides them with the opportunity to live in the country, work in the city centre and take their leisure wherever they favour. State investment in infrastructure, especially improved roads, supports their aspirations, as does private sector provision of new housing in and around the small towns and villages beyond the green belt. The good suburbs might be where some of them spend an early stage of their adult life, living in a small flat in a large old house or in a new purpose-built block, and they might also spend their leisure time there, in the pubs, wine bars and restaurants that have displaced the 'village' shops. However, they have no commitment to the area, beyond their immediate consumption of its facilities. This is similar to the processes identified in the case of Newcastle (Chapter Seven of this volume) and in the more aggregate picture of residential mobility across the country as a whole.

The changed place of suburban 'villages' like Hale and Didsbury in the housing hierarchy of younger professionals is but one of a raft of socio-economic and demographic factors that have a bearing of the future of the good suburbs. Prices of the quality houses in these areas increasingly exclude all but the very rich. Adult children of established families can no longer afford to buy, or even to rent, the sorts of properties they might aspire to in these areas. Existing home-owners are tempted to realise their property gains by selling up and moving out of the area, perhaps on early retirement. Such out-migration weakens further already tenuous community networks. The big houses in spacious grounds, built at a time when nearly all middle-class households had servants and families were larger than now, are less and less suited to modern lifestyles, although some extended families of Asian origin find them attractive, increasing the ethnic mix of the areas. Traffic congestion and parking restrictions in the 'village' centres encourage residents to forsake the suburbs' specialist shops in favour of out-of-town superstores that have dedicated car parks and can meet all their needs in one shopping trip. The older generation, fiercely protective of the localities in their current form, are not being replaced by people with the same level of commitment, as evidenced by the declining membership of the civic societies in both suburbs. Younger cohorts have more women in employment who therefore spend more time and have more interests beyond the area where they live. As a result of these and other factors, the good suburbs are inherently unstable, inhabiting a tension field between exclusiveness which attracts developers, overdevelopment which threatens their popularity, and changing social fashions in housing, shopping and leisure which undermines their prestige.

Against this background, development within the two suburbs studied has been piecemeal and has emerged from contests between the long-established residents, on the one hand, who resist every change to their immediate locality and, on the other, private developers constantly seeking opportunities to make substantial returns on investments in housing and leisure facilities. These contests are mediated by the planning system operated by the local authorities, which are heavily criticised by both parties. The local authorities are relatively unresponsive to these criticisms, not least because they are more pressed by concerns about other areas under their stewardship, including bleak housing estates with high levels of deprivation and the economic regeneration of decaying business districts. The planning system anyway is designed and regulated by central government, which has progressively eroded the powers of locally elected bodies over the past 20 years, setting the agenda for them through a flow of initiatives mostly now directed at overcoming social exclusion and achieving regeneration through partnership working.

The lack of local community involvement and desultory local authority interest means that there is a policy vacuum surrounding good suburbs. Debates prominent in the 2000 Urban White Paper over whether disused urban (brownfield) or untapped rural (greenfield) sites are the best places to provide homes for the 3.8 million new households projected to be created between

1996 and 2021 (Groom, 1999) are largely irrelevant to the suburbs, much of which do not fall clearly into either category. The establishment of Local Strategic Partnerships (LSPs) between the public, private and community sectors is one of the concrete outcomes of the White Paper. Yet the Manchester Community Strategy 2002-12, agreed by the Manchester LSP and approved by Manchester City Council, applies to the whole local authority area and its prime concern is to improve deprived neighbourhoods (Manchester City Council, 2002), which is not surprising given that the DETR's Index of Local Deprivation shows that nearly 78% of the city's residents live in wards that are among the 10% most deprived nationally (Manchester Enterprises, 2001).

Even were resources decentralised to Didsbury and Hale, it is difficult to envisage them being distributed democratically given the heterogeneity of these neighbourhoods: who would represent the community? This is a problem that has been identified by other authors: "the fragmented nature of many communities and the fact that a few key individuals sometimes dominate community groups" (Foley and Martin, 2000, p 787). The current activists who defend the status quo in Didsbury and Hale would not be the best people to take a longer-term, strategic approach.

This highlights the fact that there is no identifiable body with responsibility for exploring sustainable development strategies for the good suburbs. There is no collective interest focused on the potentially crucial contribution of the suburbs to the competitiveness of the city as a whole through the attraction and retention of key professional workers. What prevails instead are the forcefully articulated but particularistic interests of self-selected residents, the profit-seeking priorities of private developers, and the bureaucratic rigidities of the state town-planning system. At national level, the government has placed major emphasis through its 'communities plan' on managing growth in the expanding communities of southern England and addressing the problems of failing housing markets in the less buoyant midlands and north (ODPM, 2003). It has also prioritised development on previously occupied brownfield sites. Consideration of the impact of socio-economic changes on established residential areas and, especially, of the role of the good suburb in enhancing competitive advantage remains, however, a gap in recent policy debates, with potentially serious and far-reaching consequences.

References

Amin, A. and Graham, S. (1997) 'The ordinary city', *Transactions of the Institute of British Geographers*, vol 22, no 4, pp 411-29.

Castells, M. (1989) *The informational city: Information technology, economic restructuring and the urban-regional process*, Oxford, Blackwell.

Devine, F., Britton, N.J., Mellor, R. and Halfpenny, P. (2003) 'Mobility and the middle classes: a case study of Manchester and the north west', *International Journal of Urban and Regional Research*, vol 27, no 3, pp 495-509.

Florida, R. (2002) *The rise of the creative class*, New York, NY: Basic Books.

Foley, P. and Martin, S. (2000) 'Perceptions of community led regeneration: community and central government viewpoints', *Regional Studies*, vol 34, no 8, pp 783-7.

French, S. and Leyshon, A. (2003) 'City of money?', in M. Boddy (ed) *Urban transformation and urban governance: Shaping the competitive city of the future*, Bristol: The Policy Press, pp 32-51.

Groom, B. (1999) 'Households projection sparks rural plea', *Financial Times*, p 1.

Harrison, J. (2001) *Skills 2001 – Forecasting report*, Manchester: Manchester Enterprises.

Manchester City Council (2002) *The Manchester community strategy 2002-2012*, (www.manchester.gov.uk/corporate/strategy/community.pdf).

Manchester Enterprises (2001) *City pride economic development plan*, Manchester: Manchester Enterprises.

Mellor, R. (1997) 'Cool times in a changing city', in N. Jewson and S. MacGregor (eds) *Transforming cities: Contested governance and new spatial divisions*, London: Routledge, pp 56-69.

National Statistics (1999) *Annual business inquiry*, London: National Statistics via Nomis.

ODPM (Office of the Deputy Prime Minister) (2003) *Creating sustainable communities: Building for the future*, London: ODPM.

Paris, C. (1977) 'Crisis in the inner city', *International Journal of Urban and Regional Research*, vol 2, pp 160-9.

Pascall, A. (1987) 'The vanishing city', *Urban Studies*, vol 24, pp 597-603.

Pro-Manchester (2002) *Promoting professional excellence* (www.pro-manchester.org.uk/about.asp).

Pysden, E. (2002) *Deals review* (www.pro-manchester.org.uk/news.asp?PageFlag=1andNewsld=91).

Quilley, S. (1999) 'Entrepreneurial Manchester: the genesis of elite consensus', *Antipode*, vol 31, no 2, pp 185-211.

Sassen, S. (1994) *Cities in a world economy*, London: Pine Forge Press.

Turok, I. (1999) 'Employment in British cities', *Radical Statistics*, vol 71.

FIFTEEN

The middle class and the future of London

Tim Butler

As an essentially global city, London has always had a tendency towards social and economic polarisation: a 'container' for the richest and the poorest in our society. Inner London is becoming increasingly middle class – that class now accounts for approximately 20% of its population. However, the visibility and influence of this group far outstrip its physical presence. At the same time, and to an extent paradoxically, an increasing proportion of the middle class can no longer afford to live in Inner London.

There is a key distinction, however, between an 'urban seeking' and an 'urban fleeing' middle class in South East England; between those wishing to 'live the city' and those who choose to commute in from the 'Home Counties' and beyond. More recently, important distinctions have also emerged between middle-class areas *within* the city; these areas take on different meanings and associations for residents and potential residents in turn attracting and then socialising them into the norms and values of the particular area. Other cities may have gentrified areas, but issues of geographic size and population mean that there simply is not the diversity of socio-spatial difference that we have found in London.

An increasing number of today's urban middle classes operate in a world with few physical boundaries in which space and time have become compressed and distorted. At the same time, many of them are desperate to lay down some personal parameters for their lives, particularly when there are children in the household. They are often frantic about the lack of structure in their own lives and particularly those of their children. The current process of gentrification in London is an attempt to reconcile this version of present with a somewhat nostalgic view of the past. This is manifested by a desire to build a 'local community' within the global city that maps onto an individualised set of values, backgrounds, aspirations and resources. This accounts for the differences between middle-class areas that we have found in Inner London. It is also the basis of contrast with non-metropolitan centres in the UK and elsewhere. This, I term a 'metropolitan habitus'. Following Bourdieu, the distinction is made between economic, cultural and social capital, which together make up the capital assets of individuals. In Bourdieu's (1986) model, 'cultural capital' exists in various forms, expressing the embodied dispositions and resources of the habitus. It has two different strains: 'incorporated' in the form of education and knowledge; and 'symbolic', being the capacity to define and legitimise cultural, moral and aesthetic values, standards and styles (for further discussion, see Butler, 2002; Butler with Robson, 2003).

These issues are important in policy terms. Should London continue to thrive as the key European staging point in the global financial system, then it has to be a place which is attractive to the inhabitants of that system who comprise a broad spectrum of the new professions. These people are often globally mobile and are less constrained than previous generations about which city they choose to live in. The choice is often not about whether to live in London or elsewhere in the UK but whether to live in London, Paris, Frankfurt, New York or Los Angeles. A key determinant in that decision is 'quality of life': not only the cultural and transport infrastructures, but also education and the opportunities for social reproduction, which are always at the heart of middle-class anxiety. It is not clear that economic competitiveness and social cohesion are necessary correlates, but it does seem that the middle classes feel a need for cultural sustenance and secure contexts for social reproduction – both broadly defined. It is likely that the failure to provide either of these will have major implications for London's economic competitiveness. In this view, the issue of education becomes the central policy issue facing central, regional and local government for London continuing to be an attractive place in which to live. Given the centrality of London to the success of the UK economy, education becomes a matter of national policy concern. Middle-class parents may be relatively agnostic about whether this is provided on a state or private, selective or comprehensive basis so long as it meets their needs for socialising their children into the next generation of top jobs. However, the failure to provide this on a universalistic and comprehensive basis may lead to ever-greater social polarisation in Inner London and this may have, in turn, a previously un-witnessed and malign effect on social cohesion on a day-to-day basis which will effect their quality of life. Prime Minister Tony Blair was right, therefore, at least for London, to identify the key policy issue as being 'education, education, education'. One indication of this problem is that not only was *none* of our respondents in our Barnsbury study area in Islington educating their children at a secondary school, but half of them were sending their primary school-age children to private school, whereas elsewhere parents were almost universally using local state *primary* schools. In the borough of Islington more generally, only 45% of those children at its primary schools proceeded to secondary school in the borough. To this extent, it is not just a middle-class issue.

What did the project set out to do?

The general background to the research focused around issues of economic competitiveness and social cohesion and their interrelations which were core issues for the ESRC Cities programme. The particular focus of this project however, was with a group who generally do not cause policy makers much loss of sleep: the middle classes. The urban middle class tends to be seen as a problem only insofar as it causes the displacement of existing and less privileged social groups. Our own 'take' on this has been rather different, which was to ask whether the urban middle class has the *potential* at least to act as a force for social inclusion. This was partly informed by previous work I had undertaken on the gentrification of Hackney in the 1980s (Butler, 1997). An important finding of that research was that these middle classes were more socially and politically radical and committed to a form of inclusive urban living than suggested by the gentrification literature with its emphasis on displacement. In addition, the collapse of the working-class leadership of the Labour Party in London and other major cities had left a power vacuum in urban governance (Boddy and Fudge, 1984; Gyford, 1985). This earlier work indicated that the middle classes had the potential to fill this vacuum in formal political institutions and at neighbourhood levels. The research, therefore, was aimed at investigating some of these issues across London. The pan-London aspect was important because it seemed apparent that the increasing diversification of the middle classes (Butler and Savage, 1995) was likely to have a spatial dimension in relation to their settlement of Inner London. We hypothesise that we were likely to find different relationships with neighbourhoods, non-middle-class groups and social/political institutions across our chosen fieldwork areas.

Objectives

We identified the following four objectives for the project:

- to identify what are the dominant patterns of middle-class settlement of Inner London and how these are differentiated (for instance, by occupational characteristics, social background, age cohort);
- to identify the consequences of middle-class settlement, particularly in terms of networks, patterns of association, the relations between work and non-work associations;
- to investigate to what extent these social and economic interactions involve other social groups and, if so, how these variations might be explained;
- to identify what one area might learn from another; in other words, are there policy recommendations that can be made to improve an area's attractiveness while minimising its 'downsides'?

The findings were not quite as expected. Although the project found significant differences between our areas, what their middle classes shared was a general disengagement from other social groups and a lack of involvement in both formal and informal aspects of urban governance. This contrasted to my earlier research on Hackney where many respondents had expressed a desire to get involved. For whatever reason (such as disinclination or lack of time), the middle classes of London do not appear to have taken up the mantle of civic involvement. This is not to argue that they are not involved in issues of political or social concern, but rather these appear to be undertaken either as part of their formal employment or else by largely passive membership of charitable-type organizations. The main dimension of involvement, which was predicted in the original research design, concerns education. However, our finding is that this has been negotiated almost entirely instrumentally either by purchasing private educational solutions or by constructing complex educational strategies to negotiate the new market in state educational provision. This suggests that the contemporary 'downside' of gentrification is no longer displacement, but social polarisation and social exclusion.

Methods

Having undertaken an analysis of census data, initial decisions were made about where to concentrate the fieldwork. In particular, this analysis pointed us towards splitting the research between North and South London. In the original proposal for funding, although the areas were not identified, there was a discernible North London bias. The gentrification of areas of South London has been relatively recent and under-researched; carrying out fieldwork here has, we hope, gone some way to correct this bias in the literature.

The project's selection of areas was driven by a concern to reflect both the history of gentrification of Inner London over the past 30 years and to embrace the primary divisions within the middle class. The term gentrification was coined by Ruth Glass (Glass, 1964) and can be traced back to the 'upgrading' of areas of Islington, which was investigated by Peter Williams and others (Williams, 1976; see also Carpenter and Lees, 1995, for a good account). This process of 'gentrification by collective social action' (Warde, 1991) spread across North and subsequently South London from the late 1970s onwards. A more recent phenomenon, characterised by Warde (1991) as 'gentrification by capital', has been the regeneration of large swathes of London Docklands both north and south of the Thames. We set out to 'capture' aspects of this history but also to identify areas that had apparently been colonised by different sections of the middle classes.

Following earlier work (Butler and Savage, 1995; Butler, 1997), we decided to base this around Savage et al's (1992) approach to intra-class divisions within the middle class. This considers the middle classes not just in terms of occupational divisions but also those based around lifestyle and values. Savage et al identify two main groups: 'liberal ascetics' mainly, but not entirely, working in the 'welfare professions'; and 'corporate undistinctives' who are associated mainly with the managerial and senior administrative sectors. He also somewhat tentatively identifies a third group that he terms 'postmoderns', whose tastes do not easily break down into either major group. This group, it was thought, might prove to be very visible in gentrified Inner London. The strength of this approach is that it moves beyond crude splits into managers versus professionals, private versus public sector workers. This is particularly important in contemporary London where middle-class careers and occupations have undergone very rapid change in the shadow of globalisation and the creation of a so-called 'knowledge economy' based around financial services and the production and distribution of knowledge and culture in their widest forms. Following our analysis of census data, these theoretical and historical concerns, and our own observational work, we selected the following six areas in which to undertake fieldwork (Figure 15.1):

1. Telegraph Hill (New Cross, in the London Borough of Lewisham);
2. Brixton (Herne Hill and Tulse Hill, Brixton);
3. Between the Commons (Battersea, Wandsworth);
4. Barnsbury (Islington);
5. London Fields (Dalston, Hackney);
6. Docklands. This was subdivided into three areas:
   - The Isle of Dogs (Tower Hamlets);
   - Surrey Quays (Southwark);
   - Britannia Village (Newham).

We interviewed approximately 75 respondents in each of the six areas (equally divided between the sub-areas in the case of Docklands), giving a total of some 450 respondents in all. We used a questionnaire combining structured and semi-structured questions to generate both qualitative and quantitative data. Interviews were conducted face-to-face in respondents' homes. The quantitative data were analysed using Statistical Package for the Social Sciences (SPSS). The qualitative data were transcribed and analysed according to thematic issues. While not yielding a statistically representative sample in a strict sense, we believe the survey to be broadly representative of the middle class in each area.

Figure 15.1: London, showing the study areas

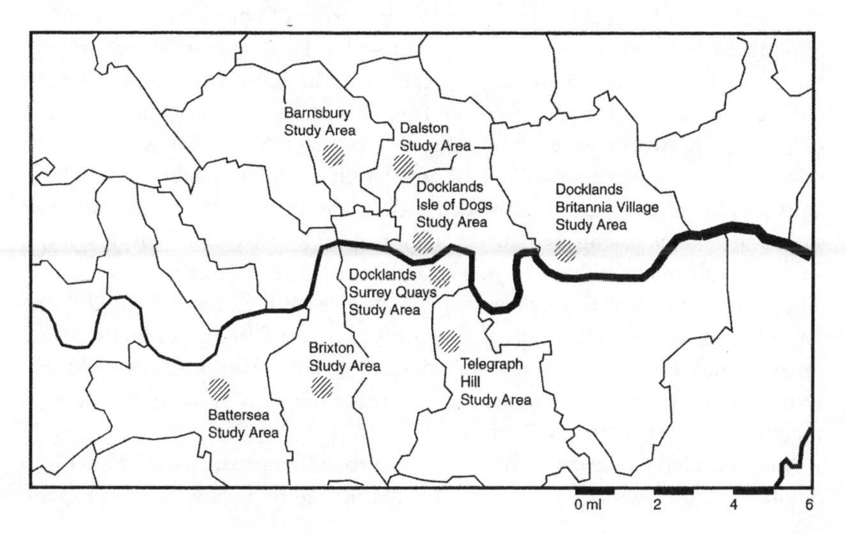

Moreover, the large-scale qualitative information generated a particularly rich resource. Findings from the study are reported in depth elsewhere (see Butler and Robson, 2001; Robson and Butler, 2001; Butler with Robson, 2003).

Summary of key findings

Given the importance that is placed in this research on the difference between the areas, the main findings are discussed in relation to the individual areas (a much fuller consideration of both the findings and the conceptual issues raised by the research can be found in Butler with Robson, 2003). The findings show that there is a metropolitan habitus (Butler, 2002) which is then subdivided socially and spatially into a series of 'mini habituses'; there is, however, a danger that we map these differences to the exclusion of what they share in common. It is likely to be the case that the differences between the various 'mini habituses' pale into insignificance compared to the contrast between the overall sense of a metropolitan habitus and that occupied by the middle class taken as a whole, whether nationally, in other provincial cities, or in non-urban settings.

None of the research areas is what might be termed middle class in a conventional understanding of the term – nearly all are ethnically mixed; home ownership is in a minority; there are more poor people than those with high incomes; and car ownership is below average. There are important nuances of difference, but it is important to stress that this is an *urban* middle class, which practises, as the journalist Nicholas Tomalin (the original model for the Marc Boxer cartoon in Islington) put it, "conspicuous thrift" (Carpenter and Lees, 1995, p 298). This is an urban middle class in the making which, much to the frustration of the marketing profession, has to be teased out from under the urban poor with whom they cohabit spatially.

Taken as a whole, our respondents were attracted to living in areas with 'people like us'; broadly, although Docklands was a notable exception, each of the areas had identifiable characteristics in terms of social background and respondents' contemporary outlook and lifestyles. Respondents identified with these and found them to be among the main attractions for living in their particular area. They tended to make friends with people like themselves and their social networks were often based around friendships that went back to university, and sometimes to school and family. Children often formed the basis for the parents' social networks, particularly in Telegraph Hill. All areas shared a general disengagement from non-middle-class social groups and a lack of involvement in both formal and informal aspects of urban governance. The main dimension of involvement for those with children was, predictably enough, education, although this manifested itself in individualised and instrumental ways. There was little evidence of what Hirschmann (1970) has termed 'voice' or 'loyalty', nor (perhaps unsurprisingly given our methodology) was there much evidence of 'exit'.

All respondents shared a commitment to urban living, partly out of a wish to distance themselves from their own upbringing and partly a wish not to spend long hours travelling to and from work, but mainly because they wanted the excitement and culture that they saw only a cosmopolitan city like London as being able to provide. The suburbs and small towns and villages from which many came were 'boring'. University had provided an escape from this and London enabled them to continue that way of life into adulthood. This, of course, also matched the transformation that had taken place in the economy, in which middle-class jobs are now to be found less in managing 'Fordist' enterprises and more in the emerging service sectors of the 'new economy' – the so-called 'weightless world' (Coyle, 1999).

The nature of the commitment to urban living varied considerably however. Most respondents in Battersea hankered after the country life, but it simply was not a practical proposition at this stage in their lives when at least one member of the household needed to work long hours in the City (of London). The ready property market and relatively good rail and road links, however, kept alive the idea of eventually making it to Wiltshire or somewhere else commutable. Respondents in Docklands were not anti-urban but felt that where they lived was largely a relationship born of convenience rather than commitment; the attraction of Docklands was its lack of commitment. Perhaps this was symbolised by the fact that, unlike the other areas, this was 'newbuild' gentrification: there was little possibility of any community 'in the mind' or sense of history with which one might form an identification with the area – in fact, quite the opposite.

It is this notion of a community 'in the mind' which both unites and separates our respondents. There were different narratives of identification in each of our areas. In nearly every case, this represented an abstracted and idealised version of community. Again, this was probably weakest in Battersea where, as I have argued elsewhere (Butler and Robson, 2001; Butler and Robson, 2003a), respondents tended to 'motor along' on their substantial stocks of economic capital whereas in other areas the gentrification process depended, at least nominally, on the deployment of varying amounts of social and cultural capital. Even in Battersea, however, it was apparent that respondents were able to draw on considerable stocks of social capital if needed, although normally this was regarded as a latent resource and relations were conducted through the market – 'eating out as opposed to joining in'. The well-developed local consumption infrastructure, as it were, mediated relationships through spending.

Given the relatively long-standing nature of gentrification in Battersea (Munt, 1987), it might even be argued that gentrification itself has become the idealised narrative – in that elsewhere respondents would go to some lengths to distance themselves from the term. This gives Battersea a peculiar cognitive map – the middle-class community is highly bounded and inward-looking, and only opens outwards to equivalent areas like Clapham and Fulham. There is no sense here of the middle classes being embedded in a more 'authentic', volatile or rounded London. This is a case of isolation based not upon the raising of the metaphorical drawbridge but in the extensive colonisation of a swathe of the city, the very fabric of which has been transformed in the image of a private/managerial/

hedonistic group. This is the creation of a new urban space, in which Battersea has been lifted out of the local, and into the global, economy. Of all the areas we studied, it conformed most closely to Neil Smith's (1996) notion of a 'revanchist' middle-class gentrification in which there has been a 'retaking' of the city.

Barnsbury has much in common with Battersea. Upper Street in Islington and Northcote Road in Wandsworth are both places to go for a night out in which restaurants, themed bars, kitchen/bathroom shops and estate agents have edged out the retailers of a past era. Both have become global spaces, servicing the international service-class diaspora in a safe environment that acknowledges the cultural capital of the customer – even if it involves a rather repetitious narrative about the life cycle of seared tuna. While Barnsbury surfs the wave of globalisation along with Battersea, it does so in discernibly different ways. Its population is an equally solid middle class but, whereas those who make up Battersea's population might be corporate financiers drawn from 'the home counties', those in Barnsbury tend to be legal and other professionals largely drawn via Oxbridge from a national, if predominantly middle-class, background.

Unlike Battersea, where a sympathetic Conservative local council has enabled gentrification, in Islington the process of re-gentrification is largely based on the idea of buying into a social capital-rich environment by a group which does not have the same time or commitment to give to the area. A once coherent narrative of a mixed-community settlement (white working-class natives, liberal middle-class incomers) is now being fractured by the presence of incomers who neither belong to, nor understand, this history. The newcomers are finding the script difficult to 'read' – even if it is in their interests to do so. The values of inner-urban community experience are being displaced by values revolving around money and market-based solutions to Inner London life, à la Battersea. This has disrupted the continuity of the established community – although this would still appear to be strong – and raised the level of unease between the 'haves', on the one hand, and 'Islington born and bred' 'have-nots', on the other. Whereas the original gentrifiers largely educated their children in the local schools at all levels, not a single respondent had a child at a secondary school in Islington. Upper Street has, almost literally, moved into another world. It has been lifted out of the local economy into the global one, as a central part of the new metropolis. This has generated the development of a peculiar virtual and privatised landscape in which, despite its apparent 'buzz', social interactions are limited, with very little possibility of accidental meetings (there being no more 'local' pubs or shops, for example).

Brixton, like Barnsbury and Battersea, has become a global space but a very different one. Long the centre for London's African-Caribbean community, what middle-class Brixton demonstrates is an identification and/or accommodation with other (non-middle-class) groups. Previously, I have described relations here between individuals and groups as 'tectonic' (Robson and Butler, 2001). This describes the ways in which they move across each other which do not apparently involve much interaction, but rather a high degree of awareness of each other's presence. The experience of rubbing along with others of different cultural, social and ethnic background is a very important element of the frisson of living in a somewhat uncomfortable and 'edgy' area. This group can be described as being, in some senses, in flight from the obligations of social capital (Butler and Robson, 2001); they are seeking out difference and not attempting to huddle around with 'people like us', so characteristic of Inner-London gentrification elsewhere (Butler, 1997). Brixton is moving on from being a site for London's African-Caribbean population to being a focus for many of the manifestations of current globalisms of people, culture and entertainment. Multicultural globalism *is* Brixton and it is this atmosphere that is attractive to our respondents here. The social and cognitive maps of the area which emerge out of this dialectical 'Brixton of the mind' make it possible for the middle classes – and particularly this ascetic fraction – to include themselves in a model of urban living which is 'vibrant', heterogeneous, informally segregated and paradoxical but 'real' – and almost entirely white.

In contrast to the celebration of different aspects of contemporary globalisation in Barnsbury, Battersea and Brixton, elsewhere we discovered a sense of withdrawal from the global city and particularly its structures of consumption. In both Telegraph Hill and London Fields, there was a conscious effort to build 'enclaves', part of whose attraction was the absence of such infrastructures and their links to the rest of the world. In their place, we found social capital rich networks of personal relationships that gave the areas their particular structures of meaning. One of the things respondents like about Telegraph Hill is a sense of permanence that gives a sense of 'belonging'; most respondents had no intention of moving in the foreseeable future. The sense of belonging is celebrated as being open-minded towards others but, in reality, it is about different groups of liberal/welfare professionals *getting on with each other* as opposed to people from different ethnic or social groups (Robson and Butler, 2001). Networking among residents begins at the gate of the local primary school, which has been systematically adopted and transformed by 'the Hill'. Parents then create sub-narratives for exploiting the 'local circuit of education', be it in the extensive provision of high-quality private schooling in the south of neighbouring Southwark or state selective schools, one of which is located in the research area. Telegraph Hill becomes an enclave, a 'village in the mind', from which forays are made into the wider city.

London Fields, while sharing some of these quasi-localist tendencies, is rather more humble in both its physical disposition and its narrative construction. This is the least formed 'group' in the study, and therefore the most difficult to typify. Of all our areas, this is the one in which some kind of 'pioneer spirit' is still easily discernible. Although it is, perhaps, both ontologically and socially fragile, it has generated a coherent narrative based on the non-normative and multicultural and, to some extent, risk or 'edge living'. Two things emerge as particularly interesting. First, a 'residue of community' narrative, in which a 'Hackney of the mind' has, as one of its characteristics, an (oppositionally inflected) attachment to communal life, of which the residual working-class population is the guarantor, and a sense of loyalty to what is seen as one of the last unique and 'authentic' places in the capital. Second, the area's connection to the new 'artistic East End' – in which a novel cognitive/cultural map connects it to Clerkenwell, Shoreditch, Old Street and Hoxton (Zukin, 1988; Foord, 1999).

Finally, over the last two decades, Docklands has been successfully transformed, despite a number of hiccups and false starts (Foster, 1999). Almost all the respondents were living in Docklands because they wanted somewhere to live that was near to work and involved minimum social and maintenance commitments. Very few had children living with them – quite a number were what are described as 'empty nesters'; often there was a second property outside London to which they went at weekends, where perhaps the family had been brought up or, in some cases, still lived there full time. Docklands' respondents were most likely to go out at night both to eat and for cultural or other leisure pursuits. They were not attracted however to the '24/7 lifestyle' which is often promoted in the new city-centre developments in Bristol, Manchester, Leeds, Newcastle and Birmingham (see, for example, Lambert and Boddy, 2002). Many were tied to working extended hours in the 'City', which often involved after-hours entertaining. They did not wish to become integrated into their neighbourhoods, or become friendly with their neighbours; rather, they simply wanted 'efficient' living arrangements with minimal commitments. With such long hours, their lives were perhaps more dominated by work than those working in other areas. It was more difficult to characterise them as coming from any particular social or regional background. They were also less sensitive to the social contradictions of globalisation than those in other areas, neither wishing to 'surf it' nor retreat from it and its attendant consumption infrastructures. Their patterns of association were less local than respondents in other areas and they were more likely to have made their friendships through work.

Having presented a very basic outline of the research areas and the main trends in our findings, which are focused around similarities and differences between the fieldwork areas, this chapter now turns to two specific issues arising from the research. The first is socio-spatial divisions and the second social reproduction and education. Lack of space prevents a fuller discussion of these or other issues but they are developed in several of the publications arising from the project, notably Butler with Robson (2003).

Socio-spatial divisions

There was broad support in the data for those sociological claims that point to increasing divisions within the middle classes (Savage et al, 1992; Butler and Savage, 1995). These divisions are not simply sectoral (public versus private) nor between managers and professionals, but rather appear to be based around lifestyle and cultural differences. The research suggests that, at least in a large metropolitan area such as London, this has spatial manifestations (that is, people live in areas they identify with and in turn this shapes the area). Table 15.1 indicates that there are associations between respondents' place of residence, their occupation and the nature of their employer. Telegraph Hill and Brixton have a higher proportion of state-sector employees than other areas while Battersea and Docklands have a greater proportion working in the private sector. Intriguingly, London Fields has a high number who are self-employed. Barnsbury respondents are more evenly divided across sectors.

Table 15.1 also considers respondents' jobs; it is immediately apparent that 'professional' employment is the dominant form. This is particularly the case in Barnsbury, Telegraph Hill and London Fields where it accounts for over two thirds of all respondents (in the case of London Fields nearly three quarters). The highest concentration of managers is found in Barnsbury and Battersea, although many of these managerial occupations are ones that require a set of professional skills. This points us back towards Savage et al's (1992) conception of 'postmodern' in which traditional notions of managers and professionals have come together in new ways. Few of these managers are old-style industrial managers, while equally few of the professionals are self-account solicitors, doctors and so on. For the most part, they are highly educated people working in small and 'flat hierarchy' teams at the interface of the state and financial sectors. The presence and absence of those working in the artistic/literary areas is interesting; in London Fields and, to a lesser extent, Telegraph Hill and Brixton, these groups are a significant presence, elsewhere less so.

A third way of characterising the nuances of these variations within the metropolitan habitus is to focus on voting behaviour. Previous research has shown that Inner-London gentrifiers have a tendency to support the Labour party compared to the middle classes generally – even when their occupations are controlled for (Butler, 1997), and this is confirmed by the present research. There are, however, interesting variations by area which are illustrated in Table 15.2. Even in Battersea, which is at the heart of Conservative Wandsworth (a

Table 15.1: Socio-demographic profile of respondents by area

	Telegraph Hill	Brixton	Battersea	Barnsbury	London Fields	Docklands	Total
Mean age	46.8	41.5	43.4	45.6	47.3	42.0	44.5
Living with spouse/not same sex partner (%)	78.6	50.0	54.7	68.9	62.1	41.3	59.8
Public sector (%)	39.7	37.9	16.4	27.9	33.3	22.6	29.5
Private (%)	18.9	25.8	47.5	36.1	21.1	56.7	34.2
Voluntary sector (%)	8.6	8.6	3.3	9.8	7.0	3.8	6.9
Self-employed (%)	32.8	27.6	32.8	26.3	38.6	17.0	29.4
Managers (%)	13.9	18.5	22.4	22.7	12.3	22.8	19.6
Professionals (%)	69.2	60.0	64.2	69.7	73.9	71.9	69.1
Admin/ Secretarial (%)	3.1	9.2	7.5	3.0	0.0	1.8	4.2
Artistic %	9.2	9.2	6.0	3.0	13.9	0.0	7.1

Table 15.2: National party political support (%)

	Telegraph Hill	Brixton	Battersea	Barnsbury	London Fields	Docklands	Total (*n*)
Labour	60.0	68.1	48.6	52.8	68.1	22.7	53.7 (227)
Conservative	2.9	2.8	14.9	8.3	2.9	25.8	9.5 (40)
Liberal Democrats	15.7	8.3	13.5	15.3	15.9	15.2	13.9 (59)
Other	17.1	18.1	20.3	18.1	11.6	27.3	18.7 (79)
Don't know	2.9	1.4	0.0	2.8	1.4	4.5	2.1 (9)
Wouldn't vote	1.4	1.4	2.7	2.8	0.0	4.5	2.1 (9)
Total (*n*)	100.0 (70)	100.0 (72)	100.0 (74)	100.0 (72)	100.0 (69)	100.0 (66)	100.0 (423)

'pathfinding Thatcherite' local authority of the 1980s, still controlled by the Conservatives), nearly half of the respondents said they would support the Labour party if there were a *general* election the next day. Only in Docklands was support for Labour weak. Significantly, respondents' support for the Labour party dropped off in most areas when asked who they would support at a *local* election.

Taken together, the data from these tables can be taken to support the view outlined above that there is a metropolitan habitus which is distinct from that of the national middle-class habitus. It is, however, one which is nuanced by socio-spatial divisions. If there is one area in which the metropolitan middle class demonstrates its fragility, however, it is in respect to education.

Education

Education remains a dominating middle-class concern for those with, or contemplating having, children. Gentrification is no longer a phenomenon largely confined to the single and childless but includes many households with children in which both parents are in paid employment. Households in different areas resolved the education dilemma, notably the primary–secondary transition, in different ways; in Brixton there was a propensity to leave London when the children reached secondary school age. These complex findings are discussed in some detail elsewhere (Butler and Robson, 2003b) but can be summarised in the following table (Table 15.3) – the figures for Docklands are included but there were so few children there (itself significant) that it is not discussed here.

The data on education and schooling show that in every area, other than Barnsbury and to a lesser extent Brixton, the overwhelming number of respondents with children were happy to educate their children at state primary schools in the area in which they lived. However, at secondary level, the

Table 15.3: School destinations of respondents' children by area

	Primary			Secondary			
	State	Private	Total (*n*)	State non-selective	State selective	Private	Total (*n*)
Telegraph Hill	89	11	100 (18)	43	29	29	100 (38)
Brixton	100	0	100 (9)	67	0	33	100 (12)
Battersea	82	18	100 (17)	18	8	77	100 (16)
Barnsbury	56	44	100 (16)	16	5	79	100 (19)
London Fields	100	0	100 (13)	45	0	55	100 (11)
Docklands	33	67	100 (3)	0	0	100	100 (2)
Total (*n*)	82 (62)	18 (14)	100 (76)	38 (37)	13 (13)	48 (49)	100 (98)

picture is very different. In both Barnsbury and Battersea, over three quarters of the children were being educated privately as were over half in London Fields. In the case of Barnsbury and Brixton, not a single child was at a secondary school in the borough of residence. It is only in Telegraph Hill that children are being educated in any great number in the state sector and even here the majority are at state selective schools. These findings reinforce those of Stephen Ball about the ways in which the middle classes in London act strategically, seeking out the best advantages for their children within the city's increasingly metropolitan-wide education markets (Ball et al, 1995; Gewirtz et al, 1995; Ball and Vincent, 1998; Reay and Ball, 1998). Only in Brixton is the state non-selective sector the most common form of secondary schooling; yet, our interviews show that it is here that parents are most likely to leave London when the children approach the transition to secondary schooling. In London Fields, which is very similar to Brixton, they are more pragmatic about using private schools or in supporting their children through non-selective state education and staying in London. There are strong parallels here with the pursuit of education strategies and residential strategies identified in a provincial urban context by Boddy et al (Chapter Four of this volume).

The data on education suggest that there is an increasingly de facto segregation between middle-class and other children. This is confirmed, spectacularly so, in Islington, which is becoming noticeably 'hollowed out' (this is particularly ironic given the attraction of its 'social capital rich heritage' to contemporary incoming gentrifiers). The policy downsides associated with gentrification have become less ones of displacement and increasingly those of social polarisation: the two groups and their children move in entirely separate worlds (Butler, 2003). This is further reinforced by an analysis of the friendship patterns of respondents and their children, which show them to be highly endogenous in social class terms (Butler, 2003). Respondents' social and leisure activities do not involve them in local areas and there is little evidence of social or political involvement (Butler and Robson, 2003a, 2003b).

Lessons and implications for policy

The research reinforces and supports the existing assumption about gentrification – that it has potentially malign consequences for less powerful groups. I would argue, however, that the focus on displacement is now mistaken because what we are seeing is a situation of polarisation operating across both economic markets and social fields, notably those of consumption, education, employment and housing. There is a remarkable symmetry about how the middle classes operate here, although the nuances are significantly and symbolically different in each of the areas (Butler with Robson, 2003). The overall effect, however, is that, increasingly, owner-occupation in Inner London is restricted to relatively wealthy incomers – those excluded comprise not only the usual suspects of key workers (nurses, police and teachers) but also doctors and university professors among others. Increasingly, only the well paid mainly in the private sector can now afford to move into many of Inner London's gentrified areas. These groups are distinguished not only by their relative wealth and cultural capital but also by their whiteness (98% of our respondents were white). It is also likely that the lack of adequate state education and indeed the pressure on high-quality private education is going to be the single largest disincentive for middle-class families to live in Inner London (Hamnett, 2003).

The findings indicate a concerning lack of involvement in civic governance. Very few respondents were involved in formal or informal organizations – as local councillors, school governors or magistrates. Their focus was work, the household and play. These are matters of concern for policy because it would appear that the middle classes are becoming less altruistic with their time. It is not clear, however, what the solutions to these problems might be except to enable further improvements in education and the availability of affordable housing. It is an instructive, if perhaps uncomfortable, finding that the area where there was most satisfaction with local state educational provision was Battersea and the areas with least were in the Labour heartlands of Lambeth and Islington. Wandsworth pioneered the building of both private schools and state selective schools precisely to encourage middle-class gentrification. It is now well provided for in both segments of the market, although overall its state schools still perform below the national average. There may be lessons here, however, particularly for Islington where those families who wish to educate their children in the state sector either seek out selective schools some distance away (Camden School for girls, Brompton Oratory or Latymer) or move elsewhere in North London (for example, to the catchment area of Fortismere School in Muswell Hill).

At present, however, it needs to be stressed most respondents enjoy living in London not just for its easy accessibility to work but because they feel themselves to be part of a metropolitan culture. Most negotiate easily, although reluctantly, the downsides of crime, grime and particularly education but there seems sufficient evidence from our research to argue that they may not always go on being able or prepared to do this. It seems particularly sad that education, which was central to the post-Second World War 'settlement' based around equality of opportunity, is increasingly becoming the instrument of growing social polarisation in Inner London.

References

Ball, S. and Vincent, C. (1998) '"I heard it on the grapevine": "hot" knowledge and school choice', *British Journal of Sociology of Education*, vol 19, no 3, pp 377-400.

Ball, S., Bowe, R. and Gewirtz, S. (1995) 'Circuits of schooling: a sociological exploration of parental choice of school in social class contexts', *Sociological Review*, vol 43, pp 52-78.

Boddy, M. and Fudge, C. (eds) (1984) *Local socialism*, London and Basingstoke: Macmillan.

Butler, T. (1997) *Gentrification and the middle classes*, Aldershot: Ashgate.

Butler, T. (2002) 'Thinking global but acting local: the middle classes in the city', *Sociological Research Online*, vol 7, no 3 (www.socresonline.org.uk/7/3/butler.html).

Butler, T. (2003) 'Living in the bubble: gentrification and its "others" in North London', *Urban Studies*, vol 40, no 12, pp 2469-86.

Butler, T. and Robson, G. (2001) 'Social capital, gentrification and neighbourhood change in London: a comparison of three South London neighbourhoods', *Urban Studies*, vol 38, no 12, pp 2145-62.

Butler, T. and Robson, G. (2003a) 'Negotiating their way in: the middle classes, gentrification and their deployment of capital in a globalizing metropolis', *Urban Studies*, vol 40, no 9, pp 1791-809.

Butler, T. and Robson, G. (2003b) 'Plotting the middle classes: gentrification and circuits of education', *Housing Studies*, vol 18, pp 5-28.

Butler, T. with Robson, G. (2003) *London calling: The middle classes and the making of inner London*, Oxford: Berg.

Butler, T. and Savage, M. (eds) (1995) *Social change and the middle classes*, London: UCL Press.

Carpenter, J. and Lees, L. (1995) 'Gentrification in New York, London and Paris: an international comparison', *International Journal of Urban and Regional Research*, vol 19, pp 286-303.

Foord, J. (1999) 'Creative Hackney: reflections on hidden art', *Rising East: The Journal of East London Studies*, vol 3, no 2, pp 38-66.

Foster, J. (1999) *Docklands: Cultures in conflict, worlds in collision*, London: UCL Press.

Gewirtz, S., Ball, S.J. and Bowe, R. (1995) *Markets, choice and equity in education*, Buckingham: Open University Press.

Glass, R. (1964) *London: Aspects of change*, MacGibbon and Kee Report no 3, London: Centre for Urban Studies.

Gyford, J. (1985) *The politics of local socialism*, London: George Allen and Unwin.

Hamnett, C. (2003) 'Gentrification and the remaking of middle class Inner London', *Urban Studies*, vol 40, no 12, pp 2401-26.

Hirschmann, A. (1970) *Exit voice and loyalty*, Harvard, MA: Harvard University Press.

Lambert, C. and Boddy, M. (2002) 'Transforming the city: post-recession gentrification and re-urbanisation', Paper delivered at the conference 'Upward Neighbourhood Trajectories: Gentrification in a New Century', Glasgow, September.

Munt, I. (1987) 'Economic restructuring, culture and gentrification: a case study of Battersea, London', *Environment and Planning A: Government and planning*, vol 19, pp 1175-97.

Reay, D. and Ball, S. (1998) '"Making their minds up": family dynamics of school choice', *British Educational Research Journal*, vol 24, no 4, pp 431-48.

Robson, G. and Butler, T. (2001) 'Coming to terms with London: middle-class communities in a global city', *International Journal of Urban and Regional Research*, vol 25, no 1, pp 70-86.

Savage, M., Barlow, J., Dickens, P. and Fielding, A. (1992) *Property bureaucracy and culture: Middle class formation in contemporary Britain*, London: Routledge.

Smith, N. (1996) *The new urban frontier: Gentrification and the revanchist city*, London: Routledge.

Warde, A. (1991) 'Gentrification as consumption issues of class and gender', *Environment and Planning D: Society and space*, vol 6, pp 75-95.

Williams, P. (1976) 'The role of institutions in the inner London housing markets: the case of Islington', *Transactions of the Institute of British Geographers*, vol 3 (new series), pp 72-82.

Zukin, S. (1988) *Loft living: Culture and capital in urban change*, London: Radius.

Part Six: Ethnicity, enterprise and social cohesion

SIXTEEN

Whose hidden assets? Inner-city potential for social cohesion and economic competitiveness

Jo Foord and Norman Ginsburg

This chapter takes up two themes within contemporary academic and policy debate on the regeneration of poor urban areas. The first theme concerns the extent of social capital within such areas. We argue that there is substantial endogenous or hidden social capital in some poor areas, but that this is often isolated from wider power structures and, hence, insufficiently recognised and used in regeneration initiatives. The second theme focuses on the emergence of multicultural and creative enclaves within some inner-city locations. Here the presence of entrepreneurialism and creativity have been identified and lauded as key elements of successful revitalisation. We suggest, however, that much of the implied optimism about the impact of newly discovered 'creative entrepreneurialism' needs to be reconsidered.

With respect to social capital development, the current local policy discourse has emphasised particular, normative types of networks and associational activity, perhaps to the exclusion of others. The networks and associations that are recognised are largely those conforming to a greater or lesser extent with norms of participatory social interaction, contributing to conventional forms of local social capital. Likewise, the forms of behaviour that are seen positively to contribute to creative entrepreneurialism fuse social networking, trust and risk taking with core values of competitive economic activity. Before discussing our findings and policy implications, a brief review of interpretations of social capital and creative entrepreneurialism is appropriate.

The presence or absence of social capital has emerged as a prominent explanation for differential levels of social and cultural cohesion found in particular areas of cities. As Stoker argues (Chapter Twenty of this volume), social capital is created out of social networks and associational activity which require reciprocal relationships, accepted norms, shared values and sanctions to be acted out between trusted individuals (Schuller et al, 2000). Social capital is now widely perceived by social scientists and policy makers as a significant asset or resource within communities of all kinds, whether they are communities of place, interest, profession or identity. Lack of social capital, it is implied, contributes to social exclusion. Hence, it is argued that sustainable regeneration of poor areas necessitates the regeneration of social capital alongside physical and economic investment in housing, employment training, job creation and so on. Outsiders' stereotypical view of poor areas is that they suffer a social capital deficit or generate the wrong sort of social capital (for example, the close associations linked to deviant or criminal activity). This is very much the Etzionian communitarian view, and the implication of Putnam's work. The development of social cohesion, however, cannot be a top-down process. As Forrest and Kearns (2001, p 2137) put it, it has to be "a bottom-up process founded upon local social capital". Anthropologists and sociologists have long recognised that there are often strong and constructive forms of social capital in poor areas in terms of, for example, ties of kinship and ethnic solidarity. Hence as Portes and Landolt (1996, p 20) have said, "there is considerable social capital in ghetto areas, but the assets obtainable through it seldom allow participants to rise above their poverty". The reasons for this are legion, of course, including institutionalised processes of discrimination and structural economic inequality. Portes and Landolt (1996, p 21) go on to bemoan the lack of "a reliable formula to produce social solidarity and trust in communities lacking them". The current policy discourse on facilitating social capital building at least has the virtue of addressing this head-on.

Useful distinctions have emerged to describe the different intensities of the social relations generating social capital. Hence the contrast between 'weak' and 'strong' ties in networks of trust is made, which has highlighted the importance of weak ties or looser networks as key resources, and has shown the limitations of inward-looking strong ties. More recently this has been expanded to 'three main types' of social capital (PIU, 2002, pp 11-12) namely: bonding, bridging and linking social capital:

- *bonding social capital* exists within tight-knit groups or communities where there are strong ties, constructed around a clear identity, obviously including kin;
- *bridging social capital* takes the form of looser ties, for example between different ethnic groups, among professionals or business associates;
- *linking social capital* is "characterised by connections between those with differing levels of power or social status" (PIU, 2002, p 12), for example links between established professional and administrative structures and local communities.

Generators of social capital in poor areas, such as ethnic minority voluntary organisations or ethnic minority small businesses, typically possess considerable bonding social capital, varying levels of bridging social capital and in many cases little or no linking social capital. These barriers to more effective use of local social capital in poor areas were addressed in our research.

Ideas of creative entrepreneurialism underpin several different commentaries on the state of inner-city economies. These include Porter's market-led advocacy of inner-city potential, Landry's appeal to economic innovation through the application of creativity and Worpole and Greenhalgh's descriptive celebration of 'rich mix' cultural diversity as a backdrop to new economic activity. In their different ways, all three commentaries imply that cultural diversity, proximity to the economic core and comparatively lower operating costs in poor areas generate significant competitive opportunities for turning around failing economies. Porter (1995, 2001) suggests that business should act out of entrepreneurial self-interest to take advantage of inner cities as places with great potential for new enterprise.

Landry (2000) outlines another key component of this creative entrepreneurial environment – creativity itself – which, he argues, has become critical to the success of city economies. He defines creativity as a *social process*. Rather than individual instances of original achievement resulting from intense moments of absorption in a task, creativity emerges out of social interaction and trusted social ties that allow experimentation and risk taking. This form of creativity enables both social and economic innovation. Mobilising creativity is seen as more likely in environments where past economic conventions and labour practices have already been dismantled. The derelict urban landscapes of inner urban areas are not presented as problems: they are recast as arenas in which innovative creative enterprise can emerge.

In an extrapolation of this argument, Worpole and Greenhalgh (1999) suggest that the 'creative city' potential of the inner areas lies in their very intensity and cultural diversity. Cities, and especially those like London which have a global reach, are home to ethnically diverse populations with a multiplicity of languages and lifestyles, behaviours and aspirations. It is in these milieu that minority ethnic businesses have emerged to serve the cultural and economic-entrepreneurial needs of mixed populations. Cultural difference and diversity become the source of inspiration and, therefore, of new ideas that can be marketed by cultural industries.

Such interpretations set a particular agenda for poor areas. Rather than universally failing, these areas are seen as having clear potential: particularly economic potential which emerges out of a mixture of underused infrastructural resources (land, buildings and symbolic landscapes), cultural assets (culturally diverse practices, ethnic goods and identities and versatile labour), and a propensity for creative working (self-directed, self motivated, networked and risk taking self-employment). Underpinning such economic potential, it is assumed, are both traditional ethnically bounded social ties and the new social networks of friendship and communities of interest that are undervalued and underused. This rethinking of the assets of inner areas of cities goes some way to countering the singular representation of these poor city locations as socially chaotic, marginal and uncompetitive.

Our research examined the contributions to social capital and creative entrepreneurialism made by neighbourhood regeneration organisations, the black voluntary sector, ethnic minority businesses and local cultural producers within inner North East London, comprising the London boroughs of Islington,

Hackney, Haringey and Tower Hamlets. Social deprivation indices rank these boroughs, and particular wards within them, as among the most socially and economically excluded areas in London and Britain as a whole (DETR, 2000). The extent of ethnic diversity in the area adds a layer of complexity to the socio-spatial dynamics of inclusion–exclusion to an extent not found anywhere else in Britain (Johnston et al, 2002). Thus, our area is one that has long been problematised (and stigmatised) with its social, creative and entrepreneurial assets left under-recognised and under-resourced. The project's first aim was to investigate the extent to which particular voluntary and private sector activities counter social exclusion, contribute to social cohesion and add to economic competitiveness, in particular, how they do this through formal networks of support, informal relationships of trust and by coalescing communities of interest with communities of place and/or communities of identity. The second aim was to evaluate the impact of local governance and regeneration agencies on these activities in terms of their support, or absence of support, with a view to commenting on more effective and appropriate interventions in the future.

The research was pursued through semi-structured interviews with small and micro-businesses and key actors in regeneration, business support and voluntary sector organisations. The project was conceived in early 1997 and the fieldwork was carried out during 1998 and 1999, before the New Labour government's plethora of regeneration initiatives came on-stream.

Neighbourhood regeneration organisations

This strand of the project focused on comparatively large, independent bodies operating within specific neighbourhoods. In most cases, neighbourhood regeneration organisations have established themselves over a long period of time, compared with the short-term existence of so many regeneration initiatives. They have developed a distinctive role in poor areas by contributing to both social and economic regeneration in a multifunctional array of activity. Their independence distinguishes them from local agencies of mainstream voluntary organisations and from statutory agencies and departments. This study of neighbourhood regeneration organisations sought to delineate their contribution to social capital and to the local economy, and to pinpoint the challenges and barriers to that contribution. While each neighbourhood regeneration organisation was unique in its range of activity and its mission, there was consistency and distinctiveness in the contribution that all neighbourhood regeneration organisations make to social cohesion and economic competitiveness.

Five prominent neighbourhood regeneration organisations in inner North East London were chosen as case studies to reflect a range of different types of organisation:

- Finsbury Park Community Trust in Islington is a training, employment and community development agency;

- Oxford House in Tower Hamlets is one of the early settlements, engaged in a wide range of activity;
- The Selby Centre in Haringey is a multicultural centre, embracing many socio-cultural projects;
- Bromley-by-Bow Centre in Tower Hamlets is a multifunctional, faith-based agency.

These four could be described as relatively holistic or broad-based in their activities.

- Newlon Housing Group in Hackney is a community based housing association with a major commitment to community and economic development programmes.

The latter is clearly an organisation with a predominant focus on social housing management and development with an appropriate funding stream, but it is a good example of a neighbourhood regeneration organisation that has developed generic regeneration activity in addition to its core business.

Unlike statutory agencies whose primary objective is to provide services to meet officially recognised needs within the community as a whole, neighbourhood regeneration organisations have developed a cocktail of projects, programmes and initiatives tailored to specific needs in their localities. The activities undertaken by the five organisations in this study ranged very widely indeed, including health and social care, housing, employment training, cultural, advice and advocacy services and projects. These neighbourhood regeneration organisations promote social inclusion by involving users and by developing activities and networks that offer them immediate practical benefit. Hence, they have contributed to the economic potential of individuals by giving practical support and counselling to improve their confidence, skills and employability.

The neighbourhood regeneration organisations also sponsored and supported the formation of social and commercial enterprises. Hence, for example, the Bromley-by-Bow centre used Single Regeneration Budget (SRB) money to purchase an adjoining building that has been developed by the local Bengali community into a restaurant and catering service. In such a project, neighbourhood regeneration organisations are able to facilitate bridging and linking social capital to otherwise isolated communities. The biggest enterprise facilitated and run by the Bromley-by-Bow centre is its integrated Healthy Living Centre that has a full range of primary health care services including alternative practices and remedies. In such projects neighbourhood regeneration organisations promote linking social capital on quite a large scale, as well as contributing to the bridging social capital between different local health care interests and campaigns.

By mediating between different stakeholders and by convening and coordinating local responses to proposals initiated by external agencies, the neighbourhood regeneration organisations provided an important mechanism for local capacity building, including acting as a training ground for community leadership. Their scale and range of projects enabled them to act in a leadership role on behalf of the community sector, providing a gear-change mechanism between slower-moving external bureaucracies and diverse and rapidly changing local needs. The evidence from our study suggests that neighbourhood regeneration organisations are vitally important in developing linking social capital as well as providing a venue and support services for community groups developing bonding and bridging social capital.

However, two particular factors constrained the effectiveness of the neighbourhood regeneration organisations studied, namely the problems of legitimacy and of funding. First, they faced particular difficulties in establishing legitimacy in the eyes of public bodies, particularly local government. They operate within realms that are conventionally seen as the domain of the boroughs and other public service providers. Neighbourhood regeneration organisations championed their local areas and claimed to represent their communities' needs in ways that challenged the mainstream structures of governance. Hence, they often experienced ambivalent and uncomfortable relationships with local government.

Second, neighbourhood regeneration organisations, particularly those with a more holistic, broad-based range of activity suffered chronic financial insecurity, despite longevity and good management. There was inadequate investment in training for staff and lay members, ICT and financial systems, internal monitoring and evaluation procedures. Lack of funding severely constrained participation in local partnerships and development of effective regional and national networks.

Such findings add to those of national studies of neighbourhood regeneration organisations (Thake, 1995, 2001). These studies point to the vital contribution that neighbourhood regeneration organisations already make to social and economic regeneration of poor areas. Thake (2001) argues for the development of neighbourhood regeneration organisations to form a major plank of future regeneration strategy as 'independent anchor organisations' to underpin neighbourhood initiatives. Thus far, however, the neighbourhood regeneration organisation contribution has been under-exploited and in some cases marginalised in the recent wave of policy initiatives such as New Deal for Communities and the Neighbourhood Renewal Fund. In the corridors of power, the alleged lack of local capacity in poor communities is frequently bemoaned and it is often suggested that the community sector cannot be trusted to deliver regeneration programmes. Neighbourhood regeneration organisations demonstrably possess that capacity and also provide an appropriate context in which to develop it further. However, the Local Strategic Partnerships (LSPs) that trigger access to the Neighbourhood Renewal Fund can be local authority dominated, as can many of the delivery plans of the New Deal for Communities projects. Communities have not been brought into the heart of the regeneration agenda, despite the policy guidelines and the existence of neighbourhood regeneration organisations as important delivery vehicles.

The London Development Agency has recently recognised the significance of neighbourhood regeneration organisations in its Economic Development Strategy and is planning to facilitate their future development. At the national level, the Neighbourhood Renewal Unit, the Department for Trade and Industry (DTI) and the Home Office have all indicated greater recognition of the neighbourhood regeneration organisation contribution. The cross-cutting review of the voluntary and community sectors as delivery agents of local services undertaken by HM Treasury also envisages a more central role for locally based anchor organisations. The working through of the social inclusion agenda will require existing public agencies to modernise their service provision functions. Enormous energy is currently being put into changing the design, funding, delivery and coordination of services. However, residents, users and alternative delivery agencies also now have a central role to play. Neighbourhood regeneration organisations similar to those included in this study will have an important role to play in the development of this agenda.

Amin et al (2002) also confirm that neighbourhood regeneration organisations form an important element in the local social economy. They suggest that organisations like the Bromley-by-Bow centre have been successful above all because of some particularly strong linking social capital with power structures in government and the professions. This should not detract from the fact that neighbourhood regeneration organisation activities start from the empowerment of individuals and of local communities of interest and identity. Amin et al (2002, p 114) suggest that "the relative absence of the local state in Tower Hamlets from direct involvement in the social economy has prompted the more successful organisations to look beyond local administrative boundaries to find the sort of supportive structures and networks that enable social enterprises to develop and thrive". Neighbourhood regeneration organisations have indeed played a key role in the development of social capital of all three kinds, which is a role that may not be appropriate or achievable for local government.

The black voluntary sector

The black voluntary sector consists of organisations managed by and for black people. Here the term 'black' is used to denote the identities of people from a diversity of ethnic backgrounds collectively identified as visible minorities. There were no comprehensive databases to draw on so the study focused on formally constituted welfare service providing and advocacy organisations. Interviews were conducted with workers, activists and users in 48 organisations across the inner North East London area. The ethnic identities of the organisations studied were: Somali, Bangladeshi, Pakistani, African-Caribbean, Ugandan, Eritrean, Ethiopian, Kurdish, Vietnamese, Chinese, Turkish and Greek. Some groups worked specifically with particular communities of interest, such as minority ethnic women, young people and people with disabilities. Forty-one organisations were asked about the number of users accessing their services either in person or through telephone inquiries. We estimated that roughly 350,000 people in some way gained access to their services over a 12-month period. Demand for services far outstripped what organisations could supply. Most organisations did not have computerised systems for calculating the number of service users accessing their services, having on average only two or three full-time workers and relying greatly on part-time, sessional and unpaid workers.

The construction of black voluntary sector organisations around communities of interest and identity has enabled them to develop considerable funds of knowledge and understanding of their communities. The management committees and workers came from co-ethnic communities; they understood the culture, spoke the same language and often lived in the same neighbourhood, contributing enormously to their degree of local accountability. All the organisations aspired to horizontal power structures within the management committee and among the workforce. They were over-dependent on volunteers, who were, nevertheless, fully recognised as workers alongside paid staff. The way these organisations are structured has a strong bearing on the relationships developed with individuals and communities. These organisations enjoyed high levels of trust with their users, many of whom refused to use more mainstream organisations because of their institutional racism. This trust formed the basic ingredient for the effectiveness of their work, and the basis for the very strong bonding social capital within these organisations.

In most cases, strong formal and informal ties existed between the organisations studied and other co-ethnic and local community organisations. Ninety per cent of the organisations studied identified themselves strongly and consciously as part of a developing black voluntary sector. According to our respondents, networking with other local and national black voluntary sector organisations was an important feature of their work. Significant formal and informal ties existed between the organisations studied, the communities they represented and other voluntary organisations. Many organisations participated in the same community forums, regeneration and local authority meetings. Groups and individuals were well known to each other and were in many of the same networks. Hence, these black voluntary sector organisations had considerable linking social capital within the black voluntary sector, although less strong linkages with more 'mainstream' voluntary sector bodies.

The links between the black voluntary sector organisations and more formal institutions were much more tenuous. Black organisations were under-represented on local regeneration bodies and felt excluded from key decision making forums. Only 16 organisations said they were involved with regeneration bodies and networks, and they found their participation limited by lack of human and financial resources, and experiences of disempowerment and tokenism when they did contribute. Many black voluntary sector organisations expressed the view that 'old' voluntary sector organisations were much better connected and represented in local decision making networks around health care, schools, housing and other elements of the regeneration agenda. The organisations expressed acute needs for capacity-building support, targeted training and informed administrative assistance. Hence, the black voluntary sector organisations we studied experienced a lack of linking social capital that in some respects limited their impact and activity.

The black voluntary sector appeared to be valued and recognised by the local authorities, but many of the organisations were ambivalent about local authority and regeneration agency support. Some said that they were well supported in kind, but then went on to criticise their funding which they said had been reduced by the borough over recent years. Eighteen out of 41 said they received core funding, but that this was not sufficient to run their organisations properly. The others were reliant on a mixture of project based funding, contracts and specific small grants from the boroughs. Most of the organisations were not participating in the new contract culture of partnerships with boroughs, leaving them feeling vulnerable and excluded. The black voluntary sector faces an increasingly acute dilemma: participation in the contract culture is likely to undermine their trust and rootedness within their communities; lack of participation is likely to mean a worsening of the underfunding situation. Driven by the need to build linking social capital to get resources, black voluntary sector organisations may undermine some of their bonding social capital, and, in competing for funding, may also threaten their bridging social capital with other organisations.

Our findings closely reflect those of two recently completed studies of black and minority ethnic voluntary organisations. McLeod et al (2001) suggest that there are around 5,500 such organisations in England and Wales, most of which have been in existence for at least ten years. They found, too, that black voluntary sector organisations in the contract culture context had great and increasing difficulty in "accessing core funding, rather than funding for the delivery of specific services" (McLeod et al, 2001, p 57). They also confirm that the current emphasis on developing local, wide-ranging partnerships between public and voluntary service providers places black voluntary sector organisations "at a disadvantage in developing 'black-led' bids" (2001, p 58). This is "compounded by a feeling that funding is moving away from 'black-only' to 'multi-cultural' uses" (2001, p 58), with white-led organisations competing more and more successfully for such funding. Similarly, Craig et al (2002) found that black voluntary sector organisations felt 'marginal to local policy debates' and 'overstretched and under-resourced'. They also identified the organisations' fears that the contract culture would be "used to reduce grant aid, impose further service level agreements and marginalize their role even further" (p 1).

In London the black voluntary sector experienced a brief period of stability and recognition during the Livingstone regime at the Greater London Council in the early 1980s. However, it also became over-dependent on grant funding, which undermined some of its autonomy and edge. Since then, it has struggled for survival as funding has disappeared and the contract culture between the voluntary and public sectors has taken root, excluding less formal, smaller groups. Rice (1999) suggested that since 1987 more than 50 black voluntary sector organisations in London had lost their funding. There are, however, distinct signs of a positive shift in the policy environment. London Boroughs Grants continues to fund more than 100 black voluntary sector organisations, and has recently expressed a renewed commitment to the sector. The Greater London Authority has made a commitment to tackling inequality and discrimination against black Londoners with the establishment of the Black Londoners Forum and a policy of prioritising regeneration funding for black and minority ethnic community organisations.

At a national policy level, too, there has been some recognition of the importance of the issues raised by findings such as ours. The Social Exclusion Unit's (2000) report, *National strategy for neighbourhood renewal*, alluded specifically to the necessity for neighbourhood renewal strategists to "work with local ethnic minority voluntary groups and faith organisations ... particular efforts may be needed to make joint working of this kind possible" (SEU, 2000, p 12). A Home Office (1999, p 103) report noted that black voluntary sector organisations feel "that they have to operate under greater scrutiny from funders [which] has sometimes led to mistrust between white-managed funding bodies and black and minority ethnic voluntary organisations". This generated an important initiative, which established regional support networks for black voluntary sector organisations.

We found that black voluntary sector organisations are generating substantial bonding and bridging social capital in inner North East London, but that there are considerable barriers to their development of effective linking social capital. This is needed to help sustain the black voluntary sector but it carries with it considerable threats to their ethnic rootedness and internal democracy which is essential to their success. The black voluntary sector can make a much greater contribution to local democracy and to local urban regeneration (Ocloo, 1999, 2000). This requires a further shift in the discourse of urban policy towards a more open local public realm and neighbourhood democracy (Amin, 2002, p 20).

Ethnic minority business

The scale and contribution of ethnic minority business to national and local economies is only just beginning to be recognised. While ethnic minority entrepreneurs own 7% of all UK business, this rises sharply to 50% in some inner-city areas of London (Lewis and Bieler, 2001). We examined the embeddedness of ethnic minority business in four case study areas of inner North East London – Finsbury Park, Brick Lane, Tottenham and Green Lanes – by looking at the relationship between co-ethnic social networks and enterprise. In total, 75 interviews were undertaken with local business owners and 60 with key actors in regeneration agencies and business support.

A high proportion of ethnic minority businesses in inner North East London is concentrated in an extremely narrow group of sectors, namely retailing, catering and clothing manufacture. This confirms an established pattern found elsewhere (Waldinger et al, 1990) and reflects histories of migration and economic exclusion. We found that Turkish and Greek owned firms predominated in clothing manufacture and Indian and Pakistani enterprises were more likely to be found in retailing. Ownership in the restaurant sector was ethnically more diverse and included recently established ethnic groups such as the Vietnamese. These low value-added sectors have minimum threshold costs, a propensity for market saturation and are highly competitive with large labour inputs. We found, as did Blackburn and Rutherford (1999), that although many of the problems faced by our respondents were sector specific, these were reinforced by a lack of weak ties that might have facilitated connections within local and national economies.

However, diverging from existing evidence, we also found that there are a growing number of ethnic minority enterprises in higher value-added consumer and personal services and in the professional and IT sectors. This reflects a new trend in ethnic minority business in inner North East London: respondents in these sectors were mostly from the Caribbean and black African communities, traditionally under-represented in ethnic enterprise. They were younger and had higher levels of educational attainment. These entrepreneurs were responding to new consumption needs of local multi-ethnic populations with growing disposable incomes. They were able to mobilise weaker, more extensive ties in creating their enterprises. Nevertheless in both the traditional and new sectors, patterns of geographical location within inner North East London remained the same. Ethnic minority enterprise was most likely to be found in the poorest and least well-resourced areas of inner North East London, with poor infrastructure and a relatively low income base.

Our attention was drawn to how co-ethnic ties enabled and 'embedded' local enterprise. In the early 1990s, a large literature emerged documenting the key role of social and cultural networks in successful clusters of entrepreneurial activity within particular regions and cities of Europe. Policy advocacy of networking followed drawing on bridging and linking social capital. Elsewhere the 'cultural' approach to ethnic minority business emphasised the use of co-ethnic networks (or bonding social capital) for support as a mark of ethnic entrepreneurial distinction.

Strong co-ethnic ties and solidarities, in some circumstances, did create particular advantages in providing informal business advice and support, practical help with labour recruitment, access to finance and entry into ethnic niche markets. However, the solidarity and trust within different ethnic groups in our four case studies varied considerably as did the significance of local co-ethnic ties. Local co-ethnic ties were particularly important in Brick Lane where the tight-knit, relatively homogeneous Bangladeshi business community facilitated close endogenous social and business networks. Social obligation and business support were interdependent. However, community loyalty and business support were also maintained through transnational networks stretching between the Sylhet region of Bangladesh and Tower Hamlets. Strongly internalised local networks matched by distanciated transnational ties, however, detracted from more immediate association through linking and bridging social capital with potentially enabling local business support networks and financial services. In Finsbury Park, where diversity of ethnicity among local business ownership predominated, local ties with dissimilar others were relatively weak. Reliance on distant co-ethnic ties for moral support proved strong but less effective in solving local and daily problems. By contrast, black Caribbean and African respondents in Tottenham and South Haringey had more confidence in generalised business values, mediated through banking and accounting institutions, as sources of trust and support. In effect, their bridging social capital was strong but their bonding social capital weak. Here, entrepreneurs were distanced from local community support structures, although they still acknowledged the potential benefits of close ethnic communities, especially where racism and socio-economic disadvantage had hindered enterprise start up. Nevertheless, African, Caribbean and Cypriot respondents in this area identified some of the limitations imposed by being locked too closely into co-ethnic ties and solidarities. This close association was perceived as limiting to enterprise, a hold on developing into wider, more profitable (and possibly risky) competitive markets.

Many minority ethnic enterprises in inner North East London fulfil the expectation of self-motivated, self-supported entrepreneurialism that is creative in Landry's sense, offering the kind of competitive advantage noted by Porter and the rich vitality observed by Worpole and Greenhalgh. These are aspects of enterprise that have been promoted as key to inner-city competitiveness, yet their recognition and impact has been weakened by the climate in which these enterprises operate. Exclusion and discrimination perpetuates concentration in underperforming sectors, encourages under-investment in new sectors and thwarts innovative potential.

It is national government policy to promote entrepreneurship, especially in poor areas where it is linked to tackling social exclusion (DTI, 1999). Business support, until recently delivered through the Business Links programme, has been its mainstay. Since the entrepreneurship of ethnic minority business predominates in poor areas, engaging with the needs of ethnic minority entrepreneurs is critical. However, Oc and Tiesdall (1999) note that ethnic minority businesses are under-represented among Business Links clients. This failure was mirrored among our respondents. Although 90% identified business support needs, very few had successfully taken advantage of business support services through Business Links or other local agencies funded by regeneration projects or voluntary agencies. Most business support agencies were perceived to be inaccessible, unapproachable and providing services that were too generic and not tailored to individual needs. Experiences of racism and lack of cultural understanding were reported as commonplace. When agencies were consulted, advisors had lacked relevant sector and market knowledge, leading to frustration.

What entrepreneurs wanted was specific, culturally sensitive, advice with good follow-up.

Fragmentation, duplication and lack of coordination of business support agencies were apparent throughout our area, reflecting to a large extent the fragmented and uncoordinated structure of funding, management and delivery of local business and regeneration strategies (Lewis and Bieler, 1999). This disorganisation did little to facilitate ethnic minority business participation in either business support or regeneration programmes, or to encourage active consultation. For most enterprises and individual entrepreneurs, this reinforced their 'self-help' reliance on the inward-looking bonding social capital of friends and family while weakening the development of more socially inclusive bridging and linking social capital (Lewis and Bieler, 2001).

Ram and Smallbone (2002) confirm many of these findings in their review of ethnic minority business policy. Although delivering culturally sensitive business support has eluded past business support agencies the wider remit of the new Small Business Service (which began in 2001) may, in their view, enable a coordinated national policy to address ethnic minority business issues. The Small Business Service is charged with improving the quality and coherence of small business support and they therefore anticipate a higher priority for ethnic minority business issues. Developing a coherent strategy can be justified in terms of both economic development and social justice. Our findings endorse their agenda for developing effective and lasting support for ethnic minority business under the new Small Business Service schema. This includes a greater clarity of objectives for business support; client focused services and sensitivity to the different business needs; increased participation of under-represented groups in decision making; closer integration of business support investment and regeneration policies; and Community Finance Initiatives. In addition the Ethnic Minority Business Forum (EMBF, 2001), which advises DTI ministers and the Small Business Service, recommends the monitoring of support service take-up and the appointment of a Minister for Ethnic Minorities.

At the regional level, Regional Development Agencies – including the London Development Agency – have been charged with ensuring local regeneration programmes to specifically address the needs of ethnic minority owned businesses. In the case of the London Development Agency, this has led to the adoption of a core strategy on developing equality of opportunity in development programmes and diversity of outcomes.

There are examples of local regeneration projects that have directly supported ethnic minority businesses. In Banglatown/Brick Lane, infrastructural investment in shop and restaurant improvement has benefited established and larger businesses serving a restaurant clientele and visitor economy. The area has become a flagship of business improvement and ethnic place marketing. However, this 'boosterism' has led to the exclusion of weaker enterprises in the clothing industry, resulting in closures and removal from the local area with the loss of employment. The outcomes of regeneration for ethnic minority business at this level can therefore be contradictory. Many local agencies hold a tension between objectives to support competitiveness and those to enhance social inclusion.

Cultural producers

Much has come to be expected of creative practices (and 'places') in inner cities, particularly when linked to entrepreneurial activity. Creative entrepreneurialism produces a reservoir of skills, knowledge, talent and ideas. It is this pool of human and social capital that potentially offers entrepreneurial ways of working, fresh attitudes to economic problems and the mobilisation of rich multicultural urban diversity.

This aspect of our research focused on the interrelationship between creativity and economic regeneration. It examined an identifiable cluster of cultural producers and creative activity in Hackney that had emerged since the 1970s and been subject to local and London-wide exposure following project funding under Single Regeneration Budget and EU programmes. This cluster contained a diverse mixture of economic activities that produced cultural products and services. A total of 71 interviews were undertaken with practitioners, suppliers, intermediaries and key policy actors. Three groups of activity were identified as particularly significant in shaping local creative entrepreneurialism: self-employed artists and designer-makers working in a wide variety of media for exhibition, commission and sale through galleries, retailers and direct to the public; small and micro-businesses delivering cultural services such as design, exhibition organisation, cultural consultancy and events management; and micro-enterprises offering web-design, network and internet services. Although the clients and markets for each group of cultural producers varied, in all three it was found that artefacts, products and services were sold in the Greater London region, nationally and internationally with little dependence on local clients and outlets. Likewise, although the geography of supply chains varied by activity or product, scant evidence was found of local supply networks. Even the most basic artists' materials or office supplies were in fact sourced by mail order or over the Internet.

Consequently, unlike the ethnic minority enterprises discussed above, there was little *local* embeddedness fusing economic and social and cultural relations among cultural producers in the inner North East London area. Their social networks stretched across the London region, the UK and internationally producing very important bonding social capital. The proximity of significant friends and colleagues was not deemed necessary. Yet, close ties between trusted, although geographically distant, individuals were protected and actively maintained over space. These networks were the main conduits for gaining creative input, accessing critical judgement of work in progress and widening 'audiences' and markets. What emerges is a pattern of well-connected but not locally embedded individuals whose reference points are not in Hackney or East London. Where individuals did have close local ties these were more often associated with their children's schooling and friendship networks. As

Butler and Robson (2001) also found, association around schooling ties middle-class professionals together because of their prioritisation of education and active parenting. By and large, however, such close locally based ties are held at arm's length from those based on shared 'professional' or economic networks.

Creative entrepreneurialism advocates flexible working practices and risk taking. Sometimes this can produce spectacular success. In our research, we interviewed internationally acclaimed creative entrepreneurs working both in the traditional arts and in new media who had established their reputations through challenging the status quo and blurring life–work. However, we interviewed far more for whom creative success was more limited, life and work were less easily blurred and economic insecurity very familiar. The expectations of creative entrepreneurialism exposed the majority of individuals and enterprises to high levels of 'failure' and long periods of low return. In these instances, creativity may be recognised but not rewarded. There is a problem, therefore, in advocating creativity and entrepreneurialism as a way forward for inner urban areas. For every creative entrepreneurial 'success' there are many everyday tensions between openness to creative ideas and practices and risks of entrepreneurial failure.

This aspect of our research also identified the key role of cultural intermediaries in ascribing not only cultural but also economic value to particular artefacts, services and practices. Often this was enacted in the context of regeneration projects or programmes aimed at promoting cultural industries in local areas. Other commentators have noted the pivotal role of intermediaries in assessing cultural value (Zukin, 1995; O'Connor, 1998). The conflation of the cultural and economic judgement found here in inner North East London, signals a new departure for cultural intermediaries and marks a further intensification of cultural commodification. In inner North East London, further impetus for this trend was derived from regeneration-funded projects which employed intermediaries to deliver a creative industries strategy as a form of economic development. The implementation programmes adopted by cultural intermediaries included identifying and profiling local creative producers, building bridging and linking social capital through formalised networks, branding local production, providing training and business support and showcasing local work through national exhibitions, open studio events, a website and trade fairs. Here, effective economic development seemed to require breaking sole reliance on strong ties of bonding social capital and replacing them with the weaker, but in this context economically more effective, ties of association with institutions and agencies that could collectively brand and promote the work of individuals. However, the cultural values and bridging and linking networks of the intermediaries plus their preoccupation with targeting markets playing to middlebrow consumer tastes, acted as a filter for creative activity and production. The types and forms of cultural production deemed acceptable by the intermediaries delivering local creative industry policy were increasingly encouraged to conform to entrepreneurial norms and behaviours.

Three related observations emerged on the link between creative entrepreneurialism and regeneration. First, there was the pivotal role of cultural intermediaries in identifying the reservoir of creative skills, knowledge, talent and ideas and in ascribing cultural value to creative outputs. Second, there was the changing role of cultural intermediaries into economic interpreters for the cultural sector. That is the way in which a self-selecting group came to be both the arbiters of taste and of marketability for creative ideas and products. As a consequence creative entrepreneurialism became normalised around business skills, attitudes and conventional organisational structures in which linking and bridging social capital was valued more than bonding social capital. Finally, the particular fusion of creative entrepreneurialism and regeneration in inner North East London paradoxically aimed to neutralise, in the name of marketability, the outward expressions of diversity and rich mix on which the creative approach to city economies is supposed to be based. Thus the middlebrow taste of cultural intermediaries flavoured with a hint of the exotic prevailed in order for products and services to appeal to the buying public (Evans and Foord, 2000).

This prioritisation of creative entrepreneurialism coincides with national, regional and local policy to focus on the creative industries in cultural policy. At ministerial level, the Creative Industries Strategy Group coordinates partnership initiatives. The Department of Culture, Media and Sport (DCMS) has repeated its Creative Industries Mapping exercise maintaining a high-profile for the creative industries activity within the national economy (DCMS, 2001). Regional Development Agencies and Regional Cultural Consortiums are now charged with encouraging creative industries within their regions. Following Policy Action Team advice to the DCMS, local regeneration agencies and local authorities have adopted creative industries strategies, including Creative Industries Development Agencies, linking objectives for economic development, physical improvement and social inclusion. Yet, in their implementation economic competitiveness tends to take precedence over cultural amenity provision.

However, the London Development Partnership's *Creative energy* (2001) outlines the need to link creative economic development to raising the quality of life for all Londoners. Likewise, the Cultural Strategy Group for London offers advice on widening participation and access, profiling and promoting a wide diversity of cultural activity. At the regional level, certainly in London, a balance is now being sought between economic development through promotion of cultural industries and cultural development.

Conclusion

Our work suggests that local networks and associations in inner North East London often did not produce the forms of robust social capital or creative entrepreneurialism advocated by national policy and regeneration practice as stepping stones to successful renewal. We found that they did not always reinforce mainstream social and cultural values, nor did they always conform to norms of economic entrepreneurialism. Nevertheless, these undervalued, everyday and 'hidden' networks have emerged over many years through local association and economic activity and have provided important mechanisms for building *particular* forms of social capital and creative entrepreneurship. Furthermore, they have engendered socially cohesive collective action in a tough urban environment. We have also traced how national policy and local regeneration strategies have sought to tap into and subsequently 'develop' these networks and associations, co-opting them as key factors in the delivery of improved local opportunities. However, a tension has been identified between the self-development of social capital and of creative entrepreneurialism in themselves, and their development and incorporation into formal organisational structures involved in regeneration. The task of regional and local agencies seems to be mediating this tension.

References

Amin, A. (2002) *Ethnicity and the multicultural city*, ESRC Cities Programme, Liverpool John Moores University.

Amin, A. and Thrift, N. (1994) (eds) *Globalization, institutions and regional development in Europe*, Oxford: Oxford University Press.

Amin, A., Cameron, A. and Hudson, R. (2002) *Placing the social economy*, London: Routledge.

Bieler, E. (2000) 'The "embeddedness" of ethnic minority business in Inner North East London', *Rising East*, vol 3, no 3, pp 22-45.

Blackburn, R. and Rutherford, R. (1999) *Enterprise for culturally diverse communities*, Small Business Research Centre, University of Kingston.

Butler, T. and Robson, G. (2001) 'Social capital, gentrification and neighbourhood change in London: a comparison of three South London boroughs', *Urban Studies*, vol 38, no 12, pp 2145-62.

Craig, G., Taylor, M., Wilkinson, M. and Bloor, K. (2002) 'Black and minority ethnic organisations experience of local compacts', *Findings* 122, York: Joseph Rowntree Foundation, available at www.jrf.org.uk

DCMS (Department of Culture, Media and Sport) (2001) *Creative industries mapping document*, London: DCMS.

DETR (Department of the Environment, Transport and the Regions) (2000) *Indices of deprivation 2000*, London: DETR.

DTI (Department of Trade and Industry) (1999) *The small business service: A public consultation*, London: DTI.

EMBF (Ethnic Minority Business Forum) (2001) *First annual report*, London: EMBF.

Evans, G.L. and Foord, J. (2000) 'Landscapes of cultural production and regeneration', in J. Benson and M. Rose (eds) *Urban lifestyles: Spaces, places, people*, Rotterdam: A.T. Balkema, pp 249-56.

Foord, J. (1999) 'Creative Hackney: reflections on *Hidden Art*', *Rising East*, vol 3, no 2, pp 38-66.

Forrest, R. and Kearns, A. (2001) 'Social cohesion, social capital and neighbourhood', *Urban Studies*, vol 38, no 12, pp 2125-43.

Home Office (1999) *Strengthening the black and minority ethnic voluntary sector infrastrucure: Report on a consultation*, London: Home Office.

Johnston, R., Forrest, J. and Poulsen, M. (2002) 'Are there ethnic enclaves/ ghettos in English cities?', *Urban Studies*, vol 39, no 4, pp 591-618.

Landry, C. (2000) *The creative city: A toolkit for urban innovators*, London: Earthscan.

Lewis, J. and Bieler, E. (1999) *Business support in the London Borough of Tower Hamlets: Final report*, London: London Borough of Tower Hamlets.

Lewis, J. and Bieler, E. (2001) 'Ethnic minority business: support policy in Inner North East London', *Rising East*, vol 4, no 3, pp 17-44.

LDP (London Development Partnership) (2001) *Creative energy: The creative industries in London's economy*, London: LDP/Government Office for London.

London TEC Council (1999) *Strength through diversity: Ethnic minorities in London's economy*, London TEC Council, London Skills Forecasting Unit.

McLeod, M., Owen, D. and Khamis, C. (2001) *Black and minority ethnic voluntary and community organisations*, London: Policy Studies Institute.

O'Connor, J. (1998) 'Popular culture, cultural intermediaries and urban regeneration', in T. Hall and P. Hubbard (eds) *The entrepreneurial city: Geographies of politics, regime and representations*, Chichester: John Wiley & Sons.

Oc, T. and Tiesdall, S. (1999) 'Supporting ethnic minority business: a review of business support for ethnic minorities in City Challenge areas', *Urban Studies*, vol 36, no 10, pp 1723-46.

Ocloo, J. (1999) 'The importance of a "black" agenda in revitalising voluntary action and local democracy', Unpublished, Applied Social Studies Department, London Metropolitan University (University of North London).

Ocloo, J. (2000) 'The importance of a "black" agenda in regeneration and revitalising voluntary action', Unpublished, Applied Social Studies Department, London Metropolitan University (University of North London).

PIU (Performance and Innovation Unit) (2002) *Social capital: A discussion paper*, London: PIU.

Porter, M. (1995) 'The competitive advantage of the inner city', *Harvard Business Review*, vol 74, no 5, May-June, pp 55-71.

Porter, M. (2001) 'Good news, not blues for the inner city', *Harvard Business School Working Knowledge* (www.isc.hbs.edu).

Portes, A. and Landolt, P. (1996) 'The downside of social capital', *The American Prospect*, vol 7, no 26, pp 18-21.

Ram, M. and Smallbone, D. (2002) 'Ethnic minority business policy in the era of the Small Business Service', *Environment and Planning C: Government and policy*, vol 20, pp 235-49.

Rice, A. (1999) *The black voluntary sector: Present concerns and future directions* (www.chronicleworld.org).

Schuller, T., Baron, S. and Field, J. (2000) 'Social capital: a review and critique', in S. Baron, J. Field and T. Schuller (eds) *Social capital: Critical perspectives*, Oxford: Oxford University Press, pp 1-38.

SEU (Social Exclusion Unit) (2000) *A National Strategy for Neighbourhood Renewal: A framework for consultation*, London: The Stationery Office.

Thake, S. (1995) *Staying the course: The role and structures of community regeneration organisations*, York: Joseph Rowntree Foundation.

Thake, S. (2001) *Building communities, changing lives: The contribution of large, independent neighbourhood regeneration organisations*, York: Joseph Rowntree Foundation.

Waldinger, R., Alrich, H. and Ward, R. (1990) (eds) *Ethnic entrepreneurs*, London: Sage Publications.

Worpole, K. and Greenhalgh, L. (1999) *The richness of cities: Urban policy in a new landscape*, Stroud: Comedia/Demos.

Zukin, S. (1995) *The culture of cities*, Oxford: Blackwell.

SEVENTEEN

Ethnic minority enterprise in an inner-city context: the case of the independent restaurant sector in Birmingham

Trevor Jones, Monder Ram and Tahir Abbas

Introduction

Government, government agencies and economic development bodies have frequently seen the role of small businesses, enterprise and self-employment as a key element of competitive strength both nationally and at local and regional scales. Enterprise and self-employment has been seen as particularly relevant in addressing the particular barriers to work and economic well-being faced by ethnic minorities (Cabinet Office Strategy Unit, 2003). This has more general relevance to the competitive strength of core urban areas, given the scale and concentration of people from ethnic minorities in such areas.

While entrepreneurial self-employment is already a conspicuous feature of the economic position of Britain's ethnic minorities, this is heavily concentrated within marginal business sectors such as corner shop retailing, catering and clothing manufacture, all of which are subject to intense competition. Of these activities, catering enjoys by far the most promising market potential, based as it is on the appeal of a specialised ethnic product to a wider market. Indeed, the 'ethnic' restaurant industry is currently one of Britain's fastest growing service sectors (Mintel, 1999) although, somewhat perversely as we shall see, this does not guarantee rich pickings for all its participants. This raises particular issues in relation to cohesion and exclusion alongside issues of competitiveness.

In this chapter, we focus on ethnic restaurants in Birmingham, a city renowned for an intense inner-city cluster of South Asian curry houses with its own distinctive brand name – the 'Balti Quarter'. This striking spatial agglomeration both expresses and influences the struggles for entrepreneurial survival, which characterise the South Asian restaurant sector. On the one hand, restaurateurs profit in this instance from membership of a high-profile cluster, whose name is widely familiar throughout and beyond the city, a veritable magnet for a growing mass of middle-class 'omniverous diners' seeking the authentic ethnic culinary experience (Warde et al, 1999). At the same time, the perceived benefits of this location have attracted a surfeit of restaurateurs, with supply outlets outrunning even a rapid expansion of demand, leading to serious over-competition and unviable returns for many of these businesses (Ram et al, 2002). Of interest here also are the implications that spatially concentrated business activity has for urban policy makers. Seeking ways of rebranding their city, they can sometimes exploit a successful 'cultural industry' without necessarily considering the wider implications of their actions for local economy and society.

This chapter opens with a discussion of the salient theoretical and empirical issues in the field of ethnic minority entrepreneurship, where there are sharply opposed views on the causes and implications of the phenomenon. The aims of the study and the issues explored are then elaborated upon, highlighting the importance of the qualitative methodological framework and the spatial and sectoral context in which the study is situated. We then discuss a range of findings, many of which go against the grain of received wisdom in the field. First, we address the problem of market saturation, by far the most important problem faced by restaurateurs in the Balti Quarter, where the struggle to attract custom has forced extreme price- and cost-cutting practices on many. Second, we examine entrepreneurs' strategies to break out of these constraints and the ways in which fast-track ethnic minority entrepreneurs are able to capitalise on the demand for upmarket restaurants. Third, we spotlight the ways in which such development impinges on the business family, customarily portrayed as the minority business owner's decisive advantage but placed under considerable strain by the kind of change and modernisation demanded by 'breakout'. Related to this is the question of how far family members and other co-ethnic workers in ethnic minority firms use the skills, knowledge and experience gained in order to start their own business ventures. The prevailing assumption that this is one of the predominant means by which the ethnic minority business economy reproduces itself, is an assumption not in fact upheld here. Finally, we assess the relevance of existing policy approaches towards ethnic minority entrepreneurs.

Ethnic entrepreneurship: universalistic versus particularistic explanations

Since the first systematic study of ethnic enterprise three decades ago (Light, 1972), researchers have grappled with the seemingly intractable question of how disadvantaged racialised minorities such as Chinese in the US or Pakistanis in the UK can occupy such an apparently enviable position in the field of business ownership. In the case of South Asians in Britain, we are confronted with a migrant-origin group who have positioned themselves at the forefront of the post-Fordist 'entrepreneurial revolution', with a self-employment rate one and a half times that of the general population by the early 1990s (Ram and Jones, 1998). The enormity of this strikes home when we remind ourselves that these communities originated as immigrant workers entering the very bottom of the British economy as replacement workers, victims both of racist discrimination and of the job cuts subsequently wrought by deindustrialisation (Brah, 1996).

Prominent among the explanatory theories constructed to explain these contradictions is the 'cultural resources' perspective (Metcalf et al, 1996), which argues that the cultural attributes of some (but by no means all) ethnic minorities can, Midas-like, transform dross into gold. According to Metcalf et al (1996, p 7), "minorities may be vulnerable and oppressed, but they can create resources that offset the harshness of the environment they encounter". Recently, it has been recognised that economic activity is firmly grounded in social networks and the term *social capital* has been coined to describe "the resources that are available to a person through his or her social relations with others" (Flap et al, 2000, p 147). Since many migrant-origin communities tend to comprise cohesive, mutually loyal networks centred on shared ethnic identity, it may readily be argued that their entrepreneurs enjoy superior access to social capital and hence an actual advantage over non-members of their group. Immediately applicable to British South Asians, the argument would be that their entrepreneurialism derives its competitive strength from ready access to familial and communal sources of low-cost, loyal, flexible labour, pooled savings, customer loyalty, shared information and all manner of insider supply linkages (Werbner, 1990; Metcalf et al, 1996).

Persuasive as it may be as a neat resolution of an otherwise paradoxical situation, this culturalist paradigm has never held unchallenged sway, presented as it is in a historical, geographical and socio-economic vacuum. How can it be that the Calvinist Methodism of yesterday is the new Sikhism/Hinduism/Islam? Not surprisingly, then, this one-dimensional insistence on ethno-cultural particularism has been subject to a constant critique from those who, in the interests of a common humanity, regard it as reductionist. They instead prioritise the essentially hostile external context of racism and capitalist market forces in which the ethnic minorities must perforce operate (Aldrich et al, 1981; Jones et al, 1992, 1994, 2000; Ram, 1992, 1994). More recently, growing weight has been accorded to the notion of 'mixed embeddedness' (Kloosterman and Rath, 1999), which insists on viewing such entrepreneurs as being essentially grounded in the larger political-economy as well as in their own communal social capital. For the most part, writers of this school insist on contextualising these entrepreneurs in terms of their economic, political, institutional and spatial environment, which sets the ultimate parameters within which they must operate (Freeman and Ogelman, 2000; Jones et al, 2000; Rath and Kloosterman, 2000). While it is vital to accord due analytical significance to the ethnic community and the entrepreneurial social capital it undoubtedly unlocks, it is equally vital to avoid presenting this as a self-encapsulated state, which somehow immunises its participants from the tribulations of membership of a universal entrepreneurial community (Ram et al, 2000).

Research design, aims and methodology

The research approach explicitly acknowledges Rath and Kloosterman's (2000) insistence that ethnic minority businesses must be seen as economically as well as socially embedded. In this perspective, business outcomes are seen as shaped by the *strategies* employed by individual entrepreneurs, and the deployment of resources in relation to market potential, both actual and latent. Vital here is the question of whether business owners adopt a proactive approach to maximising their position in the market or a passive 'survivalist' stance (Blackburn et al, 1990). We also pay explicit attention to the comparative dimension by including African-Caribbean and white firms as well as Indians, Bangladeshis and Pakistanis, thereby avoiding the pitfall of explaining certain characteristics as specifically 'ethnic', when they are in reality economic, and broadly common to all small independent restaurant operators.

In addition to its explicit sectoral focus, the present study is also distinct in addressing the experiences of growing and developing firms, using as a framework the concept of 'breakout' (Ram and Hillin, 1991). This term was introduced to underline the need for ethnic minority firms to escape from their incarceration within narrow and highly competitive market segments into more lucrative markets. Here, a key argument is that the success of such a transition is contingent upon the availability of human and financial capital and other 'class resources' (Light and Bonacich, 1988): firms can no longer rely principally upon the informal social capital of family and co-ethnic workers if they are to achieve breakout.

The city of Birmingham, with its large diverse ethnic minority population, provides a particularly apt setting. Based on the 1991 Census, Bangladeshis comprise 6.2% of the city's population, African-Caribbean 1.3%, Indians 5.3%, and Pakistanis 6.9% (BEIC, 1993). These figures reflect the settlement of numerous migrant groups in Birmingham in the post-war era (Back and Solomos, 1992), giving rise to heavily segregated clusters in different parts of the city. Thus, "Sparkbrook became a largely Pakistani area, Handsworth became the Caribbean centre of Birmingham, alongside the Soho area which was overwhelmingly Indian" (Rex, 1987, p 104). It is also historically significant as the venue for the infamous Enoch Powell 'Rivers of blood' speech in 1968 and, as Back and Solomos (1992, p 329) observe, the city has been seen as an important "test case for the future of race relations in British society".

Qualitative interviews were conducted with owners and workers in 37 restaurants (eight Bangladeshi; eight Pakistani; eight white; seven Indian; and six African-Caribbean). The business owner was interviewed on at least two occasions and, in the majority of cases, it was possible to interview other family members who were directly involved in the case of family businesses. Typically, this would be the spouse of the usually male owner of the restaurant, who would often be involved in paid employment outside of the restaurant. In the case of South Asian Muslims, owners' wives rarely had any direct involvement in the restaurant (although they performed key tasks in the domestic sphere that helped to maintain the ethnic micro-business household) and hence it was not possible to interview these women. A number of male family members, however, who were often involved in the South Asian restaurants – brothers, uncles and cousins (blood relatives) – were interviewed. In addition, interviews were undertaken with at least one worker in each firm (more, in many cases). During the course of the interviews with owners and workers, many wide-ranging issues were discussed. For the purposes of this chapter, however, the emphasis is upon three issues:

- market limitations and strategies for breakout;
- labour market practices and the role of the family;
- the politico-institutional, regulatory environment.

Market saturation

Turning now to the findings from these interviews, we begin with a review of the market environment, in many senses the fountainhead from which all else flows. Undoubtedly the principal limitation on the performance and development of restaurateurs of all ethnic origins in Birmingham is the size and nature of the customer base, a limitation operating with particular severity on South Asians in the Balti Quarter where there are around 60 curry houses (UCECS, 1998). Throughout the interviews, one of the recurring complaints was the intense competitiveness of the trade, stemming from the excessive number of outlets in relation to the market – actual and potential. Indeed, more than one South Asian respondent forecast an eventual decline in what has up to now been a highly expansionary sector, since a large number of restaurants were operating below viable margins. In the South Asian case, the industry has in a sense become the victim of its own initial success, with the invention of 'Balti' food, a novel style of presentation which gave Birmingham's curry houses a national reputation in the 1980s. Initially successful in attracting white custom from a very wide radius, the Balti trade was an even greater magnet for entrepreneurs, thus bringing about the current surplus of supply outlets over demand, with restaurateurs engaging in destructive price competition in a struggle for a viable share of an inadequate (and, according to one respondent, 'fickle') customer base. While the catering trade has presented South Asian entrepreneurs with an excellent opportunity to address a wide market beyond the bounds of their own community, this has proved insufficient to accommodate the explosive growth in numbers of those seeking to supply it. Non-South Asians, too, are frequently placed in similar difficulties with customer recruitment, with 'English' restaurants struggling to establish a definite and recognised identity for their cuisine; and African-Caribbeans often trapped in low-income, inner-city areas.

Among restaurateurs in the Balti Quarter, extreme price-cutting is the common response to hyper-competition, a highly self-destructive and short-termist strategy, as acknowledged by one of the Pakistani proprietors interviewed:

> Well there are just too many people. So what they do, they put their prices down, so they kill the market. You know, they have got 20% off or 50% off, you buy one and get one free, it's just killing the market.

In a similar vein, a neighbouring Indian owner declares, "Sometimes it's better to close up and stay at home" (Ram et al, 2002, p 27).

Not surprisingly in view of such hostile market conditions, Balti firms tend to be characterised by low aspirations, being oriented towards basic survival rather than profit-maximisation. Consistent with this, the notion of 'success' is evaluated in an extremely modest way, a typical response being "If you can pay the bills and make a living, that's it, that's success". Here we note that such modest independent survivalism is actually much more representative of small business culture than are the go-getters discussed in the following section. Independence rather than material gain has always been the small entrepreneur's cardinal motivation (Bechofer and Elliott, 1978; Storey, 1994), an orientation completely unaffected by ethno-cultural identity. Indeed the most explicit proponent of these values among our interviewees is actually a white restaurateur for whom "Success has never meant growth and I've never wanted to be a millionaire; it's just having a restaurant with customers who enjoy coming here".

Alongside the survivalists, the present sample also contains numerous intensely proactive operators not content with passive coasting on the edge of survival. In Ram and Hillin's (1991) original concept of breakout, the emphasis was on the need for ethnic minority firms to shift into higher-order sectors of the economy but the present respondents demonstrate the alternative possibility of repositioning within an existing sector so as to take better advantage of its potential. At the broadest level, our respondents' common strategy is designed to distinguish themselves from competitors and create an individual niche for themselves. We are able to identify four broad variations on this theme.

Product differentiation

Given its essential creativity, the restaurant trade offers obvious scope for any individual firm to blunt the hard edge of competition by promoting its own uniqueness. Creating a personal monopoly by doing something no one else does is perhaps the surest way to flourish in a hyper-competitive market. In a trade based in the most literal sense on catering to consumer taste, the most obvious strategy for winning and retaining custom is to create a unique style and content of cuisine, and several of our South Asian respondents have taken a conscious decision to stand apart from the dominant undifferentiated Balti cuisine. One Indian owner plumped for 'traditional Punjabi' cuisine and goes so far as to prepare meals to customers' specifications when requested. Another South Asian respondent defined the personal market niche thus: "I don't copy other people, so I don't regard anybody as my competitor at all". This approach had also been followed by one of the African-Caribbean owners who offered 'authentic Jamaican food with live entertainment', while a white restaurateur claimed to serve food 'unique to this restaurant'. This last owner also emphasised customer care as part and parcel of this approach: "We spend more time socialising with the diners than we do cooking for them". A key feature of this group, this approach enabled proprietors to become aware of changing customer preferences and adjust their service accordingly.

Upmarket shift

While the above strategy is well designed to cultivate a loyal core of customers and to maximise the owner's own job satisfaction, it is not necessarily consistent with fast-growth money-making. More oriented in this direction area are those whose strategy is based on a shift towards high-quality food in expensive surroundings tapping into customers prepared to pay a premium price. Among our sample this was best exemplified by the Indian owner of 'a very high class restaurant', the culmination of two decades of restaurant ownership, with accumulated profits ploughed back into constant growth. This was a capital-intensive and highly professionalised venture undertaken by an unusually well resourced individual, with a business family background and a business studies degree. As such it was well beyond the reach of the mass of capital-starved ethnic minority entrepreneurs.

Portfolio breakout

Much the same applies to this strategy, the acquisition of multiple outlets and/or additional activities supplementing the core business (13 employers owned more than one business). Representative of this approach is a Bangladeshi owner-manager who held partnerships in several restaurants dotted across the West Midlands, while retaining sole ownership of his headquarters business in inner Birmingham. What sets him apart from the average is his early start in the 1970s and a long-term policy of accumulating capital by selling businesses as going concerns to new entrants, a strategy not open to newcomers with few resources. A cheaper version of this diversification strategy was adopted by a Pakistani eatery, which has developed a supplementary line supplying other restaurants with starters. Unhappily, this is a very labour-intensive undertaking, and effectively traps the entrepreneur in the very situation from which breakout is supposed to be an escape.

Locational breakout

Recently Rekers and van Kempen (2000) have made a convincing case for according greater analytical priority to the spatial context of minority ethnic enterprise. As a consumer service, restaurant catering is a classic example of a locationally sensitive activity, whose outlets need to be positioned strategically in relation to the uneven distribution of market potential within the city. Certainly our own respondents appear conscious of this factor, being for the most part strategically rather than randomly located. One potentially rewarding strategy is to locate within an agglomeration of similar businesses, whose reputation guarantees pulling power over a wide radius. In effect, businesses benefit from collective economies of scale. Thus, a concentrated swarm of Balti houses has beneficial cluster effects because, as one of our Pakistani respondents notes, "You are getting more people into the area and picking up passing trade". Indeed, more than one of the interviewed owners mentioned customers attracted from as far as Wales and North West England, a truly impressive travel-to-eat hinterland. Given Birmingham's current policy of rebranding itself as a multicultural city of spectacle and leisure, we would anticipate a further boost in this direction from tourists and other visitors, especially if the Balti Quarter is assiduously promoted as a cultural and leisure experience.

However, as we have seen earlier in this chapter, such spatial niches are finite and beyond a certain point diminishing returns set in. Spoilt for choice, diners tend to flit in fickle fashion from one Balti house to another, with several owners complaining about what they see as a lack of customer loyalty. Not surprisingly, then, several of the most commercially successful firms in the sample are those who have consciously (re)located in potentially rewarding areas such as affluent residential suburbs and city-centre spaces. Two of our Indian respondents are lucratively established in Birmingham city centre, profiting from their role as part of the general night-out experience. Others, like the successful owner ensconced in leafy Solihull have opted to put literal distance between themselves and the competition by tapping into a high-income local market. In a market where the principal competitive threat stems from fellow South Asians, the benefits of being the only – or even the first – curry house are inestimable.

Despite the success of these breakout firms, we nevertheless need to face the reality that these strategies are a strictly rationed option, open only to an elite minority. With the exception of product differentiation, all these approaches are necessarily capital-intensive, in some instances extremely so, given the expense of acquiring and equipping premises in prime locations. Bearing in mind that access to adequate financing is a perennial problem for ethnic minorities, with recurrent complaints about the stickiness of bank funding (Deakins et al, 1994; Ram et al, 2002), such strategies are beyond the means of the average South Asian or African-Caribbean entrepreneur. Certainly the scale of investment required – comfortably into six figures for several respondents – places it well beyond the range of the family and community social capital on which ethnic entrepreneurs supposedly depend. What we are now witnessing here is a quantum shift in scale and modus operandi, one that switches the onus gradually away from informal resources and on to mainstream market sources of labour and capital. In effect, market breakout also entails a degree of breakout from dependence on the family, a change that will become evident in the following section.

Labour market practices, family and co-ethnic labour

Let us now turn our attention to the ways in which the role of the business family and of co-ethnic employees has both influenced and been affected by these strategies. Advantageous access to labour power from family and community has been seen as a key element in ethnic small business, with the entrepreneur's family accorded critical importance as a business resource (Werbner, 1990; Barrett et al, 1996; Sanders and Nee, 1996; Ram and Jones, 1998). From the very outset, the family has been presented as the primary source of the rich social and economic capital, which so benefits the ethnic minority business owner. Usefully summarised by Sanders and Nee (1996), the argument states that immigrant-origin entrepreneurs gain decisive advantages from their embeddedness in the large, extended, often patriarchal families typical of their cultural traditions. For most writers, the key element in the family firm is *trust*, which not only helps to ensure a ready supply of low-cost willing labour and of pooled savings (Werbner, 1990) but also eliminates the capital versus labour antagonism typical of pure capitalist organisations. Extending this logic, many accounts present the ethnic business family as essentially harmonious, cemented together by the mutual reciprocity and stakeholder status of all its members. Essentially the family is the business and vice versa (Baines and Wheelock, 1998).

Although change is very definitely afoot, we would stress that the involvement of family members continues in almost all of the minority ethnic firms interviewed in the present study and in some cases remains absolutely crucial. It is also the case, however, that its role assumes its greatest importance among the survivalist firms, whose social relations come closest to those customarily depicted for ethnic catering (see Bailey, 1987; Parker, 1994). Labour power is the key resource supplied here, with many of these entrepreneurs enjoying contributions from spouses, siblings, older children, cousins and other blood relatives. As well as sheer weight of numbers, family members were qualitatively distinguished, tending to occupy senior positions, with routine paid jobs more often filled by fellow Asian non-family members.

In such key positions of responsibility, where the incumbent's reliability needs to be automatically assumed, the trust factor assumes maximum potency. Following from Weidenbaum's (1996) observation that few workers beyond the blood relative circle can inspire such trust levels, it is hardly surprising that the tendency to keep managerial functions within the family dies hard. Indeed, in the present sample, this practice continues even in some of the most progressive breakout firms, with one multiple outlet proprietor using mainly relatives to manage his five eateries.

Apart from management, however, most firms are obliged to recruit beyond family boundaries. Exceptions to this are one or two unusually large families, such as the Bangladeshi restaurant where the availability of four adult sons obviates the need to farm out any full-time jobs beyond the family circle. This is not the general rule, however. Even among the survivalists, the nature of the catering trade with its division of labour between manager, chefs, waiters and kitchen hands makes it necessary for recruitment beyond the family circle. In the South Asian firms, this takes the form of co-ethnic workers recruited through informal word-of-mouth networks, where recommendation, personal acquaintance and reputation take the place of formal credentials and references. Once again we see trust playing a key role here.

Although so often presented as some kind of unique South Asian cultural trait, family labour power turns out to be a vital ingredient among other groups too. Striking here was the woman proprietor of a Caribbean restaurant, whose start-up was only made possible by building work contributed by her brother and the culinary skills of her mother, thus belying the standard image of African-Caribbeans as bereft of social capital. Alongside this, one of the white restaurateurs declares that his long-term survival has been utterly dependent on his wife's contributions and she herself notes that "The business requires me to put money in and help out to reduce the staff costs". All this fits with Jones et al's (1994) finding that many labour practices are common right across the ethnic spectrum, with informality and trust-based relationships emerging as shaped more by the exigencies of small entrepreneurialism than by cultural values.

Unproblematic as the restaurant labour process may appear, there is the potential for tensions. For example, a gendered division of labour was in evidence, particularly in the South Asian firms. Among our own respondents this took several forms: women's unpaid work within the restaurant itself; women engaging in outside employment to supplement household income; or, that most gendered female role of all, responsibility for the domestic sphere, as was the case in almost all the South Asian Muslim firms. As well as its obvious child-rearing and housekeeping functions, this latter activity could involve cultivating links with other families and the wider co-ethnic community, networks which have been shown to be of benefit to business activity (Kibria, 1994). Here we see one instance of a very definite intra-Asian differentiation and Muslim–non-Muslim entrepreneurial contrasts have been remarked upon by several writers (Rafiq, 1992; Metcalf et al, 1996). In the present survey, Muslim owners tend to be unequivocal on this issue, as with the Bangladeshi respondent who maintained, "Most of the restaurateurs' wives have never worked. This is common in the Bangladeshi community; we do not like our wives to work". Whatever its cultural origins, this gendered division of labour is one in which women's contributions tend to be invisible and unacknowledged, even though they were absolutely critical to the viability of several of the surveyed firms.

Further possible clashes of interest also arise at the inter-generational level, where the evidence from our survey suggests that the involvement of second-generation South Asian family members cannot be regarded as an example of uncomplicated family collectivities at work. Rather, their presence was more a product of limited labour market choices, socialisation and power relations within the household. Revealing here is our interview with the son of a Pakistani owner, whose reluctance is palpable: "I wouldn't say I wanted to work here; I was just told by my dad to come round and give it a try". Similarly, the brother of a Pakistani owner speaks of being "obliged" to work as a chef for him.

For some, there is no doubt that restaurant employment acts as a last resort safety net or, as one Bangladeshi family member puts it, "The restaurant is for when you can't do anything else". In some instances, children wishing to escape from the comforting but confining womb of the family business have found themselves thwarted by lack of sufficient qualifications for satisfactory entry into the external labour market. Consequently what might appear as a positive vote for joining the family firm is frequently the result of labour market push – accompanied in some instances by parental arm-twisting.

The politico-institutional environment

So far, then, we have established a picture of ethnic minority restaurateurs and workers operating in a highly pressurised commercial environment, with various forces conspiring to drive the number of restaurants well beyond the support capacity of a fast growing but ultimately limited and unstable consumer demand. Yet, as Rath (2000) argues, the ethnic entrepreneurial environment is not composed purely of market forces but is influenced in all manner of ways (often unintended) by national and local state activity. Most immediate in the priorities of our own respondents are the effects of local planning practices and in particular the general relaxation in urban land-use controls instigated by the Thatcher administrations of the 1980s (McEvoy, 2000). Although this deregulation was philosophically consistent with the Thatcherite aim of releasing enterprise from bureaucratic bondage, it has actually subjected them to new competitive pressures. In firms in the Balti Quarter, for example, the readiness of the local authority to grant land-use change permission is widely blamed for encouraging the excessive numbers of restaurants that respondents see as their chief problem (UCECS, 1998):

> It seems like you can just walk in and just do whatever you want. When we started up we had to wait months and months before we got the permission but nowadays you can just [get it]. But they should realise that there is not enough business to cover everybody, there is only a limited amount you can do.... Like this block, they could have given permission for a restaurant, for

> a clothes shop … for any other retail business and they would have done better than have 20 restaurants saturated in one place, and it attracts people as well, to come for different things. People will only come here if they want a restaurant, if they are eating out or whatever, and that is the only kind of clientele you are going to get. (Sahid, owner/manager, *Tandoori express*, Pakistani)

Offsetting this is the role of business support agencies to assist small firms with funding, business planning and other problems. However, owners were usually very sceptical:

> I did go to Business Link for advice, but I don't think – they were just writing letters backwards and forwards, they came for a visit and Business Link said they didn't know anything about it. I already know about it and I think it was just a waste of time. (Hussain, owner/manager, *Desh Pardesh*, Pakistani)

This scepticism is consistent with evidence suggesting that ethnic minority employers, particularly South Asians, do not use business services to the degree expected (Marlow, 1992).

Summary

This chapter has attempted to show how the competitive survival and development of ethnic restaurants is shaped by a combination of the market orientation of the enterprise, the deployment of family/community resources and the regulatory framework. Undoubtedly the most important general conclusion to emerge from our findings is that family/community resources do not operate in some kind of autonomous vacuum. While family and co-ethnic labour certainly does comprise an absolutely vital resource for many, success is more likely to stem from strategic market positioning than from labour-intensive working. In essence, our most dynamic, profitable businesses are those that have broken out in some way from the hyper-competitive markets, which typically bedevil ethnic restaurateurs (especially South Asians) in Birmingham. Unhappily, because successful breakout is usually a capital-intensive affair, it is open only to those with generous class resource endowments.

Although ethnic social capital must never be downplayed, a sense of proportion is necessary nevertheless. When we consider that small businesses are very small fish in a vast dangerous ocean, it comes as no real surprise that the ethnic business household is rarely able to dictate the terms of its own entrepreneurial activity. Important as the aspirations of the business family may be, the operation of the firm has to be seen more as a reaction to wider economic forces than as an autonomous process in its own right. Apart from this, the internal workings of the firm are riddled with their own (usually) hidden contradictions along generational, gender and status lines. Such contradictions become heightened in breakout firms and all the signs are of a decreasing reliance on family social capital as part of a general thrust towards modernisation on the part of such enterprises.

In addition to their extreme exposure to naked market forces, our respondents see the regulatory environment as increasingly impinging upon them. At present, the problem of hyper-competition is widely perceived as being aggravated by under-regulation, a failure on the part of local planners to curb the excessive proliferation of Asian restaurants in the Balti Quarter. Although the classic forces of demand and supply ought, in the long run, to restore equilibrium, sensitive planning controls might be thought less painful than a bloody cull via market forces. The apparent detachment of business support agencies seems to have exacerbated this situation.

This emphasises the importance of improving the effectiveness of business support agencies including the Small Business Service. As the recent Cabinet Office report observed, what is needed is a strategy to deliver a service that is focused on and tailored to the needs of different ethnic minority groups and closer working relations with those institutions that are utilised by ethnic minority entrepreneurs (Cabinet Office Strategy Unit, 2003). Business Link operators should aim to overcome the specific barriers and problems faced by ethnic entrepreneurs and to set and meet targets to achieve this. As this study demonstrates, there is a clear need to re-engage business support agencies with ethnic entrepreneurs, particularly if they are to break out of the particular niche markets and competitive market forces within which they tend, currently, to be confined.

References

Aldrich, H., Cater, J., Jones, T. and McEvoy, D. (1981) 'Business development and self-segregation: Asian enterprise in three British cities', in C. Peach, V. Robinson and S. Smith (eds) *Ethnic segregation in cities*, London: Croom Helm, pp 170-90.

Back, L. and Solomos, J. (1992) 'Black politics and social change in Birmingham, UK: an analysis of recent trends', *Ethnic and Racial Studies*, vol 15, no 2, pp 327-51.

Bailey, T. (1987) *Immigrant and native workers*, Boulder, CO: Westview.

Baines, S. and Wheelock, J. (1998) 'Reinventing traditional solutions: job creation, gender and the micro-business household', *Work Employment and Society*, vol 12, no 4, pp 579-601.

Barrett, G., Jones, T. and McEvoy, D. (1996) 'Ethnic minority business: theoretical discourse in Britain and North America', *Urban Studies*, vol 33, no 4/5, pp 783-809.

Bechofer, F. and Elliott, B. (1978) 'The voice of small business and the politics of survival', *Sociological Review*, vol 26, pp 57-88.

Birmingham Economic Information Centre (1993) *1991 Census topic reports: Ethnic groups in Birmingham*, Birmingham: Birmingham City Council.

Blackburn, R., Curran, J. and Woods, A. (1990) 'Exploring enterprise cultures: small service sector enterprise owners and their views', in M. Robertson, E. Chell and C. Mason (eds) *Towards the 21st century: The challenge for small business*, Macclesfield: Nadomal Books, pp 138-49.

Brah, A. (1996) *Cartographies of diaspora: Contesting identities*, London: Routledge.

Cabinet Office Strategy Unit (2003) *Ethnic minorities and the labour market*, London: Cabinet Office.

Deakins, D., Hussain, G. and Ram, M. (1994) *Ethnic entrepreneurs and commercial banks: Untapped potential*, Birmingham: University of Central England Business School.

Flap, H., Kumcu, A. and Bulder, B. (2000) 'The social capital of ethnic entrepreneurs and their business success', in J. Rath (ed) *Immigrant businesses: The economic, political and social environment*, London: Macmillan, pp 142-61.

Freeman, G. and Ogelman, N. (2000) 'State regulatory regimes and immigrants' informal economic activity', in J. Rath (ed) *Immigrant businesses: The economic, political and social environment*, London: Macmillan, pp 90-106.

Jones, T., McEvoy, D. and Barrett, G. (1992) *Small business initiative: Ethnic minority component*, Swindon: ESRC.

Jones, T., McEvoy, D. and Barrett, G. (1994) 'Labour-intensive practices in the ethnic minority firm', in J. Atkinson and D. Storey (eds) *Employment, the small firm and the labour market*, London: Routledge, pp 172-205.

Jones, T., McEvoy, D. and Barrett, G. (2000) 'Market potential as a decisive influence on the performance of ethnic minority business', in J. Rath (ed) *Immigrant businesses: The economic, political and social environment*, London: Macmillan, pp 37-53.

Kibria, N. (1994) 'Household structure and family ideologies: the dynamics of immigrant economic adaptation among Vietnamese refugees', *Social Problems*, vol 41, pp 81-96.

Kloosterman, R., van Leun, J. and Rath, J. (1999) 'Mixed embeddedness: (in)formal economic activities and immigrant businesses in the Netherlands', *International Journal of Urban and Regional Research*, vol 23, pp 252-66.

Light, I. (1972) *Ethnic enterprise in America*, Berkeley, CA: University of California Press.

Light, I. and Bonacich, E. (1988) *Immigrant entrepreneurs*, Berkeley, CA: University of California Press.

McEvoy, D. (2000) 'Support and regulation: two faces of British government and ethnic minority businesses', Paper presented at the 12th International Conference of Europeanists, Chicago, 31 March.

Marlow, S. (1992) 'Take-up of business growth training schemes by ethnic minority owned small firms', *International Small Business Journal*, vol 10, no 4, pp 34-46.

Metcalf, H., Modood, T. and Virdee, S. (1996) *Asian self-employment: The interaction of culture and economics*, London: Policy Studies Institute.

Mintel (1999) *Food and drink: Indian food*, London: Mintel International Group Ltd.

Parker, D. (1994) 'Encounters across the counter: young Chinese people in Britain', *New Community*, vol 20, pp 621-34.

Rafiq, M. (1992) 'Ethnicity and enterprise: a comparison of Muslim and non-Muslim-owned businesses in Britain', *New Community*, vol 19, pp 43-60.

Ram, M. (1992) 'Coping with racism: Asian employers in the inner city', *Work, Employment and Society*, vol 6, pp 601-18.

Ram, M. (1994) *Managing to survive: Working lives in small firms*, Oxford: Blackwell.

Ram, M. and Hillin, G. (1991) 'Achieving "break-out": developing mainstream ethnic minority business', *Small Business Enterprise and Development*, vol 1, pp 15-21.

Ram, M. and Jones, T. (1998) *Ethnic minority business in Britain*, London: Small Business Research Trust.

Ram, M., Jones, T., Abbas, T. and Sanghera, B. (2002) 'Ethnic minority enterprise in its urban context: South Asian restaurants in Birmingham', *International Journal of Urban and Regional Research*, vol 26, pp 24-40.

Ram, M., Sanghera, B., Abbas, T., Barlow, G. and Jones, T. (2000) 'Ethnic minority business in comparative perspective: the case of the independent restaurant sector', *Journal of Ethnic and Migration Studies*, vol 26, pp 495-510.

Rath, J. (2000) 'Immigrant businesses and their economic, politico-institutional and social environment', in J. Rath (ed) *Immigrant business: The economic, political and social environment*, Basingstoke: Macmillan, pp 1-19.

Rath, J. and Kloosterman, R. (2000) 'Outsiders' business: research on immigrant entrepreneurs in the Netherlands', *International Migration Review*, vol 34, no 3, pp 657-81.

Rekers, A. and van Kempen, R. (2000) 'Location matters: ethnic entrepreneurs and the spatial context', in J. Rath (ed) *Immigrant businesses: The economic, political and social environment*, London: Macmillan, pp 54-69.

Rex, J. (1987) 'Life in the ghetto', in J. Benyon and J. Solomos (eds) *The roots of urban unrest*, Oxford: Pergamon, pp 103-10.

Sanders, J. and Nee, V. (1996) 'The family as social capital and the value of human capital', *American Sociological Review*, vol 61, pp 231-49.

Storey, D. (1994) *Understanding the small business sector*, London: Routledge.

UCECS (University of Central England and Cooper Simms Consulting) (1998) *The Balti experience feasibility study*, Birmingham: Economic Development Department, Birmingham City Council.

Warde, A., Martens, L. and Olsen, W. (1999) 'Consumption and the problem of variety: cultural omniverousness, social distinction and dining out', *Sociology*, vol 33, no 1, pp 105-28.

Weidenbaum, M. (1996) 'The Chinese family business enterprise', *California Management Review*, vol 38, pp 141-57.

Werbner, P. (1990) *The migration process: Capital, gifts and offerings among British Pakistanis*, New York, NY: Berg.

EIGHTEEN

Youth employment, racialised gendering and school–work transitions

Sophie Bowlby, Sally Lloyd Evans and Clare Roche

Since the 1980s, government policy has aimed to increase the participation of young people in education and training, in parallel with the withdrawal of welfare support to those not in education and training or employment. This trend has continued under New Labour. Education, training and integration of young people into the world of work have been central to policies addressing social exclusion and social cohesion with high-profile programmes, such as the New Deal, helping young people combine paid work with education and training (DfEE, 2001). The expansion of places in further and higher education and encouragement to stay on into the sixth form means that less than 10% of young people now enter the labour market full-time at 16. More than 30% of all 18 year olds now participate in higher education and the aim is to increase this to 50%. These policy transformations are bound up with major changes in the structure of the UK youth labour market, which has become increasingly part-time, casualised and driven in most localities by the growth of urban service economies (Roberts, 1995; McDowell, 2002). Not surprisingly, with social exclusion high on the agenda, policy research has tended to focus on disadvantaged and socially excluded youth in depressed urban economies (Armstrong, 1997; Williamson, 1997, 1998; Johnston et al, 2000). A focus on gender, ethnicity and discrimination and on inadequate demand for labour have been central to analyses of the multifaceted problems that groups of excluded youth face in such depressed labour markets (Britton et al, 2002).

Less attention has been paid to understanding the school and labour market experiences of more 'included' or 'ordinary' youth from different ethnic and class backgrounds in localities that are seen to be 'on the up'. How does the policy environment work for these young people? In such buoyant labour markets, do problems of racial and gender inequality in employment become insignificant? Do such labour markets offer all young people a realistic chance of secure and adequately paid employment?

This chapter explores the school–work transitions of young men and women, aged 16-25, from different ethnic and class backgrounds in the two prosperous towns of Reading and Slough at the end of the 1990s. First, here we discuss the context of our research; second, we describe the research methods; third, we detail our findings; and, finally, we discuss the policy implications of our research.

Over the last 30 years, youth school–work trajectories have become longer, more complex and highly differentiated (McDonald, 1997). Furthermore, the shift to a service economy has changed the mix of skills demanded of young workers and the opportunities offered by employers. The skills demanded in service occupations are mainly the 'soft' skills of interpersonal communication, self-presentation and self-motivation that reflect a person's social persona rather than the task-related skills that were dominant in a manufacturing economy (Duster, 1995). Moreover, urban labour markets present the young job seeker with increasingly polarised opportunities. There is a proliferation of part-time, low-paid and relatively insecure jobs in retail, finance and leisure alongside the growth of highly paid and highly skilled professional and managerial occupations. In prosperous towns like Reading and Slough, high house prices make it almost impossible for young people in their early 20s (except university entrants) to leave home without parental support. Thus, the processes of 'growing up' are being extended well into a young person's mid-20s.

The combinations and timing of education, training and paid work during the school–work transition depend on factors including parental and school support, peer pressure, personal aspirations and the state of the local labour market (Bynner, 1991; Roberts et al, 1994; Morrow and Richards, 1996; Evans and Furlong, 1997; Furlong and Cartmel, 1997). Educational achievement is a key influence on the shape of the school–work transition. It is an important predictor of later economic success and is strongly linked to class background. For example, 80% of the children of professional and managerial workers go to university, but only 10% of the children of unskilled workers (Machin, 1998; Sparkes, 1999; Hobcraft, 2000; McDowell, 2002). Those who go to university or gain qualifications through further education may do part-time work alongside their education. This is seen as a useful experience of the world of work, but not as direct training for future employment. However, for those with poor or no qualifications, these early work experiences may simply provide a taste of the work they will continue to do full time.

In addition to their class – and, hence, education and qualifications – a young person's gender and ethnicity may have an important influence on the school–work transition. First, the adult labour market is strongly differentiated by gender and ethnicity. Women have formed a high proportion of recruits entering the expanding service sector while male participation rates have fallen. Moreover, women have being doing better than men in secondary school exams, prompting fears of a 'crisis of masculinity' and alarm about the possibility that (some) young men may find themselves less employable than women. However, women's increased participation in paid work has not yet resulted in their lifetime earnings matching those of men except for a tiny minority of successful middle-class women. Women form the overwhelming majority of part-time workers and are found disproportionately in low-paid occupations. Women with children have lower lifetime earnings than women without children and men with children (Bradley, 1996; Walby, 1997; Cabinet Office, 2000).

There are also marked differences in the success of different ethnic groups in the labour market. In general, non-white groups have higher unemployment rates, lower earnings, and lower occupational achievements than their white counterparts. Although second-generation minority ethnic immigrants seem to do better than their parents, inequalities between them and their white peers persist even after allowance for differences in human capital and local economic prosperity. African-Caribbeans, Pakistanis and Bangladeshis stand out as faring least well of all minority ethnic groups (Modood et al, 1997; Cabinet Office, 2002).

Second, in the past, paid work was not thought to be so important to British white young women as to British white young men; for women, marrying and having a family were seen as more important goals and markers of adulthood than financial independence. Women were not expected to become 'breadwinners'. Such gendered expectations have been changing, although having a family is still regarded as a reason for many women, but not men, to reduce their involvement in the labour market. However, not all groups in Britain share in the view that gaining paid work is the main or even a desirable marker of adulthood for women. A common generalisation is that, among Pakistani Muslims in Britain, the primary role of women is to marry, have children and care for family members and that doing paid work may be frowned upon (Lloyd Evans and Bowlby, 1996, 2000). In contrast, a dominant stereotype of African-Caribbean women is that they expect and are expected to work full time for their working lifetime. These differences in expectations are reflected in respectively low and high rates of participation in paid work for all women of working age in both groups. One key question addressed in our research was whether these gendered and racialised differences in labour market behaviour and expectations are being challenged or are being reproduced in the youth labour markets of prosperous towns.

Our research is centred on the concept of 'racialised gendering' (Brah, 1994). The term refers to the way in which ideas of the characteristics of men and women from different ethnic groups come to be held within and impact on the labour market. Usually, several competing versions of racialised gender characteristics are in circulation, and are formulated, negotiated, articulated and spread through social networks in situations in which different groups have varying degrees of power and conflicting interests. Local differences in economic, political and community organisation may therefore influence these representations and understandings. We have addressed two interrelated questions:

- how do young people's ideas of their own racialised and gendered identities affect their labour market behaviour as they move from full-time education into the world of paid work?
- how can racialised and gendered ideas held by employers about young people influence their employability?

Researchers on youth transitions have suggested that the structure of education and training allows today's youth to experiment with different combinations of education, training and paid work – a mix-and-match approach to the transition from school to work (MacDonald, 1997). There is said to be a 'fragmentation of youth transitions' (Furlong and Cartmel, 1997) that gives individual young people more choice and control over their futures. Some authors, however, criticise this view (Coles, 1995, 2000), arguing that it overemphasises young people's ability to create individual paths to the labour market. Instead, they suggest that many young people are increasingly constrained by a casualised and insecure labour market that no longer guarantees a job for life or a 'living wage'. They argue that the growth of mass further education and higher education, decreased welfare support for young people, the rise in youth training schemes and virtual collapse of apprenticeships and other trainee roles has led to an extended and more insecure youth transition for less educated men and women. Our evidence suggests that the second view is more persuasive; that is, young people's choices are indeed structured and constrained, although individuals do have some power to map out different paths to full-time paid work.

In the next section, we briefly describe our research. We then examine three overlapping, interconnected phases in the transition from school to paid work that most young people pass through between 16 and 25 years of age in the process of potential integration into the full-time labour market:

- *Imagining careers.* In childhood and adolescence, young people start to build up ideas about possible paid work careers and to imagine what full-time involvement in the labour market will be like. Although thinking about work happens from a much earlier age, 16 years of age is a key formal turning point for young people as they are faced with options that shape their careers; thus one element of our research focused on the information about work and careers gained by 16 year olds.
- *Apprenticeships in employability.* Engagement in education and training can now extend many years beyond secondary school. During this period, many young people combine 'full-time' or part-time study with regular part-time work that can involve substantial hours of employment. In the process, they experience the world of paid work and of agencies concerned with employment. This experience may improve their 'employability' and develop their ideas about the labour market.

- *Finding long-term, full-time employment.* Most young people seek long-term, full-time work, but some young people may never achieve reasonably secure or adequately paid employment.

In the following sections, we focus on the role that gender, ethnicity and class play in shaping the opportunities and barriers young people face during each of the three phases.

Our research

Interviews with young people and employers

We focused on young people aged 16-25 who had undertaken all their secondary education in Britain, and were from three ethnic groups: those of Pakistani and African-Caribbean background and white young people. The first two groups were selected because they have high levels of youth unemployment nationally. White young people were included in order to focus on the situation of the ethnically dominant group in Britain. We chose two localities for our study which differed in the size and mix of their minority ethnic populations but which both had buoyant economies: Reading and Slough. We conducted in-depth, qualitative interviews with 230 young people. Table 18.1 gives details of the ethnic and gender characteristics of our respondents. We included some young people with Indian, other Asian, African and mixed race backgrounds, because we wished to examine the appropriateness of the 'standard' ethnic boundaries we were using to define our groups. Contacts with young people were made via schools, colleges, youth clubs, advice centres, hostels, careers centres as well as on the street.

We also undertook in-depth interviews with human resource managers from 23 firms in Slough and 20 in Reading to identify the explicit and implicit ideas about skills, ethnicity and gender embedded in employers' recruitment

Table 18.1: Characteristics of the sample (%)

Characteristic	
Gender	
Male	45.7
Female	53.9
Ethnic background	
White	46.5
African-Caribbean	15.2
Pakistani	18.3
Mixed Race	6.1
Indian	6.5
Other Asian	3.0
African	2.2
Total number in sample	230

processes. Eighteen agencies were contacted during the research, including: agencies involved in youth and community work, the job centres and careers centres in both places, the Training and Enterprise Council (TEC), the Slough Foyer, agencies providing drop-in centres, the local Race Equality Councils and the Education-Business Partnerships.

The two towns

Slough and Reading provide somewhat different contexts for the construction and reconstruction of ideas about work and labour markets. The 1991 Census showed Reading's socio-economic composition to be "a near microcosm of England's as a whole ... around seven percent of its population define themselves as Asian or black or belonging to some other minority ethnic group" (Hill, 1996, p 34). While the local authority and many of the public and voluntary agencies in the town are aware of and sensitive to issues of ethnicity and race, these issues are not at the forefront of most people's consciousness. In contrast, the 1991 Census showed the minority ethnic population in Slough as 28% of the town's population. Twenty-three per cent recorded themselves as from different Asian backgrounds (13% Indian, 9% Pakistani, 0.1% Bangladeshi and 1.3% other Asian), and 3% from African-Caribbean backgrounds; categories of 'Other Black' and African accounted for the remainder. Slough sees itself and is widely perceived as a multi-ethnic town, one in which issues of race are at the forefront of the political agenda. In both towns, the South Asian groups have a far higher proportion of young people than do other ethnic groups. In 10 years' time, it is estimated that they will make up more than 30% of the 16-year-old population in Berkshire (BLSC, 2001). The 2001 Census shows that the differential between the ethnic minority populations in Reading and Slough still remains although the proportion of the population made up by ethnic minorities has increased in both (to 13.2% for Reading and 36.3% for Slough).

Both Reading and Slough are prosperous towns on the M4 corridor west of London, with very low levels of recorded unemployment. Both once had substantial manufacturing sectors which have given way to service employment although Slough has retained a larger manufacturing sector and it was into these factories that many of the first Asian immigrants to Slough were recruited. Most recruitment to these manufacturers is now of highly skilled engineering and white-collar employees. Large office complexes lie on the outskirts of both towns and both places have seen significant growth of employment in IT (especially software development) over the last two decades. There is also substantial employment in the public sector (health, education and local government) and in retailing and distribution. Young people face essentially a two-tier labour market: jobs for those with graduate qualifications or training in specialised skills for which recruitment is national or even international; and a lower tier of less well paid jobs, ranging from part-time and full-time work in retailing and distribution to factory and office work, for which recruitment is primarily local.

The majority of respondents (93%) had done some form of paid work, which was unsurprising given the favourable economic conditions in both localities. In a pattern that mirrors national labour market participation rates, 97% of our African-Caribbean respondents had done some form of paid work, compared to 92% of the white and 91% of the Pakistani young people. There were only limited variations in labour market participation rates in terms of ethnicity, gender or class. However, this apparent similarity masks differences in the type and quality of this work and in young people's aspirations, as the next section shows.

School–work transitions: different phases, different paths

Imagining careers

The majority of young people start to explore and understand the world of work through:

- interactions with family and friends who are in paid work;
- classroom discussion;
- careers advice;
- work-experience placements;
- 'Saturday' jobs and other casual jobs.

For most of the young people we interviewed, school-based work experience was a positive experience that helped them construct ideas about the labour market and imagine their role within it. Seventy-two per cent had done work experience at school:

> [It was] the first kind of proper place of work with proper adults doing important things. (White man, 21)

> Yeah, it was useful yeah because it actually started me off and made me want to do it even more than I wanted to do. (White man, 17, talking about work experience in motor trades)

> Not very well in the first years but then when you do work experience you get a taste of it but it's [school] not, nothing good, they don't show you the real world. (African-Caribbean woman, 17, talking about why school did not prepare her for work)

However, participation in work experience among our sample was not as widespread as national educational objectives might imply. While there were similar participation rates for white men (68%) and women (75%), African-Caribbean men had very much lower rates (44%) than African-Caribbean women (75%); Pakistani men and women have similar participation rates (57%

and 62%) that are markedly lower than those of white men and women. Discussions with agencies involved in work-experience placements in Reading and Slough suggest that it is becoming more difficult to find employers willing to take on work-experience students. Moreover, there were specific problems in finding placements for pupils from ethnic minority backgrounds. For example, we were told of difficulties in arranging partnerships between employers and schools with a high number of Asian students, while stereotyped views of young African-Caribbean men resulted in them being offered unsuitable placements.

Despite these reported problems, we did not identify any differences between the types of placement held by young people from different ethnic groups. We did, however, identify clear gender differences (Table 18.2). This is especially marked in relation to jobs involving the 'care' of children (done almost entirely by women), and in jobs relating to sport or mechanical/manual jobs (strongly dominated by men). Moreover, the category 'professional', which appears gender neutral, hides a gendered allocation to different types of professional work experience (for example, it was women who tried out nursing and teaching), although some categories of professional work such as legal work were as common among the young men as the young women we interviewed.

Other institutions can provide important steps into the paid labour market both through the experiences and encouragement they provide and because involvement in voluntary work, clubs and sport is seen positively by employers. Forty-two per cent of our respondents had done voluntary work. However, this activity seems to be more common among women (61% of volunteers were women) and those who had, or were aiming for, A levels and degrees.

Table 18.2: Work experience and gender (White, African-Caribbean and Pakistani respondents)[a]

	Female		Male	
	n	%	*n*	%
Nursery/childcare	23	36.0	1	2.1
Office	8	12.5	3	6.4
Hairdressing	1	1.6	0	0.0
Catering/hospitality	2	3.1	2	4.3
Vet	3	4.5	0	0.0
Professional	14	21.9	12	25.5
Retail	3	4.7	5	10.6
IT	1	1.6	2	4.3
Sport and leisure	1	1.6	3	6.4
Mechanical/manual	2	3.1	7	14.9
All other	2	3.1	4	8.5
No work experience	4	6.3	8	17.0
Total	64	100	47	100

Note: [a]All respondents for whom work experience was known – 28 women and 40 men did not give us this information.

Young people, particularly those from less privileged backgrounds, spoke warmly about the encouragement they had received through the voluntary sector:

> There was a couple of youth workers in there … she was so interested in our lives and … she gave me the kick-start I needed. (Pakistani man, 19)

> Yeah, because since I was on that, my whole life, my whole life has changed. Opportunities have opened up and my whole attitude to life has changed. (Mixed-race man, 19, talking about The Prince's Trust).

Careers advice, both from school-based careers advisors and the local careers centre can also play an important role in suggesting training and career opportunities to young people. There were mixed responses to our questions about careers advice, but on the whole they were negative. Young people who had established ideas about their future found the careers service a useful provider of factual information, but for the remainder it did little to enlighten or enthuse them about the options available. Some had not realised the potential value of careers advice while others found the advice given stereotyped and unimaginative:

> She told me to be a builder or a taxi-driver. (Pakistani man, 19)

> I never went to any careers interviews in school, that was my fault but I didn't know where the careers centre was to be honest, when I left school I didn't know anything, so like. (Pakistani man, 19)

> Because they were saying, "Oh, where do you think you could get the information from?" and you were like, "Well, you're the careers advisor, you should be telling me". "Now, what do you think you want to be doing with your life?" – give me some help! (Pakistani woman, 19)

> We didn't really speak to the careers officer so, we don't seek any advice from you know there's a careers place in town somewhere isn't there? (African-Caribbean woman, 17)

For some young people with low qualifications, careers advice consisted of teachers advising them to remain in school so they would 'get a better job'. We interviewed a number of reluctant and unhappy sixth-formers, many of whom were male, who were questioning the value of staying on at school when it had failed to translate into better job opportunities for older friends and family. In contrast, more young women believed that education was a route into a better job.

About half of 16-18 year olds had used the careers centre, but women in this age group from all ethnic groups were more likely to use the careers centre than men. Interestingly, although the numbers are small, there is an indication that young Pakistanis and African-Caribbeans are more likely to use the careers centre than white young people, perhaps reflecting more difficulties in finding out about work opportunities from family and friends than is the case for the other two groups.

Only 45% of our overall sample had done 'Saturday' jobs or casual paid work and young people aiming for A levels and university were less likely than those aiming for lower qualifications to involve themselves in such paid work. Among 16-17 year olds, women of all ethnicities were more likely to have tried Saturday work than their male counterparts (just as they were more likely to have visited the careers centre). However, this gender differential had disappeared by the age of 18-19. It seems that young men may be a little slower to start out in the labour market than young women.

Most young people felt parents played a positive role in discussing job options and training and education decisions. The majority of both parents and children believed that gaining qualifications was important to a successful working life although, as expected, those of middle class and minority ethnic background expressed these attitudes more strongly:

> You, like, need qualifications, you have to have qualifications; if you don't have that then you won't get nowhere in life. (Pakistani man, 17)

In particular, mothers were often cited as giving encouragement and support and young women's aspirations often involved doing better than their mothers and 'not having to scrape around for money' or do menial jobs. Young Pakistanis talked about the pressure from parents for them to stay at school to improve their job chances. With the exception of the few interviewees who were estranged from their parents or who had difficult home backgrounds, parents were reported as encouraging their children to make their *own* choices of training and career. However, this enabling role was limited by parents' lack of knowledge about the youth labour market and training and career options.

We asked young people to discuss what they thought of as 'good' and 'bad' jobs and 'men's' and 'women's' jobs. The responses of the majority of the interviewees related either to their own (or family and friends') immediate experience or to very general stereotypes of jobs. There were no significant ethnic, class or gender differences in attitudes. The majority of 'bad' job types mentioned were concerned with dirt (cleaning and refuse collection), working with food or manual labour; 'good' jobs are white-collar occupations. Traineeships for skilled manual work are not seen as attractive both because of what is seen as 'low pay' and because they do not fit the 'good' job image. Although many respondents thought that jobs done largely by men were more likely to involve 'heavy' tasks, there was little trace of any positive association between skilled or unskilled manual work and a desirable version of masculinity. Young people felt the most important characteristics of jobs were whether you enjoyed doing them and the social quality of the working environment. Money earned was important but far less important than these first two characteristics.

The prospects offered by a job were mentioned far less frequently than the other three factors while only a tiny 5% mentioned that ethical considerations would affect their evaluation of a job. It is clear that young people value work as a social experience; most have not yet thought about issues such as pensions and long-term pay and promotion prospects, and they imagine a desirable job as one involving 'white-collar' work.

During this first phase of the school–work transition, involvement in work experience and paid work is differentiated by gender, ethnicity and academic trajectory. Furthermore, it is plain that, with the important exception of work experience, the majority of information about training and career possibilities comes from parents, schools and careers advisors – few employers are directly involved.

Apprenticeships in employability

Almost three fifths (58%) of our interviewees had done part-time work and a third (32%) had done temporary paid work. Part-time jobs in the buoyant service economies of Reading and Slough are abundant, and few young people reported long-term problems in finding part-time work.

The social networks of parents and friends were very important to finding the first part-time job – over half had found their first job by this route. These networks were usually focused around the neighbourhood and school. Most other young people had found their first part-time jobs through 'cold-calling' on potential employers, usually shops or restaurants. Young Pakistanis in both towns were more likely to find their first jobs through peers or cold-calling than through family – perhaps reflecting the lack of employment of mothers and the perceived unsuitability of fathers' occupations as a source of employment (Lloyd Evans and Bowlby, 1996). Using peer group friends for job search biases information flows since such friends often share the same gender, ethnicity, class and neighbourhood. In both towns we found some employers had become the preserve of a particular ethnic, gender and class group for part-time work. These biases in information about part-time jobs are of little significance to the careers of young people who continue their education, but, for the minority who enter work straight from school, such sources remain highly significant.

The interviews showed that most young people and their parents regard part-time work as a 'normal' activity for older teenagers and some parents were reported as strongly encouraging their children to do it. Rates of participation in part-time work among young people from different ethnic backgrounds were similar, as was the type of work. Table 18.3 shows that retail work accounted for nearly half of all part-time work and appears to be equally available and attractive to young men and women. However, there were differences in the types of shop in which men and women worked. Young men were more likely to work in bike shops, sports shops and menswear and young women in all other retail outlets. The exception is supermarkets, where we found no evidence of a gendered pattern of employment although there may be gendered differences

Table 18.3: Part-time work and gender (White, African-Caribbean and Pakistani respondents)[a]

	Female		Male	
	n[b]	%	*n*[b]	%
Nursery/childcare	2	1.9	0	0.0
Office	5	4.7	2	2.6
Hairdressing	4	3.8	0	0.0
Catering/hospitality	16	15.1	15	19.5
Professional	15	14.2	6	7.8
Retail	50	47.2	33	42.9
IT	1	0.9	0	0.0
Sport and leisure	1	0.4	5	6.5
Mechanical/manual	4	3.8	8	10.4
All other	8	7.5	8	10.4
Total	106	100	77	100

Notes: [a] Based on the 1st and 2nd part-time jobs they had held; [b] Number of jobs.

in the type of work done within the store. In other occupations there is evidence of familiar gendered divisions.

Most of the young Muslim Pakistani women interviewees were doing or had done paid work and had plans to continue working full-time when they had finished their education. However, several of these young women told us of friends whose parents did not allow them to do part-time work or who were placing restrictions on their career choices:

> I'm quite lucky to work as well because I'm Asian and there's a lot of Asian people that are not allowed to work, like my friends here; hardly any of them work. (Pakistani woman, 16, interviewed at school)

It is possible that the young Pakistani Muslim women who were willing to talk to us were those whose parents encouraged participation in paid work or that these young women wanted to present their parents as doing so. Although there are young Pakistani Muslim women whose parents restrict their ability to do paid work or take up the career of their choice, it is important to challenge the stereotype that this is the case for all or that only 'westernised' young women wish to do paid work. Some Pakistani women we interviewed counterposed a religious identity based on an informed reading of the Koran, which they endorsed, to a 'cultural' identity as Pakistani, which they wished to challenge. This strategy allowed them to question codes of behaviour that could be construed as 'cultural' rather than religious, including the undesirability of paid work for women. Many of these women wore the hajib with western dress that conformed to Islamic principles. Dwyer (1999) reports similar findings.

We have seen that there are differences in the part-time work done by men and women. In addition, in the interviews, young people suggested both that employers preferred women to men and that those from ethnic minorities often faced discrimination. More particularly, Pakistani youth in Slough suggested that Pakistani men faced negative stereotypes when seeking work:

> One thing, it's harder for boys to get jobs than girls ... because boys, especially Asian boys, Pakistani boys in Slough. Haven't you heard of them, Slough boys? They've got bit of a reputation for being trouble.... (Pakistani woman, 17)

This negative reputation seemed to be stronger in Slough than in Reading. However, in both towns, young African-Caribbeans believed that African-Caribbean men have a problem in getting work "cos it's how they're seen, innit? It's like they think they're all bad and whatever" (African-Caribbean woman, aged 19, Slough). The impact of such images of young African-Caribbean men was evident in their accounts of negative reactions to their appearance by employers.

In our interviews, both young people and employers said part-time jobs provide experience and skills that will help young people in future employment. Certainly these jobs provide experience of timekeeping, of social interaction within the workplace and, often, with the public. They frequently require some degree of financial responsibility. With some notable exceptions, however, they offer rather limited training opportunities. Young people tend to work alongside other young people and we found little evidence of mentoring or training that would allow them to enhance their job status. The jobs are often low-paid, low-status service sector jobs or 'stop-gap jobs' (Tannock, 2001) that offer few opportunities for long-term career development. Moreover, in buoyant labour markets such as Slough and Reading, many young people flit between these jobs according to short-term pay differentials and peer group influences – a tendency that does not encourage employers to invest in training.

Views on the quality of opportunities in the part-time youth labour market differed quite markedly between young people of different educational and class background and between Reading and Slough. Those who are still studying for qualifications perceive both Reading and Slough to be good places to find the part-time work they require. Typical comments were:

> Reading's a good place to get jobs. (White woman, 16)

> I mean not full-time but part-time work there's a lot going. (White woman, 17)

> There's so many jobs out there for everybody. (Pakistani woman, 24)

These young people did not think of these jobs as relevant to their later careers. They were content to see them as a source of money and 'life' experience because "they're not proper jobs anyway".

In contrast, among those who did not hope to gain more than the equivalent of one or two GSCEs, there was a feeling that the labour market consists of an abundance of low-paid, part-time service sector jobs or 'stupid jobs' that offer few opportunities for career advancement and movement to full-time positions. Some young workers already felt part of a 'stop-gap' work cycle which breeds negative views for the future:

> If you get the job you're very lucky and it's usually terrible pay. (White woman, 16)

> Cos at my age there's not many possibilities ... at the moment you're stuck at the bottom thinking "Oh, I can't be bothered", y'know? "Stupid job". (White woman, 16)

> Lots of retail and nothing else. (African-Caribbean woman, 18)

Young people were less positive about Slough than Reading. In particular, Slough was perceived as offering particularly few good job opportunities for those with lower qualifications and as offering a two-tier labour market stemming from its selective secondary education system:

> Going to grammar or secondary modern can change the whole course of your life... It's really unheard of for kids on council estates to manage to get into grammar schools ... feel like you've failed at 12. (White man, 17, Slough)

During this phase of the school–work transition, young people become more clearly divided into those who are working for academic and non-vocational qualifications and those who think their chances of gaining good qualifications to be small. While the former find the buoyant labour markets of Reading and Slough a valuable source of paid work, some of the latter become discouraged:

> All good jobs [are] taken by people who have sort of got brains above C. (African-Caribbean man, 17)

It appears that, from the point of view of young people, employers fail to engage adequately in the first and second stage of the school–work transition. They are not proactive in seeking links with schools, in providing work experience or in offering innovative training to young part-time workers. How do employers see it? Our interviews with agencies and employers suggest that employers are increasingly reluctant to take work experience placements and to become involved in educational programmes. They say they lack suitable jobs, that health and safety concerns limit the jobs young people can do and that economic uncertainty and the internal restructuring experienced by many businesses reduces their ability to engage with 'peripheral' activities. Furthermore employers do not see this as their responsibility – employers often blamed inadequate teaching and poor parenting for the failure to produce adequately skilled or 'employable' young people for the labour market.

Most employers and public sector agencies believe there is a skills mismatch in the local labour market and that the skills levels of young people are failing to keep up with the demands of local employers (Khan and Lloyd-Evans, 2000). Employers suggested that young people in Slough and Reading are not 'hungry for work' and that high local housing costs prevent young people making the transition to independence from parents and gaining employability attributes such as 'responsibility' 'maturity' and 'motivation'. Firms had not dropped their standards in response to such problems or increased their involvement in the training of young people. Rather, many had decided not to employ under-18 year olds, and sought older employees or skilled workers outside the local labour market.

Underemployment of particular groups of youth, especially African-Caribbean young men and Asians, is also seen as an important issue in the Thames Valley (BSLC, 2001). Underemployment, where paid workers are not using their full training and experience potential or where they are working fewer hours than they would like, is key to equality issues in the youth labour market. Three barriers that may hinder the third (final) transition to full-time work for young people from different backgrounds are: firms' recruitment practices; the explicit attitudes of employers to the employability of men and women, Pakistani, African-Caribbean and white young people; and employers' lack of awareness of the need for, or implementation of, equal opportunities and diversity policies. These are discussed in the next part of this chapter.

Finding long-term, full-time employment

Recruitment and employability

Although hiring practices varied, a majority of firms favoured both word-of-mouth recruitment and the use of recruitment agencies for non-graduate vacancies. Word-of-mouth recruitment is prevalent for the second-tier part-time and full-time jobs in offices, retail outlets and warehouses. About two thirds of the firms (17 out of 23 in Slough; 13 out of 20 in Reading), used word-of-mouth recruitment as a significant element of their recruitment procedures. Bonuses or rewards in kind were offered to existing employees for recruiting (for example, £30 for a part-time post or £1,000 or a holiday for full-time recruitment). There was also widespread and increasing use of private recruitment agencies by major firms, especially by the large national or international firms we interviewed. 'Temp to perm' strategies were also favoured as low-risk ways of recruiting candidates who might fit a firm's corporate culture with permanent positions generally filled from those employed initially on a temporary basis. Most of these firms claimed that public agencies, such as the Job Centre, do not provide recruits who are either 'employable' or 'suited'

Table 18.4: The five skills most highly rated by the firms surveyed

Skill	% of companies listing each skill in top five skills
Communication/interpersonal skills	84
Willingness to learn	55
Reliability	42
Enthusiasm	42
Motivation	39
Total number of companies	155

to the employer. The notion of 'suitability', in relation to both the firm's identity and to fellow employees, is of particular salience in understanding the employability and skill criteria used by many firms.

In collaboration with the Windsor-Slough Education Business Partnership, we carried out a questionnaire survey of the skill requirements of firms in the Slough labour market in 1999, to which 155 companies responded. Employers were asked to identify the ten most important skills in order of priority from a given list of skills and key competencies. These results were combined with the insights gained through the in-depth interviews with employers. Five skills stood out as the most desired (Table 18.4). Only a small proportion of companies did not list these five skills in their top ten. Some skills were seen as valuable, but teachable through employment and work-based training: negotiation skills; IT skills; resilience; anticipating change; learning quickly; and compromise. Many employers thought part-time paid work and involvement in clubs and voluntary work helped young people acquire these skills and favoured candidates with such experience.

For all but the least skilled jobs, employers required qualifications or ability to pass their own numeracy and literacy tests, but these qualifications alone are not sufficient to make a young person employable. Employers also assess candidates on a range of 'soft skills' and personal attributes. Most employers believed these soft skills were attributes rather than skills that could be learned. Judging a young person's possession of these attributes was a highly subjective process and respondents had considerable difficulty in defining what it was they sought in employees' personalities. Table 18.5 shows some of the words

Table 18.5: Employers' selection criteria: words used to describe desirable personal attributes

'Fitting in'	Interpersonal skills	Motivation
the right person	composure	driven
a good personality	maturity	motivation
someone who fits in	a buzz	something inside
behavioural issues	the bubble	the X factor
right appearance	likes people	
nicely spoken	gets on with people	
right attitude	a people person	
our style		

and phrases used by employers and indicates the high value placed on 'fitting in' and 'good' communication styles as well as motivation.

Employers' requirements for 'soft skills' imply demands for socially learned, acceptable self-presentation and communication styles that act against those who appear strongly 'different' in dress, speech or behaviour. This not only includes many young people of ethnic minority background but also some young white working-class women and, especially, men. Many employers were explicit about their preference for employing young women. Young women were said to be more mature and responsible and more likely than men to possess communication and facilitation skills. However, there is little evidence to suggest that employers' preferences for young women are being translated into better long-term opportunities. Young women just appear to be more sought after in the buoyant part-time phase of the school–work transition and for second-tier full-time jobs.

The desire to recruit young people who are socially acceptable to co-workers tends to perpetuate the gender, ethnic and class characteristics of existing employees. The desire to ensure that employees communicate well with customers leads to a move towards socially 'safe' employees – in the South East of England we suggest these will be people who can use broadly middle-class, 'English' styles of communication. In some circumstances, for example, retail firms serving a diverse local population, the desire for acceptability to customers can promote ethnic, class or gender diversity in firms. In general, however, our findings support the argument that the pressures are for employers of people in service occupations to select people whose social behaviour and presentation fit dominant ideas of social acceptability (Duster, 1995). In a white dominated society, this will incline employers towards those who either are white or who can 'play for white'. Furthermore, the comments by employers on women's possession of communication skills, suggest that the image of the 'good' young employee is not only white English and 'middle class' but also 'feminine'. This leaves non-white young men in a situation where they are especially likely to have difficulties in obtaining employment and associated work experience. As we have seen from our interviews with young people, this issue is recognised among young people themselves. Despite the promotion of equal opportunities and campaigns such as the Commission for Racial Equality's Leadership Challenge, many employers have not thought about or are unaware of the implications of adopting particular recruitment and hiring practices.

Equal opportunities and embracing diversity

The majority of firms in our study had a limited understanding of equal opportunities. Ideas about embracing diversity were even more vague. When ethnic difference was raised in the interview many employers became wary and claimed that they were 'colour-blind' in their employment practices and equated this with operating an equal opportunities policy:

> Ethnicity is not an issue here ... we treat everyone equally. (Engineering firm, Reading)

Implicit in many employers' discussions of equal opportunities is the notion that employees from ethnic minority backgrounds can achieve 'whiteness' in their work behaviours and self-presentation, and thus employers can and should be 'colour-blind'. A minority of smaller employers showed a lack of awareness of equal opportunities issues by voicing stereotyped ideas about ethnic minorities. However, there were striking differences in the way in which employers in Reading and Slough talked about the issues.

In Reading, many employers said they were unable to talk about ethnic difference either because they had little experience of employing Asian or African-Caribbean people or because they were 'colour-blind'. Employers had to be prompted to talk about issues such as provision for religious worship or appropriate dress and, while most said they would be willing to accommodate such differences, many clearly had never done so. Firms explained low proportions of ethnic minority employees as the result of a lack of applicants. They were very reluctant to talk about ethnicity as if mentioning ethnicity or difference might lay them open to accusations of racism. In contrast, in Slough, especially among the larger firms, there was a high degree of awareness of the potential sensitivity of the issue and many had a well-rehearsed policy approach and stressed that they implemented equal opportunities. Here, a more common explanation for low ethnic proportions in their labour force was "they lack the skills". In most firms, this was regarded as a 'fact of life' even in those who had severe difficulties in recruitment. Firms were not attempting to devise or adopt policies to recruit, and support and train non-standard applicants – for example, to use methods advocated by the Commission for Racial Equality.

In Slough, most employers believe they understand cultural differences and claim to be happy to make provision for religious practices and appropriate dress, although they were far more alert to issues concerning young Asians than young African-Caribbeans. However, their recognition of cultural difference sometimes slipped into stereotyped and negative views about employing ethnic minorities. Many employers talked about three 'problems' posed by employing young Muslim Asians:

- that the demands of the family take precedence over the demands of the job, especially for women, and that parents did not take daughters' employment seriously;
- that young Pakistani men and women were not committed to employment;
- that young Pakistanis often want to take a large amount of leave to return to Pakistan at short notice or take leave too often for religious celebrations.

We do not wish to deny that employers had experienced such problems with particular employees, but these comments suggest a negative stereotyping of all young Pakistanis, especially women, by some employers.

In both Slough and Reading, few firms actively monitored the ethnic composition of their labour force. Although nine of the firms we interviewed had signed up to the Commission for Racial Equality's Leadership Challenge, only four were actively monitoring. Only one firm employed a proportion of ethnic workers equivalent to the proportion in the local population. A common view was "if you're following a diversity policy you don't need to monitor ethnicity" (Manufacturing firm, Slough). In Reading, only five of the 17 larger firms could easily find for us their proportion of ethnic minority workers.

Three firms from Reading and two from Slough did actively monitor the ethnic composition of their labour force and implemented policies specifically intended to increase recruitment of such groups. One human resource manager stood out:

> We compare the branch with the census information for Great Britain and then the census information for Reading ... when I saw our figures for last year, I thought "I can't justify this". I feel uncomfortable, and when we're struggling to recruit anyway there must be no excuse for not, you know, using that as one of the areas we need to look at. So we're making a concerted effort. (National retailer, Reading).

Conclusions

Our interviews with young people and employers raise a number of important questions about the changing nature of school–work transitions, the crucial roles played by schools, agencies and employers, and the extent to which gender and ethnicity still shape labour markets in modern urban economies. Our discussion of young people's labour market experiences has implications for a range of policy issues, but here we focus on two fundamental policy strategies: first, the need to reaffirm the importance of equality in education, training and the labour market, not only in relation to ethnicity and diversity, but also in relation to gender; and second, the need to induce a greater synergy between the home, youth-related education and agencies and the workplace in order to help young people make more informed decisions about their lives.

Re-emphasising equality of opportunity

Although many of our young interviewees no longer believe in the existence of a gender division of labour, it is clear from our research that the school–work transition is a highly gendered process, and one that is strongly inflected by ethnicity and class. Young women's desire to 'do better' than their mothers often leads to increased educational and work aspirations, but such hopes are unlikely to be fulfilled as they still seek work in traditionally 'female' occupations that remain low paid with limited career opportunities. Among employers and agencies, there was some complacency about issues of gender inequality. However, we contend that from the classroom to the workplace, there should be a renewal of attempts to encourage young women and men to break out of gendered career paths, trajectories that neither help young women to fulfil their long-term career aspirations nor assist young men in finding work in the new service economies.

The transition to full-time work is one of the most difficult for young people to negotiate. It is here that racialised and gendered notions of skills and employability attributes shape young people's career opportunities. Since the Race Relations (Amendment) Act of 2000, the government requires that equality of opportunity should be centrally integrated into the culture and organisation of public sector bodies, including education and training providers (see Bhavnani, 2001). Based on our experience of employers' poor equal opportunities practice, we would advocate the extension of this legislation to incorporate private businesses. Organisational cultures that maintain subjective notions of 'employability' need to be challenged to implement effective equal opportunities policies that embrace diversity and equality.

Closing the loop in the school–work transition

Transitions from childhood to adulthood are constructed around formal education and learning in schools and colleges, and informal socialisation in the household and family sphere. Entry into the spaces of the labour market is seen as undesirable for children until they become adolescents, although, by the age of 13, some young people have already had experiences that condition their ideas about jobs and adulthood (Johnston et al, 2000). Such an arrangement does little to help children, particularly those from working-class and minority ethnic backgrounds, to develop positive aspirations and ideas about different work and training opportunities. School-based careers advice needs to be provided earlier, the boundaries between school and business need to be more permeable and parents should be brought more centrally into each phase of the school–work transition. Employers, particularly small- and medium-sized enterprises, should be offered incentives to invest in the youth labour market. This would require addressing the tensions in the current relationship between school and further education providers, partly based on competitive funding arrangements for sixth-formers, which do not help to foster more constructive linkages.

In 2000, when our field research ended, the government introduced the Connexions service, a new focus for youth training and employment, which aims to 'join up' the rather fragmented provision of career advice and training that we have highlighted in this chapter. While this service is still in its infancy, we are optimistic that a more integrated policy approach will improve the quality of advice and information available to young people. However, it is important that this is focussed not only on the most disadvantaged young people but on all in order to avoid perpetuation of gendered and racialised inequality in the labour market.

In our introduction, we asked whether problems of racial and gender inequality in employment become insignificant in buoyant labour markets, and whether such markets allow successful challenges to gendered and racialised differences in labour market behaviour. The answer, clearly, is 'no'. Gendered and racialised expectations remain very significant to young people's career chances and choices. Moreover, although such labour markets do offer almost all young people the opportunity to take up part-time paid work, they do not offer all a career path to adequately paid full-time work. Class background also affects young people's career opportunities. It strongly influences educational performance. Educational performance in conjunction with inadequate understanding of labour market opportunities limits many less academically able young people (who are not in other ways 'disadvantaged') to a future of insecure and poorly paid employment. This disadvantage is intensified for young people from ethnic minority backgrounds. Thus *under*employment of certain groups of young people rather than their *un*employment still limits the effective use of labour and hence competitiveness of buoyant urban labour markets.

References

Armstrong, D. (1997) (ed) *Status 0: A socioeconomic study of young people on the margin*, Belfast: Northern Ireland Economic Research Council.

Berkshire Learning and Skills Council (2001) *Draft inclusion and equality strategy, 2001-2004*, Berkshire Learning and Skills Council.

Bhavnani, R. (2001) *Rethinking interventions in racism*, Stoke-on-Trent Commission for Racial Equality with Trentham Books.

Bowlby, S., Lloyd Evans, S. and Mohammad, R. (1997) 'Becoming a paid worker: images and identity', in T. Skelton and G. Valentine (eds) *Cool places: Geographies of youth cultures*, London: Routledge, pp 229-48.

Bradley, H. (1996) *Fractured identities*, Cambridge: Polity Press.

Brah, A. (1994) '"Race" and "culture" in the gendering of labour markets', in H. Afshar and M. Maynard (eds) *The dynamics of race and gender: Some feminist interventions*, London: Taylor and Francis, pp 151-71.

Britton, L., Chatrick, B., Coles, B., Craig, G., Hylton, C. and Mumtaz, S. with Bivand, P., Burrowa, R. and Convery, P. (2002) *Missing connexions: The career dynamics of black and minority ethnic young people at the margins*, Bristol/York: The Policy Press/Joseph Rowntree Foundation.

Bynner, J. (1991) 'Transitions to work: results from a longitudinal study of young people in four British labour markets', in D. Ashton and G. Lowe (eds) *Making their way: Education, training and the labour market in Canada and Britain*, Milton Keynes: Open University Press, pp 171-95.

Cabinet Office (2000) *The female forfeit – The cost of being a woman*, London: Women's Unit, Cabinet Office.

Cabinet Office (2002) *Ethnic minorities and the labour market: Interim analytical report*, London: Cabinet Office.

Coles, B. (1995) *Youth and social policy*, London: UCL Press.

Coles, B. (2000) *Joined-up youth research, policy and practice: A new agenda for change?*, Leicester: Youth Work Press.

DfEE (Department for Education and Employment) (2001) *New Deal for young people and long-term unemployed people aged 25+*, London: DfEE.

Duster, T. (1995) 'Postindustrialisation and youth employment: African Americans as harbingers', in K. McFate, R. Lawson and W.J. Wilson (eds) *Poverty, inequality and the future of social policy: Western states in the new world order*, New York, NY: Russell Sage Foundation, pp 461-86.

Dwyer, C. (1999) 'Veiled meanings: young British Muslim women and the negotiation of differences', *Gender, Place and Culture*, vol 6, no 1, pp 5-26.

Evans, K. and Furlong, A. (1997) 'Metaphors of youth transitions: niches, pathways, trajectories or navigations', in J. Bynner, L. Chisholm and A. Furlong (eds) *Youth, citizenship and social change in a European context*, Aldershot: Ashgate, pp 17-41.

Furlong, A. and Cartmel, F. (1997) *Young people and social change: Individualisation and risk in late modernity*, Milton Keynes: Open University Press.

Hobcraft, J. (2000) *The roles of schooling and educational qualifications in the emergence of adult social exclusion*, CASE paper no 43, London: London School of Economics and Political Science.

Irwin, S. (1995) *Rights of passage: Social change and the transition from youth to adulthood*, London: UCL Press.

Johnston, L., MacDonald, R., Mason, P., Ridley, L. and Webster, C. (2000) *Snakes and ladders: Young people, transitions and social exclusion*, Bristol/York: The Policy Press/Joseph Rowntree Foundation.

Khan, J. and Lloyd Evans, S. (2000) *Slough skills audit report*, London: Windsor Slough Education Partnership and Slough Education Action Zone.

Lloyd-Evans, S. and Bowlby, S.R. (2000) 'Crossing boundaries: racialised gendering and the labour market experiences of Pakistani migrant wives in Britain', *Women's Studies International Forum*, vol 23, no 4, pp 461-74.

Lloyd-Evans, S., Bowlby, S.R. and Mohammad, R. (1996) *Pakistani Muslim women's experiences of the labour market in Reading: Barriers, aspirations and opportunities: Part II*, Research report prepared for Reading Borough Council and the Government Office for the South East.

McDonald, R. (1997) (ed) *Youth, the underclass and social exclusion*, London: Routledge.

McDowell, L. (2000) 'Learning to serve: employment aspirations and attitudes of young men in an era of labour market restructuring', *Gender, Place and Culture*, vol 7, pp 389-416.

McDowell, L. (2002) 'Transitions to work: masculine identities, youth inequality and labour market change', *Gender, Place and Culture*, vol 9, no 1, pp 39-59.

Machin, S. (1998) 'Childhood disadvantage and intergenerational transmission of economic status,' in A. Atkinson and J. Hills (eds) *Exclusion, employment and opportunity*, CASE paper no 4, London: London School of Economics and Political Science, pp 55-64.

Morrow, V. and Richards, M. (1996) *Transitions to adulthood: A family matter*, York: York Publishing Services/Joseph Rowntree Foundation.

Roberts, K., Clark, S.C. and Wallace, C. (1994) 'Flexibility and individualism: a comparison of transitions into employment in England and Germany', *Sociology*, vol 28, no 1, pp 31-54.

Sparkes, J. (1999) *Schools, education and social exclusion*, CASE paper no 29, London: London School of Economics and Political Science.

Tannock, S. (2001) *Youth at work: The unionized fast-food and grocery workplace*, Philadelphia, PA: Temple University Press.

Walby, S. (1997) *Gender transformations*, London: Routledge.

Williamson, H. (1997) 'Status zero, youth and "underclass"', in R. Macdonald (ed) *Youth, the underclass and social exclusion*, London: Routledge, pp 70-82.

Williamson, H. (1998) *Youth and policy: Contexts and consequences*, Aldershot: Ashgate.

Part Seven: Leadership, governance and social capital

NINETEEN

Leadership and partnership in urban governance: evidence from London, Bristol and Glasgow

David Sweeting, Robin Hambleton, Chris Huxham, Murray Stewart and Siv Vangen

A new leadership agenda has emerged in UK local governance. A community leadership role for local government has been articulated by central government and, following the Local Government Act 2000, new decision making structures have been introduced to support individual municipal leaders (Hambleton, 2000). In London, the first directly elected mayor in the UK was elected in 2000 to lead the Greater London Authority (GLA) (Sweeting, 2002). Beyond local government, community leaders are drawn into various partnerships, including those related to urban regeneration, creating a new generation of partnership leaders (Purdue et al, 2000). The Prime Minister himself has highlighted the importance of leadership at the local level (Blair, 1998), and the Local Government Association (LGA) has encouraged its members to adopt a much more outgoing approach to local leadership emphasising collaboration with other local stakeholders.

In a period that is witnessing a proliferation of urban partnerships and the emergence of a new elite of partnership leaders, the existing UK literature on leadership is lacking in several respects. In particular, UK research on local political leadership, while it has revealed insights into the relationships between party politics and the management of local authority bureaucracies, has tended to focus on the 'internal world' of the town hall (Leach and Wilson, 2000). Research on city leadership and elected mayors in other countries has focused on the relationship between the mayor and the council (Svara, 1990, 1994), or on the role of the chief executive (Klausen and Magnier, 1998). The relationship between the political leader and local governance is one that is only starting to be addressed (John and Cole, 1999; John, 2001). Research in the field of community development studies has examined ways of strengthening local participation in partnerships (Atkinson and Cope, 1997; Purdue et al, 1999), while issues relating to leadership have received less attention (Purdue et al, 2000), with little on the exercise of leadership in city-wide, multi-sector partnerships. Research in the field of management and organisational studies, while advancing understanding of the impact of organisational cultures on leadership within organisations, has neglected, with some exceptions (Bryson and Crosby, 1992; Chrislip and Larson, 1994), inter-organisational settings. In short, there has been a lack of focus on leadership for partnership in the 'leadership' literature, and a lack of focus on leadership in the 'partnership' literature. This chapter outlines our approach to researching leadership in urban governance. We go on to present summaries of some of the key findings from a recently completed research project. We provide brief reports on our research in London, Bristol and Glasgow, and we conclude with some thoughts for the policy agenda.

The research project

This project involved examination of aspects of leadership in three UK cities: Bristol, London and Glasgow. It did not attempt a comparison of these cities per se. Instead, different research methods were used in each city in order to develop a comparative understanding of the exercise of leadership. Our focus, therefore, is on differences in the way leadership can be manifested rather than in differences between the cities themselves.

The research in London focused on mayoral leadership (the Mayor of London and the new GLA) using documentation, attendance at meetings and interviews with key London actors. The research in Bristol examined leadership in a complex web of urban regeneration partnerships using participant observation and extensive interviewing of key actors. In Glasgow, research related to the extent to which leadership can be identified from the working of partnerships in action. Thus, an action research mode – working with partnerships – was appropriate to the identification and definition of leadership issues in the Glasgow case.

Understanding local leadership

> Leadership over human beings is exercised when persons with certain motives and purposes mobilise, in competition or conflict with others, institutional, political, psychological, and other resources so as to arouse, engage, and satisfy the motives of followers. (Burns, 1978, p 18)

Leaders can be identified either in terms of position or of behaviour (Edinger, 1975, pp 255-6). A 'positional' perspective argues that leaders may be identified, and their behaviour studied, in the light of the formal positions that they hold. This contrasts with the reputational perspective which starts from identification of who are thought (by others) to be the key leaders in the locality. The focus here is on the 'behaviour' of these individuals, regardless of their position. In partnership working, the positional leaders are those who represent the major sectors that engage in partnership working – the public sector, the private sector and the voluntary/community sectors – and those who hold formal leadership positions, such as chair or manager. However, there is no simple model of the way in which leadership behaviour in partnerships may be explained. Moreover, our research suggests that adopting an approach which seeks to characterise expected behaviour by analogy with the leadership roles and styles found in traditional sectors is likely to be unproductive, given the variety in the circumstances of these sectors and the differing conceptions of leadership which exist.

We have sought to develop, therefore, a framework which might explain the way in which leadership in partnership is exercised without prejudice to the sector from which leaders come (Purdue, 1999; Purdue and Razzaque, 1999; Purdue et al, 2000). It draws on several sources of literature on leadership and provides a framework that highlights the multiplicity of influences on and approaches to leadership. This framework, developed over the course of the project, provides a useful heuristic device for enabling comparison of diverse forms of leadership using common criteria. It has four elements:

- the policy environment;
- the institutional arrangements;
- personal characteristics;
- followers and supporters.

We conceptualise these as combining in a diamond-shaped model of leadership (Figure 19.1).

Figure 19.1: The diamond of leadership

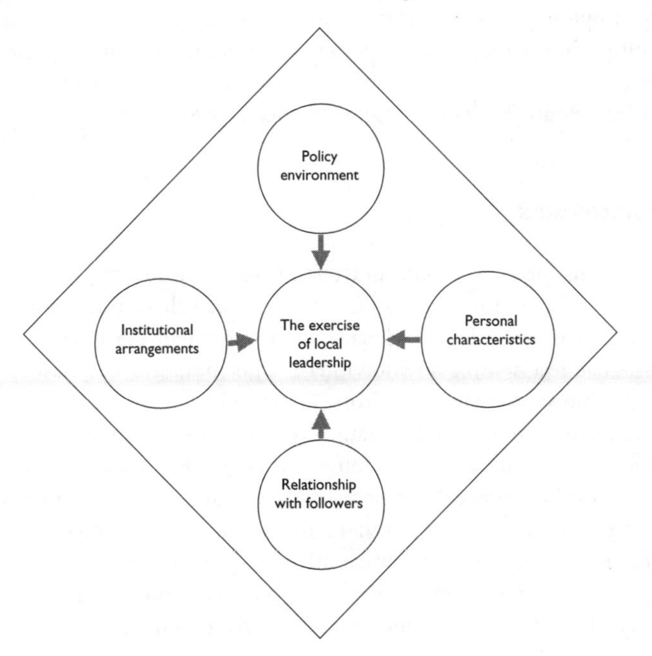

The policy environment

The policy environment within which leaders operate shapes and constrains the exercise of local leadership. At one level, the policy environment is international. Increasingly, city leaders position themselves in a global context that imposes constraints and opportunities (Hambleton et al, 2002). In the UK context, the central state imposes significant limits on local leadership; for example, elected councils have relatively limited financial power. In urban regeneration, challenge bidding and competition also demarcate the scope for the exercise of local leadership. Effective local leaders must negotiate with this environment – they understand the policy conditions that limit local discretion, and they work to identify and expand the political space within which they can operate. The academic literature would recognise this as contingent leadership, as their leadership is dependent on a given context. It follows that leadership behaviour may be partially explained in terms of theories of contingency (Bryman, 1992; Chemers, 1993).

The institutional arrangements

The institutional arrangements of formal decision making structures and informal networks, partnerships, and collaboration within which area regeneration strategies are developed and implemented, provide a second set of factors influencing local leadership. In particular, leadership in partnership rests on the leader's capacity to negotiate with other actors in the inter-organisational setting in order to generate 'collaborative advantage' (Huxham, 1996). The complexity of inter-organisational partnership working coupled with the multiplication of partnerships puts a premium on the capacity of leaders to negotiate fruitful transactions. There are links with theories of transactional leadership (Hollander, 1993; Melucci, 1996).

Personal characteristics

Local leaders bring their own skill and energy to the leadership task. Any analysis of leadership, therefore, must refer to the personal characteristics evident in the leader(s) reflecting the degree of charisma, commitment, persuasive abilities and ambition that rest within an individual. The literature emphasises the variety of leadership styles that exist. Stone (1995) adapted what Burns (1978) had termed 'collectively purposeful causation' towards a more explicit discussion of power relations and the ability to initiate change. His classic distinction between power 'over' and power 'to' reflected a new awareness of the importance of influence (as opposed to authority) in the exercise of leadership. Gray (1996) also focussed on those who 'entice others to participate' in joint action, and developed the role of the 'convenor' of collaborative action. This recognition of the capacity of the leader to mobilise collaborative advantage echoes Svara

(1994) who pointed to the tendency for many US mayors to move towards a more facilitative style of leadership, and of those who emphasise facilitative leadership as the basis for transformational collaboration (Chrislip and Larson, 1994; Himmelman, 1996).

It is possible to go further and identify leadership styles. For example, Skelcher et al (1996) suggest that network participants may be 'enthusiasts', 'activists', 'pragmatists' or 'opponents'. These general attitudes towards network participation affect the potential emergence of individuals as leaders. Skelcher et al (1996) also identify three leadership roles – the charismatic, the fluid and the coordinating roles. Building on this typology we have identified a number of (non-exclusive) roles, or leadership styles, which might be adopted (Hambleton and Stewart, 2000; Stewart, 2002):

- *champion* (taking forward the goals of the partnership);
- *salesperson* (selling the partnership and its achievements to others in order to generate more resources and support for partners);
- *interpreter* (moving between networks to carry the message of one set of interests to another);
- *broker* (again moving between networks but in the capacity of negotiator, bringing together resources, putting together packages or multi-organisational projects);
- *coordinator* (mediating, bringing partners together, ensuring information is shared);
- *manager* (ensuring the effective operation of the partnership, the delivery of outputs, and the fulfilment of contractual obligations);
- *visionary* (inspiring the partnership to think long term);
- *representative* (reflecting the feelings and wishes of particular interests and ensuring that their voices are heard in the debates of partnership);
- *agent provocateur* (seeking to provoke action where it is felt unlikely to happen, generating controversy and/or conflict).

Followers and supporters

The relationship with followers and supporters can determine the legitimacy and influence that the leaders can carry into the negotiating and bargaining arenas of inter-organisational relations. This aspect of our framework highlights, for example, the importance of party group relations for councillors (Leach and Wilson, 2000) and also fosters an appreciation of the broader relationships with constituents or local populations. The relationship with followers can be crucial as leaders seek to generate support. This relationship is in part a function of the role that leaders choose to play or are forced into, but is also a function of their personal attributes and capacity to generate change by virtue of their own leadership. In this sense, there is a further linkage to the ideas of charisma generated from Weber (1968) and developed through Bryman (1992) and

Moscovici (1993), for example. Here, leaders can generate trust among their followers and give a forceful, transformational lead. This leading from 'in front' can help to forge alliances and it may develop, through moral leadership, a stance which brings a distinctive local response welcomed, supported and sustained by local followers. It may also be attractive to the media and this can enhance the visibility of local leadership.

This framework – or 'diamond of leadership' – helps to map the variety of influences on local urban leadership, and allows an assessment to be made between the relative strength of influences on local urban leadership. It is the interaction of leaders with the four variables that helps to explain the exercise of local leadership. However, leaders are not helpless victims of wider forces. They can influence – as well as be influenced by – their surroundings. For example, leaders can help to change the policy environment, and can change the attitudes of their followers.

Summary of key findings

This section briefly presents some key results from each of the case studies.

London

With the creation of the GLA, the government promised "a directly elected executive Mayor with the power to make a real difference to London on the issues that matter to Londoners" (DETR, 1998, p 8). The government seemed to promise a strong mayor, inspired in part by American examples (Pimlott and Rao, 2002, pp 62-3). Using literature on American mayors, a continuum between 'strong' and 'weak' mayors can be constructed against which examples of city executive can be analysed. The five features that are commonly used to form a continuum between strong and weak mayors are:

1. control over budget;
2. control over policy;
3. powers of appointment of senior staff;
4. direction of lines of authority and accountability;
5. existence of other elected officials (Svara, 1990, pp 47-8; Ross et al, 1991, pp 84-9; Judd and Swanstrom, 1994, pp 92-4; Svara, 1994, pp xxi-xxiv; Hambleton, 1998, pp 3-5).

Power in strong mayor systems is concentrated in the mayor. Strong mayors usually manage the budget, direct the policy making process, appoint senior staff and have authority over the work of departments. The mayor and council are generally the only elected officials in strong mayor systems. Alternatively, diffused power between the mayor, council and other elected actors, characterises 'weak' mayor systems. Budget and policy decisions are shared between the mayor, council and senior officers, and it is possible for the council to veto mayoral initiatives. Department heads usually report to the full council.

The spotlight in this model is largely on the powers of mayor and council. The model tends to disregard the informal powers of mayors, and does not take into account the relationships between levels of government. Thus the terms 'strong' and 'weak' are only relevant within city hall, rather than in governance more generally. But it is possible for both 'strong' and weak' mayors to be influential in governance. To extend the model to the UK context, it is necessary to consider how mayors gain influence outside city hall (Sweeting, 2003).

In France, the *cumul des mandats*, allowing mayors to hold more than one elective office, gives them access to networks and contacts in central government in order to promote local interests (Humes, 1991, p 27; Norton, 1994, p 132). In the US, mayors rely heavily on party networks and work hard to foster productive links with business (Ross et al, 1991). A study comparing Britain and France suggests that leaders who are adept at inspiring others can work within the complexity of urban governance to extend their influence (John and Cole, 1999). In addition to the particular activities of mayors, consideration must be paid to the autonomy of the system of local government within the national political system. Mayors in systems where municipalities are largely autonomous from other levels of government have more power than mayors in authorities where other bodies retain political sovereignty. Assessment of mayoral strength needs to take into account both the formal powers of mayors within the local authority, and the formal and informal powers that they can draw on in leadership of the locality. Using the discussion so far as a base for analysis, how strong is the Mayor of London, both within and beyond city hall?

Within the GLA, the Mayor of London is very much a strong mayor. The mayor controls the budget, as it is mayoral prerogative to propose the budget, and the assembly requires a two thirds majority to overturn the budget (even then it must substitute another). With regard to policy making, again the mayor is clearly dominant. The strategies of the mayor, while subject to assembly scrutiny, do not need assembly approval. The mayor appoints many (but not all) senior staff, including 12 people to the mayor's office, and many board members of the functional bodies – although the assembly appoints the chief executive of the GLA. The GLA is the only elected London-wide body, though its powers are not substantial.

Outside the GLA, and in contrast to the powerful position within the institution of the GLA, the mayor is far more constrained, and can only be described as weak. The autonomy of local government in the UK is slight as local councils are dominated by central government (Carter, 1996). The GLA is no different. Created by parliament, the GLA could be reformed or abolished by parliament. The GLA has no direct tax raising powers, though congestion charging will provide a small income stream in the future. While there is a power of general competence for the GLA, it is prohibited to spend money on matters such as housing, health and education. The policies of the GLA must have regard to national policies, and there are reserve powers for the government in many aspects of the GLA's functions (Pimlott and Rao, 2002, pp 72-5).

Ken Livingstone, the first directly elected mayor of London, and former Labour politician, was expelled from the Labour Party because he stood as an independent candidate in the mayoral election. For a time, therefore, he could not count on exercising influence through party connections. He also gave up other elective offices. Alliances within the GLA involving the mayor and the assembly members can be uncomfortable, but given the strength of the mayor in relation to the GLA this was not so critical as the lack of party support, either upwards to central government, or downwards to London boroughs. Relations with the Association of London Government have been fractious and conflictual (Pimlott and Rao, 2002, pp 166-7). The issue of funding the London underground railway system led to court, with the government successfully defending itself in actions brought by Livingstone and his transport team. Such difficult relations may go some way towards explaining why Livingstone has tried to, and succeeded in, rejoining the Labour Party. Damaging exchanges that were once played out in public arenas can now be kept private, and the mayor will be more likely, through party loyalty, to gain the support of other governmental bodies.

Livingstone has been unexpectedly 'pro-business' – for example, being in favour of tall buildings, advocating membership of the Single European currency, and having city interests represented in his advisory cabinet. His approach is, nevertheless, some way from one of forming a coalition between big business and the mayor in order to achieve collective action to work towards common goals.

The discussion so far indicates that, in creating the GLA, the government has delivered half of what it promised. The Mayor of London is powerful within the institution of the GLA. In relation to London governance as a whole, however, he is weak and these constraints serve to undermine the possibility of effective political leadership by the mayor in the capital.

Bristol

In Bristol, where there was a situation of complexity surrounding the relationship of the key regeneration partnership (the Bristol Regeneration Partnership) to a myriad of other partnerships, identification of any clear leadership role is extremely difficult. Different sectors of local governance (public, private, voluntary and community) and different levels of government (from neighbourhood to region) have all put forward 'leaders'. The fact that a number of local leaders held membership of more than one partnership may have helped the sharing of information and the integration of otherwise disparate initiatives. However, it was often unclear how those sitting on more than one partnership divided their loyalty between the different partnerships, and whether other partnership participants were aware of the range of partnerships that some members sat on.

The arrangements for partnership working move through successive phases as their role and functions evolve (Snape and Stewart, 1996; Lowndes and Skelcher, 1998). The shifting pattern of partnership working in the Bristol city-region emphasises this point as new regional and sub-regional and neighbourhood partnerships supplement the more long-standing city partnership arrangements. A number of partnership phases can be identified in Bristol in each of which collaborative leadership played a particular role.

In Bristol, five phases in partnership working can be discerned. In the early 1990s, some individual leaders sought to *promote* the idea of public–private partnerships in Bristol, and by doing so established the normative framework that enabled partnerships to occur. Thus, the task included 'selling' the philosophy of partnership, alongside or in preference to more conventional methods of working.

Once this cultural framework was established, leaders were evident in this mid-1990s phase in the *establishment* of partnerships by identifying areas of common interest, 'sounding-out' prospective participants, establishing structures and working out common goals. Both 'power brokers' and 'managers' (Stewart, 1998) contributed to this function which consists of carrying the dominant culture into the operational aspects of collaborative working and creating the specific circumstances within which collective action will occur.

A third phase of leadership (late 1990s-early 2000s) required many of the same skills as the second phase in order to *maintain* and *support* the partnership. Partnership participants will still need some reason to remain part of the partnership after formation. However, members of partnerships in Bristol suggested that additionally a managerial type of leadership is needed at the third phase. Thus, while the power brokers may remain nominally members of any one partnership as it moves into the implementation stage, their active involvement may wane as their energy is transferred either to the maintenance of the partnership culture in general or to the construction of new partnership structures.

The fourth phase of partnership working shows evidence of partnership fatigue associated with leadership *attrition*. Motivation falls and leaders become more wary of joining partnerships, less inclined to attend meetings other than those they deem to be crucial and more willing to send alternates to keep a watching brief on partnerships rather than to actively participate.

It is unsurprising, therefore, that a fifth stage is visible, nationally and locally. This occurs where the protection of the partnership philosophy is combined with a drive to consolidation, and *rationalisation*. This last tendency is captured in the government's latest thinking on Local Strategic Partnerships (LSPs) (DTLR, 2001).

How far is it possible to relate these observations about the evolution of the leadership role (from promotion, to establishment, to maintenance and support, through attrition, to rationalisation) to the framework of leadership influences (policy environment, institutional arrangements, personal characteristics, followers and supporters), and to roles and styles of leadership? Table 19.1 sets out one set of relationships that appears to emerge from the Bristol data.

At the outset, in the *promotion* phase, strong personal styles are important as those organisations unused to or suspicious of joint working are hesitant about

Table 19.1: Leadership influence and partnership phase: the Bristol conclusions

Partnership	Leadership influence
1 Promotion	Policy environment crucial but personal style also central; Followers provide legitimacy *Leader as champion or visionary*
2 Establishment	Policy environment continues as driver; Institutional arrangements become important; Personal style gives way to systems; Membership defines role of followers *Leader as broker or negotiator*
3 Maintenance and support	Personal style subservient to arrangements as partnership bureaucracy takes over *Leader as manager*
4 Attrition	Partnership matures; Follower fatigue sets in; Arrangements become routine; Leadership succession becomes an issue *Leader as absentee*
5 Rationalisation	Policy environment demands rationalisation; Strong leadership demanded; Leaders establish strategic roles; New arrangements/protocols required; Followers seek accountability *Leader as coordinator*

new forms of collaboration and need leaders to convince them of the benefits of becoming involved. Followers are uncertain, but are willing to put their faith in new ways of working if a convincing vision can be articulated. However, the behaviour of leaders is heavily dependent upon the policy environment set by central government. Central government establishes the strategic framework for partnership working – the LSP. That such partnerships will be accredited emphasises the force of the external environment on local autonomy and leadership (DTLR, 2001).

The policy environment continues to dominate during the *establishment* phase. Central government has reinforced the requirement for partnership and indeed prescribed the form and working of partnerships that receive public money. Individual leaders become less significant as the systems and institutional arrangements for partnership working are established. But partnerships have to be put together and brokerage, negotiation and packaging of bids become the premium skills. Followers are rewarded (or not) by membership and status within the partnership structures.

Partnership management and *maintenance* then becomes crucial. A bureaucratic style of partnership working dominates, and 'the system' imposes itself on leaders. Transactional behaviour becomes a kind of juggling process, as leaders seek to hold together a wide variety of interests and public, private and community constituencies overlap.

In a fourth phase as the partnership matures and its procedures become routinised, many of those involved begin to experience partnership fatigue and a process of leadership *attrition* commences. The initial leaders become less central, either because they are tired and wish to move on or because the partnership has built the capacity of new leaders. Thus, succession becomes a major organisational (and sometimes inter-organisational) issue as new leaders emerge.

Less clear are the leadership features that might characterise the emergence of a *rationalisation* agenda such as that required for LSP. The environment demands rationalisation; strategic and collaborative leadership is expected; and new arrangements and protocols need to be put in place to make sense of the current complexity. The requirements of LSPs suggest leaders will need to revisit the vision for governance of the locality. How can partners be drawn into the process? How can inclusiveness be achieved? At the same time rationalisation can be threatening to existing power structures and a sophisticated leadership is needed to steer the local governance in a new era.

Glasgow

The Glasgow team's work focused on gaining a conceptual understanding of the nature and relevance of the concept of leadership to the practice of partnership working (Huxham and Vangen, 2000). It concentrated on the detail of the workings of a small number of partnerships with the theory being drawn in the main from data taken from health promotion partnerships in the city. Since the attention of the work was strongly centred on practice, the conception of leadership that emerged characterised it as being connected with 'making things happen' in the partnership. Leadership in this context is seen, therefore, as related to the influences upon the outcomes of partnership activity. In formal terms, this perspective defines leadership as being concerned with *the mechanisms that lead a partnership's policy and activity agenda in one direction rather than another.*

The study, however, demonstrates clearly, that much of what does happen in partnerships is influenced by factors other than just the participants in the system. This leads to a conceptualisation of collaborative leadership that views it as being enacted not only by those participants who may be identified as leaders, but also by the structures and communication processes embedded within the partnership. The conceptualisation therefore identifies three leadership '*media*': structures, processes and participants.

The study also reveals that the three media are often, to a large extent, outside of the immediate conscious control of the members of the partnership. For example, *structures* and *processes* are often imposed upon a partnership by funders or legal requirements. Alternatively, they may emerge from the activities of the partnership and members can be unconscious of the structural and processual changes that are implicit in their actions. Similarly, the most influential *participants* in partnerships are not always the members of the partner organisations. For example, in many cases, partnership managers, whose role is formerly to support the partnership and who are not usually employed by any of the member organisations, spend much more time driving partnership activities forward than do the members themselves.

Conceptually, the three leadership media are grouped under the heading of *contextual leadership* because they affect the outcomes of individual leadership initiatives. The study shows individuals – both members of partnerships and other participants who interact with partnerships – becoming involved in 'informal leadership' activities (Hosking, 1988) that are intended to lead the partnership forward. Examples of such activities include: managing power and controlling the agenda; representing and mobilising member organisations; and, enthusing and empowering those who can deliver partnership aims. The study also demonstrates many inherent challenges in such activities. For example, moving the collaborative agenda forward is inherently difficult in partnership situations because members' incentives for participating often pull in different directions. Similarly, it is likely to be hard work to energise members because they will by definition have different levels of commitment to the partnership's activities. Furthermore, discontinuities such as changes in personnel or government policy frequently get in the way of even the most carefully nurtured plans.

The important general conclusion to be drawn from this study is that, while individuals' activities clearly do affect the outcomes of the partnership, those aiming to 'lead' are frequently thwarted by dilemmas and difficulties so that the outcomes are not as they intend. Wherever the findings show 'leaders' achieving the outcomes they wished for, they also show them devoting very significant personal attention to championing the cause. This highlights the paradox that the single-mindedness of 'leaders' appears to be central to collaborative success. Research that extends this conceptualisation of leadership practice in partnerships has demonstrated that 'leaders' *simultaneously* manage partnerships in a facilitative way that involves *embracing*, *empowering*, *involving* and *mobilising* and in a directive way that involves *manipulation* and *politicking* (Vangen and Huxham, 2003).

At the most general level, the practical implication that we draw from this conceptualisation is that leading any one 'leadership activity' through to completion requires a very large amount of resources in the form of energy, commitment, skill and continual nurturing (both facilitative and directive) on the part of the 'leader'. Leading across the full range of activities and processual concerns that need to be addressed to drive forward a partnership holistically, is thus highly resource consuming.

The shaping of local leadership

In the light of this empirical material from the three cities, we are able to identify three approaches to leadership in urban governance:

- designed and focused;
- implied and fragmented;
- emergent and formative.

Designed and focused leadership is explicitly built (or designed) into institutional structures, and clearly identifies and focuses on the contribution of individuals in exercising leadership. The Mayor of London is an example of this sort of leadership. This represents a highly visible and transparent approach to leadership within the systems of government. Designed and focused leadership provides a clear vision of future direction, a firm manifesto and a dedicated budget. The leader can also be expected to be high-profile. They impose influence and leverage on others, rely on a dedicated staff, offer patronage to supporters, hold office by virtue of personal election/appointment, derive authority from position and are directly accountable to a constituency of followers. In the directly elected mayor model, this leadership is personal and individualised, although it is possible to also envisage designed and focused leadership by a small group, as in the cabinet model now prevalent in UK local government.

Implicit and fragmented leadership exists in a situation of loose governance where multi-organisational partnerships coexist in a fragmented system, and where no single organisation or person offers clear direction. Instead, a number of potential leaders hold multiple membership of several partnerships which may imply the presence of integrated leadership but in practice may fail to offer it. Bristol exemplifies this tendency. Implied and fragmented leadership provides a consensual (and often confused) view of direction, operates on an implicit rather than explicit forward plan and puts together packages of resources through joint funding arrangements. Leadership can lack visibility, can depend on a team of temporary staff, have delegate and often shifting membership, derive authority from collective sanction and be less transparently accountable.

Emergent and formative leadership emerges as a consequence of the behaviour of partners within the structures and processes of partnership working. It rests on pragmatic and formative organisational and inter-organisational learning about what it is possible to achieve. In this approach, leadership means 'making things happen'. Evidence from the Glasgow partnerships exemplifies this mode of leadership. Emergent and formative leadership relies on implementation to shape policy, reflects pragmatism in developing future direction, uses ad hoc resources to make progress, emphasises learning as the basis for further action, derives authority from getting things done and is accountable for what is done not what is said.

The research considered the relationship between the forces shaping local leadership (the 'diamond' discussed earlier) and the three approaches to urban leadership uncovered in the case studies. How important are the various shaping influences in explaining the exercise of local leadership? The significance of each of the four influences lies along a strong–weak continuum. Note, however, that in some cases, leaders can influence as well as be influenced by the elements in the framework. Understanding the nature of urban leadership in any particular

Figure 19.2: Factors shaping local leadership in the case studies

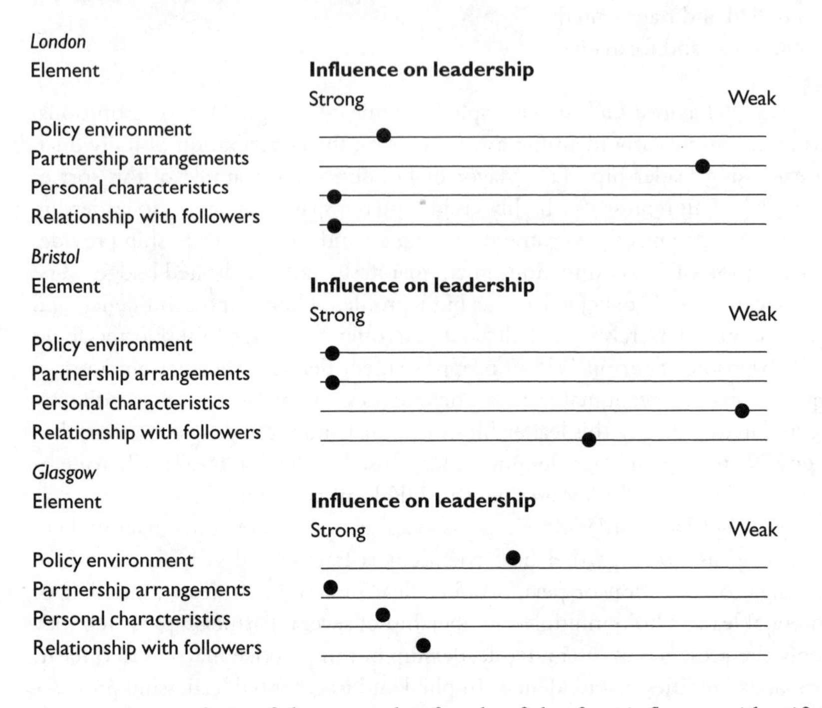

city requires analysis of the strength of each of the four influences identified earlier, and what elements of focused, fragmented or formative leadership are entailed. In Figure 19.2, we provide an outline of the influences at work in our three case studies during the period of our research.

Designed and focused leadership – typified by our analysis of the mayoral leadership in London – was clearly dependent on external policy as reflected in the powers of the Mayor of London and the GLA. Certainly, the mayor is able to shape policy and influence the policy environment; but in the context of UK local government legislation, Whitehall is able to impose strict limits on the exercise of mayoral leadership. This leadership is not constrained by partnership arrangements. Much stronger is the influence of personal style which an individual leader may bring, and the relationship with followers upon whom the single leader depends. In the London case, Mayor Livingstone has been particularly successful in generating support from Londoners for many of his policies.

Implied and fragmented leadership – typified by Bristol at the time of the fieldwork – is highly dependent on the external policy environment and the formal requirements of partnership working. The arrangements for partnership working, which are complicated and bureaucratic, soak up the enthusiasm of local leaders. Personal style counts for little, and managers and brokers struggle to achieve consensus in a situation of fragmented multi-organisational bargaining. Followers are largely missing since few are clear what the partnership is doing or where the leadership is going.

Emergent and formative leadership (such as was evident in Glasgow) is less dependent on the policy environment. Indeed, local leaders prefer to set their own agenda and may even be able to ignore the external policy environment. Conversely, leadership behaviour is strongly influenced by the structures and processes of partnership working. Personal style (building networks and trust) is important as is the relationship with followers, in this case those who were willing to forge alliances for the delivery of action. However, action is driven by the exigencies of implementation rather than policy statements; strategic direction is weak.

Policy implications

Several conclusions can be drawn for current policy and practice. Some of these are particularly relevant to the development of LSPs. First, the mayoral model has the potential to provide autonomous local leadership. This form of leadership, which depends heavily on leadership style, can enhance representational legitimacy. However, should the powers of the mayor and the organisation he or she leads be hedged in by central government, the potential of the model to deliver effective leadership will be undermined.

Second, the fragmented, multi-organisational model, which implies a collaborative approach to leadership, can result in weak leadership that is subservient to external policy influence and dominated by bureaucratic arrangements. There is a danger that partnerships may slip to a position where there is effectively no leadership driving strategy or action. Implicit and fragmented leadership is the undesirable consequence. The research suggests that in situations of multi-organisational collaboration – such as LSPs – the need is for a leadership which articulates and structures the relationship between stakeholders to ensure clarity, rather than confusion, in joint working.

Third, the tasks associated with leadership in partnership change according to the maturity of partnership working in the particular area or sector. The active promotion of partnership working by leaders to create a culture of partnership is a necessary task where partnerships have been rare or absent. The establishment of a partnership can carry the culture of partnership working from the policy level to the operational level of collaborative working. Again, however, leadership is required, as well as training and staff development, should partnership working achieve the desired innovations and breakthroughs in day-to-day practice. As understanding between partners grows, leadership tasks can then move on to consolidation and rationalisation.

Fourth, structure and process are as central to partnership working as participants. Those involved with partnerships are obliged to work within the 'media' of partnerships. Since partnerships are ostensibly collaborative, strong leadership may be perceived as inimical to joint working. Nevertheless, identification of leadership from partnership members is crucial – who holds the chair, who sets the agenda, who attends, who influences whom? These are all key questions. Leaders in partnership arrangements carry out apparently contradictory roles – generating understanding, collaboration and inclusiveness – while pragmatically steering and shaping the behaviour of participants.

References

Atkinson, R. and Cope, S. (1997) 'Community participation and urban regeneration in Britain', in P. Hoggett (ed) *Contested communities: Experience, struggles and policies*, Bristol: The Policy Press, pp 201-21.

Blair, T. (1998) *Leading the way: A new vision for local government*, London: Institute for Public Policy Research.

Bryman, A. (1992) *Charisma and leadership in organisations*, London: Sage Publications.

Burns, J. (1978) *Leadership*, New York, NY: Harper Row.

Carter, C. (1996) *Members of one another: The problems of local corporate action*, York: Joseph Rowntree Foundation.

Chemers, M. (1993) 'An integrative theory of leadership', in M. Chemers and R. Ayman (eds) *Leadership theory and research*, London: London Academic Press, pp 293-319.

Chrislip, D.D. and Larson, C.E. (1994) *Collaborative leadership: How citizens and civic leaders can make a difference*, San Francisco, CA: Jossey Bass.

DETR (Department of the Environment, Transport and the Regions) (1998) *A mayor and assembly for London*, Cm 3897, London: HMSO.

DTLR (Department for Transport, Local Government and the Regions) (2001) *Local strategic partnerships: Guidance*, London: DTLR.

Edinger, L. (1975) 'The comparative analysis of political leadership', *Comparative Politics*, January, pp 253-69.

Gray, B. (1996) 'Cross sectoral partners: collaborative alliances among business, government and community', in C. Huxham (ed) *Creating collaborative advantage*, London: Sage Publications, pp 57-79.

Hambleton, R. (1998) 'Strengthening political leadership in UK local government', *Public Money and Management*, January-March, pp 1-11.

Hambleton, R. (2000) 'Modernising political management in local government', *Urban Studies*, vol 37, no 5-6, pp 933-52.

Hambleton, R. and Stewart, M. (2000) *Leadership in urban governance: The mobilisation of collaborative advantage*, Urban Leadership Working Paper no 1, Bristol: Faculty of the Built Environment, University of the West of England.

Hambleton, R., Savitch, H.V. and Stewart, M. (2002) *Globalism and local democracy*, London: Palgrave.

Himmelman, A. (1996) 'On the theory and practice of transformational collaboration: from social service to social justice', in C. Huxham (ed) *Creating collaborative advantage*, London: Sage Publications, pp 19-43.

Hollander, E. (1993) 'Legitimacy, power and influence', in M. Chemers and R. Ayman (eds) *Leadership theory and research*, London: London Academic Press, pp 29-47.

Hosking, D. (1988) 'Organizing, leadership and skillful process', *Journal of Management Studies*, vol 25, pp 147-66.

Humes, S. (1991) *Local governance and national power*, Hemel Hempstead: Harvester Wheatsheaf.

Huxham, C. (1996) *Creating collaborative advantage*, London: Sage Publications.

Huxham, C. and Vangen, S. (2000) 'Leadership in the shaping and implementation of collaboration agendas: how things happen in a (not quite) joined up world', *Academy of Management Journal*, vol 43, no 6, pp 1159-75.

John, P. (2001) *Local governance in Western Europe*, London: Sage Publications.

John, P. and Cole, A. (1999) 'Political leadership in the new urban governance: Britain and France compared', *Local Government Studies*, vol 25, no 4, pp 98-115.

Judd, D. and Swanstrom, T. (1994) *City politics: Private power and public policy*, New York, NY: Harper Collins.

Klausen, K. and Magnier, A. (1998) *The anonymous leader: Appointed CEOs in Western local government*, Odense: Odense University Press.

Leach, S. and Wilson, D. (2000) *Local political leadership*, Bristol: The Policy Press.

Lowndes, V. and Skelcher, C. (1998) 'The dynamics of multi-organisational partnerships: an analysis of changing modes of governance', *Public Administration*, vol 76, pp 313-33.

Melucci, A. (1996) *Challenging the codes: Collective action in the information age*, Cambridge: Cambridge University Press.

Moscovici, S. (1993) *The invention of society: Psychological explanations for social phenomena*, Cambridge: Polity.

Norton, P. (1994) *International handbook of local and regional government: A comparative analysis of advanced democracies*, Aldershot: Edward Elgar.

Pimlott, B. and Rao, N. (2002) *Governing London*, Oxford: Oxford University Press.

Purdue, D. (1999) 'Community leadership in area regeneration: a theoretical review', *Urban Leadership*, Working Paper 4, Bristol: Faculty of the Built Environment, University of the West of England, pp 1-21.

Purdue, D. and Razzaque, K. (1999) 'Leadership: the missing ingredient in social capital', *Urban Leadership*, Working Paper 5, Bristol: Faculty of the Built Environment, University of the West of England, pp 1-15.

Purdue, D., Razzaque, K., Hambleton, R. and Stewart, M. with Huxham, C. and Vangen, S. (2000) *Community leadership in area regeneration*, Bristol/York: The Policy Press/Joseph Rowntree Foundation.

Ross, B., Levine, M. and Stedman, M. (1991) *Urban politics: Power in metropolitan America*, Itasca, IL: F.E. Peacock.

Skelcher, C., McCabe, A. and Lowndes, V. (1996) *Community networks in urban regeneration: 'It all depends who you know'*, York: Joseph Rowntree Foundation.

Snape, D. and Stewart, M. (1996) *Keeping up the momentum: Partnership working in Bristol and the West*, Report to the Bristol Chamber of Commerce and Initiative, Bristol: University of the West of England.

Stewart, M. (1998) 'Partnership, leadership and competition in urban policy', in N. Oatley (ed) *Cities, economic competition and urban policy*, London: Paul Chapman Publishing, pp 77-90.

Stone, C. (1995) 'Political leadership in urban politics', in D. Judge, G. Stoker and H. Wolman (eds) *Theories of urban politics*, London: Sage Publications, pp 96-116.

Svara, J. (1990) *Official leadership in the city: Patterns of conflict and cooperation*, Oxford: Oxford University Press.

Svara, J. (1994) *Facilitative leadership in local government*, San Francisco, CA: Jossey Bass.

Sweeting, D. (2002) 'Leadership in urban governance: the Mayor of London', *Local Government Studies*, vol 28, no 1, pp 3-28.

Sweeting, D. (2003) 'How strong is the Mayor of London?', *Policy & Politics*, vol 31, no 4, pp 465-78.

Vangen, S. and Huxham, C. (2004) 'Enacting leadership for collaborative advantage: dilemmas of ideology and pragmatism in the activities of partnership managers', *British Journal of Management*, vol 15, no 1, pp 39-55.

Weber, M. (1968) *Economy and society*, New York, NY: Bedminster.

TWENTY

'Pathways to integration': tackling social exclusion on Merseyside

Richard Meegan

As clearly demonstrated elsewhere in this volume (Chapters Two to Five for example), marked spatial concentration of disadvantage is a significant feature of major urban areas across the UK both prosperous and less buoyant. Problems of social exclusion and a lack of social cohesion persist despite considerable variation in competitive strength. At the same time, as earlier chapters make clear, such problems are particularly intractable in those urban areas where the overall economic context is particularly weak. The research reported here focused on Merseyside, which would fall into this category of less buoyant areas. It focuses more specifically on one particular regeneration initiative being carried out on Merseyside to address issues of social exclusion and concentrated disadvantage[1]. A distinctive feature of this programme was the targeting of a significant tranche of spending on areas of the city-region experiencing particularly marked concentrations of disadvantage. This spending, in the shape of the so-called 'Pathways to Integration' priority, was channelled through specially formed partnerships in the targeted areas that were required to involve representation from local residents and community organisations alongside representatives of public agencies, the private sector (where it existed) and voluntary organisations. In the context of the ESRC Cities Research programme, the initiative offered the opportunity to explore the relationship between core research themes – governance, social exclusion/inclusion, participation and social capital – in a major 'real time' experiment in partnership working in urban regeneration[2].

Objective One and Pathways: multi-level social governance?

The research traced the genesis of the Pathways initiative to the negotiations over the Single Programming Document for delivery of the structural funds. It had not featured in the original proposal, *Merseyside 2000* (Government Office for Merseyside, 1993), but was promoted by EC officials who had picked up on some of the arguments in the ex ante evaluation of *Merseyside 2000* over the relative silence in the original plan on the city-region's socio-economic geography (Lloyd and Meegan, 1994). The original proposal had made no reference to the marked spatial disparities in industrial development, social and economic well-being and environmental conditions that existed across the city-region. Nor had it made any prior assessment of either the spatial implications of the implementation of the programme as a whole or of the potential spatial impact of its detailed measures. Bringing together the aim of tackling social exclusion and the recognition of the marked spatial concentrations of disadvantaged individuals and groups suggested to the EC's negotiating team the need to introduce a spatially targeted measure within the broader set of Pathways to Integration measures. After what were, by all accounts, sometimes quite difficult discussions, a final Single Programming document was agreed. With national and local 'matched funding', some £1.6 billion was to be spent over the five-year programming period (1994-99). One of the five priority areas for spending, 'Action for the People for Merseyside', recognised that a key 'driver for change' in the economic and social conversion of the area was the people of Merseyside themselves, including, of necessity, groups and individuals hitherto excluded from or in danger of being excluded from mainstream economy and society. 'Pathways to Integration' contained the additional spatial targeting element of the programme. People living in areas with particularly pronounced economic and social problems were also to be eligible for a raft of measures aimed at providing 'pathways' to education, skills, training, jobs, a better quality of life and assistance to secure community involvement in designing, implementing and monitoring the initiatives funded in their areas. They were to be given something extra from the programme and, as already noted, this extra resource was to be delivered with the involvement of people living in the areas themselves. Thirty-eight areas, containing just fewer than 500,000 people, were eventually targeted to receive the extra tranche of funding (15% of the total 'matched' programme spend, some £240 million) (Figure 20.1).

The research showed that the EC's view of Pathways was, in principle if not in practice, relatively clear. It regarded spatial-targeting as providing a focus for the social inclusion elements of the programme in terms not simply of concentrating spending but also for broadening participation in the governance process. The aim was to push 'subsidiarity' in this aspect of the Objective One Programme down below city-regional level. As such, it exemplified a growing shift towards what can be seen as 'multi-level social governance' in European social and economic policy (Geddes and Bennington, 2001).

The formal governance structure of the programme, however, was the responsibility of the local partners and early negotiations clearly revealed differing institutional powers and capacities as representatives of local authorities, Training and Enterprise Councils (TECs), the private sector and Further Education (FE) and Higher Education (HE) sought to influence this structure. What these negotiations revealed was the continuing importance of government in the partnership structure: central government for reasons of overall public accountability for the public expenditure that acted as 'matched funding' and local government for delivery of the Pathways element of the programme

Figure 20.1: Objective One Programme on Merseyside (1994-99)

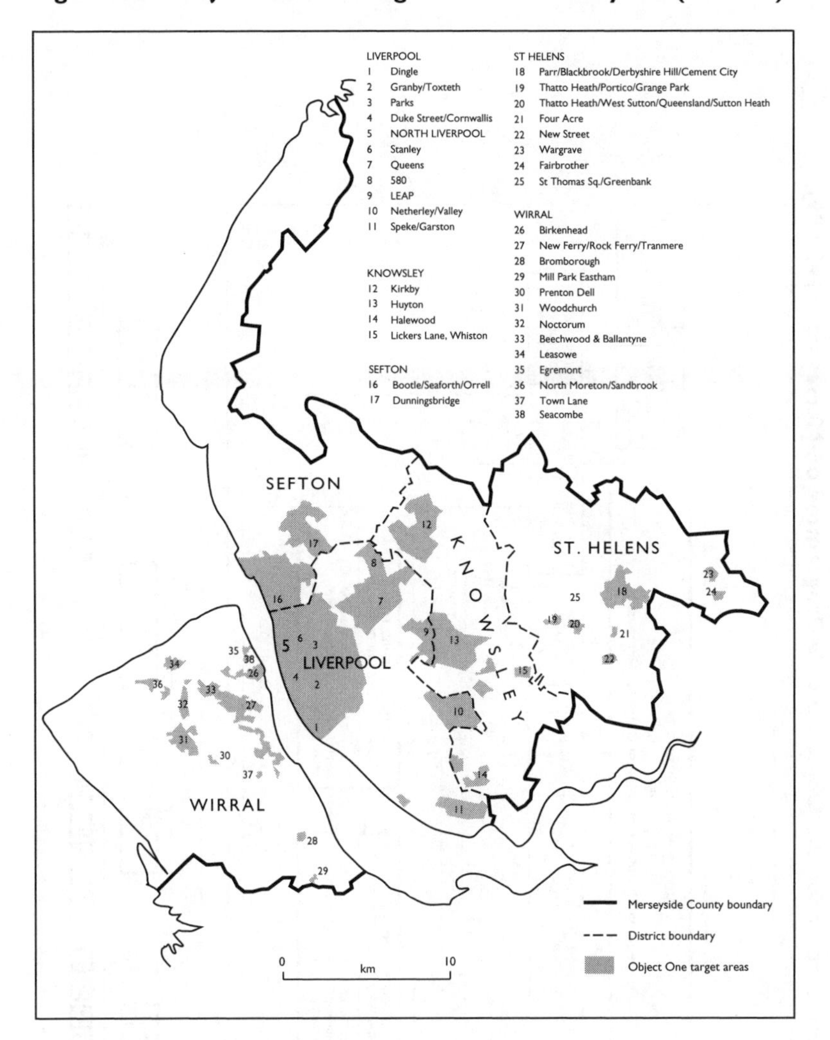

(Figure 20.2). Reports of the demise of the state, as far as urban regeneration programmes like Pathways are concerned, remain exaggerated. As Pathways confirmed, however, what are not exaggerated are the reports of the changing role of the local state and of the multi-purpose local authority being replaced by one that has to work in partnership with other agencies and actors (Stoker, 1999, 2000).

The responsibility for defining the 'Pathways Areas' and for setting up the Area Partnership Boards was assumed by local government and the research revealed considerable variation in the ease with which this could be achieved. Some areas had existing community groups and partnership structures; others had none. One local authority, St Helens, was hindered by its previous political

Figure 20.2: The governance architecture for the Objective One Programme on Merseyside (1994-99)

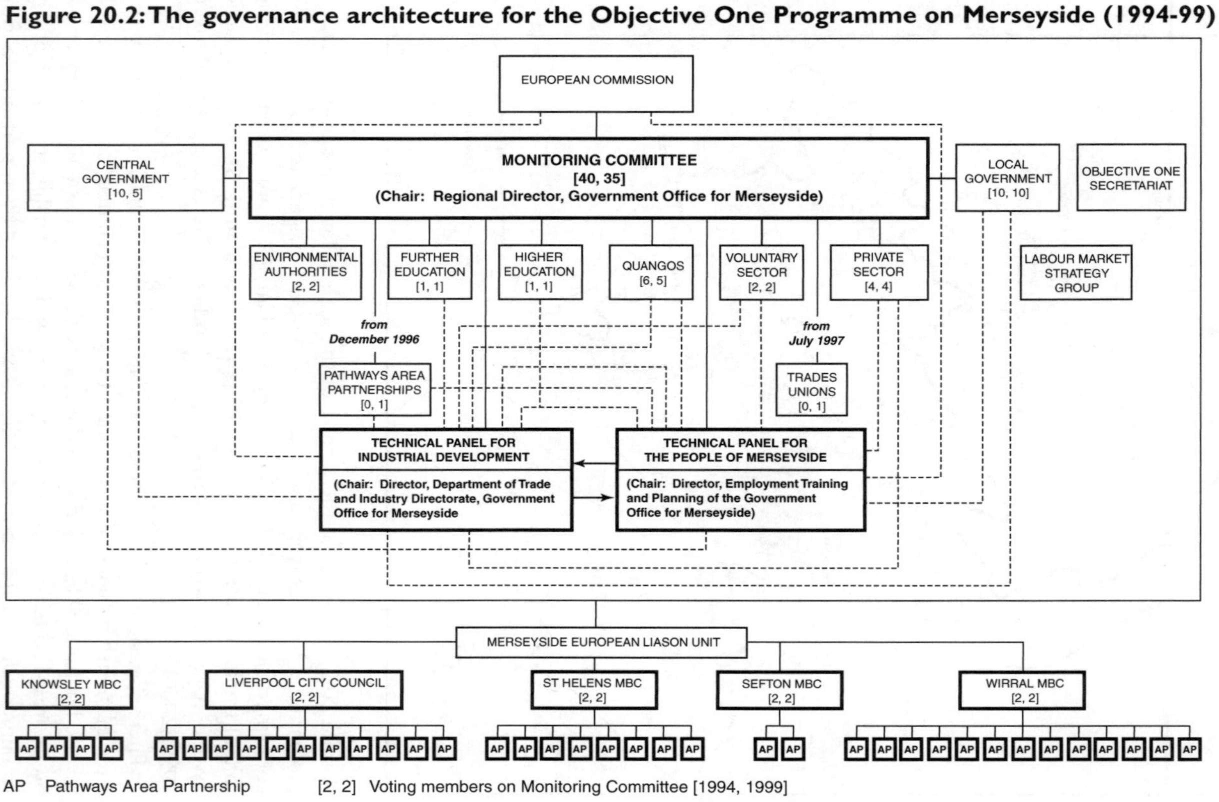

decision to run down its community development activity and chose, politically, to administer the Pathways initiative through an intermediary body (a local housing association). There were differences in approaches to the exercise across the five local authorities – on a spectrum ranging from 'hands on' to 'arm's length' (with Liverpool being the most interventionist, St Helens the least, and the others located in-between). The support structures varied accordingly. This variation in community development and political and policy support structures inevitably influenced operation of the initiative and outcomes, both between and within local authorities. Case studies of individual 'Pathways Area Partnerships' revealed this variation and underscored the need for policy to be sensitive to 'locality', to specific local social, political and economic circumstances and the different historical trajectories and 'path dependencies' of different areas even in the same local authority districts.

Social exclusion and Pathways

'Social exclusion' has become a key element of the political and policy discourses of European economic and social policy and is at the centre of the tension in these discourses between the agendas of 'competitiveness' and 'cohesion'. Combating social exclusion in Europe can justifiably claim to be the 'new urban policy challenge' (Atkinson, 2000). Given the political nature of 'social exclusion', there are inevitably a number of different approaches to understanding it, which are themselves based on very different theoretical perspectives and political ideologies. It is essential, therefore, that those using the concept explicitly define it. This definition needs to be multidimensional (and not simply income related), dynamic and processual (emphasising the processes causing social exclusion, as well as seeing it as a state), with a focus on the mechanisms, actors and institutions operating at societal level to cause disadvantage (Silver, 1994; Atkinson, 1998; De Hann, 1998; De Haan and Maxwell, 1998; Parkinson, 1998; Percy-Smith, 2000).

The European Foundation definition of the term as "the process through which individuals or groups are wholly or partially excluded from full participation in the society in which they live" (cited in De Hann and Maxwell, 1998, p 2) captures the meaning to some extent but what came out from interviews with community activists involved in Pathways was the need to extend this definition to incorporate notions of social justice and social and political citizenship rights (Fraser, 1997; Young, 1999):

> I honestly think [the aim of Pathways] it's about giving the most basic right to those communities that are in need and by basic right I mean the right to help themselves, to be involved and not to be excluded, to make decisions, to move on upwards and to fix the things that they feel need to be fixed in whatever way ... whether it's with European funding or non-eligible activities with non-European funding or whatever. But I think it's about basic rights.

(Executive member, Merseyside Pathways Network, interview December 2000)

The Pathways Areas are classic examples of the geographical concentrations of disadvantage that result from what Allen and Cars (2002) have called 'disjointed structural change'. Their 'everyday life-worlds' are produced by the disjointed operation of economic, political and welfare state structures. Structural economic change impacting on aggregate employment patterns through broad sectoral and occupational shifts produces new demands (in terms of the provision of education, housing and social insurance) on welfare states that are increasingly limited in their capacity to adjust by financial constraints operating on them as part of the political adjustment to the changing role of the state in global economic management. The loss of (manual) employment and long-run increase in unemployment accompanied by the growth of flexible labour in service sectors demanding particular accredited and personal skills have detached groups and individuals from the labour market who are also experiencing welfare state provision that is struggling to cope. Macro-structural processes then interact with micro-local factors in the form of labour, land and property markets to produce geographical concentrations of disadvantaged groups (Glennerster et al, 1998; Madanipour, 1998; Byrne, 1999), as exemplified by the Pathways Areas on Merseyside.

Our interviews with both policy makers and practitioners and community representatives involved in Pathways showed the wide range of interlocking causes of social exclusion (fragmenting local labour markets, the 'poverty trap', caring responsibilities and poor health linked, in turn, to poor quality housing) and its often 'hidden' effects (high dependence on tranquilisers, debt and coping with declining local shopping provision). What came out strongly from the interviews and discussion groups was a virtual consensus that social exclusion on Merseyside was heavily conditioned by exclusion from the labour market. Employment on Merseyside reached a post-war peak in 1966. Since then, it has fallen by some 30% and in Liverpool the loss of employment has been even more pronounced with nearly half of its jobs disappearing in just three and a half decades. Other research in the Cities Research programme (Turok and Edge, 1999) demonstrated the endemic problem of demand deficiency in local labour markets on Merseyside. By the late 1990s, the city-region stood out as having the highest levels of 'worklessness'/economic inactivity in Britain, with an economic inactivity rate of just over 30% compared with the corresponding figure of 17.5% in the South East of England. And, as the mapping of Pathways Areas itself revealed, this worklessness was highly spatially concentrated.

Data relating to Pathways Areas graphically revealed the multidimensional nature of social exclusion (MIS, 1998, 2000). Rates of claims for council tax rebates and free school meals are almost universally higher in Pathways Areas compared to non-Pathways Areas. So, too, are rates of claim for income support which, when added to the high numbers of people on unemployment benefit, underline their low levels of income. Educational attainment (measured by GCSE qualifications) – a key indicator of social exclusion – is also predominantly lower in Pathways Areas in relation to the averages at local authority district, city-region, region and national levels. Electoral turnouts in Pathways Area wards were also consistently lower than in non-Pathways Areas and with one of them, Abercromby in inner Liverpool, setting a record low level (6%), suggesting considerable disillusion with formal politics.

Tackling that scale and depth of social exclusion is asking a lot of one or even two rounds of Objective One funding. However, what the Pathways approach did provide was an experiment in developing policies to address the problems of disadvantaged neighbourhoods and a philosophy of intervention, elements of which have subsequently been pursued in national policy and specifically in relation to the current government's Neighbourhood Renewal Strategy (Social Exclusion Unit, 1998).

As already noted, a central issue was jobs and how to make these accessible, both physically and socially, to people distanced from the labour market. One of the important things that the Pathways focus revealed, especially in the areas made up of 'outer estates', was the central importance of transport and physical access to areas of new employment opportunities. This reinforces Meadows' (2001) argument that transport needs to be viewed as an integral part of employment policy. Thus, Pathways saw Merseytravel, the local Passenger Transport Authority, experimenting with supported bus services linking Pathways Areas to growing employment centres. Pathways also underlined the need for active employment policies. Access to employment is more than just physical, of course, and the social distancing of Pathways residents from the local labour market means that while generating new jobs is necessary it is not in itself sufficient to address the needs of those most 'distanced' from the labour market. Labour market policy has to be sensitive to this and the research identified a range of Pathways-based employment and training policies and projects that demonstrated this sensitivity, including:

- customised training programmes involving one-to-one mentoring of the *voluntary* trainees;
- non-vocational training operating on a non-formal basis being used as a 'bridge' to orthodox training programmes generally perceived by potential trainees as being distant and "not for us";
- outreach delivery of computer training (using laptop PCs) in community venues (again geographically and socially distanced from orthodox training provision);
- outreach educational provision for young children and, through them, their disadvantaged young parents;
- in Liverpool, Jobs, Education and Training (JET) Centres, based in Pathways neighbourhoods, have been set up to combine individual-centred educational and employment guidance with active labour market placement.

These projects recognised the social and geographical dimensions of exclusion from the labour market and were 'closer' in both a social and geographical sense to those excluded. The projects also recognised the multidimensional nature of exclusion. One example, a project targeting young homeless people, perhaps best captures this sensitivity. Homelessness was not seen as the 'problem' but as a symptom of a range of interrelated problems (such as family break-up, alcohol/other drug dependency and unemployment), which needed to be addressed in a holistic manner for inclusion to be achieved. Housing is just one element in the individually tailored package. Employment is another (in this case, the recycling of old furniture), which can provide, for the individual concerned, income and self-confidence and an opportunity and incentive to break away from alcohol dependency, offending and other associated problems.

The last example was of a firm operating in the 'social economy' or 'third sector', the sector operating in the spaces between market and state and 'formal' and 'informal' economies (Lipietz, 1992; Amin et al, 1999). The growing importance of this sector on Merseyside in general and in the Pathways Areas became evident in the research, which identified:

- an evolving *institutional diversity* with social businesses, consolidating their position alongside more hybrid organisations operating, under one umbrella organisation, trading activities and charitable operations funded through a mix of market and non-market sources;
- examples of *intermediate labour market projects* offering (social) enterprise-led training for individuals and groups particularly prone to exclusion from formal labour markets and with employment outputs better than those from orthodox training schemes;
- examples of *environmental projects* which are particularly important in a local context in which Local Agenda 21 is struggling;
- the formation of *a network of social economy practitioners*, the 'Social Enterprise Network' to support and promote the sector locally. The network, an important example of 'social capital' (see later in this chapter), emerged out of an initiative by Liverpool City Council to establish a community-based economic development unit to promote the social economy locally. With practitioners operating predominantly in what became Pathways Areas in the Objective One programme, Pathways funding helped to consolidate the unit's activities and widen its geographical scope. The network has gone from ten founding members to 170 at the time of writing.

The research also identified some of the difficulties that the 'third sector' faces, most notably those related to promoting social entrepreneurialism in the context of depressed local economies and labour markets and funding and sustainability.

Participation and Pathways

Pathways was about citizen participation. The politics of participation, however, is chaotic and disorderly and, if power is genuinely at stake, conflictual. Reaching particular rungs on Arnstein's classic (1969) ladder of participation (symbolising the hierarchy of different elements of non-participation, tokenism and citizen power) is dependent, then, on the negotiation of political interests. And the complexity and contradictory nature of political intervention offer spaces for engagement, which communities can potentially exploit to their advantage. Thus, Taylor cites Abbott's (1996) argument that the amount of influence communities can have on government policy depends on the degrees of openness of government and complexity of decision making. Where government is closed and where the issues surrounding decision making are simple, communities are excluded[3]. As government becomes progressively more open and decision making more complex, community participation can shift to an arena of consensus or 'negotiated development' that transcends confrontation or manipulated involvement. The impact of participation is not determinate but dependent on the way in which its politics is played out. In relation to area-based initiatives, in participation like Pathways, what is important is what Allen and Cars (2002) describe as the 'micro-politics of neighbourhood governance'. The institutional structures and governance of participation are crucial in this context and especially the degree to which they create webs between the informal networks of representatives of community organisations, tenants' associations and other local interest based activities with the formal networks of the professional officers and representatives of local authorities and statutory agencies (Allen and Cars, 2002).

Accepting the political contingency of participation emphasises the need to recognise that the 'interests' of participants and facilitators and the participatory structures adopted have always to be critically interrogated (Jones, 1999). First is the need to be sensitive to the discourses of participatory exercises (Atkinson, 1999). These discourses reflect the asymmetrical power relations involved and can set limits to what can be achieved by participation and steer action in particular directions that do not necessarily benefit those participating. Second is the vexed question of defining 'community' and the need to recognise that communities are not homogeneous and are often riven with divisions and conflicts (Taylor, 2000, 2002). Again, the politics of participation (when genuinely open and transparent) will bring these divisions to the fore and provide an arena for conflict resolution. Time is crucial. It is very difficult, for example, for self-interested cliques to dominate local community politics over a sustained period of time if the arena in which they are operating is open to general public scrutiny and offers opportunities for other groups to form.

A third issue relates to levels of participation. Participation historically has been low and particularly so for the least advantaged whose capacity to participate is systematically undermined by their disadvantaged situation (Parry et al, 1992). If intervention is to address that situation – and involve representatives of those affected in it – then there is clearly a need for the development of participatory capacity. This, again, is a political choice and involves 'capacity building' of all those engaged in the participatory process, not just the disadvantaged. This capacity building needs to be a political goal of participation. It is also necessary to be clear about the nature of participatory democracy. Chanan's (1997) notion of a pyramid (rather than the orthodox ladder) of participation by local people in partnerships and development programmes is helpful in capturing this difficulty. At the base of the pyramid is the general population of the areas who could potentially benefit from local development programmes. The pyramid progressively narrows as a result of the degree to which smaller and smaller proportions of this population participate: from people who use community groups but do not actively help; to people who occasionally use them and are willing to help but are not initiators of activity; to people who are regularly active and influential; to the higher, and narrower, levels that make up the apex of the pyramid in the shape of elected or nominated representatives of community groups on community fora from which representatives are elected or nominated to serve on partnerships. The pyramid thus shifts from the 100% population base to something like less than 1% active participation at the apex. Pathways was a good example of this model.

At the end of the first programming period, there were some 260 residents/ representatives of community organisations sitting on the boards or area groups of the 38 Area Partnerships. The constituencies of these community representatives varied significantly in size, from small neighbourhood fora or church groups to large Residents Associations. The Area Partnerships have also held public meetings, which, from our observation, have had attendances numbered in tens or, on occasion with controversial issues, hundreds. Overall, it is clearly not mass participation but there has been citizen participation in the programme and arguably at unexpected levels for an area like Merseyside in which the political climate in the years leading up to the Pathways initiative had veered between outright hostility to citizen participation (outside of political party organisation) to only lukewarm encouragement of it.

Of 90 residents that we interviewed who were active in 11 case study Pathways areas, 26 (29%) were in paid (full- or part-time) employment, 25 (28%) were registered unemployed (and participating despite all the complications produced by the benefits system and the need to be 'available for work'), 10 (11%) were receiving disability/sickness benefit (unemployment benefit by another name in some cases) and 18 (20%) were retired. The remainder described themselves as (unpaid) volunteers. The great majority was relatively old: of the 81 interviewees who gave their age, 86% were over 35 years of age, and 54% over 45. Only three were in their early 20s. They were split evenly between males and females.

While it could be argued that this profile is weak on relatively young residents (but then, local representative democracy also has difficulty in involving and/ or representing these) it is strong on gender balance and the economically inactive. The high proportion of registered unemployed residents shows that exclusion from the labour market does not necessarily signify exclusion from active citizenship. Individuals who were actually identified by the Objective One spending programme as members of a targeted 'socially excluded' group (the unemployed) were actively participating in the delivery of it.

Those interviewed gave a wide range of reasons for wanting to participate, varying from a concern with housing issues (which are not eligible for support from the Structural Funds), unemployment and associated social problems (especially as these impact on the future prospects of children in the areas) and general environmental and quality of life concerns. The perceived barriers to participation included, not least, the bureaucracy and language of 'partnership working'. Time demands were also important, with participants claiming to spend between a half-day and a full 'working week' on Pathways activities – and it is unpaid work. Support varies across the Pathways Partnerships. Some pay travel and subsistence expenses; others provide childcare, but none pay for time commitment. This adds weight to the arguments for the introduction of some form of 'community wage' or 'credit' that can be offset against public services (in the shape, for example, of a discount on council tax payment) in recognition of participation.

Pathways also demonstrated the important role of neighbourhood in relation to participation with neighbourhood-based organisations playing a significant role. The challenge for the partnerships was to balance the strengths of 'natural neighbourhoods' (their rootedness in 'place-communities') and their representative organisations with their potential weaknesses (fragmentation and competition). This issue came to a head in Liverpool towards the end of the first round of Pathways, with a proposal by the local authority to change the geography of Pathways Areas. This proposal met with a considerable degree of opposition from some of the Pathways Areas. The episode revealed the tensions between operational definitions of regeneration areas and neighbourhood-based ones and emphasised the need for area definition to be part of an evolutionary process of community engagement. To be effective, the areas defined need to make social sense to the neighbourhoods and neighbourhood-based organisations within them (Meegan and Mitchell, 2001).

Social capital and Pathways

Participation is clearly linked to the notion of 'social capital'. The research focused on definitions of social capital from writers such as Coleman et al (1988) and Putnam (1993) emphasising the networks, norms and, especially, trust that enable individuals and groups to engage in cooperative activity. It reinforced the argument in the literature (mainly from a developing-world perspective: Evans, 1996; Harriss and de Renzio, 1997; Woolcock, 1998; Ostrom, 2000) that orthodox usage of the term underplays power relations and emphasises horizontal links within communities at the expense of linkages between communities and between the state and society.

It was clear that, running throughout the Pathways process, were issues of trust between the partners. Our research revealed the pronounced degree of mistrust historically between residents and 'outside' agencies yet we also found evidence of a transformation of relationships as networks of trust and channels of communication between them develop (Hibbitt et al, 2001). Transparency and information exchange play a vital role in this context and the research underlined the variability of these across the Pathways areas.

It is possible to point to examples of the way in which Pathways is strengthening different types of social capital within neighbourhoods by helping to build relations of trust between members of local communities and between them and outside agencies. Newly forged relationships are acting to reduce some of the mistrust of professionals that has developed in neighbourhoods over time and which has also acted as a barrier to community involvement. This process, however, is slow and fragile, and must be accompanied with appropriate support for local residents and within an open and transparent process where agendas are clarified and, importantly, language is not divisive. While a consensus model of partnership is not always to the benefit of communities, a partnership approach to building social capital would appear a particularly useful step in breaking down barriers between residents and policy makers. Trust in these partnerships cannot be taken for granted and assumed to emerge spontaneously – it needs to be a political objective and the building of trust relationships needs to be a core element of the regeneration process.

In this context, local authority support units and outreach workers had a key role to play in the governance of Pathways and much depended on the quality of the relationships that they were able to form with the Area Partnerships and, given the initiative's focus on inclusion, especially with representatives of community organisations. It was these who were crucial in creating the webs that could combine the informal networks of local 'communities' with the formal networks of local authorities and statutory agencies and help establish the trusting relationships and institutional flexibility that implementation of partnership initiatives like Pathways requires (Cars et al, 2002). It is at this level that community participation is encouraged or discouraged. It was not easy for council officers, especially those operating in the areas themselves, to balance the demands placed on them by the community members of the partnerships and the constraints of local government accountability for the funding of the partnership. The legacy of mistrust of local authority motives, more marked in some areas than others, only compounded these difficulties.

It needs to be emphasised that partnership relationships are fragile and there were occasions where outcomes appear to have been adversely affected by the failure to develop strong working relationships, where the arena of consensus referred to earlier in this chapter was not reached. For example, community groups in one inner-city partnership in Liverpool have had a history of conflict with the local council that pre-dated and conditioned Pathways. When it came to allocating the partnership to directorates, it also became a case of what can only be described as 'pass the parcel', with the area having three different directors in fairly rapid succession. The Pathways Partnership also had a somewhat ambiguous relationship to an already established Single Regeneration Budget programme that encompassed the Pathways Area but was not designed around it. Revealingly, at the end of the programme, it was the area with the largest single 'underspend' on its European Regional Development Fund (ERDF) allocation. While issues of accessing 'matched funding' loomed large in this, the legacy of strained political relationships did little to help[4].

In terms of social capital, an important development was the creation, by community activists, of the Merseyside Pathways Network (MPN), a network of residents and representatives of community organisations involved in the Area Partnerships. It is an unassociated organisation with six board members elected at annual general meetings by voting members of the MPN who are mandated representatives of community organisations active in the Pathways Areas and on the Pathways Area Boards. It has bi-monthly members meetings that are open to anyone who 'works, lives or plays' in the Pathways Areas and the board also meets every two months. It successfully lobbied for representation on the monitoring committee and network directors also became voting members of the Technical Panel for the People of Merseyside, which had specific responsibility for Pathways.

And this small group of activists has been particularly influential in developing the programme. Representatives of the MPN were involved in internal assessment of the first programme and in the group responsible for drafting the single programming document for the second round of Objective One funding[5]. A representative from the Pathways Network co-chaired (with the North West Trades Union Congress [NWTUC] representative) the 'People and Communities' Working Group which was chiefly responsible for Pathways Mark II in the new Single Programming Document. There had been general agreement among the partners, and the community participants in particular, that while Pathways had performed better than expected (not least in its ability to spend its financial allocations), it had tended to operate in isolation from the rest of the programme. Consequently, two priorities were combined in the new programme: one, Developing Locations, concerned with concentrating investment in eight areas identified as having the greatest potential for economic growth (Strategic Investment Areas) and the other, Developing Pathways Communities, concerned with ensuring that the jobs that this investment creates are accessible to Pathways residents. Central to this linkage, was the awkward question that had been constantly raised throughout the programme by community representatives at individual partnership level and through the MPN on the monitoring committee: 'Who is benefiting?' This critical role did not always make for comfortable relationships between the MPN and agencies and local authorities, as might be expected from a network that at root was contesting the 'ownership' of Pathways (Box 20.1). However, in practice, a generally positive 'negotiated consensus' was reached.

Box 20.1: Participation

Well, I mean he [senior Local Goverment Official] actually screamed at me at the Monitoring Committee and said to me "How dare you say that about my Pathways areas? You and your bloody Network". And I just said, "I don't care what you've got to say, they ain't *your* Pathways areas, they belong to the Pathways residents themselves" and turned heel and walked away. But, I mean, that was the attitude from the ... Council, "*my* Pathways areas". I'm sorry ...! I think there was culture shock right the way across the local authorities about "Oh my God, this lot have got themselves organised and what are they going to do to us?" And it wasn't like that. It was about: *we're* getting *ourselves* organised so we can do for *us* and, you know, in partnership or without, or whatever the case may be. (Executive Member of MPN, interview December 2000).

Urban regeneration as a learning process

Atkinson (2000) argues that, in the current context of multi-level governance, regeneration initiatives need to be treated individually as learning exercises in their own right. What emerged strongly from our interviews and discussions with community activists, policy makers and practitioners (at all levels, from Europe through national to local) was that the Pathways initiative was very much a learning process. References were repeatedly made, unprompted, to terms and phrases like 'learning curves', 'learning experience', 'learning exercise', 'building up expertise', 'learning the language', 'learning the lessons', 'learning from our mistakes', 'cultural change', 'knowledge' and 'understanding'.

It was also evident that the initiative had itself produced institutional change and experiment in the governance of the programme. Individuals and groups were engaging with each other in different ways, new relationships were being formed and new skills and capabilities were being developed. The more we thought about these changing institutions and relationships, the more relevant the literature on 'learning' in economic geography (Braczyk et al, 1998; Cooke and Morgan, 1998; Mackinnon et al, 2002) became with its focus on 'localised learning'. The emphasis is on learning and knowledge transfer in and between firms, technological development and allied institutional structures. The policy focus is on networks and linkages between firms, regional innovation clusters, technology transfer, education and training at regional and local levels and the learning economy at national level. The basic concepts, however, seem to be clearly applicable to broader economic and social policy and, as the Pathways initiative appeared to show, regeneration policy.

Learning, from an institutionalist perspective, is an interactive, action-oriented process (Lagendijk and Cornford, 2000; Lakendijk, 2001). Three forms of learning can be distinguished and these are all visible in Pathways. First, there is the *cognitive learning* that allows understanding of context (in this case, of regeneration). This form of learning revealed itself, for example, in the 'jargon busters', the plethora of briefing papers produced for community representatives by the Area Partnerships and the computer-based guide to Objective One funding produced by the MPN. Second, there are clear instances of the interactive process of *social learning* that improves understanding between those involved. This process was played out generally in the day-to-day interactions of partnership business. Finally, there are examples of the *institutional learning* in which attitudes, routines and behaviour within institutions change as a result of the learning process. This could be seen, for example, in the experience of (senior) local authority officers directly linked to some of these partnerships. In the partnerships there was also evidence of partners changing their behaviour as power relationships shifted. Thus, for example, there were cases of Training and Enterprise Councils (TECs) changing their institutional structures and general approach in response to the changing expectations of local partnerships (strengthened, it has to be said, by the granting of 'scoring' powers for project bids to partnership level).

A key strand in the literature on learning is the distinction between tacit knowledge and explicit or codified knowledge (knowledge that can be communicated in a formal, systematic manner). The interviews and discussion groups showed the depth of tacit knowledge (knowledge derived from direct experience) that participants had gained of the regeneration process as it progressed. They were very much 'learning by doing' and, in the process, learning how to learn; but there were no obvious institutional mechanisms for ensuring that this knowledge was consolidated and codified. The learning process has been fragmented and ad hoc and there are real dangers that the knowledge and learning to date remain unconsolidated, particularly as new policy agendas emerge. To avoid this loss of 'collective memory', there does appear to be a pressing need for some form of institutional structure in major policy initiatives like Pathways that can act as a knowledge and learning base: retrieving, documenting and disseminating experience.

The imminent establishment of a Merseyside Social Inclusion Observatory is a very positive step in this direction, but there does also appear to be a strong argument for a separate institution performing the 'ombudsperson' role, perhaps at regional level. Finally, while the development of the neighbourhood learning strategy set out in the Neighbourhood Renewal Unit's (2002) *The learning curve* is also unquestionably a very positive development in this context, the Pathways experience would strongly suggest that emphasis in the strategy needs to be placed on 'co-learning', bringing together representatives of community groups and local authorities and public agencies in 'action learning'.

Conclusion: 'Pathways to integration' – learning the lessons

Pathways was a learning exercise; so, what was learned? Pathways certainly showed the difficulties involved in reconciling representative and participatory democracy and of moving participation into a negotiated arena of consensus. It underlined all that we already knew about the difficulties of 'partnership' and 'community participation' (unequal power relations, the clash between formal/

professional cultures and their informal/community-based counterparts, resource and cultural constraints on participation and difficulties of 'reflecting' heterogeneous communities) and 'social capital' (its 'goods' and 'bads', the need for horizontal networks to be 'scaled-up' to vertical ones and the centrality of trust). And coming out of all this, the crucial importance of time and political commitment – for building the knowledge and human capital and the trusting networks that social capital and participatory policy intervention require (Taylor, 2000).

Pathways did show that communities are willing to engage in policy if genuine spaces for engagement are provided. It showed that this process of participation is sustainable where power is devolved (as, for example, with the scoring and appraisal of project bids), informal institutional capacity is developed to encourage collaborative working and trusting relationships are developed between local authorities, agencies and participating citizens. In terms of the latter, the role of officers acting as intermediaries and brokers appears to be crucial. Opening up strategy development and monitoring and evaluation to community representatives consolidates this. The fragility of this process of social learning, however, cannot be overstated[6]. It needs continually renewed political commitment to flourish.

Table 20.1: Lessons from Pathways Round One (1994-99)

Positive	Negative
Programme issues • 'Pathways' was the best performing element in the Objective 1 programme in terms of meeting its overall funding allocation • 'Pathways' ERDF allocation actually spent – despite difficulties of project development and funding	*Programme issues* • Not achieving linkages between 'Pathways' and the remainder of the Objective 1 programme • Failure to link 'Pathways Areas' to areas of development opportunity • Not getting sufficient 'bending' of mainstream Council spending programmes into 'Pathways Areas' • Lack of clear objectives and targets for 'Pathways' • Bureaucracy/form-filling, slow speed of decision making on bids • Time constraints – unrealistic time frame for achieving programme aims • Non-flexibility in terms of facilitating finance • Variations in the size of partnership areas • Difficult boundary issues – the issue with all area-based regeneration initiatives • Pressure on small numbers of support staff • Conflicting roles of support staff/ contractual problems • Staff turnover in agencies and in particular in government office for Merseyside • Frustration at complications of funding rules and processes • Variable degree of political commitment across (and within) local authorities • Variable private sector involvement

Table 20.1: contd.../

Positive	**Negative**
Capacity building and community engagement • Amount of capacity building in local communities and Area Partnerships • Local people getting involved and maintaining their enthusiasm, including unemployed people and people with experience of, and empathy with, individuals experiencing 'social exclusion' • Turnover in community membership of 'Area Partnerships' • Some innovative efforts to engage 'hard-to-reach groups', most notably young people • Emergence of Merseyside Pathways Network and role in delivery of Round One and helping to frame 'Pathways' in Round Two	*Capacity building and community engagement* • No real baseline for measuring community capacity • Variability in training • Inadequate capacity building for 'suits' and agencies • Variations in community development and engagement • Issue of matched funding – especially for capacity building and development (needs more EU resources) • Jargon and bureaucratic culture deterring community involvement • Initial Action Planning exercise raising undeliverable expectations (especially regarding housing issues) • General lack of engagement of young people • Tensions between 'stakeholders' (eg between local authorities and the Merseyside Pathways Network)
Nature of projects • Community-based nature of the projects being developed/decentralisation of 'service' delivery • Producing projects/programmes more 'user focused' • Locally developed projects to meet local needs • Key role of social economy	*Nature of projects* • Problems with matched funding and cash flow for genuine community projects • ESF (largely training) projects remained essentially provider led • Time pressures to get projects developed shifting power towards public agencies/ local authorities • Inadequate support for the funding of business plans/feasibility studies prior to project approval • Shortage of project management skills • Time taken to deliver projects affecting community participation • Requirement for guarantor bodies (usually local authorities) for some projects • Poorly developed monitoring and evaluation • Lack of policy framework for development of social economy activity at city-regional level

Table 20.1: contd.../

Positive	Negative
Learning process • Important learning process in 'bottom-up' regeneration – put disadvantaged communities at the heart of regeneration • Important for changing perceptions and attitudes to urban regeneration placing communities more at the centre of the way urban programmes are developed • Acceptance of long-term nature of regeneration and need for a holistic approach to it • Importance of effective strategic partnerships demonstrated • Helping to change the culture and way in which local authorities operate • Opportunity to 'shift the agenda' of agencies with bidding organisations beginning to respond to community needs rather than organisational requirements (helped it needs to be emphasised by the granting of project scoring powers to Pathways partnerships) • Signs of willingness to adopt a 'risk' culture and accept failure • Need for flexible, informal governance structures – like the 'Driver 5' group in Liverpool – to develop trust and broker agreement between participants • Need for realism on levels of (and limits to) participation • Need for supportive structures to ensure the effectiveness of 'participatory democracy'	*Learning process* • Regeneration jargon • Reluctance to share practice/exchange of information across 'Pathways Areas' • Local marketing/publicity of achievements • Initial failure to influence the key mainstream agencies (particularly the FE sector and TECs) • Some partners acting more as observers than active/positive participants • Lack of any (independent) institutional structure or mechanisms for consolidating knowledge and resolving conflict

Notes

[1] The project formed part of the city-region's social and economic conversion programme under Objective One of the EU's Structural Funds (initially for the period 1994-99 but subsequently extended until 2006).

[2] The research used mainly qualitative research methods based on over 200 semi-structured interviews with 'key informants' and community representatives on the Area Partnerships in 11 case study Pathways Areas, policy makers/practitioners and managers of community-based economic development initiatives and 'Pathways' projects specifically targeted at excluded groups. It also involved participant observation in the form of attendance at meetings of Pathways Area Partnerships, community public meetings, training days, project steering groups and a New Deal for Communities focus group and focus group discussions with community representatives from the Pathways Area Partnerships, trainees on Pathways Area-based training courses, managers

of community-based economic development projects and local authority coordinators of the Pathways Area Partnerships. Fieldwork was undertaken in 1999 and 2000.

[3] The discussion specifically relates to geographical communities but the argument could equally apply to communities of interest.

[4] This strained relationship was carried over into the second round of the programme but there does appear to be recent promising signs of reconciliation with the direct intervention of the Council's chief executive.

[5] The MPN also came up with a scoring system for project funding under the Pathways priority in the second programme. Central to the system is consultation over bids at the level of partnerships which is built in to the 'quality threshold' score that all bids need to exceed. The quality threshold criteria include a range of essential and desirable requirements. The key essential ones are that the proposed project fits with the Pathways Partnership Action Plan, that there is community participation in the design of the project, that the applicant in question agrees to regular monitoring and evaluation (with regular feedback to Pathways partnerships), that the project is appropriate for the Pathways priority and is complementary to existing services/activities.

[6] This fragility was underscored in a discussion group we held bringing together policy makers and practitioners and representatives of the MPN at the end of the research and early in the second round of the Objective One programme. A key theme was the importance of time, the need to recognise that addressing the social and economic problems that people in the Pathways Areas are facing and consolidating the participatory arena of consensus will take time, and certainly more than one or even two rounds of Objective One funding. Yet, there were still political pressures for 'delivery' and 'outputs' from a process of participation that itself needs to be seen as a key 'output' of the programme and one that needs continuing support to 'bring on board those who haven't bought into it yet'. There was a concern expressed by the MPN participants that training support for residents and representatives of community organisations was not being sustained into the second programme and, from policy makers, that a renewed political mandate for participation was needed.

References

Abbott, J. (1996) *Sharing the city: Community participation in urban management*, London: Earthscan.

Allen, J. and Cars, G. (2002) 'The tangled web – neighbourhood governance in a post-Fordist era', in G. Cars, P. Healey, A. Madanipour and C. De Maghalhães (eds) (2002) *Urban governance, insititutional capacity and social milieux*, Aldershot: Ashgate, pp 90-105.

Amin, A., Cameron, A. and Hudson, R. (1999) 'Welfare as work? The potential of the UK social economy', *Environment and Planning A*, vol 31, pp 2033-51.

Atkinson, A.B. (1998) 'Social exclusion, poverty and unemployment', in A.B. Atkinson and J. Hills (eds) *Exclusion, employment and opportunity*, CASE Paper no 4, London, Centre for Analysis of Social Exclusion, London School of Economics, pp 1-20.

Atkinson, R. (2000) 'Combating social exclusion in Europe: the new urban policy challenge', *Urban Studies*, vol 37, nos 5-6, pp 1037-55.

Braczyk, H.-J., Cooke, P. and Heidenreich, M. (1998) *Regional innovation systems: The role of governances in a globalized world*, London: UCL Press.

Chanan, G. (1997) *Active citizenship and community involvement: Getting to the roots*, Dublin: European Foundation for the Improvement of Living and Working Conditions.

Coleman, J.S. (1988) 'Social capital in the creation of human capital', *American Journal of Sociology*, vol 94, Supplement, pp 95-120.

Cooke, P. and Morgan, K. (1998) *The associational economy: Firms, regions and innovation*, Oxford: Oxford University Press.

De Haan, J. (1998) '"Social exclusion": an alternative concept for the study of deprivation?', *Institute of Development Studies Bulletin*, vol 29, no 1, pp 10-19.

De Haan, A. and Maxwell, S. (1998) 'Poverty and exclusion in North and South', *Institute of Development Studies Bulletin*, vol 29, no 1, pp 1-9.

DTI (Department of Trade and Industry) (2002) *Social enterprise: A strategy for success*, London: DTI.

Evans, P. (1996) 'Government action, social capital and development: reviewing the evidence on synergy' *World Development*, vol 24, no 6, pp 1119-32.

Four Cities (2002) *Firing the imagination: A guide to learning for participation in urban planning*, Four Cities Project, Maynooth: National University of Ireland.

Fraser, N. (1997) *Justice interruptus: Critical reflections on the 'postsocialist' condition*, London: Routledge.

Geddes, M. and Bennington, J. (eds) (2001) *Local partnerships and social exclusion in the European Union: New forms of local social governance?*, London: Routledge.

Glennerster, H., Lupton, R., Noden, P. and Power, A. (1999) 'Poverty, social exclusion and neighbourhood: studying the area bases of social exclusion', CASE Paper no 22, London: Centre for Analysis of Social Exclusion, LSE.

Government Office for Merseyside (1993) *Merseyside 2000*, Liverpool: Government Office for Merseyside.

Harriss, J. and de Renzio, P. (1997) '"Missing link" or analytically missing? The concept of social capital,' *Journal of International Development*, vol 9, no 7, pp 919-37.

Hibbitt, K., Jones, P. and Meegan, R. (2001) 'Tackling social exclusion: the role of social capital in urban regeneration on Merseyside – from mistrust to trust', *European Planning Studies*, vol 9, no 2, pp 141-61.

HM Treasury and Department for Work and Pensions (2001) *The changing welfare state: Employment opportunities for all*, London: HM Treasury.

Jones, P. (1999) 'Researching "participation": methodological issues for the Pathways project', Pathways to Integration Project Working Paper no 3, Liverpool: Department of Geography, University of Liverpool.

Lagendijk, A. (2001) 'Scaling knowledge production: how significant is the region?', in M. Fischer and J. Frohlich (eds) *Knowledge, complexity and innovation systems*, Berlin: Springer-Verlag, pp 79-100.

Lagendijk, A. and Cornford, C. (2000) 'Regional institutions and knowledge – tracking new forms of regional development policy', *Geoforum*, vol 31, pp 209-18.

Lipietz, A. (1992) *Towards a new economic order*, London: Polity Press.

Lloyd, P.E. and Meegan, R.A. (1994) *Appraisal of the development plan for Merseyside, United Kingdom*, Final Report to Directorate-General XVI, Commission of the European Communities, CRED Research Unit, Liverpool; Department of Geography, University of Liverpool.

Mackinnon, D., Cumbers, A. and Chambers, K. (2002) 'Learning, innovation and regional development: a critical appraisal of recent debates', *Progress in Human Geography*, vol 26, no 3, pp 293-311.

Madanipour, A. (1998) 'Social exclusion and space', in A. Madanipour, G. Cars and J. Allen (eds) *Social exclusion in European cities*, London: Jessica Kingsley Publishers, pp 75-89.

Meadows, P. (2001) *Lessons for employment policy*, Review of Work and Opportunity Research Programme, York: Joseph Rowntree Foundation, December.

Meegan, R. and Mitchell, A. (2001) 'It's not community around here, it's neighbourhood', *Urban Studies*, vol 38, no 12, pp 2167-94.

MIS (Merseyside Information Services) (1998) *Pathways impact monitoring: Baseline study and progress report*, Liverpool: MIS.

MIS (2000) *Pathways impact monitoring: Baseline study and progress report*, Liverpool: MIS.

Neighbourhood Renewal Unit (2002) *The learning curve: Developing skills and knowledge for neighbourhood renewal*, London: Neighbourhood Renewal Unit, ODPM.

Ostrom, E. (2000) 'Social capital: a fad or a fundamental concept?', in P. Dasgupta and I. Serageldin (eds) (2000) *Social capital: A multifaceted perspective*, Washington, DC: The World Bank, pp 172-214.

Parkinson, M. (1998) *Combating social exclusion: Lessons from area-based programmes in Europe*, Bristol: The Policy Press.

Parry, G., Moyser, G. and Day, N. (1992) *Political participation and democracy in Britain*, Cambridge: Cambridge University Press.

Percy-Smith, J. (2000) 'Introduction; the contours of social exclusion', in J. Percy-Smith (ed) *Policy responses to social exclusion: Towards inclusion?*, Buckingham: Open University Press, pp 1-21.

Putnam, R.D., Leonardi, R. and Nanetti, R.Y. (1993) *Making democracy work: Civic traditions in modern Italy*, Princeton, NJ: Princeton University Press.

Silver, H. (1994) 'Social exclusion and social solidarity: three paradigms', *International Labour Review*, vol 133, pp 531-98.

Social Exclusion Unit (1998) *Bringing Britain together: A national strategy for neighbourhood renewal*, London: HMSO.

Stoker, G. (ed) (1999) *The new management of British local governance*, London: Macmillan.

Stoker, G. (ed) (2000) *The new politics of British local governance*, London: Macmillan.

Taylor, M. (2000) 'Communities in the lead: power, organisational capacity and social capital', *Urban Studies*, vol 37, no 5-6, pp 1019-35.

Taylor, M. (2002) 'Is partnership possible? Searching for a new institutional settlement', in G. Cars, P. Healey, A. Madanipour and C. de Maghalhães (eds) (2002) *Urban governance, institutional capacity and social milieux*, Aldershot: Ashgate, pp 106-24.

Turok, I. and Edge, N. (1999) *The jobs gap in Britain's cities: Employment loss and labour market consequences*, Bristol: The Policy Press.

Woolcock, M. (1998) 'Social capital and economic development: towards a theoretical synthesis and policy framework', *Theory And Society*, vol 27, pp 151-208.

Young, J. (1999) *The exclusive society: Social exclusion, crime and difference in late modernity*, London: Sage Publications.

TWENTY ONE

Voluntary organisations and the generation of social capital in city politics

Gerry Stoker, Graham Smith, William Maloney and Stephen Young

There is considerable common ground between debates around social cohesion on the one hand and somewhat more specific ideas of social capital (Boddy, 2002). This is particularly the case where social cohesion is seen in terms of participation in different forms of social relations or associational activities. The debate around social capital directs attention in particular to oft-neglected features of the civic infrastructure of cities and promises an explanation of why in some localities political activity (and more broadly social and economic activity) displays greater vitality and appears to be more effective. Research on social capital has been dominated by the work and approach of Robert Putnam (1993, 2000). In much of his early work, Putnam laid a great emphasis on the number and density of voluntary organisations in an area as a good predictor of the presence or absence of social capital. 'The more voluntary organisations the better' was the broad message. As levels of social capital increase, then this is said to have a significant positive impact on important policy outcomes in areas such as education, health, crime, welfare, economic growth, the performance of political institutions and the development of effective and democratic governance.

In the light of such claims, it is not surprising that "in a little over a decade the topic of social capital has moved from the pages of obscure journals to the forefront of policy debate" (Leigh and Putnam, 2002, p 15). Yet we are not convinced that the creation of social capital can have a beneficial public effect in as straightforward a manner as some policy makers and advocates would have us believe. Social capital does or fails to do its work in particular contexts and whether it does so depends on a variety of factors other than the levels and intensity of social capital. Putnam deserves considerable credit in bringing the concept of social capital to the attention of social scientists and policy makers. His own work is impressively constructed and executed but we believe that Putnam's approach is limited on a number of counts.

First, particularly in his early work Putnam takes a 'bottom-up perspective': he focuses on the affect of the attitudes and behaviour of individuals on the performance of social and political institutions. Putnam perceives the nature of the state as an exogenous factor (Tarrow, 1996, p 395). This neglects the role played by political structures and institutions in shaping the *context of associational activity* and hence the creation of social capital. The governance of an area is affected by social capital, but is itself an influence on social capital. Political institutions have a significant role, at least in helping to sustain civic vibrancy and probably also in stimulating its growth. Public authorities are deeply implicated in the shape and activities of voluntary associations[2], whether it be in terms of the institutions created to encourage engagement and participation, the form of grants and service level agreements or the nature of capacity building programmes. The political system does not determine civil society nor vice versa; rather, there is an interpenetration of state and civil society.

Second, given this interpenetration, Putnam's claim that it is possible to read off the implications for governance from knowledge about associational activity and 'stocks' of social capital becomes deeply problematic. Knowledge of civic organisations and a generic understanding of their civic vibrancy expressed through their numbers and their access to information and networks does not enable us to make immediate comment on the quality of governance in a given locality. Nor does the identification of a certain set of values and attitudes held by individuals in a community provide a sufficient basis for ascertaining the performance of governance arrangements.

Finally, Putnam limits his analysis of the presence or absence of social capital to the relationship between individuals: he neglects the variety of *locations* in which social capital is generated, accessed and inhibited. Social capital can equally be conceived as the property of relations between *corporate actors* as well as persons (Coleman, 1988, p 98). We should not only study the relationship between individuals, but also between associations and institutions.

We think that social capital is a useful concept but that its application needs to be placed within an appreciation of the particular context in which social capital effects are being observed. Social capital does its work in particular locations and works through particular relations. To understand how social capital can make a difference in the politics of cities we do not need general information about the amount of social capital in a city but a detailed way of judging its presence or absence in particular relations.

Our analysis of associational life in four UK urban areas highlights the importance of investigating social capital as a *relational* concept. In particular, we focus on the relationships between voluntary associations and between voluntary associations and the local authority. What becomes clear is that there is an uneven distribution of social capital and that different actors have differential access to social capital resources. Social capital is context specific. Only by being sensitive to the different locations in which social capital is created or inhibited is it possible to judge its impact on governance. In this chapter, we initially explore the nature of social capital within Birmingham by focusing in particular on the activities of voluntary associations, their relationships with each other and with the City Council. Comparisons are then drawn with our research in Glasgow, Southampton and Stockport. To begin our analysis, however, we present a brief review of the concept of social capital and how it makes collective action more effective.

Social capital and collective action: understanding the relationship

Our own investigation rests on James Coleman's formulation of social capital which stresses its relational nature:

> Social capital is defined by its function. It is not a single entity but a variety of different entities, with two elements in common: they all consist of some aspect of social structure, and they facilitate certain actions of actors whether persons or corporate actors within the structure. Like other forms of capital, social capital is productive, making possible the achievement of ends that in its absence would not be possible. Like physical capital and human capital, social capital is not completely fungible but may be specific to certain activities. A given form of social capital that is valuable in facilitating certain actions may be useless or even harmful for others.... Unlike other forms of capital, social capital inheres in the structure of relations between actors and among actors. (Coleman, 1988, p 98)

Coleman's conception highlights at least two important factors. First, social capital is a *relational* concept; second, there are a variety of *locations* in which social capital is generated, accessed and inhibited. Social capital is a property of relations between *corporate* actors as well as persons. What such a definition points us to is the importance of not only studying the relationship between individuals, but also between organisations and institutions.

Social capital can be constituted in a variety of ways, as Coleman notes. It is a complex resource available to individuals and organisations that facilitates the achievement of collective action. The components of social capital include:

- the context of obligations, expectations and trustworthiness in which actors operate;
- the quality of the information channels to which they have access;
- the availability of norms and effective sanctions to discipline relationships.

Unlike physical or human capital, it is not the property of individuals or institutions. Social capital inheres in the relations between actors and is a resource that is drawn upon to facilitate collaborative activities. It is the shared knowledge, norms and sense of trust that is brought to activity that in turn makes that activity more likely to succeed. As Elinor Ostrom comments "social capital is created and maintained by the very process of working together" (Ostrom, 1997, p 178).

The launching point for our understanding of social capital as a relational concept is to see it as a particular solution to a general problem (perhaps *the* problem) confronted by political science, namely how people "undertake collective action to resolve social dilemmas" (Ostrom, 1998, p 1). For Ostrom, the key to understanding how collective action dilemmas are overcome lies in understanding the way in which sustainable relations are constructed between people. She uses the concept of social capital as one ingredient in what she refers to as a second generation model of understanding rationality that recognises "all humans as complex, fallible learners who seek to do as well as they can given the constraints that they face and who are able to learn heuristics, norms, rules and how to craft rules to improve their achieved outcomes" (Ostrom, 1998, p 9).

It is now possible to see the various elements of social capital that at first sight seem to be disparate features as a set of connected phenomenon. Trust begets exchange that in the context of a free flow of information can provide the framework for building norms and sanctions that make collective action sustainable in the long run. The connections can in turn flow in the other direction and feed back on one another. The quality and nature of these relationships are articulated through social networks whose efficacy varies according to their nature and intensity. In short, social capital matters but it does so in the context of particular relations where it is converted into a capacity to act together effectively. We need to examine not whether a city or urban area has social capital or not but in what situations that social capital is created and put to work.

Patterns of civic engagement in Birmingham

Putnam (2000) holds that in general terms civic organisation has declined in the US: the 'bowling alone' phenomenon. He argues that people are less inclined to establish formal and informal social contact with each other and as a result social capital has declined. One particularly striking piece of evidence, according to Putnam in some versions of his argument, is that the number of civic associations or voluntary organisations has reduced over the last two or three decades. There are many who question Putnam's 'civic deficit' thesis, but in the case of Britain, Peter Hall concludes that "levels of social capital, at least on most indicators, have not declined significantly in recent decades" (Hall, 1998, p 32). He further argues that there is strong evidence that government policies "have made a major contribution to sustaining the kind of associations that augment the level of social capital in Britain" (1998, p 21).

The national level policy environment has been well disposed towards associational activity but so too has local government. Indeed, it has been argued that the late 1970s and 1980s saw a general opening out of local authorities and a strengthening of the diversity and capacity of local group politics (Stoker, 1988; Stoker and Wilson, 1991). There is much general evidence to support the view that the 1990s saw the continuation of such local trends with increased support for local voluntary associations and more avenues for engagement with local authorities (Lowndes et al, 1998; Young, 2000).

An analysis of levels of associational activity in Birmingham provides an excellent opportunity to pursue the debate and move from a general level of evidence to a particular illustration of trends in an individual city[1]. In *Second city politics*, a study of Birmingham in the late 1960s and early 1970s, Ken Newton (1976) records 4,264 groups, which are classified (using his original classification system) in Table 21.1. We carried out a similar mapping exercise of voluntary and community activity in Birmingham in 1998. Inevitably, there are some problems with direct comparisons given the different forms that directories and listings take and the counting procedure adopted by Newton. In spite of such problems, we have attempted to follow Newton's 'rules' in our data collection.

While both sets of data are very much partial analyses and an underestimation of activity, there nevertheless appears to be an increase of at least a third in the number of voluntary associations in Birmingham over the last three decades. If we were to disregard sports clubs where the figure for 1998 is a substantial underestimate, then there is at least a doubling in the number of groups: in 1970 there were 2,120 non-sport voluntary associations; in 1998 this figure is up to 4,397. While not wanting to make a direct correlation between numbers of groups and levels of social capital, this simple analysis of associational activity across three decades suggests that the 'civic decline' thesis is misplaced. Also, it is suggestive that we need to be sensitive to the wider political context within which associations operate.

Table 21.1: Comparison of number of voluntary associations in Birmingham in 1970 and 1998[a]

Type of association	Number in 1970	Number in 1998
Sports	2,144	1,192
Social welfare	666	1,319
Cultural	388	507
Trade Associations	176	71
Professional	165	112
Social	142	398
Churches	138	848
Forces	122	114
Youth	76	268
Technical and Scientific	76	41
Educational	66	475
Trade Unions	55	52
Health	50	309
Not classified	–	75
Total	4,264	5,781

Note: [a] For 1998 sources see Maloney et al (2000); for 1970 sources see Newton (1976).

Many of the shifts in the numbers of associations across different fields of operation reflect changes in the political environment of the last 30 years or so (Stoker, 1997; Taylor, 1997). For example, as local government powers and functions have been progressively eroded in traditional service delivery areas such as housing, existing or new voluntary and community organisations have taken over some of these responsibilities and developed new areas of work. This in turn has opened up new opportunities for arm's-length providers. In other areas, there has been a shift to a more enabling role rather than direct provision of social services. The doubling of the number of groups in the social welfare category reflects the impact of such trends. This category includes not only social care providers but also associations within the areas of community economic and social development, housing, employment and training as well as civic advocacy groups. The growth in education groups reflects a rise of parent–teacher associations, and of nurseries, play schemes and after-school clubs. A similar trend can be observed in the youth sector. Health is another area where we see dramatic rises in numbers which include 'friends' of hospitals and other support groups.

Local government has also moved into new policy fields such as economic development, environmental protection and crime prevention and has done so in cooperation with a range of 'third force' organisations (Stoker and Young, 1993). The impact of these trends is reflected in the growth in the social welfare, social and health categories. Again, while Newton did not record environmental associations as a separate category, our analysis recorded 44 groups.

Shifts in the type of voluntary associations over time is suggestive that the changing political environment, and specifically the changing role played by local authorities, has had a significant impact on voluntary activity, and inevitably the creation of social capital. On the other hand, the steady state of trade unions and declines in professional and trade associations probably reflect wider shifts in the economic and industrial base of Birmingham. Finally, the category 'churches' has expanded rapidly. This can be accounted for by the emergence of new Christian denominations and the rise of other faith-based associations in Birmingham's expanding black and minority ethnic communities.

The results of a postal survey of voluntary and community organisations in Birmingham in November 1998 provide more details of the relationships between voluntary associations and between associations and the local authority[2]. The belief that a new range of associations has emerged is supported by the finding that two thirds of our sample of groups were established after 1970. More than that, our data on the current dynamics of Birmingham's voluntary sector reveals evidence to suggest not only that there are more groups but also that they are more politically active, better connected and generally positive about associational life in Birmingham.

In the early 1970s, Newton found a relatively quiet world of connections between established groups and officialdom, underwritten by close contacts and grant provision arrangements that enabled useful social care and other public service objectives to be achieved. Most groups remained politically inactive – only about 30% of all voluntary organisations in Birmingham had asked about a decision or contacted the local authority or another public body in the city in the previous year. The active groups tended to work with the permanent officials in departments rather than councillors or other political figures. When asked about the operation of the local political system, the secretaries of the active groups reported a general view that they were paid sufficient attention (60% of the sample) and the secretaries reported their dealings with both councillors and officers as helpful. General interview material confirmed for Newton that groups were 'well satisfied with their relationships with public bodies and officials in the city'. Some interests, such as those of Birmingham's already substantial black and minority ethnic communities, were largely sidelined.

In 1998, we see a relatively healthy picture of civic life in Birmingham. Many associations are involved in extensive networks of organisations both inside and outside the geographical boundaries of Birmingham. Some 85% of respondents claimed to have 'contact with other voluntary and community groups in Birmingham' and 54% say that they have 'contact with other voluntary and community groups outside Birmingham'. Over half the sample (56%) indicate they have regular contact with officers and/or councillors in the city council. The importance and variety of information networks is also apparent (see Table 21.2). Although the single most important source of information for many groups is their own members and users, almost 70% of associations in Birmingham place a high premium on contact with other associations and public authorities, pointing to the importance of networking and information exchange to civic activity in the city. Information flows and networks are typically seen as an important element of social capital (Coleman, 1988).

There is also evidence of the impact of financial support from the city council. Just under a third of the sample (31%) have a grant from Birmingham City Council as a main source of funding. Some 22.5% of groups report that they are involved in a service level agreement with the council. Newton found that in 1971 the city council was spending £1 million of grant funding and support for service provision by voluntary organisations. The figure for 1998 was £17 million. Between 1970 and 1971 and between 1997 and 1998, prices went up

Table 21.2: Main sources of information for voluntary organisations in Birmingham

	Very important (%)	Important (%)	Fairly important (%)
Members of own group	51.4	24.8	7.8
Birmingham City Council	27.6	23.5	17.6
Other public body	17.8	25.3	17.8
Other local voluntary organisation	25.1	28.2	19.6
National organisations	26.1	24.3	17.3

Table 21.3: Trust in Birmingham

	Agree/strongly agree (%)	Neither agree nor disagree (%)	Disagree/strongly disagree (%)
Our organisation trusts other voluntary and community groups in the city (*n*=357)	70	27	3
There is a high level of trust between our organisation and the city council (*n*=355)	44	35	21
Trust between the city council and voluntary and community groups is essential for a healthy city (*n*=357)	90	10	0

by 8.6 times, so in real terms there has roughly been a doubling of grant funding provided to the voluntary sector[3].

If information flows and networks are one element of social capital, trust is typically seen as another. In response to a series of statements about their relationship with other associations and the city council, some interesting insights into social capital in the city emerge.

Against a backdrop of high trust levels between voluntary associations (some 70% of organisations agree that they trust other voluntary groups in Birmingham), the drop in the perception of the trustworthiness of relations between voluntary organisations and the city council is marked: 44% of voluntary groups in Birmingham agreed that there are high levels of trust. About half that number (21%) disagreed with the statement. This drop in trust may be of some concern given that the overwhelming majority of the sample (90%) agree that trust between Birmingham City Council and voluntary and community groups is essential.

Although these findings raise some interesting questions for social capital analysts, overall frequencies tell us nothing about the *type* and *activities* of voluntary associations that are more likely to trust the city council. If trust is an indicator of social capital, where is it more likely to be found? Are there specific characteristics of organisations that are related to their perceptions of the trustworthiness of relationships? Table 21.4 begins to unpack some of the characteristics of the more and less trusting voluntary associations.

Cross tabulating a series of different group characteristics against levels of trust, three specific factors emerge as statistically highly significant ($p<0.001$): regular involvement in council forums; regular contact with councillors and/or council officers; and a city council grant as a very important source of income (Table 21.4). No other characteristics – including the size of the voluntary organisation (indicated by income level), the primary area of operation (neighbourhood to national) or the function of the group (service provision, advocacy, and so on) – which intuitively might be expected to affect perceptions

Table 21.4: Who trusts in Birmingham?

There is a high level of trust between our organisation and the city council		Agree/strongly agree (%)	Disagree/strongly disagree (%)
All organisations		44	21
Regularly involved in council forums	Yes	50	19*
	No	29	25*
Regular contact with councillors/ officers	Yes	57	19*
	No	24	24*
City council grant is *very* important income source	Yes	60	15*
	No	35	24*

*p<0.001

of trust, displayed a similar level of significance (see Table 21.6 for a fuller analysis of characteristics). What this suggests is what the social capital literature predicts: mechanisms for bringing organisations together are important in facilitating the development of social capital. Typically, it is those organisations that have some form of regular contact with, and/or significant financial support from, the city council that feel that there is a high level of trust between them and the council. The relationship between funding and trust also raises some interesting questions for those such as Barbara Misztal who argues that trust "Neither can be purchased nor bribed, as an old-age truth – immortalized by King Lear – illustrates, any attempt to 'buy' trust can only destroy it" (Misztal, 1996, p 20). It seems that Birmingham City Council's attempts to 'buy' trust have not been so disastrous.

Civic engagement in other locations: a comparison with Birmingham

We were unable to undertake a comparative counting exercise of voluntary organisations in any of our other three locations of study because there was no prior work to draw on comparable to that undertaken by Newton in Birmingham. However, we were able to conduct survey work of voluntary organisations using the same set of statements in these other locations[4]. We expected to find some differences in the structure of the relationships between voluntary organisations and local authorities as we chose to look at places that would contrast with Birmingham. First, we looked at Glasgow because that has a similar urban scale to Birmingham but it is located in Scotland. In comparison with Birmingham, it suffers from a greater degree of urban deprivation and has a relatively small black and minority ethnic population. Stockport is a relatively well-to-do suburban authority. Southampton is a medium-sized city in the more prosperous South of England with a relatively more recent experience of industrialisation than the other locations. Table 21.5 presents a comparison of the sense of trust felt by voluntary organisations in the four locations.

Table 21.5: Trust held by voluntary organisations in four urban areas

a) Our organisation trusts other voluntary and community groups	Agree/strongly agree (%)	Neither agree nor disagree (%)	Disagree/strongly disagree (%)
Birmingham (*n*=376)	70	27	4
Glasgow (*n*=301)	72	25	3
Southampton (*n*=120)	74	22	4
Stockport (*n*=96)	81	18	1
b) There is a high level of trust between our organisation and the city council	**Agree/strongly agree (%)**	**Neither agree nor disagree (%)**	**Disagree/strongly disagree (%)**
Birmingham (*n*=374)	44	35	21
Glasgow (*n*=301)	38	42	20
Southampton (*n*=129)	36	42	22
Stockport (*n*=96)	45	47	8

What is immediately striking is the similar broad trend between the two trust statements. In all four locations, voluntary organisations are significantly more trusting of each other than they are of their local authority. Stockport emerges as the area where trust both among voluntary organisations and between voluntary organisations and the local council is at its highest. It is an interesting finding that the levels of trust between voluntary organisations actually rise as the size of the urban area decreases (Table 21.5a). One obvious explanation is that there are less organisations in the smaller urban areas and thus that they are more likely to be aware of each other's existence and activities – a precursor for the development of trust.

Where the data begin to raise more interesting questions is in the response to the second statement (Table 21.5b). Here, voluntary organisations in Stockport and Birmingham report significantly higher levels of trust in the city council than the other two cities. It is particularly interesting that the responses from the cities with the most similar characteristics vary to a significant extent: in Birmingham, 44% agree that there are high levels of trust, in Glasgow 38%. Both cities have had to face a range of different and often severe urban problems, many related to inner-city deprivation and regeneration. One tentative explanation for the difference in trust is the relative success that the two city councils have had in their policies and funding towards the voluntary sector. In the mid-1990s, Glasgow faced a 'funding crisis' following local government reorganisation in Scotland and consequently withdrew resources from a number of voluntary organisations and projects. Many organisations believe that the city council unfairly targeted the voluntary sector: against such a backdrop, it is difficult to build trusting relationships. In comparison, Birmingham City Council has to a greater extent managed to protect its voluntary sector from savage funding cuts and arguably has a more effective infrastructure for engaging with voluntary organisations.

The apparent 'success' story from Birmingham does need to be tempered to a degree, however. Although voluntary organisations in Birmingham and Stockport have relatively positive perceptions of their relationships with the council, it is significant that, in Birmingham, 21% disagree with the statement compared to only 8% in Stockport. The results suggest that Birmingham City Council has been successful in developing positive relationships with a large proportion of voluntary organisations (44%), but that a fairly significant number remain distrustful. This should not be unexpected: given the sheer number and diversity of voluntary organisations in Birmingham (Table 21.1), it would be a Herculean task on the part of the local authority to effectively engage them all.

Do the characteristics of 'trusting' voluntary organisations differ across cities? An analysis of Birmingham and Glasgow produces quite striking results (Table 21.6). Even though there are differences in overall levels of trust between voluntary organisations and the city council, it is the same three factors that are statistically highly significant ($p<0.001$): groups regularly involved in council

Table 21.6: Who trusts? Birmingham and Glasgow compared

		Agree %	Disagree %	Agree %	Disagree %
All organisations		**44**	**21**	**38**	**20**
Group has contact with other groups in city	Yes	45	21	41	18
	No	41	17	26	29
Group is member/affiliated to umbrella group in city	Yes	48	19	40	20
	No	37	23	38	18
Group regularly involved in city council forums	Yes	50	19***	53	15***
	No	29	25***	19	28***
Group has regular contact with councillors/officers	Yes	57	19***	52	18***
	No	24	24***	13	22***
City council grant/SLA very important source	Yes	60	15***	57	16***
	No	35	24***	21	23***
Annual income above/ below £50,000	Above	53	18*	46	18**
	Below	36	25*	23	22**
Primary area of operation					
Neighbourhood		45	23	41	22
Area/district of city		38	30	33	22
City-wide		40	22	51	16
Region		57	9*	47	11
Scotland		–	–	27	20
UK		39	13	33	20
Primary function of group					
Finance/resourcing		47	21	45	25
Buildings/facilities		52	14	49	26
Services		51	19	38	14
Advocacy/info/research		30	27[a]	30	19
Representation		32	32	41	30

Notes: *$p<0.05$; **$p<0.01$; ***$p<0.001$

forums, in regular contact with officers and/or councillors and in receipt of significant resources from the council. It appears that, in Birmingham, these relationships are simply more effective. Although the size of the organisation measured in terms of annual income is more significant in Glasgow ($p<0.01$), no other characteristics appear to be good indicators of trusting relationships. It makes little difference whether the group operates on a city-wide or neighbourhood basis, for example; nor does the function of the group appear to make any difference to the likelihood of it having a trusting relationship with its council. Again, these findings are in a general sense very supportive of the social capital case that regular contact can smooth the path towards effective relations. What works for generating social capital for individuals – informal and formal contact – appears also to work for organisations.

Conclusions: inter-organisational social capital in cities

Three initial conclusions can be drawn from this brief analysis of relationships between organisations in cities. First, social capital can be most easily created in conditions where there is shared identity among those constructing the relationship, hence the relative ease with which trust characterises relations between voluntary organisations. Second, the results suggest that inter-organisational social capital can be actively generated and promoted by local public authorities through the use of mechanisms such as consultation forums, outreach work, capacity building and funding regimes. Third, there is a distributional quality to social capital: certain groups may be excluded from accessing inter-organisational social capital. This last observation we regard as characteristic of the way that social capital works: it adheres to particular relationships.

One of the structures that Coleman (1988) highlights as generally facilitating social capital is 'closure of social networks'. Such closure creates the conditions for both the emergence of effective sanctions that can monitor and guide behaviour, and trustworthiness of social structures that allows the proliferation of obligations and expectations. We speculate that such closure may occur more straightforwardly where the groups forming the relationship view each other as similar types of organisation that share values, norms and common expectations. In contrast, in the case of building 'cross-sectoral' social capital, it will be necessary for closure to be more actively constructed. In cities such as Birmingham and Glasgow, 'closure' is achieved for voluntary organisations through access to forums, relationships with councillors and officers and funding regimes. As our results show, regular contact is related to higher levels of trust.

The social capital generated through closure is recognised by voluntary organisations. We asked in all four urban areas whether voluntary organisations felt that their respective local authority was even-handed in its treatment of them. In response to the statement 'The Council favours certain voluntary and community groups', only 8% disagree with the statement in Southampton and Birmingham. In Glasgow, only 5% disagreed. In comparison, 17% in

Stockport disagreed with the statement, which is a finding that fits in with the slightly more positive response to trust statements within that city. Local authorities simply do not have the resources or even the will to engage with all groups in the city. Thus, in urban areas, inter-organisational social capital is "neither brokered equitably nor distributed evenly" (Foley and Edwards, 1998).

Local authorities face the quandary that selective engagement (and thus 'closure' in Coleman's terms) is likely to lead to a perception of distrust in the system more generally. Social capital can be built up across sectors, but typically only when 'closure' or restricted access is present. This restricted access is likely to be noticed by other groups and indeed perceived as favouritism, which will in turn have a negative impact on their perception of the city council. Social capital, therefore, can be generated by 'enlightened' policy intervention, but that generation is likely to be able to draw in only a limited number of groups in a set of relations that have limited boundaries. The more generalised generation of social capital across cities may be undermined to a degree by the exclusiveness demanded by the dynamics of effective social capital building between government agencies and particular groups.

Our evidence leads us to the view that there is only so much that social capital can do. It works best in face-to-face settings or in the context of regular communication and in arenas where a limited group of participants are attempting to construct the conditions for effective action. It may be that the wider commitment to collective action within society rests less on construction of networks of social capital and more on some of the more traditional ingredients of democratic politics: leaders, parties, the media and effective officialdom. In short, the presence of a vibrant set of civic organisations is not necessarily the panacea presented by the Putnam-school. At the very least, the achievement of good governance conditions requires the effective working of the traditional political institutions of representation as much as it does the arrival of a new participative form of politics.

Notes

[1] The definition of 'voluntary association' used in this chapter also encompasses local and neighbourhood community-based associations which other definitions sometimes overlook.

[2] Questionnaires were sent out to voluntary and community associations using the Birmingham Voluntary Sector Council mailing list supplemented by additional environmental, professional and trade union lists. The response rate was 30% (n=387). The data set covers the variety of different types, functions and geographical focus (neighbourhood to international) of associations in Birmingham.

[3] The figure of £17 million does not include all the service level agreements – as such the financial support currently provided to the voluntary sector will be substantially higher.

[4] We used the same survey instrument in Stockport, Southampton and Glasgow as we did in Birmingham. The survey was distributed using much the same types of mailing list.

References

Boddy, M, (2002) 'Linking competitiveness and cohesion', in I. Begg (ed) *Urban competitiveness: Policies for dynamic cities*, Bristol: The Policy Press.

Coleman, J. (1988) 'Social capital in the creation of human capital', *American Journal of Sociology*, vol 94 (supplement), pp 95-120.

Foley, M. and Edwards, B. (1998) 'Is it time to disinvest in social capital?', Paper presented at the American Political Science Association Annual Conference, Boston.

Hall, P. (1998) 'Social capital in Britain', Paper presented at the American Political Science Association Annual Conference, Boston.

Leigh, A. and Putnam, R. (2002) 'Reviving communities: what policy-makers can do to build social capital', *Renewal*, vol 10, no 2, pp 15-20.

Lowndes, V., Stoker, G., Pratchett, L., Leach, S. and Wingfield, M. (1998) *Enhancing public participation in local government*, London: DETR.

Maloney, W., Smith, G. and Stoker, G. (2000) 'Social capital and urban governance: adding a more contextualised "top down" perspective', *Political Studies*, vol 48, pp 823-41.

Maloney, W., Smith, G. and Stoker, G. (2001) 'Social capital and the city' in B. Edwards, M. Foley and M. Diani (eds) *Beyond Tocqueville. Civil society and the social capital debate in comparative perspective*, Hanover: Tufts, pp 83-96.

Misztal, B. (1996) *Trust in modern societies*, Cambridge: Polity Press.

Newton, K. (1976) *Second city politics*, Oxford: Clarenden Press, pp 153-81.

Ostrom, E. (1997) 'Investing in capital, institutions and incentives', in C. Clague (ed) *Institutions and economic development*, Baltimore: Johns Hopkins Press.

Ostrom, E. (1998) 'A behavioural approach to the rational choice theory of collective action', *American Political Science Review*, vol 92, pp 1-22.

Putnam, R. (1993) *Making democracy work*, Princeton: Princeton University Press.

Putnam, R. (2000) *Bowling alone: The collapse and revival of American community*, New York: Simon and Schuster.

Stoker, G. (1988) *The politics of local government*, Basingstoke: Macmillan.

Stoker, G. (1997) 'Local government reform in Britain after Thatcher', in J. Lane (ed) *Public sector reform*, London: Sage, pp 225-34.

Stoker, G. and Wilson, D. (1991) 'The lost world of British local pressure groups', *Public Policy and Administration*, vol 6, pp 20-34.

Stoker, G. and Young, S. (1993) *Cities in the 1990s*, Harlow: Longman.

Tarrow, S. (1996) 'Making social science work across space and time: a critical reflection on Robert Putnam's *Making Democracy Work*', *American Political Science Review*, vol 90, pp 389-97.

Taylor, M. (1997) 'The impact of local government changes on the voluntary and community sectors', in R. Hambleton et al (eds) *New perspectives on local government*, London: Joseph Rowntree Foundation, pp 74-117.

Young, S. (1999) 'Participation strategies and local environmental politics: local agenda 21', in G. Stoker (ed) *The new politics of British local governance*, Basingstoke: Macmillan, pp 181-97.

Conclusions

TWENTY TWO

Competitiveness, cohesion and urban governance

Martin Boddy and Michael Parkinson

This final chapter provides a summary of key findings from the research programme and explores policy implications. The first part of the chapter draws on the individual studies presented in this volume. The second part reflects on some of the wider issues relating to the main programme themes of competitiveness, cohesion and urban governance.

The four 'integrated city studies' that comprised Part One of this volume each covered a wide range of topics. Each also focused, from differing perspectives, on the core themes of competitiveness, cohesion and governance and on the relations between them. Key conclusions relating to these core themes are summarised here. Looking at the case study areas themselves, London is clearly distinctive given its sheer scale, complexity and its intensely internationalised economy. Bristol represents a free-standing city-region in prosperous southern England. The Scottish case study included direct comparison between Glasgow, with its history of severe decline, and more prosperous and increasingly buoyant Edinburgh. The final case study included comparative study of Liverpool, with, again, a history of severe economic problems, and Manchester, commonly perceived to have done better than its near neighbour – and to have done so in part through its own efforts.

Looking first at competitive advantage, a number of common messages emerge from the city case studies. Land, property and the planning system are clearly critical factors. In the case of London, it is argued that the region's overall growth record has been constrained by lack of space and also planning constraints rather than any lack of demand. In both Edinburgh and Bristol, the availability of land and property have shaped and sustained competitive success in the past but now threaten to constrain continuing expansion. The balance between provision of employment growth and residential development and the overall effectiveness of strategic planning at a sub-regional scale are critical. Planning reform, as set out in the Planning and Compulsory Purchase Bill, 2002 (currently expected to come into force in June 2004), and new regional structures including in England Regional Spatial Strategies are likely to have important implications for the long-run competitiveness of urban areas.

In terms of 'urban assets' the city studies in general emphasise the importance of a relatively traditional set of urban agglomeration economies to competitive strength and the ability to attract investment. These include market size and diversity; shared services, amenities and infrastructure including transport, communications and connectivity; and a shared labour pool and skill base. In the case of London, this was reflected in the willingness of firms to meet high market rents and operating costs in order to realise the benefits of locating within the metropolitan area. There was little evidence, however, to support the importance in general of 'industrial clusters' with their stress on inter-firm linkages, collaboration, trust and non-market relations. Detailed analysis in the Scottish, Bristol and London case studies in particular found little evidence of agglomeration based on these sorts of processes – the one so-called 'agglomeration economy' which did emerge as particularly significant was the size and diversity of the shared pool of labour represented by the major urban areas.

In this sense, the capacity to attract and retain a more skilled and highly qualified labour force alongside more routine inputs was identified as a key contributor to competitive success. Here, quality of life, the local environment and educational provision are critical factors, reinforcing the messages from a number of the other projects in the programme. New housing both in peripheral locations and in core urban areas can be a positive factor here. The impact on core urban areas can, however, be limited. Increased employment in the high value knowledge economy can simply generate increased levels of inward commuting from what are seen as more attractive residential locations.

In terms of social exclusion and social cohesion, the London and Bristol studies both point to the scale and persistence of spatially concentrated poverty and deprivation in parts of these urban areas despite their overall prosperity. These spatial concentrations reflect processes of housing allocation, both market and non-market, which generate patterns of residential segregation. But they point as well to patterns of change in the labour market and the dependence of particular groups on benefit levels, which emphasise increasing polarisation of incomes and wealth. This is reinforced in Glasgow and Liverpool for example, which suffer from low overall demand for labour and low levels of labour market participation as a result.

In terms of possible links between competitiveness and cohesion, much of the population of more prosperous urban areas such as London, Bristol or Edinburgh clearly benefits from higher levels of demand, better incomes, lower unemployment and attendant social problems. The more severe economic and social problems of places such as Liverpool, Manchester and Glasgow clearly do reflect lower levels of demand for locally produced goods and services and lack of demand for labour. What the more prosperous urban areas show, however, is the persistent coexistence of relatively high levels of poverty, deprivation and social exclusion with competitive success. Ensuring levels of demand in the urban economy and labour market is necessary in order to address issues of social exclusion. It is not sufficient, however, to eliminate persistent and spatially concentrated poverty and social exclusion even in the more buoyant areas.

Employment is clearly a critical link between competitiveness and cohesion.

In policy terms, specific measures are needed to reconnect excluded populations to the labour market including those in more prosperous urban areas. The government's welfare-to-work and related policies are very relevant in this respect and evaluation indicates that they have had significant impacts. Evidence suggests, however, that they do not go far enough to address the needs of those who are most disadvantaged in the labour market.

It is crucial as well to address issues of educational exclusion and educational performance given the evidence we now have of their major implications for future exclusion from the world of work. The importance of pre-school education and activities is also now known to have major implications for subsequent performance and the government's national child care strategy, Sure Start programme and related measures are very relevant here.

Employment and work-related measures are not relevant, however, to major elements of excluded populations in the short term at least and possibly the long term and who will be dependent on state benefits and other measures. These include older people, the long-term sick, children in workless households and those with caring responsibilities. Particularly for these groups, issues of cohesion and inclusion thus need to be addressed in their own right on the basis of social justice, independently of the competitiveness agenda.

Also at issue is the possible impact of social exclusion or a breakdown of social cohesion on competitiveness. High levels of social exclusion reflected in levels of crime or threats to social order, for example, might potentially impact on business investment, the attractiveness of urban living and hence on the capacity to attract and retain more highly skilled professional and technical staff within major urban areas. Here there is in fact no real indication from any of the case studies that business performance or investment and location decisions had been affected by concern over the levels or effects of social exclusion or lack of cohesion. Similarly, there was no real evidence that the overall supply of more skilled workers had been affected by concerns over quality of life, crime or social order at a general level. These issues, together with the quality (including social mix) of local schooling are major concerns for middle-class households in general. However, strategies in terms of residential location and educational choice generally allow such households to distance themselves physically from what are perceived to be the more immediate threats.

Turning to the specific impacts of policy and governance on competitiveness and cohesion, all four studies unsurprisingly emphasise the overriding importance of long-term structural factors including industrial structure and of economic forces external to any particular urban areas. In this sense they downplay the potential or capacity of governance to play a major part, particularly at the local level. However, the overriding conclusion is that governance can make a significant if relatively marginal impact.

The Manchester and Liverpool study does provide a very useful test case of the role of governance. It concludes that the supposed advantages of the former over the latter in terms of performance have been overstated and to an extent reflected good fortune rather than good governance. In more subtle respects, however, the local council and other actors in Manchester were able to trade more effectively on real but relatively small advantages. It was possible for the council to construct better quality relationships of trust and credibility with stakeholders and to derive cumulative benefit from demonstrating the capacity to deliver. In contrast to Liverpool, stable leadership in Manchester at a critical period was able to take a long-term view, to generate and to pursue the 'big idea' with the failed Olympic bid that was transformed into the major success of the Commonwealth Games in 2002. Manchester was also able to construct around these initiatives an effective approach to intergovernmental and public–private sector partnership. At the level of area-based regeneration, on the other hand, both Liverpool and Manchester achieved considerable success through effective partnership working and community involvement.

The London case study points to lack of effective governance at the level of the functional metropolitan region as a whole. This weakens capacity to influence the location of economic activity, address infrastructure and environmental needs and enhance the possibility of the benefits of a dynamic and competitive economy being shared more widely by the region's population and its localities. At a more detailed level, the dominant message to emerge is that actual service delivery by local government is central not only to the quality of life for residents but also to both competitiveness and cohesion. They also point to the supply of low- and moderate-income housing, improved public transport and raising the performance of the weakest state schools as policy areas in relation to both cohesion and competitiveness.

Both Bristol and Glasgow point to the negative impacts of spatially fragmented governance structures with administrative responsibility for a functionally coherent city-region split between a number of local authority units. This can promote unproductive competition for resources, population and jobs between adjoining administrative areas. It can inhibit strategic planning, decision making and infrastructure provision. It can also lead to duplication of facilities, fragmentation of services and additional costs of coordination. The core area can bear additional costs through servicing the needs of those who come into the centre for employment, retail or leisure purposes. Where there are significant differences in educational quality between adjoining units, as in Bristol, for example, this can drive patterns of residential decision taking and reinforce patterns of social segregation.

Competitiveness and urban change

Part Two of this volume changes scale to that of the urban system as a whole, as well as broad patterns of urban change. In this sense, these chapters complement the more detailed and fine-grained analysis undertaken in the city studies and make an important contribution to the overall evidence base. Shifts in the level of population and employment have been seen as key indicators of the competitive strength of different urban areas (Begg, 2002). As Moore and Begg demonstrate in Chapter Six of this volume, there have been significant shifts in the overall distribution of population and employment across Britain as a whole in recent decades: from urban to more rural areas, from the larger cities to the smaller cities and finally, an increasing concentration of successful cities in the south of the country which have attracted a disproportionately large share of growth and investment in new and expanding industries.

The performance of different cities across the country as a whole measured in terms of growth or decline in population and employment, however, has changed little relative to one another over recent decades. Rankings have changed little over time with few cities significantly changing their place in the urban hierarchy. Nor has there been significant change in relative levels of unemployment or in the distribution of unemployment across different types of area – unemployment remains concentrated in the major conurbations and larger free-standing cities.

There are clearly, therefore, powerful long-run trends favouring the south over more peripheral areas and driving the shift in population and employment from the conurbations and larger urban areas towards smaller towns and cities and more rural areas. As Moore and Begg conclude, this means that policy must address these deep-seated and persistent trends across the country as a whole. 'Urban policy' which simply focuses on the regeneration of specific local areas will have little hope of success. The obstacles to raising urban competitiveness, moreover, go well beyond the concerns of the Urban Task Force with improvements in design and quality of urban living. Policy, therefore, needs to engage with mainstream national government spending programmes and their impacts on different parts of the urban system rather than resources devoted to narrowly defined urban policy. It should concentrate on enhancing the 'investability' of different urban areas, recognising the diversity of characteristics and potential competencies. Policy must also consider cities in their sub-regional and regional context and the appropriate spatial scale for any intervention.

Champion and Fisher (Chapter Seven of this volume) confirm the continuing strength of the 'urban exodus', the loss of population from the major conurbations to the rest of the country through net migration. This is despite three decades of urban policy initiatives. It also involves the loss in particular of better-off households and those from professional and managerial occupations. Policy goals in terms of urban renaissance, of retaining or attracting households back to the major urban areas, thus face a difficult task. Searching for more positive messages, Champion and Fisher point out that the net loss of population represents the difference between what is in fact a large inflow of population to the main urban areas but an even larger outflow.

London, moreover, manages to attract and retain people in professional and technical occupations much better than other major urban areas – understanding why and how this might be further encouraged across urban areas as a whole offers some hope. International in-migration tends to favour the larger urban areas and in the case of London has largely compensated for losses to the rest of the country. The net impact of migration flows from overseas could be a factor in the future. There is also some evidence from the study that reducing crime and unemployment and ensuring the availability of suitable housing including newly built private homes, good quality schools and other amenities can go some way towards redressing the balance. The policy goal of increasing housing density may however be something of a threat given the reported attachment of potential residents to open-space, parks and peace and quiet. Overall, however, in the light of the 2001 Census of Population, the hoped-for demographic recovery in Britain's urban areas and the optimism this had inspired for urban renaissance has proved to be weaker than was thought. Continuing urban exodus remains, therefore, a deep-seated structural trend confronting policy thinking on the future of our towns and cities.

Cheshire et al (Chapter Eight of this volume) report on a piece of research which is technically complex but which has potentially important implications for understanding why some cities prosper at the expense of others. Working at the European scale, they observe that some of the worst performing cities and regions of Europe are located in close proximity to some of the most dynamic and prosperous ones in what has been termed a 'patchwork of disparities'. On the basis of the study, they suggest that this outcome is not simply a matter of chance or a statistical quirk but a more systematic feature of the European space economy. It arises because commuting patterns change over time and respond to the patterns of opportunity generated by processes of urban growth.

The more successful, faster growing urban areas attract in additional commuters. This boosts their apparent total output relative to the size of their resident population (because the number of employed workers rises relative to the number of residents). There are also real economic effects in addition to this statistical effect. Increased commuting flows tend to include a high proportion of more highly skilled and more productive workers – who are more likely to travel further to take up job opportunities – boosting levels of output. Growth may also generate increasing economies of scale, further boosting output growth. In other words, the findings present some evidence of the positive effects of urban agglomeration – larger urban areas tend to be more efficient because they can offer larger markets, a wider range of specialist goods and services and bigger and more varied pools of skilled labour.

The study suggests, therefore, that there are specific processes generating the observed disparities between urban areas in close proximity one to another. This may actually lead to greater disparities in income and unemployment between individuals and urban areas. However, these differences may actually increase the overall efficiency and level of output of the urban cluster as a whole. The difficult implication is that intervening in order to achieve a greater degree of equity may damage the competitiveness of the more prosperous urban areas or regions. This has clear policy implications in terms of the potential trade-off between equity and efficiency. And one could speculate, at least on the implications of these findings for the relative performance of neighbouring urban areas such as Manchester and Liverpool or Edinburgh and Glasgow, as described in Part One of this volume.

Competitiveness, innovation and the knowledge economy

It is widely accepted that levels of innovation have been key drivers of competitiveness and economic growth at national and international levels. Innovation has also been seen as a critical influence on competitive strength at regional and city-region level. A variety of factors, it is argued, combine to create a virtuous circle of innovation spatially concentrated in a small number of internationally competitive city-regions. In Part Three, Simmie's analysis (Chapter Ten of this volume) shows that innovation is encouraged by the concentration in particular urban areas of high-quality labour pools, specialist and general business services and transport and communications infrastructure particularly hub airports linked to national road networks. The crucial asset he argues, however, is access to cutting-edge knowledge, which may include spillovers from large firms to smaller firms locally, other forms of face-to-face contact but also ready access to international suppliers, customers and collaborators.

In policy terms, this emphasises the importance of core metropolitan cities, hub airports and high capacity communications systems focused on them. For non-metropolitan cities it suggests the need to support networking and supply chains between urban areas and the metropolitan core. Policy should also seek to promote permanent institutional arrangements to facilitate personal contact between key players in different innovative centres including international networks. Support for international exports by innovative sectors is also crucial, expanding markets, promoting knowledge exchange and further innovation in a virtuous circle. In turn, this can attract inward investment. It can attract in younger and better-educated workers from less successful regions together with intellectual capital in the form of technical and professional workers as a basis for further learning and innovation. This will be reinforced by policy measures which support a high-quality urban environment, housing, cultural and leisure facilities. Having said that, there is, as Simmie observes, no one pattern underlying the development of successful and innovative European city-regions. Each has reflected a particular history of development and specific institutional arrangements.

Cooke's work on the knowledge economy (Chapter Nine of this volume) further emphasises the crucial relationship between competitiveness at both local and regional levels and the concentration of knowledge-based industries. His analysis clearly demonstrates the difference in this respect between the best performing parts of the UK and those lagging well behind the national average. He also suggests that these differences will if anything widen over time as the better-off, more competitive regions reap the rewards of their concentrations of innovative, knowledge-based businesses. He further argues that competitive success is, paradoxically in a sense, driven by collaborative behaviour, by networking and cohesion within the innovative small- and medium-sized enterprise (SME) sector in particular of a type captured in some notions of social capital. More competitive localities may be better able to generate and exploit these forms of socio-economic interaction. Small- and medium-sized enterprises in the knowledge-based sector are also demonstrably more active in terms of networking and collaboration than in other sectors. Significantly, this is the case whether they are in the less buoyant parts of the country or the more booming areas – the latter simply have higher concentrations of well-networked, innovative, knowledge-based SMEs.

The implications in policy terms do, at one level, simply reinforce the now commonly accepted need to stimulate and support an innovative, knowledge-based economy as the core of development strategies. Recognising the centrality of non-market processes of collaboration and interaction and potential means of fostering such linkages is clearly important. In this respect, Cooke's work makes it very clear that the success of boom areas of southern England such as the Thames Valley sub-region is far from a model of independently operating competitive enterprises. It has been heavily underpinned and supported by a range of institutional structures that foster forms of collaboration and social capital which have been very significant to the success of individual business units. The overall competitive strengths of southern England do, on the basis of this analysis, look deeply embedded in the spatial structure of the knowledge economy and in this sense, shifting the balance in favour of the lagging regions and localities would seem a difficult task. The analysis does, however, point to some of the areas that need to be addressed by Regional Development Agencies (RDAs) and their strategic partners. The recent trajectories of Scotland, Northern Ireland and the Republic of Ireland suggest that there is potential for raising competitiveness and innovation.

Housing, property and economic performance

Planning, housing and commercial property development are key influences shaping patterns of population and employment change. They impact, therefore, on overall patterns of urban change but also on competitiveness and urban development across individual towns and cities. Guy and Henneberry (Chapter Twelve of this volume) examine the particular role of property developers and, in particular, institutional investors in shaping the urban property market, the way these institutional actors view development opportunities and the patterns of development that result. They stress the importance of difficult to shift values and assumptions based on past experience to the way in which institutional investors operate. This has important implications for attempts to intervene in the process of development from a policy perspective. It leads, they argue, to a homogeneous view on the part of institutional investors and mainstream national developers who aim to identify those opportunities which conform to institutional investment criteria. Institutional investors are only interested in 'institutional property'. They only 'see' or take an interest in those parts of the city that conform to these criteria.

Clearly, institutional investment should not be discouraged where it can take an active role in urban regeneration. The scope or scale of involvement is likely, however, to be quite limited, falling well short of the goals of regeneration policy both nationally and on the ground in particular cities. Extending Guy and Henneberry's argument, it can also lead, by implication, to a narrow definition of what becomes thought of as 'urban regeneration', meaning essentially large-scale 'flagship' projects often developed on the back of significant public investment.

As their detailed case studies demonstrate, however, urban property markets, particularly outside of London, are characterised by much greater diversity of investment opportunity than is seen by the institutional investor. They identify different models or development pathways in provincial property markets leading to 'islands of development'. These reflect often locally based developers operating with different and possibly competing perspectives on development opportunities, different cultures or ways of seeing these opportunities. They might typically work with more peripheral sites and smaller lot sizes, place more emphasis on design, seek to realise the distinctive potential of particular sites or neighbourhoods, relating risk to future potential rather than past trends. To an extent they may operate as 'pioneers' demonstrating and opening up new development opportunities. The policy implication is that national and local efforts at urban regeneration need to recognise the importance of the way in which property markets are structured and to work with and encourage independent and locally based forms of investment and development.

Meen and Andrew (Chapter Eleven of this volume) examine the role of housing in the economic performance of cities, focusing on the critical relationship between housing supply and spatial preferences in the housing market expressed in patterns of residential location. They look at the factors behind the locational decisions of households and the implications in particular for patterns of household movement and the skills base of cities. Their conclusions, as they say, are rather stark. Their work suggests that there is likely to be further erosion of the skills base in inner-urban areas and increasing segregation as those with higher incomes move to areas of low unemployment and low deprivation. The movement of existing households away from core urban areas and cities more generally is, moreover, likely to continue. And there is little real possibility of attracting back to the cities households that have already left. Some commute back but are increasingly likely to seek jobs nearer home.

Government policy aims to concentrate development on brownfield sites in urban areas, to promote good design, to enhance the urban environment and to create mixed communities, however, will run up against deep-seated demands for suburban and ex-urban locations which they have little hope of shifting. This in turn means that restraining greenfield development will be difficult. It is also, on the evidence presented, unlikely that mixed communities will readily emerge. Quality of the environment, as Meen and Andrew's work demonstrates, is very important in determining location and could in principle help to reduce movement out of urban areas. The challenge in terms of improving the physical infrastructure, raising educational standards in core urban areas and reducing crime are, however, very significant and there is, as yet, little evidence that policies aiming to address these have delivered significant and long-lasting change.

New households and, particularly in the case of London, international in-migration, however, are a source of potential growth and skills. Younger, high-income households do seem to be attracted to the facilities and employment opportunities that cities offer and have generated some growth in population. From a policy perspective, the challenge is to retain these households as they grow older and avoid (or delay) them following the movement of traditional households out of the urban areas. The policy implication is not that we should be building new homes, which attempt to attract back traditional families with children. We should instead concentrate on building houses and facilities attractive to young, high-income households who will add to the skill base. As Meen and Andrew observe, there is evidence, internationally as well as from the UK, that though small in number they can act as a valuable engine of growth and may well be increasingly important in the future. To the extent that urban regeneration initiatives can in practice secure real improvements in the urban environment, this might also contribute to a reduction in the outflow of population.

Space, place and social cohesion

Major variation in levels of social and economic disadvantage and the concentration in particular neighbourhoods of high levels of persistent disadvantage are evident across UK cities. There are persistent concentrations of high levels of disadvantage and social exclusion even in the more prosperous urban areas. Successive policy initiatives over past decades have responded with spatially targeted, 'area-based initiatives', including most recently the national strategy for neighbourhood renewal. One argument for this approach has been that living in areas of concentrated disadvantage has adverse impacts on individuals over and above their own personal characteristics and family circumstances. It is widely assumed that living in such areas adds an extra dimension of disadvantage. There has, however, been little in the way of real evidence, particularly for the UK, of such 'area effects', their impact on individuals or their importance relative to other factors.

Detailed analysis reported on by Buck and Gordon (Chapter Thirteen of this volume) did find some evidence of area effects. There was not, however, a clear link from area deprivation to adverse impacts on individuals. The main finding was that the chances of escaping from poverty were slightly lower for those living in more deprived areas. The magnitude of these area effects is not however large particularly compared with the effects of individual characteristics. This suggests that the case for spatially targeted policy based on the impact of specific area effects is not, as Buck and Gordon put it, entirely without foundation. But the effects are weak and so too is the case for spatial targeting. Nor are the effects of living in the *most* disadvantaged areas particularly bad – there is not a step change in area effects associated with the worst areas. So, concentrating policy measures on the worst areas in particular is not, on this basis, justified.

The project also demonstrated that it is in practice very difficult to find conclusive evidence for area effects and how they operate. It is difficult, therefore to come up with positive policy conclusions. At the very least, it is important to avoid simple assumptions as to the existence and operation of area effects. This places particular importance on addressing the causes of social exclusion regardless of where people live. By implication, these findings also suggest that if area-based initiatives are to be justified this must be done on grounds other than the importance of area effects as discussed, for example, by Lupton and Turnbull (Lupton, 2003; Lupton and Turnbull, 2003).

While much of the focus of urban policy has been on the 'problem areas' of the inner city, the role of very different sorts of neighbourhoods is equally significant to wider issues of competitiveness and cohesion, whether traditional middle-class suburbs, edge-of-city development or new brownfield housing schemes in core urban areas. As Halfpenny et al argue (Chapter Fourteen of this volume), traditional suburbs from the Victorian and Edwardian era have long provided for the middle-class professional workers who have underpinned the competitiveness of the larger provincial cities such as Manchester. Providing an environment and quality of life that will attract and retain new generations of high level service industry professionals remains fundamental in terms of continuing competitive strength. And where these groups choose to live will have important implications for the dynamics of urban change and on the future of these traditional 'good suburbs' as 'urban assets'. Halfpenny et al find in their case study of Manchester that these areas no longer fulfil the role they once did. Younger generations of professionals in finance and business services for example live or aspire to live beyond the traditional suburbs in the surrounding villages and small towns. This is their preference, as well as new central area residential developments, which appeal more to younger, single and childless rather than older, more established professionals.

There is also something of a policy vacuum in relation to the traditional suburbs. Older residents are resistant to change but represent a declining proportion of residents as a whole. There is increasing pressure from developers for redevelopment and subdivision on a piecemeal basis. Major policy debate, following the Urban White Paper, focuses on the development of brownfield sites elsewhere in the city and managing pressures for greenfield development. The city's 'Community Strategy', understandably, focuses on the most deprived neighbourhoods. Lack of community involvement or of a coherent community of interest in the suburbs compounds this. The local authorities as well have more pressing concerns including both inner areas and outer social housing estates. There is a vacuum, therefore, in terms of any form of strategy for the sustainable development of these good suburbs or for their future role in the overall structure of the city and its urban assets. This points to a significant gap in current policy debates and the measures that have emerged from these debates.

Butler (Chapter Fifteen) again focuses on the middle class, but in the context of metropolitan London. He focuses in particular on the 'urban seeking' middle class who choose and can afford to live in particular gentrified neighbourhoods of inner London. The scale of the metropolitan urban region, in contrast to provincial cities such as Manchester, is such that it can support a range of such distinctive neighbourhoods. There were significant differences between these including contrasts between areas in North and South London, between more recently gentrified areas and also new developments in Docklands. There was also, however, a shared commitment to some form of 'urban living'. They also found that the issue in terms of 'gentrification' in now less one of the displacement of lower-income groups but of an increasingly marked social polarisation between the wealthy middle class and other urban residents in or adjacent to these neighbourhoods. This polarisation is evident in terms of consumption patterns, employment and housing. Only the well off can now generally afford inner London's gentrified areas.

Polarisation is particularly evident however in terms of education where the well off and other groups in many cases inhabit essentially separate worlds. Households develop a range of strategies for ensuring what they see as an appropriate education and process of socialisation for their children. For large numbers, this involves private education. For others it involves sending children some distance to better, selective, state schools or moving into the catchment areas of such schools. For some, it involves moving out of London as children reach secondary school age. As Butler observes, from a policy perspective, if London is to continue to operate as a competitive node in the global financial and economic system it has to be attractive to a broad spectrum of the new professions which underpin this system. These particular neighbourhoods represent part of that attraction. Key determinants are quality of life, the cultural infrastructure but also in particular education both of itself and as a milieu for social reproduction. Education is therefore a central issue in policy terms for local, regional and central government if London is to continue to be attractive to key labour market groups. The downside is likely to be increasing polarisation, and this, extending Butler's argument, may be reinforced by current strategy which sees the solution to London's housing shortage in general and more specific issues of affordability as lying in large-scale provision for the less well off middle class on the fringes of the conurbation and beyond.

Ethnicity, enterprise and social cohesion

Current urban policy initiatives commonly assume that the richness of local networks and associations, or social capital is a significant asset or resource within communities. Lack of social capital in areas with high levels of deprivation is seen as contributing to social exclusion and an obstacle to regeneration. At the same time, it has been argued that the cultural diversity and creative potential of inner-city areas can provide the basis for what has been termed creative entrepreneurialism. Focusing on inner-North London, Foord and Ginsburg (Chapter Sixteen of this volume) found that a range of networks had formed over the years through local association and economic activity through a process of self-development. These have proved important in building particular forms of social capital and creative entrepreneurship.

From a policy perspective, national and local strategies for neighbourhood renewal have typically sought to incorporate and subsequently develop these networks and forms of association into policy delivery at local level. Self-developed forms of social capital and creative entrepreneurialism have, however, proved inaccessible to such incorporation. They remain, as Foord and Ginsburg put it, 'hidden assets'. Thus, while assumptions that social capital are lacking in such areas are to an extent unfounded, this does not provide an immediate basis for more formal regeneration initiatives to build on. And while there was indeed found to be considerable creative entrepreneurialism locally, again, this did not link readily into the formal organisational structures involved in regeneration. Local and regional agencies, it is argued, need actively to work to make these connections if regeneration initiatives are to capitalise on the potential of local social capital and entrepreneurialism.

Social capital has also been seen more specifically as the basis for ethnic entrepreneurialism reflected in high levels of self-employment among particular ethnic minorities. The immediate and extended family and broader co-ethnic community are seen as sources of low-cost, loyal, flexible labour, pooled savings, customer loyalty, shared information and supplier linkages. Such factors are to some extent significant, albeit not in such a straightforward fashion as sometimes presented. However, as Jones et al argue in relation to the concentration of South Asian restaurants in Birmingham (Chapter Seventeen of this volume), it is vital to look at the broader economic, social and policy context within which such ethnic businesses operate. Not least is the evidence that the scale and characteristics of ethnic entrepreneurialism are at least as much a reaction to the external context of racism and of market forces as they are a reflection of inherent cultural traits and resources.

While self-employment and enterprise are commonly promoted by government, ethnic minority businesses are heavily concentrated in more marginal business sectors including cornershop retailing, clothing manufacture and catering and subject to intense competition. As Jones et al found in Birmingham, ethnic restaurants are generally faced with market saturation and are oriented more towards basic survival than profit maximisation, development and expansion. Planning policies that have failed to control the entry of new businesses into an already saturated market have not helped this. And while Birmingham's 'Balti Quarter' may be promoted as one of the city's cultural attractions, that very concentration of businesses fighting for a limited overall market itself constrains business survival and development. There are businesses that have successfully 'broken out' into the mainstream restaurant trade with more upmarket appeal, product differentiation, business expansion and new locations, and with less dependence on informal resources and family labour. Such a strategy generally, however, requires considerable financial resources and has only been achieved by a small minority of ethnic entrepreneurs.

At a more general level, government policy has come to emphasise entry into paid employment as central to social inclusion. Evidence points to the very different labour market experience of different ethnic groups. Increased participation of young people in training and education has generally, however, been seen as a key route into paid employment. Bowlby et al (Chapter Eighteen) focus specifically on the transition from school to work which represents a crucial part of the process. The process of transition has become more complex over time. There have also been significant changes in the labour market with a proliferation of part-time, low-paid and relatively insecure jobs alongside more highly paid, better quality jobs in professional and managerial occupations. Some have argued that young people are now more able to combine education, training and work in different and more flexible ways such that they have greater choice and greater control over the transition to work. Others have argued that many young people are increasingly constrained by a casualised and insecure labour market and that transitions to work and choices for the future are in fact increasingly structured and constrained. Labour market behaviour and the choices available are also shaped and constrained by race and gender.

Bowlby et al show how young people's ideas of their own racial and gendered identity shapes their behaviour in the labour market and how their employability is in turn shaped by the racialised and gendered ideas held by employers. As their research shows, these factors remain highly significant in buoyant labour markets where the level of demand might have been thought to allow gendered and racialised labour market differences to be successfully challenged. The impact of these differences on transitions from school to work has major implications, therefore, for the choices and outcomes facing young people and for their future roles and trajectories in the labour market. In policy terms, it becomes crucial to reaffirm the importance of equality of opportunity in education, training and the labour market and renewed efforts to encourage and support young people in breaking out of gendered and racialised career paths and trajectories. Attention is needed to the quality and timeliness of advice and information provided to young people across the labour market as a whole – which the government's new Connexions service may go some way to address. Bowlby et al also argue the need to extend the Race Relations (Amendment) Act 2000 to private businesses in order to challenge organisational cultures which maintain subjective notions of employability.

Leadership, governance and social capital

As indicated in the introduction, the role of governance is now deeply embedded in urban policy and practice from regional to neighbourhood levels.

Emphasising the inter-organisational dimension, partnership working has become embedded as a key principle of urban policy and urban governance in recent decades – most recently with the introduction of Local Strategic Partnerships (LSPs). Sweeting et al (Chapter Nineteen) emphasise the vital and in some senses contradictory roles played by leadership in the context of partnership working and the different forms that it can take. Understanding local leadership is crucial to understanding and supporting the effective operation of partnerships in different contexts. The personal characteristics of individual local leaders are significant but the wider structures within which they operate including the policy environment, formal and informal institutional arrangements and the relationship between leaders and followers are important influences.

Different approaches to leadership in partnership and urban governance are possible. Leadership may be 'designed in' as with elected mayors, although the power and influence of the role is likely to be strongly shaped by the policy and institutional environment and may be hedged in by central government. Leadership may inhere in the structure of multiple partnerships in an implicit form but is likely, therefore, to remain fragmented and lacking in strategic direction. The danger, as Sweeting et al point out, is that this form of leadership may be subservient to external policy influence and dominated by bureaucratic arrangements.

This is the danger with LSPs where multi-organisational working may lead to confusion and lack of direction. Leadership may also be exercised in a practical sense deriving its authority from a capacity to get things done. In a policy context it is also important to recognise that partnership and urban governance, and the role of leadership within this, evolves and develops over time. There is the capacity, therefore, to shape and develop leadership at the local level and the role that this plays. Leadership is potentially contradictory in the context of partnership working with its emphasis on collaboration. The roles of leadership will at times be contradictory. However, as this work makes clear, it is nevertheless a vital – and somewhat neglected – component of effective urban governance, particularly given the centrality of partnership working to the current urban policy agenda.

Meegan's (Chapter Twenty) detailed analysis of a particular spatially targeted regeneration initiative in Liverpool demonstrates how central government remains highly influential even when formal responsibility is devolved to local partners. The need for local government to work through partnership with a wide range of other agencies and actors is also, however, very evident. The case of Merseyside shows how macro-structural processes interact with micro-local factors on the ground to produce the sorts of geographical concentrations of disadvantage which the initiative sought to address. The project also demonstrated the central importance of access to employment including physical access and transport for many households. Generating new jobs is thus necessary but not sufficient to link to those most 'distanced' from job opportunities.

In terms of process, the project demonstrated the value of a partnership approach to building social capital. It also demonstrated, however, that the process is slow and fragile. It has to be accompanied by appropriate support for local residents within an open and transparent process. It is clear that issues of trust are central to building social capital and that transparency and information exchange play a vital role. Trust cannot be taken for granted but needs to be worked on and built in as a core element of the regeneration process at the local level. This can make it difficult to reconcile representative democracy and the role of elected councillors and their representatives on the one hand and truly participative democracy and policy intervention on the other. An overriding lesson is also the timescale needed to develop trust-based participatory processes on the ground. There are important lessons here for LSPs and New Deal for Communities, as well as the operation of other area-based initiatives on the ground.

Stoker et al (Chapter Twenty One of this volume), finally, take issue more generally with some aspects of the debate around social capital. In particular, they question whether social capital has beneficial effects in quite the straightforward way that policy makers and proponents of the idea sometimes assume. Its impacts and effectiveness depend on context and a variety of factors other than the scale or intensity of social capital itself. Putnam in particular, they argue, neglects the role of the state, political structures and institutions in shaping the context for the creation of social capital. He also underplays the extent to which social capital is a property of relations between associations and institutions rather than just individuals. Their own research on Birmingham also contradicts one of Putnam's key arguments to the effect that civic organisation has declined. They find that the overall number of voluntary associations has in fact increased significantly over recent decades. There have, at the same time, been significant shifts in the nature of these associations reflecting shifts in the social and political environment.

In line with their argument as to the locus of social capital, they go on to focus in particular on the relationships between voluntary associations and between voluntary associations and the local authority. Local authorities have come to play an increasing role in associational relations and hence in shaping the context for social capital, particularly through their funding of organisations in the voluntary and community sector. Social capital, they conclude, can be generated by enlightened policy interventions. This is, however, likely to operate only on a limited basis, leaving other organisations feeling isolated. Selective engagement on the part of local authorities is necessary in order to build effective relations but is likely to generate distrust on the part of other organisations. Social capital, they argue, is most effectively generated in face-to-face settings, where there is regular communication and where a limited group of participants are attempting to build the context for effective action. This may be valuable in certain contexts. It is unlikely, however, to provide the more general context for civic engagement and democratic governance across the board that some proponents of social capital have seen it providing.

Competitive advantage, cohesion and territorial governance

This second part of the chapter, steps back from the detail of the individual projects and reflects more generally on the broad themes of the research programme. It looks in turn at the roots of competitive advantage; the potential for change in terms of competitive strength and the potential, therefore, for policy leverage; links between competitiveness and social cohesion; the rationale of area-based initiatives and the spatial targeting of urban policy; and, finally, issues of territory, governance structures and the pursuit of competitive advantage.

What makes for competitive advantage?

As outlined in Chapter One of this volume, there have been many different attempts to define competitiveness and the factors that underpin competitive success at the level of cities or city-regions. Based on the research programme's findings and other evidence, we can start to identify a number of characteristics associated with competitive success. These include economic diversity, skills and human capital, broadly defined quality of life and environment, innovation and finally connectivity.

Economic diversity

As Moore and Begg's study among others suggests (Chapter Six of this volume), cities which have a broad industrial base rather than being dependent on a single sector or small number of related sectors tend to be more successful in responding to economic change and in reinventing themselves economically, over time. Building from where they are, this suggests that cities should be constantly seeking to push into new areas of economic activity rather than simply seeking to specialise or lock in their existing structure. Many successful cities including those in Germany and other parts of mainland Europe, for example (Parkinson et al, 2003), are those that have retained and modernised their traditional manufacturing sectors as well as developing strengths in new areas of economic activity.

Skills and human capital

There is also a strong relationship between the skills base of city-regions and their competitive performance in terms of innovation and levels of output per head. To an extent this is dependent on locally generated skills and human capital via the educational infrastructure and further and higher education institutions in particular. Evidence from mainland Europe and elsewhere points to the role of institutional structures and relationships. What is important is not simply the number of university students but the nature and quality of the relationships between universities, industry and those engaged in economic development. And there is increasing recognition of this in the UK.

Quality of life and environment

There is an important relationship here as well with a set of factors that can be summed up in terms of quality of life and environment. This includes some combination of the distinctiveness of core urban areas, architectural and housing quality and the diversity and the nature of the built environment, cultural facilities, the access to the natural environment and amenities. The more competitive cities are those which are able to attract in – or retain – those professional, managerial and technical workers for whom lifestyle and environment is an increasingly important consideration, those termed by Richard Florida (2003), 'the creative classes'. Quality of life is also an increasingly important consideration for key decision makers themselves that can impact on investment decisions. This is particularly the case for those contemplating moving out from London and the South East, the core area for many such workers.

This points to the importance of urban renaissance – measures which secure improvements in the overall quality of the urban environment and cultural development. In the UK, Bristol and Edinburgh are examples of places that have perhaps particularly benefited from these sorts of factors while many other places have been actively seeking to enhance what they have to offer. Urban renaissance is not, however, the same as urban competitiveness. Success in terms of physical regeneration, cultural development and international profile is not the same, necessarily, as competitive success and the one does not automatically lead to the other. Barcelona is sometimes cited as an example of a city that has achieved much in terms of urban renaissance but which still nevertheless lags behind in terms of sheer economic performance. It has, nevertheless, maximised its assets in this respect and made it much more likely that it can attract investment and improve its skills base and competitiveness in the long run. The UK government's urban renaissance agenda is thus potentially of considerable and increasing importance to the more focused goal of competitive success in economic terms.

Innovation

Cooke and Simmie (Chapters Nine and Ten of this volume, respectively) add to the growing volume of evidence confirming the importance of innovation and innovative capacity to competitive success. Their more detailed findings are summarised earlier in this chapter. As with competitiveness more generally, a wide range of indicators or composite 'scorecards' has been developed to measure innovative capacity or innovative performance. The OECD estimates that between 1970 and 1995 over half of total output growth in the developed world resulted from innovation. The EC has similarly estimated that over 40% of the variation in per capita regional income can be explained by variations in innovative performance. As Cooke's own study shows, there is considerable overlap with similar indicators used to capture and quantify the concept of the 'knowledge economy' or competitive strength more generally. Innovation in the sense of new products, processes, services or forms of organisation that typically drive increased output and productivity is crucial, however, to the competitiveness of urban areas.

Simmie points to the significance of innovative activity in the London region. Different indicators of innovative capacity based for example on a combination of high level skills, high-technology industry and research and development (R&D) expenditure and patents, confirm the ranking of the London region among the top ten or so performers in Europe, albeit some way behind the leaders. However, of the English core cities, for example, only Bristol features in the top half of the 50 highest scoring regions, with the remainder well down the table.

Much attention has focused on the performance and characteristics of innovation at the national level. More recently, however, it has increasingly been argued that structures and relationships at regional or city-region scales – regional or local 'innovation systems' – can make a difference to the scale and impact of innovative activity. One can point to the success of a range of city-regions in mainland Europe. And the evidence here points to the much more developed nature of such locally rooted innovation systems (Parkinson et al, 2003). In the case of Stuttgart, for example, there are well-developed links between industry, public and private research institutions, laboratories, banks and different levels of government that have sought to promote innovation over an extended time period. In the case of Toulouse, national government investment decisions including aerospace, telecommunications and computing activities have been reinforced by private investment and R&D facilities and local institutional structures that set out both to attract such activities and to lever in additional public funds in support of them.

It is hard to separate out the crucial factors that really make a difference. It may be, for example, that the most innovative firms tend to cluster together not to be close to each other as such, but because they share a common interest in recruiting the type of professional and technical labour attracted to urban centres with a high quality of life. The UK system of support for innovative activity at the local and regional level does typically, however, remain underdeveloped by comparison with parts of mainland Europe. It is essentially market-driven with private businesses taking decisions and driving processes of innovation in an essentially autonomous manner marked by the absence or public–private sector partnership and collaboration or close links between industry and higher education. Only very recently have the RDAs been seen as potentially playing a greater role in supporting innovation, and the UK government has started to put some effort into encouraging stronger links between universities and private business at regional and sub-regional levels. Local innovations systems thus lag two or even three decades behind developments in some of the more competitive cities of mainland Europe.

Connectivity

Finally, the most successful cities also have the physical or electronic infrastructure to move people, goods and information quickly and efficiently. There is a basic level of communications infrastructure that is essential to the efficient functioning of any given urban area. It is hard to quantify this or measure its effects, but it is apparent that most UK cities lag behind the best examples on mainland Europe in this respect. Crucially important, as well, are air transport and the extent of international connectivity by air. This facilitates the face-to-face contact which has grown with, rather than been replaced by, the massive increase in electronic connectivity. London is clearly very well served by international standards in this respect, reinforcing and supporting its role as a world city but also the differentials in terms of connectivity between London and the south east and the rest of the UK. In the UK, only Manchester, 13th out of the top 50 European airports by passenger numbers, ranks among the better-connected cities (Birmingham is next in 35th place).

Capacity for change

A wide range of characteristics associated with competitive advantage can be identified, even if their precise role and importance cannot be very precisely measured. A critical question, however, is the extent to which competitive advantage can change over time – and more importantly, how far there is scope, therefore, for policy leverage, to make a difference. Evidence on the hierarchy of different towns and cities in terms of performance, measured by change in population or employment or per capita gross domestic product (GDP) points to the relative stability of rankings over time. Even in the longer term, there is in general, not dramatic change in the performance of urban areas comparing one with another. Cities that performed well a decade ago or two decades ago have generally continued to do well, and those that have struggled generally still do so. This suggests that the set of factors that determine the relative competitiveness of different places are deep-rooted and themselves relatively stable. Evidence underlines the fact that there are structural characteristics of competitiveness, whether favourable or unfavourable, which are acquired over a long period of time and which persist over time.

Industrial structure in terms of sector-mix is clearly a major determinant of competitive strength and its effects are relatively persistent over time. Many major urban areas continue to suffer from their legacy of manufacturing industry while those that have an established presence of more dynamic service activities and new manufacturing sectors have done well over a period of some years. Economic diversity also emerges as a critical feature underpinning urban competitiveness in the longer term – Bristol's adaptive capacity, that is, its ability to reinvent itself over time, is a case in point. Again, diversity of economic structure is not something that can be readily created in the short term.

Other features critical to urban competitiveness also tend to be relatively fixed or stable in the short to medium term. This is obviously the case with basic geographical location – Moore and Begg emphasise the importance of the simple fact of proximity to London in explaining economic performance over time. Connectivity in terms of road, rail, air and IT infrastructure also tends to be relatively stable – new investment and innovation tends if anything to reinforce the centrality of already well-connected places. Education and skill levels do not tend to change much in the short term at least. Other features considered central to urban competitiveness including quality of life, the strategic capacity to win support for and to mobilise long-term development strategies and the innovative capacity of firms and organisations are complex and multidimensional. Again, they are not generally amenable to significant change in the short to medium term at least. This means that the potential leverage over features critical to competitiveness at the level of the city or city-region is limited in the short term at least.

This is not, however, to say that nothing can be done. As we have pointed out elsewhere (Parkinson et al, 2003), there are examples of cities that have significantly changed their economic fortunes over a relatively short period of time. Helsinki, faced with the collapse of its main trading partner, the Soviet Union, faced deep recession. The city leaders, working with Nokia and with the universities, were able, however, to build a new economic strategy built on communications. It is now highly rated by the private sector and scores highly in terms of innovation. Barcelona has also been widely cited as a model for economic development. City leaders pursued a long-term strategy, starting with the Olympics and aiming to reconstruct much of the city's physical environment along with its international image. In terms of economic competitiveness as such, as suggested earlier, it still lags behind many urban areas. However, in terms of physical renewal or urban renaissance and reinvention, it has come a long way – and this is likely to have positive effects in the longer term. On a somewhat smaller scale, this is the sort of approach pursued in the UK by Manchester (described in Chapter Three of this volume) or Birmingham for example, and there are many other cases where renaissance, important in its own right, has also been seen as a route to securing improvements in competitive strength.

Over a longer time scale one can point to the history of the three most successful non-capital cities in Europe, Frankfurt, Stuttgart and Munich, which totally reinvented themselves in the wake of wartime destruction. The success of the UK new and expanded towns which, as Moore and Begg demonstrate, lead the leagues tables in terms of population and employment growth over recent decades, is an example of the policy-led creation of competitive urban places. There are obvious lessons here for the implementation of the government's Communities Plan (ODPM, 2003a), including new and expanded settlements. Experience also points to the importance of edge-of-city development in Bristol and Edinburgh for example. Creation of places considered by the private sector to confer significant competitive advantage has been important to securing continued economic success – issues of quality and sustainability notwithstanding.

This points to the need to identify early achievable wins in the short term while seeking to secure more fundamental structural improvements in the longer term. The former might, for example, include physical renewal, cultural development and measures to improve the quality of urban living which in the longer term might impact on the skills base, business investment or creativity. There are examples where infrastructure investment has resulted in significant improvements in connectivity – the French TGV is much cited, but the contrast with the UK is self-evident. Airport and airport-related development outside of the London region remains underdeveloped compared with many parts of mainland Europe. Working towards more effective strategic capacity at the sub-regional or city-region scale, however, is a long-term process and a process that can be frustrated by shorter-term and more local interests. It is, however, likely to pay dividends in the longer term.

Competitiveness, cohesion and social exclusion

Competitive strength is commonly seen as a self-evident policy goal and the benefits that flow from it as taken for granted. Overall levels of unemployment and social deprivation measured in terms of a range of indicators are clearly worse in relative terms in less economically competitive and less successful cities across the UK – this much is in a sense a truism in that unemployment levels are one self-evident measure of success or otherwise. Tackling issues of social deprivation and social exclusion are always likely to be easier in a context where the overall level of prosperity is higher and there are more opportunities and better paid employment available locally.

As discussed earlier in this chapter, however, it is clear that competitive success is far from incompatible with persistent concentrations of unemployment and social deprivation and high levels of economic and social inequality. The examples of Bristol, London, Leeds or Edinburgh, arguably the UK's most successful larger urban areas, make this clear. Competitive success does not eliminate inequality or concentrated disadvantage. The very success of these places if anything makes the contrasts starker. Their overall success and level of prosperity serves to emphasise that there is no automatic link from economic competitiveness to beneficial social outcomes.

The operation of the housing system will itself lead to spatially concentrated disadvantage. Inequalities of purchasing power whether in terms of money or 'points' will tend to concentrate those who are most disadvantaged in the worst of the housing stock. However, as we have argued elsewhere (Boddy, 2002), the evidence points as well to social exclusion as an active process, setting up barriers which distance some within the local population from participation in mainstream society. Social exclusion, we would conclude, is thus more than simply a synonym for poverty or deprivation. It reflects among other things, 'early years' underdevelopment, lack of educational attainment and the sorts of barriers faced later by those most disadvantaged in the labour market. Disparities in income among those who are in employment also point to the growing polarisation of the labour market between better paid 'knowledge workers' and low-paid 'service workers'. This sort of polarisation is likely to be more marked in the more successful city-regions that are further down the road towards a dynamic, knowledge-based economy.

Area-based initiatives and spatial targeting

There has been a succession of different urban policy initiatives stretching over the years, starting with Education Priority Areas and the Urban Programme in the late 1960s, which have been targeted on specific areas of towns and cities. These areas have typically been identified by some form of index of deprivation or broadly defined need and project funding allocated according to some combination of criteria and a bidding process. New Deal for Communities and Health Action Zones are among the most recent examples. There has equally been an ongoing debate as to the effectiveness of such area-based initiatives. The government's Action Plan for neighbourhood renewal set out what it claimed to be a new approach to address the true scale of the problem through an integrated approach involving all key areas of government policy and harnessing the government's main spending programmes rather than relying on one-off regeneration initiatives. The vision, according to the Prime Minister, was that of "a nation where no-one is seriously disadvantaged by where they live" (SEU, 2001, p 5). Taken at face value, this suggests that it is where people live that matters, not their particular characteristics, history or family background.

In the previous section of this chapter, we identify the implications of social exclusion and social polarisation. Programme findings, and the work of Buck and Gordon in particular (Chapter Thirteen of this volume), suggest that living in areas of concentrated disadvantage does not add significantly or in any simple way to disadvantage suffered by an individual on the basis of their own individual circumstances. What matters, therefore, is not where people live but, more specifically, their own individual characteristics and that of their household circumstances. And as the various longitudinal studies now available demonstrate, it is the cumulative effects of these over time which are the most damaging in terms of deprivation and social exclusion later in life. In this respect, then, the focus of Prime Ministerial concern is misconceived, or at the least badly expressed. The broader case for area-based initiatives on the grounds that reducing spatially concentrated disadvantage will, in itself, serve to reduce deprivation and social exclusion at the level of individuals and households is also, on this basis, ill conceived.

We would argue on the basis of research programme findings, that it is the government's main funding programmes, and how these are targeted, that will have by far the greatest impact on levels of social exclusion rather than specifically 'urban policy' measures such as New Deal for Communities. These would include in particular, the minimum wage and the child tax and working tax credits. They would also include key national programmes including the various New Deal 'welfare-to-work' programmes, Sure Start and 'early years' initiatives. Critical as well, will be the targeting of main programme spending on health, education, children, policing and other major policy areas – as the government itself argued in its Action Plan. So far, however, the evidence for significant shifts at this fundamental level is very limited. And ironically, indeed, even in New Deal for Community neighbourhoods, where area-based action has had the bending of main programmes in favour of deprived communities as a key objective, there is as yet only limited sign of success. There is considerable potential to learn from initiatives such as New Deal. To the extent that they succeed, they can have a very real impact on the lives of people in the areas on which they are targeted. Their potential impact on overall levels of deprivation and exclusion at a more general level is, however, very limited.

Territory, governance and competitive advantage

A final key issue which emerges from the research programme and other sources of evidence is the relationship between formal administrative structures and governance on the one hand, and competitive advantage and social cohesion on the other. It is now widely argued that spatial planning, economic strategy and many aspects of governance and service provision need to operate at the scale of the city-region if they are to be effective in terms of competitiveness, cohesion and quality of life. Cheshire et al's findings (Chapter Eight of this volume) add further weight to this argument.

In practice, however, formal administrative responsibilities in the UK are commonly fragmented between a number of local councils. There is often competition and tension if not actually conflict between adjoining local councils over a range of issues including economic development, house building, planning and environment, transportation and fiscal and financial issues. These can be made worse by differences in political control. Central city councils are typically responsible and have direct influence over only part of the physical urban area and even less over the overall functional city-region. They are also unable to represent and work on behalf of the city-region as a whole in wider regional, national and international arenas.

The same is generally the case across mainland Europe and the US – where fiscal and financial divisions make conflicts between administrative areas even more stark (Conant and Myers, 2002; Parkinson et al, 2003). City-regions everywhere have struggled to establish an effective spatial architecture of governance at the appropriate scales. Smaller administrative units have been unwilling to cede power and influence and national governments reluctant to impose on the existing political and administrative structures. There have been some attempts to set up second-tier, city-region or metropolitan-scale political and administrative structures. In the case of the UK the last attempt at this for the major cities proved politically unpopular, generated considerable tensions between first- and second-tier authorities and were abolished by Conservative central government with little opposition. The last round of local government reform replaced 'two-tier' local government with single-tier 'unitary' councils in many other areas. As elsewhere, the picture in different parts of the UK is now very mixed, with different places devising different sorts of ad hoc joint collaborative arrangements for different services typically including planning, transport, waste and the environment.

Again, in the case of mainland Europe, the situation is mixed. There are few examples of formal sub-regional structures being created. Most places have decided that it is not worth attempting to create formal institutional structures. However desirable in theory, as in the UK, it is acknowledged that administrative reform or new institutional structures are unlikely to be secured in practice. It is generally recognised, however, more clearly than currently in the UK, that in order to be competitive in the global marketplace it is vital to organise and act at a wider sub-regional or metropolitan scale. Many places are setting up important albeit less formal strategic alliances at city-region scale often led by powerful mayors as in Lyon, Barcelona and Helsinki. The common view is that strategic alliances between willing partners, mobilised around a strategic vision, agreed powers, resources and territories are the way forwards.

In the case of the UK, the major emphasis on the part of central government in terms of the spatial architecture of governance has been towards an expanded role for the regions. Following devolution in Scotland and Wales, the English RDAs have had an increasing role, particularly in relation to the government's competitiveness agenda. Parallel developments have boosted the role of regional government offices and regional assemblies have been set up to provide a new political and policy focus at regional level. Under current arrangements, the role of regional structures will be further strengthened in some regions at least through the creation of elected regional assemblies. Important though such developments may be at regional scale – and their true significance waits to be seen – they do not address directly the argued need for a focus at city-region scale. Whatever, their merits, new regional-scale structures are too large to address directly at least, issues of spatial strategy and strategic planning at city-region scale.

There is, however, considerable scope for agencies and institutional structures at regional scale to reinforce strategic alliances and the spatial architecture of governance at the crucially important level of the city-region. Particularly so given the reforms and new provisions included in currently proposed planning provisions (ODPM, 2003b, 2003c). These powers do away with the current system of broad 'structure plans' and more detailed local plans. Regional Spatial Strategies (RSS), building on, but potentially going much further than, existing Regional Planning Guidance, will set the overall context. Through RSS, the RDA, regional assemblies, regional government offices and other bodies can establish the requirement and framework for strategic planning at city-region or metropolitan scale. Regional Spatial Strategies will be delivered on the ground through a more flexible system of Local Development Frameworks.

There will also be the requirement for 'area action plans' covering areas of change including growth areas and regeneration initiatives.

Existing local councils will still be centrally involved in the process. Collaboration, joint planning and shared vision will be crucial to the process. But the new structures and powers give regional level bodies the opportunity to put strategic thinking at city-region scale at the core of the spatial planning framework and to tie this into broader, integrated regional strategy in terms of planning, economic development, transport, housing and the environment. Implementation of the government's Communities Plan (ODPM, 2003a) will also be relevant here. Exactly how this will all operate in practice is not yet clear. Much remains uncertain and different bodies at regional and sub-regional scales are still struggling to make sense of rapidly changing powers and institutional structures across a broad range of policy fronts. What is clear, however, is that the current situation provides the opportunity to embed metropolitan-wide or city-region level strategic thinking at the heart of the new national spatial architecture of governance, with far-reaching implications for competitiveness and cohesion across our towns and cities.

References

Boddy, M. (2002) 'Linking competitiveness and cohesion', in I. Begg (ed) *Urban competitiveness: Policies for dynamic cities*, Bristol: The Policy Press, pp 33-54.

Conant, R. and Myers, D. (2002) *Towards a more perfect union*, Novato, CA: Chandler and Sharp Inc.

Florida, R. (2002) *The rise of the creative class*, New York: Basic Books.

Lupton, R. (2003) '"Neighbourhood effects": can we measure them and does it matter?', CASE Paper no 73, London: London School of Economics and Political Science.

Lupton, R. and Turnbull, R. (2003), 'Is targeting deprivation an effective means to reach poor people?', CASE Paper no 70, London: London School of Economics and Political Science.

Parkinson, M., Hutchins, M., Simmie, J., Clark, G. and Verdonk, H. (2003) *Competitive European cities: Where do the core cities stand?*, Final report to core cities working group, October 2003, mimeo.

ODPM (Office of the Deputy Prime Minister) (2003a) *Sustainable communities: Building for the future*, London: ODPM.

ODPM (2003b) *Planning policy statement 12: Local development frameworks*, (draft), London: ODPM.

ODPM (2003c) *Draft consultation paper on new planning policy statement 11 (PPS11) – Regional planning*, London: ODPM.

Social Exclusion Unit (2001) *A new commitment to neighbourhood renewal: national strategy action plan*, London: Cabinet Office.

Index

C

F

J

K

L

M

S

Celtic First Names